Caroline Lapuise
12/12/99

National Library of Canada
ISBN 0-9685847-0-5

Canadian Cataloguing in Publication Data
Roy Laprise, Caroline, 1919,
Mon héritage, ma culture, mes souvenirs : 1898-1998=
My heritage, my culture, my memories : 1908-1998

Text in English and French
Includes index.
ISBN 0-9685847-0-5

1. Roy Laprise, Caroline, 1919-   . 2. Canadians, French-speaking - Ontario - Chatham Region- Social life and customs - 20th century.* 3. Chatham Region (Ont.)- Social life and customs - 20th century. 4. Canadians, French-speaking - Ontario - Chatham Region - Biography.* 5. Chatham Region (Ont.) - Biography. 6. Women - Ontario - Chatham Region- Biography. I. Title: II. Title: My heritage, my culture, my memories.

FC3099.C45Z49 1999   971.3 '33   C99-932057-2E
F1059.5.C45R69 1999

Données de catalogage avant publication (Canada)
Roy Laprise, Caroline, 1919-
Mon héritage, ma culture, mes souvenirs : 1898-1998 = My heritage, my culture, my memories:
1898-1998

Textes en français et en anglais.
Comprend un index.
ISBN 0-9685847-0-5

1. Roy Laprise,Caroline, 1919-   . 2. Canadiens français - Ontario - Chatham, Région de - Moeurs et coutumes - 20e siècle. 3. Chatham, Region de (Ont.) - Moeurs et coutumes - 20e siecle. . 4. Canadiens français - Ontario - Chatham, Région de - Biographies. 5. Chatham, Région de (Ont.) - Biographies. 6. Femmes - Ontario - Chatham, Région de - Biographies. I. Titre. II. Titre: My heritage, my culture, my memories.

FC3099.C45Z49 1999   971.3 '33   C99-932057-2F
F1059.5.C45R69 1999

Written and Published by: Caroline Roy Laprise

Printed by: AGMV Marquis

Sur la photo, trois générations en 1944

Debout à droite : Adolphe Roy.
      1ère rangée : Anne-Aline Roy, Loretta Roy, Gérard Laprise,
          Yvonne Roy Lucier, Léontyne Roy.
      2e rangée : Edmond Roy, Raoul Roy, Bernard Roy.
      3e rangée : Trefflé Laprise, Félix Lucier.
      Photo par : Caroline Roy Laprise

      On the photo are three generations in 1944

Standing to the right : Adolphe Roy.
      1st row: Anne-Aline Roy, Loretta Roy, Gérard Laprise,
          Yvonne Roy Lucier, Léontyne Roy.
      2nd row: Edmond Roy, Raoul Roy, Bernard Roy.
      3rd row: Trefflé Laprise, Félix Lucier.
      Photo taken by: Caroline Roy Laprise

Cover designed by Paul Richer
La couverture du livre à publier est la conception de Paul Richer

A word from Paul: It's very special that Mrs. Laprise allowed me to produce this cover.
I feel in a small way connected to the project, to making this dream come true.   I
perused some early drafts last summer, if they are any indication, this will be an
incredible book.   Can't wait to see it.

Table des Matières - Table Of Contents

Mon Héritage
Ma Culture
Mes Souvenirs

1898 - 1998

My Heritage
My Culture
My Memories

Caroline Roy Laprise

Dédicace

Je dédie ce modeste volume en témoignage de mon affection et de ma reconnaissance envers mon époux, Trefflé Laprise.

À toutes les mères chrétiennes du passé, du présent et de l'avenir, vous qui façonnez l'âme de vos enfants à votre image, vous qui semez dans les jeunes coeurs les principes chrétiens, vous qui devinez que le renoncement de soi-même est la clef du succès autant pour l'homme que pour la femme qui aspirent laisser en héritage une oeuvre durable, je désire vous saluer d'une manière tout à fait spéciale.

Je veux témoigner, d'une manière tangible, en faveur de mes enfants, mes petits-enfants et enfin à toute la postérité qui suivra. Vous êtes liés l'un à l'autre par héritage . . . laissez-vous guider par la Providence qui donne la vie, qui vous nourrit et vous fait vivre.

C'est avec amour que j'ai choisi de vous fournir, à ma façon, une continuité de votre patrimoine, à l'aide d'un communiqué permanent qui pourra se transformer, tour à tour, en disquette évocatrice et vivante pour tous ceux et celles qui voudront, au besoin, créer des liens et attiser les souvenirs du bon vieux temps.

Dedication

"It's great to be alive."

This milestone is a tribute to my husband, Trefflé Laprise, who originally had the idea that I write this book. So, I went about this task with a good grace and carried out his wishes to the best of my ability.

I'm privileged to be able to share with you my love, my research, my memories, my values and also our culture.

To my children and grandchildren who so tenaciously but kindly convinced me to go forward, this testimony is for you.

To every woman, past, present and future, to my friends and most importantly to an elite group of persons who already have passed on to their eternal rest but had a lasting influence on my life and spurred me on to greater heights of accomplishments, this labour of love is for you.

Wholeheartedly, to everyone whose life's friendly path I've shared and enjoyed, I am most grateful. May your light shine forever on your children's children.

Caroline Roy Laprise

Avant-propos

Un centenaire d'héritage,
Un centenaire de dévouement,
Un centenaire de valeurs humaines,
Un centenaire de patriotisme,
Un centenaire d'amour et de fierté,
un défi en soi mais tâche encore plus méritante d'amasser environ un siècle de connaissances et d'expériences vécues pour ensuite pouvoir les compiler dans un livre que j'ai mis sur pied en ce jour ensoleillé d'octobre 1995.

Je suis heureuse de pouvoir vous communiquer à ma façon les trésors du passé, les visages des ancêtres, parler des gens que j'ai connus et qui ont laissé leur marque, ou encore vous permettre de contempler à votre guise une quantité de photos en plus de vous faire découvrir les mille facettes d'histoire et de valeurs humaines qui vous ont été léguées à travers les années.

Tout comme octobre annonce l'automne des saisons, de même, j'envisage avec confiance l'automne de ma vie qui passe rapidement, raison prémonitoire de vous transmettre au meilleur de mes connaissances mes souvenirs de quatre-vingts années d'existence, une vie richement vécue. C'est une tentative onéreuse, puisqu'ici, remarquez bien, il s'agit d'un siècle environ.

Vous trouverez des étapes spéciales de ma vie, de ma famille ainsi que des événements mémorables de votre paroisse et des communautés avoisinantes.

C'est ainsi que je veux commencer ma retraite bien méritée. C'est peut-être aussi la satisfaction d'une sorte de joie de vivre, d'une joie de donner, de voir grandir en âge et en sagesse la génération future. J'anticipe être témoin de l'évolution scientifique, technologique et économique du siècle, à l'égard de diverses institutions.

Même si les temps changent et que le progrès évolue, il est toujours bon de connaître son appartenance. Donc, j'espère pouvoir attirer votre attention en y insérant les généalogies des familles Roy, Caron, Laprise, Charron, Faubert et autres. Mon but principal est de rejoindre autant que possible les personnes de tous les âges: petits, adolescents, parents, grands-parents et vieillards. Le tout pourra fort bien vous intéresser et même vous fasciner un peu . . . mais mon plus grand désir est celui-ci : de vous inciter à protéger jalousement votre patrimoine culturel . . . votre seul lien avec le passé.

Embarquez donc dans le courant du troisième millénaire, le vent dans les voiles, aplanissant la voie du futur pour ceux qui vous suivront.

FORWARD

My Ancestors
My Children's Children
Preserving Family Histories
For Future Generations.

Inspired by family, friends and community, this book illustrates a century of adventure, a spectrum of cultural and historical events, and a lifetime of memories.

The autumn days have been enchanting, and inspiring. Lake Erie can deploy its fury at times but my peaceful haven, sheltered by the shimmering oaks bordering Lakeshore Road and cloaked in a multiple display of colours, remains a refuge of serenity. Yes, autumn 1995, in all its splendour and tranquillity, entices me, in the golden days of my life, to recapitulate a century while paying tribute to our ancestors, our culture, our churches, our schools, our relatives and our friends.

A Century of Heritage
A Century of Dedication
A Century of Values and Love
Our Pride for Generations to Come.

Hommage à la femme

Voici le message que je veux transmettre à toutes ces femmes militantes et géniales qui ont fait fructifier dans l'ombre de leur foyer leur ingéniosité et leurs talents dans les belles paroisses de Saint-Pierre, de Pain Court et de Grande Pointe depuis plus d'un siècle environ.

C'est par l'entremise de vos aspirations et de votre dévouement que nous avons vu grandir et fleurir notre petit coin de pays. Vous devez vous enorgueillir et je vous en félicite;

Vous avez épaulé
vos maris dans leurs
entreprises.

Vous avez rayonné
comme élites de
notre société.

Vous avez propagé
la foi de nos
ancêtres.

Vous avez vu
grandir nos familles
en âge et en sagesse.

Fondatrices et anges
de nos foyers, vous
avez contribué à l'éducation
des enfants ainsi
qu'à leurs besoins
ordinaires.

Vous avez invoqué
l'aide du Seigneur
en le priant de
bénir et de protéger
vos familles et
par là, vous avez pu voir
couronner l'accomplissement
de vos désirs et de
vos idéals.

Je vous invite donc, chères dames, à venir remercier tous ceux et celles qui ont collaboré dans vos entreprises et qui vous ont secondées et appuyées dans vos efforts. Par là, j'entends les maris, les bienfaiteurs, le clergé, les instituteurs et institutrices, les communautés religieuses, les conseils municipaux, les associations franco-ontariennes, les commissions scolaires et enfin, tous les compatriotes qui vous ont côtoyées. Ensemble, mes dames, vous avez cheminé dans l'espérance, malgré maintes tribulations, pour l'avancement de vos familles.

Je garde des souvenirs bien vivants du passé, souvenirs pleins de vie, de chaleur et d'amitié. Je souhaite que vous continuiez à rayonner avec ce goût de lumière, de vie et d'amour qui vous habitent. Je sens que c'est là votre force et la source de votre fécondité.

Que Dieu prenne toutes vos vies pour les transformer en des êtres de paix, de bonheur, de compassion et de tendresse.

"Sème la joie dans le jardin de ton frère et elle fleurira dans le tien."

Caroline Roy Laprise

Au-delà d'un tricentenaire et demi
de patrimoine historique et religieux.

"Et c'est ainsi qu'un peu plus que trois siècles et demi,
dans les régions marécageuses de notre péninsule d'Essex et Kent,
habitée alors par la tribu des Attawandarons, on retrouve le
Père Jean de Brébeuf et son confrère
Père Joseph-Marie Chaumonot plier bagages
et quitter pour de bon ces régions inhospitalières
en passant par la petite rivière-aux-cornes-de-cerf,
aujourd'hui la Thames . . ." [1]

Et jetant un dernier regard vers la petite
mission de Saint-Joseph déserte mais non oubliée,
dans les broussailles du comté de Kent d'alors.
Et traçant une large bénédiction . . . signe d'un aurevoir . . .
Et fidèles à la voie mystique qui les appelle.
Le courant les emporte vers la Huronie,
gibet de supplices agonisants,
terre ensanglantée et bénie du Fort Sainte-Marie.

1. Fragment tiré du spectacle centenaire de Pain Court (1854-1954), intitulé
"Sous le sourire de Notre Dame" s. g. c.

Les Martyrs Canadiens

Saint Jean de Brébeuf   (1593 - 1646)

Echon, comme l'appelaient les Hurons, était le vrai leader des apôtres de la Huronie. Il jouissait d'un grand prestige, qui venait en partie de la prestance de sa haute stature mais surtout de sa vie intérieure. Depuis longtemps, il vivait mystiquement la passion douloureuse de la nation huronne. Son martyre fut très cruel; il fut longuement charcuté et brûlé, avant de rendre le dernier soupir.

Saint René Goupil   (1607 - 1642)

Ce "donné" était chirurgien de son métier et connu pour sa charité et son entregent. Fait prisonnier avec le Père Jogues, alors qu'il était en route pour la Huronie, il fut emmené en Iroquoisie. Il fut abbatu d'un coup de hache alors qu'il faisait une croix sur le front d'un jeune Indien. À Auriesville, dans "Le Ravin", on peut suivre pas à pas les dernières heures du médecin.

Saint Isaac Jogues   (1607 - 1646)

Ce prêtre Jésuite avait un don exceptionnel d'adaptation à la vie des Indiens; il en était admiré et apprécié. Arrêté une première fois avec saint René Goupil, il fut torturé puis adopté par une famille indienne. Il s'évada par New Amsterdam. Après un court séjour en France, il revint au pays et fut envoyé comme ambassadeur en Iroquoisie; il fut mis à mort, à Auriesville.

Saint Jean de la Lande   (+ - 1646)

Il était lui aussi un "donné" de la Compagnie de Jésus. Il accompagna le Père Jogues en Iroquoisie. Il vit mourir son compagnon, fut torturé puis abattu d'un coup de tomahawk.

Saint Antoine Daniel   (1601 - 1648)

Il a séjourné 14 ans, en Huronie. Il avait un don spécial pour évangéliser les jeunes. Il venait de célébrer l'Eucharistie, quand on attaqua son village; il fut abattu devant la chapelle.

Saint Gabriel Lalemant   (1610 - 1649)

Autant Brébeuf était vigoureux, autant Lalemant était malingre, mais il y avait en lui une grande force intérieure. À peine arrivé en Huronie, il est fait prisonnier avec le Père de Brébeuf. Son supplice fut interminable; il commença en même temps que celui de saint Jean de Brébeuf et ne prit fin que le lendemain.

Saint Charles Garnier   (1610 - 1649)

Il avait reçu en partage le charisme de l'entregent et de l'amabilité; il était chez les Pétuneux, quand il fut abattu alors qu'il prêtait assistance à un Indien mourant.

Saint Noël Chabanel   (1613 - 1649)

Il éprouvait une répugnance naturelle pour tout ce qui a trait à la vie indienne; il fit le voeu de rester missionnaire auprès des Indiens, selon la volonté de ses Supérieurs. Alors qu'il accompagnait le Pétuneux en fuite devant les Iroquois, il fut tué par un Huron apostat.

Articles: Almanach Populaire Catholique 1992,
      Revue Sainte-Anne p. 108, 109, 110, P. 108 - 110

Saint Jean de Brébeuf et Joseph Chiwatenwa
André Leprise, 1999

**À l'aube de ce nouveau millénaire je suis privilégiée de
vous présenter mon patrimoine ancestral.**

Mon père
Adolphe Roy
né le 13 août 1895
fils de Thomas Roy et Charline Ouellette
et descendant d'André Roy et de Bridget Hickey

Ma mère
Délia Caron
née le 13 février 1899,
fille de Médéric Caron et de Elmire Faubert
et descendante de Moïse Caron et de Antoine Faubert.

Le prologue "La paroisse de Pain Court" est une causerie donnée au 18e congrès annuel de la Société Canadienne d'Histoire de l'Église Catholique à Windsor, Ontario, en septembre 1951, préparée par le Père Vincent Caron (1906 - 1971) un descendant de Moïse Caron.

En mai 1968, à Ottawa, j'avais organisé une fête de reconnaissance pour le Père Vincent Caron en témoignage d'admiration et de remerciement pour ses trente années et plus comme professeur de théologie morale à la Faculté de Théologie de l'Université d'Ottawa. À cette occasion, il me présente quelques-uns de ses écrits y inclus le prologue en me disant tout bonnement:

"Ça pourrait te servir plus tard pour rehausser, en sorte, notre patrimoine."

FÊTE DE RECONNAISSANCE – Une vingtaine d'étudiants de la région de Pain Court, Ontario, se sont réunis, mardi, pour fêter le R. P. Vincent Caron, o.m.i. Le Père Caron, originaire lui-même de Pain Court, est professeur à l'Université d'Ottawa et a enseigné la théologie morale pendant plus de 30 ans. Les étudiants et les étudiantes qui participaient à la fête suivent tous des cours dans des institutions d'Ottawa. On reconnaît, en avant, de gauche à droite, Mlle Marguerite Bélanger, de l'École normale d'Ottawa, le Père Caron, et Mlle Claire Faubert, du collège Bruyère; en arrière, Louis Blais, de l'École normale, et Louis Caron de l'Université d'Ottawa.

(Photo Champlain Mercil)   Mai 1968

LA PAROISSE

DE

PAIN COURT

Ottawa, Ont.

1951

La paroisse de Pain Court

Origine du nom: Pain Court est un nom français bien savoureux dont l'origine remonte à l'établissement des premiers colons dans cette partie du pays. « C'est la misère extrême de nos ancêtres qui a donné le jour au nom de Pain Court ». Au début du siècle dernier, quelques colons canadiens-français étaient établis du côté nord-ouest de la rivière à La Tranche, à une courte distance de son embouchure, le long d'un petit ruisseau. Ils étaient très pauvres et le blé qu'ils avaient récolté parmi les souches dans de petits «abbatis» était peu abondant. Le moulin à farine le plus rapproché était à Détroit et ils n'avaient d'autres moyens de s'y rendre qu'en canot en été ou sur la glace en hiver, une distance d'environ 50 milles. Souvent ils se trouvaient forcés de moudre leur blé à la main avec un pilon de bois sur une pierre ou une buche creusée. La farine était substantielle et le pain nourrissant, mais il n'y en avait pas toujours pour que toute la famille puisse en avoir chaque jour de l'année. En ce temps-là, l'église la plus rapprochée et la seule pour toute la région était l'Assomption de Sandwich. Il arrivait à ces bons colons d'avoir le bonheur, l'une ou l'autre fois durant l'année, d'une visite du missionnaire, qui ne pouvait pas facilement s'annoncer. Cette visite coïncidait souvent avec une période de disette où on n'avait plus de pain. « Pour s'excuser de leur pauvreté les chefs de famille disaient aux missionnaires: nous n'avons pas de pain, le blé a péri, ou, nous avons tout mangé ». D'autres fois ils conservaient pieusement un peu de farine pour en faire un petit pain au missionnaire lorsqu'il viendrait et ils lui disaient: « notre pain est court, tout petit, mais nous vous le donnons de bon coeur ». L'histoire se répétait souvent et quand le missionnaire partait pour la mission de la rivière à La Tranche, il disait: « Je m'en vais dans la mission du pain court », on tout simplement : « Je m'en vais à Pain Court ». Le nom prit bien dans tout le pays car il était expressif ; il faisait comprendre la grande disette chez nos pères. Comme la paroisse n'avait pas encore de nom officiel on s'habitua tranquillement à appeler cette partie du pays: Pain Court, et ce nom prit racine pour toujours. [1.] »

Dès 1829, le nom de Pain Court était reconnu au moins officieusement quand Charles Rankin vint faire l'arpentage de ce qu'il appela le « Pain Court Block ». Il est aussi reconnu par le conseil municipal de Dover dont le livre des minutes rapporte que, dès la première année, 1848, les réunions mensuelles du conseil avaient lieu le plus souvent dans l'école de Pain Court ; quelques fois cependant dans l'hôtel de Louis Bétourney. Jusqu'en 1860, il n'y avait pas d'autre nom pour désigner Pain Court.

Vers 1852, la première année de l'existence de la paroisse, les gens avaient demandé au Gouvernement de leur accorder un bureau de poste et de le nommer «L'Immaculée-Conception » ; mais il n'était pas trop porté à accorder des faveurs aux Canadiens français. Ce n'est qu'après huit ans qu'une réponse arriva : le bureau de poste était accordé, mais le nom demandé était rejeté et celui de « Dover South » imposé, à la grande déception des gens. La raison en était, rapporte un certain M. Bourassa, député de Saint-Jean, que le nom « L'Immaculée-Conception » était trop français et trop catholique pour un bureau de poste. Les gens du Gouvernement étaient persuadés alors que cette minorité de Canadiens français émigrés et tout entourés d'Anglais, finirait par disparaître comme les naturels du pays. Ils se sont trompés. Le nom de Pain court est resté enraciné et a survécu, bien que ce ne soit qu'en 1911 qu'il ait été reconnu officiellement pour le nom du bureau de poste, grâce au patriotisme du regretté Père Emery. Et Pain Court en est arrivé à son centenaire d'existence, et l'Immaculée-Conception, notre patronne, l'a toujours gardé catholique et canadien-français.

Les premiers missionnaires; La paroisse de Pain Court est située dans le township actuel de Dover, comté de Kent. Rattachée originairement à celle de Saint-Pierre, elle avait pour limites, avant la fondation de la paroisse de Grande Pointe, toute cette partie de territoire comprise entre la rivière Thames, le lac Sainte-Claire et la Little Bear Line, dans toute sa longueur.

Il n'est pas impossible d'admettre le passage du saint martyr Jean de Brébeuf en notre paroisse ; et ce qui est encore plus probable c'est sa présence prolongée dans un village sauvage situé autrefois près de l'église actuelle de Saint-Pierre. En effet, les Relations des Jésuites nous apprennent que les Pères Jean de Brébeuf et Joseph-Marie Chaumonot, alors qu'ils étaient à la mission Sainte-Marie, en Huronie, près de la baie Georgienne, firent un voyage du 2 novembre 1640 au 19 mars 1641, se rendant dans cette partie de la péninsule. Ils avaient résolu d'établir la mission des Saints-Anges parmi les Attiouandarons, surnommés Nation Neutre, afin de leur annoncer la parole de Dieu et les mystères de notre sainte foi. Tout le pays ontarien au nord du lac Erié, depuis Niagara jusqu'au Détroit, était alors habité par cette nation qui avait une population d'au moins 12,000 âmes, établie dans une quarantaine de bourgades.

« *Les Pères ont parcouru en leur voyage dix-huit bourgs ou bourgades, à toutes lesquelles ils ont donné un nom chrétien... Ils se sont arrêtés particulièrement à dix* » contenant « *cinq cents feux et 3,000 personnes auxquelles ils ont proposé et publié l'Évangile... En ces dix-huit bourgs qu'ils ont visités, il ne s'en est trouvé qu'un à savoir Khioetoa, surnommé de saint Michel, qui leur ait donné l'audience que méritait leur ambassade* » et où « *les Pères firent le premier baptême d'adulte en la personne d'une bonne vieille qui avait déjà presque perdu l'ouïe [2].* »

Le Père Chaumonot dessina une carte de leur tournée missionnaire. Elle n'existe plus, mais en 1656 Sanson, géographe du roi, et en 1664 Du Creux, l'historien jésuite, s'en seraient inspirés pour faire leurs cartes géographiques de la région des grands lacs, sur lesquelles sont indiqués ces dix villages que visitèrent les missionnaires ; deux de ces villages sembleraient avoir été situés dans le comté actuel de Kent : Saint-Joseph et Saint-Michel. D'après plusieurs historiens [3] Khioetoa ou Saint-Michel aurait été situé du côté sud de la rivière Thames, à l'est de Jeannette's Creek, sur le lot 5 de Tilbury East, dans le voisinage de l'église de Saint-Pierre, (située sur le lot no 1) et Saint-Joseph, probablement près de Clearville dans le township d'Orford, à 3 milles du lac Erié, ou bien, près du cimetière de Chatham. Un troisième village se trouvait dans les environs de Sarnia. Il est donc vraisemblable que notre paroisse ait été visitée par ces saints missionnaires deux siècles avant sa fondation.

Moins de dix ans après ce voyage des missionnaires, les Attiouandarons avaient cessé d'exister comme nation, les Iroquois les ayant défaits immédiatement après avoir exterminé la nation huronne, incendié toutes les missions, et torturé le Père de Brébeuf et plusieurs de ses compagnons. Cependant, le pays ne cessa pas d'être habité par des groupements épars de diverses tribus sauvages, ou de servir de terrain de chasse à celles des contrées voisines. Durant de longues années, pour s'y rendre, les Indiens sillonnèrent en canots d'écorce les eaux calmes de l'Escunnisepe, la rivière aux Cornes de Cerfs, à laquelle les explorateurs français ont donné le nom pittoresque de rivière à La Tranche puisqu'elle semblait trancher à travers la forêt majestueuse; nom trop français, que Lord John G. Simcoe substitua sans raison pour celui de River Thames en 1793, la troisième année qu'il était lieutenant gouverneur de la Province.

Cession et arpentage des terres : Après la révolution américaine, un grand nombre de loyalistes et d'autres personnes qualifiées de Détroit, désireux d'avoir des terres dans cette région fertile du pays, firent pression auprès du Gouvernement, l'obligeant d'acquérir pour la couronne tout ce territoire situé entre les lacs Erié et Sainte-Claire et le long de la rivière à La Tranche, et qui, de par le droit naturel, appartenait encore aux Indiens, afin de pouvoir ainsi le repartir parmi les nombreux appliquants.

Le 19 mai 1790, un grand conseil fut convoqué à l'Assomption de Sandwich par le Colonel Alexander McKee, auquel prirent part les représentants de la Couronne et les chefs des Chippewas, des Hurons, des Ottawas et des Pottawatomies. Le 21 mai, un document sur parchemin était préparé par lequel ces chefs indiens s'engageaient à céder au Roi Georges III la majeure partie du territoire comprenant les comtés actuels de Kent, Essex, Elgin et une partie de Middlesex, ne se réservant que deux petits carrés de terre de 6 par 7 milles, le long de la rivière de Détroit, l'un aux environs de la rivière aux Canards et l'autre près de l'église de l'Assomption. Les agents du Roi y apposèrent leurs signatures et les chefs indiens leurs totems. Tout ce territoire fut acheté pour la somme de £1,200, payée en marchandises.

Deux jours après la signature de ce traité, le ministère des terres ordonnait à l'arpenteur-adjoint Patrick McNiff de commencer à délimiter les townships, les concessions et les lots de terre. Il entreprit d'abord de faire l'inspection générale de la contrée, ébaucha une carte de la rivière à La Tranche et des terres qu'elle traverse, depuis son embouchure jusqu'au delà du site actuel de Chatham, prenant soigneusement en note toutes ses observations. Remontant la rivière par le lac Sainte-Claire, il remarqua que de chaque côté, pour une distance d'environ six milles il ne se trouvait que quelques touffes dispersées d'arbres, mais des marais et de vastes prairies naturelles généralement asséchées et s'étendant à perte de vue du côté gauche (de Dover) vers le N.N.E., jusqu'au Chenail Ecarté; tandis que du côté droit, elles s'étendaient à moins de distance. Il admira la nature du sol : une terre noire avec un fond glaiseux, excellente pour la culture du blé et du maïs. La limite de ces six milles serait à peu près là où se trouve l'église de Saint-Pierre aujourd'hui, le lot No 1 de Tilbury East. Au delà commençait, des deux côtés de la rivière, la forêt dense de bois franc, chêne, noyer noir, érable, frêne, entrecoupée de marécages et de quelques prairies ouvertes.

M. McNiff trouva 27 habitations construites en pièces sur pièces, huit sur la rive nord et toutes les autres sur la rive sud: quelques unes vacantes, la plupart habitées; et il indiqua sur sa carte le nom de chaque propriétaire. La plupart était des « squatters », quelques-uns détenaient leurs propriétés en vertu de contrats privés avec les Indiens. Il est probable que les rives de la rivière de La Tranche aient été habitées dès 1775 ou 1780. En 1781, McNiff fit l'arpentage des terres du devant, des townships actuels de Dover Est et de Raleigh, puis en 1793 continua dans les cantons de Dover West et Tilbury Est. De 1795 à 1803, Abraham Iredell continua le travail d'arpentage du comté de Kent et fut assisté par W. Hambly en 1804. Il délimita, au milieu de presque tous les townships des réserves connues sous le nom de « Crown Reserves » et de « Clergy Reserves ». Les profits de ces dernières étaient destinés à la sustentation du clergé anglican. Dans Dover la Clergy Reserve comprenait près de 9,000 acres, presque tous les lots entre le Ticky Tacky (Jacob) Road et la ligne Cul de Sac (Winter's Line) depuis la 5e jusqu'à la 11e concession inclusivement. Elle était administrée par George Thomas, un banquier de Chatham. La Crown Reserve comprenait presque tous les lots entre la Little Bear Line et la ligne Cul de Sac depuis la 5e jusqu'à la 11e concession, presque 10,000 acres de terre. Entre 1840 et 1846 elle passa à la Canada Land Company.

Nous avons la liste des noms de tous ceux qui appliquèrent pour des lots de terres le long de la rivière à La Tranche: 19 en 1789, 66 en 1790 et 36 en 1791. Entre 1792 et 1804 toutes ces terres longeant les deux rives, depuis l'embouchure de la rivière jusqu'au village de Chatham, avaient été distribuées à des colons dont il serait trop long ici d'énumérer la liste des noms. Presque tout l'arpentage de Dover fut terminé en 1809 et 1810 par Thomas Smith, à l'exception du « Pain Court Block » dont les lots ne furent mesurés qu'en 1829 par Charles Rankin. [4]

Pionniers de Pain Court : Il semble bien qu'en 1829, notre localité avait déjà été habitée depuis au moins une quinzaine d'années et que les pionniers s'y étaient établis comme « squatters » au milieu de la forêt vierge, le long du petit ruisseau depuis le Jacob Road en montant vers l'est. Nous apprenons leurs noms d'après un document du 13 septembre 1827, date où ils prêtèrent le serment de fidélité devant John Dolsen, commissaire :

Jean-Baptiste Faubert Sr (62 ans, natif du Bas Canada, habite sur son lot depuis 20 ans ; a une famille de 7 enfants dont 2 filles encore avec lui ; a une maison, une grange, 10 acres de terrain défriché). Jean-Baptiste Martel (45 ans, natif du Bas Canada, servit durant la guerre ; a une maison, 10 acres de terre cultivée ; a un fils et 3 filles, 1 enfant décédé ; 9 ans de résidence). Pierre Réaume (43 ans, natif de Dover, a 7 acres de terre cultivée avec une maison, une étable ; a 4 fils, 3 filles; 8 ans de résidence). Gabriel Bergeron (53 ans, natif du Bas Canada ; a 3 ½ acres de terre cultivée avec maison; a récolté du blé d'Inde en 1826; 2 ans de résidence). Isaac Charron (a 6 acres clôturées avec une maison; 3 ans de résidence). Michel Deloge (26 ans, natif de Dover). Louis Dézilet (30 ans, né en Bas Canada). André Charron (33 ans, natif de Dover).
Jean-Baptiste Primeau.

Ils avaient tous porté les armes, à l'exception de trois, (probablement les derniers parce que trop jeunes alors) dans la Kent Militia, pour la défense du Canada contre l'invasion américaine ; c'est pourquoi ils espéraient que le Gouvernement ne les dérangerait pas et leur accorderait un jour les propriétés qu'ils occupaient de bonne foi. Mais un certain James Askin de Détroit, capitaine durant la guerre de 1814, ayant appris, à leur insu, que ces terres étaient à distribuer par le Ministère des terres, en obtint les papiers d'allocation et se rendit auprès d'eux, les avertir de cesser l'amélioration de leurs terres puisqu'il en était devenu le légitime propriétaire. Ils n'étaient pas hommes à s'en laisser imposer si facilement ni à se départir des quelques arpents qu'ils avaient défrichés de peine et de misère. Bien qu'illettrés, ils firent préparer une pétition signée de leurs marques et adressée au lieutenant gouverneur, Sir Peregrine Maitland, réclamant justice. Justice leur fut rendue par le Gouvernement le 25 octobre 1825. L'allocation de M. Askin fut annulée, pour la raison que les terres étaient antérieurement occupées par des habitants du pays, à l'insu du Governement, mais apparemment au su de M. Askin. Permission lui fut accordée cependant de réclamer ailleurs son allocation de terrain de dimension égale. Quant aux supliants, il leur fut recommandé de fournir, à leurs propres frais, un rapport d'arpenteur de leurs propriétés respectives, qui leur seraient définitivement octroyées, n'excédant pas 100 acres chacune.

L'arpenteur Charles Rankin vint mesurer les propriétés du Pain Court Block en 1829, et le plan qu'il traça l'année suivante, y indique quelques autres propriétaires, en outre des pionniers mentionnés : John McDonald, Edmund Baby, Alexis Urquhart, Ladéroute, Jean-Baptiste Cadieux, Robert Crow, Léon Matte et Wm. McCrea. En examinant attentivement ce plan, il ne semble pas que tous ces propriétaires habitaient leurs lots, car on ne compte que treize maisons construites le long du ruisseau, onze du côté nord et deux du côté sud. Le Pain Court Block comprenait 15 lots d'inégales dimensions, numérotés de 1 à 15, avec une superficie de 695.3 acres, auxquels

s'ajoutaient 4 autres lots d'environ 50 acres chacun ; soit en tout 895 acres. [5]
Le Registre du township de Dover indique les noms d'autres Canadiens français établis dans le voisinage de Pain Court : dans Dover est, sur la 1ère concession, No 3 Rémi Campeau, 1797 ; No 4 Fontenay Dequindre, 1805 ; No 5 Marie-J. Gouin, 1804 ; 2e Conc., No 10 Jean-B. Bénéteau, 1802 ; No 11 Jean-B. Riché, 1825. Dans Dover ouest, 1ère Con., No 1 Paul Caron, 1797 ; No 7 Esther Trudell, 1809 ; No 9 André Bénéteau, 1798 ; No 10 André Lafleur, 1802 ; No 11 J-B. Marsac, 1798 ; 2e Conc., No 4 Pierre Langlois, 1802 ; No 5 Alexis Langlois, 1798 ; No 6 Pierre Demers 1802.

Paroisses de l'Assomption et de Saint-Pierre :

L'histoire de la paroisse de l'Immaculée Conception de Pain Court est inséparablement reliée à celle des paroisses de l'Assomption de Sandwich et de Saint-Pierre sur la rivière à La Tranche. La première église de toute la région fut celle de Sainte-Anne de Détroit dont la fondation coïncide avec l'établissement du Fort Pontchartrain par le Chevalier de La Mothe Cadillac et une centaine de soldats et de colons français. Les Pères Récollets en furent les missionnaires durant 80 ans. La paroisse de l'Assomption a commencé vers 1728, n'étant d'abord qu'une petite mission pour les Hurons, et fut desservie durant plus d'un demi siècle par les deux Pères Jésuites Armand de la Richardie (1728-46) et Pierre Potier (1746-81). Leurs successeurs furent l'abbé Jean-François Hubert (1781-85) qui devint le neuvième (deuxième Canadien) évêque de Québec, et les Sulpiciens F. X. Dufaux (1786-96) et J.-B. Marchand (1796-1825) .

M. le curé Marchand, tout en étant curé de l'Assomption, fit construire deux chapelles ; celle de Saint-Pierre sur la rivière à la Tranche fut bénite le 8 juillet 1802, et celle de Saint-Jean-Baptiste de Malden (Amherstburg) en 1803. Il fut seul à les desservir pendant vingt ans. M. l'abbé Joseph Crevier lui fut envoyé comme vicaire à l'automne de 1816 et devint curé (1819-31) de l'Assomption, des deux missions déjà mentionnées, ainsi que de celle de Maidstone fondée en 1823. Il remplaça la première chapelle de Saint-Pierre devenue insuffisante. La nouvelle église, construite en bois et peinte en blanc, bien que modeste, était plus spacieuse. Elle fut ouverte au culte le 28 novembre 1824 et servit jusqu'en 1895, alors qu'elle fut détruite par le feu. M. Crevier eut comme vicaire M. l'abbé Joseph Fluet, jeune prêtre de 24 ans, dont on rencontre le nom dans le registre de Saint-Pierre, depuis le 19 octobre 1825 jusqu'au 2 mai 1831. Du 30 janvier 1832 au 27 août 1834, nous y trouvons les noms des prêtres suivants : Angus McDonnell, P. Foley, Charles-François Fitz-Maurice, George A. Hay et de l'évêque coadjuteur de Kingston R. Epps Tob. À l'automne de 1834, l'abbé Jean-Baptiste Morin, déjà âgé de 61 ans, est rappelé d'une mission au Kamouraska, et chargé de la paroisse de Saint-Pierre, qui embrassait alors le vaste territoire, dont furent détachées plus tard les paroisses de Belle Rivière, Saint-Joachim, Pointe-aux-Roches, Staples, Tilbury, Raleigh, Chatham, Pain Court, Grande Pointe, Wallaceburg, Lambton, Dresden, Thamesville, Bothwell et Blenheim. Le 16 septembre 1843, son nouvel évêque, Mgr Michel Power de Toronto, vient faire la visite pastorale, accompagné de l'abbé J.J. Ray. En 1846, l'abbé Jh. Billon succède à l'abbé Morin, qui s'en va recevoir sa récompense, le 10 décembre 1847, âgé de 74 ans. Ses restes reposent sous le sanctuaire de l'église de Saint-Pierre.

Il vaut la peine de noter quelques détails intéressants inscrits au registre de la paroisse : « Le 10 août 1847, bénédiction de la cloche à qui on a donné le nom des patrons de la paroisse (Saint-Pierre et Paul) par le R. P. Jaffré, missionnaire résidant à Sandwich. Le parrain a été Joseph Marie Billon, la marraine Mme George Jacob. Certifié par Jh. Billon, curé». Pour les années suivantes on remarque les signatures des prêtres suivants: Jean Vincent Jaffré, S.J. (fondateur de l'église de Chatham) 1848-50, J. Grimot, P.S.S. 1851 et Claude-Antoine Ternet 1851- 53. Le registre rapporte aussi que le 16 juillet 1851, Mgr de Charbonnel, évêque de Toronto, fait sa première visite à Saint-Pierre et administre le sacrement de confirmation à 289 personnes : 151 femmes et 138 hommes, dont tous les noms sont inscrits.

Chapelle à Pain Court :

À l'occasion de cette visite pastorale en juillet 1851, l'évêque s'était rendu compte de l'état exact de la paroisse de Saint-Pierre, de son immense territoire et de sa population nombreuse de l'autre côté de la rivière, (dans Dover). Sans tarder il avait nommé un nouveau curé, M. Claude-Antoine Ternet, P.S.S., âgé de 57 ans environ, « vicaire général avec des pouvoirs extraordinaires», qui arriva en septembre. Mais Monseigneur y revint lui-même, le 10 décembre de la même année, et chargea M. Ternet de faire construire une chapelle à Pain Court, en ajoutant certaines recommandations que le curé inscrit dans son nouveau registre le 1er janvier 1852 :

« Nous recommandons très expressément à M. Ternet de ne commencer une chapelle à Pain Court qu'après... avoir obtenu des intéressés une souscription en bonne forme équiva lente à la dépense nécessaire à la construction . . .»

Le site choisi pour l'érection de cette chapelle fut le lot No 13, en face du cimetière actuel. Les travaux ne languirent point et la construction fut très simple. Dans deux mois, ce modeste temple dont saint Joseph fut choisi comme patron, était inauguré, comme nous l'indique le document suivant :

« Le premier mars, mil huit cent cinquante deux, nous soussigné, Claude Antoine Ternet, curé de la Paroisse de Saint-Pierre de Raleigh, par le pouvoir reçu de Monseigneur de Charbonnel, Evêque de Toronto, avons fait la bénédiction solennelle de la petite chapelle que nous avons dédiée à Saint Joseph pour l'invoquer comme patron à Pain Court où nous avons fait nous même construire cette chapelle, dans l'heureuse espérance que dans la suite on y bâtira une église.»

Le petit sermon que l'abbé Ternet prononça en cette circonstance est inscrit au registre de la paroisse. Faute d'espace, il n'est pas possible de le transcrire ici.

D'après le recensement de 1851, le canton de Dover du comté de Kent, comptait plus de 1100 catholiques, environ 200 familles, la plupart canadiennes-françaises, une vingtaine de familles catholiques de langue anglaise et une quizaine de familles protestantes.

Canadiens français : Allaire 8, Alexandre 7 (2 fam.), Antaya 5, Baby 9, Bachand 8, Ballard 5, Béchard 26 (5 fam.), Bélanger 8 (2 fam.), Belleau 4 (2 fam.), Benoit 9 (2 fam.), Bernier 29 (5 fam.), Bertrand 8, Blais 8, Boucher 9 (2 fam), Bourrett 2, Brouillet 8, Campbell 22 (4 fam.), Carron 13 (2 fam.), Cassidy 5, Champagne 1, Charron 33 (5 fam.), Delant 1 (hôtelier), Deloge 14 (2 fam.), Drouillard 1, Dragon 1, Dubuque 5, Dumas 9, Emery 32 (4 fam.), Faubert 22 (3 fam.), Gervais 9 (2 fam.), Hébert 25 (4 fam.), Jubinville 18 (3 fam.), Labadie 26 (4 fam.), Ladéroute 4, Laiguille 7, Lamarche 8, Larch 4, Létourneau 17 (3 fam.), Lauzon 45 (7 fam.), Leboeuf 19 (2 fam.), Maillet 17 (2 fam.), Martin 7, Métivier 18 (3 fam.), Moran 2, Ouellette 17 (4 fam.), Paquette 8, Peltier 28 (4 fam.), Phaneuf 3, Poisant 3, Primeau 21 (3 fam.), Réaume 55 (10 fam.), Richer 19 (4 fam.), Robert 7 (2 fam.), Roy (King) 24 (3 fam.), Saint-Amour 10 (2 fam.), Saint-Germain 16 (2 fam.), Saint-Pierre 20 (3 fam.) , Sterling 27 (4 fam.), Toulouse 18 (2 fam.), Trudeau 1 (scribe), Trudell 8 (2 fam.), Turcotte 5, Urquhart 7 (2 fam.), Wood 17 (2 fam.), Yacks 7.

Catholiques de langue anglaise : Baker 6, Boyle 6, Crump 6, Dolsen 24 (4 fam.), Dunavan 6, Flood 1, Foster 6, Hock 3, Jacob 9, Bridget Hickey (adoptée), Lawless 7, McCart 2, McNamara 7, Morisson 6, Murphy 3, Tim Mulgeen âgé de 22 ans, maître d'école, O'Neil 9, Peck 7, Perry 3, Smith 7, Crow 20 (4 fam.).

Familles protestantes : Andrew, Bagnall, Babbitt, Carr, Clements, Clarke, Adam Crow, Cook, Jackson, Merritt, McLeod, McMullin, Murdoch, Peterkin, Smith, Thackeray.

Les habitations de toutes ces familles à cette époque, à part quelques rares exceptions, étaient des maisons construites de troncs d'arbres à un étage. La grande majorité des pères de familles étaient cultivateurs, quelques-uns de simples journaliers. Les jeunes gens, dès l'âge de 12 ans, étaient inscrits comme journaliers.

Chapelle à Grande Pointe : Deux mois seulement après l'inauguration de la nouvelle chapelle à Pain Court, une autre cérémonie semblable avait lieu à la Grande Pointe, présidée par le même curé Claude-Antoine Ternet. Il a soin de le noter au registre de la paroisse:

«Le 11 mai 1852, nous soussigné, Claude-Antoine Ternet, curé de la paroisse de Saint-Pierre de Raleigh, ayant fait construire une petite chapelle à la Grande Pointe, en avons fait la bénédiction solennelle et l'avons dédiée à Saint-Antoine Solitaire. »

Année jubilaire – Érection de Croix : L'année 1852 était une année jubilaire, que le Pape Pie IX, pour signaler son retour à Rome d'exil, annonça par une encyclique le 21 novembre 1851, publiant une indulgence plénière et invitant tous les fidèles de l'univers à la prière et à l'action de grâce. Le pieux et dévoué curé Ternet prépara ses paroissiens à gagner cette indulgence, organisa des processions extérieures avec l'érection et la bénédiction solennelle de trois Croix : le vendredi, 3 septembre 1852, à la Grande Pointe ; le 10 septembre à Pain Court et le 17 septembre à Millerode.

L'abbé Raynel – Première église : Peu de temps avant le départ de M. Ternet (27 juin 1853) l'abbé Jean-Thomas Raynel, Français, âgé de 31 ans, vient prendre charge de la paroisse de Saint-Pierre et de ses deux missions annexes, le 11 juin 1853. Sa première attribution est la construction d'une église à Pain Court. Dans une lettre du 28 juillet, Mgr de Charbonnel lui communique quelques précisions à ce sujet :

« 150 pieds de long sur 50 me paraissent être trop pour Pain Court présent et futur. . . Cependant faites pour le mieux ; mais point de dettes . . . Vous ne pouvez rien faire avant de m'avoir envoyé un contrat en bonnes formes donnant le terrain à la corpora tion épiscopale catholique et romaine du diocèse de Toronto en Canada . . . et ainsi de toute opération semblable . . . »

Le terrain choisi se trouvait à l'endroit du cimetière actuel : une partie du lot 12ᵉ de la 2ᵉ concession. Ce lot complet de 200 acres avait été cédé par la Couronne, le 6 novembre 1841, à Thomas C. Street, qui en avait vendu la moitié du côté est à Isaac Gauthier pour £500, le 10 juin 1845. Cette propriété passa à Edouard Bertrand le 18 juillet suivant; il fit deux contrats avec la Corporation Episcopale du Diocèse de Toronto, cédant d'abord 4 ½ acres de la partie N.E. de son terrain pour £12,10 d, le 16 août 1853 et 3 ¾ acres de la partie est pour £ 15, le 27 avril 1854. Cette première partie de terrain avait été achetée pour un cimetière, dont le Père Raynel traça les limites, conformément à l'autorisation de l'Evêque. Depuis le 8 octobre 1852 jusqu'au 7 mars 1855, trente-trois adultes et un enfant y furent enterrés et l'acte de leur sépulture est inscrit dans le registre de l'église de Saint-Pierre.

Le samedi, 8 avril 1854, il y eut une assemblée paroissiale à l'entrée de la chapelle Saint-Joseph pour délibérer au sujet de la construction de la nouvelle église, et de l'adjudication des bancs. Depuis quelques années, il était beaucoup question de la définition du dogme de l'Immaculée Conception. Sa sainteté Pie IX avait envoyé une encyclique « Ubi primum » à tous les évêques et fidèles de l'univers, le 2 février 1849, demandant leur avis au sujet de l'opportunité d'une définition solennelle de cette croyance généralement reçue dans l'Eglise. Les réponses de toute la chrétienté furent joyeuses et enthousiastes et le Saint Père avait fixé la date de la proclamation de ce dogme au 8 décembre 1854. La patronne de notre église était tout désignée ; ce serait « L'Immaculée Conception », mais on conservait saint Joseph comme second patron.

Les travaux de construction commencèrent aussitôt au printemps et « le 31 août 1854 le très révérend Père Point, vicaire général du diocèse de Toronto, en remplaçant de Monseigneur de Charbonnel qui ne pouvait pas se rendre à Pain Court lui-même vient bénir les fondations et la

pierre fondamentale de l'église de l'Immaculée Conception, en présence du Père Jaffré, missionnaire de Chatham et de M. Moncoq, missionnaire de la rivière Sainte-Claire, et d'un grand nombre
de fidèles de Dover. »

Huit mois après, le dimanche 29 avril 1855, le très révérend Père Point retournait pour la
bénédiction solennelle de la nouvelle église terminée en présence d'une grande foule de fidèles
accourus des environs. Mais elle n'était terminée que grosso modo. Pratiquement il n'y avait de fini
que les murs et le toit. La voûte ne fut construite qu'en 1857 et 58, et les travaux continuèrent en
1861 et 62. Au dire des anciens de la paroisse, cette première église n'était pas orientée dans le
même sens que l'église actuelle, mais façait le ruisseau.

Entre temps toute cette partie sud-ouest de l'Ontario avait été détachée du diocèse de
Toronto par l'érection du diocèse de London, le 21 février 1856, et était passée sous la juridiction de
Mgr Adolphe Pinsonneault, qui fut sacré le 16 mai 1856. Le 4 septembre de cette même année, le
nouvel évêque vint visiter les églises de Saint-Pierre et de l'Immaculée Conception. Il donna le
sacrement de confirmation à 15 garçons et 12 filles à Saint-Pierre, et fit quelques ordonnances relatives aux limites de toute la paroisse y compris les missions qui en dépendaient: l'Immaculée
Conception, Saint-Antoine, Saint François-Xavier et Saint-Patrice ; relatives aussi à leur desserte
alternative, aux droits du curé, au comité paroissial et à la réserve du Saint Sacrement. En 1858, le
Père Raynel s'absente de sa paroisse pour deux mois (du 4 février au 31 mars) et est remplacé
par M. Barthélemy Boubat.

Peu après son retour, le 10 avril 1858, Mgr L'Evêque lui annonce par lettre qu'il « sépare de
Saint-Pierre de Raleigh toute la partie de cette ancienne paroisse qui se trouve dans le town
ship de Dover et en forme la nouvelle paroisse de l'Immaculée Conception, qui a pour limite
Sud la Rivière La Tamise, Ouest et Nord le Lac Sainte-Claire et Est la ligne appelée Bearline
entre les Nos 18 et 19. D'après la même décision sa grandeur choisit Saint Joseph pour sec
ond patron de la dite église et la dite paroisse. —Jean Raynel ptre. »

Jusqu'à date il ne semble pas qu'il y ait eu de presbytère à Pain Court pour habiter le curé.
Cependant il dut en avoir fait bâtir un récemment, puisque le 8 novembre 1858, il fait la « liste des
objets appartenant au presbytère de Saint-Pierre de Raleigh, qui, sur l'avis du Père Point, vicaire
général et de M. Musart, prêtre, ont été transportés dans le presbytère de l'Immaculée Conception».

Départ du Père Raynel, 1er octobre 1859 : Il y avait plus de six ans que le curé Raynel était
dans notre région. Il avait été un véritable missionnaire au coeur sensible, charitable et dévoué ; il
avait connu et partagé les peines et les misères de ses paroissiens. Souvent ces cultivateurs
n'avaient pas de blé pour la semence, ni même pour donner chaque jour du pain à leurs familles.
N'osant pas leur demander l'argent qu'ils ne possédaient pas, il avait payé de ses propres sous
une partie de la dette de l'église de l'Immaculée Conception. La paroisse lui était redevable de
$2,833,68. Il avait tenu son évêque au courant. Considérant les difficultés inconcevables que le
bon curé devait endurer, Monseigneur le retira de la paroisse et le fit curé de sa cathédrale à
Sandwich, où il avait transféré son siège épiscopal en février 1859. Mais avant de partir, M. Raynel
avait offert de substituer cette dette par une fondation de messes et de prière qui seraient dites à
ses intentions par ses successeurs et les paroissiens. L'évêque approuva le tout en substance, y
faisant néanmoins quelques réserves.

Durant deux ans, la paroisse est desservie par l'abbé Gilbert-Victor Girard (2 oct. 1859 au 10
déc. 1860) et M. Joseph Grimot, P.S.S. (25 déc. 1860 à avril 1861). Mais ces prêtres sont déjà
surchargés par ailleurs et ne peuvent rendre aux paroissiens de Pain Court les services auxquels ils
étaient accoutumés. C'est pourquoi ces pauvres paroissiens ne tardent pas à regretter le départ de

leur bon et dévoué curé Raynel et demandent avec instance à l'évêque de le leur renvoyer.

Retour de M. Raynel : Après une longue attente, Mgr Pinsonneault se rend à leur demande à condition qu'ils soient plus fidèles à remplir leurs devoirs et leurs obligations envers l'église et envers leur pasteur. Monsieur le curé Raynel est donc renvoyé à Pain Court, le 1er septembre 1861; mais les paroissiens oublièrent bientôt leur promesse et le pauvre prêtre eut encore beaucoup à souffrir, comme le laisse soupçonner les lettres de réprimande que leur adressa l'évêque. Malgré les peines et les misères qu'il eut à endurer, l'abbé Raynel continua à administrer la paroisse de Pain Court durant huit autres années, ne s'absentant que l'espace d'un an, où il fut remplacé par un Oblat de Marie Immaculée, le Père Paul Andrieux (25 déc. 1863 — 10 nov. 1864). Durant ces huit années, peu d'événements remarquables sont inscrits au registre de la paroisse sinon l'érection de la neuvaine de Saint François-Xavier, la bénédiction d'une cloche et la nomination de nouveaux marguilliers. Le curé Raynel est un des grands curés qui sont passés à Pain Court. Durant ses quatorze années de ministère, il a accompli énormément pour la paroisse de l'Immaculée Conception. Exténué et à bout de force, il résigna le 17 octobre 1869. Après quelques années de soin et de repos à Montréal, il entra chez les Jésuites. Il continua à faire du ministère, et c'est en revenant de porter la communion à quelques malades, qu'il mourut subitement, le 13 avril 1888, âgé de 66 ans, après avoir été, pendant plusieurs années, un modèle d'édification à toute sa communauté. Il fut inhumé au Sault-au-Récollet.

Incendie de la première église : La première église de l'Immaculée Conception que le Père Raynel avait construite avec tant de peine, et qui était considérée comme un beau monument d'architecture dans le temps et pour le pays, n'exista pas longtemps. Elle fut détruite par le feu au mois de mai vers l'année 1874.

Deuxième église de Pain Court : L'abbé J.-Calixte Duprat, qui était curé depuis le 9 novembre 1869, commença immédiatement avec courage à faire des plans et à rassembler des fonds pour la construction d'une nouvelle église en brique. Le matériel fut fourni en partie par Edouard Fontaine, qui avait une briqueterie florissante dans le voisinage. L'architecte fut S.-M. Goddard et l'entrepreneur Antoine Delisle. L'église fut suffisamment terminée pour permettre au curé d'y célébrer

« la première grand-messe le dimanche 30 mai, 1875. Monseigneur John Walsh vint faire la bénédiction solennelle le mardi 8 juin 1875. Les prêtres suivants étaient présents, à part du curé J.C. Duprat : Jas. Murphy, Dean, Irishtown, B. M. Gauran de Québec, E. L. McFahan de Belle Rivière, P. Villeneuve de St. Francis, Jos. Girard de Biddulph, P. Fauteux de Stony Point, B. J. Walters de Corunna, J. Hours, C. S. B. de Chatham, P. Andrieux de Sainte-Anne, Grand de Chatham, J. A. Caissé de Montréal, J. Boubat de Sarnia et D. Flannery de St. Thomas. »

Ce n'est qu'en 1885, que l'intérieur de l'église fut terminé et la cloche installée dans le clocher par l'abbé Joseph Bauer. Mais de fait cette église ne fut jamais une construction bien faite et solide. Le curé Duprat ne put pas précisément faire bombance durant son séjour à Pain Court ; car, d'après le livre de compte, ses quêtes du dimanche étaient plutôt lamentables. Voici le montant de quelques unes de ses collectes du dimanche en 1876 :

« le 23 janvier : 38 sous; 13 fév.: 54 sous ; 27 fév.: 29 sous ; 12 mars : 26 sous ; 26 mars : 18 sous ; 16 avril: 35 sous., 30 avril: $1.66 ; 23 mai : 33 sous ; 4 juin : 42 sous ; 30 juil. : 67 sous ; 20 août : 52 sous ; 10 sept. : 15 sous. En tout la quête du dimanche en 1876 lui rapporta la somme de $104.88. L'année suivante il eut $1. 47 à la quête de Noël.»

En 1882, (le 26 janvier) M. Duprat fut obligé de se retirer du ministère, à cause d'une grande surdité qui le rendait inapte aux fonctions du ministère. Il se retira à l'hospice de la Providence à l'Assomption. Quelques années avant de mourir, il retourna à Pain Court où il est décédé, le 20 mars 1901, à l'âge de 72 ans, et fut enterré dans le cimetière de Pain Court.

Les curés Bauer et Villeneuve : M. Joseph Bauer (né en Alsace-Lorraine en 1839) devint curé en janvier 1882. Ce fut un homme énergique, et les anciens se souviennent que peu de temps après son arrivée à Pain Court, il avertit les paroissiens : « J'ai été envoyé pour vous tondre et je vais vous tondre ; et ils ajoutent : « Il nous a tondus aussi.» Il fit ériger un presbytère en brique, qui existe encore aujourd'hui. Il termina l'intérieur de l'église de Pain Court, et fit construire, en 1884, l'église de Saint-Philippe, à la Grande Pointe qu'il deservait alors. M. Bauer ne semble pas avoir été très prudent en affaires cependant ; car son successeur, l'abbé A.P. Villeneuve, (13 mars 1886 au 2 août 1888) hérita d'une dette considérable, qu'il acquitta en assez peu de temps. Trois ans avant la construction de l'église de Saint-Philippe, le curé de Pain Court avait environ 325 familles inscrites dans son registre. Mgr John Walsh, en une lettre du 26 juin 1886, détermina que la route entre la 6e et la 7e concession du township de Dover servirait de limite entre Pain Court et Grande Pointe.

Les curés Andrieux et Courtois : Le successeur de l'abbé Villeneuve fut le Père Paul Andrieux, o. m. i., qui connaissait déjà la paroisse, pour y avoir exercé le ministère durant l'année 1863-64. Né en France en 1825, ordonné prêtre à Ottawa par Mgr Guigues, o.m.i., il avait passé les dix premières années de sa vie sacerdotale (1850-60)chez les sauvages, puis vint dans le diocèse de London desservir les centres canadiens-français. Pendant quinze ans, (1873-88) il fut curé de Sainte-Anne de Tecumseh où il bâtit une église ; curé de Pain Court durant plus de douze ans, (8 août 1888 au 16 janvier 1901) et enfin de Belle Rivière, de 1901 à 1904. Âgé et malade, il dut se retirer à Windsor, où il est décédé le 15 décembre 1919, à l'âge de 94 ans, dont 69 passés au service de Dieu et de l'Eglise. Ses restes reposent dans le cimetière de Tecumseh.

Le dixième curé de Pain Court fut l'abbé Joseph-Edouard Courtois, né à Gentilly, diocèse de Nicolet, le 21 août 1862, ordonné prêtre à London le 25 août 1889 par Mgr John Walsh. Après une année de ministère à Windsor, il devint curé de French Settlement, durant onze ans. Il arriva à Pain Court le 16 janvier 1901.

L'église qui n'était vieille pourtant que de 25 ans, avait besoin d'être remplacée. Les intempéries des saisons avaient endommagé prématurément cette construction, dont la maçonnerie était de qualité inférieure : les murs se désagrégeaient, les plâtrages tombaient. L'évêque de London, Mgr McEvay, l'avait jugée dangereuse, et en avait averti le curé et les gens. Cependant, le Père Courtois ne se sentit pas la force d'entreprendre une nouvelle construction, et fut nommé curé de Saint-Joachim, où il est décédé l'année suivante, le 14 avril 1912, après une courte maladie.

M. le curé A.D. Emery : Peu de temps après son élévation au siège épiscopal de London, Mgr Michael F. Fallon nomma le Père Alfred-David Emery curé de Pain Court, précisément pour y construire une nouvelle église et un nouveau presbytère. Ses talents d'organisation et son savoir-faire manifestés durant sept ans à Kinkora, ainsi que son succès dans la construction d'une école et d'un presbytère, la rénovation à neuf de l'église et l'établissement d'une école séparée, le désignèrent aux yeux de l'évêque comme étant l'homme qu'il fallait pour la paroisse de Pain Court. Originaire de la Grande Pointe, où il naquit le 22 mai 1873, le Père Emery connaissait bien notre population et ses besoins. Arrivé à Pain Court le 25 janvier 1911, il gagne vite l'estime et la confiance de tous les paroissiens, et les intéresse aussitôt à la construction de l'église. En peu de temps, ses plans sont faits et tout est organisé. Le transport des matériaux commence vers la fin du mois de mars, les fondations le 10 mai, et le dimanche, 11 juin, Mgr Fallon, en présence d'un grand nombre de prêtres et de fidèles, accourus des paroisses environnantes, bénit la pierre angulaire. Le dimanche, 3 mars, de l'année suivante, l'église est terminée, bénite et ouverte au culte divin ; dix mois seulement après le commencement des travaux.

Cette église était de style roman. Elle était surmontée d'un clocher et de deux clochetons que l'on pouvait voir de toute la campagne environnante. Au-dessus de la porte d'entrée à une hauteur assez élevée, une niche contenait une statue de l'Immaculée Conception, patronne de la paroisse ; une autre semblable se trouvait au-dessus du maître-autel. Les statues des douze apôtres, de saint Jean-Baptiste, de saint Joseph, de sainte Anne, de saint Dominique et de sainte Thérèse avaient leur place dans le sanctuaire, au-dessus des autels latéraux, ou autour de la nef. Les stations du chemin de la Croix étaient de grands tableaux encadrés, de la Passion de Notre-Seigneur. Le jubé était spacieux. Cette église, pouvant asseoir environ 600 personnes, était claire et belle ; elle inspirait la piété et élevait les coeurs vers Dieu. Elle avait coûté $ 44,000. et le presbytère, qui fut construit la même année, en avait coûté $ 6,000. Mais les paroissiens en étaient fiers et avaient déjà payé la moitié de cette dette en 1921.

Au mois de janvier 1914, le Père Emery fonda le Bulletin Paroissial, qu'il fit paraître régulièrement tous les mois, tout le temps qu'il fut à Pain Court. Pour commémorer le 65e anniversaire de la première messe célébrée dans la paroisse, le 1er mars 1852, il fit ériger à l'entrée du cimetière un calvaire en bronze, qui fut béni le 25 mai 1917. Dès le commencement de la première guerre mondiale et de la terrible épidémie de grippe qui sévit à travers le monde, notre bon curé consacra la paroisse au Sacré-Coeur et faisait chanter en choeur tous les dimanches l'invocation : «Protégez nos familles par votre Sacré-Coeur». Pas une seule personne de la paroisse ne fut victime d'aucune de ces calamités. En actions de grâces et en souvenir de cette faveur, le Père Emery, avec la généreuse coopération des paroissiens, fit ériger, dans la cour de l'église, une magnifique statue en bronze représentant le Sacré-Coeur et installée sur un monument en pierre portant l'inscription : « Sacré-Coeur de Jésus, protégez nos familles. 1919 ». Cette statue fut dévoilée et bénite par Mgr D. O'Connor, vicaire général du diocèse, immédiatement après la grand-messe, le 1er juin 1919.

Le Couvent — Les Soeurs de Saint-Joseph : Il manquait encore une oeuvre de prime importance dans la paroisse, une oeuvre qui collaborerait avec le ministère du prêtre, en faciliterait la tâche et en assurerait l'efficacité permanente : l'établissement d'une communauté religieuse d'institutrices à laquelle serait confiée l'éducation des enfants. Toutes les démarches que notre dévoué curé dut entreprendre pour la réalisation de ce désir ne nous sont pas encore connues ; mais il avoue lui-même que des difficultés innombrables se dressèrent de tous côtés, et faillirent lui faire perdre tout espoir de réussite à certains moments. Il devait à la fois négocier avec l'évêque, les religieuses et la commission scolaire. Sous son initiative, les commissaires firent construire un couvent, qui fut terminé en 1923, et la Supérieure Générale des Soeurs de Saint-Joseph accepta l'invitation d'y envoyer des religieuses, avec l'approbation de Mgr Fallon. Mais comme le couvent était construit sur la propriété de l'église, on ne voulut pas permettre aux Soeurs d'y habiter, avant que ce terrain ne fut vendu à la commission scolaire, par un contrat en forme. Cependant, en septembre 1923, les deux permières religieuses, soeurs Hilaire et Anna-Marie commencèrent à enseigner à l'école du village, voyageant matin et soir entre Pain Court et l'hôpital Saint-Joseph de Chatham, où elles résidaient temporairement. Le jour de l'ouverture des classes, elles firent l'inscription de 70 élèves dont 40 dans la classe inférieure et 30 dans la classe supérieure. Finalement le contrat fut signé, par lequel la Corporation Episcopale du diocèse de London vendait le terrain du couvent à la commission scolaire, et le 4 décembre 1923, Soeur Scolastique, supérieure, accompagnée des soeurs Hilaire, Laurentia et Anna-Marie, vint prendre possession du beau couvent qui leur avait été préparé, et le lendemain le Père Emery disait la messe dans leur chapelle pour la première fois.

Envers les Soeurs il manifesta toujours une sollicitude paternelle, de même que les paroissiens, une bienveillante générosité et les enfants une grande docilité respectueuse. Dès les premières années, le progrès des enfants fut remarquable à l'école, aux examens et dans leur conduite en général. Plusieurs fois ils remportèrent les premiers prix et le trophée dans les concours oratoires français ou anglais, avec les autres écoles. Les Soeurs de Saint-Joseph furent dans la paroisse une source de bénédiction continuelle, telle que l'avait prévue le Père Emery.

Jubilé de diamant de la paroisse : Durant les années 1925 et 1926, en plus de son travail ordinaire, le Père Emery assume la tâche considérable de composer un livre de 300 pages sur l'histoire de Pain Court, un livre bien illustré et documenté et d'une grande valeur, au moins locale, qui sera terminé pour la célébration du 75e anniversaire de la fondation de la paroisse. En même temps il se dépense à l'organisation de cette grande fête, à laquelle il invite tous les anciens paroissiens. Il n'y eut jamais dans l'histoire de Pain Court, une fête aussi grandiose que celle des 5 et 6 juillet 1926, qui réunit une foule d'environ 3,000 personnes, anciens et anciennes de la paroisse, venus de toute part de l'Ontario, du Québec et des Etats-Unis : fête religieuse et patrio-tique à la fois, avec messe solennelle, distribution du pain bénit, sermon et discours de circon-stance, et un programme intéressant commémorant les anciens costumes et amusements, les procédés agricoles de nos ancêtres, le martyre du Père de Brébeuf, etc. et offrant une occasion de réjouissance pour tous, jeunes et vieux.

Voyage à Rome : Durant l'été de 1927, le Père Emery prend une vacance en Europe. La compagnie Cook organise un voyage dont une soixantaine de Canadiens français font partie. Doyen d'âge parmi les prêtres, il est choisi chapelain du groupe. Le pèlerinage arrive à Rome pour la fête des saints apôtres Pierre et Paul. Le curé admire beaucoup les grandes basiliques romaines. L'audience publique du Saint-Père lui cause la plus vive impression, surtout, quand après lui avoir fait baiser son anneau le premier, Pie XI l'invite à l'accompagner autour de la grande salle d'audience, pour se faire introduire à chaque pèlerin. Jamais plus grand honneur n'avait été rendu au curé de Pain Court.

École Sainte-Catherine : Le nombre des enfants d'école avait tellement augmenté depuis quelques années que l'école du village était devenue insuffisante pour les contenir tous commodé-ment. Elle avait vieilli et avait besoin de réparations considérables. En 1928, la commission scolaire décide d'en bâtir une nouvelle. Le Père Emery présente des plans magnifiques qui sont acceptés. Les travaux de construction commencés de bonne heure se poursuivent durant tout l'été, et le 15 octobre on inaugure, sous le patronage de sainte Catherine, une belle école moderne à quatre classes bien éclairées, meublées et décorées.

Départ du Père Emery : Ce fut la dernière oeuvre du Père Emery. Quelques semaines plus tard, il apprenait par lettre sa nomination à la paroisse de Saint-Joachim, en même temps que plusieurs autres curés étaient changés de paroisses. Durant ses dix-huit années de ministère, il a complètement renouvelé, presque recréé la paroisse de Pain Court. Ceux qui ont connu le Père Emery peuvent témoigner de son zèle sans limite, de son dévouement à toute épreuve, de sa grandeur d'âme. Il a employé tous ses talents, ses ressources et ses énergies pour faire prospérer matériellement toute la paroisse, et relever le niveau moral et intellectuel de toute la population. Pour les gens de Pain Court il a donné tout son coeur, le meilleur de lui-même. Il a semé la bonne semence de la parole divine, infusé la piété, la dévotion, stimulé la communion fréquente, encour-agé les vocations religieuses et sacerdotales, développé le bon esprit paroissial et patriotique. Il aimait les jeunes gens, chérissait les enfants et savait gagner tous les coeurs.
Tout le monde était bienvenu au presbytère et les paroissiens aimaient à le visiter comme il aimait à visiter ses paroissiens. Il est passé en faisant le bien. De son vivant on n'a peut-être pas su l'apprécier suffisamment, mais comme il se plaisait à le dire, on saurait l'apprécier plus tard. Et de fait on ressent encore les bienfaits de son influence. Et si en ce 30 novembre 1928, en route

pour Saint-Joachim, acompagné du Père Ducharme qui l'avait assisté quelques semaines durant sa paralysie, le Père Emery avait le coeur gros, toute la population qu'il venait de quitter, de son côté, le regrettait déjà amèrement.

R. P. Vincent Caron, o.m.i.
Nihil obstat :
A. CHALOUX, ptre,
Ottawa, le 11 oct,. 1951.
Imprimatur :
† ALEXANDRE VACHON,
 Archevêque d'Ottawa, le 11 oct., 1951.
1   A.-D. Emery, Paroisse de Pain Court, 1851-1926.
2   Reuben G. Thwaites, the Jesuit Relations & Allied Documents, Cleveland, 1898, Vol. XXI, pp. 222, 230, 232.
3   George F. Macdonald, Windsor — F. C. Coyne, The Valley of the Lower Thames, 1640-1850, Toronto 1951, p. 5.
4   W. G. McGeorge, Early Settlement and Surveys along the River Thames in Kent County, Kent Historical Society, Papers and Addresses, Chatham, Ont., 1924 — F. C Hamil, The Valley of the Lower Thames, 1640 to 1850, University of Toronto Press, 1951, Chap. 1 & 2.
5   Survey Records, Department of Lands, Toronto, No. 20, Survey April 26, 1830, C. Rankin " Sketch showing the situation of the inhabitants of Pain Court agreeably to the way in which their side lines are extended & c. Lots and names.

Causerie donnée au dix-huitième Congrès annuel de la Société Canadienne d'Histoire de l'Église Catholique, à Windsor, Ont. en septembre 1951.

Père Vincent Caron o.m.i.

"CARON, Vincent, fils d'Eugène Caron, cultivateur, et de Philomène Bourassa, né à
Pain Court, Ontario, le 19 mai 1906; décédé à Ottawa, Ontario, le 27 juillet 1971."

Vincent fit ses études classiques à l'Université d'Ottawa (1919-1922) et au Juniorat du Sacré-Coeur à Ottawa (1922-1924), puis entra au noviciat de Ville LaSalle le 1er août 1924 où il fit profession le 2 août 1925. Il poursuivit ses études cléricales au scolasticat Saint-Joseph à Ottawa (1925-1926) et au scolasticat de Rome (1926-1932), fit profession perpétuelle à Roviano, Italie, le 2 août 1928; il fut ordonné prêtre à Rome le 6 juillet 1930 par le cardinal Basilio Pompili, vicaire de Rome et évêque de Velletri. Docteur en philosophie et en théologie, il fut nommé professeur de philosophie au scolasticat de Natick, Massachusetts (1932-1933), puis passa à l'Université d'Ottawa (1933-1937). Lors de la fondation du séminaire universitaire à Ottawa, le père devint l'un des premiers membres du personnel (1937) et y demeura toute sa vie.

Professeur de théologie morale à la faculté de théologie de l'Université d'Ottawa, il fut élu vice-doyen (1945-1955), et lorsque son mauvais état de santé le força à quitter l'enseignement (1964) on le nomma professeur émérite. Il fut également chargé de l'Association des anciens du séminaire (1937-1971).

Le père a été inhumé dans le cimetière Notre-Dame de Hull. [1]"

Gracieuseté des "Archives Deschâtelets" 175 Main, Ottawa, Canada KIS 1C31.

Jean-Charles LAFRAMBOISE, o.m.i. Père Vincent Caron, o.m.i. 1906-1971, dans Notices
nécrologiques. Province Saint-Joseph, (1973), 7p.; archives du séminaire universitaire, Ottawa. #245

River Heritage

The Thames River played an important role in the settlement of Chatham,
Pain Court and Prairie Siding. At one time, ferries traveled the river to Detroit.
This is the steamer "Ossifrage" on the Thames at the turn of the century.

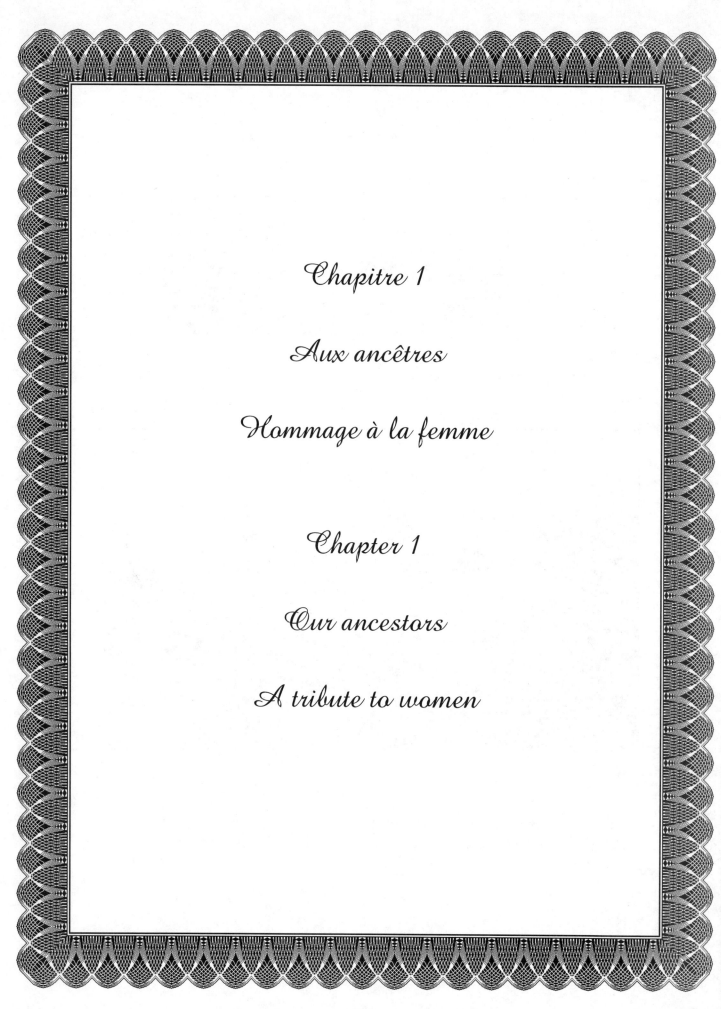

Chapitre 1

Aux ancêtres

Hommage à la femme

Chapter 1

Our ancestors

A tribute to women

1898 - 1998
Hommage aux Femmes
Reconnaissance
aux fondatrices de nos foyers
de St-Pierre,
de Pain Court
et de Grande Pointe.

Remerciements
pour vos travaux inlassables,
vos peines, vos joies, vos ennuis, vos contributions.

Admiration
pour votre vaillance,
votre courage,
et votre clairvoyance.

Salutation
aux gardiennes assidues
de notre foi, de notre langue,
et de notre patrie.

Louange
femmes intrépides,
femmes comblées d'amour,
femmes persévérantes,
femmes fières et nobles.

A Tribute To Women
1898 - 1998

JOURNAL DIOCÉSAIN DE LONDON
NOËL 1995

Lettre ouverte aux femmes
du monde entier

(Par le pape Jean-Paul II)

Signée le 29 juin 1995, la lettre aux femmes du pape Jean-Paul II a été rendu publique le 11 juillet 1995. Dans cette lettre, écrite à l' occasion de la quatrième Conférence mondiale sur la femme, qui s'est tenue à Péquin en septembre, le Pape s'adresse "directement à chacune des femmes pour réfléchir avec elles sur les problèmes et les perspectives de la condition féminine en notre temps", s'arrêtant "particulièrement sur le thème essentiel de la dignité et des droits des femmes."

Après avoir adressé un merci à la femme-mère, à la femme-épouse, à la femme-fille et à la femme-soeur, à la femme-au-travail, à la femme-consacrée, et à la femme "pour le seul fait d'être femme!", le Pape reconnaît ensuite que "le merci ne suffit pas" à cause des conditionnements et des nombreuses difficultés vécus par les femmes et les obstacles qu'elles ont rencontrés au cours de l'histoire de l'humanité. Reconnaissant "la responsabilité objective de nombreux fils de l'Église dans certains contextes historiques", le Pape déclare le regretter sincèrement.

"Il est urgent, dit-il, d'obtenir partout l'égalité effective des droits de la personne et donner la parité des salaires pour un travail égal, la protection des mères qui travaillent, un juste avancement dans la carrière, l'égalité des époux dans le droit de la famille, la reconnaissance de tout ce qui est lié aux droits et aux devoirs du citoyen dans un régime démocratique."

Le Saint-Père condamne "la longue et humiliante histoire - fréquemment souterraine - d'abus commis à l'encontre des femmes dans le domaine de la sexualité" et dénonce le "masochisme agressif". Il rappelle cependant que, même dans ces conditions, l'avortement "reste toujours un péché grave". Mais, "avant même d'être une responsabilité à faire endosser par les femmes, (il) est un crime qu'il faut mettreau compte de l'homme et de la complicité du milieu de vie". Le Pape lance ensuite un "appel pressant" pour que soit redonné "aux femmes le plein respect de leur dignité et de leur rôle".

Jean-Paul II manifeste sa gratitude envers les femmes engagées dans divers domaines de la société et de l'Église, soulignant qu'elles "accomplissent une forme de maternité affective, culturelle et spirituelle, d'une valeur vraiment estimable". Louant ce qu'il appelle "le génie de la femme", le Pape souhaite qu'on y réfléchisse à la lumière du dessein de Dieu sur la création, et en s'inspirant aussi du modèle de la Vierge Marie.

Dans la perspective de l'engagement des femmes dans l'Église, Jean-Paul II déclare qu'il "est aussi possible d'accueillir une certaine diversité de fonctions, sans conséquences désavantageuses pour la femme, dans la mesure où cette diversité n'est pas le résultat d'un ordre arbitraire, mais découle des caractères de l'être masculin et féminin." Le Pape déclare ensuite que "l'exercice du sacerdoce ministériel" a été confié par le Christ aux hommes seulement, et que la femme, à l'instar des autres laïcs, participe au sacerdoce commun enraciné dans le baptême.

En terminant, le Pape "invite les communautés ecclésiales à faire de l'année en cours un temps de profonde action de grâce au Créateur et au Rédempteur du monde pour le don d'un aussi grand bien que la féminité; dans ses multiples expressions, elle appartient au patrimoine constitutif de l'humanité et de l'Église". (R. Parrot)

L'Église canadienne
Vol. 28. numéro 8-sept. 1995

Hommage chères dames pour une décennie de dévouement.

Sous la présidence de Mme Ida Bourassa, la société des dames de Ste-Anne et les paroissiens de Pain Court ont participé à une fête pour honorer les anciennes présidentes de 1930 à 1940.

Les anciennes présidentes à l'honneur sont:
Assisses: g.à d. Philomène Caron (Edouard), Mary Pinsonneault, Emélie Caron, _____ , _____ ,
Debout: g. à d. Eulalie Gagner, Vitaline Daniel, Bella Martin, Joséphine Primeau, Délima Peltier.

Gratitude for a Decade of Services and Leadership.

I dedicate this eulogy to my aunt
Mrs. Marie-Louise Cheff

God hath not promised skies always blue.
Flower strewn pathways.
God hath not promised suns without rain.
Days without sorrow, peace without pain.
But God hath promised
Strength for the day
Rest for the labor
Light for the way
Grace for the trials
Help from above
Unfailing sympathy, Undying love.

Poem chosen by aunt Marie-Louise for her obituary souvenir card.

Marie-Louise Caron was born on November 25, 1989, in Pain Court, Ontario to Médéric Caron and Elmira Faubert. She thrived gracefully among 14 other siblings, namely eight sisters and six brothers. She attended the parochial school in Pain Court and married Ovilla Cheff of Grande Pointe on November 28, 1905.

In 1906, sixteen year old Marie-Louise embarked on a long journey to western United States and settled in Anaconda Montana where her husband was employed by Anaconda Copper Mines. A child was born in 1906 but died a year later on his birthday.

In 1910 they moved to Ronan Montana when the Flathead Reservation was opened to settlement. There, she raised fourteen children in a log style home they built together.

They owned and operated the Star Bottling Firm and did some farming and hunting as well. They operated a soda pop fountain and an ice cream parlor in Ronan, Montana. Rex was born on November 4, 1910 and later married Mae Demers of Grande Pointe, born May 8, 1918. He became the eldest son as Leo died in infancy. A sister, Bernida, was born in 1918.

In 1915, another son, Bud became part of the wonderful family. To this day, he has two books published in the States "Indian Trails" and "Grizzly Tales," a family history. A second book appeared in 1996, "The Woodman and His Hatchet." These books are of utmost importance to those interested in their family histories and to all those interested in back country survival. Copies of these books are in the "Pain Court Secondary School Community Library."

The other children born to Ovilla and Marie-Louise were Floyd of Missoula, Montana, Chris of California, Louis and Herman of Michigan, Ovilla of Ronan, Montana, James and Clarence of Bloomfield Hills, Michigan, Raymond and Harry both of Columbia Falls, Montana, Grace Tuumala of Michigan, and Josephine Schwach of The Republic of Missouri.

Marie-Louise was one of fifteen children and repeated the feat by having fourteen of her own inheriting a legacy of offsprings namely 131 grandchildren, 31 great grandchildren, 19 great great grandchildren.

"Growing old gracefully while living every day to its fullest is what life is all about," said aunt Marie-Louise.

Aunt Marie-Louise adhered to her motto and convictions. In 1937, the family moved to Detroit, Michigan in the hope of a better life. At 88, and still going strong, Mrs. Cheff owned and operated a residence for women for thirty-two years, quite a task but undertaken with such strength, compassion and dignity, personally seeing to the cooking of meals, the washing of linen, the scrubbing of floors, the ironing and most of the general upkeep of the residence.

"I'm the oldest in this house and I can do a day's work better than the youngest," she said. "I raised my children on an Indian reservation in Montana. It was hard work. We were awfully poor . . ."

She admitted that during these hard years in the wilderness and later on in life she frequently relied on the power of prayer. "It seems as if prayers always help," she said. "When someone is sick, it's the only hope that pulls them through."

Her husband, Ovilla, predeceased her in 1956. For the next 25 years or so, her courage, her tenacity, her exemplary life touched many souls who came in contact with her. Always smiling, always forgiving, always full of compassion for all those who surrounded her, she was a woman who gave continuously without reserve. She understood how to reach out and soothe the anguish of the soul. It's a credit to her power of healing through love that ten of her offsprings, all registered practicing chiropractors, have learned to relieve the agony of pain and distress of the body.

Aunt Marie-Louise conceded she had much to be thankful for, but without prayer you will never get anywhere. I loved her dearly and eventually tried to follow in her footsteps. She was dedicated to alleviating the pains, the sorrows of all who crossed her path. Mrs. Cheff was visited regularly by her family who kept her constant company. Father Thomas Krell, co-pastor of "Visitation Parish" in Detroit visited her home's residence once a month.

"When I was younger, she said "you had the memories of your family and the time you spent together. You didn't have all the things you have today to distract you away from the things and from the people that should be of the utmost importance to you."

A few years before retiring she was decorated, "Mother of the Year" for the city of Detroit, Michigan. Later when she officially retired in 1979, she was named "Women of the Year " for the state of Michigan.

Before leaving for her last journey to Montana in 1980 she returned to Pain Court accompanied by her oldest son, Rex, to bid a final farewell to my mother, Délia, her much beloved sister, a reunion though sad but memorable of which I was privileged to attend.

"My dear sister, I will not see you again," she said in a quivering voice, "but I know you will have the courage to continue to live your life to the best of your knowledge and I will return to Montana to die where I have lived and toiled with my family. I'm now 91 years old. I had a hard life but a very happy one. God was my guiding light. I was certainly rewarded with a very fulfilling life. I had help from above. I have received unfailing sympathy and undying love.

Marie-Louise Cheff, a cherished mother, a beloved aunt, and a well-respected citizen died on September 30, 1981, two months before reaching her 92nd birthday.

She will always be remembered as a great humanitarian, a precious jewel whose shining example of goodness will lead the way for those who aspire to embrace the weary and the home-less.

Caroline Roy Laprise

.

Mme Hélène St-Pierre

Atteindre l'âge de cent ans ou plus est un phénomène rare. C'est donc dire qu'ici, à Pain Court, on s'enorgueillit de compter une des nôtres, Mme Hélène St-Pierre, qui vient d'atteindre cent années d'existence.

Quels riches souvenirs et quelles douces mémoires ont dû envelopper son coeur en ce grand jour de fête le 3 janvier 1975 lorsqu'elle reçut les hommages et félicitations de ses enfants, de ses petits-enfants, de la part de nombreux parents et amis lors d'une rencontre intime dans sa demeure. M. Darcy McKeough (M.P.P. Chatham - Kent) vint lui présenter une plaque souvenir au nom du ministre provincial William Davis.

Elle lui dit : "Je vivrai peut-être jusqu'à 103 ans ..."

Épouse de feu James St.Pierre décédé en 1933 et mère de six enfants dont cinq vivants : Oscar de Plymouth Michigan, Léopold de Pain Court, Léona Loyer de Chatham Ontario, Blanche et Anna qui demeurent avec elle et Wesley, l'aîné de la famille, décédé en 1947 à l'âge de 46 ans.

Mme St-Pierre attribue sa longévité à sa grande foi en Dieu, au travail ardu et au soin délicat de ses enfants qui lui ont aidé à surmonter maintes difficultés au cours de sa vie. Depuis quelques années, à la suite d'une fracture aux deux hanches, elle doit se fier à une chaise roulante mais rien ne l'empêche de jouir de la vie. A maintes reprises elle se promène en fourgonnette avec ses filles mais c'est la télévision avec toutes ses merveilles qui semble l'intriguer le plus.

Une messe fut concélébrée, à son domicile par le Père Léo Charron et Mgr. A. Caron. Un souper servi pour la famille termina une journée mémorable pour la "Centenaire" qui a dit lors d'une visite: "Ce fut pour moi une des plus belles journées de ma vie."

Que Dieu vous bénisse et vous accorde de longs et heureux jours, chère dame et acceptez nos plus sincères félicitations.

Mme Hélène St-Pierre est décédée à Pain Court le 15 décembre 1977 âgée de 102 ans.

Blanche St-Pierre

Mrs. Elizabeth Reaume

Mrs. Elizabeth Reaume, of Jeannette's Creek, on Monday, observed her 97th birthday. Mrs. Reaume, who lives with her son, Wilfred Reaume, is in remarkably good health and takes a keen interest in the affairs of her family and of the community.
Tilbury Times, 1958

Ninety seven years ago, Mary Elizabeth Hamlin was born in a log cabin on Tecumseh Road in 1861, six years before confederation. She died November 6, 1961, she was 100 years old.

Married to Claude Reaume when she was nineteen years old, she moved one half a mile up the road to his parents log cabin home on the west side of the Jeannette's Creek bridge and two years later when their home was completed, moved across the road to the home where she is still living.

Now at 97 years, Mrs. Reaume has 179 direct descendants, she had 12 children, seven of them living, 33 grandchildren living, 83 great grandchildren and 56 great great grandchildren.

A life-long and faithful attendant of St. Peter's church, Mrs. Reaume has been unable to attend her church the past couple of years. Making her home with her son, Wilfred Reaume, she is very active, making her own bed, and cooking.   She still dresses her own hair, using rag curlers and indeed still presents a dainty appearance.

Looking back over the years, Mrs. Reaume remembers homesteading on 10 acres of usable land and having to build up the dykes and clearing the land of the forest. She remembers her father, an Irishman, working for the CNR when they originally laid the tracks through that district. She remembers her parents making a dugout canoe from an oak tree and making straw hats, which they had woven out of wheat straw, along the lake to Detroit where her mother sold them. She remembers acting as a midwife for Dr. Sharpe and helping to bring many of the local residents into the world. She remembers the wonderful occasions when twice a year her family went by horse and buggy to Chatham to do their half-yearly shopping.

There were 15 Hamlin children, four of them still living and one sister, Mrs. Albert Cassidy who is ninety years old and lives in Tilbury in 1958.

At the time of her ninety seventh birthday, 125 direct descendants gathered together to celebrate this occasion.

– Tilbury Times

STATEMENT.

Tilbury Centre, Ont., May 2 1898

Mr. Claud Reaume

IN ACCOUNT WITH

THE TIMES.

WM. A. SHAW, - PUBLISHER.

$1.00 PER YEAR—IN ADVANCE.　　$1.50 PER YEAR IF NOT SO PAID.

To 1 Year's sub
to April 1/96　　　*$1 00*
Paid
Wm. Shaw

KIPPEN & SCARFF
BANKERS.
No. 02088
TILBURY, ONT.

16 66 *Tilbury, Ont., Dec 13 1898*

Ten Months after date, for value received O promise to pay to

the order of _____

at the office of **Kippen & Scarff Bankers,** *here the sum of*

Sixteen _____ **Dollars**

with interest at the rate of twenty per cent per annum after due until paid

Claude Reaume

PAID OCT 26 1899 KIPPEN & SCARFF TILBURY ONT.

BANK OF CAN.

Mr. Claude Reaume

Mr. Claude Reaume, born May 11, 1859 and Elizabeth Hamlin, born in 1861, had a family of twelve children. Mr. Wilfred Reaume, in this picture, was the youngest son, while Israël Reaume, married to Rose Gabrieau, was the eldest of the family. Three of his children were Jean (Reaume) Béchard, married to Seville Béchard, a widower, Clement Reaume married to Marie-Jeanne Martin, February 16, 1957, and Gérard Reaume married to Kay MacLeod.

Wilfred Reaume married Muriel Murphy February 11, 1929 and lived at the old homestead all his life. They shared the house with his parents and built a new one on the same farm in 1963 after his mother Elizabeth passed away. Muriel, his wife, is still living in the new house built in 1963, while their son Irwin is living at the old homestead. Irwin's father, Wilfred, passed away in 1988 at 90 years old. His mother Muriel is now 87. In 1998 Mr. Irwin Reaume, is building a new home for his family on the original property of Claude and Mary Elizabeth Reaume, his grandparents.

Wilfred and Muriel had taken very good care of his mother Elizabeth for at least 19 year's after Claude, his father passed away, on October 6, 1943 at 84.   They are buried in St. Peter's Church cemetery.

I remember visiting Mary Elizabeth at least once a year with my father Becca Roy at the old homestead. She was an amazingly interesting woman for her advanced years. Elizabeth's father worked as a railroad engineer all his life and they had 15 children. Many of her brothers also worked on the railroad when living in the Jeannette's Creek area and later moving either to Windsor or Detroit. Francis Hamlin was the baby of the Hamlin's. Losing her mother in infancy, Francis was raised by Charline and Thomas Roy, my grandparents. Unfortunately this is the extent of my research, and I do wish I could elaborate more. I hereby extend my congratulations to all relatives.

Caroline Roy Laprise

St. Peter's Church 1802 - 1952
Église St-Pierre "de Raleigh" 1802 - 1952

St. Peter's

In preparing a history of the Catholic Church in Kent our thoughts are carried back more than a century, to the year 1802, when Rev. J. B. Marchand, of the congregation of St. Sulpice, Montreal, built a small chapel at St. Peter's which was dedicated on the 8th day of July that same year. Father Marchand was stationed at Sandwich and visited St. Peter's about once a month. The church records date back to this chapel's dedication on the 8th day of July on which day the first baptism is registered, being that of Michael Deloge, an infant of ten months. Father Marchand attended the little parish until about the year 1819 in which year Rev. Father Crevier took charge and it was during his pastorate that the first Catholic church in the County of Kent was built in 1823. It was a modest structure, plain and simple in outline, but it meant so much to the sturdy pioneers who made many sacrifices to reach St. Peter's on Sundays. Father Crevier remained in the parish until 1827 and from that year until 1835 the names of Father's Fluett, McDonell, Fitz-Maurice and Hay signatures arose off the records of baptisms, marriages etc.

Kent, like all the rest of Ontario in these early days, was in the diocese of Kingston. The first Bishop of this see was the Rt. Rev. Alexander McDonell, who in the year 1832 received from the government a lot of 210 acres surrounding St. Peter's church which is the property of the church today and which brings in yearly quite a revenue for the support of the church and pastor. In 1835 Rev. John Baptiste Morin was called from a mission in Nova Scotia to take charge of St. Peter's parish where he laboured faithfully until the year 1846. As the missionary territory allotted to Father Morin was very extensive and his flock so scattered, he, despite his zeal and energy, could seldom visit them all. He would however hold missions through the district in private houses. Word would be sent throughout the county that on a certain day Father Morin would hold a mission at a certain house and thither would flock the neighbours, happy indeed to have the privilege of receiving the sacraments. From 1847 to 1859 the following priests in turn had charge of St. Peter's. Father's Fitz-Maurice, Durand, Fernet, Kaynelt and Boubat. From 1859 to 1872 there was no resident priest at St. Peter's and the records during that time are signed by Father's Ferard, Grimot, Raynell, Andrieux and Delabaysse of Chatham who said mass about once a month. From 1872 to 1885 St. Peter's was attended by Father Villeneuve of Tilbury; from 1885 to 1886 by Father Fauteux of Pain Court and from 1886 to 1892 by Father's Leveque, Carriere and Langlois of Big Point. In 1892 St. Peter's again had a resident priest, Rev. Charles Parent, who had charge of one parish until 1900. During his pastorate the historic old wooden church built in 1823 was burned to the ground on the evening of October 28, 1895. It is thought by many that in this fire the records of the church were destroyed but this is not the case. All the books containing the records of the church since its inception in 1802 were saved and are still preserved at St. Peter's. Preparations for building were commenced at once and on May 26, 1896 Bishop O'Connor of London laid the corner stone of the new church. It was finished that same year, a fine brick structure, that today, as it were, keeps guard over the plains not far from the Thames. Father Parent also built the fine presbytery at St. Peter's in 1892. Father Rocheleau took charge of the parish in 1900, remaining only a few months and was succeeded by Father Ladouceur who laboured earnestly in the parish until his death in 1910, raising sufficient money to pay off the balance of the debt incurred in building church and presbytery.

There are in the parish of St. Peter's about 115 families, nearly all of French extraction. In 1902 the centenary of St. Peter's was duly celebrated under the late Bishop, Rt. Rev. F.P. McEvay and late Father Ladouceur. There was Pontifical high mass in the morning at which the whole parish and their friends assisted and a monster picnic at Bagnell's grove across the river in the afternoon.

The present pastor of St. Peter's, Rev. Father Martin, took charge in 1910. He is an old Kent boy born in Dover Township in 1877, educated at Assumption College, Sandwich, St. Thérèse,

Quebec and Montreal and was ordained priest at St. Philippe church, Big Point, in 1901. He has already built new sheds, cement sidewalks etc. and made many other improvements all tending toward the general welfare of the parish.

R. P. Vincent Caron o.m.i.

Parish Histories of London Diocese

St. Peter's Tilbury East

Oldest daughter of a venerable mother, the parish of St. Peter's Raleigh in Tilbury East is, her 196th year, the second oldest parish in the Diocese of London.

Upper Canada was a small and scarcely explored part of the Diocese of Quebec when the Sulpician, Father J.B. Marchand on a trip to Montreal from his parish church, Assumption in Sandwich discovered 12 French families living along the River Thames. Determined to give them the consolation of their Catholic religion he began the construction of a chapel. In July 1800 he reported to his bishop that he hoped it would soon be completed. Several months were to elapse before the hewn log building on a tortuous bend of the River Thames 11 miles west of Chatham was ready for Divine service.

ROOTS DEEP

Built on land which historians now claim was part of the village of Saint-Michel founded by Saint John de Brébeuf and Father Chaumonot during their visit to the Neutral Indians in 1640, the little log church was completed in June 1802 with 36 French and Indian families constituting its congregation. The first baptism was recorded in the parish register on July 7 and was the first of nine that year.

The limits of the parish in its earliest day were not well defined. The surrounding country was a relentless tangle of forest and swamp. Pioneer settlers found their way to the district by boat from Montreal or Detroit. There were no roads until 1804 and these, never kept in repair, were practically useless. Early missionaries had the choice of foot travel, horseback or canoe. Settlers were unable to get through to Sandwich with loaded carts or wagons until 1807. Later, when there was a semblance of roads, members of the infant parish of St. Peter traveled three or four days by ox-drawn carts or charrettes to reach Sandwich.

VISITED BY BISHOP

Travel conditions were crude and defiant when Msgr. Joseph-Octave Plessis, 11th Bishop of Canada, visited Upper Canada. One of the great doctors of the Catholic Church in Canada, he was responsible for the independence of religious practices and education of civil power and authority. Early in his episcopate, Bishop Plessis determined to visit every section of his immense diocese, an accomplishment which required 10 years. In 1816 he came within the limits of the present province of Ontario with its four missions: Kingston, Malden, Sandwich and Tilbury East. After 16 days travel from Kingston he arrived in Sandwich and on July 1 was at St. Peter's. Details of his pastoral stay are not recorded. As was the custom in that day, he probably conducted a mission, gave religious instructions and examinations and administered Confirmation.

After his visit the parish grew and prospered. By 1824, the log church was too small to accommodate its congregation. During the pastorate of Father Joseph Crevier who had succeeded Father Marchand as the second pastor in 1819 a large frame church was built and blessed by Father Crevier, who like his predecessor served both in Sandwich and St. Peter's.

MISSION OF ASSUMPTION

Following the death of Father Marchand at Assumption in 1825, Father Crevier who had been his curate and in charge of St. Peter's was named rector of Assumption and was succeeded by Father I.F. Fluet who served until 1832 when Father Angus McDonnell, rector of St. Raphael's in Glengarry took charge of St. Peter's. At the same time he was rector at Assumption.

He remained only a short time after his coming to St. Peter's, on January 30, 1832. Three who followed him, Fathers P. Foley, Charles-François Fitz-Maurice and George Hay guided the congregation until August 27, 1834. In the Fall of that year Father Jean-Baptiste Morin, 61 year old priest of the mission of Kamourssa in Nova Scotia took charge of St. Peter's. The parish was then so extensive that Father Morin was required to hold Divine Service and missions in private homes in Chatham and Raleigh and Dover townships. The first parish with its roots in St. Peter's was established at Belle River in 1834 and in the following years 14 other parishes and missions of the Diocese claimed St. Peter's as their mother church. They include in addition to Belle River, St. Joachim, Tilbury, Stoney Point, Raleigh, Staples, Chatham, Pain Court, Big Point, Wallaceburg, Thamesville, Bothwell, Lambton, Dresden and Blenheim.

A little more than a year after he was consecrated the first Bishop of Toronto, the Rt. Rev. Michael Power paid a pastoral visit to St. Peter's on September 16, 1843. Eight years later on July 16, 1851, Bishop Power's successor Rt. Rev. A.F. Marie de Charbonnel confirmed 289 members of the parish on the Thames.

Father Morin was pastor in 1846. He remained a year. No less than three pastors officiated from 1847 to 1851; they were Fathers J. B. Dillon, P. Voin and J. W. Joffroi. Father Morin died in 1847 and was buried under the sanctuary of St. Peter's on the Epistle side of the altar as he had requested.

During the pastorate of Father Dillon a bell given the names of the parish patrons. St. Peter and Paul were blessed by Father R. P. Jaffre, missionary resident at Sandwich. The ceremony, impressive and largely attended, was held August 20, 1847.

NAMED VICAR-GENERAL

On the occasion of his pastoral visit in July of 1851, Bishop de Charbonnel, aware of the huge extent of the parish and the large number of Catholics living on the other side of the river, named the new pastor Father Claude Ternet, "vicar-general with extraordinary powers." He also instructed him to build a mission church at Pain Court, an assignment which was completed early in 1852.

Father Ternet remained only a short time at St. Peter's and was succeeded in 1853 first by Father J. A. Raynell and then by Father M. B. Boubat. A few months after he had taken possession of his episcopal chair as first bishop of the Diocese of London, the Rt. Rev. A. P. Pinsonneault visited St. Peter's where he confirmed 15 boys and 12 girls and set forth the boundaries of missions of St. Peter's.

Sixteen pastors followed Father Boubat in the 97 years which followed the appointment of his immediate successor Father Girard in 1850. They include Fathers Paul Andrieux, o.m.i., 1864, Joseph Delallys, F. A. Raynell who served in 1853 and 1872, A. P. Villeneuve 1872, P. Fauteux 1884, L. M. Leveque 1884, A. Carriere 1886, P. Langlois 1888, Charles Parent 1892, E. C.

Ladouceur 1900, Theo Martin 1910, A. A. Rondot 1928, R. J. Lefaive 1933, A. F. Scalisi 1945 and the present pastor L. L. Ouellette who was appointed in 1953.

In 1895 during the pastorate of Father Parent the frame church was destroyed by fire. Only a chalice remained. Fortunately the direction of the wind kept the flames from the new presbytery and the barn built the previous year.

Following the destruction of the church, Mass was said in the presbytery until the completion of the new brick church opened for Divine services in 1896. Of modified Gothic design and measuring 80 by 40 feet, the church stands in a rural setting with its windows overlooking the cemetery.

TREASURE HOUSE

Severely plain in its early construction, the building has been considerably improved during the past 60 years. Extensive decorations were made in 1920 by the pastor Father Martin who secured for the church its greatest art treasures— 10 mural paintings by George Delfosse of Montreal. If any choice were to be made of these costly and beautiful works of ecclesiastical art, it would probably be the mural over the main altar depicting an incident in the life of St. Peter.

Father Martin also secured new stations of the cross for his church and made extensive improvements to church grounds and the presbytery. The work of improvement was continued by pastors who followed Father Martin.

Father Scalisi began the task of upgrading the cemetery on the church grounds shortly after he went to St. Peter's. Pine trees, planted in the form of a cross many years before had grown high and made the cemetery a place hard to keep in order. There were few monuments and the graves were elevated mounds hidden by high grass. The trees were cut down, the ground leveled and God's acres became beautifully dignified and serene.

The rectory was renovated and modernized. The renovation of the mural paintings, the greatest task of all, was also completed. Church walls were reinforced, and urgent repairs to walls and roof completed.

ANNIVERSARY 1952

In 1949 parishioners and priests built a parish hall, digging its foundation one cold November month. But the greatest plan of all was made for the celebration of the 150th anniversary, July 1952. Church organization planned and carried out every type of program designed to obtain money for the redecoration of the church. Four months of constant work finally gave the interior its simple and artistic decor which makes it one of the most beautiful of God's houses of the province.

Almost free of debt, the church was ready for the anniversary services held on July 6 when His Excellency the Most Rev. John Cody preached at the Mass celebrated by Father Pierre Boudreau, native son of the parish.

One problem which has plagued the parish almost from the time of its inception has not yet been resolved. Each year the raging Thames chews away a little more of the land in front of the church. In the days of the old frame church a swooping lawn stretched 300 feet toward the river Thames. This land has entirely disappeared. A bank was constructed and re-enforced as a protection against floods but year by year the Thames flows on, and in early Spring grows deeper and wider.

Although it has mothered the parishes and missions in this long history, the number of families has grown from 36 in 1882 to 150 in 1962. Indians have disappeared from the congregation and most of the congregation is of French and Irish origin.

Published for 150th anniversary, 1952
Chatham News

THE LIVES AND TIMES OF OUR ANCESTORS IN THE AREA.

Excerpts From
"History of St. Peter's Parish"
1802 - 1947

LOT 1, RIVER ROAD
TILBURY EAST TOWNSHIP

Compiled and written by Rev. Théophile Martin.
Born in Pain Court in 1877, he was the son of
Lévi Martin and Caroline Faubert.

Nestling quietly and unobtrusively opposite an elbow point, in one of the numerous and tortuous bends of the River Thames, eleven miles west of Chatham, an unpretentious, though picturesque, brick church, built in 1896, marks the spot where early history on the crooked stream is accurately trace for the past 126 years.

Numerous motorists from the Border cities and Michigan whirl by this neat Catholic Church with only an admiring glance, little realizing that in the ancient church yard adjoining, lie many of the pioneers of Kent, Essex and Lambton counties, in fact, the first white settlers of that part of the Western Ontario peninsula.

For considerably more than a century, the present church grounds have been the site of St. Peter's Roman Catholic Church, a church that holds the distinction of being the second oldest Catholic place of worship in Western Ontario. Its only rival and predecessor is Assumption Church, Sandwich. So closely linked is the history of the two churches that the first pastor of St. Peter's Church, the Rev. Father J. P. Marchand, also served at the identical time as the Pastor of Assumption. His arduous dual charge was made possible by this pioneer priest making hurried trips on horseback along the river and lake trail, at least once a month.

That was the day before buggies, automobiles or aeroplanes. It was even a time before roads, worthy of the name, existed. The hundred and one adjuncts, of present day civilization, lying at the very doors of this generation, were undreamed-of possibilities to those early faithful settlers who struggled to wrest a livelihood from the little clearings and product of the hunt. It was a day when, after long and arduous hours of toil on the little clearings bordering the Thames, parents and their children would trudge miles to receive blessings and encouragement, always cheerfully given by catholic spiritual leaders in Ontario's pioneer settlements.

It may be said to the credit of the early Roman Catholic Clergy, that they were unceasingly ready to undergo the hardships of the primeval forest with their parishioners, and to share with them their dangers, privations and trials in time of sickness.

For the past eighteen years, as Pastor of this historic church, I have been privileged to guide the destinies of one hundred or more families. I am glad to say that St. Peter`s has certainly proved a source of great pride and interest to me. During my service as its pastor I have endeavoured to place this Church among the most beautiful and interesting Catholic Churches of old Ontario. (This work has necessitated much manual labour which, personally, I have often performed.)

It is interesting to note that every birth, christening and marriage that have taken place in St. Peter`s Parish since 1802, is chronicled in well preserved books, the pages of which are written in ink in the handwriting of the Church Pastor at the time of their happening. Among these names, are recognized those of many French families of Lambton, Kent and Essex counties today. Descendants from these early families have multiplied, in Biblical terms, as the sands of the seashore.

The great dream of Father Hubert, regarding the future of St. Peter, has since become a reality far greater in its fulfilment than even the zealous and devoted disciple of God had anticipated. As a mother church, St. Peter's gave birth later to fifteen parishes or missions. Already three pastors have faithfully kept this precious flock so dear to Father Hubert (later Bishop Hubert).

So energetic and zealous a priest was destined by God for even greater responsibilities that those associated with his great vicariate at Detroit. While in the midst of his organization projects in our country, he was named Assistant Bishop of Quebec, with future succession. In the fourth year of his episcopate, Rome took from him almost half of his diocese. Pius VI formed an apostolic vicariate in what is the United States of today, having Baltimore as its chief centre. In this division, the immense diocese of Quebec lost what is now Oregon, Illinois, Michigan, Louisiana, Mississippi and all the New England States up to Baltimore. News travelled so slowly in those early times that it was four years before Msgr. Hubert learned of this momentous change. While witnessing his great diocese being taken from him in large sections of territory, he had one consolation in being able to keep what is the Canadian part today, including the parish of St. Peter's, for which he had planned wisely and well. This beautiful parish has since given birth to fifteen parishes and missions including Belle River, St. Joachim, Tilbury, Stoney Point, Raleigh, Staples, Chatham, Pain Court, Big Point, Wallaceburg, Thamesville, Bothwell, Lambton and Dresden. Attending these today are twenty-one priests.

Father Hubert believed that the Parish of St. Peter's would prove an inexpugnable fort. St. Peter's, accordingly became the fortress of the Catholic Church in Canada West in those days. The office of a Catholic missionary in those early times was not an enviable post. This path was beset with dangers both physical and spiritual.

Despite the fact that Father Hubert visited all this part of the country during his four years' administration as Vicar General at Detroit, it was not possible for him, because of a long illness, to realize the entire fulfilment of his projects, following his elevation to the Episcopacy. The immensity of his diocese combined with his ill health, greatly curtailed the prosecution of his many projects. Realizing his inability to carry out his plans, he entrusted their execution to Msgr. Denaut, his successor.

The Parish of St. Peter's has the distinction of having been visited by Msgr. Plessis, the eleventh Bishop of Canada, 1816. The parish at that time was known as St. Pierre sur La Tranche, the name La Tranche having been applied to the tortuous and beautiful stream now commonly known as the Thames. St. Peter's was honoured in the Bishop's visit by his determination in 1806 to visit every part of his immense diocese from the Atlantic to the Pacific. The great contrast in pioneer travel in the early part of the century to that of today is best exemplified in the fact that the immense itinerary planned by the bishop took him ten years to complete. Today a similar journey could be accomplished within a few months at the most.

Following visits to the many parts of his great diocese in the east, including Nova Scotia (then Acadia), New Brunswick, Boston, New York and Albany, it was not till the year 1816 that he undertook to visit the western part of his diocese, travelling by way of the St. Lawrence River by boat and portage. At the time there were only four missions in Ontario: Kingston, Malden, Sandwich and St. Peter's. He visited St. Isodore of Kingston on May 28 to June 4; Notre Dame of Assumption, Sandwich, from the 20th to the 29th of June. During his stay at Notre Dame of Assumption he visited St. John of Malden (the Amherstburg of today), and returned in time to arrive at St. Peter's for July 1, 1816. Just what activities he engaged in at the Parish of St. Peter's at the time of his visit is not definitely recorded; but it is certain that he gave Confirmation to numbers of souls there. This deduction is made from his memoirs which record having given Confirmation to 33, 725 people during the general visit to his immense diocese. Msgr. Plessis, eleventh Bishop of Canada, was the first to visit the Province of Ontario. Travel was so arduous and difficult in those days that the journey from Kingston to Sandwich consumed 16 days. Msgr. Plessis is regarded as the greatest Bishop of Canada, up to his time.

We owe to Msgr. Plessis the liberty of freely practising our religion in this country independently of the civil power. For his great services he was well named the great Canadian Athanasius, one of the Fathers of the Church in Canada. It was under his regime that the big diocese of Canada was divided into four parts, the division taking effect on December the 5th, 1822, six years after his memorable visit to the whole of his diocese. The division was as follows: No. 1 district: Upper Canada, under the administration of Msgr. Alexander McDonald; No 2, district of Montreal, under Msgr. Lartigue; No. 3 District of the gulf of St. Lawrence under Msgr. McEachern; No.4 District of the Northwest Territories, under Msgr. Provencher. The four administrators of as many districts were under the dependence or supervision of Msgr. Plessis, the British Government having consented to the arrangement but wishing to settle matter with the Bishop, Msgr. Plessis, alone.

The parish books, referred to above, often contained the complete cycle of life`s major events of those early settlers, including birth, christening, marriage and death. Due to the continual migrations of all parts of the country, especially to the great lumber forests of Michigan there are many instances where the death of early parishioners are not therein recorded. Records of their demise would doubtless be found in the parish books of some distant Catholic Church in the country to which the early inhabitant had wandered.

The history of the Parish of St. Peter's, of the diocese of London, is inseparably linked with the history of what was later Upper Canada, in 1780. In that year there was but one diocese in the whole of Canada. Its precincts stretched from Halifax to Vancouver. It was named the diocese of Quebec. In addition to all Canadian territory, the diocese stretched far into what later became the United States. It included Michigan, Illinois, Oregon, Ohio, Mississippi, Louisiana and, in the New England States, up as far as Baltimore.

Up to 1780, Father Hubert (later Bishop of Quebec, and 12th French Canadian Bishop) had filled many posts of confidence in the eyes of his Bishop, His Lordship D`Englis. Father Hubert had been director of his Grand Seminary, and Apostolic Visitor of the Vicars General, located at various points of the North American continent which comprised that immense diocese of New France.

Destinies of certain men are foreordained in a peculiar way. One day Father Hubert was sent by his Bishop to Illinois to fulfil a very delicate mission with the Vicar General Gibeault. On his return, by way of Fort Detroit, he arrived at the pioneer post just in time for the funeral of Father Bocquet, Recollet Order. Following the funeral, Father Hubert, of necessity, replaced the deceased as parish priest of Fort Detroit and as Vicar General of all the regions of the immense Detroit district. That great vicariate embraced all Michigan, the Province of Ontario and the State of Ohio. Such an immense territory was surely enough to occupy the full services and time of such a Vicar General who, by his very nature, was the soul of zealousness and devotion to his charge. If the various missions in his care were not numerous, they were far distant from one another and sufficient to tax the energies and devotions of the strongest of men.

Because the principal centre (noyau) of Father Hubert`s administration was Detroit and its adjacent territory, that pioneer spiritual leader constructed a church and presbytery there. Immigration to the Detroit district, including what is now Western Ontario, had already gotten well under way. The great fertility of the soil, the admirable climate and wealth of natural resources, had already become known to distant inhabitants of the old and New France. Feeling a great tax on his strength, because of the increasing numbers of settlers under his spiritual care, Father Hubert asked his Bishop in Quebec for several priests to assist him in his mission yet to be established in the immense Detroit field of labours.

Taking the great wooded Detroit River as a natural division, the Parish of Detroit soon became divided into two parts; one a church, L'Assomption at Sandwich, and the other at Detroit, Ste. Anne. On each bank of the river the population, swelled by continual immigration, was growing very rapidly. That tide of growth on the Canadian shores stretched from Bois Blanc Island as then named, to near Sarnia of today. Again, from Amherstburg to Chatham, French Canadians came from Quebec to establish their homesteads along the shores of the rivers and lakes. For all this great territory there were only two churches and two missionary priests.

Following 126 years of early settlement, in the beautiful counties of Essex and Kent alone, we find today more than 35,000 Catholic French Canadians. This number is entirely separate from the English speaking people of other nationalities. All this territory formerly formed a part of the Parish of Assumption Church at Sandwich and was a second division of the parish of Detroit. In 1870, at Detroit, the Vicar General, Father Hubert, administered all this region which comprised part of the colony of Detroit. On what is now the Canadian side of the river, Father Pothier (Jesuit)was the only missionary parish priest under the administration of Father Hubert.

Illustrative of the natural increase of French Canadians in this territory, Father Hubert relates that the Campeau family alone counted 3,000 souls. Because of its numerous members this family had erected for itself a little chapel in Detroit, the parish priest conducting mass in it periodically.

Zealous and devoted to his charge, Father Hubert, on observing the continued immigration of French Canadians to the Detroit district, conceived the project of establishing new missions in the most populated sections of his vicariate. With this in view he visited all the region between Amherstburg and Chatham, now known as the Canadian side, but, which at that time, formed a part of the Detroit vicariate. The parish of St. Peter's owes its inception to that memorable trip of Father Hubert. On passing the quaint spot along the Thames, he was impressed with its natural charm and geographical position, the ideal centre for a great mission. He determined that the day would not be far distant when a missionary priest would be sent to minister to Catholic souls along the beautiful shores of Lake and River St. Clair.

The erection of the Parish of St. Peter's is fairly accurately traced to the month of June, 1802, since the first act of baptism is dated July 7th, 1802. The limits of the parish at that time were not well defined between the region of what is now East Kent and the Detroit River. Our ancestors had come to establish themselves in this virgin forest by travelling by boat from Montreal to Detroit, water being the only accessible route. Our missionaries of the time visited the far scattered missions in one of three ways; by foot, canoe or horseback. Roads were unheard of in those pioneer days. The missionaries were content to make the sign of the cross before starting on their long pilgrimages, and placed their respective voyages under the protection of God and the Blessed Virgin.

Detroit was only a little village, the only place for several hundred miles where one could get his grain ground, or get mail from a post office. These hardy ancestors of ours for a number of years came to Detroit by canoe pushed forward by strong arms. They experienced the peculiar joy of splitting the waves of St. Clair Lake en route to Detroit. Later, when a semblance of a trail had been blazed along the river and lake banks, they journeyed from the Parish of St. Peter's to opposite Detroit by slow plodding oxen hitched to that rare carriage of the day - the charrette. The trip to Detroit took from three to four days; a trip now accomplished by motor car in a couple of hours or less. When night fell on them, they slept in the open air along the shores of Lake St. Clair. Their food was extracted chiefly from the hunt by the wayside. It consisted often of fish, wild duck, partridge or other game. By making a smudge to drive away the troublesome mosquitos, they slept peacefully under the canopy of heaven.

Further changes occurred as the years passed.   The first store in the Parish of St. Peter's was situated about one mile from the actual church toward Lake St. Clair, where a post office was established named Dolsen. A little later a hotel was erected near the post office and store, where travellers who made the trip from London to Detroit by canoe or stage - according to the season and passability of roads - enjoyed the rest provided by the pioneer half-way house.

Several years later, another small store appeared below Prairie Siding, together with a small elevator, where grain was brought from the little farms cleared with great labour of heavy forest growth, as well as from those farms nearer what is now Chatham. Another post office, named `Williams` was established about a mile and a half east of what is Prairie Siding today.

The present Church of St. Peter's, a substantial brick structure, is the third edifice to grace the site of the pioneer parish church yard. It was opened for service in 1896, just 32 years ago. Church history of St. Peter's`s parish starts with the erection of a chapel in 1802 - which undoubtedly was constructed of hewn logs, no trace of which remains today. It is known that when this pioneer church became too small for the rapidly growing congregation, it was replaced by a larger frame church in 1824, the edifice being blessed by the then parish priest, Father Joseph Crevier, on the 28th of Nov., 1824. The former chapel was used for a number of years after the building of the new frame church as a school. The latter church, which served St. Peter's`s Parish for close to a century, was destroyed by fire in 1895 - an old chalice alone being rescued from the ashes of the venerable edifice.

Many were there whose cycle of life began and finished at old St. Peter's. There they were born, christened, married, had their children christened; and when life's span was terminated the impressive funeral services were held in the old frame church. In 1833, Rev. Father Jean-Baptiste Morin 1, a native of Lower Canada, was called from a mission in Nova Scotia and stationed at St. Peter's's, where he laboured faithfully in the discharge of his sacred ministry until the Lord called him to his reward at the ripe age of 70. He was buried on the 17th of December, 1849, under the sanctuary of St. Peter on the Epistle side of the altar, as he had requested.

It is most interesting to note the effect of the ever changing banks of River Thames, especially in the vicinity of St. Peter's Church. The site of the older frame church, since burned, is so near to the present river bank that were the edifice there today it would stand in the middle of the present highway. So deeply has the river cut into the land that the days of the frame church there was a beautiful sloping lawn in front for more than 300 feet towards the river. This land has since entirely disappeared before the mad spring rushes of the turbulent Thames. At the time of its construction the present brick church was built some 200 feet back from the site of the former church. The bank in front of the present church was first constructed thirty years ago as a protection against the spring floods induced in great measure by the gradual drainage of more and more land extending towards Chatham. This great rush of water in the spring caused the river bank to be built from Prairie Siding to a couple of miles west of the church. Flood waters necessitated this bank being rebuilt, straightened and strengthened several times, while the river became wider and deeper each succeeding year. Because of its meandering course, the early French settlers knew the present Thames only by its name of the period, "River La Tranche."

Topography of land along the route of the Thames has formed a most colourful page of history. One hundred years ago Indians were plentiful along its North bank in what is now Dover Township. The river traversed a thick forest through almost all of Kent county and broke into open land in the vicinity of Lake St. Clair, from Mitchell's Bay to the lighthouse at the mouth of the river. Indians in their boats and canoes were to be often seen travelling down the river towards Lake St.Clair, the only route of travel available through the heavily forested country. In a few days these Indians would return, their boats and canoes laden down with the trophies of the hunt and assurances of a well stocked larder for the family board. When stores were replenished, it would mean another voyage downstream to the better hunting grounds along the shores of beautiful Lake St. Clair.

One of the greatest aids to travel is found today in the fine government bridge over the Thames, built in 1924, which connects Dover and Raleigh Townships. Recognized as a crying necessity for many years, it remained for this fortunate generation to see the ultimate fulfilment of a long cherished dream of quick transport over the Thames. Situated two miles east of the church the new bridge has enabled parishioners from the north bank to drive to Mass each Sunday under far more favourable conditions of travel.

In concluding the history of my parish I may say that although St. Peter's occupies a comparatively secluded and isolated site, it is by peculiar coincidence, on direct route of all important lanes of travel today between the Border Cities and Eastern Canada. These include railroad, motor car and even aeroplane routes. In fact, many notables in world history, including members of royalty, government and high ecclesiastical officials of the Roman Catholic Church, have passed frequently through the actual grounds of St. Peter's Church property while unaware of the fact. As they whirled along the rails of the now Canadian National Railway, which for nearly a century has bisected the property of this venerable church, they have been unconscious of the fact that only a stone's throw distant was situated this second oldest Catholic Church in Western Ontario.

1 The priest who baptized M.T. David Roy, in 1837. See the 150th souvenir book for proof.

Excerpts From "The Valley of the Lower Thames"
FRED COYNE HAMIL

"River Thames: The branches of the river perhaps reminded the Chippewa of the prongs of a deer's horn, for they named it the Escunnisepi or Horn River. To the French its trench-like appearance suggested the name La Tranche, by which it was known for nearly a century. Lieutenant-Governor John Graves Simcoe gave the river its present name soon after his arrival in the province in 1792."

P.4: "When the Jesuit Fathers appeared there in the winter of 1640-41 the total white population of Canada numbered about 200, and Montreal had yet to be founded. Late in the year 1640 Jean de Brébeuf and Joseph Marie Chaumonot set out on the forest trail along the head of Lake Ontario and along the shore of Lake Erie. They visited 18 villages of the neutrals . . . another, near the mouth of the Thames River, may have been the village of Kiostoa or St. Michael, Brébeuf and Chaumonot lived for four months among these Indians." A footnote from the Dept. of Lands and Forests, survey office map of the Thames River 1790 stated that the village near Jeannette's Creek was on Lot 5, East of Tilbury.

In 1787 the land was then covered with forest and swamp. "The great marshes and plains of Dover and Tilbury spread eastward along the banks of the river for six miles from Lake St. Clair." P. 14. The lands that were cultivated only a few acres here and there, once Indian cornfields "which had been won with great toil by chopping down trees."

P. 113: - "By an act of the provincial legislation of 1803 the tax on cultivated land was set at one penny per acre, while that on wild land was but one-twentieth of a penny."

P. 119: - After the war of 1812 - "the farmers of the Lower Thames in 1817 still grew principally quantities of oats, peas, barley, hemp, flax, potatoes and turnips . . . Much of the soil was so rich that good crops were obtained without the use of manure for ten years and in some cases for twenty-five years."

P. 120: - "Cheese and butter sold for about 18¢ a pound and wool from 30 to 46¢ a lb. A four-year-old workhorse cost from $33 to $38, a cow from $12 to $15, a good ox $25 and a sheep $2.50 or less . . . Farm labourers in 1817 were paid about $6 a month in the winter time and $8 in the summer; and harvest labourers 60 cents a day . . . masons averaged $1.25 per day and carpenters and blacksmiths 60 to 90 cents per day. Board and lodging could be had for less than 25¢ a day. Bricks sold at the kiln in Raleigh for $4.68 a thousand."

P. 130-31: - "In 1831 Tom McCrea's apple orchard in Raleigh sold apples for 12¢ a bushel. They were plentiful and going to waste. Potatoes sold at 25¢ a bushel."
"Near the mouth of the Thames River and along the shores of Lake St. Clair, were the French Canadian farmers who had settled around the great marshes (1831). Their chief occupation was in

keeping herds of cattle and horses, which found pasture in the marshes during the summer and were fed on wild hay in the winter.

In 1835 wheat and peas were selling for about 34¢ a bushel, barley and corn for 30¢ and oats for 23¢."

P. 158 -"district government built roads in 1804 but they were not kept in repair. Loaded wagons and carts were unable to get through to Sandwich until 1807. There were primitive log bridges over Baptiste's and Jeannette's creeks."

P. 160 - "The township line between Raleigh and Tilbury East was not cut for a wagon until 1835" - One described it as the worst road he had ever been on.

P. 164 - "Stagecoaches came in 1828 along the Thames - in 1797 Matthew Dolsen operated his tavern in Dover East, two or three miles below the Forks at Chatham. Each of the four sons of Thomas Crow had his own tavern. (1834) Corn Whiskey cost 3¢ and meals 12-½ ¢."

P.168 - "A post office was established on the Thames in Raleigh in 1816 with Thomas McCrae as postmaster. Steamboats were running between the Detroit River and Chatham in 1830, making connections with the stagecoaches twice a week."

P. 187 - "Except for the Moravian Chapel at Fairfield (began in 1792) there were no churches on the lower Thames until 1802, when a Roman Catholic chapel was built in Tilbury East to serve the French people of that area. It was named St. Peter's, and once a month a priest came from Sandwich to officiate. In 1835, the parish was then so extensive that Father Morin had to hold missions in private homes in Raleigh and Dover and in Chatham at the home of Elias Dauphin."

P. 150-251: "Around the mouth of the Thames River the many hundreds of acres of flat, treeless prairie still remained the resort of ducks and old wildfowl. (1845) In the summer time many cattle might be seen, half hidden in the tall grass. Sir Richard Bonnycastle likened the sight of this unbroken sea of verdure to the pampas of South America. Droves of wild horses and cattle, stretching as far as the eye could reach, especially on the south side of the river, roamed . . . when wanted, they were caught with a noose . . ." Many of the French inhabitants raised flocks of geese.

p. 263 - Chatham had 812 inhabitants in 1841 - 1500 in 1845, and 2000 in 1850.

P. 298 - St. Joseph's Roman Catholic Church was begun on May 30, 1847, when the foundation was laid by Bishop Lefèvre of Detroit, on the land secured in 1836 . . . completed the following November, under the supervision of Rev. Father Jos. V. Jaffre of the Society of Jesus, who had come to Chatham in 1845 as the first parish priest. Before that time services had been conducted in private houses, among them Elias Dauphin's, by priests from St. Peter's in Tilbury or from Sandwich. When Father Jaffre first came he celebrated his first mass in Reardon's wagon-shop in 1845. A group of 25 families got together, stones were brought from Amherstburg, brick obtained in Chatham, and oak and walnut timber from the vicinity. Mass was said two Sundays a month in Chatham, and on the other Sundays in such places as Wallaceburg, Blenheim, Tilbury, Thamesville and Bothwell.

St. Joseph's
History of Parish before 1913.
Rev. Father Vincent Caron o. m. i.

In the year 1836 the plot of ground known as the Catholic Church land was received from the government of that day by Right Rev. Dr. McDonell, Bishop of Kingston, with the understanding that a Catholic Church be built thereon. To Mr. Peter Paul Lacroix, Government Land agent here at that time, and who for two terms had the honour of representing this district in the parliament at Quebec, was left the selection of the land and he certainly exercised excellent judgment in the matter. The government surveyor, Mr. McIntosh, surveyed the plot which comprised all that land bounded now by Wellington, Raleigh, Richmond and Queen streets. It was not however until 1847 that the realization of this contract began to take form and shape. In the meantime however divine services were held at long and irregular intervals in private homes by missionaries from St. Peter's and Sandwich. In 1835 Rev. Father Morin celebrated mass in the house of Mr. Eli Dauphin in Chatham as well as in Raleigh and other places throughout the County. Later Rev. Rather Raynell of St. Peter's used to visit Raleigh about once a month and say mass in the homes of Mr. John Finn and Mr. Timothy Dillon. But the strong faith of the settlers was not satisfied with this, to them, meager service to God and Sunday after Sunday would see them wending their way to St. Peter's church in Tilbury East. Many interesting stories are told of the hardships endured and the sacrifices made by the settlers in order to hear mass on Sundays. People living in Raleigh and Harwich would start on their pilgrimage to St. Peter's on Saturday staying over night in Chatham. Then early on Sunday morning with their co-frères in Chatham, they would start out on their long walk to St. Peter's, carrying a lunch with them. After mass Father Morin would take them into a room provided with chairs, table and a stove where they could prepare and eat the lunch they brought. This finished, they would start on the return journey home. And such a journey as this, was through dense forests, the paths impeded with tangled underbrush and ever and always with them the terrible fear of the wolves that prowled through the forest.

As the Catholic population of Ontario had been steadily increasing during these years it was found necessary to make a division in the diocese of Kingston and in 1842 all that portion of the Province west of the Eastern boundary of the Province of Ontario was erected into a new diocese with Toronto as the Episcopal see and Rt. Rev. Dr. Power was appointed the first bishop. In 1843 Bishop Power undertook a trip through his large diocese and among other places visited Chatham saying mass in a small frame storehouse that stood in the rear of the present Bank of Commerce.

About the time the Catholics in the district began to think seriously of having a church of their own and all that was needed was a man filled with courage, energy and zeal should come forward to guide and encourage by word and example the efforts of the people. Such a man was the first parish priest of Chatham, Rev. Father Joseph Vincent Jaffre, of the Society of Jesus, who came here from Sandwich in 1845. He said his first mass in a small wagon shop belonging to Mr. Reardon, situated where now stands Stone`s dry goods store. Later services were held in a small school on the corner of Wellington and Sixth streets, then for a short time in a small house of Mr. Tobin`s where the present Canadian Pacific Railway depot stands and then for nearly two years in the home of Mr. Patrick O'Flynn across from the Tecumseh Park, until the first part of St. Joseph's church was enclosed in 1847. For two Sundays in the month Father Jaffre said mass in Chatham, the rest of the time he visited neighbouring places forming new missions. Wallaceburg, Blenheim, Tilbury, Thamesville and Bothwell are all the fruits of his untiring zeal and energy. Father Jaffre laboured incessantly to organize the parish and to collect funds from the settler in Howard, Raleigh, Dover and Chatham in order to build a church. He was nobly assisted in this work by Mr. Patrick

Kelly who spent much time going about the country with Father Jaffre and another very staunch friend and helper was Mr. J.B. Williams. Between 25 and 30 families were thus gathered together forming, as it were, the nucleus of the splendid congregation of over 600 families who today worship at St. Joseph's and the same names that adorn the record of these early days today stand out bright and clear as staunch, true friends of the Church. Kelly, Williams, Doyle, Reardon, Lacroix, O'Keefe, O'Flynn, Donovan, Downey, Forhan, Early, Dooling, O'Hare, Reaume, Ryan, Tobin, O'Neill, Waddick, Dillon, Hogan, Lamb, Taff, Quinn, Robert, Finn and Sullivan. Thus, with willing hearts and willing hands was the work for St. Joseph's church commenced. The settlers accustomed to using spade and axe, hammer and pick went to work in earnest and Father Jaffre began to see his cherished plans realized. Stones were brought from Amherstburg, timbers were cut form the neighbouring forests of oak and walnut and some brought from St. Thomas, brick was made in a small brickyard where now stands St. Joseph's hospital and on the 30th day of May in the year 1847 the corner stone of St. Joseph's church was laid by Right Rev. Monseigneur Lefèvre, administrator of the diocese of Detroit. Father Jaffre laboured in the parish till 1860 building in 1857 the first presbytery. In 1860 he was sent by his Superior to Brooklyn N. Y. to look after the spiritual needs of the immigrants who about that year began to swarm into the country. From 1860 to 1878 priests of the Jesuit order continued to look after the interests of St. Joseph's parish and the following names seem quite familiar yet to the older settlers, Fathers Grimott, Petit, Ferard, McQuaid, Comilleau, Gockeln, Dumortier, Bayard, Delabaysse, Sherlock, Holzer, Baudin and Marshall.

In 1853 Sandwich was erected into a diocese with Bishop Pinsonneault in charge. On August 1st, 1873 the Basilian Fathers of Assumption College, Sandwich, took charge of St. Joseph's parish and many of the older residents remember well the kindly and gentle Fathers Hours, Grand and Ferguson who at different times resided here.

As a great number of Germans settled in the parish about this time, coming direct from the Fatherland, and as there were no German priests among the Basilians, they appealed to Bishop Pinsonneault to send here a priest who understood their language. This resulted in the Basilians withdrawing from Chatham and Bishop asked the Franciscans to take charge of the parish. Coming as they did from the German Province of Cincinnati, they were conversant with the language and on January 25th ,1878 we find Rev. Father Eugene settled here as parish priest of Chatham. Father Eugene holds at the present time, the important office of Superior General of the Franciscan order in America. He remained here not quite a year and was succeeded by Rev. Father William in Dec. 1878 who remained as pastor of St. Joseph's until 1889.

About the year 1880 the Episcopal see was changed from Sandwich to London, the latter being so much more central and the Archbishop Walsh of Toronto was the first Bishop of London.

It was during Rev. Father Williams pastorate that the present magnificent temple on the corner of Wellington and Queen streets was erected at a cost of about $65,000. It stands on the site of the humble church erected in earlier days by the heroic Father Jaffre. From 1889 to 1897 Rev. Father Paul had charge of the parish, and during his stay the parish held an unique and interesting celebration commemorating its golden jubilee. It was a three days function commencing on Sunday Oct. 8th and continuing on Monday and Tuesday the 9th and 10th, and it was a joyous and happy congregation that assisted at the services. While at the first mass in Chatham in 1835 there were but five persons assisting, at the time of the celebration of the golden jubilee there were 2200 Catholics in the parish and the congregation today numbers over 3000. From 1897 to 1901 Rev. Father Solanus had charge of the parish and in 1901 came Rev. Father James, the present honoured pastor of St. Joseph's. In 1909 the parishioners oversaw a thorough overhauling and the walls and ceilings were decorated, the work costing in the neighbourhood of $10,000, occupied about eight months, but it was beautifully done and the church was formally reopened for services on December 12th, 1909. It holds the record today of being one of the most beautifully decorated churches in the country. To Rev. Father James is due the credit of collecting the money for paying for this work as well as for paying off a debt of about $20,000 on the church proper, the balance of the latter being wiped out only this year.

The present bell in the tower of St. Joseph's rang out the hours of service in the old church as well. There is a story told of a Mr. Flanigan, on whom devolved the duty of ringing the bell in the old church, that one day the rope broke and down crashed the bell through the roof to the floor. Mr. Flanigan escaped unhurt but the picture he made crawling out through the door in his fright with a couple of boards on his back, was talked of by some of his old chums for long afterward. The tone of the bell was somewhat injured in the fall but it was sent to Detroit to be recast and today does excellent service in the bell tower of the new church.

There was a time
by Lisa and Jim Gilbert

According to much research, the first religious services in Chatham, Pain Court, St. Peter's on the Thames and surroundings were conducted by Jesuits.

I hereby wish to acknowledge the following article published by Jim and Lisa Gilbert on July 22, 1992 relating to early churches.

Page 20, Chatham This Week, July 22, 1992

First religious services in Chatham conducted by Jesuits

Pioneer life in the Chatham area may have been a bit crude and rough at times, but that did not mean the spiritual side of their existence was ignored nor taken lightly.

Probably the first religious services in Kent County were conducted by the Jesuit missionaries, who visited the Neutral Indian camp site of the present day Maple Leaf Cemetery.

The first actual religious structure in the area was a small Roman Catholic chapel built, facing the Thames River, in Tilbury Township on the present day site of St. Peter's Church. The church records date back to the chapel's dedication on July 8, 1802.

Within the City of Chatham, the first church was built in 1819. It was called St. Paul's Anglican Church and was erected on the north side of Stanley Street, almost opposite present day Victoria Residence. It had a rectory on one side and Chatham`s first burying ground on the other side.

In 1841, the Wesleyan Methodists erected a church on King Street where the CPR Station once stood in recent years. The building, seating about 400, continued in use until the erection of Park Street Methodist Church . . . 1871.

In 1845, the first Roman Catholic Church began construction on the present day site of St.

Joseph`s Church. Rev. Father Joseph Vincent Jaffre was the pastor and was rewarded for his effort, in later years, by having a street in the area (Jeffrey Street) named after him.

In 1867, the Methodists erected a little brick church on Wellington Street and, remarkably, it still survives today although few people know is as a church.

It was, until a few years ago, the home of M. J. Smith Feeds. If one looks carefully at the structure today, the bricked-in outline of the church windows can be clearly seen.

In 1837, a 10-acre tract of land bounded by William, Wellington, Prince and Park Streets was reserved for the benefit of the Church of Scotland. A permanent structure, however, was not built on this tract until 1847 due to the schism in the parent Church of Scotland at the time.

The Free and United Presbyterian Churches which, in 1875, had become connected with the Presbyterian Church in Canada, four years later united in Chatham under the name of the First Presbyterian Church with Rev. Angus McColl and Rev. William Walker as joint pastors.

In 1889, when Rev. F. H. Larks became minister, the first steps were taken to build a first Presbyterian Church, which opened in May of 1893. Today, it's the last of three beautiful structures that grace the corners of Fifth and Wellington Streets - the other two being Harrison Hall and Central School.

An attempt to outline the development of each and every church in Chatham is certainly well beyond the scope of this column; however, since many of the churches in town have written their own histories, it`s a project that has interesting possibilities.

It would certainly be an exciting research project and one would reveal much about our pioneer ancestors who, along with their hard life, hard drinking and rough ways never forgot their spiritual roots.

*Jim and Lisa Gilbert are local award-winning broadcasters, educators and historians.

Deuxième église de Pain Court, érigée en 1874 et remplacée en 1911, par un temple au style roman.

Source: Pro-f-ont, Pain Court et Grande Pointe,
Paul François Sylvestre   p. 107

Pain Court

The origin of the name Pain Court may be of interest here before entering into the history of the parish. When the first settlers came to that part of the country early in the last century, the nearest flour mill to them was in Detroit. Those who had neither horses nor wagons to drive to Detroit found it very hard to procure flour and in summer time would often risk going to Detroit in canoes in order to get flour and provisions. These trips would occupy often over a week, so we can well imagine the misery and suffering endured in bad weather when it was impossible to get to Detroit. The expression "Bread is Short" became quite a familiar one among the settlers expressed more simply in French by the words Pain Court, a name which still clings to the little village in the now rich and prosperous township of Dover.

Until the year 1845 there is no record of a church at Pain Court. In that year Rev. Father Morin of St. Peter's visited the district and held services in a small chapel built where the cemetery stands today, but as he had several missions under his charge he could seldom visit Pain Court, although there were quite a number of settlers in that district, mostly of French origin, who had come there from the Province of Quebec. In 1854 the people of Pain Court signed a petition and sent it to Msgr. Adolphe Pinsonneault, Bishop of Sandwich, asking permission to build a church as the congregation was increasing and they felt that they could afford both to build a church and support a pastor. The Bishop encouraged them in their undertaking and gave the desired permission, appointing the Rev. Father Raynell of St. Peter's, to look after the interests of the new parish. The building was begun in 1854 and the corner stone of the new church was blessed on the 30th of August the same year by Rev. Father Point, vicar-general of the diocese. Though the church cost only about $2000 it was a heavy debt for the young parish for in those days the splendid farms that are today the pride of Dover were either low-lying marshes or forest lands. It was not until 1862 that the church was finished and plastered. Father Raynell remained in charge of the parish until 1869 when he entered a Jesuit monastery. In the same year Father Duprat was sent to the parish. In 1874 the church was destroyed by fire but the little congregation was not daunted. They at once set to work to build a new brick church, material for which was made by Mr. Edward Fountain who had a flourishing brickyard along Pain Court Creek. This church was never well built, however, and was really not finished until 1885. Its poor construction was noticed all the time for plaster, stones and brick were often falling from the walls.

Father Baeur succeeded Father Duprat as parish priest of Pain Court and proved himself most energetic in the district. In 1884 he established a mission at Big Point and built St. Philippe church and rebuilt the parsonage. Father Villeneuve then took charge of the parish for a couple of years and was succeeded by Rev. Father Andrieux, who is still living in Windsor retiring on account of poor health and old age. Father Courtois then took charge until 1911 when the present pastor, Father Emery was sent there by Bishop Fallon. The church so poorly constructed in 1874 was considered unsafe by many and the late Bishop McEvay warned the people of this. Bishop Fallon on his first visit to the church condemned it outright and preparations were made to build a new church just as soon as Father Emery took charge of the parish. The foundation was laid on May 10, 1911, on the 13th of June the corner stone was blessed by Bishop Fallon and on March 3rd, 1912, the church was formally opened, just ten months after the foundation was laid. The building is a magnificent Gothic structure costing about $44,000, more than $12,000 of which has already been paid off. During the same year a fine brick parsonage was built costing about $6000. Father Emery, the present pastor was born and baptized in Grande Pointe and received his early education there studying later for the priesthood at the Grand Seminary, Montreal.

To pass through the village of Pain Court today and ask the names of the residents we would find that they are identical with the names of those sturdy pioneers through whose energy and zeal the first church was built, Thibodeau, Emery, Robert, Blais, Ouellette, Goudreau, Faubert, Béchard, Primeau, Caron, Bélanger, Houle, Pinsonneault etc.

On Good Friday of this year, March 21, 1913, the splendid new church in Pain Court suffered severely from the hurricane that swept over this district. The two big chimneys were blown down crashing through the roof of the church, one chimney passing through the main floor into the basement and doing altogether about $2,500 damages.

–Père Vincent Caron

Le "faîte" de notre héritage patrimonial

A. D. Emery, Curé
Pain Court, Ont.   19 août, 1926.

Alfred -David Emery, onzième curé de Pain Court. (1911- 28) naquit à la Grande Pointe le 22 mai 1873, de François Emery et de Rosalie Tétrault. Il fit ses études classiques au collège de Sainte-Thérèse de Blainville, ses études philosophiques à Sandwich et sa théologie au grand séminaire de Montréal. Il fut ordonné prêtre à London par Monseigneur McEvay le 20 décembre 1902. Après son ordination il fut nommé immédiatement vicaire à la cathédrale où il exerça le ministère sacerdotal jusqu'au mois de mars 1901 alors qu'il fut nommé administrateur de Kinkora. A la mort du curé O'Neil, juin 1901, if fut nommé curé de cette paroisse et y demeura jusqu'au mois de janvier, le 21, 1911. A Kinkora, il construit un presbytère, une école, répara l'église, puis établit une école séparée catholique. Enfin, le 25 janvier 1911 il prend charge de la paroisse de Pain Court où il avait été envoyé. Pourquoi?

"Where there is church and house to be built at once." Voilà la tâche qui lui était assignée. Tout était à faire et refaire. La tâche pouvait décourager n'importe quel curé qui connaissait les conditions de la paroisse d'alors. Le nouveau curé mit tout l'ouvrage à faire entre les mains du Sacré-Coeur, et se contenta de travailler de toutes ses forces. En quelques années la paroisse fut complètement renouvelée. Le Sacré-Coeur a bien conduit les affaires. En quelques années furent construits à Pain Court: église, presbytère, couvent, deux monuments religieux, un trottoir en ciment entre les deux extrémités du village, garage, appentis, érection de deux croix. Un Bulletin Paroissial fut fondé et paraît régulièrement tous les mois depuis1911. Ses récréations se passent au bien de la jeunesse et à l'école des langues."

A. D. Emery - Album souvenir de la paroisse de Pain Court   p. 62 - 63

Former Pain Court priest gave valuable contribution

One of the best contributors to the history of Kent County with the arrival of the first French families in the area was the late Rev. A. D. Emery, the parish priest of Immaculate Conception Church at Pain Court from 1911 to 1928.

Father Emery had a passion for research of many types. He spent the best part of two years and more, tracing back the histories of many families whose descendants had settled in Québec and later immigrated to Southwestern Ontario and settled in Dover Township.

Father admitted later, it was a task even if it was a labour of love. Numerous trips were made to Montréal, Québec, Île d'Orléans and points east.

One of the early settlers on record was believed to be Robert Caron who was born in Lyons, France in the year 1612. He arrived at Québec in 1637 and his immediate descendants were in the Pain Court block about the year 1705 or 1706.

Nicholas Gourde born 1610 in Belisac, province of Roussillon, France landed in Trois-Rivières Québec in 1665. The family was in Dover Township shortly after the year 1710. According to Father Emery's painstaking research, he was able to establish the most important fact that no less than 52 basic families from France had their progeny listed as descendants and settlers in the Southwestern part of Ontario.

To go into details regarding these numerous families who left their motherland in France to brave the rigours of our cold Canadian winters would take much time.

Descendants of families who left their native land to come to Canada in the17th century could be traced to some 15 provinces of France. Those included were Guillaume Antaya, Louis Béchard, Henri Bélisle, François Bélanger, Jacques Bernier, Pierre Blais, Gaspard Boucher, François Bourassa, Pierre Bourdeau, Mathurin Cadotte, Thomas Chartrands, Olivier Charbonneau, Claude Charron and Maximillien Couture.

Among those who came from French provinces bordering the Atlantic and the Bay of Biscayne included Guillaume Lauzon, Guillaume Couture, Léonard Leblanc, Claude Philippe Gauthier, Charles Demarais, Antoine Emery, probably one of the forefathers of Father Emery, Jean Goudreau, Abel Turcotte, Julien Laplante, René Ouellette, Martin Provost, Jean Pinsonneault, and Philip Robert. There were several families of Primeau, a few Pilotte and at least four had the surname of Faubert. As the years moved on and the numbers of settlers grew, there were several families with the name of Martin, Laplante, Roy who settled along the North bank of the Thames River.

Two families with the name of Daigneau dit Laprise, arrived about the year 1755. Their parents came from Angers, province of Anjou, others came from Mort, évêché de Poitiers, France.

Some of Father Emery's observations indicate that he followed some of the historical system that appeared in the "Jesuit Relations" which was the product of Historian Parkmanon.

Father Emery supplied considerable information from his notes to the Kent Historical Society. A former pastor also supplied some of the early data concerning the parish when the first Volume of the Society's articles was published several years prior to the first World War.

Father Emery was an entrepreneur of his era. Film was a passion and relatively new in the early twentieth century. After his departure for St. Joachim in 1928 worthwhile memorabilia were discovered in the rector's attic in 1930 by Father Loiselle. By 1938 with Father Zotique Mailloux who was parish priest from 1933 - 45, we found hundreds of feet of film. By 1944, with the assistance of the equipment of the National Film Board and l'Office National du film in Ottawa, I started the task of editing some one hundred bobbins of film valued as keepsake films. The National Film Board was already supplying our schools with French and English versions of educational films as well as adult entertainment films in both languages. As of 1950 a two-hour bobbin of film exists depicting the early lives of our settlers in Pain Court. Other films are also registered such as the celebrations of the Pain Court centennial (1954) as well as its 125th anniversary. Two additional videos were produced, one French, one English in 1995.

According to Victor Lauriston`s "Romantic Kent" published in 1952, Reverend Father Alfred Emery "wrote exhaustively on the pioneers and about the church of Pain Court."[1] In his "Album souvenir de la paroisse Immaculée Conception de Pain Court." published in 1926, Father Emery commemorates a 75 year span of historical facts and events allocated to the community's foundation and growth from 1851 to 1926.

It is also noteworthy to mention Fred Coyne Hamil's critique recorded in "The Valley of the Lower Thames (1640 - 1850)" published in 1951 concerning Father Emery's meticulous historical presentations of the period :"Undoubtedly, it is the finest and most workmanlike production in the field of Kent History."[2]

1° Victor Lauriston, Romantic Kent 1952 p. 728
2° A. D. Emery, Album souvenirs de la paroisse de Pain Court 1851 - 1926
3° Fred Coyne Hamil, Valley of the Lower Thames 1951, p.

Mgr F.M. Fallon bénit la pierre angulaire de la 3e église accompagné
du curé A.D. Emery et de ses paroissiens - 13 juin 1911.
L'ouverture officielle eut lieu le 3 mars 1912

Église Immaculée Conception de Pain Court, Ontario érigée en 1911.
Elle fut la proie des flammes le 2 janvier 1937.

Intérieur de l'église Immaculée Conception
de Pain Court, érigée en 1911

Une bénédiction providentielle.

Le Frère André à Pain Court.

Frère André, l'humble portier du Collège Notre- Dame à Montréal, l'apôtre infatigable et bras droit de Saint Joseph, était âgé de 76 ans lors de sa visite à Pain Court en 1921.

Quelle profusion de grâces accordées aux paroissiens! Ensemble, ils ont pu solidifier le patronage du deuxième patron et protecteur de leur paroisse..

Ce prodigieux guérisseur d'âmes et de corps fit éclat chez nous. La messe du 23 octobre a été célébrée en présence du Frère André y compris les membres du clergé des paroisses avoisinantes accompagnés d'un cortège d'enfants de choeurs de la paroisse. Cependant pour quelques privilégiés, sa visite était encore plus significative; Napoléon Roy et Roland Gagner, avec leurs copains, Armand Roy et Alfred Pinsonneault, p'tits bonhommes de sept ou huit ans, étaient servants de messe pour la célébration liturgique.

De dire Roland Gagner: "Ce jour-là, je m'en rappelle encore."

Qui peut oublier la croix du Mont-Royal? Dressée au faîte du dôme de l'Oratoire Saint-Joseph de Montréal, elle resplendit, à perte de vue, douce et féconde, attirant par milliers les pèlerins vers ce lieu saint, un chef-d'oeuvre d'architecture et un projet longtemps rêvé par le visionnaire et vigilant "Bienheureux André Bessette" (1845 - 1937).

L'Église canadienne du 20e siècle a choisi le 6 janvier pour honorer le Bienheureux André Bessette. Cette date figure au calendrier liturgique.

Dover Hotel - Dieudonné Gagner
Chemin de fer électrique, Chatham à Pain Court
Electric car terminal open 1910
Le p'tit char débarquant passagers devant l'hôtel Dover.
On peut reconnaître le propriétaire D.D. Gagner Sr. (en chemise blanche)

     Salut à M. Narcisse Béchard. "Il naquit à Pain Court en décembre 1862, fils de Calixte Béchard et Marie Houle. Il épousa Thérèse Daniel en 1897. De 1892 à 1902, il devient maître de Poste à Pain Court suivi par M. Alphy Cheff de Grande Pointe. Il remplit plusieurs fonctions, assesseur, percepteur de taxes, conseiller, préfet, Juge de paix ainsi que commissaire d'école pendant de nombreuses années. Il fut président du comité chargé d'intéresser une compagnie de chemin de fer électrique afin de construire une voie ferrée de Pain Court à Chatham. Ses efforts furent couronnés de succès. Cette nouvelle voie fut terminée en 1910. If fut aussi président d'un comité chargé d'établir un système de téléphone dans la municipalité de Dover." Merci à M. Béchard pour sa contribution à l'évolution de notre belle région.

1. A.D. Émery, Album souvenir de la paroisse de l'Immaculée Conception de Pain Court, page 95.

Attention! La parade va bientôt défiler.

Un tombereau chargé de gens de la place qui attendent
le signal pour le déroulement de la parade du 75ᵉ anniversaire en1926.

Sur la photo ci-dessus, on aperçoit:

      Debout en avant - Alphy Caron
      Assis dans le tombereau - Dieudonné Gagner Sr. (qui tient les guides)
      Chapeau à la main - Adélard Caron
      En avant des boeufs - Hercule Trahan

The Church of the Immaculate Conception in the heart of Pain Court

This church was erected after the previous church was destroyed by fire and is a reminder of the early days of struggle in "short bread." (Star Staff Photo) 1938

Interior of Immaculate Conception in 1938

Pain Court Landmark Changes Hands

According to Pain Court resident, Amédée Emery, the Central Hotel was constructed in 1893 by his grandfather the late Alphy Cheff. A native of Grande Pointe, the late Mr. Cheff moved a small hotel off the site in order to build what was considered a show place at the time.

He also operated a sawmill at the rear of the Hotel and sawed all the wood that went into the construction of the building. Mrs. Cheff, the former Catherine Yott, worked alongside her husband in the hotel business and she was known far and wide for her excellent "cuisine."

A few years prior to Mr. Cheff's death in 1936, Francis and Jacob Roy, along with their wives, operated the hotel as well as the grocery store.

For a decade or more, Mrs. Marie Emery managed the Post-office and resided at the hotel with her husband and family. All were part of the establishment which progressed well. After Mr. Alphy Cheff's death, Francis Roy owned and operated the grocery store with his family while Jacob continued with the hotel for a very short period. Much later Joseph Roy, Jacob's son and his wife Frances, operated the business until it was sold to a new proprietor.

It has changed hands many times but the Central Tavern, as it is known today, is still thriving under the management of Bob and Rose Branquet, the owners for 19 years.

THIS OLD PHOTO SHOWS CENTRAL HOTEL IN 1915
...building was one of the showplaces in Pain Court

73

Vocation sacerdotales des paroisses de Pain Court, Grande Pointe et Saint Pierre de Raleigh.

1854 - 1900

Alfred Béchard	fils de	Moïse Béchard et Lena Rémillard
Hubert Robert	fils de	Pierre Robert et Julienne Gaudreau
Philippe Daigneau . . .	fils de	Hubert Daigneau et Eugénie Pilotte
Théophile Chapelain .	fils de	Antoine Valentin et Josephine Wagnes
A. D. Emery	fils de	Francis Emery et Rosalie Tétreault
Théophile Martin	fils de	Lévi Martin et Caroline Faubert
Joseph Emery	fils de	Joseph Emery et Martha Yott
Ovila Charbonneau . . .	fils de	Edouard Charbonneau et Cordilia Philion
Dominat Caron	fils de	Joseph Caron et Hermine Laplante
Pierre Bourdeau	fils de	Thomas Bourdeau et Orise Lanoue

1900 - 1990

Vincent Caron	fils de	Eugène Caron et Philomène Bourassa
Oscar Martin	fils de	Narcisse Martin et Bella Bachand
Augustin Caron	fils de . . .	Solomon Caron et Roseanne Faubert
Raoul Yott	fils de	Alexandre Yott et Théotiste Lemoyne
Adrien Roy	fils de	Léo Roy et Ursule Trudell
Léo Dénommé	fils de	Télesphore Dénommé et Antoinette Laporte
Jacques Carron	fils de	Alphonse Carron et Gertrude Pinsonneault
Eugène Roy	fils de	Norman Roy et Helen Tremblay
Robert Couture	fils de	Lionel Couture et Eileen Labadie
Marcel Caron	fils de	François Caron et Mae Bastien

Les religieuses des paroisses de Pain Court, Grande Pointe et St-Pierre de Raleigh.

Les Soeurs des Saints Noms de Jésus et de Marie

Marie Demers . . . . Soeur Marie Romuald
Elmire Thibodeau . . . . Soeur Antoinette de Marie
Pamela Gauthier . . . . Soeur Marie Zacharie
Claire Goure . . . . Soeur Marie Gérard Majella
Edna Caron . . . . Soeur Gérard-Marie
Anna Caron . . . . Soeur Marie Claire-Thérèse
Clara Caron . . . . Soeur Marie Rosa-Edna
Léona Caron . . . . Soeur Augustin-Marie
Marie-Thérèse Caron . . . . Soeur Marie Bernard-Adrien
Césarine Thibodeau . . . . Soeur Marie Cécile-Antoinette
Marie-Louise Caron . . . . Soeur Marie Blanche-Alma
Annette Caron . . . . Mère Provinciale, Soeur Marie Ubaldine
Marie-Louise Béchard . . . . Soeur Marie Anne-Eva
Anna Daniel . . . . Soeur Marie Lucie
Edna Daniel . . . . Soeur Marie Rita du Crucifix
Pauline Trahan . . . . Soeur Marie Jean-Victor
Marie-Thérèse Caron . . . . Soeur Marie du Crucifix
Lucille Caron . . . . Soeur Marguerite-Aline

Les Soeurs Ursulines

Hélène Trudell . . . . Mère Marie Rosalie
Nellie Trudell . . . . Mère Marie Eucharia
Della Daniel . . . . Mère Marie Ethelbert
Vivienne Caron . . . . Mère Marie Anne Geneviève
Rose-Rita Roy . . . . Mère François-Xavier
Béatrice Benoit . . . . Mère Marie Phyllis

Les Soeurs de St. Joseph

Rosanna Bourassa . . . . Soeur Marie Joachim
Loma Laprise . . . . Soeur Marie Rufina
Viola Gagner . . . . Soeur Marie Yvonne
Evéline Gagner . . . . Soeur Marie Evéline
Agnès Martin . . . . Soeur Gervais
Eva Faubert . . . . Soeur Jean-Marie
Edna Faubert . . . . Soeur Marie Léocrita
Ursuline Roy . . . . Soeur Marie Rosaire
Marguerite Trudell . . . . Soeur Marie Rosamond

Les Soeurs Grises de la Croix, d'Ottawa

Laurette Gagner . . . . Soeur Marie Zacharie
Claudia Gagner . . . . Soeur Marie Gérald
Rose-Marie Trahan . . . . Soeur Claire-Pauline
Evéline Pinsonneault . . . . Soeur Jean-Roméo
Anne-Louise Gagner . . . . Soeur Anne-Louise Gagner

Les Soeurs Missionnaires de l'Immaculée Conception

Jeanne Roy . . . .   Soeur Anna-Marie
Marguerite Roy . . . .   Soeur Marie-Angélique
Marie Roy   . . . .   Soeur Joseph-Marie
Louise Roy . . . .   Soeur

Les Filles de la Sagesse

Laurette Roy . . . .   Soeur Laurette de l'Assomption

Les Soeurs de Loretto

Marie-Anne Caron (Adélard Caron) . .   Soeur Marie Lucina

Les Soeurs de l'Immaculée Coeur de Marie

Cécile Campbell   (Joseph Campbell) . Soeur

Les Soeurs de l'Hôtel Dieu

Bella Goure . . . . .Soeur Goure
Cécile Laprise . . . . .Soeur Cécile Laprise
Cécile Cartier . . . . Soeur Cécile Cartier
Florida Cadotte   . . . . .Soeur St. Augustin
Mae Cartier . . . . .Soeur Mae Cartier

Les Soeurs Dominicaines du Rosaire

Simonne Pinsonneault . . . . .Soeur Marie-de-Fatima

Hommage aux bâtisseurs de notre héritage
religieux et culturel

Antoine-Claude Ternet	1851 - 55
Thomas Raynel ....1855 - 58, 59, 1861-63, 1864-69	
Barthelémy Boubat	1858 - 58
Gilbert Girard	1859 - 60
Joseph Grimot	1860 - 61
Paul Andrieux ....1863 - 64, 1886 - 1901	
Calixte Duprat	1869 - 82
Joseph Boule	1882 - 86
Philias Villeneuve	1886 - 1901
Joseph-Emélien Courtois	1901 - 11
Alfred David Emery	1911 - 28
Joseph A. Loiselle	1928 - 33
Zotique Mailloux	1933 - 45
Charles Laliberté	1946 - 50
Joseph Isaac Ducharme	1950 - 54
Mgr W. Boudreau	1954 - 55
Euclide Chevalier	1955 - 64
Léo Charron	1964 - 80
Charles Sylvestre	1980 - 89
Gilbert Simard	1989 - 95
Alexandro Costa	1995 - 97
Robert Champagne	1997 -

Vicaires de la paroisse de Pain Court

Zotique Mailloux	1930 - 32
Philip Mugan	1932
Césaire Levaque	1941
Laurent Lacharité	1945
Pierre Boudreau	1945
Charles Sylvestre	1948
Paul Bénéteau	1951
Ulysse Lefaivre	1951 - 54
Pierre Boudreau	1956 - 64

Grande Pointe

Première église bâtie en 1882
et démolie en 1949

Église St-Philippe de Grande Pointe
bâtie en 1949.

Photos -Livre Centenaire -Grande Pointe. 1886 - 1986

Première école de Grande Pointe - 1873
L'édifice sert aussi de chapelle jusqu'au moment où l'église
Saint-Philippe est construite en 1882.

Historique du nom "Grande Pointe"

Les pionniers français appelaient cette partie nord de Dover, "la grande pointe," en raison de la pointe de terre irrégulière qui s'étendait dans le lac Ste- Claire. Dans les dernières années, le Département des postes a reconnu ce fait et on accorda un bureau de poste à ce district en 1882. Comme l'histoire se répète, en 1964, le Département a renommé le district en lui donnant un nom officiel.

Dans les premiers registres trouvés dans l'Église de Pain Court pour les années 1850 à 1882 lorsque St-Philippe était une mission de Pain Court, toutes les entrées concernant les paroissiens de Dover Nord étaient sous le nom de "Grande Pointe."

Dans son livre "Romantic Kent," M. Victor Lauriston, écrivain et historien du Comté de Kent, écrivait sur la page 357, ch. 32, intitulé "Later Days of Dover," et imprimée en 1952, il fait allusion à l'établissement de la nouvelle paroisse de "Grande Pointe" communément connue comme "Big Point" dû à l'augmentation de 2000 âmes ou presque dans la mission de La Tranche en 1871.

History of the name "Grande Pointe"

The first early French settlers referred to this part of North Dover as "la grande pointe" referring to the jagged point of land which extended into Lake St. Clair. As a result, a Post Office was granted to the district in 1882, and history repeated itself when in 1964 the Department renamed the district giving it an official name.

In the original registers kept at the Pain Court Church, for the years 1850 to 1882 when St. Philippe was a mission of Pain Court, all entries concerning parishioners of North Dover were referred to as of "la Grande Pointe."

In his book "Romantic Kent," Victor Lauriston, Kent County's well known writer and historian, writing on page 357, chapter 32 entitled "Later Days of Dover," printed in 1952, when describing days circa 1871 of the Pain Court district, makes allusion to the establishment of the new parish of "Grande Pointe," popularly known as "Big Point."

Ref.   Livre Centennaire Page 8 - Grande Pointe 1886 - 1986

Alphy Cheff

At the Chatham Library re- Commemorative Biographical Record - I found this interesting piece of information relating to one of the pioneers of Grande Pointe.

ALPHY CHEFF, proprietor of the "Central Hotel," and postmaster, Pain Court, Dover township, county of Kent, and one of the leading men of the community, was born at Big Pointe, same township, six miles from his present home, Aug. 1862, a son of Joseph and Mary Ann (Martin) Cheff, of Montreal.

Joseph Cheff was born in St. Jacques le Mineur, county Laprairie, Quebec, June 30, 1826, and his wife was born at St. Philippe, in the same county, Oct. 6, 1845, settling at Big Point, where Mr. Cheff purchased and operated a farm, and a few years later built a sawmill where he did an extensive business. He made that place his home until 1877, when he retired. Since 1883 he has been postmaster of Big Point, most ably discharging the duties of the office. In politics he has always been a member of the Reform party. Both he and his wife are consistent members of the

Roman Catholic Church. The children born to this union were as follows: Delaise, who married Joseph Pinsonneault, a farmer of Dover township: Eva, deceased; Josephat, a farmer, at Frenchtown, Montana; Liza, who married Theo. Bourassa, a hotel keeper at Chatham, On; Sifros, deceased; Edmond, a farmer in Dover township; Alphy Zephire, a farmer and merchant of Big Point, Dover township; and Eva, deceased, who married Joseph Thibodeau.

Joseph Cheff was a son of Joseph Cheff, Sr., of Montreal, who came to this county a few years prior to his son. He was an hotel keeper and settled in Dover township. During the Rebellion in 1837-38 he took an active part.

In 1888, in Big Point, Mr. Alphy Cheff was married to Catherine Yott, and their children are: Mary, Melina and Georgina, Twins. Mrs. Chef was born at Kingston, Ont., on Wolf Island, Nov. 25, 1862, a daughter of Frank and Mattie (Yott) Yott, who although bearing the same name, were of no known relationship. Mr. Yott was a sailor for many years, coming to County Kent in 1865, and settling in Pain Court. He died in 1873, aged forty years, and his wife died in September, 1894, aged sixty years, and both are buried in Pain Court cemetery.

Mr. Cheff remained with his parents, upon the farm until his marriage, when he embarked in a mercantile business at Big Point, continuing in the same from 1883 - 1890, being in the meantime deputy postmaster. He then engaged in operating an hotel and sawmill at Pain Court. After three years he erected his present hostelry, six miles from Chatham — a brick building containing eleven rooms, well appointed with every convenience, where pleasant and comfortable entertainment is afforded the traveling public. The table is an excellent one, doing credit to the management of Mrs. Cheff, and the "Central Hotel" is patronized by the very best people who come to Pain Court, Ontario. Mr. Cheff also owns a fine farm of 100 acres at Big Point, which he rents. In October, 1902, he was appointed postmaster, and has since that date held the office, proving very acceptable to his constituents. In politics, like his father, Mr. Cheff is a member of the Reform party, and takes an active part in local affairs. In religious matters, both he and his wife are members of the Catholic Church. Genial, enterprising, public-spirited, Mr. Cheff is a man who wins many friends, and is justly recognized as one of the representative business men of Dover township.

This church stood on the ninth concession in Dover.
Today this is known as the parish cemetery.

Bulletin Paroissial.

"Un journal catholique dans une paroisse, c'est une
mission continuelle."—Paroles du Pape Léon XIII.

Vol. VII, No. 3   GRANDE POINTE, ONT.   Mars 1920

OBJETS A PREPARER POUR L'ADMINISTRATION DES SACREMENTS AUX MALADES.

Nous croyons rendre service aux familles en leur indiquant les préparatifs à faire pour l'administration des sacrements aux malades. Ce n'est pas aussi compliqué qu'on pourrait le croire.

Il faut préparer:

1o.—**Une table** couverte en entier d'une nappe blanche et placée près du malade.

2o.—**Un crucifix** sur la table.

3o.—**Deux chandeliers** avec cierges.

4o.—**Une assiette** contenant six boules de coton et un morceau de mie de pain. La ouate sert à essuyer les onctions sur le malade et le pain à purifier les doigts du prêtre.

5o.—**Un verre d'eau bénite** et un rameau bénit.

6o.—**Un autre verre d'eau ordinaire**, avec une serviette pour purifier et essuyer les doigts du prêtre après les onctions.

7o.—**Un linge pour servir de nappe** de communion au malade.

8o.—**Une petite cuillère.**

Remarque: 1o.—Tout ce qui reste dans l'assiette après la cérémonie doit être consumé par le feu.

2o.—Si le prêtre ne donne pas l'Extrême-Onction, les préparatifs sont les mêmes, moins l'assiette et son contenu.

Devoirs des personnes qui assistent un malade en danger de mort.

1o.—Inviter les parents et les amis du malade à assister à son administration afin de prier pour lui.

2o.—Se mettre à genoux depuis l'arrivée du prêtre jusqu'à son départ et s'unir aux prières de l'Eglise et à celles du malade.

3o.—Aider souvent le malade à produire des actes de Foi, d'Espérance, de Charité et de soumission à la volonté de Dieu; lui faire demander souvent pardon de ses péchés; lui faire invoquer fréquemment Jésus, Marie, Joseph son ange gardien.

4o.—L'exhorter à la patience par la considération de Jésus en croix et par l'union de ses souffrances à celles du Divin Sauveur. Lui faire baiser souvent le crucifix.

5o.—A l'approche de la mort, allumer la chandelle bénite et lire les prières des agonissants avec la plus grande piété.

ST-PHILIPPE - GRANDE POINTE
1886 - 1992

Le nom Grande Pointe vient de la situation géographique de cette partie de Dover Nord : une grande pointe de terre qui s'étendait dans le lac Ste-Clair dans le comté de Kent sur la Rivière Thames.

En 1882, le Département des postes accorde un bureau de poste à ce district. Dans les premiers registres trouvés dans l'église de Pain Court, pour les années 1850 à 1882 lorsque St-Philippe était une mission de Pain Court, toutes les entrées concernant les paroissiens de Dover Nord étaient sous le nom de "Grande Pointe."

Le 5 mars 1829 les habitants de Dover pétitionnent le Lieutenant-Gouverneur pour l'allocation des lots sur lesquels ils sont installés. Ils font cette demande en guise de reconnaissance pour avoir participé à la dernière guerre avec les États-Unis; les personnes suivantes ont signé la pétition :

Simon Lauzon	Thomas Réaume
Antoine Labadie	Luc Emery (junior)
Jean-Baptiste St-Pierre	Jean-Baptiste Leguille (senior)
Olivier Hébert	Thomas Hébert
Luc Emery (senior)	Pierre Toulouse
Joseph Mailloux	Jean-Baptiste Leguille (junior)
Jean-Baptiste Renaud	Jean-Baptiste Lauzon (senior)
Antoine Dragon	Jean-Baptiste Lauzon (junior)
Augustin Dubé	Jacques Toulouse
Simon Drouillard	

Le 11 mai 1852 Claude-Antoine Ternet, curé de la paroisse de St-Pierre de Raleigh fit ériger une petite chapelle à Grande Pointe et la dédia à St-Antoine. Le 3 septembre 1852, il fait la bénédiction officielle de la croix publique.

Il y a eu de ces jours pionniers. De vastes étendues de terre ont été défrichées et les marécages asséchés. Du matin au soir ils préparaient la terre pour la cultiver. La famille se nourrissait de chasse, de la pêche et du peu de nourriture récoltée sur les éclaircis. C'était assez normal de trouver une famille de 12 à 21 enfants qui habitait une cabane à rondins. Chaque maison avait sa grange où l'on hébergeait une vache, quelques porcs et quelques poules.

Des sites de terres familiales ont été choisis par ces nouveaux-venus de la province de Québec, notamment St-Jean-d'Iberville, St-Jacques-le-Mineur et St-Rémi. Un pionnier pouvait obtenir une région boisée gratuitement de la Couronne et il s'engageait à la défricher. On invitait un membre de la parenté ou un ami avec leur famille et on échangeait 25 arpents de terre pour une vache, un taureau ou même un traîneau.

Comme tout autre secteur en voie de développement, la vie était dure mais simple. De temps à autre, on attelait les taureaux ou des chevaux à une charrette ou wagon pour transporter le blé d'Inde à Chatham, une distance d'environ 10 miles parcourus entre 1 à 5 heures dépendant de la condition des routes. On transportait aussi le sirop d'érable et la potasse pour vendre ou échanger contre des produits nécessaires à la survie. Les femmes tissaient la laine de leurs moutons et fabriquaient les vêtements d'usage. La région était dotée de six ateliers de forgerons. On y fabriquait des instruments agricoles et des wagons.

La vie sociale des pionniers était très active. Presque tous les soirs on faisait la musique et la danse qui divertissaient ces braves gens. Dans la famille des St-Pierre même il y avait "10 frères violoneux."

En 1850, le comté de Kent a été divisé en cantons dont le 10e étant "Dover." En 1851, le recensement a révélé que la municipalité de Dover comptait 1100 catholiques et à peu près 250 familles. En 1882, la région s'est tellement développée qu'on avait besoin d'une église pour accommoder la population catholique. Alors, le curé de Pain Court, le Père Bauer, autorisé par l'évêque Walsh, fait construire une église au coût de $6000.00 sur un lopin de terre mesurant 150 pieds de façade. Ce terrain fût donné par Moïse Martin et Joseph Cheff. A la demande des ces familles le nom de la paroisse a été changé à St-Philippe. Ces deux familles étaient originaires de St-Philippe, Québec. Les briques ont été fabriquées sur place. Le bois et le travail de charpenterie ont été donnés par les paroissiens. Cette église a servi pendant 67 ans. Le cimetière de la paroisse, situé à l'arrière de l'église, a été béni en 1882. Le premier enterrement a été celui de Théodore Emery inhumé le 29 octobre 1884. Avant cette date, les sépultures avaient lieu soit dans le cimetière de St-Pierre ou celui de Pain Court.

En 1949, une nouvelle église de style gothique fut construite à un mille plus loin au carrefour est de la neuvième concession et de la Winter Line. L'église St-Philippe est un édifice imposant.

Les curés de la paroisse :
1886 - 1887 : Père A. Carrière
1887 - 1891 : Père Pierre Langlois
1891 - 1894 : Père Charles Antoine Parent
1894 - 1904 : Père Joseph Loiselle
1904 - 1908 : Père Rémi Prud'homme
1908 - 1918 : Père Lucien Landerville
1918 - 1928 : Père Joseph Emery
1928 - 1939 : Père Wilfred Roy
        Père Jean Noël. Celui-ci avait été envoyé comme vicaire pendant la maladie du Père Roy.
Ce vicaire capable et zélé a laissé un excellent souvenir de ses quelques mois à St-Philippe.
1939 - 1945 : Père Pierre Boudreau
1945 - 1949 : Père Oscar Martin
1949 - 1955 : Père Euclide Chevalier. Celui-ci s'est vêtu de salopettes et avec son énergie et son savoir-faire, il s'est joint aux paroissiens pour la construction de la nouvelle église.
1955 - 1966 : Père Laurent Paquette
1966 - 1970 : Père Roger Bénéteau
1970 - 1977 : Père Charles Lanoue
1977 -   : Père Henri Masse
1977 - 1992 : Père Louis Rivard, qui est, jusqu'à ce jour, curé de St-Philippe, et reconnu pour son sens d'organisation et de motivation; c'est un homme d'affaires. Il est le grand responsable pour les grandes rénovations de la salle paroissiale et de l'intérieur de l'église, l'embellissement du cimetière, la réintroduction des pique-niques paroissiaux. Le Père Rivard est un vrai père de famille ; il aime bien voir ses fidèles réunis ; c'est un grand consolateur et un fervent prêcheur des principes de la foi

catholique. On raconte aussi que le Père Rivard est un bon pêcheur et chasseur.

La paroisse de St-Philippe de Grande Pointe se veut une paroisse rurale agricole. Une faible minorité de personnes travaillent à salaire à Chatham ou à Wallaceburg. La population juin 28, 1998 est composée de 92% de gens d'origine française. Les paroissiens sont bilingues en grande majorité.

Les premières récoltes étaient le blé, le blé d'Inde et la pomme de terre. Au début du 20e siècle les fermes de Grande Pointe produisaient de l'avoine, du maïs, de l'orge, de la betterave à sucre, du sarrasin et du foin.

Durant les années 50, 60, 70, le développement d'hybrides et l'amélioration des instruments aratoires et des techniques agricoles ont énormément accru le rendement des fermes. Le maïs et la fève soya réclament la plus grande part des récoltes ; viennent ensuite la betterave, le pois, le maïs sucré et la tomate ; le blé d'hiver est également semé ; l'avoine et le foin sont devenus choses du passé. La fermeture de la raffinerie Dominion de Chatham a mis fin à la production de betteraves à sucre.

Bien que l'agriculture fut toujours considérée l'industrie principale de cette région, il nous faut mentionner l'établissement de plusieurs entreprises par des entrepreneurs locaux. En 1845 Joseph Cheff gérait une des premières scieries à Grande Pointe. En 1928 Ovilla Tétrault acheta la scierie de Calixte Benoit; Ovilla et son fils Édouard ont géré leur scierie jusqu'au début des années "40"; la pénurie d'arbres dans la région les oblige à fermer boutique. Le forgeron était aussi un entrepreneur précieux de la communauté; en plus de ferrer les chevaux, il polissait les patins des traîneaux, mettait des jantes de métal sur les roues et réparait beaucoup d'objets; parmi les forgerons de Grande Pointe notons Ferdinand Létourneau, Alfred Alexandre, Francis Emery, Rodolphe L'Écuyer, Francis Ducèdre, Ovilla Tétrault. Le magasin général était le supermarché de l'époque; on y vendait de tout : l'étoffe, les provisions alimentaires, la quincaillerie, les drogues, les souliers, les vêtements, les harnais, les fers à cheval, l'essence, l'huile et même des pièces de rechange pour automobile; on vendait en gros : des sacs de 100 livres odes barriques. On échangeait aussi des oeufs, du beurre, de la laine et autre; les propriétaires de ce genre de magasins: M. & Mme Arthur Houle, M. & Mme Calixte Benoit, Joe Couture, Clément Charron, Trefflé Emery. En 1930, Édouard Emery et Wilfrid Normandin entreprirent la transportation du gravier; cette entreprise s'est développée du fait que les "chemins de rodins" devenus légendaires, étaient devenus impassables à cause du gel et dégel de la terre; aussi l'arrivée de l'automobile nécessitait la mise à jour du système routier. En 1945 M. Normandin cessait son association avec Édouard et par la suite Édouard vendait sa part à Trefflé. L'entreprise est devenue la compagnie de construction T-Emery Ltée. La compagnie a étendu ses services en ajoutant des gravières locales, des chasse-neige; la compagnie construisait des routes, des ponts et beaucoup d'autres projets de construction lourde. Parmi les entrepreneurs électriciens : Esdras Mallette, Adrien Emery et ses frères Bernard, Montfort et Léonard, Rhéal Charron, Al VandenEnden et les frères Kehoe. La famille de Homer Martin commença en 1934 la fameuse récolte de maïs soufflé. Rodolphe L'Écuyer établit la compagnie de foreuse de puits. La station-service Benoit a ouvert ses portes en 1943 et opère encore sous ce nom. En 1947 Arthur Daniel établit un atelier de soudure; il faisait des réparations générales, construisait de petits bateaux de métal, des vaporisateurs de récoltes et pendant les périodes moins occupées, il installait des systèmes d'écoulements des eaux sur les fermes.

L'éducation des enfants à Grande Pointe s'est développée comme celle de tout autre petit village. Les enfants obtenaient leur éducation au foyer; les parents leur enseignaient leurs prières, les dix commandements de Dieu, la vie chrétienne: les garçons devenaient apprentis en très bas âge de métier de charpentier, maréchal forgeron, cultivateur; les filles se formaient en économie-domestique, filage, tissage.

Ce ne fut qu'en 1860 que la première école fut construite à Grande Pointe; ce bâtiment de modèle "cabane à rondins" était situé sur le lot 7 du 9e rang, terrain acheté de François Luc Emery.

Les enseignants pionniers des premières écoles de Grande Pointe:
M. Théophile Sylvain, Mlle Aurore Odette et M. Ducharme. La premiè école de briques fut construite en 1912 et nommée sous le nom S.S.#9 Dover mais reconnue comme l'école St-Philippe. En 1957 à cause du grandissement croissant des inscriptions scolaires, la construction débuta pour l'école actuelle de St-Philippe. La bénédiction solennelle et l'ouverture officielle eurent lieu le 12 juin 1958. Cet édifice "ultramoderne" remplace les deux autres écoles; ses premiers enseignants : Mlle Jeannette Emery, Mme Florine Griffore, M. Amédée Emery, M. Georges Gagnon. Plusieurs ajouts se sont faits à l'école: une maternelle en 1958, deux salles de classes ainsi qu'une bibliothèque en 1963, un gymnase en 1971.

Pour la réalisation de ce répertoire, de sincères remerciements sont adressés à Monseigneur Jean Z. Noël pour son support constant dans tous nos projets, au Père Louis Rivard pour sa grande coopération dans ce projet, à Soeur Theresita, archiviste de London pour son aide précieuse, à Amédée Emery et Omer Charron pour les nombreuses heures de recherches, à Claudette (Piquette) Bibeau pour l'excellent travail de recherches et dactylographie de ce répertoire.

Extrait du livre "Centenaire de Grande Pointe" pages 18 - 19.

The Halfway House

In 1897, Francis Dubuque built the Halfway House on the 8th concession. It was one of Grande Pointe's most important meeting places. Here the folks gathered to exchange information and opinions and to discuss their problems over a glass of ale or whisky. The travellers also found shelter for the night and ate generously and not expensively at the common table.

After the death of Francis Dubuque, it was operated by Mr. Philippe Belle. It was during the war and at this time all the hotels were closed in Ontario because of prohibition. Mr. Belle then opened a service garage. It became a prosperous business but he relocated to Detroit. Mr. Rose turned it into a general store. Mr. Rose did not have a good clientele and eventually Mr. Fred Ouellette took it over and petitioned the government so he could reopen it as a hotel; he won and from that day forward it served as a pub.

Early Wednesday morning on June 13, 1984 one of Kent County's oldest and best known landmarks was destroyed by fire.

Chapitre 2

Les généalogies

Chapter 2

Geneological Studies

Fêtes jubilaires du 75ᵉ à Pain Court - 1926

Roland Bélanger, petit St-Jean-Baptiste, Joseph Roy, le petit ange
À l'arrière plan de droite à gauche: M. David Bélanger,
grand-père de Roland et M. Calixte Faubert.
Photo: Gracieuseté de Roland Bélanger

Extrait du bref de Pie X, en date du 25 février 1908

1°   Pour le grand bien, le bonheur et la prospérité de l'Église canadienne et de tous les catholiques du pays, nous proclamons Saint Jean-Baptiste patron spécial auprès de Dieu des fidèles franco-canadiens, vivant soit au Canada soit en terre étrangère.

Canadiens français, vous avez une double mission:

1°   La mission de conserver intact votre héritage religieux et national;

2°   La mission de répandre cet héritage. J'ajoute que c'est votre droit de garder votre héritage, et votre devoir de le répandre.

        Son Excellence Mgr. Antoniutti, ex-délégué apostolique au Canada

We remember . . .

Marie-Hélène Gagner

As I search my memory to recall my experiences of a woman I loved dearly, vivid images of faith, hospitality, courage, family love, compassion, generosity, mothering, and many more tumble into view. Her name is Marie-Hélène Gagner, better known as Helena, (née Caron).

Born in 1887 in a log house in Pain Court, Ontario, and deceased in 1991, this woman lived through more than a century of revolutions in industry, technology, communications, and yes, even in Church life. She was able to adjust to these phenomenal changes with amazing serenity.

The only girl in a family of eight boys, her education was necessarily curtailed after grade eight, but she never lost her desire to learn more. Farm life in those early pioneer days required much hard work and she did not shirk the tasks. In 1908 she married her childhood sweetheart, Dieudonné Gagner, with whom she shared her love, her work, her faith , her joys and her sorrows, her work and her play. Together they established a small business, raised a family of 2 boys and 3 girls, participated in Church projects, municipal affairs, school board responsibilities, and travelled to widen their horizons.

Helena's deep faith, especially manifested in her love of the Eucharist and her fidelity to the Family Rosary, sustained her and her family in health and in sickness, in trials and successes, in work and play. With her husband and family she worked tirelessly and took part in all parish activities.

Always a welcoming hostess in the Gagner household Helena never shirked the requirements of hospitality. Family, friends and relatives as well as her husband's involvement in municipal, educational, and cultural affairs called for an "Open door" to the family home.

Early appreciative of the importance of education in both English and French, though herself deprived of advanced studies, she worked with her husband to provide an education for their five children: Raoul and Roland both graduated from University of Ottawa, Viola (Sister Yvonne, c.s.j.) and Eveline (Sister Eveline, c.s.j.) became teachers and Yvonne (Mrs. Percy Nugent) graduated as a nurse.

Widowed at age 66, Helena's faith and family were her solace in her grief and her source of courage to move on. Shortly after her husband's death in 1954 she left the family home in Pain Court to live in an apartment in Chatham. Her daily participation in the Eucharist and her daily prayers were still her mainstay. In 1978, at ninety-one years of age, after the death of her eldest, Raoul, she moved to Marian Villa, a retirement home in London. Here, the chapel was for her a hallowed place. In August, 1988, nearly one hundred friends, relatives and family gathered in thanksgiving to celebrate her 100th birthday. Three years later, in March, 1991, at 103 years, 7 months, the God she loved dearly all her life called her Home. To her 5 children, 13 grandchildren, 32 great grandchildren and 6 great great grandchildren she left her legacy of love and faith. May we all treasure it!

In loving memory,
Sister Eveline Gagner, c.s.j.

Bella Charron

Sa vie fut humble, laborieuse et remplie d'actes de charité faits dans le secret: prières ardentes, paroles pleines de foi et exemples de vie chrétienne.

Après avoir été la joie de sa famille, elle en sera l'ange gardien.

Maintenant que la mort a fermé ma paupière, que le dernier chant du prêtre du Seigneur s'est fait entendre, que la terre a couvert mon corps, vous tous que j'ai aimés, priez pour moi.

Jésus, Joseph et Marie, je vous donne mon coeur, mon esprit et ma vie, etc.

(300 jours d'indulgence chaque fois.)

Bella Charron, the daughter of Toussaint Campbell and Josephine Laprise of Pain Court, was born October 18, 1890. She was the second youngest of six children. When she was about twelve years old, she lived in a house built by her father on the fourth concession in Pain Court. What a coincidence that her daughter, Thérèse, would live in that very same house when she married Rosaire Sterling. Bella lived in the Pain Court area until she married, except for two years in River Rouge, Michigan, where she moved with her family. It was there that she worked in a sewing factory, which was beneficial in acquiring the skills of a wonderful seamstress, making her own wedding dress and that of her sister for a double wedding and later on, many of her children's clothing.

At the age of twenty-one, she married Napoléon Charron of Grande Pointe and lived on a fifty acre farm on the eighth concession. In the next twenty-five years, she gave birth to fifteen children, five dying at a very early age, three withing two weeks. Through it all, she always had a deep faith and never gave up.

As most people at that time, they had no modern conveniences, no electricity, no running water etc. Other than sewing, she made bread every other day to feed her large family and was well known for her delicious doughnuts. She also had to help her husband in the field many times until her older children were old enough to help.

Her husband Napoléon died in 1944, when the youngest child was only six years old. At the time, the family was quarantined with scarlet fever and no one could come to pay their respects to the house where he was exposed. After his death, she stayed in Grande Pointe until 1947, when they moved to St. Joachim where her son Gérard kept farming. In 1977, she moved to Windsor where she lived until she was ninety-seven years old. She then had to go into Tilbury Manor where she died in her one hundredth and first year.

After her husband's death, there wasn't one day that went by that she didn't say a rosary for him. In her last years especially, she said many rosaries every day. She had a deep love for God and the Blessed Virgin. She died very peacefully on September 8th, 1991. She was truly a great lady and a wonderful mother.

Daughter,
Jeanne Florida Dupuis

Patrimoine Ancestral

André Roy Sr. was a parishioner of
St-Rémi de Napierville in Richelieu Valley,
south of Montréal, Québec in 1837.

In 1837,André Roy Sr.
came to Pain Court Ontario
with his family, in the spring
of 1837. After 155 yearshis
descendants are still
numerous in the area.

Hebreux 11, 1-2

Notre Patriarche André Roy, père.
Our Patriarch André Roy, Sr.

En 1874 à l'age de 82 ans il fut tué par un boeuf enragé. Son épouse Josephte Schreiber l'avait précédée dans
la tombe en 1860. Tous deux furent enterrés à Pain Court, sur l'emplacement du *nouveau monument*.

In 1874 at the age of 82 André was killed by a raging bull. His wife Josephte Schreiber had preceded him
in death in 1860. Both were buried where the new monument now stands.

Arbre généalogique des "ROY"

FRANCE   Louis LeRoy   marie   Anne LeMaistre
le 27 avril, 1638 à Dieppe, Normandie, France

1e   Nicholas LeRoy 1   marie   Jeanne LeLièvre
février, 1658,   à Dieppe, France
ARRIVENT AU CANADA le 22 septembre, 1663

2e   Nicolas LeRoy II   marie   Marie-Madeleine Leblond
le 18 novembre, 1686, paroisse Ste Famille, Île d'Orléans

3e   Alexis LeRoy   marie   Marie-Madeleine Leclerc
le 20 juillet, 1716, paroisse St. Laurent, Île d'Orleans

4e   Jean-Baptiste LeRoy   marie   Véronique Desfourneaux
le 26 novembre, 1753, à St. Vallier,   Dit Nouel, dit St-Jean   Québec

---

5e   Jean Alexis Roy   marie   Marie-Anne Dupille
le 12 juillet, 1790, à Lacadie, Québec

6e   André Roy 1   marie   Josephte Schreiber
le 8 juillet, 1811, à Lacadie, Québec

7e   André Roy II   marie   Bridget Hickey
le 23 février, 1855, à St. Pierre, Ontario

8e   Thomas Roy   marie   Charline Ouellette
le 14 novembre, 1882 à St. Pierre, Ontario

9e   Adolphe Roy   marie   Délia Caron
le 12 novembre, 1918 à Pain Court, Ontario

10e   Caroline Laprise   Raoul Roy   Edmond Roy
Yvonne Lucier   Bernard Roy   Anne-Aline Barrette
Léontine Roy   Loretta Roy   Raymond Vincent Roy

Anne-Aline Barrette (en partie)

Caroline Roy   marie   Trefflé Laprise
le 18 janvier, 1938, à Pain Court, Ontario

11e   Caroline -   Gérard, Roger, Claude, Florent,
Caroline, Guy, Jean-Marie, Colette

Yvonne -   Robert, Rosaire, Marc, Claudette

Léontine -   pas mariée

Raoul -   Yvette, Denise, Mariette, Simonne

Bernard -   Becky, Germaine, Kathy

Loretta -   pas mariée - religieuse

Edmond -   Vincent, Raymond, Colette

Anne-Aline - Paul, Roch

Raymond -   décédé à l'âge de 5 ans

12e   Gérard -   Jean-Marc, Jeannine Laprise

Roger -   Richard, Lucien Laprise

Claude -   Renée, Nicole Laprise

Florent -   Phyllis, née le 20 nov.1965 - décédée le 27 nov. '65
Maurice, André Laprise

Caroline -   Jamie, Christie Trudell

Guy -   Vincent, Jason, Jeremey Laprise

Jean-Marie - Chantal, Julie, Joël et Mélanie Laprise

Colette -   Robert et Joey Crow

13e   Maurice Laprise - Mathieu, Dominique, Rebecca

André Laprise - Chad, Amanda, André James

Jamie Trudell - Matthew, Natasha, Joshua

Nicole Brown - Kira et Ian

Lucien Laprise - Madison

Julie Simpson - Justin

Joël Laprise - Mélanie

Caroline Roy Laprise
Mes recherches 1950

Père Adrien Roy, o.m.i., né le 16 septembre, 1922

1ère messe à Pain Court le 20 juin, 1949, décédé le 2 mai, 1968
fils de Léo Roy et d'Ursule Trudelle.

C'est au début des années '50 que Père Adrien Roy o.m.i. entreprit des recherches généalogiques. Il était alors professeur à l'Université d'Ottawa. Mais ce fut vraiment dans les années `60 qu'il put s'adonner à loisir à son passe-temps préféré. Il habitait Ville LaSalle près de Montréal et de cet endroit stratégique il put pendant plus de six ans poursuivre ses recherches de paroisse en paroisse avec toute la ténacité que nous lui connaissons. Tous les registrés paroissiaux depuis Détroit jusqu'à Québec où il y avait quelques possibilités de traces de nos ancêtres furent examinés à fond par Adrien.

J'en fus témoin à plusieurs reprises l'ayant accompagné dans des randonnées surtout celles de la région de Québec. Un jour d'automne en 1965, j'accompagnais Adrien à la Paroisse de St. Vallier près de Québec. En descendant de voiture un monsieur d'un certain âge attira l'attention d'Adrien et celui-ci de me souffler à l'oreille: "Regarde donc comme il ressemble à mon oncle Becca! Remarque ses oreilles surtout. Des vraies oreilles de Roy." De fait, c'était bel et bien un Roy (le bedeau de la paroisse) et lui de nous dire au cours de la conversation : "Oui, ça fait longtemps qu'on est par icite nous les Roy. On vient tous de l'autre bord du fleuve. Nos ancêtres sont débarquées là-bas en 1663." En même temps il nous indiquait du doigt la côte de Beaupré et plus précisément les paroisses de l'Ange-Gardien et de Bois-Châtel où le premier Roy (Nicolas LeRoy) s'installa en terre canadienne. Vous pouvez imaginer la joie qu'Adrien aurait éprouvée s'il avait pu m'accompagner jusqu'à Dieppe en mai 1984, et fouiller avec moi dans les archives de la Paroisse de Saint-Remy, et enfin trouver et lire avec moi dans les vieux registres paroissiaux, maintenant conservés aux Archives départementales de Rouen, le message suivant en vieux français de l'époque -1639: 25 Mai fut bapt. Nicolas fils Louis LeRoy & Anne Le Maistre, noe par Jacques Baudoinj et Françoise Priaux.

C'est dommage que 1968 mit fin à sa vie et à tous ses projets de généalogiste. Hommage, gratitude et fidélité à ce vaillant chercheur. Il était de "Chez Nous."

~   ~   ~

Father Adrien Roy, o.m.i. began his genealogical research during the early fifties. He was then a professor at the University of Ottawa. However, it was not before the sixties that he began to pursue his favourite pastime in earnest. He was living then at Ville La Salle near Montréal. For the next six years, he pursued his research in the surrounding parishes. From Detroit to Québec, not one parish register escaped his scrutiny. Thus, he found many records relevant to the history of our ancestors.

I have witnessed his untiring work as I often accompanied him in his meanderings in the region of Québec. In the autumn of 1965, I drove with him to the parish of St-Vallier situated on the south shore of the St. Lawrence River, near the Île d'Orléans. As we came out of the car, we noticed a middle-aged man. Upon seeing him, Adrien whispered to me, "Notice how this man looks like uncle Becca! Look at his ears . . . Roy ears!" In fact, this gentleman was a Roy: the caretaker of the parish. During our conversation, he said, "Yes, the Roys have been here for a very long time." And pointing to Beaupré on the north shore of the river, where the parishes of l'Ange-Gardien and Bois-Châtel are located, he continued, "We all come from over there. It is there that the first Roy – Nicolas LeRoy– came off the ship in 1663."

You can imagine what would have been Adrien's joy if he could have accompanied me to the parish of St-Rémy of Dieppe, in Normandie, France, in May of1984. He and I could have searched together in the archives of that parish and finally read from the old parish registers (now kept at the

National Archives in Rouen) the following record written in the French of that era - 1639; 25 May fut bapt Nicolas fils Louis LeRoy & Anne LeMaistre, noe par Jacques Baudoinj et Françoise Priaux.

In 1968, death put an end to his life and to his genealogical research. Homage, gratitude and fidelity to this untiring researcher. He was one of us; he was from "Chez Nous."

Rosaire Roy
fils de Léo
frère d'Adrien

Revue 150e anniversaire p. 16-17, 1989

La famille Roy

Au-delà d'une douzaine de branches différentes de Roy, aucunement apparentées entre elles, s'établirent au Canada, aux débuts de la colonie, prétendent les "experts" en généalogie canadienne-française. Pour les différencier, dès les débuts, on ajouta des surnoms au nom régulier de famille. Ainsi on eut des Roy dit Desjardins, Roy dit Laliberté, Roy dit Audy, Roy dit Piédalue, Roy dit Roiroux, Roy dit Châtellereau, etc. De leurs descendants, nombreux sont ceux qui, aujourd'hui, portent le nom de Desjardins, Laliberté, Audy, Piédalue, etc. comme nom de famille, alors que leur véritable nom de famille , autrefois, était bien Roy.

Aux débuts de la colonie, en fait, les Roy étaient des LeRoy. La branche dont descendent les Roy venus à Pain Court, se distingua des autres en n'ayant pas de surnoms "dit. . ." et en étant la dernière à laisser tomber l'article "Le", cela vers 1760, au moment de la conquête du Canada par l'Angleterre.

Nicolas LeRoy, l'ancêtre canadien des Roy de Pain Court, était originaire de la Normandie, en France, plus précisément de la ville de Dieppe, du diocèse de Rouen. Fils de Louis LeRoy et de Anne Lemaistre de la paroisse Saint-Rémi de Dieppe, il y fut baptisé le 25 mai 1639, et au début de février 1658, il y épousait Jeanne Lelièvre, fille de Guillaume Lelièvre de la paroisse Sainte-Thérèse de Dieppe, dont les parents, Jacques Lelièvre et Antoinette Bougard, étaient cependant de Saint-Léonard de Honfleur.

Avec sa mère, veuve depuis peu, et sa propre petite famille, Nicolas émigrait au Canada et débarquait à Québec le 22 septembre 1663. Il y était reçu par son beau-père Guillaume Lelièvre, veuf, au pays depuis trois ans environ. Ce M. Lelièvre se remariera à Québec, le 21 août 1666, à Marie Milliet (Contrat Audouard). Le 7 novembre 1663, Anne Lemaistre, mère de Nicolas, épousait à Québec, un compatriote, Adrien Blanquet, d'Auquemesnil, près de Dieppe.

Nicolas s'établit d'abord sur la Côte de Beaupré, près du Saut-Montmorency, dans la paroisse de l'Ange-Gardien mais sur le territoire qui deviendra plus tard la paroisse actuelle de Sainte-Marguerite de Bois-Châtel. Il avait comme voisins immédiats, Jean Trudelle et sa famille, le premier Trudelle au Canada. Nicolas LeRoy demeura 16 ans sur la Côte de Beaupré.

Le 30 mars 1679, il vendait sa terre et transportait sa famille sur la rive sud du Fleuve Saint-Laurent, pour s'établir dans la Seigneurie de La Durantaye où l'appelait Olivier Morel, seigneur de ces vastes domaines. En 1696, cette Seigneurie de La Durantaye avait une superficie totale de 70,560 arpents carrés et correspondait en largeur aux terres comprises entre Beaumont et Berthier-en-Bas d'aujourd'hui.

M. de La Durantaye plaça Nicolas LeRoy, en qualité de fermier, à la tête de ses vastes domaines où s'élève, aujourd'hui, la paroisse de Saint-Gabriel de La Durantaye. Il y mourut vers 1690, laissant sa veuve qui se remaria à François Molinet de Beaumont, le 8 février 1695, et neuf enfants : Louis, marié à Marie Ledran, eut 10 enfants: NICOLAS, marié d'abord à Madeleine Leblond dont il eut 11 enfants, puis à Marie-Renée Rivière qui lui en donna un; NOËL, marié deux fois, d'abord à Jeanne-Thérèse Cassé dont il eut 2 enfants, puis à Marguerite Rabouin qui lui en donna 13 enfants; MARIE, épouse de Jean Gautreau et mère de 3 enfants; GUILLAUME, époux de Angélique Bazin et père de 13 enfants; ANNE; JEAN marié à Catherine Nadeau qui lui donne 9 enfants; ÉLIZABETH épouse Zacharie Turgeon et devint mère de 13 enfants; JEAN-BAPTISTE marié d'abord à Marie-Marguerite Bazin qui lui donne 1 enfant, puis Claire Cadrin qui lui en donne 11. Nicolas fut donc grand-père de 87 petits-enfants.

On retrouve aujourd'hui les descendants de Nicolas LeRoy et de Jeanne Lelièvre établis surtout sur la rive sud du Saint-Laurent, à partir de Lévis, face à la ville de Québec, jusqu'à la Rivière-du-Loup. Dans la Seigneurie de La Durantaye, les Roy semblent s'être déplacés vers l'est de ce grand domaine, spécialement dans les paroisses actuelles de Saint-Michel de Saint-Vallier et de Berthier-en-Bas.

Les Roy de Pain Court descendent du deuxième fils de Nicolas LeRoy et de Jeanne Lelièvre. IL portait lui aussi le nom de Nicolas. Né en 1661, décédé à Saint-Vallier le 4 février 1727, il avait épousé, à Sainte-Famille de l'Île d'Orléans, le 18 novembre 1686, Madeleine Leblond qui lui donna 11 enfants, puis le 18 avril 1724, à Québec, Marie-Renée Rivière dont il eut une fille. Il était lieutenant de milice. Trois fils, Étienne, Alexis et François, perpétuèrent son nom. C'est Alexis, son troisième enfant, qui doit retenir notre attention.

ALEXIS, né le 8 mars 1693 et décédé le 5 septembre 1746 à Saint-Vallier, épousa Marie-Madeleine Leclerc, à Saint-Laurent de l'Île d'Orléans le 20 juillet 1716, et fut père de 12 enfants dont Jean-Baptiste-Alexis. Celui-ci, né le 8 avril 1730, épousa, le 26 novembre 1753 à Saint-Vallier, Véronique Nouel dit Desfourneaux dit Saint-Jean, qui mourut le 11 août 1761, lui ayant donné 4 enfants. L'année suivante, Jean-Baptiste-Alexis se mariait de nouveau à Françoise-Osite Beaudoin dont il eut au moins un enfant, Germain, marié à Christine Dodier à Saint-Vallier, en 1794.

Jean-ALEXIS, seul fils survivant de Jean-Baptiste-Alexis Roy et Véronique Nouel dit Desfourneaux, naquit le 19 mai 1755 à Saint-Vallier. Jeune homme, il quitta Saint-Vallier et vint s'établir au sud de Montréal, dans la vallée du Richelieu, plus précisément dans la paroisse de Saint-Philippe de Laprairie. C'est à Saint-Philippe qu'il contracta un premier mariage. En effet, le 15 janvier 1781, Marie-Agathe Rémillard, fille de Joseph-Marie et de Clotilde Denis dit Lapierre, devenait sa femme. Elle lui donna 5 enfants avant de mourir à Lacadie le 16 novembre 1789 à 24 ans. Lacadie était une toute nouvelle paroisse, fondée en 1784 et détachée de Saint-Philippe. L'année suivante, le 12 juillet 1790, Jean-Alexis mariait Marie-Anne Dupille, fille de Michel et de Marie-Louise Leclerc, qui lui donna 17 enfants dont huit moururent en bas âge. Trois de ses garçons, André, Joseph et Médard, sont responsables de la présence de descendants de Nicolas LeRoy et Jeanne Lelièvre dans le comté de Kent, en Ontario.

Le premier à venir par ici fut André, deuxième enfant et aîné des survivants du deuxième mariage. Né à Lacadie le 11 juin 1792, il y épousa, le 8 juillet 1811, Marie-Josephte Schreiber, fille de Marie-Anne-Madeleine Dumas et de Henry Schreiber, un soldat allemand en service dans l'armée anglaise du Canada et qui s'était décidé à demeurer au pays une fois son service terminé. André et Josephte eurent 16 enfants, 8 garçons, 8 filles, mais purent en réchapper 8 seulement, 6 filles et 2 garçons. Tous naquirent en Bas-Canada excepté le tout dernier, Michel-Théodore-DAVID, né à Pain Court et baptisé à Saint-Pierre de Raleigh le 21 août 1837, peu de temps après l'arrivée de la famille dans le comté de Kent. En émigrant dans l'Ontario, les époux Roy étaient accompagnés de leurs enfants, Zoé, Salomé, Marie-Anne, Esther, Marie-Cézarie et André âgé de 8 ans. Leur fille aînée, Victoire, ayant épousé Paul Lériger dit Laplante, le 12 janvier 1829, à Saint-Constant, ne viendra les rejoindre que plus tard, vers 1850.

La famille Roy était-elle, oui ou non, accompagnée d'autres familles en venant par ici?

Il y a deux opinions à ce sujet:

La première les fait quitter Saint-Rémi de Napierville où la famille demeurait depuis quelques années, au printemps de 1837, avec les familles de Joseph Bélanger et Alexandre Campbell. Trois mois de pénible voyage en charrette à boeufs et par barge, et ils parviennent à Pain Court où ils établissent leurs demeures.

L'autre opinion traditionnelle veut que seule la famille Roy soit venue en 1837 et ait accueilli les deux autres familles amies, les Bélanger et les Campbell, au printemps de 1838. Celles-ci seraient parties de Saint-Rémi à l'automne de 1837 et auraient hiverné sur la rive nord du Lac Érié dans les environs de Cedar Springs pour rejoindre leurs amis, les Roy, au printemps de 1838. Les trois familles se connaissaient bien déjà, étant toutes de Saint-Rémi de Napierville. Toujours est-il que les Campbell, les Bélanger et les Roy, grâce sans doute à cette amitié de colons et à des mariages subséquents, ont toujours gardé entre elles des affinités qui ne se sont jamais démenties.

Quelques 5 ans plus tard, le jeune frère d'André, MÉDARD ROY, né à Lacadie le 11 août 1812 et marié à Saint-Rémi le 4 février 1834 à Zoé Campbell, fille du pionnier Alexandre, venait rejoindre son frère, de 20 ans son aîné, à Pain Court.

MÉDARD ROY et Zoé Campbell eurent au moins 13 enfants, les 4 premiers nés et baptisés en Bas-Canada, les autres nés à Pain Court et baptisés d'abord à Saint-Pierre, puis à Pain Court après l'érection de cette paroisse, en 1854. Joseph fut le premier à naître dans Kent, ayant vu le jour le 14 novembre 1843. Il fut baptisé à Saint-Pierre. Médard a dû rester à Pain Court jusqu'aux débuts de 1861 au moins, peut-être même jusqu'en 1863, car le 9 octobre 1860, il y fait baptiser son dernier enfant, Médard Jr., et le 4 mai 1863, il y marie son deuxième garçon, Louis-David, à Marie Gaudreau. Toujours est-il que vers ce temps, Médard et sa famille déménagèrent à Tilbury et des environs.

JOSEPH ROY, né le 11 mai 1797, cinquième enfant et deuxième fils survivant de Jean-ALEXIS et de Marie-Anne Dupille, épousa Marguerite Poutrée à Lacadie le 10 octobre, 1814. Ils eurent au moins 9 enfants. Leur troisième enfant JOSEPH; l'aîné des garçons, épousa Marie-Flavie Surprenant à Lacadie, le 11 février 1839; il mourut à Pain Court le 21 octobre 1903. C'est ce deuxième JOSEPH ROY, né à Lacadie le 2 avril 1819, qui, après un séjour de quelques années aux États-Unis, dans les usines, arrivait à Pain Court en 1859 avec sa famille et y faisait baptiser aussitôt sa fille Julie qui ne l'avait pas été en Amérique. Cette Julie mariera plus tard Julien Béchard Sr., fils de Cyprien et de Mathilde Plantier. Neveu de André Sr. et de Médard, ce deuxième Joseph Roy vint donc établir dans Kent une troisième branche de Roy, rattachée, comme les deux autres, au même tronc commun, celui de Jean-ALEXIS, descendant à la quatrième génération née au pays, de Nicolas LeRoy et Jeanne Lelièvre, le couple ancêtre en terre canadienne.

Joseph Roy et Marie-Flavie Surprenant virent 6 de leurs 8 enfants se marier à Pain Court et y élever des familles.

Joseph-Marc, l'aîné, né le 25 avril 1842, à Saint-Jacques-le-Mineur, nouvelle paroisse détachée de Lacadie, épousa à Pain Court le 6 septembre 1864, Olympe Faubert, fille de Pierre (Pierriche) et de Marie Touchette, qui lui donna 9 enfants. Charles, né aussi à Saint-Jacques-le-Mineur le 7 mai 1843, maria Adélaïde Béchard, fille de Chrysanthe (Crisan) et Adélaïde Plantier, sa première femme, le 22 novembre 1864. Il eurent 13 enfants. Lucien, né vers 1845 aux États-Unis, épousa Marcelline Béchard, soeur de Adélaïde, le 3 mai 1864 et en eut 10 enfants. Julie, née aux États-Unis vers 1847, maria Julien Béchard Sr. et fut mère de 10 enfants au moins. Théodule naquit aux États-Unis vers 1849 et épousa Julienne Béchard, fille de Calixte et de Marie Houle, le 23 août 1873, et en eut 6 enfants. Flavie, née aux États-Unis en 1854, devint l'épouse de Henry Duquette, fils d'Étienne et de Marguerite Bonneau, le 26 novembre 1872. Henriette et Adélaïde semblent être mortes enfants.

Grâce à Joseph Roy et Marie-Flavie Surprenant et à leurs enfants, innombrables sont les gens de Pain Court et environs qui peuvent se reconnaître des liens de parenté entre eux.

ANDRÉ ROY Sr., époux de Josephte Schreiber, premier rejeton de Jean-Alexis Roy et Marie-Anne Dupille à s'établir en Ontario, vit sa fille aînée, Victoire, épouser Paul Lériger dit Laplante, à Saint-Constant, quelques années avant d'émigrer à Pain Court. Vers 1850, ce couple Laplante sera la première famille de ce nom à s'établir dans Kent.

Trois ans à peine après son arrivée à Pain Court, André Sr. voyait ses 5 autres filles commencer à se marier, toutes à Saint-Pierre car Pain Court n'existait pas encore comme paroisse.

Ce fut d'abord ZOÉ qui épousa Michel Saint-Germain, le 16 juin 1840; puis ce fut SALOMÉ qui devint épouse de Frédéric Talbot dit Gervais, le 3 novembre 1841; vint ensuite MARIE-ANNE qui maria Moïse Béchard, fils de Basile, premier Béchard à Pain Court, le 5 février 1844; puis ESTHER devint Mme François-Edouard Goudreau, le 19 août 1845; MARIE-CÉZARIE devint Mme François Benoit le 27 janvier 1846 et mourut le 21 mars 1847 quelques jours après avoir mis au monde son premier bébé. Son veuf se remaria quelques années après. Pendant ce temps, ANDRÉ Jr. et DAVID avançaient en âge et pensaient au mariage. Ils étaient les deux survivants des 8 garçons nés à André Sr. et Josephte Schreiber. Pour ANDRÉ Jr., né à Saint-Constant le 1er août 1829, l'heure sonna le 12 février 1850 à Saint-Pierre où il épousait Lucie Campbell, fille du pionnier Alexandre et Marie Surprenant. Lucie lui donna 2 enfants avant de mourir à 22 ans, le 9 avril 1852, deux jours après avoir donné naissance à son deuxième enfant, William, qui mourut bébé. L'autre enfant, Alexandre épousera, le 9 novembre 1875, à Pain Court, Mary Bélanger, fille de Léandre et Geneviève Houle, qui lui donnera 10 enfants dont 3 garçons, Henri, Alphée et Eugène qui survécurent pour laisser ses descendants. Henri maria Anna Pinsonneault qui lui donna 9 enfants, dont Napoléon, fondateur de "King Grain & Seed Co. Ltd." de Pain Court, et Gérard. Alphée épousa Oliva Caron qui fut mère de 6 enfants dont Roland et Gérald. Eugène épousa Delphine Caron qui fut mère de 7 enfants dont Ernest, Wilfred et Normand.

Veuf, André Jr. liait sa destinée, le 23 février 1855 à Saint-Pierre, à Bridget Hickey, née en Irlande en 1836 du mariage de Thomas Hickey et de Ellen Gleeson, du comté de Limerick. Thomas Hickey était décédé en mer alors qu'il immigrait au Canada, en 1846, avec sa femme et ses enfants Bridget, Mary et Patrick. Il fut enseveli à Saint-John, Nouveau-Brunswick. Mary épousa Hubert Gaudreau et mourut à 37 ans; Patrick se maria plus tard et mourut sans laisser de descendants mâles. Bridget qui décéda le 6 décembre 1931 à l'âge de 95 ans, donna 7 enfants à André Roy Jr. dont 2 qui moururent en bas âge. Les survivants furent Thomas, Hélène, Joseph, Anna et James.

Hélène maria Crisan Béchard Jr. et eut 5 enfants. Joseph épousa Geneviève Béchard, soeur de Crisan Jr. et n'eut pas d'enfants. Anna, maria Ambroise Thibodeau, fils de José et Adèle Bélanger, et fut mère de 3 enfants. James maria Mary Fairbanks et eut 6 enfants.

THOMAS, l'aîné, naquit le Jour de l'an 1856 et se maria deux fois. Adélaïde Daniel, fille de Pierre et de Adélaïde Tétreault, devint sa femme le 25 novembre 1878 à Pain Court et mourut le 23 mars 1881 à 21 ans, 3 jours après avoir mis au monde son premier-né, Thomas-William, qui ne vécut que 7 mois. Thomas se remaria à Pain Court, le 14 novembre 1882, à Charline Ouellette, née à Jeannette's Creek (paroisse de Saint-Pierre) le 14 octobre 1857 du mariage de François-Xavier et Julie Primeau. Charline lui donna 10 enfants. Rose (Rosie) maria Maurice May de Pike

Creek et lui donna 5 enfants dont Thérèse qui entra chez les Ursulines de Chatham.

Léo, né le 16 novembre 1886 et décédé le 25 juillet 1965, épousa Ursule Trudelle, fils de Régis et d'Euphrasie Béchard, et fut père de 10 enfants: Ursuline devint une soeur de Saint-Joseph sous le nom de Soeur Marie-Rosaire; Armand maria Lorette Cadotte et eut 7 enfants, dont Robert, seul garçon; Aurèle épousa Laurienne Caron et eut 8 enfants, 6 garçons et 2 filles; Lionel maria Léona Pinsonneault et en eut 4 enfants dont un garçon, Adrien ; Étienne épousa Claire Pinsonneault et eut 10 enfants, dont 4 garçons; Bernadette, institutrice, ne se maria pas; Adrien, prêtre, fut d'abord Oblat de Marie-Immaculée puis revint dans le Diocèse de London comme prêtre séculier; Rose-Rita se fit Ursuline à Chatham; Alma épousa Joseph Ménard de Windsor et fut mère de 2 enfants; Rosaire maria Denise Bissonnette de Welland et eut 4 enfants dont Daniel.

André épousa Rose Thibodeau et fut père de 3 enfants dont Lucille, Jules. Marie-Brigitte (Monette) et Théodore-Donat restèrent célibataires; Jacob et Françis (F.- X.) épousèrent le même jour les jumelles Cheff, Georgina et Mélina respectivement, et eurent 3 enfants chacun. Marie, fille de Jacob, devint une Soeur Missionnaire de l'Immacullée-Conception, à Montréal; Joseph et Robert assurent une postérité à Jacob, et Thomas en a fait autant pour Françis.

Jean-Berchmans-Adophe (Becca) maria Délia Caron et fut père de 9 enfants, dont Raoul, Bernard et Edmond pour assurer la transmission du nom familial, et Laurette qui se fit Fille de la Sagesse, à Eastview, Ontario. Napoléon mourut à 11 ans, accidentellement. Agnès maria Réal Caron et fut mère de 3 filles.

Thomas Roy mourut le 27 avril 1930 et Charline Ouellette, sa femme, l'avait précédé dans la tombe, le 30 décembre 1926.

DAVID ROY, fils d'André Sr. et de Josephte Schreiber, a la distinction d'être le premier Roy de notre branche à naître en Ontario, quelque temps après l'arrivée de ses parents dans le comté de Kent. Né à Pain Court le 21 août 1837 et baptisé à Saint-Pierre, il se maria deux fois. Le 19 janvier 1858, à Pain Court, il épousait Euphémie Pinsonneault, fille de Jacob, le premier Pinsonneault dans Kent, et Claire Tétreault. Née à Saint-Jacques-le-Mineur le 23 août 1840, Euphémie lui donna 12 enfants, et à 41 ans, le 9 octobre 1881, elle mourait peu après avoir mis au monde son dernier enfant. David se remaria l'année suivante à Chatham à Mary Jane Young qui lui donna 8 enfants. Vers 1900, David et sa famille quittèrent Pain Court, allèrent d'abord à Détroit puis finirent par s'installer définitivement à Sault-Sainte-Marie. Ses descendants semblent tous être aux États-Unis surtout dans la région du Sault-Sainte-Marie.

On retrouve d'autres Roy dans la péninsule de Kent-Essex, mais ils ne sont pas descendants de Jean-ALEXIS et Marie-Anne Dupille. Ce sont les Roy de Pointe-aux-Roches et de Técumseh qui, jusqu'à date, ont donné trois prêtres à l'Église du diocèse de London. Ce sont Wilfrid qui mourut curé de Grande-Pointe, son neveu Hubert, et son petit-neveu, Paul, fils d'Hiram.

Ces Roy sont venus de Joliette, Québec, et se disent descendants de Nicolas LeRoy et de Jeanne Lelièvre. Jusqu'à date, cependant, les recherches de l'auteur de ces notes se sont avérées sans résultats objectifs et définitifs quoique tout indique qu'ils le sont vraiment. Chose certaine, c'est qu'ils sont venus par ici à peu près 50 ans après les fils d'Alexis et de Marie-Anne Dupille.

Les recherches de l'auteur, à Windsor et à Saint-Pierre, ont révélé aussi la présence de Roy dans la région dès avant 1778. En effet, un certain Augustin Roy épouse Élizabeth Bélanger à

Détroit, le 15 juillet 1793, et est dit fils d'Augustin et de Marie-Louise Beaumont de Saint-Vallier. Quelques-uns de ses enfants contractent mariage à Saint-Pierre après 1820 et se disent descendants de Nicolas LeRoy et de Jeanne Lelièvre mais jusqu'à date les recherches de l'auteur à leur sujet se sont avérées sans résultats concluants et objectifs, quoique tout indique qu'ils le sont vraiment. Si tel est le cas, tous les Roy de la péninsule sont rejetons de cet ancêtre commun et sont dès lors parents.

Son Éminence le Cardinal Maurice Roy, Archevêque de Québec, soit dit en passant, est un descendant, à la huitième génération canadienne, de Nicolas LeRoy et de Jeanne Lelièvre, le couple pionnier venu de France en 1663.

Adrien Pascal Roy, prêtre
Revue 150e anniversaire des Roy à Pain Court 1989   p. 18 - 25

THE ROY FAMILY

According to research in French-Canadian genealogy, more than one dozen different and unrelated branches of the Roy family settled in Canada in the early 1600's. From the very beginning, in order to distinguish them, surnames were added to their regular family names. In this way we had "Roy dit Desjardins", Roy dit Laliberté", Roy dit Audy", Roy dit Piédalue", "Roy dit Roiroux", "Roy dit Châtellereau", etc. Many of their descendants carry the family name of Desjardins, Laliberté, Audy, Piédalue, etc., but in fact their real family name used to be Roy.

In these early days, Roy was in fact Leroy. The branch from which are descended the Roys who settled in Pain Court distinguished itself by not adding a surname "dit . . ." and by being the last to drop the article "Le", in the 1760's, at the time when Canada was conquered by England.

Nicolas LeRoy, Canadian ancestor of the Roy family of Pain Court, came from Normandy in France, more specifically form the city of Dieppe, in the diocese of Rouen. He was the son of Louis LeRoy and Anne Lemaistre from the parish of Saint-Rémi in Dieppe where he was baptized on May 25, 1639, and where in early February 1658, he married Jeanne Lelièvre, daughter of Guillaume's parents, Jacques Lelièvre and Antoinette Bougard, were from the parish of Saint-Léonard in Honfleur.

Accompanied by his recently widowed mother and his own small family, Nicolas emigrated to Canada and set foot in Québec on September 22, 1663. He was greeted by his father-in-law, Guillaume Lelièvre, then a widower who had lived in Canada for approximately three years. On August 21, 1666, Mr. Lelièvre remarried, this time to Marie Milliet (Audouard Contract). On November 7, 1663, Anne Lemaistre, Nicolas' mother, married in Québec a fellow countryman, Adrien Blanquet, from Auquemesnil, near Dieppe.

Nicolas first established himself on the coast of Beaupré, near the Saut-Montmorencey, in the parish of l'Ange-Gardien, on the land which was later to become the present site of the parish of Sainte-Marguerite-de Bois-Châtel. His immediate neighbours were Jean Trudelle and his family, the first Trudelle family in Canada. Nicholas LeRoy remained 16 years on the shores of Beaupré.

On March 30, 1679, he sold his land and with his family, he moved to the South Shore of the Saint-Lawrence to settle in the Seigneurie de La Durantaye at the invitation of Olivier Morel, lord of this vast domain. In 1696, the Seigneurie de La Durantaye covered a total area of 70,560 square acres and was equal in width to the lands between Beaumont and Berthier-en-Bas as we know them today.

M. de La Durantaye appointed Nicolas LeRoy, a farmer, as manager of his vast domain where stands today the parish of Saint-Gabriel de La Durantaye. He died in the 1690's leaving his wife who later remarried François Molinet of Beaumont, on February 8, 1695. Nicolas also left 9 children: LOUIS, married to Marie Ledran, had 10 children; NICOLAS, had 11 children from his first marriage to Madeleine Leblond; his second wife Marie-Renée Rivière gave him one child; NOËL was also married twice - his first wife Jeanne-Thérèse Cassé gave him 2 children and his second wife Marguerite Rabouin gave him 13 children; MARIE, wife of Jean Gautreau and mother of 3 children; GUILLAUME, husband of Angélique Bazin and father of 13 children; ANNE; JEAN married Catherine Nadeau and had 9 children; ÉLIZABETH, wife of Zacharie Turgeon was the mother of 13 children; JEAN-BAPTISTE was first married to Marie-Marguerite Bazin who gave him one child; his second wife Claire Cadrin gave him 11 children. Nicolas was therefore the grandfather of 87 grandchildren.

Today, the descendants of Nicolas LeRoy and Jeanne Lelièvre are to be found in most parts of the South Shore of the Saint-Lawrence, from Lévis, across from Québec City, as far as Rivière-du-Loup. In the Seigneurie de La Durantaye, the Roy family seems to have moved to the easterly section of this vast domain, particularly where we today find the parishes of Saint-Michel, Saint-Vallier and Berthier-en-Bas.

The Roys of Pain Court are descendants of the second son of Nicolas LeRoy and Jeanne Lelièvre. He also carried the name of Nicolas. He was born in 1661 and died in Saint-Vallier on February 4, 1727. On November 18, 1686, he married, in the parish of Sainte-Famille of l'Île d'Orléans, Madeleine Leblond with whom he had 11 children. His second wife, Marie-Renée Rivière, whom he married on April 18, 1724, in Québec, gave him one daughter. Nicolas was a lieutenant in the militia. Three sons, Étienne, Alexis and François, carried on his family name, but the third son, Alexis, is of particular interest in this case.

ALEXIS was born on March 8, 1693, and died on September 5,1746, in Saint-Vallier. On July 20, 1716, he married Marie-Madeleine Leclerc in the parish of Saint-Laurent of l'Île d'Orléans and was the father of 12 children, one of whom was Jean-Baptiste-Alexis, born on April 8, 1730, and on November 26, 1753, he married Véronique Nouel dit Desfourneaux dit Saint-Jean in the parish of Saint-Vallier. From this marriage, 4 children were born. Véronique died on August 11, 1761 and the following year Jean-Baptiste-Alexis remarried, this time to Françoise-Osite Beaudoin with whom he had at least one child, Germain, who married Christine Didier in Saint-Vallier in 1794.

Jean-ALEXIS, the only surviving son of Jean-Baptiste-Alexis and Véronique Nouel dit Desfourneaux was born on May 19, 1755, in Saint-Vallier. As a young man, he left Saint-Vallier and settled to the South of Montréal, in the Richelieu Valley, more precisely in the parish of Saint-Philippe of Laprairie. His first marriage, on January 15, 1781, to Marie-Agathe Rémillard, daughter of Joseph-Marie and Clotilde Denis dit Lapierre, was blessed in the parish of Saint-Philippe. Marie-Agathe gave him 5 children before her death in Lacadie on November 16, 1789, at the age of 24. Lacadie was a very young parish, founded in 1784 and detached from the parish of Saint-Philippe. On July 12 of the following year 1790, Jean-Alexis married Marie-Anne Dupille, daughter of Michel and Marie-Louise Leclerc, and from this marriage, 17 children were born. However, 8 of these children died at a young age. Three of the sons, André, Joseph and Médard, are responsible for the presence in the county of Kent in Ontario, of descendants of Nicolas LeRoy and Jeanne Lelièvre.

The first to come to the area was André, second born and the eldest of the surviving children of the second marriage. He was born in Lacadie on June11, 1797, and on July 8, 1811, he married Marie-Josephte Schreiber, daughter of Marie-Anne-Madeleine Dumas and Henry Schreiber, a German soldier who had decided to settle in the country at the end of his military service in the British army of Canada. André and Josephte had 16 children, 8 boys and 8 girls, but unfortunately, only 8 survived, 6 girls and 2 boys. All were born in Lower-Canada except the youngest, Michel-Théodore-DAVID, born in Pain Court and   baptized in the parish of Saint-Pierre in Raleigh on August 21, 1837, shortly after the family's arrival in the county of Kent. When they emigrated to Ontario, the Roy couple was accompanied by their children, Zoé, Salomé, Marie-Anne, Esther, Marie-Cezarie and André who was 8 years old. Their eldest daughter, Victoire, who had married Paul Lériger dit Laplante on January 12, 1829, in Saint-Constant, came to join them later, around 1850.

Did other families accompany the Roy family when they came to this area? There are two opinions on this issue.

The first maintains that in the spring of 1837, the family left Saint-Rémi of Napierville, where they had lived for several years, with the families of Joseph Bélanger and Alexandre Campbell. After a difficult journey by oxen-drawn cart and by barge, they reached Pain Court where they settled.

The traditional opinion claims that the Roy family came alone in 1837 and that their friends, the Bélanger and the Campbell families joined them in the spring of 1838. It is thought that these two families left Saint-Rémi in the fall of 1837 and after spending the winter on the North shore of Lake Erie in the Cedar Springs area, joined their friends, the Roys, in the spring of 1838. The three families knew each other well as they were all from Saint-Rémi of Napierville. This early settlers' friendship and the subsequent marriages are probably at the root of the affinities the Campbell, the Bélanger and Roy families have always maintained.

Approximately 5 years later, André's young brother, MÉDARD ROY, came to join him in Pain Court. Médard, who was 20 years younger than André, was born in Lacadie on August 11, 1812, and married to Zoé Campbell, daughter of the pioneer Alexandre, on February 4, 1834.

MÉDARD ROY and Zoé Campbell had at least 13 children; the first 4 were born and baptized in Lower-Canada, the others were born in Pain Court and baptized first in Saint-Pierre and then in Pain Court after the founding of the parish in 1854. Joseph was the first to be born in Kent, on November 14, 1843. He was baptized in Saint-Pierre. Médard probably remained in Pain Court until the early 1861's, possibly until 1863, because on October 9, 1860, his last child, Médard Jr. was baptized in this parish and on May 4, 1863, his second son, Louis-David, married Marie Gaudreau, also in Pain Court. We do know that at about that time, Médard Roy is the ancestor of the Roys of Tilbury and its surrounding area.

JOSEPH ROY 1, born on May 11, 1797, fifth child and second surviving son of Jean-ALEXIS and Marie-Anne Dupille, married Marguerite Poutrée in Lacadie on October 10, 1814. They had a least 9 children. Their third child JOSEPH 2, eldest of their 4 sons, married Marie-Flavie Surprenant in Lacadie on February 11, 1839, and died in Pain Court on October 21, 1903. It is this second JOSEPH ROY, born in Lacadie on April 2, 1819, who arrived in Pain Court with his family in 1859 after having spent several years in the factories in the United States. He immediately had his daughter baptized as Julie who later married Julien Béchard Sr., son of Cyprien and Mathilde Plantier. Therefore, this second Joseph Roy, nephew of André Sr. and of Médard, came to establish in Kent a third branch of the Roy family, related as the other two to a common lineage, that of Jean-ALEXIS, thus extending to a fourth generation born in Canada the descendants of Nicolas LeRoy and Jeanne Lelièvre, the first Roy couple on the Canadian soil.

Out of the 8 children of Joseph Roy and Marie-Flavie Surprenant, 6 were married in Pain Court where they also raised their family.

The oldest, Joseph-Marc, was born on April 25, 1842 in Saint-Jacques-le-Mineur, new parish detached from Lacadie, and on September 6, 1864, he married in Pain Court, Olympe Faubert, daughter of Pierre (Pierriche) and Marie Touchette. They had 9 children. Charles, also in Saint-Jacques-le-Mineur, on May 7, 1843, married Adélaïde Plantier, his first wife, on November 22, 1864. They had 13 children. Lucien, born around 1845 in the United States, married Marcelline Béchard, sister of Adélaïde, on May 3, 1864. They had 10 children. Julie, born in the United States around 1847, married Julien Béchard Sr. and was the mother of at least 10 children. Théodule was born in the United States around 1849 and on August 23, 1873, married Julienne Béchard, daughter of

Calixte and Marie Houle. The couple had 6 children.

Flavie, born in the United States in 1854, married Henry Duquette, son of Étienne and Marguerite Bonneau, on November 26, 1872. It appears that Henriette and Adélaïde died at a young age.

Because of Joseph Roy and Marie-Flavie Surprenant and their children, it is interesting to note that many inhabitants of Pain Court and its surroundings are related to each other.

ANDRÉ ROY Sr., husband of Josephte Schreiber, first child of Jean-Alexis Roy and Marie-Anne Dupille to settle on Ontario, married his eldest daughter, Victoire, to Paul Lériger dit Laplante, in Saint-Constant, a few years before he emigrated to Pain Court. The Laplante couple became the first family carrying this name to settle in Kent, around the 1850.

Barely three years after his arrival in Pain Court, André Sr. began marrying off his daughters, all in the parish of Saint-Pierre as Pain Court did not yet exist as a parish.

First, ZOÉ married Michel Saint-Germain, on June 16, 1840; then, SALOMÉ became the wife of Frédéric Talbot dit Gervais, on November 3, 1841; on February 5, 1844, MARIE-ANNE was married to Moïse Béchard, son of Basile, the first Béchard in Pain Court; on August 19, 1845, ESTHER became Mrs. François-Edouard Gaudreau; and finally, on January 27, 1846, MARIE-Cézarie married François Benoit, son of Pierre and of Sophie Bisaillon. She died on March 21 of the following year, a few days only after giving birth to her first baby. Her widower remarried several years later.

During this time, ANDRÉ Jr. and DAVID were growing up and of age to consider marriage. Out of the 8 sons born to André Sr. and Josephte Schreiber, they were the two surviving sons.

On February 12, 1850, the wedding bells rang for ANDRÉ Jr., born in Saint-Constant on August 1, 1829. He married Lucie Campbell, daughter of the pioneer Alexandre and Marie Surprenant, in the parish of Saint-Pierre. Lucie gave André Jr. 2 sons before she died on April 9, 1852 at the age of 22, two days after giving birth to her second child, William, who died when he was still a baby. On November 9, 1875, the other son, ALEXANDRE, married Mary Bélanger, daughter of Léandre and Geneviève Houle. This wedding took place in Pain Court and from this union 10 children were born, three of which were sons, Henri, Alphée and Eugène who survived and left many descendants.

Henri married Anna Pinsonneault who gave him 9 children, two of which were sons, Napoléon, founder of the company "King Grain and Seed Co. Limited" in Pain Court, and Gérard. Alphée married Oliva Caron who gave him 6 children, two of which were sons, Roland and Gérald. Eugène married Delphine Caron who gave him 7 children, three of which were sons, Ernest, Wilfrid and Normand.

On February 23, 1855, André Jr., now a widower, was remarried in the parish of Saint-Pierre to Bridget Hickey, born in Ireland in 1836, daughter of Thomas Hickey and Ellen Gleeson, of the County of Limerick. Thomas Hickey lost his life at sea in 1846 during the voyage which was to lead him, his wife and his children, Bridget, Mary, and Patrick, to the shores of Canada. He was buried in Saint-John, New Brunswick. Mary married Hubert Gaudreau and died at the age of 37; Patrick married later and died without leaving any male descendants. Bridget died on December 6, 1931 at the age of 95. She and her husband, André Roy Jr., had 7 children, two of which died at an early age. The surviving children were Thomas, Hélène, Joseph, Anna and James.

Hélène married Crisan Béchard Jr. and had 5 children. Joseph married Geneviève Béchard, sister of Crisan Jr. The couple had no children. Anna married Ambroise Thibodeau, son of José and Adèle Bélanger and was the mother of 3 children. James married Mary Fairbanks. They had 6 children.

THOMAS, the oldest, was born on New Year's Day, 1856, and was married twice. Adélaïde Daniel, daughter of Pierre and Adélaïde Tétrault, became his wife in Pain Court, on November 25, 1878. She died on March 23, 1881, at the age of 21, three days after giving birth to her first-born, Thomas-William, who lived for seven months only.

Thomas married for the second time in Pain Court on November 14, 1882. His wife was Charline Ouellette, daughter of François-Xavier and Julie Primeau, born in Jeannette's Creek (parish of Saint-Pierre), on October 14,1857. Charline gave him 10 children. Rose (Rosie) married Maurice May from Pike Creek and had 5 children, one of whom was Thérèse who entered the Ursuline Order in Chatham.

Léo was born on November 16, 1886, and died on July 25, 1965. He married Ursule Trudelle, daughter of Régis and Euphrasie Béchard and was the father of 10 children: Ursuline became a sister in the religious order of Saint-Joseph and took the name of Sister Marie-Rosaire; Armand married Loretta Cadotte and had 7 children, with Robert being the only son; Aurèle married Laurienne Caron and had 8 children, 6 sons and 2 daughters; Lionel married Léona Pinsonneault and had 4 children, including one son, Adrien; Étienne married Claire Pinsonneault and had 10 children, four of whom were sons; Bernadette became a teacher and never married; Adrien, a priest, was first an Oblate of Mary Immaculate and later returned to the Diocese of London to serve as a secular priest ; Rose-Rita became an Ursuline nun in Chatham; Alma married Joseph Ménard from Windsor and was the mother of 2 children; Rosaire married Denise Bisonnette from Welland and had 4 children, with one son, Daniel.

André married Rose Thibodeau and was the father of 3 children, with one son, Luc; Marie-Brigitte (Monette) and Théodore-Donat remained single; Jacob and Francis (François-Xavier) married the Cheff twins, Georgina and Mélina, respectively. Both couples were married on the same day and both had 3 children. Marie, Jacob's daughter, became a missionary Sister of the Immaculate Conception in Montréal; Joseph and Robert gave Jacob many descendants, as did Thomas for his father, Francis.

Jean-Berchmans-Adolphe (Becca) married Délia Caron and was father of 9 children, with three sons, Raoul, Bernard and Edmond to ensure the survival of the family name. Laurette joined the religious order of Les Filles de la Sagesse, in Eastview, Ontario. Napoléon died accidentally at the age of 11 years. Agnès married Réal Caron and was the mother of 3 daughters. Thomas Roy died on April 27, 1930. His wife, Charline Ouellette, had predeceased him on December 30, 1926.

DAVID ROY, son of André Sr. and Josephte Schreiber, had the distinction of being the very first Roy of our branch to be born in Ontario, a short time after his parents' arrival in the County of Kent. He was born in Pain Court on August 21, 1837, and baptized in Saint-Pierre. He married twice. On January19, 1858, in the parish of Pain Court, he married Euphémie Pinsonneault, daughter of Jacob, the first Pinsonneault in Kent, and Claire Tétreault. Euphémie was born at Saint-Jacques le Mineur on August 23, 1840, and gave David 12 children. She died on October 9, 1881, at the age of 41, a short time following the birth of her last child. David remarried in Chatham the following year, to Mary Jane Young who gave him 8 children. Around 1900, David and his family moved away from Pain Court; they first went to Detroit and finally settled definitively in Sault-Saint-Marie. It appears that all his descendants are in the United States, particularly in the area of Sault-

Saint-Marie.

We find other Roys in the Kent-Essex peninsula, but they are not the descendants of Jean-Alexis and Marie-Anne Dupille. They are the Roys of Pointe-aux-Roches and Tecumseh who, to this day have given three priests to the Diocese of London. These are Wilfrid who died as parish priest in Grande-Pointe, his nephew Hubert, and his grand-nephew, Paul, son of Hiram.

This Roy family came from Joliette, Québec, and claims to be descendant of Nicolas LeRoy and Jeanne Lelièvre. To date, however, the research done by the author of this text have shown no objective and definite results to this fact, although everything points to the validity of this claim. We know for a fact that the family came to the area approximately 50 years after the sons of Alexis and Marie-Anne Dupille.

The findings of the author, in Windsor and in Saint-Pierre, also reveal the presence of Roys in the area before the year 1778. In fact, a certain Augustin Roy married Elizabeth Bélanger in Détroit, on July 15, 1793. He was supposedly the
son of Augustin and Marie-Louise Beaumont of Saint-Vallier. Some of his children were married in Saint-Pierre after 1820, and claim to be descendants of Nicolas LeRoy and Jeanne Lelièvre. However, the research of the author has not to date proven this assertion as absolutely objective and conclusive, although everything points to the truth of the claim. If such is the case, all the Roys of the peninsula are the descendants of this common ancestor and are therefore related.

In closing, it is noteworthy to add that His Eminence Cardinal Maurice Roy, Archbishop of Québec, is an eighth Canadian generation, descendant of Nicolas LeRoy and Jeanne Lelièvre, the pioneer couple who left France in 1663.

Adrien Pascal Roy, priest

Revue - 150ᵉ anniversaire des Roy à Pain Court 1989   p. 26 à 33

Thomas Roy   ~   Charline Ouellette
fils de   fille de
André Roy,   François Xavier Ouellette
et   et
Bridget Hickey   Julie Primeau
N. 01-01-1856   N. 14-10-1857
S. 29-04-1930   S. 30-12-1926

Mariage: 14-11-1882

Commemorative Biographical Record

THOMAS A. ROI (sometimes called King), one of the successful farmers of Dover township, in the County of Kent, has passed his entire life in that township, and is accounted one of its most worthy citizens. He is a grandson of Andrew Roi, who was of French extraction, and who migrated from the Province of Québec to the County of Kent, Ont., in 1836. He took up 250 acres of land in Dover township, 200 of which were Lot 114, Concession 3, the remaining fifty being part of Lot 19, Concession 3, Dover East, in what is known as Pain Court Block. He became a successful farmer and one of the prominent citizens of the day, and there passed the remainder of his life he was a devout Roman Catholic in religious faith. Pain Court Block is a tract comprising several thousand acres in Dover township, and though the name given is by a French priest as appropriate at the time - means "short bread" it is one of the richest farming districts in the world at the present time. It is thickly settled by French families.

Andrew Roi, father of Thomas A., was born in the Province of Québec, and came to the County of Kent with his parents in 1836, in childhood. They located on the south side of the river previously stated, the father took up land, first 200 acres, later another fifty. Like his father, Andrew Roi was a prosperous farmer. He was twice married. His first wife, Lucy Campbell, of Montréal, died May 4, 1853, aged twenty-three. To this union came two children, Alexander and William, the latter dying young. For his second wife Andrew Roi married Bridget Hickey, who was born in the County Limerick, Ireland, Nov. 15, 1836, daughter of Thomas and Ellen (Gleason) Hickey. Thomas Hickey was a farmer and died in October 1846 aged forty-one, while on the voyage to Canada with his family. He was buried at St. John, N.B. His wife died Dec. 26, 1865, at the home of one of her sons at Lake Superior, and was also buried at St. John. Both were communicants of the Catholic church. Their children were : Bridget, Mrs. Roi: Mary, deceased wife of Ebert Boudreau: Catherine, who died young: and James P., who died in 1895, leaving a widow, Janie Larks, and six daughters. To Andrew and Bridget (Hickey) Roi were born the following children: Thomas A., who is mentioned farther on: Ellen, who married Crysen Béchard, of Chatham, Ont.: Mary, who died young, Joseph, a farmer of Dover township: James, a merchant in Chatham and Annie wife of Ambroise Thibodeau, a farmer of Dover township. The father of this family passed away April 11, 1878, aged fifty years, and is buried in Pain Court cemetery. He was a member of that church, and his widow, now aged sixty-seven, is also a faithful Catholic. She still resides on the old homestead, which is on Lot N 19, 3rd concession, and whither she removed in 1857.

Thomas A. Roi was born Jan. 1, 1836, in Dover township, received his education there and remained with his parents until his marriage, after which he farmed on Lot N 19, in Dover Township, on his won account until 1886. In that year he purchased 100 acres of his present place, and later traded his lot, No. 19 for a farm of fifty acres adjoining same, and across the road from his other purchase, these holdings now comprising 150 acres of excellent farming property. In 1903 he purchased the place known as the Foot farm, the west half of Lot 16, front concession, on the river Thames. Mr. Roi had displayed unusual ability as a manager, and this quality, combined with industry and thrift, has won for him not only a place among the most prosperous farmers of his township, but has also caused him to be the choice of his fellow citizens for various positions of trust within their gift. He has taken a prominent part in the local civil administration, having served six years as deputy reeve of the township, one year as reeve, and for nearly twenty years as trustee, secretary and treasurer of the school board. In politics he supports the Conservative party.

In November, 1878, in Pain Court, Mr. Roi married Adelaide Daniel, and they had one child, Thomas J., who died young. Mr. Roi's second marriage, in November, 1882, was to Charline Ouellette, who was born in October, 1857, in Tilbury township. She was the daughter of Francis Xavier Ouellette of Tilbury and Julia Primeau of Pain Court. Mr. Ouellette was a farmer during his active years, but is now living retired. Then children have been born to Thomas A. and Charline (Ouellette) Roi, namely are Rosie, Léo, andrew, Bridget, Théodore, Jacob, Frank, Adolphe, Napoléon and Agnes. The family are Roman Catholics in religious faith.

1 J.H. Beer Co. 1904

150

" Et quand l'Écriture rend témoignage aux anciens,
c'est à cause de leur foi."

Hébreux, 11, 2

Pain Court, Ontario

Histoire du monument généalogique de la Famille Roy

Il naquit il y a plusieurs années dans le coeur et l'âme de quelques descendants qui devinrent gênés de la pauvre condition des vieilles pierres tombales sur le lot de nos ancêtres.

En octobre 1983 une première réunion eut lieu chez "King Grain". Étaient présents : Napoléon, Gérard, Lionel, Roland, Ernest, Raoul, Bernadette, Normand et Rose Rita. C'est à cette rencontre que la 5e génération de Roy à Pain Court, dont nous étions tous des représentants, décida d'agir. Un monument sera érigé pour honorer tous nos ancêtres. Le travail de recherches d'Adrien o.m.i. nous inspira d'en faire un monument généalogique.

Nous avions rêvé alors de compléter ce projet afin qu'il coïncide avec le 150e anniversaire de l'arrivée des Roy à Pain Court en 1837. Toutefois le temps requis pour sa réalisation fut plus long que projeté. Voici donc qu'aujourd'hui toutes les difficultés sont du passé et nous pouvons tous dire ensemble avec vous: "C'est notre monument; c'est notre merci à nos ancêtres; c'est notre acte de foi dans leur mission à Pain Court; c'est le symbole de l'héritage que nous voulons léguer aux générations de demain."

Aujourd'hui marque le début d'un pèlerinage des descendants Roy éparpillés aux quatre vents. Ils reviendront un jour à leur source. C'est alors qu'il vous diront à leur tour un merci sincère de leur avoir préservé le patrimoine et l'histoire des anciens.

Ce monument Roy sert de lien entre le passé et l'avenir.

Ce fut pour nous un privilège et un plaisir de rendre service et d'avoir été avec vous tous les artisans de ce projet.

Le comité du monument: Napoléon Roy
Raoul Roy
Roger Roy
Rose Rita Roy

History of the Roy Family Memorial

The idea originated many years ago in the heart and soul of a few descendants who were simply bothered by the deteriorating condition of the old tombstones in the family plot. More recently the Cemetery committee gave the last good shove when it asked the parishioners to repair damaged tombstones on their family plots.

In October 1983, the seed was sown at a meeting held at "King Grain". Present that night were: Napoléon, Gérard, Lionel, Ernest, Roland, Bernadette, Raoul, Normand and Rose Rita. At that meeting we all agreed to erect a beautiful monument to the memory of our pioneers. We were all of the 5th generation of Roys in Pain Court and so it became our project. The research work of Father Adrien inspired us to have a genealogical monument.

We had hoped at that time to complete the project in time for the 150th anniversary of the arrival of the Roys in Pain Court in 1837. There was ample time but unforeseen circumstances made it altogether impossible. Hence the 1989 date. We can all say that it is our Monument because we all had a share in it. It is our thank you to our forefathers; it is our act of faith in their mission in Pain

Court; it is a symbol of the heritage that we wish to leave to future generations.

More than likely in years to come many from far and wide will return to Pain Court to find their roots. We hope that this genealogical monument will serve them well and that our small contribution will be for them a legacy of our love that will increase in them the pride of belonging to a tradition of brave and tenacious people.

It has been a pleasure and a privilege to have served on this committee and to have had a hand with you all in bringing this project to a happy ending.

Revue - 150e anniversaire des Roy à Pain Court 1989 p.4

150 Années d'Héritage Ancestral

Je m'empresse de venir saluer les responsables pour la réalisation des fêtes grandioses du 150e anniversaire des "Roy" à Pain Court. Des sincères remerciements à l'équipe:

Napoléon Roy	Raoul Roy
Roger Roy	Jules Roy
Mariette Faubert	Rose Rita Roy

Pour l'aménagement du parterre qui entoure la pierre tombale, nos félicitations et remerciements vont surtout aux deux architectes paysagistes: Raoul Roy et son compagnon Ernest Roy.

Un merci spécial pour le support financier concernant le monument Roy attribué aux familles bénévoles du descendant patriarche André Roy. C'est grâce à vos dons monétaires qu'on a pu tenter d'entreprendre un projet de telle envergure.

To the committee who contributed so much to the success of the Roy's 150th celebration, a note of thanks goes to Napoleon Roy, Rose Rita Roy, Raoul Roy, Roger Roy, Mariette Faubert and Jules Roy.

A special tribute to Raoul Roy, the chief landscape designer of the cemetery plot surrounding the Roy Monument and second in command, his faithful companion, Ernest Roy.

We owe a debt of gratitude to all the families of the descendant for your monetary donations towards the monument. To everyone who contributed in any way, we owe a debt of gratitude. I thank you.

Caroline Roy Laprise

~~~~~~~~~~~~~~~~~~~~~~~~~~~

C'est à souligner qu'une deuxième réunion eut lieu à Pain Court du 8 août au 9 août 1992. Celle-ci pour célébrer, en particulier, la descendance de David Michael Théodore Roy, le benjamin de André Roy et de Josephte Schreiber, né à Pain Court en août 1837 et commémorant ainsi le 155e anniversaire de sa naissance.

André Roy
Oldest Son of André Sr. and Josephte Schrieber

André Jr.

Since our celebration of the 150th in 1989 these photos were discovered in the attic of a descendant. They must be shared with every one.

Bridget Hickey

Youngest son of André Sr. and Josephte Schrieber

Michael Theodore David Roy

Born in Pain Court in 1837, he died in 1919 at 82 in N. Zephyr Hills Florida

Revue - 155e Roy reunion '92

Euphémie Pinsonneault

Daughter of the pioneer Jacob, married M.T. David on January 19, 1858 in Pain Court. She died in 1881 at 41 in Pain Court, Ontario.

Patrimoine Ancestral
Moïse Caron

*Moïse Caron décédé le 25 juillet 1907 âgé de
83 ans. Son épouse Marie Thibodeau décédée
le trois janvier 1907 à l'âge de 73 ans.*

Photo: gracieuseté du 75e anniversaire,
Album – Souvenir de Pain Court, A.D. Emery.

MOÏSE CARON. Among the prominent and substantial retired farmers of Pain Court Block, Dover Township, County of Kent, Ont., is Moïse Caron, whose residence in this part of the country dates from 1866. He was born Feb. 4, 1845, in St. Jacques Le Mineur, Québec, a son of Augustin and Mary (Gourdenet) Caron.

Augustin Caron passed his life as a farmer, in Québec, where he died in 1844, at the age of forty-eight. His wife, Mary (Gourdenet), died in 1889, aged eighty-seven years. Their children were: Florence, deceased wife of Jacob Roy; Melie, deceased wife of Alexis Godfois; Moïse ; Romain, of Massachusetts; Rémi, a retired farmer of Massachusetts; Prudent, a farmer at Montréal; and Toussaint, also a farmer of Montréal.

As previously stated Moïse Caron came to Dover Township in 1866. Purchasing a partially cleared tract of 100 acres, on Pain Court Block, he located thereon, and at once began to clear and cultivate his land. His industry and frugality met with deserved reward; his land became highly productive, and his means accumulated. He became an influential man among his neighbours, all of whom, like himself, are French, and his advice is often sought.

Moïse Caron has been three times wedded. By his first wife, Flevia Pinsonneault, he became the father of two daughters: Flevia, who married August Lever, a prominent farmer of St. Edward; and Mathilda, who died young. For his second wife Moïse Caron married Célina Tétreault, who died in Pain Court in 1872, aged forty-five years, and is buried in the consecrated ground of Pain Court Church Cemetery. This union was blessed with six children: Médéric, mentioned below; Joe, Edward and Napoléon, all farmers at Pain Court; Edwidge, who married Alex Sterling; and Cordelia, who died young. The third wife of Mr. Caron was Mrs. Mary (Thibodeau) Béchard, and to this union have come Denise, who married Adolphus Trahan, a farmer of Dover Township; and Solomon, who manages the home farm, now consisting of 150 acres. The family — all communicants of the Church of Rome — are members of Pain Court Parish.

Médéric Caron, son of Moïse, and a man of prominence in his community, was born in Montréal Aug. 4, 1857. He remained with his parents until his marriage. At the age of seventeen he entered Sandwich College, from which he was graduated in 1878, and then returned to the farm. Two years later he began teaching school at Mt. Clemens, Michigan, and after a year and a half there returned to Dover Township, where he also taught for the time. He began farming on his present place of 100 acres in 1882. This farm, at the time of its purchase, was all covered with brush, but with the application characteristic of his race he bent his energies to the task, and in a comparatively few years had the land cleared and under cultivation. It has now, by his wise management and progressive methods, become one of the finest in this county of rich farms.

In November 1882, in Chatham, Mr. Caron was united in marriage with Elmire Faubert, who was born in Chatham in October 1865, a daughter, of Anthony and Olive (Robert) Faubert, of Montréal 1. Anthony Faubert came from Montréal to the County of Kent in1850, and for a few years lived in Dover Township, thence moving to Chatham, where he and his wife yet reside. Their children, besides Mrs. Caron, were: Rose, who married Marcel Marshall, a farmer of Chatham; Marguerite, who married Peter Yott, a farmer of Chatham; David, a farmer of Dover; Nelson, a farmer of Chatham; Louise, who married Philip Lucier, a farmer of Grande Pointe, County of Kent; Napoléon and Alfred, at home; and James, John and Salina, all three of whom died young. Anthony

Faubert was a school trustee for a number of years. The families are all Roman Catholics in religious belief.

To Médéric Caron and his wife have been born the following children: Josephine, who married Wilfrid Béchard, a farmer in Dover Township; Salina, who died young; Dennis, who died young; Rémi, Alfred, Marie-Louise, Célina, Olive, Alphonse, Mélina, Délia, Magdalena and Cecilia, all at home; and Albert, who died young. Alcide born 1905.

Médéric Caron is a believer in the principles of the Conservative party, and he takes an intelligent interest in public affairs, and has been honoured by election to a number of local offices.

For four years he has been treasurer of Dover proving himself an efficient and acceptable public servant. He has been careful in the management of his own affairs, and equally so in the care of the trusts reposed on him. Like all his family he is a communicant of the Roman Church. His life has been an exemplary one, and no man in the community is more highly esteemed; few men in any community are so deserving of unstinted regard from their fellow men.
Médéric was treasurer of Dover township 1888 - 1918. (30 years)

1. Antoine Faubert was born August 8, 1839 in Ste-Martine.

M. Médéric Caron - dame Elmire Faubert
marié 14 novembre 1882 à Chatham

ROBERT CARON fille de Pierre Crevet et Marie Lermercie	marié le 25 octobre 1637 à Québec	MARIE CREVET de La Rochelle, France
ROBERT CARON né le 10 février, 1647 à Québec. décédé le 30 avril 1714	marié le 14 novembre 1674 à Château-Richer	MARGUERITE CLOUTIER fille de Jean Cloutier et Marie Martin
JOSEPH CARON né le 7 avril 1686 à Ste-Anne-de-Beaupré	marié le 27 février 1713 - à Cap St-Ignace	MARIE-MADELEINE BERNIER fille de Pierre Bernier et Françoise Boule
PIERRE NOËL CARON né le 27 décembre 1735	marié le 4 juillet 1757 à St-Thomas-de-Montmagny	MARIE-GENEVIÈVE THIBAULT veuve de Louis Lemieux fille de Jacques Thibeault et Marie-Anne Proulx
CHARLES CARON né vers 1762 décédé le 6 mars 1842	marié le 24 juillet 1786 à St-Thomas-de-Montmagny	MARIE-JOSEPHTE BONNEAU fille de Zacharie Bonneau et Josette Noël
AUGUSTIN CARON né vers 1790 à St-Thomas-de- Montmagny	marié le 31 juillet 1815 à Lacadie	MARIE JOURDONNAIS fille de Pierre Jourdonnais et Marie- Françoise Rémillard
MOÏSE CARON né le 5 février 1825 à Lacadie, décédé le 23 juillet 1907à Pain Court, Ontario	marié le 15 janvier 1849 à St-Jacques-le-Mineur	CÉLINA TÉTREAULT fille de Albert Tétreault et Marie-Rose Rémillard
MÉDÉRIC CARON né le 4 août 1857 à St-Jacques-le-Mineur	marié le 14 novembre 1882 à Chatham (St. Joseph)	ELMIRE FAUBERT fille de Antoine Faubert et Marie-Olive Robert
DÉLIA CARON le 12 novembre 1918 à Pain Court, Ontario	mariée né le 13 février 1899 à Pain Court, Ontario	ADOLPHE ROY fils de Thomas Roy et Charline Ouellette

Adolphe Roy et son épouse Délia Caron

Enfants de Adolphe Roy et Délia Caron

CAROLINE, mariée à Trefflé Laprise

YVONNE, mariée à Félix Lucier

LÉONTINE, célibataire

RAOUL, marié à Theresa Denomy

BERNARD, marié à Irene Bourdeau

LORETTA, religieuse Filles de la Sagesse d'Eastview, Ontario

EDMOND, marié à Yvette Delrue

ANNE-ALINE, mariée à Roger Barrette

RAYMOND-VINCENT, décédé à l'âge de 4 ans

~~~~~~~~~~~~~~~~~~~~~~~~~~~~~~~~~~~~~

Petits-enfants de ADOLPHE ROY et DÉLIA CARON

Caroline Roy et Trefflé Laprise	- Gérard, Roger, Claude, Florent, Caroline, Guy, Jean-Marie, Colette
Yvonne Roy et Félix Lucier	- Robert, Rosaire, Marc, Claudette
Raoul Roy et Theresa Denomy	- Yvette, Marietta, Denise, Simone
Bernard Roy et Irene Bourdeau	- Becky, Kathy, Germaine
Edmond Roy et Yvette Delrue	- Vincent, Colette, Raymond
Anne-Aline Roy et Roger Barrette	- Paul, Roch

Caroline Roy Laprise

GENEALOGY STUDY

CARON

THIRTEEN GENERATIONS

1636 - 1994

Roland Gagner 1993

GENEALOGY STUDY
CARON

(The French Canadian Society of History and Genealogy)

Many Caron arrived from France to Canada. Some came from Auvergne, in the south of France, others from Picardie or the Parisian region, and others finally from La Rochelle on the western coast of France on the Atlantic Ocean. Among these last ones, the one who has our most attention is Robert Caron not only because he left many descendants but because his life was very active.

1st GENERATION

CARON, Robert - In 1636, Robert Caron was already in Canada. He had left Rennes and La Rochelle, his native city, to go among the first pioneers establishing himself on the shore of Beaupré, near Québec, near the Montmorency Falls, at Longue- Pointe on the Seigneurie of Pierre le Gardeur de Repentigny.

Was it because he witnessed the wedding of his friend Jamin Bourguignon that winter, that he desired to establish himself also? On October 25th, 1637 at Québec, he married a young Normande, Marie Crenel, originally from Benouville. Right away he continued to clear his land and finish the little house which would ensure their happiness. Five years later, he could sell everything for 150 pounds and establish himself better near Québec at Côteau Sainte-Génevieve. Many children were born.

Working exhaustively, Robert Caron attracted the consideration of the Compagnie des Cent Associés that gave him 40 acres, a large farm partly cleared. It was a lot easier.

The four boys and three girls of the family grew up and were promising to become worthy successors of their parents.

July 28th, 1656 was a great day: the oldest daughter, Marie, was married in Notre Dame de Québec Church to a Normand son, born in Canada, Jean Picard, a boy with a future who would become, like his father, merchant and bourgeois.

But only a few days after the tragic death of Dollard des Ormeaux, Marie was taken by the Indians, tied and taken away into their canoes and she was never seen again.

Even after the pain and anxiety of this troubled period, the Caron family went back to work without falling into discouragement. The children established themselves close to Québec, at Château-Richer, at Cap Saint Ignace, at Sainte Anne, on l'Île d'Orléans. Today their descendants are in great numbers. There is among them a man who gave honour to his country Réné Édouard Caron, who was Lieutenant Governor of the Province of Québec in 1873.

2nd GENERATION

Robert II - second son of the pioneer, has the Caron of Pain Court among his direct descendants. He was born at Québec on July 30th, 1647 and died at Sainte-Anne where he established himself after his wedding, November 14th, 1674 at Château Richer, near Québec to Marguerite Cloutier, daughter of Jean and Marie Martin, who gave him at least twelve children of which seven boys who transmitted the name Caron, all who had large families.

3rd GENERATION

Joseph - son of Robert II, born April 7th, 1686 at Sainte Anne, married on February 27th, 1713 at Cap Saint Ignace, Marie-Madeleine Bernier, daughter of Pierre and Françoise Boulet who gave him thirteen children among which eight boys.

4th GENERATION

Pierre-Noël - the youngest, was born at l'Islet on the 27th of December, 1735 and married Marie Proulx on July 4th, 1757 at Saint Thomas de Montmagny. He must have had a nice large family as was the custom at that period when Canada had just become a colony of England. Unfortunately, our research has only permitted us to trace only three of which Charles who died at 80 years old at saint Jacques le Mineur on March 6th, 1842. He was therefore born in 1762, probably at Saint Thomas de Montmagny.

5th GENERATION

CARON, Charles - July 24th, 1786 at Saint Thomas de Montmagny, married Josette Bonneau, daughter of Zacharie Bonneau and Josette Noël who gave him at least seven children which we are certain. Among them there were four boys who continued his name after they were married at Lacadie south of Montréal in the neighbouring parishes.

Charles Caron and Josette Bonneau seem having moved to Lacadie a few years after their marriage in 1786. They probably established in the part of the parish which later was detached to form the new parish of Saint Jacques le Mineur, because right after its establishment, we find in the parish registers the names of the members of this family. In fact, it is there that Charles died in 1842 and also Augustin, the youngest of his sons in 1844.

6th GENERATION

Augustin - must have been born at Saint Thomas about 1790. He accompanied his family at Lacadie and married July 31st, 1815 Marie Jourdanais, minor daughter of Pierre and Marie Françoise Remillard who gave him not less than 13 children of which 10 established a household, 2 died babies and one it seems remained a spinster. In order, these are the 13 children: Florence(1816), Esther(1818), Prudent(1819), Marie(1821), Émilie(1822), Moïse(1825), Romain(1827), Lulienne(1829), Jérémie(Rémi-1832), Augustin-Prudent(1834), Toussaint(1836), Aglace(1839), Denise(1841).

7th GENERATION

Moïse - seems to have married soon after the death of his father to Flavie Pinsonneault of Saint-Édouard who gave him two children of which one survived and became Mrs. August Levert of Saint-Édouard.

Moïse remarried January 15th, 1849 at Saint-Jacques, to Célina Tétreault, daughter of Albert and Marie-Rose Remillard who gave him six children, five who survived and brought to Pain Court.

Already married and established at Saint Édouard, Mrs. Levert did not accompany her father to Pain Court in 1866. As we shall see, Moïse remarried in Pain Court Marie Thibodeau, widow of Chrysanthe (Crisan) Béchard and had three children of which two survived.

Moïse Caron arrived therefore in Pain Court in 1866 with his wife and their five children:

Joseph, Médéric, Édouard, Napoléon and Hedwidge. On February 4th, 1870 at the age of 37, his second wife Célina Tétreault died. Fourteen months later, on April 21st, 1871, Moïse Caron married for the third time the widow of Crisan Béchard, Sr. who had herself five living children. By the wink of an eye, Moïse and Marie saw their family doubling and it was not over. In fact, they had three children of which Denise and Salomon survived.

Moïse saw all his children get married and raise large families mostly his boys. They were all well established on beautiful farms on the 4th concession east and west of the Bear Line in Pain Court.

8th GENERATION

1. Joseph - first married Marie Gagnon, daughter of Pierre and Lucie Yott on October 14th, 1879, who before dying gave him two children of which Lucie who married Joseph-Pierre Faubert and raised a large family in Detroit.

A second time he married Hermine Laplante, daughter of Jean-Baptiste and Marie Béchard, on April 29th, 1884 and they had five children: Eugène, Délina, Hector, Dominat and Delphine. Dominat became a priest Oblat de Marie Immaculée and Eugène married Philomène Bourassa and was father of twelve children, 7 boys and 5 girls.

The oldest Vincent followed his uncle at the Oblates and like him passed his life teaching at the University of Ottawa. The other six boys, married, succeeded to perpetuate the name Caron. Hector married Hélène Jubenville and they had four children. Délina married Zacharie Gagner and Delphine married Eugène Roy.

2. Médéric - married in November, 1882 to Elmire Faubert, daughter of Antoine and Olive Robert and became the father of fifteen children: Josephine who married Wilfrid Béchard; Célina who died young; Dennis who died young; Rémi who married twice, 1st in 1906 to Regina Béchard, 2nd in 1920 to Maria Laprise, widow of Trefflé Blais; Alfred who married Lucie Béchard; Marie-Louise who married Oliva Cheff; Célina who married Mr. McBride; Olive who married Alphy Roy; Alphonse who married Edith Belle; Mélina who married Eugène Thibodeau; Délia who married Adolphe Roy; Magdelèna who married Paul Ouellette; Cécilia who remained celibate; Alcide who married Alexina Ouellette and Albert who died young. Médéric was a graduate of Assumption College in Windsor.

3. Édouard - on May 2nd, 1881 married Philomène Sterling, daughter of William and Rosalie Dubois and they had fourteen children equally divided between girls and boys. One boy died as a baby and all the others married except Armand and Cécile. The children were: Alphy, who married Élizabeth Fisher, widow of Jim Gamble; Willie, who married Nelida Desmarais; Amédée who married Marie-Louise Barrette; Zéphyre who married Corinne Houle; Hervé, who married Yvonne Béchard; Armand, who remained celibate; Cécile, celibate; Délia, who married Léopold Gagner; Célina, who married Joseph Robert; Alma, who married Wilfrid Bélanger; Victoria, who married Henri Bélanger; Rosa, who married Steven Jubenville; Ovila who married Édouard Antaya.

4. Napoléon - the last of the sons of Moïse Caron and Célina Tétreault married on February 25th, 1884 Émilie Béchard, daughter of Calixte and Marie Houle and they had six boys and one girl: Louis, who married Annie Sterling, widow of Willie Bourdeau; Hélèna, who married Dieudonné Gagner, Jr., son of Dieudonné, Sr. and Olevine Lucier; Adélard, who married Annie Gamble; Ozias, who married Rose Démarais, daughter of Pierre and Ida Laplante; Ladislas, who married Alma Trudell, daughter of Régis and Euphrasia Béchard; Wilfrid, who remained celibate; Réal, who married Agnès Roy, daughter of Thomas and Charline Ouellette.

Napoléon was established on 100 acres that was covered with trees in the beginning. In three years he had cleared 50 acres and built a nice large brick home and beautiful barns. He also had a threshing business with grain thrasher and steam engine. He was well respected and lived in Dover Township. His wife, Émilie was an intelligent and loving woman and strong and always working towards the progress of the farm.

Napoléon established all his sons on beautiful farms.

5. Hedwidge - married Alex Sterling, son of William and Rosalie Dubois, on May 11th 1886 and they had several children: William, who married Alice Houle at Grande Pointe on January 21st, 1919; Célina, who married Philippe Pinsonneault on November 25th, 1907; Alma, who married Alfred Belisle on April 27th, 1914; Victoria, who married Danus Pinsonneault on May 10th, 1920; Velarie, who married a Mr. Poissant from Wallaceburg.

6. Denise - daughter of Moïse and Marie Thibodeau, married Delphis Trahan, son of Julien and Éléonore Poutré on April 7th, 1891. They had three children: Hercule, who marreid Eva Yott, daughter of Alex and Théotiste Lemoyne on October 18th, 1915; Alphore, who married Irene Lucier at Grande Pointe; Victor, who married Marie-Anne Gagner, daughter of Dieudonné Gagner, Sr. and Olivine Lucier on July 23rd, 1928.

7. Salomon - son of Moïse and Marie Thibodeau was the baby of the eleven children that "Le Vieux Moïse" had from his three wives. At Pain Court, November 9th, 1897 he married Rosanna Faubert, daughter of Pierre and Sophie Sterling who gave him ten children, only one dying very young. The five girls were Edna, Anna, Clara, Léona and Marie-Thérèse became nuns of the Holy Names of Jesus and Marie to which they exercised their apostolate in Windsor and vicinity. The oldest of the four boys, Augustin became a priest and was in the parishes of Rivière-aux-Canards, Saint-Joachim and McGregor.

He also received the title of Monseigneur as a recompense for his zeal and charity for the people. Réginald married Lucille Adam and had a nice family; Gérard married Florence Bénéteau and was the father of six children; Adrien, the youngest, married Antoinette Brisson and they had three boys and one girl.

9th GENERATION

HÉLÈNA - daughter of Napoléon and Émilie Béchard, married Dieudonné Gagner, Jr. at Pain Court on June 8th, 1908 and they had five children: Raoul, married Edna Lauvray at Ottawa who died after one year of married life of tuberculosis and in a second marriage he took for his wife Irene Daniel at Pain Court on September 11th, 1933; Viola entered the convent with the Sisters of St. Joseph in London and became Sister Évéline Gagner; Yvonne, married Percy Nugent of Bad Axe, Michigan, U.S.A. at Pain Court on August 22nd, 1950.

Hélèna was a very loving mother and very religious and she had the constant support of her good and generous husband Dieudonné.

The father of Dieudonné, Dieudonné Sr. established them in a beautiful store at the corner of the 4th concession and the Winter Line in Pain Court, just across the road of his hotel the "Dover Hotel". They raised their family in this store close to the church and the school where they learned the good Christian principles. Hélèna was also a neighbour to her parents Napoléon and Émilie.

Roland Gagner

GÉNÉALOGIE "CARON"

Au début de la nouvelle colonie, beaucoup de familles se dirigent vers le Canada, entre autre, les "Caron". Plusieurs viennent d'Auvergne, situé au sud de la France d'autres de Picardie et finalement de La Rochelle sur la côte ouest de la France dont notre ancêtre Robert Caron, de qui nous sommes les descendants.

1ère Génération
Robert Caron

En 1636, il était déjà au Canada. Il est venu de La Rochelle, sa place natale, pour s'établir avec d'autres pionniers sur les côtes de Beaupré, près de la ville de Québec et des Chutes Montmorency. Il entreprit une vie très active. Après le mariage de son ami, Jamin Bourguignon, il constate que lui aussi désire se faire une place.

Alors, le 25 octobre 1637 à Québec, il épousa une jeune de la Normandie, Marie Crenel, originaire de Benouville. Il continue de défricher le terrain, se construit une demeure modeste pour assurer leur bonheur. Cinq ans plus tard, ils prennent la décision de tout vendre pour mieux s'établir près de Québec, à la côte Sainte-Geneviève. Ils avaient plusieurs enfants.

La Compagnie des cents associés lui procura 40 arpents de terre demi-clairée. Leurs enfants, quatre garçons et trois filles, semblaient tous capable de suivre les traces de leurs parents.

Le 28 juillet 1656, l'aînée de la famille, épousa Jean Picard à l'église Notre Dame de Québec. Son père était un marchand.

Quelques jours seulement après la mort tragique de Dollard des Ormeaux, Marie est devenue prisonnière des Indiens. Elle est disparue, sans y retrouver aucune trace d'elle.

Ce fut une grande épreuve pour la famille. La peine les envahit mais ils reprennent leur courage et continuent. Leurs familles s'établissent près de Québec, à Château-Richer, à Cap Saint-Ignace, et à Ste-Anne, sur l'Île d'Orléans.
Parmi eux, René Édouard Caron devient Lieutenant-Gouverneur de la province de Québec en 1873. Bravo!

2e Génération
Robert II

Deuxième fils du pionnier devient l'ancêtre des descendants à Pain Court.
Né à Québec, le 30 juillet 1647, à Château-Richer, près de Québec. Il contracte mariage avec Marguerite Cloutier, fille de Jean et Marie Martin. Elle lui donna au moins 12 enfants. Le nom "Caron" fut transmis par au moins 7 garçons qui tous ont eu de belles familles.

3e GÉNÉRATION
Joseph

Fils de Robert II, né le 7 avril 1686 à Ste-Anne. Il se marie à Cap St. Ignace, le 27 février, à Marie Madeleine Bernier, fille de Pierre et Françoise Boubt. Ils ont eu treize enfants, dont 8 garçons.

4e Génération
Pierre Noël

Était le plus jeune de la famille - Joseph. Il est né à l'Islet, le 27 décembre 1735. Il épousa Marie Gèneviève Thibault, fille de Jacques et Marie-Anne Proulx, le 4 juillet 1757, à St. Thomas de Montmagny. Vers cette période, le Canada devient colonie de l'Angleterre. Nous pouvons retracer seulement trois des enfants, dont Charles est mort à 80 ans à St-Jacques- le-Mineur, le 6 mars

1842. C'est dire qu'il est né en 1762.

5e GÉNÉRATION
Charles Caron

Il est né vers 1762, épousa Marie-Josephte Bonneau, fille de Zacharie Bonneau et Marie-Josephte Noël, le 24 juillet 1786. Elle lui donna au moins 7 enfants. Parmi ceux-là, 4 garçons qui continueront sa progéniture. Charles et Josephte semblent avoir déménagé à l'Acadie après quelques années. La nouvelle paroisse de Saint-Jacques le Mineur devient une paroisse détachée de l'Acadie, car nous retrouvons les noms des membres de sa famille au registre. Charles est mort à Saint-Jacques le Mineur, le 6 mars, 1842, ainsi que son fils, Augustin, en 1844.

6e GÉNÉRATION
Augustin

Il est né vers l'an 1790 à St. Thomas, Montmagny. Il accompagna sa famille à l'Acadie. Épousa le 31 juillet, 1815, Marie Jourdanais, fille de Pierre Jourdanais et Marie-Françoise Rémillard. Elle lui donna au moins treize enfants. Parmi eux, dix ont établi un foyer, deux meurent bébé et une n'est pas mariée. Voici les enfants:

Florence (1816)	Esther (1818)
Prudent (1819)	Marie (1821)
Émélie (1822)	Moïse (5 février 1825)
Romain (1827)	Lulienne (1829)
Jérémie (1832)	Augustin-Prudent (1834)
Toussaint (1836)	Aglace (1839)
Denise (1841)	

Augustin, décédé le 22 janvier 1844, à Sant-Jacques the Mineur.

7e GÉNÉRATION
Moïse

Il est né le 5 février 1825.

1er mariage

Il épousa Flavie Pinsonneault de St. Édouard. Ils eurent deux enfants. Flavie survécut mais Mathilda est décédée à un jeune âge. Flavie épousa Auguste Levert de St. Édouard.

2e mariage

Le 15 janvier 1849 à Saint Jacques, il épousa Célina Tétreault née à l'Acadie 1833, fille d'Albert Tétreault et de Marie-Rose Rémillard. 1. Ils eurent 6 enfants dont 5 ont survécu. Cordelia meurt très jeune. Alors ils se dirigent vers Pain Court avec 5 enfants en 1866. Le 4 février 1870, Célina meurt à 37 ans.

1. Née 1833 à l'Acadie - décédée le 4 février 1870 à 37 ans.

1-	Joseph Caron	marié	1-Marie Gagnon
			2-Hermine Laplante
2-	Médéric Caron	marié	Elmire Faubert
3-	Édouard Caron	marié	Philomène Sterling
4-	Napoléon Caron	marié	Émélie Béchard

| 5- | Hedwidge Caron | marié | Alex Sterling |

3e mariage

Le 20 avril 1871 à Pain Court, après quatorze mois, il épousa Marie Thibodeau, veuve de Chrysan (Crisan) Béchard. Ils eurent trois enfants. Deux ont survécu;

| 1- | Salomon Caron | marié | Rosanna Faubert |
| 2- | Denise Caron | mariée | Delphys Trahan |

Moïse a le bonheur de voir tous ses enfants se marier et avoir de belles familles, spécialement beaucoup de garçons. Il les établit sur de belles fermes fertiles, dans le 4e rang, à l'est et à l'ouest de la Winter Line, à Pain Court.

8e GÉNÉRATION
Joseph

1er mariage - Marie Gagnon, fille de Pierre Gagnon et Lucie Yott. Elle a eu deux enfants donc Lucie épousa Joseph-Pierre Faubert. Ils ont élévé leur famille à Détroit.

2e mariage - Hermine Laplante, le 29 avril 1884. Ils eurent cinq enfants, Eugène, Délina, Hector, Dominat, et Delphine. Père Dominat était membre des Oblats de Marie Immaculée et professeur à l'université d'Ottawa.

Eugène	marié	Philomène Bourassa
Délina	mariée	Zacharie Gagner
Delphine	mariée	Eugène Roy
Hector	marié	Hélène Jubenville

Le fils d'Eugène, Père Vincent Caron suivit dans les traces du Père Dominat, chez les Oblats. Lui aussi était professeur à l'université d'Ottawa. Il a enseigné la philosophie et la théologie morale pendant plus de 30 ans.

Médéric

Né le 4 août 1857 à Saint Jacques le Mineur. Il se marie, le 14 novembre 1882, à l'église St. Joseph de Chatham, à Elmire Faubert, fille d'Antoine Faubert et Marie-Olive Robert. Père de quinze enfants;

Joséphine	mariée	Wilfrid Béchard
Célina	morte jeune	
Denis	mort jeune	
Rémi	marié	1-Régina Béchard 1906
		2-Maria Laprise 1920
		Veuve de Trefflé Blais
Alfred	marié	Lucie Béchard
Marie-Louise	mariée	Ovila Cheff
Célina	mariée	M. McBride
Alphonse	marié	Ida Belle
Mélina	mariée	Eugène Thibodeau

Délia	mariée	Adolphe Roy
Magdelèna	mariée	Paul Ouellette
Cécilia	morte jeune par le feu	
Alcide	marié	Alexina Ouellette
Albert	mort jeune	

Médéric était diplômé de l'université de l'Assomption - 1878, il est fermier comme son père. En 1880, il est professeur à l'école de Mt. Clemens au Michigan. Vers l'an 1882, il retourne à la ferme où il y demeure le reste de sa vie. En peu de temps, il défriche 100 arpents de terre.

Le 14 novembre 1882, il épousa Elmire Faubert. En politique, il était conservateur, toujours intéressé dans les affaires municipales. Il fut commissaire d'école pendant 4 ans et trésorier du canton de Dover pendant 30 ans. Il était aussi Juge de paix. Il a vécu une vie exemplaire et gardait l'estime des ses concitoyens.

Édouard

Épousa Philomène Sterling le 2 mai, 1881, fille de William et Rosalie Dubois. Ils eurent 14 enfants, donc 7 garçons et 7 filles :

Alphy	marié	Elizabeth Gamble
		Veuve de Jim Gamble
Willie	marié	Nelida Desmarais
Amédée	marié	Louise Barrette
Zéphyre	marié	Corinne Houle
Hervé	marié	Yvonne Béchard
Armand	célibataire	
Cécile	célibataire	
Délia	mariée	Léopold Gagnier
Célina	mariée	Joseph Robert
Alma	mariée	Wilfrid Bélanger
Oliva	mariée	Édouard Antaya
Rosa	mariée	Steven Jubenville
Victoria	mariée	Henri Bélanger

Un garçon mort très jeune.

Napoléon

Dernier des garçons de Moïse Caron et Célina Tétreault. Il épousa Émélie Béchard le 25 février 1884, fille de Calixte Béchard et Marie Houle. Ils eurent 6 garçons et une fille.

Louis	marié	Annie Sterling
		Veuve de Willie Bourdeau
Hélène	mariée	Dieudonné Gagner Jr.
		Fils de Dieudonné Gagner Sr.
		et Olivine Lucier
Adélard	marié	Anne Gamble
Ozias	marié	Rose Démarais
		fille de Pierre et Ida Laplante

Ladislas	marié	Alma Trudell fille de
		Régis et Euphrasie Béchard
Wilfrid	célibataire	
Réal	marié	Agnès Roy fille de
		Thomas et Charline Ouellette

Ils habitaient une ferme de 100 arpents couvert de forêt. Dans l'espace de trois ans, déjà 50 arpents étaient défrichés. Une belle maison était construite ainsi qu'une grange. Il était reconnu et aimé de ses concitoyens. Pendant des années, il opérait un moulin à battre le grain, avec la vapeur (steam engine). Il parvient à mettre sur pieds tous ses garçons, chacun sur une belle terre.

Hedwidge

Mariée le 11 mai 1886 à Alex Sterling, fils de William et Rosalie Dubois. Ils eurent 5 enfants:

William Jr.	marié	Alice Houle à Grande Pointe
		le 21 janvier, 1919
Célina	mariée	Philippe Pinsonneault
		le 25 novembre, 1907
Alma	mariée	Alfred Bélisle
		le 27 avril, 1914
Victoria	mariée	Danus Pinsonneault
		le 10 mai, 1920
Vélrie	mariée	Poissant de Wallaceburg

Denise

Fille de Moïse et Marie Thibodeau a marié Dolphis Trahan, fils de Julien et Éléonore Poutré, le 7 avril, 1891. Ils eurent 4 enfants:

Hercule	marié	Eva Yott fille de Alex et Théotiste Lemoyne, le 18 octobre, 1915
Alphore	marié	1. Irene Lucier à Grande Pointe
		2. Fébronic Blais
		veuve de Willie Blais
Victor	marié	Marie-Anne Gagner fille de
		Dieudonné et Olivine Lucier
Hector	mort à 8 mois	le 23 juillet, 1928

Salomon

Fils de Moïse et Marie Thibodeau. Il était le dernier des enfants de Moïse, le onzième. Il épousa Rosanna Faubert, fille de Pierre et Sophie Sterling. Enfants de ce mariage: cinq filles dont Edna, Clara, Anna, Léona et Marie-Thérèse, tous religieuses Jésus-Marie de Windsor.

Augustin - L'aîné des garçons. Augustin devient prêtre, diocèse de London et curé de Rivière-aux-Canards, St. Joachim et McGregor. Il reçoit aussi le titre de Monseigneur.

Réginald - Marié à Lucille Adam. Ils eurent plusieurs enfants, Pierre, Hélène, Claire, François, Michel, Denise, Louise.

Gérard -   Marié à Florence Bénéteau. Ils eurent 3 garçons: Jérôme, Jean, Clément, et 3 filles: Rose-Marie, Agnès, Thérèse.

Adrien -   Marié à Antoinette Brisson. Ils eurent 3 garçons et une fille: Bernard, Louis-Paul, Gérard, Anne-Marie.

Trahan family

FIVE GENERATIONS – 100-year-old Delphis Trahan, Pain Court (front-left) had his first look at his three-week-old great great grand-son Robert Jean on the weekend when the five generations met at a family gathering. Holding Robert is his father, Bernard. His great-grandfather, Hercule Trahan, Pain Court (rear-left) and grandfather Alex, R R 1 Pain Court (rear-right) and father Jean-Bernard Trahan. "Mr. Delphis Trahan, husband of the late Denise Caron who died in 1946. He was born May 5, 1869 and died October 21, 1972. He was 103 years old."

Narcisse Laprise et son épouse Adée Roy

Laprise Coat of Arms

This biography was prepared individually for
the Laprise surname on January 12, 1976 at the request of
Caroline Laprise, Pain Court, Ontario

EXTRAIT DU RÉGISTRE DE NOTRE-DAME DE QUÉBEC

ACTE DE MARIAGE

Acte de Mariage de Jean Daniaux & Marie Michault en l'église Notre-DamedeQuébec, en date du 10 septembre 1670.

Le dixième jour du mois de septembre de l'année mil six cent soixante et dix, après les fiançailles et la publication de deux bans de mariage faite les septième et huitième du même mois d'entre Jean Daniaux, fils de deffunct Jean Daniaux et de Renée Brunet, ses père et mère , de la paroisse de St. André, de la ville de Niort évêché de Poitiers, d'une part; et Marie MICHAULT, fille de defunct Brésil Michault et de Marguerite Tessier, ses père et mère, de la paroisse de Bourg Levilay, Archevêché de Sens, d'autre part. Monseigneur Evesque s'estant que de Pétrée les ayant dispensé du troisième ban et ne s'entant découvert aucun empêchesment. Je sousigné prestre curé de cette Église paroissiale de Notre-Dame de Québec, les ay en la dite Église solennellement par paroles de présent, conjoints en mariage, et leur ay donné la bénédiction nuptiale selon la forme prescrite par la Ste Église en présence de Pierre Renard, Jacques La Croix, Pierre Braban, Jacques Tomie de Beaumont, etc.

H. De Bernières.

Note :- 1er mariage

(Mariage du 1er ancêtre en l'Église de Notre-Dame de Québec, le mariage est célébré par le Curé De Bernières.)

142

Selon 1er volume Mgr. Tanguay

JEAN DANIAUX

Baptisé -   1637 fils de Jean Daniaux et de René Brunet, de St. André, ville de Niort, évêché de Poitiers, France.

Décédé -   6 janvier 1709 à St. Michel de Bellechasse.

Son 1er mariage-

10 septembre 1670, Marie-Louise Michault, baptisée 1647 fille de Brésil Michault et Marguerite Tessier du Bourg-Levilay, évêché de Sens en France.

Enfants issus de ce mariage:

Jacques baptisé 21 janvier 1672

Marguerite baptisée 15 février 1674

Marie-Françoise baptisée 31 juillet 1676

Joseph baptisé 2 avril 1679

Québec, le 29 septembre 1953.

M. et Mme Trefflé Laprise,
R. R. No. 7
Chatham, Ont.

Cher monsieur et chère Madame,

     Je vous remercie infiniment pour les renseignements que vous avez été assez bons de m'envoyer. Ils concordent bien avec les détails que j'ai. Il y a plus de 30 ans, un de mes oncles avait fait préparer une généalogie par les Drouin, et je vous envoie copie de leurs notes. Vous y trouverez le nom des parents du premier ancêtre. L'endroit, d'où il venait en France, etc. De plus, je trouve dans un dossier spécial à l'Archevêché à Québec , que Jean Daniau a fait abjuration de la religion calviniste à Québec quatre jours avant son premier mariage. Cela ne change rien, mais ce sont des détails intéressants à savoir.

     J'aurais aimé à vous rencontrer lors de votre passage à Québec, nous aurions pu échanger des renseignements "on the spot". J'espère qu'à votre prochain voyage dans nos murs que j'aurai le plaisir de vous rencontrer.

     J'ai inclus aussi une copie de ma lignée directe. Je descends de Jean-Baptiste, second fils du second lit, et vous descendez de son frère François. La parenté n'est pas très grande . . . Je connais une famille à Québec qui porte encore le nom Dagnault et qui descend de Jacques, le fils du premier mariage.

     J'ai plus de 400 mariages dans mes notes . . . Dagneau-Laprise, les deux noms sont portés indifféremment par ici.

     Je vous remercie encore une fois et vous prie de me croire.
          Votre bien dévouée,
          L. Dagneau

              Mlle Léda Dagneau,
              103½ rue Ste-Anne, app.25
              Québec.

Québec, le 5 mars 1954.

M. et Mme Trefflé Laprise
R.R. No. 7
Chatham, Ont.

Monsieur et Madame,

J'ai réussi à obtenir les mariages des comtés de Montmagny, Bellechasse et L'Islet de la famille Dagneau-Laprise.

Je vous envoie une copie des familles que j'ai pu organiser. Je crois que je vous ai donné les détails de la première famille de Jean Daniau et M. Louise Michaud et Françoise Rondeau.

Comme vous verrez, les familles mentionnées aux pages 6, 7, 8, et 9 ne sont pas complètes. J'ai seulement les notes que vous m'avez données. Pouvez-vous les compléter? Donnez les dates de mariages, les parents des épouses, et les autres enfants s'il y en a. . . .Autrement il me faudra les chercher au greffe d'Ontario, en quelque part.

En un mot, donnez-moi les détails que vous pourrez et je tâcherai de les compléter plus tard. Vous pouvez garder les cinq premières pages pour vos notes et me retourner les autres avec vos notes.

J'espère vous intéresser avec ces détails. J'ai pu collectionner plus de 600 mariages, et j'en attends d'autres du Lac St-Jean, de Roberval, de l'Évêché de St-Jean d'Iberville, près de Montréal, etc. etc. C'est un travail bien long.

Veuillez m'excuser si je vous dérange encore, et je vous prie de me croire.

Votre bien dévouée,
L. Dagneau

Mariage à l'Église : - Acte de Mariage à l'Église

MARIAGE

**à St. Jean, Île d'Orléans - Québec
en date du - 7 -juin -1686
Mariage de Jean Dagneau   &   Françoise Rondeau**

L'an- 1686, le septième jour du mois de Juin, après la publication des trois bans de mariage faiete le premier, conquiesme et douziesme du mois de mars précédent, d'entre JEAN DANIO dit Laprise âgé de quarante-huit ans, habitant de Bellechasse dans la comte du Sud et veuf de defunct Louise Michaud d'une part; Et Françoise Rondeau âgée de quinze ans fille de Brésil Rondeau et de défunte Catherine Verrier --- ses père et mère, de cette paroisse d'autre part, vûle certificat de Messire Jean Pinguet faisant les fonctions curiales au dit lieu de Belle-chasse, par lequel il déclare avoir publié les trois bans dans le lieu de la mission et ne s'estant découvert aucun empêchement. Je prestre soussigné faisant les fonctions curiales dans cette paroisse, ay pris leur mutuel et réciproque consentement par paroles de présent les ai mariés et ensuite donné la bénédiction nuptiale solon la forme prescrite par l'Église en présence de Nicolas __ dit Lapointe, René Auclair, Estienne Corriveau et Charles Antelin qui ont avec les dites époux et épouse, déclaré ne savoir escrire ny signer de ce interpellés suivant l'ordonnance.   -- Signé

Francheville

146

Le 1ᵉʳ ancêtre au Canada

Jean Daniaux
En deuxième Mariage, a épousé.

Françoise Rondeau

Cette Françoise Rondeau a eu pour père;

Pierre Rondeau, fils de Jean Rondeau et de Jacquette
Pallereau, de la ville de Maroilly,
évêché de Maillezaie, en France,
dans le Poitou.

Pierre Rondeau, père de Françoise Rondeau à eu
comme mère;

Catherine Verrier, fille de Jean Verrier et d'Agnès
Briquet, de la paroisse de
Crostieul, évêché d'Avrances, en France.

****

J'ajoute que ce Pierre Rondeau, le père de votre arrière ancêtre,
s'est marié deux fois : une 1ᵉʳᵉ fois à Catherine Verrier, et une
2ᵉ fois à Marie Ancelin, avec plusieurs enfants en première et
deuxième noces.

JEAN DANIAUX DIT LAPRISE
Première génération au Canada

1er Mariage

Baptisé -   1637 le 6 janvier, 1709 décédé à St. Michel à l'âge de 72 ans.
Marié -   le 10 septembre 1670 Marie-Louise Michaud baptisée 1647

2e Mariage

Nous sommes descendants de ce mariage à Françoise Rondeau, née 1671.
Mariée 7 juin 1686 à St. Jean, Île d'Orléans. Selon l'acte de mariage, elle avait 15 ans. Lui, était âgé de 49 ans.
        Enfants de ce mariage: Jean, Guillaume, Laurent, Joseph, François, Jean-Baptiste et Françoise.

Jean-   Né vers 1687, décédé 20 juin 1759 après 4 mariages.

Guillaume -   Né 1689 - 4 mariages

Laurent -   Baptisé 18 octobre 1694, mort 19 mai 1716

Joseph -   Baptisé 1700, mort 22 juillet 1795, 2 mariages.

Françoise -   Baptisée 24 mars 1702, décédée 14 mai 1723
                 Mariée 18 août 1722
Jean-Baptiste - Marié à Claire Blanchet 1728, ancêtre de Léda Dagneault de Québec.
                 Grâce à elle pour beaucoup de renseignements reçus
François -   Notre ancêtre - marié le 11 février 1725 à St. Pierre du Sud
                 contrat   C. Michon

FAMILLE DAGNEAU – LAPRISE

Jean Daniau et Renée Brunet, de St-André de Niort,
évêché de Poitiers. Poitou. France.
Jean Daneau - né 1637, mort 6 janvier 1709
à St. Michel de Bellechasse – 72 ans.

1ère génération au Canada:

1.) Jean Daniau mariés Marie-Louise Michault - 4 enfants issus de ce mariage.
2.) Jean Daniau et Françoise Rondeau (son 2e mariage)
  mariés le 7 juin 1686 à St-Jean, Île d'Orléans. 7 enfants issus de ce mariage.

2e génération: François Dagneau et Marie Rousseau
Mariés à St-Pierre du Sud le 11 février 1725
(Contrat C. Michon).

3e génération: Jean-Baptiste Dagneau et et Marie-Josephte Morin
mariés à Berthier le 5 février 1753

4e génération: Jean-Baptiste Dagneau et Marie-Josephte Blais
mariés à St-Pierre du Sud le 27 janvier 1783

5e génération: Jean-Baptiste Dagneau et Marie-Agathe Destroismaisons
mariés à St-Pierre du Sud le 11 juin 1820

6e génération: Édouard Laprise et Henriette Minville dit Gagné;
1ère génération à Pain Court
mariés à St-Thomas de Montmagny en 1855

7e génération: Narcisse Laprise et Adée Roy
mariés à Pain Court le 16 novembre 1884

8e génération: 1) Josephat Laprise et Délia Charron
mariés à Grande Pointe le 21 mai 1912
2) Josephat Laprise et Laura Rose Corriveau (veuve de
Ernest Corriveau) mariés à Chatham en 1961.

9e génération: Trefflé Laprise et Caroline Roy
mariés à Pain Court le 18 janvier 1938

2e Génération

François Dagneau, fils de Jean1 et Françoise Rondeau
  mariés à St-Pierre du Sud, le 11 février 1725 (Contrat Michon, notaire).

Marie Rousseau, fille de

Jean-Baptiste, 1 marié à Berthier, le 5 février 1753, avec Marie-Josephte Morin, fille de
        Pierre-Noël Morin et de Thérèse Pelletier;[2] marié à St-Pierre du Sud le 27 février 1775,
        avec Marie-Euphrosine Lizotte, fille de Joseph Lizotte et de Marie-Joseph Miville.

Madeleine, baptisée à St-Pierre du Sud 1730; inhumée le 25 novembre 1755 à St-Pierre.

Marie-Geneviève, mariée à St-Pierre du Sud, le 9 février 1756, avec Pierre Morin,
        fils de Jacques Morin et de Thérèse Quemleur-Laflamme.

François, marié le 14 janvier 1748 (C. Rageot, Notaire) avec Marie-Geneviève
        Morin, fille de Pierre-Noël Morin et de Thérèse Pelletier.

Charles, 1.   marié à St-Thomas de Montmagny, le 9 février 1750, avec Françoise
        Fournier, fille de Louis Fournier et de Angélique Bossé.
        marié à St-Pierre du Sud, le 17 novembre 1760, avec Marie-Louise
        Destroismaisons, fille de Louis Destroismaisons et de Anne Proulx.

Marie-Reine, mariée à St-Pierre du Sud, le 22 février 1762, avec Joseph Talbot, fils de
        Jacques Talbot et de Angélique Mercier.

Prisque, 1 marié à St-François du Sud, le 11 janvier 1762, avec Geneviève Plante, fille
        de Charles Plante et de Marie-Madeleine Avare; veuve de Nicolas Boissonneau.
        [2] marié à Ste-Marie, le 2 juillet 1793 avec Marie-Claire Rolandeau, fille de
        Louis Rolandeau et de Thérèse Picard.

Pierre, marié en 1770, à St-Pierre du Sud, avec Marie-Geneviève Rousseau, fille de
        Jean Rousseau et de Marie Picard.

3e Génération

Jean-Baptiste Dagneau, [2] fils de François Dagneau et de Marie Rousseau.
        A marié 1. à Berthier, le 5 février 1753.
        B marié 2. à St-Pierre du Sud, le 27 février 1775.

        A) Marie-Joseph Morin, fille de Pierre-Noël Morin et de Thérèse Pelltier.

1. Marie-Joseph, baptisée le 7 décembre 1753 à St-Pierre du Sud; mariée
        à St-Pierre du Sud, le 10 juillet 1780, avec Antoine Gagné et de
        Marie-Catherine Boucher.

2. Jean-Baptiste, [3] baptisé à St-Pierre du Sud, le 28 décembre 1754; marié
        à St-Pierre du Sud, le 27 janvier 1783, avec Marie-Joseph Blais, fille de
        Jean-Baptiste Blais et de Marie-Joseph Rémillard.

3. Joseph-Marie, baptisé à St-Pierre du Sud, le 8 avril 1758; marié à
St-Pierre du Sud, le 19 août 1782 avec Marie-Josephte Pellerin, fille
de Louis Pellerin et de Geneviève Huart.

   B) Marie-Euphrosine Lizotte, fille de Joseph Lizotte et de Marie-Joseph Miville. Baptisé
   le 2 septembre 1749 à Ste-Anne de la Pocatière.

1) Marie-Louise, baptisée le 10 août 1775 à St-Thomas; mariée en 1797
à St-Pierre du Sud, avec Antoine Dassylva, fils de Pierre Dassylva et
de Ursule Dupuis.

2) Marie-Charlotte, mariée à St-Pierre du Sud, le 11 janvier 1802, avec Pierre Caman, fils
de Pierre Caman et de Marie Gagné.(fils d'Écossais).

3) Jules-Simon, baptisé le 24 juin 1790.

4) Catherine, mariée le 30 octobre 1809, à Notre-Dame de Québec, avec Joseph Duval,
fils de Pierre Duval et de Marie-Louise Gauvreau.

Références dans les livres de Mgr. Tanguay.

4e Génération

Jean-Baptiste Dagneau,	fils de Jean-Baptiste Dagneau et de Marie-Joseph Morin. Baptisé à St-Pierre du Sud, le 28 décembre 1754. Marié à Berthier, le 27 janvier 1783 avec Marie-Joseph Blais.
Marie-Joseph Blais,	fille de Jean-Baptiste Blais et de Marie-Joseph Rémillard.
Marie-Françoise,	mariée à St-Pierre du Sud, le 8 novembre 1803 avec François-Germ Guimont, fils de Jean-Gabriel Guimont et de Reine Lemieux.
Marie-Josette,	mariée à St-Pierre du Sud, le 5 août 1806, avec Marcel Thibault, fils de Basile Thibault et de M. Geneviève Dupont, de l'Islet.
Euphronine,	mariée à St-Pierre du Sud, le 15 octobre 1811, avec Jacques Bernier, fils de Isidore Bernier et de Geneviève Dupont, de L'Islet.
*Jean-Baptiste,	baptisé à St-Pierre le 25 septembre 1790; 1) marié à Cap St-Ignace, le 4 novembre 1817, avec Marie-Rose Méthot, fille de Jean-Baptiste Méthot, et de Marthe Breux. 2) marié à Cap St-Ignace, le 11 juin 1820, avec Marie-Agathe Destroismaisons, fille de Pierre-Noël Destroismaisons et de Rosalie Brie.
Marie-Angèle,	mariée à St-Pierre du Sud, le 27 janvier 1824, avec Abraham Anctil, fils de veuve Christine Bélanger.

Geneviève,	mariée à St-Pierre du Sud, le 19 octobre 1824, avec Joseph Fontaine, fils de Joseph Fontaine et de Marie-Marguerite Picard.
Marie-Julie,	mariée à St-Pierre du sud, le 7 novembre 1826, avec Charles Lemieux, fils de Ignace Lemieux et de Élizabeth Dion, de Cap St-Ignace.
Marie-Chantal,	mariée à St-Jean-Port-Joli, le 2 février 1830, avec Henri Chouinard, fils de Julien Chouinard et de Marie-Ange Chouinard.

5e Génération

Jean-Baptiste Dagneau, fils de Jean-Baptiste et Josephte Blais. Baptisé à St-Pierre,
    Montmagny le 25 septembre 1790;
    1) marié à Cap St-Ignace, le 4 novembre 1817 avec Marie-Rose Méthot,
    fille de Jean-Baptiste Méthot et de Marthe Breux.
    2) marié à St-Pierre de Montmagny le 11 juin 1820 avec Agathe
    Destroismaisons, fille de Pierre-Noël Destroismaisons et de
    Rosalie Brie.

Honoré,	marié à St-Thomas, le 9 avril 1847, avec Marie Morin, fille de Louis Morin et de Julie Thibault. Venu à Pain Court 1867
Prudent,	marié à St-Pierre de Montmagny, le 22 avril 1851, avec Émélie Mainville, fille de François Mainville et de Marguerite Roy.
Jean-Baptiste,	marié à St-Jean, Port-Joli, le 4 octobre 1853, avec Arthemise Anctil, fille de François Anctil et de Rosalie Dessin dit St-Pierre. En 1867 s'établit à Wallaceburg.
*Édouard,	baptisé à St-Thomas 1829. Marié à St-Thomas de Montmagny, le 19 février 1855, avec Henriette Minville, fille de Jacques Minville et de Suzanne Emond. Il s'établit à Pain Court en 1867 – "Narcisse l'accompagne, il a 9ans."
Paul,	marié à Cap St-Ignace, le 1er février 1859, avec Eliza Gagné, fille de Louis Gagné et de Esther Lemieux.
André,	marié à Ste-Louise de l'Islet, le 8 novembre 1859, avec Virginie Bélanger, fille de Jean-Marie Bélanger et de Constance Bélanger. Venu à Pain Court, Ontario.
Joseph,	marié à Buckland, le 21 juin 1864, avec Josephte Nicole, fille de Francis-Xavier Nicole et de Marie-Berthelet. Il était tailleur et s'établit à Détroit.
Onésiphore,	marié à St-Thomas, le 21 septembre 1858, avec Célina Goudreau, fille de Prosper Gaudreau et de Marguerite Bouchard.

Archange,   mariée à St-Pierre du Sud, le 4 février 1846, avec Alfred Létourneau,
                 fils de Eustache Létourneau et de Catherine Gagné.

Clémentine,   mariée à St-Pierre du Sud, le 19 août 1851, avec Germain Guimont,
                 fils de Alexis Guimont et de Esther Fournier.

Quatre générations:
Au centre, Narcisse Laprise 81 ans avec le petit Gérard, 1 an.
À gauche, Josephat Laprise 50 ans, à droite, Trefflé Laprise 27 ans.

LAPRISE - DIT DAGNEAU
EN ONTARIO - 1867

Nos ancêtres se sont dirigés vers la Nouvelle France - le Canada vers 1650.

Cinq générations se sont établis au Québec de St. Thomas de Montmagny. Ce fut la 6e génération qui se dirige vers l'Ontario en 1867. Parmi ceux-là nous remarquons :

Édouard Laprise   et Henriette Mainville mariés à St. Thomas, 19 février 1855.
                     Édouard décédé le 28 novembre 1902, à l'âge de 72 ans.

Honoré Laprise   marié à St. Thomas le 9 avril 1847 avec Marie Morin.
                     1.André Laprise et Virginie Bélanger mariés le 8 novembre 1859, mort le 11 janvier 1915 à 53 ans.

LES DESCENDANTS À PAIN COURT

Jean-Baptiste   et Arthemise Anctil, région de Wallaceburg.

Joseph Laprise   et Josephte Nicole, région de Détroit.

Les Laprise de l'Ontario sont les descendants d'Édouard Laprise et Henriette Mainville. Il y a, à Pain Court et à Wallaceburg une lignée de Laprise qui sont les descendants d'André Laprise et Virginie Bélanger. C'est à remarquer qu'il y a aussi les Faubert qui sont leurs descendants.

Nous comptons aussi André Laprise marié à Philomène Campbell. Henri Laprise, leur garçon, épousa Ida Normandin le 7 janvier 1919. Leurs descendants sont à Wallaceburg.

Édouard Dagneau dit Laprise est né en 1829 à St-Pierre du Montmagny. Ses parents sont Jean-Baptiste Laprise et Marie-Agathe Destroismaisons dit Picard. Il quitte le Québec pour venir s'établir à Pain Court, lot 15, 7e rang, Dover, avec sa femme et ses enfants. Deux frères l'accompagnent, Jean-Baptiste et Honoré, chacun avec leur famille. Un troisième frère, André, s'établit lui aussi à Pain Court. Édouard arrive à Pain Court en 1867 et se construit une maison à la hâte, puisque c'est déjà l'automne. Il était âgé de 38 ans et Narcisse notre descendant, avait 9 ans. Il nous a raconté les démarches qu'il a dû entreprendre dès son arrivée en 1867. Il eut bien des défis à envisager. Il épousa sa femme Henriette Minville dit Gagné à St-Thomas de Montmagny en 1855.

1ère Génération de Laprise à Pain Court - Ontario

6e génération

Edouard Laprise - Henriette Minville dit Gagné, mariés à St-Thomas Montmagny en 1855.

7e génération

Narcisse Laprise et Adée Roy mariés en 1884 à Pain Court le 16 novembre.

8e génération

Josephat Laprise et Délia Charron mariés le 21 mai 1912 à Pain Court.

9e génération

Trefflé Laprise et Caroline Roy mariés le 18 janvier 1938 à Pain Court.

10e génération, 11e génération, 12e génération

Tous descendants de Narcisse Laprise et Adée Roy

En 1997, notre lignée compte 12 générations au Canada et 7 générations dans le Sud Ontario.

6e Génération

Édouard Dagneau dit Laprise, fils de Jean-Baptiste né 1829, décédé à Pain Court le 28 novembre 1902, marié le 19 février 1855 à Henriette Minville dit Gagné, fille de Jacques Minville et Suzanne Edmond. Les enfants issus de ce mariage sont:

Narcisse - né le 30 mai 1859 à St-Thomas Montmagny, mariage à Pain Court le 16 novembre 1884 à Adée Roy née 1869 le 7 février, décédée à Pain Court le 10 mars 1944.

Joséphine - née au Québec, épousa Toussaint Campbell le 25 novembre, 1879. Elle meurt le 8 mai 1934.

Joseph - né le 19 mars 1897, épousa Hélène Roy, fille de Joseph et Hélène Faubert le 27 octobre 1891.

Délima - née le 15 décembre 1872. Elle meurt le 19 décembre 1872.

Angéline - née 1859, épousa William Boyer le 8 mars 1886. Ils demeuraient sur la rue St-Clair à Chatham. Ils étaient propriétaire de "Boyer Electric." Angéline meurt le 24 février 1955 à 87 ans. William meurt le 5 juillet 1933. William, frère de Mathilda Boyer et mariée à Thomas Onésime Béchard, parents de Thomas Béchard marié à Roseanna Bélisle.

Albert - épousa Marcelline Roy le 10 novembre 1890. Il est décédé le 16 septembre 1917.

Émélie - épousa Jean-Baptiste Richer le 19 novembre 1889 à Pain Court.

7e Générations

Narcisse Laprise -   fils d'Édouard Dagneau dit Laprise et Henriette Minville dit Gagné, né à St-Thomas du Montmagny le 30 mai 1859. Il est décédé le 12 mars 1944 à 85 ans. Il épousa Adée Roy le 16 novembre 1884 à Pain Court, née le 6 février 1868. Elle est décédée à Pain Court le 14 juin à 81 ans.

Enfants de ce mariage:

Eugène -   célibataire, né le 31 octobre 1886, décédé le 13 avril 1943.

Rosanna -   mariée à George Reaume, le 9 octobre 1911.

Délima -   mariée à Josephat Roy (Lucien) le 24 novembre 1908.

Josephat -   né le 21 janvier 1890, décédé le 9 janvier 1980, marié le 21 mai 1912 à Grande Pointe à Délia Charron, née le 19 février 1892, fille de Théodore Charron et Phébée Hébert, décédée le 8 octobre 1959 à 67 ans.

Lucien Jos -   né le 21 janvier 1890 jumeau, décédé le 21 septembre 1891.

Ida -   mariée à George Emery le 21 mai 1918.

Maria -   mariée à Rémi Caron le 9 avril 1920. Veuve de Trefflé Blais.

Louisa -   mariée à Théophile Marchand le 20 février 1922.

Délia -   mariée à Harry Bourdeau le 3 décembre 1923.

Donat -   marié à Marie-Louise Therrien le 3 décembre 1923, décédé le 29 mai 1964.

Gilbert -   né le 22 avril 1896, décédé le 29 novembre 1970, marié à Lorraine Comeau née 1900.

Prudent -   marié à Dorothy Giroux

8e Génération

Josephat Laprise - fils de Narcisse Laprise et Adée Roy, né le 21 janvier 1890, décédé le 9 janvier 1978 à 88 ans, marié le 21 mai 1912 à Délia Charron à Grande Pointe, fille de Théodore Charron et Phébée Hébert. Elle est née le 18 février 1892.

Enfants de ce mariage:

Trefflé - né le 16 mai 1903 à Pain Court, décédé le 20 mars 1980, marié à Caroline Roy le 18 janvier 1938, fille d'Adolphe Roy et Délia Caron.

Loma - née le 14 février 1914, entre en communauté à 17 ans chez les Soeurs St-Joseph de London.

Cécile - née le 18 janvier 1917, entre en communauté à 19 ans chez les Soeurs St-Joseph Hospitalières de Windsor.

Anna - née le 18 juin 1919, mariée à Alex Trahan le 18 novembre 1942.

Wilfrid - né le 23 mars 1923, marié à Carmel Mailloux de Pointe-aux-Roches, le 24 septembre 1945.

Jeanne - née le 28 février 1925, mariée à Johnny Haslip de Chatham le 29 septembre 1951.

9e Génération

Trefflé Laprise - fils de Josephat Laprise et Délia Charron, né le 16 mai 1913 à Pain Court, décédé le 20 mars 1980 à Pain Court, marié le 18 janvier 1938 à Pain Court à Caroline Roy, fille d'Adolphe Roy et Délia Caron.

Enfants de ce mariage:

Gérard - né le 14 mars 1939.

Roger - né le 13 août 1940.

Claude - né le 25 novembre 1941.

Florent - né le 19 mars 1943.

Caroline - née le 27 août 1946.

Guy - né le 23 septembre 1950.

Jean-Marie - né le 21 juin 1954.

Colette - née le 22 août 1955.

10e Génération

Gérard Laprise -	marié à Aline Cartier de Grande Pointe.
Roger Laprise -	marié à Rose-Marie Houle de Tilbury.
Claude Laprise -	marié à Marie-Reine Masse de Tilbury.
Florent Laprise -	marié à Bernadette Pinsonneault de St-Joachim.
Caroline Laprise -	mariée à David Trudell de Thamesville.
Guy-Vincent Laprise -	marié à Penelope McDonald de Chatham.
Jean-Marie Laprise -	marié à Lucille Benoit de Grande Pointe.
Colette Laprise -	mariée à Malcolm Crow de Nova Scotia.

11e Génération

Gérard -	Jean-Marc, Jeannine Laprise
Roger -	Richard, Lucien Laprise
Claude -	Renée, Nicole Laprise
Florent -	Phyllis, Maurice, André Laprise
Caroline -	Jamie, Christie Trudell
Guy -	Vincent, Jason, Jeremey Laprise
Jean-Marie-	Chantal, Julie, Joël, Mélanie Laprise
Colette -	Robert, Joey Crow

12e Génération

Maurice Laprise -   Mathieu, Dominique, Rebecca

André Laprise -   Chad, Amanda, André James

Jamie Trudell -   Matthew, Natasha, Joshua

Nicole Brown -   Kira, Ian

Lucien Laprise -   Madison

Julie Simpson -   Justin

Joël Laprise -   Melanie

Édouard Dagneau dit Laprise, né en 1829 à St-Pierre-de-Montmagny, quitte le Québec pour venir s'établir à Pain Court lot 15, 7e Concession, dans le canton de Dover, avec sa femme et ses enfants. Deux frères, Jean-Baptiste et Honoré l'accompagnent avec leur famille. Ces deux frères s'établissent dans les environs de Wallaceburg. Un autre frère, Joseph, un tailleur de renommée s'établit à Détroit. Quelques années plus tard, André vient rejoindre ses frères, et s'établit à Pain Court avec sa femme.

Édouard arrive à l'automne, 1867, et se construit une maison pour passer l'hiver. Il était âgé de 38 ans et Narcisse, notre descendant avec qui nous avons vécu et bien connu, n'était alors qu'un p'tit bonhomme de 9 ans.

En 1953, accompagné de mon époux Trefflé, j'ai visité les belles terres arpentées de St-Thomas-de-Montmagny qui longent la rive du fleuve St-Laurent. Sur le terrain où habitait les "Laprise" nous avons bel et bien découvert cette source d'eau naturelle décrite par nos ancêtres. Il paraît que cette source prodigieuse, au pied de la montagne, servait de puits communautaire pouvant abreuver toute la région environnante.

Pour ceux qui désirent se renseigner davantage concernant ces propos, adressez-vous à Wilfrid Laprise. Ils serait en mesure d'élaborer davantage.

Caroline Roy Laprise

Patrimoine Ancestral
Famille Théodore Charron

Phébée Hébert, Emma Charron,
Théodore Charron, Délia Charron,
Napoléon, Elizabeth, Alphée Charron

GÉNÉALOGIE - FAMILY TREE

Ancêtre Charron - France

Pierre Charron - 1 - marié Judith Martin
Paroisse St. Martin, diocèse de Meaux en France
Dictionnaire Généalogique Tanguay
1608 - 1700 féf. 929. IVI

1ère Génération au Canada

Pierre Charron - 2 -   venu au Canada 1640
marié à Montréal le 19 octobre, 1665 à Catherine Pilatte
(Pillard), née 1651
fille de Pierre et Marguerite Molinet de Notre-Dame de Cogne
échêvé de La Rochelle. Il est décédé à Montréal le 26 décembre
1700, 12 enfants issus du mariage
Re Tanguay 1608 - 1700

2e Génération

Nicholas   né le 9 avril 1676 à Boucherville Québec
marié Marie Viau le 15 juin 1703 à Longueil, fille de
Jacques Viau et Marie-Thérèse Robin
15 enfants issus du mariage

3e Génération

Jacques   né le 1 septembre 1710 Longueil Québec
marié Marie Audet - dit Lapointe - le 16 septembre 1743
fille de Innocent Audet - dit Lapointe - et
Geneviève Lenclin à Boucherville

4e Génération

1ère Génération à Windsor

Pierre Charron - 3 -   né à Montréal, venu à Windsor, 1er mariage le 10 mars 1777 à
Charlotte Campeau à L'Assomption Windsor,veuve de Toussinait
Grenon et fille de Charles Campeau et Marie-Charlotte Juillet -dit-
Montreuil.
2e mariage le 7 mars 1791 à Windsor à Marie-Jeanne Pelletier,
veuve de Nicolas Goyeau et fille de André Pelletier et Catherine
Meloche.

5e Génération

André Charron -   né février 1793 à Windsor, Ontario, fils de Pierre Charron - 3 - et Marie-Jeanne Pelletier, marié Marguerite Desloges fille de Michel Desloges et Thérèse Grenon le 11 janvier 1813 à St-Pierre sur la rivière La Tranche (Thames).
Décédé le 29 janvier 1873 à Pain Court.

6e Génération

1ère génération à Grande Pointe et Pain Court

Pierre Charron -4-   né et baptisé à St-Pierre 16 décembre 1826
marié à Sarah Lauzon 17 janvier 1852, fille de Clément Lauzon
et Émélie Deslongchamps décédé le 3 août 1908 à Grande Pointe

7e Génération

Théodore Charron -   né 16 août 1855, 1er Charron baptisé à Pain Court,
marié à Phébée Hébert le 6 novembre 1877 à Pain Court,
fille de Gédéon Hébert et Marie Boutin
décédé le 21 mars, 1925 à Grande Pointe

8e Génération Enfants

Joseph   -né le 20 septembre 1879, décédé le 3 novembre 1880

Emma-   -née le 16 août 1881, décédée le 4 mars, 1965
marié Zéphir Emery le 22 octobre 1901
décédée le 4 mars 1965

Napoléon-   né le 6 août 1883
marié Bella Campbell le 7 novembre 1911
décédé le 10 décembre 1944 à 61 ans.

Alphée-   né le 26 juin 1886
marié Alphonsine Dubuque le 19 octobre 1909
décédé le 30 mars 1970, 83 ans

Élizabeth-   née le 15 octobre 1888
mariée Alphie Maillet le 18 janvier 1910
décédée le 2 octobre 1965, 76 ans

Délia-   née le 19 février 1892
mariée Josephat Laprise le 21 mai 1912
décédée le 8 octobre 1959

Philippe-   né le 18 juin 1895
décédé le 8 septembre 1895

Zéphir-   né le 15 juin 1895
                             décédé le 6 décembre 1897

– FAMILY TREE –

1. Pierre Charron[2] son of Pierre Charron 1 , & Judith Martin, in the parish of St-Martin, Diocese of Meaux, in France, came to Canada in 1640. He married in Montréal, on Oct. 19, 1665, to Catherine Pilette, daughter of Pierre Pilette, & Marguerite Moulinet, of the parish Notre-Dame de Gogne, Diocese De La Rochelle, in France, died Dec. 26, 1700, in Montréal, Qué.

2. Nicolas Charron born April 9, 1676, in Boucherville, Qué. Married Madeleine Viau, June 15, 1703, daughter of Jacques Viau & Marie-Madeleine Plouart.

3. Jacques Charron born Sept. 1, 1710, in Longueil, Qué. Married Marie Audet-dit-Lapointe, in Boucherville, Qué. Sept. 16, 1743, daughter of Innocent Audet-dit-Lapointe, & Géneviève Lenclin.

4. Pierre Charron [3] born in Montréal, came to Windsor, Ont. Died Oct. 14, 1824, married first, to Charlotte Campeau, March 10, 1777, at Assumption, Windsor, widow of Toussaint Grenon, daughter of Charles Campeau, & Marie-Charlotte Juillet-dit-Montreuil. Second, to Marie-Jeanne Pelletier, March 7 1791, in Windsor, widow of Nicolas Goyeau, daughter of André Pelletier, & Catherine Méloche.

5. André Charron son of Pierre Charron, & Marie-Jeanne Pelletier, born Feb. 1793, Windsor, died Jan. 29, 1873, buried at Pain Court. Married Marguerite Desloges, Jan. 11 1813, at St-Pierre sur la rivière La Tranche, (Thames) daughter of Michel Desloges, & Thérèse Grenon.

6. Pierre Charron 4 born Dec. 16, 1826, baptised at St-Pierre, died Aug. 3, 1908, Grande Pointe. Married Sarah Lauzon, Jan. 17, 1852, daughter of Clément Lauzon, & Émélie Deslongchamps.

7. Théodore Charron born Aug. 16, 1855, first Charron baptized at Pain Court, died March 21, 1925, Grande Pointe, married Phébée Hébert. Nov. 6, 1877, Pain Court. Daughter of Gèdéon Hébert, & Marie Boutin.

Family of André Charron & Marguerite Desloges - St. Peter's

Thérèse, born Oct. 11, 1813, died July 10, 1837, age 23, married Jean Métivier, May 19, 1835, son of Joseph Métivier & Margaret Robertson.

André, born Aug. 29, 1815, died June 24, 1897, age 81, first married Jeannette Lehon, Sept. 5, 1836, second marriage to Julie Champagne, Jan. 22, 1861, widow of Clovis Bernier, daughter of François Champagne & Julie Soucy.

Véronique, (Charlette), born June 10, 1817, married Lambert Dubois, Jan. 7 1836, son of Hyacinthe Dubois & Geneviève Cardinal.

Jean-Baptiste, born Feb. 15, 1819, died Jan. 7, 1906, age 86, married Hermine Champagne, Aug. 30, 1841, daughter of François Champagne, & Julie Soucy.

Michel, born Jan. 16, 1821, married Clémence Champagne, Feb. 7, 1843, daughter of François Champagne & Julie Soucy.

Jeanne, born Oct. 1, 1822, married John Crow, Nov. 17, 1840, son of Robert Crow & Rebecca Everet.

Marguerite, born Dec. 15, 1824, married Hilaire St-Amour, Nov. 4, 1850, son of Narcisse St-Amour & Angélique Dubois.

*Pierre, born Dec. 16, 1826, died Aug. 3, 1908, age 83, married Sarah (Sally) Lauzon, Jan. 17, 1852, daughter of Clément Lauzon & Émélie Deslongchamps.

Julienne, born Feb. 20, 1829, married Charles Paquin, July 13, 1850, son of Jean-Baptiste Paquin & Hélène Ligner.

Antoine, born Feb. 6, 1831, married Rosalie Béchard, July 8, 1851, daughter of Basile Béchard & Josephte Giroux.

Jacques (James), born Sept. 19, 1833, died Oct. 29, 1916, age 83, married 1st. Euphémie Létourneau, May 5, 1852, daughter of Eustache Létourneau & Zoé Raymond, 2nd to Martha-Jane Drouillard, daughter of Thomas Drouillard & Minnie Béchard, 3rd to Zoé Genaw, widow of Charles Lozon. Athanase, born Jan. 28, 1836, married Maria Wade, later went to Port Huron, and changed his name to Dennis Sharrow.

Olivier, born Feb. 26, 1838, died Oct. 7, 1927, age 89, married Philomène Martin.

-Omer Charron

An interesting note on Pierre Charron 4

He was of St. Pierre. He was on the first independent County Council of Kent. The inaugural meeting was held in the New Court house in Chatham, February 27, 1851. He was 25 years old and not married. He represented Tilbury West. On the same council was Robert Mitchell. He was representing Dover East and West. Incidently, Mitchell's Bay was named in his honour

Ref. P. 136 Romantic Kent

Pierre Charron 4 was the son of André Charron and Marguerite Desloges of Windsor. He was born December 16, 1826 at St. Pierre. He married Sarah Lauzon January 1852, daughter of Clément Lauzon and Émélie Deslongchamps. He died August 3, 1908 at 82 years.

Pierre Charron & Sarah Lauzon

DAVID,   born Aug. 2, 1853, died Oct. 18, 1935, age 82, not married.

*THÉODORE,   born Aug. 16, 1855, died March 21, 1925, age 69 married Phébée Hébert, Nov. 6, 1877.

JULIENNE,   born Feb. 9, 1858, died April 10, 1935, age 77, married William Sterling, Nov.6, 1877.

AURÈLE-VITALIE,   born May 3, 1861, died March 10, 1862, age 10 months.

CLÉMENCE,   born May 1, 1863, died April 7, 1934, age 70, married 1st Noé Martin, Oct. 20, 1885, 2nd Jean-Baptiste Rose, Oct. 12, 1890.

EMMA,   born April 10, 1867, died Jan. 30, 1907, age 42, married Aristide Hébert, Oct. 19, 1897.

SOPHIE,   born May 25, 1870, died July 19, 1927, age 57, married Charles Trudell, July 3, 1900.

Théodore Charron & Phébée Hébert

JOSEPH,   born Sept. 20, 1879, died Nov 3, 1880, age 14 months.

ÉMMA,   born Aug. 16, 1881, died March 4, 1965, age 83, married Zéphire Emery, Oct. 22, 1901.

NAPOLÉON,   born Aug. 6, 1883, died Dec. 10, 1944, age 61, married Bella-Marie Campbell, Nov. 7, 1911.

ALPHIE,   born June 26, 1886, died March 30, 1970, age 83, married Alphonsine Dubuque, Oct. 19, 1909.

ÉLIZABETH,   born Oct. 15, 1888, died Oct. 2, 1965, age 76, married Alphie Maillet, Jan. 18, 1910.

DÉLIA,   born Feb. 19, 1892, died Oct. 8, 1959, age 67, married Josephat Laprise, May 21, 1912.

PHILIPPE,   born June 18, 1895, died Sept. 8, 1895, age 3 months.

ZÉPHIRE,   born June 15, 1897, died Dec. 6, 1897, age 6 months

-Omer Charron

Napoléon Charron & Bella-Marie Campbell

OMER,   born April 6, 1913, godparents Toussaint Campbell & Josephine Laprise married Clara Tétrault, Aug. 25, 1959, widow of Harvey Provost.

BLANCHE,   born July 29, 1915, godparents Théodore Charron & Phébée Hébert.

VÉLINA,   born Nov. 19, 1916, died April 11, 1927, age 10, godparents Aphie T. Charron & Alphonsine Dubuque.

ARMAND,   born Sept. 27, 1918, died April 16, 1927, age 8, godparents Josephat Laprise & Délia Charron.

HECTOR,   born May 18, 1920, died April 2, 1924, age 3, 11months, godparents Joseph Campbell & Souphronie Maillet (Myers).

LAURETTE,   born March 20, 1922, godparents Dollard Maillet (Myers) & Alma Campbell, married Rhéal Boucher, Aug. 3, 1946.

GÉRARD,   born Feb. 19, 1923, godparents Alphie J. Maillet (Myers) & Éliza Charron, married Maria Forza, Feb. 20, 1960.

LÉOPOLD,	born March 2, 1925, died April 23, 1927, age 2, godparents Fred Charron & Oliva Sterling.
ROLAND,	born March 6, 1926, godparents Fred Campbell & Arvella Sterling, married Lauria Duperron, Oct. 25, 1952.
FLORENCE,	born Oct. 10, 1927, godparents Joseph Sterling & Roseanna Campbell.
THÉRÈSE,	born Jan. 13, 1930, died July 13, 1994, age 64, godparents Henri L Martin & Josephine Campbell, married Rosaire Sterling, Aug. 26, 1950.
CÉCILE,	born Aug. 31, 1932, died age 8 days, godparents Dieudonné Maillet (Myers) & Virginia Couture.
FLORIDA-JEANNE,	born July 23, 1933, godparents Clément Charron & Florida Gagnier, married John Dupuis, Sept. 11, 1954.
ANNETTE,	born Nov. 5, 1936, godparents Oscar Sterling & Marie-Anne Lucier, married Augustin Martin, June 2, 1956.
ÉVELINE,	born April 10, 1938, godparents Gérard Charron & Laurette Charron, married Clifford Quinlan, Oct. 18, 1958.

-Omer Charron

EMMA CHARRON,
- born August 16, 1881
- married Zéphir Emery October 22, 1901
- died March 4, 1965

They had 5 children;

Homer	married	Antoinette Martin
Bertha	married	Jim Haden
Florida	married	Leroy La Framboise
Alma	married	Elmer Dillon
Orville	married	three times ?

JOSEPH
- born September 20, 1879
- died November 3, 1880 (14 months)

PHILIP ARCHILLES
- born June 18, 1895
- died December 6, 1897 (6 months)

ZÉPHIR
- born June 15, 1897
- died December 6, 1897 (6 months)

ÉLIZA
- born October 15, 1888
- married Alphy Maillet January 18, 1910
- died October 2, 1965

They had six children;

Donné	married	Virginie Couture
Laura	married	Willie Marchand
Eddie	married	Betty Carter
Alma	married	Félix Poissant
Arsène	married	Rita Ouellette
Beulah	married	Gérard Ouellette

Alphy Charron

- BORN June 25, 1886 Grande Pointe
- died March 30, 1970 Grande Pointe
- November 19, 1909 married Alphonsine Dubuque, daughter of Jules Dubuque
     and Joséphine Rose.
- Alphonsine, born January 30, 1890 and died February 7, 1953.
They had eight children;

Clément	- born December 25, 1910, died December 2, 1974 married Florida Gagner, November 22, 1932
Joséphine	- born November 25, 1912 married July 14, 1937 to Oscar Poissant
Dorothée	- born December 23, 1914 died March 22, 1926 (11 years)
Orville	- born May 29, 1917, died October 3, 1983 at 66 married Ida Quenneville February 5, 1971
Maria	- born September 21, 1919 married June 30, 1942 to Orville Pinsonneault
Aurore	- born September 26, 1922 married June 30, 1942 to Hector Tétreault
Oscar	- born May 16, 1925 died May 31, 1987, 62 years
Rita	- born July 11, 1927 married November 20, 1948 to Clifford Cadotte

N.B.   Joséphine (Rose) Dubuque died at 27 yrs old, leaving three children namely Alphonsine, Alphy and Annie. Alphonsine and Alphy Dubuque were raised by their aunt and uncle, Marie Tharsile (Rose) and François Dubuque. Annie Dubuque was raised by another aunt, Arméline (Rose) Benoit in River Rouge Michigan. She married Joe Garner of Michigan.

Délia Charron

She was born February 19, 1892. She married Josephat Laprise May 21, 1912. She died October 8, 1959. Josephat Laprise was the son of Narcisse Laprise and Adélaïde Roy. They were blessed with six children;

Trefflé Laprise
- born May 16, 1913
- married Caroline Roy January 18, 1938
- died March 20, 1980
- Caroline Roy was born May 21, 1919, daughter of Adolphe Roy and Délia Caron

Loma
- born February 14, 1915
- she is a member of the St. Joseph Order in London.

Cécile
- born January 18, 1917
- she entered with "Soeurs Hospitalières" de St. Joseph in Windsor, Hotel-Dieu Hospital.

Anna
- born June 18, 1919
- married Alex Trahan

Wilfrid
- born March 23, 1923
- married Carmel Mailloux, Pointe-aux-Roches

Jeanne
- born February 28, 1925
- married John Haslip

IN REFERENCE BOOK AT THE LIBRARY TENANTS AND FARMERS IN DOVER 1881

Pierre Charron owner of lot 9, Concession 7
Eli Charron owner of lot 6, Concession 7
Alphy Charron owner of lot 7, Concession 7
Théodore Charron owner of lot 5, Concession 8

THÉODORE

He was a renowned house builder. He built homes, log cabins, modest little homes and elaborate square, two storey homes. Some of his work was the Arthur Martin dwelling on the Winter Line, another one was Eddie Maillet's home and Joseph Béchard's home on the 8th Concession in Dover. He also built Alphy Maillet's home. Eliza was his daughter. He was repairing a roof there after he returned from Chatham at 5 o'clock at night the 21st of March, 1925. That same night, as he was playing cards, he died instantly . He was 69 years old.

Théodore Charron was born August 16, 1855. He was the first Charron to be baptized in Pain Court. He married Phébée Hébert November 6th 1877. Phébée was born July 20, 1857. She was baptized at St. Pierre and she died in 1920.

It is interesting to note that Gédéon Hébert of Lacadie, Québec was the great great grandfather of two brothers, Wilfrid Hébert and Gédéon Hébert who came to St-Pierre and later to Grande Pointe. After a few years the two brothers decided to move on to Kansas with their families, leaving behind one son and Phébée, who was married by then to Théodore Charron, son of Pierre Charron and Sarah Lauzon. They never returned to this area, so Phébée never saw her family again. She was extremely sad and broken hearted.

Mr. Omer Charron accompanied by Alphy Charron, his uncle, made a trip to Kansas in 1954 in order to visit and acquaint themselves with some relatives there. Omer made a second trip in 1955 with his wife, Clara Tétreault. They also visited a brother of his grandmother, Phébée, in Sue City, Iowa. Mr. Aristide Hébert. A cousin, much later, visited Grande Pointe and Pain Court to acquaint themselves with some relatives in Canada. For relatives in Kansas, it was a form of communication from their relatives in Canada.

Fred Charron

I'm sure you might be interested in a rare phenomenon that was inherited by Mr. Fred Charron of Grande Pointe. He was born February 27, 1885, baptised in Pain Court, was married to Oliva Sterling January 24, 1911 and died October 4, 1982. He was 96 years old.

Apparently this gift has been transmitted from one generation to another. It is known to be transmitted from woman to man and man to woman. It was his aunt who bestowed upon him this gift, together with prayers that accompany this phenomenon. Hundreds have witnessed his special powers.

He was an illiterate person who could neither read or write but nonetheless it was remarkable that he was able to prescribe and prepare his own medicine for diseases or complications. He was known to be the best veterinarian around for matters relating to horses and livestock. Of great importance was his powers to stop blood instantly. There could be no remuneration for such services as this would nullify the benefits. Many more citizens relied upon him also for detecting the sources of water supply for wells.

Possibly many more special notations could be made in surrounding areas but sometimes getting to the right sources are practically impossible as years go by.

-Réal Charron

FIVE GENERATIONS ALIVE – EXTRAORDINARY RECORD

Jacob Pinsonneault of Dover and his descendants
Among the most respected in the county
Aged head of the family, born in 1818
Saw Parliament Buildings burn in Montréal, in 1837
(Revolution in Lower Canada)

"Five generations living" is a most remarkable record, one rarely equalled anywhere. It is the record of the descendants of Jacob Pinsonneault of the fourth concession of Dover. Mr. Pinsonneault is just about to complete his 88th year.

Four of the generations are shown in the picture. Besides Mr. Pinsonneault himself, the picture shows his son, Joseph - 64 years of age, his grandson, Joseph A. -37 years of age, and his great grandson, Harvey, who is now in his fourteenth year. All reside on the fourth concession of Dover. The representative of the fifth generation, born only last spring, is Baby Thibodeau, a great grandson of Mr. Pinsonneault's oldest daughter, the late Mrs. David Roy. (Euphémie Pinsonneault).

Mr. Pinsonneault first saw the light of day on August 20, 1818 at the village of St-Jacques le Mineur in the county of Laprairie, Québec. On August 20 next, he will have completed his 88th year.

Mr. Pinsonneault spent the first 40 years of his life in his native village of St-Jacques le Mineur. He married Miss Claire Tétrault, of the same place, in1838 at the age of 20. She was a sister of the late Mr. Tétrault who was many years ago a prominent shoe merchant in Chatham and who has passed away only last spring. Mrs. Pinsonneault died 32 years ago in 1865.

It was in 1854 that Mr. and Mrs. Pinsonneault and their family came to Dover. In those days, railway facilities were very poor. The party travelled by train as far as Lachine, to Niagara Falls by boat, thence by rail to Chatham. The Great Western railway, later the western division of the G.T.R., had just been extended to Chatham. Chatham in those days was very unlike what it is today. The only businessmen whom Mr. Pinsonneault remembers from that far off time were McKeough Bros., Eberts and Northwood, and Mr. Rice. The first man he met when he struck Chatham was a compatriot, the late James Lake, who formerly conducted a hotel opposite Tecumseh Park, where the Park house now stands. Mr. Lake spoke French and helped Mr. Pinsonneault in becoming settled in his new surroundings.

The first week after he settled in Dover - it was in the month of May that the party arrived - Mr. Pinsonneault was engaged with a team of oxen hauling stone from the river to Pain Court. The stone was used in the building of the foundations of the first church in Pain Court. The residents of that vicinity, previous to the building of this church, attended St. Peter's on the south side of the river, which, save for the chapel at Chatham and the church at Sandwich, was then the only Roman Catholic edifice in the western peninsula.

In those days, a great many of the Dover settlers were half breeds who engaged largely in the braiding of straw, which they conveyed by canoe to Detroit where it was traded for flour, sugar and other necessities of life. Chatham, with its smaller population and cruder civilization, did not in those days afford much of a market for braided straw. The trip to Detroit by canoe customarily took three days.

When Mr. Pinsonneault came to this part of the country, it was all heavily timbered and very wild. The Winter Line was only a corduroy road to the river and the River Road, though the best in Dover, was not very good. The country, round about, was largely uncleared and wild animals of earlier days had not yet vanished from the face of the earth. In the first year that he was in Dover, Mr. Pinsonneault more than once saw deer going through his barn yard; and during the night time, wolves could be heard howling in the bush around the house. The house of those days was a small affair, constructed of logs. It can still be seen at the old Pinsonneault homestead on the fourth concession of Dover, where, after the lapse of more than half a century, it has been reduced to serve as a pig pen.

It is on this old homestead that Mr. Pinsonneault has lived ever since coming to Dover. He started with practically nothing save honesty, integrity and industry. In the intervening years he has prospered. Industry has earned enough to make the family comfortable; and honesty and integrity have made the name of Pinsonneault one of the most respected in the township of Dover.

Sixteen children were born to Mr. and Mrs. Pinsonneault, of whom 10 lived to be married, the others dying in infancy. The 10 children who attained maturity were: the late Mrs. David Roy, Joseph Pinsonneault, Mrs. David Goure and the late Mrs. Ambroise Thibodeau, all of Dover, Napoléon Pinsonneault, of the customs staff, Chatham, Mrs. Anthony Masse of Dunseth, North Dakota, Mrs. Arthur Masse of Dover, Alfred Pinsonneault with whom Mr. Pinsonneault Sr. now resides on the old homestead, the late Mrs. Geoffrey LeBoeuf of Ruscom River, Essex County and Mrs. Eugene LeBoeuf of Tilbury.

There are also 62 grandchildren, 62 great grandchildren and one great great-grandchild. This representative of the fifth generation was born only last spring, being a descendant of the oldest daughter, the late Mrs. David Roy of Dover (Euphémie Pinsonneault).

Despite his advanced age, Mr. Pinsonneault's health is remarkably good. Always a worker, he still does many chores about the place when his son is away, doing the work around the barn and taking care of the stock in a manner that would bring credit to a much younger man. From his early years, his health had been exceptional. Save for an attack of rheumatism some 15 years ago, he has scarcely experienced any sickness.

A remarkable fact is that Mr. Pinsonneault can both hear well and see well. Many a man of 50 would envy him his eyesight. His memory too is splendid and he can discuss with vividness the scenes attending the burning of the Parliament Buildings in Montréal in 1837.

That the aged pioneer is not without a sense of humour is shown by a little story. A grand daughter from Montréal visited last winter and had occasion to remark that she was pleased that he was able to hear so well. The old man rejoined that he sometimes heard too well - heard too much noise, indicating as he said so, the playful young members of his son's large family.

Mr. Pinsonneault hopes, with a continuance of his present good health, to round out the century - a hope in which a multitude of friends heartily and fervently join.

Jacob Pinsonneault died in Pain Court July 12, 1910 at 92 years old.

Journal Royunion `92   Back to our Roots.

Patrimoine Ancestral
Pinsonneault Family

On May 18, 1856, in Montréal, Pierre-Adolphe Pinsonneault was consecrated bishop for the new diocese of London, Ontario. He was the first and only French-Canadian bishop ever to serve that diocese even though the first inhabitants were French and their descendants numbered over 70,000 comprising about 1\3 of the catholic population.

Msgr. Pinsonneault came from St-Philippe de Laprairie where he was born on November 25, 1815, the son of Paul-Théophile Pinsonneault and Clotilde Raymond. After completing his secondary education, he was admitted in the Company of St-Sulpice at Issy, near Paris, France. On December 19, 1840, in that same city, he was ordained priest. He then returned to Montréal where he taught in the seminary from 1841 to 1843. From 1843 to 1849, he served the Irish congregation of Montréal. At that time, he left the society of St-Sulpice and was named canon for the Cathedral from 1849 to 1856.

Mgsr. Pinsonneault was a distant cousin of Jacob Pinsonneault, the first Pinsonneault to come to Pain Court in 1854. In fact, they were cousins by fourth or fifth degree.

François Pinsonneault dit Lafleur was born in 1646 in Anjou, France. He arrived in Canada in September 1665 as a soldier in the Carignan Regiment, Company of St. Ours with his wife Anne Leper. They were married at St. Ours, Québec, Canada in 1673. They lived in Sorel, Contrecoeur, Ville Marie (Montréal) and Laprairie where they died; François in 1731 and Anne in 1732. They had 7 children, 1 of them dying in infancy. The oldest, Pierre, was born in Sorel in 1674. On October 19, 1700, in Montréal, he married Marie-Charlotte Lecours, daughter of Michel Lecours and widow of Benoit Bisaillon. They had 10 children; Paul, the oldest, became Msgr. Pinsonneault's great great grandfather while his brother Pierre became the grandfather of Jacob, the first Pinsonneault in Pain Court.

Pierre, the son of François Pinsonneault and Anne Leper, was born in 1704. He was married twice, each time in Laprairie. Marie-Catherine Bisaillon, became his first wife on January 14, 1725. She gave him two sons before she died: Pierre and François-Michel. On April 21, 1732, Pierre was married to Françoise Robert.

Pierre Pinsonneault, son of Pierre and Marie-Catherine Bisaillon, was born on September 15, 1726. At Laprairie, on January 29, he was married to Geneviève Deneau. She gave him at least 5 children before dying in 1758 in St.-Philippe. On October 22, 1759, in St-Philippe, he was remarried to Marie Josephte Dupuis. One child was born of this second marriage.

Joseph, son of Pierre and Geneviève Deneau, was born in 1755 and died in Lacadie on December 22, 1833. He married three times but had children only by his first wife. On February 12, 1781, in St-Philippe, he married Marie-Josephte Robert, daughter of Joseph Robert and Marguerite Longuin, who gave him 11 children. She died in childbirth on April 9, 1802 in Lacadie at the age of 36. In 1805, in Lacadie, Joseph was married for the second time to widow Julie Thuot, who died on July 14, 1823. Still in Lacadie, he was married for the third time to widow Suzanne Desmarteaux. His sons Joseph and Jacob deserve our attention.

Isaac, son of Joseph Pinsonneault and Marie-Josephte Robert, was born in 1794. On January 31, 1814, he married Marie-Louise Rémillard. He had a son, Paul, who married Anne Trudelle on January 10, 1871, in Pointe-aux-Roches. It is unknown if the Pinsonneaults from Pointe-aux-Roches today, are his descendants.

Joseph Pinsonneault, son of Joseph and Marie-Josephte Robert, was born on January 22, 1785 in Lacadie where he died on May 23, 1832. Appoline Tremblay, daughter of Étienne Tremblay and Marie Rainville, became his bride on October 26, 1801. She gave him at least 10 children. Célina (Lina), married Moyse Béchard who came to Pain Court in 1870. She was the mother of Father Alfred Béchard. Joseph married Josephte Bouchard, Isaac married Catherine Bouley, Sophie married Isaac Comeau Sr., who died in Pain Court, Olive married Jules Beaudin, Alfred married Florence Roy, Lambert married Marguerite Langevin, Julienne married Athanase-Moyse Martin. Toussaint's brother, whose two sons Moïse and Levi, established themselves in Grande Pointe and Pain Court. After the death of her husband, Appoline Tremblay was remarried to Joseph Beaudoin in 1832 and ended her days at St-Jacques le Mineur. She died in 1860 at the age of 75 years old.

In 1854, **Jacob Pinsonneault** arrived in Pain Court accompanied by his wife and 5 of his eleven children. Born in 1818, he married Claire Tétrault on February 6, 1838 in Lacadie. She was the daughter of Albert Tétrault and Marie-Rose Rémillard. Jacob died in Pain Court on July 9, 1910 at the age of 92. Claire
Tétrault had given him 16 children before dying in Pain Court on June 26, 1865 at the age of 43. Eleven children were born at St-Jacques le Mineur and the last five were born in Pain Court. Six of the first eleven children died in infancy before Jacob and Claire's departure for Ontario.
On December 28, 1867, in Pain Court, Jacob was remarried to Lucie Caron, daughter of François Caron and Catherine Lemerise. They never had any children but Lucie was a real mother to Jacob's children.

One after another, the children of Jacob Pinsonneault and Claire Tétrault were married. On January 19, 1858, in Pain Court, Euphémie married David Roy, son of André Roy Sr. and Josephte Schreiber. She had 12 children before dying at 41 years old. Marguerite married Jean-Baptiste Goure son of Joseph Ambroise Thibodeau, son of Hubert Thibodeau and Esther Rémillard. She also died young after giving birth to 6 children. Olive married Antoine Masse, son of Antoine Masse and Virginie St-Jacques in 1871. Delphine married Antoine's brother Arthur Masse in 1876 and died at childbirth in 1885 at the age of 28. Eloise married Joseph Leboeuf from St-Joachim in 1885 and Rose married Eugène Leboeuf, Joseph's brother, son of Nazaire Leboeuf and Hedwidge Demers.

Joseph Pinsonneault, oldest son of Jacob, was born at St-Jacques on July 22, 1843 and married Eloise Cheff on October 1, 1866. She was the daughter of Joseph Cheff Jr. and Marie-Anne Martin. She had 11 children of which 5 died at a young age. Alma married Antoine (Tony) Ouellette, son of Antoine Ouellette and Margaret O'Neil and Anna married Henri Roy, son of Alexandre Roy and Mary Bélanger. Anna was the mother of two nuns. Her son, Napoléon Roy, was the founder and principal shareholder of "King Grain and seed Company limited" of Pain Court.
Josephat married Mary Daniel, daughter of Pierre Daniel and Archange Tétrault and had 5 children of which Hervé and Jean's numerous sons actually assure a masculine posterity and a guarantee of the Pinsonneault name to continue. Pierre (Dominat) married Anna Daniel (Mary's sister) who gave him 9 children: eight girls and one son, Wilfrid. He married Bertha Breault, daughter

of Joseph Breault and Hermine Morin in Tilbury. Wilfrid's sons and grandsons are assuring the continuation of the Pinsonneault name. Emile married Adeline (Déline) Normandin, daughter of Appolinaire Normandin and Josephine Thibodeau. They had 12 children; 4 daughter and 8 sons. Philippe, the youngest son of Jacob married Celina Sterling, daughter of Alec Sterling and Hedwidge Caron. They had 4 sons and 4 daughters.

Napoléon, the first Pinsonneault to be born in Pain Court in 1855, was married 3 times in Pain Court but ended up establishing himself in Chatham where we can meet his descendants. In 1878, he married Marie Sterling who gave him 4 children. In 1887, he married Philomène Thibodeau, daughter of Ambroise Thibodeau, son of Hubert. They had one child in 1891. He was married for the third time to Zulma Rémillard who gave him 4 children.

Alfred, the youngest and also the third son of the pioneer Jacob Pinsonneault to be born in Pain Court in 1860, married Hélène Daniel, daughter of Pierre Daniel and Archange Tétrault on November 16, 1880. They had 11 children. There were 6 boys to continue the Pinsonneault name in our area; Arcade, Danus, Amédée, Jacob, Ovide and Léopold. Unfortunately, we don't find one of them in Pain Court today. The majority of them settled in Grande Pointe, Chatham and Windsor.

If the "old Jacob Pinsonneault" were to return in our region, he would certainly be proud to see the very great number of his descendants who are members of the two French parishes of Pain Court and Grande Pointe, without counting those who went elsewhere to find fortune. Like their ancestor, the pioneer Jacob, the Pinsonneaults have multiplied and are prosperous. Their presence in the peninsula is a precious contribution.

There are also other Pinsonneaults in the Kent-Essex Peninsula, those in Pointe-aux-Roches and St-Joachim. No doubt, by looking back to our deep roots, we would succeed in tracing them to the descendants of Jacob, who came to Pain Court in 1854. Unfortunately, the researches were limited to the Pain Court pioneers. It was impossible to retrace their parentage with the distant cousins established in the county of Essex.

GÉNÉALOGISTE   Rev. Adrien P. Roy
translated by Marguerite Pinsonneault-Gagnier

Journal 155e Royunion `92

Patrimoine Ancestral
Famille Thibodeau

Le 16 octobre 1835, on baptisait, à St-Pierre de Raleigh, Salomé Thibodeau. Cette enfant était le premier Thibodeau à faire son apparition dans les records paroissiaux de notre région. Elle était la fille de Hubert Thibodeau et d'Esther Rémillard arrivés depuis quelques mois seulement du Bas-Canada, de St-Cyprien de Napierville plus précisément. Hubert Thibodeau peut donc à juste titre être appelé le pionnier des Thibodeau de notre péninsule sud-ontarienne. D'autres Thibodeau sont venus par ici plusieurs années après lui. Ils semblent avoir été des cousins plutôt lointains. N'ayant pas été aussi prolifiques qu'Hubert et ses fils, il est normal de soutenir que leur postérité en souffre dans une comparaison avec les descendants d'Hubert, du moins, au point de vue nombre.

Les Thibodeau sont descendants d'Acadiens, c'est à dire de ce groupe spécial de Français au Canada, ceux qui sont venus coloniser les Provinces Maritimes et qui ont développé un langage et des traditions bien à eux, et bien différents des Canadiens-Français proprement dits. Si vous voulez insulter un acadien, essayez de le convaincre qu'il est un Canadien-Français proprement dit. Si vous voulez insulter un Acadien, essayez de le convaincre qu'il est un Canadien-Français comme les autres, ceux du Québec par exemple.

Le peuple acadien a été, à juste titre, appelé le peuple martyre, à cause de l'ignoble déportement dont ils ont été victimes quelques années seulement avant la conquête définitive par les Anglais. Peuple heureux, fier, entreprenant, tenace devant l'épreuve, profondément attaché à son sol et à son dieu, il dût tout quitter, voir ses foyers et ses églises en ruines fumantes et partir pour l'exil. Ils s'égrenèrent pour ainsi dire, tout le long de la côte américaine de l'Océan Atlantique jusqu'en Floride et surtout en Louisiane, où beaucoup recommencèrent à neuf. Beaucoup d'autres furent pourchassés jusque dans les bois du Nouveau-Brunswick et heureusement échappèrent ainsi au plus gros du carnage qui s'abattait sur leur petite patrie. Après la conquête définitive du Canada et le calme revenu, ils reparaîtront et par la revanche des berceaux, reprendront possession d'une partie de leur ancienne patrie.

Après de pénibles pérégrinations, de nombreux exilés aboutirent dans bien des endroits de la province de Québec et s'y installèrent. C'est ainsi qu'on en trouvera en 1784, établis au sud de Montréal, dans la Vallée du Richelieu, en nombre suffisant pour fonder une nouvelle paroisse à même la paroisse de St-Philippe de Laprairie. Naturellement, on l'appelle Lacadie, en souvenir de leur ancienne patrie. Cette paroisse était tout simplement immense et avec les années, elle donna naissance à plusieurs autres paroisses. Mentionnons entr'autres St-Jacques le Mineur, St-Rémi et St-Cyprien de Napierville, St-Luc et St-Blaise, autant de paroisses qui, avec Lacadie et St-Philippe fournirent tant de colons aux paroisses naissantes de Pain Court et Grande Pointe par ici.

Parmi les Acadiens revenus d'exil et installés à Lacadie, et qui nous enverront des descendants dans le Sud de l'Ontario, mentionnons les Hébert, les Trahan, les Bourgeois, les Comeau, les Breault et, naturellement les Thibodeau.

Notons bien qu'un seul Thibodeau vint de France en Acadie, aux débuts de la colonie: c'était Pierre né en 1631 et qui mourra à Port Royal le 26 décembre 1704.
Originaire du Poitou, il arriva en Acadie en 1654 avec Emmanuel LeBorgne de Belle-Isle. Il était meunier de son métier, à Prée Ronde, dans le haut de la Rivière Port Royal. En 1698, il fonda Chipoudi (Hopewell, N. B.)

Vers 1660 il épousa Jeanne Terriot, fille de Jean et de Perrin Bourg, et elle lui donna 16 enfants, 8 filles, 8 garçons dont 7 continueront le nom de Thibodeau avec chacun une nombreuse famille.

Les Thibodeau de Pain Court descendent du deuxième fils du pionnier JEAN, né en 1673 à Port Royal, alla s'établir à Rivière-aux-Canards (il y en a une en Acadie!) après s'être marié, le 17 février 1703 à Port Royal, à Marguerite Hébert, fille d'Emmanuel et d'Andrée Brun. En 1714, il transporta sa famille à Grand-Pré où ses enfants et leurs famille furent pris dans la tourmente de 1755. Jean mourut le 9 décembre 1746, père de 11 enfants, à Rivière-aux-Canards. Cinq de ses fils perpétueront son nom.

CHARLES, né en 1711 à Port Royal, le 21 février 1735 à Grand-Pré, épousait Anne-Marie Melanson, veuve de Charles Babin et fille de Philippe et de Marie Dugas. Ce couple avait une dizaine d'enfants quand ils prirent le chemin de l'exil. Toute la famille fut déportée au Maryland où Mme Thibodeau est décédée. Le 19 juillet 1764 à Philadelphie, Charles se remariera à Madeleine Boiron, veuve de Joseph Poirier et fille de Charles et Françoise Gaudet. Il réussit à revenir au Canada et s'établit à Bécancour où il meurt le 28 novembre 1779.

Ses 3 fils qui survécurent à l'exil, finirent par s'installer à Lacadie et moururent dans les environs. C'était Olivier, Pierre et Jean-Baptiste. Olivier est celui qui doit retenir notre attention.

Né en 1753 à Grand-Pré probablement, et décédé à Lacadie le 21 mars 1812 à 59 ans, **OLIVIER** avait épousé avant 1778, on ne sait où ni quand au juste, Marie Cyr, fille de Joseph et de Marie-Josephte Cormier, qui lui donna 10 enfants. A Lacadie Olivier Thibodeau était aubergiste. Quatre fils perpétueront son nom: Henri, Olivier, René et Jean-Baptiste. Le premier doit nous intéresser particulièrement car il est le père d'Hubert venu à Pain Court.

HENRI Thibodeau, décédé le 29 août 1871 à St-Athanase, près de St-Jean d'Iberville, à l'âge de 93 ans, est donc né en 1778. A Lacadie, le 2 août 1802, il épousait Marie-Anne Coupal, fille de Joseph et de Marie Jourdannais qui lui donna 16 enfants au moins, dont 9 survivants et 5 garçons pour perpétuer son nom: Hubert, Ambroise, Médard, Julien et Moyse.

HUBERT Thibodeau naquit en 1805 à Lacadie et mourut à Pain Court à 55 ans le 23 novembre 1860. Le 11 janvier 1825 à Lacadie, il avait épousé Esther Rémillard, fille mineure de Michel Rémillard et de Rose Monet. Dès son mariage il s'établit à St-Cyprien de Napierville, paroisse voisine de Lacadie et y élève sa famille jusqu'en 1834 probablement, alors qu'il émigre dans le comté de Kent, où 9 autres enfants verront le jour. Nous sommes certains que Hubert et Esther eurent 15 enfants au moins, 13 vivants 5 garçons et 8 filles qui tous se marièrent. Voici les 15 dont nous reconnaissons l'existence grâce à des records précis, mais à en juger d'après les écarts entre les premiers enfants nés dans le Bas-Canada, il est fort possible qu'il y ait eu quelques enfants de plus et qui seraient morts bébés avant que la famille n'émigre en Ontario. Hubert, né le 31 mars et mort le 3 août 1827 à St-Cyprien de Napierville; Joseph (surnommé José) né à St-Cyprien le 13 mai 1828; Ambroise né probablement à St-Cyprien et mort à Pain Court le 14 octobre 1910 à 78 ans; Euphanie née vers 1830 à St-Cyprien aussi, probablement: Rémi né vers 1831; Marie née le 21 février 1834, probablement à St-Cyprien aussi et décédée à Pain Court le Jour de l'An 1907; Salomé née le 16 octobre 1835 et décédée le 21 septembre 1909; Henri né à St-Pierre le 3 août 1837 et décédé le 2 mars 1916 à Pain Court; Rose née le 1 juin 1839; Esther née le 17 avril 1841; William né le 21 avril 1843; Arcange (Cangette) née le 24 juillet 1845 et décédée le 18 décembre 1880; Julienne née le 7 juillet 1847; Lucie-Félicité née le 28 octobre 18 et décédée le Jour de l'An 1927; Philomène née en août 1851 et morte à 9 mois le 6 mai 1852.

Grâce aux 13 survivants de cette nombreuse famille qui se sont mariés et eurent tous de grosses familles, on peut s'imaginer qu'il s'en trouve des gens de Pain Court et environs qui ont des liens de parenté entre eux par le sang Thibodeau qui leur coule dans les veines.

Huit des 9 filles connues de Hubert Thibodeau et d'Esther Rémillard semblent toutes avoir eu d'assez grosses familles, après s'être mariées toutes à Pain Court, excepté la plus vieille qui le fit à St-Pierre avant que Pain Court ne soit érigée en paroisse.

EUPHANIE épousa d'abord le veuf Joseph Cheff Sr. le 16 janvier 1849 à St-Pierre et lui donna une deuxième famille de 8 enfants dont Hubert qui maria Agnès Lucier et Adélaide qui devint la femme de Francis Gaudreau et eut une grosse famille; devenue veuve, Euphanie épousa un autre veuf, Richard Réaume Sr. le 18 novembre 1885 à Pain Court.

MARIE, maria d'abord le veuf Chrysanthe (Crisan) Béchard et lui donna 8 enfants dont Crisan Jr., Joséphine, Euphrasie, Isaie et Geneviève qui survécurent et se marièrent; puis elle épousa Moïse Caron, 2 fois veuf, le 20 avril 1870 et lui donna 3 enfants dont Denise qui maria Delphis Trahan et Salomon qui maria Rosanna Faubert et fut père de 5 religieuses et d'un prêtre, Mgr Augustin Caron. Parmi ses autres descendants on compte aussi un autre prêtre et au moins 6 autres religieuses.

SALOMÉ épousa Louis Tétreault (Louison) le 9 septembre 1856 et demeura au "Grand-Bois" près de Tilbury. Elle eut plusieurs enfants parmi lesquels une religieuse. Au nom de ses descendants on compte 2 prêtres, le Père Philippe Tétreault, un Père Blanc d'Afrique, et le Curé Félix Bézaire, et au moins une religieuse, Soeur Anne Bézaire, Ursuline.

ROSE (Rosalie) maria Étienne Girardeau le 7 janvier 1856, eut plusieurs enfants aussi et alla demeurer à Kansas City puis à Fort Wayne, Indiana.

ESTHER épousa Richard (Tatlou) Hébert le 7 octobre 1865 et alla demeurer à Bay City, Michigan et dans l'Indiana.

ARCANGE (Cangette) épousa Léon Charron le 16 février 1863 et mourut à 35 ans ayant eu au moins 6 enfants dont Joseph, Cyrille et Désiré qui élevèrent de grosses familles à Pain Court.

JULIENNE épousa Désiré Robitaille le 23 octobre 1866 et demeura à Windsor.

LUCIE-FÉLICITÉ maria Moïse Bourassa, le 28 février 1870, eut 12 enfants dont une religieuse et parmi ses autres descendants, compte un prêtre, le R. P. Vincent Caron, o.m. i. et au moins 2 religieuses connues.

Quant aux 6 garçons connus, 5 laissèrent des rejetons.

JOSEPH (Joe) eut au moins 9 enfants de sa première femme, Adèle Bélanger, fille de Joseph et de Catherine Schmidt, (premier couple Bélanger à Pain Court) qu'il épousa le 14 juillet 1851 à St-Pierre. Une de ses filles devint religieuse et au moins deux petites-filles et autres aussi. Ses garçons Ambroise et Cyrille se sont chargés de ne pas laisser mourir la descendance masculine du "Vieux José" Thibodeau, à Pain Court et ailleurs.

AMBROISE se maria 3 fois: la première, le 23 mai 1854 à St-Pierre, à Cézarine Laplante fille de Paul et Victoire Roy dont il eut 10 enfants; la deuxième, le 4 mai 1868 à Eugénie Pinsonneault, fille de Jacob et Claire Tétreault, premiers Pinsonneault à Pain Court, qui lui donna 6 enfants; la troisième, le 28 septembre 1887, à la veuve d'Isaac Comeau, Rose Bourassa fille de Félix et de Céleste Boutin. De ses nombreux enfants soulignons que Joseph eut des fils qui fondèrent la Compagnie de Transport par camions qui a fait énormément pour faire connaître le nom de Thibodeau dans tout le sud de l'Ontario, avec siège social à Windsor, et Alfred qui devint courtier très prospère à Détroit. Joseph était fils de sa première femme, Alfred de sa deuxième.

RÉMI se maria à Sara Emery qui lui donna plusieurs enfants. Nous ignorons ce qui est devenu de cette famille et où se trouvent les descendants de Rémi.

HENRI, le 14 janvier 1862, épousa Sophie Robitaille fille de Michel et de Henriette Roy qui lui donna pas moins de 12 enfants dont 7 au moins moururent bébés. Joseph, Ambroise et Henri Jr. se marièrent et eurent des enfants pour assurer la postérité masculine de Henri Sr., fils du pionnier Hubert. William, le benjamin des garçons, eut deux femmes. Le 23 juin 1863 il épousa Hélène

Emery, fille de Luc et de Charlotte Hébert qui lui donna au moins 5 enfants dont Francis qui sera connu dans les environs comme propriétaire de "moulins à battre le grain" et éleva sa famille surtout à Chatham où il mourut de façon atroce, brûlé vif dans un incendie. Sa deuxième femme, Lucie Hébert, fille de Grégoire et Arcange Trudelle, eut 3 enfants. Il l'avait mariée le 2 décembre 1876.

Il est indéniable que Hubert Thibodeau et ses fils furent des plus prolifiques et en con-séquence, on a peine à compter leurs descendants qui semblent maintenant éparpillés aux 4 coins de la Péninsule du Sud-Ontario, et plus encore, semble-t-il, aux États-Unis. En considération de ce fait, l'historien ne peut que voir avec un certain serrement de coeur la disparition presque totale des Thibodeau, de la scène de Pain Court. Des 5 fils du pionnier Hubert, seul "le vieux José" compte maintenant des descendants dans la paroisse, ses fils Ambroise et Cyrille ayant des petits-fils qui semblent s'être chargés de ne pas laisser mourir le nom. Bravo!! Quant aux autres, ils sont allés chercher fortune ailleurs, et, dans la plupart des cas, semblent avoir réussi haut la main.

Dans l'ensemble, l'histoire ou la destinée des Thibodeau de Pain Court, les premiers du nom à faire leur apparition dans notre région, paraît avoir suivi une courbe aussi intéressante et variée que celle des ancêtres d'Acadie. Parce qu'Acadiens d'origine, ils ont connu les beaux jours comme les heures moins intéressantes. Mais ils font partie d'une race qui ne connaît pas la véritable défaite et qui ne sait mourir. Leur contribution au développement et à la vie de notre paroisse fut un apport précieux et notre localité doit en être fière et reconnaissante.

Thibodeau Family

On October 16, 1835, Salomé Thibodeau was baptized at St. Peter's Raleigh. This child was the first Thibodeau to make an appearance in the parish records of our region. She was Hubert Thibodeau and Esther Rémillard's daughter. They arrived a few months earlier from Lower Canada, more precisely St. Cyprien de Napierville. Therefore, Hubert Thibodeau could be called the pioneer of the Thibodeaus in the peninsula of southern Ontario. Other Thibodeaus arrived in this area several years after him. They were probably distant cousins.

The Thibodeaus are of Acadian descent, that is, of a special group of French people in Canada, those who came to settle in the Maritime Provinces and who developed a language and tradition all their own, and quite different from the French Canadians as such. If you want to offend an Acadian, try to convince him that he is a French Canadian like the others, for example, those of Québec.

The Acadian people were rightly called a people of martyrs because they were victims of an ignoble deportation only a few years before the definitive conquest by the British. A happy and proud people, enterprising, tenacious in trials, profoundly attached to their land and their God, they had to leave for exile with British bayonets at their backs to say the least. An incalculable number of them, especially children, perished from misery en route to exile. They scattered all along the Atlantic Ocean on the American coast down to Florida and especially in Louisiana, where several of them began a new life all over again. Several others were pursued into the woods of New Brunswick and fortunately escaped most of the carnage befalling their colony. After the conquest of Canada and a relative peace having been restored, they reappeared and due to their numerous large families took possession again of part of their former territory.

After painful wanderings, several exiled people appeared in many areas of the province of Québec and settled there. That is how, in 1784, a sufficient number of then established south of

Montréal, in the Richelieu Valley, and founded a new parish from St. Philippe de Laprairie parish. Naturally, they called it Lacadie, in remembrance of their former land in New Brunswick. This parish was simply immense and with time, gave birth to many other parishes such as St. Jacques le Mineur, St. Rémi and St. Cyprien de Napierville, St. Luc and St. Blaise. It is from these parishes of St. Luc, St. Blaise and St. Philippe de Lacadie that came many settlers of the parishes of Pain Court and Grande Pointe.

Amongst the Acadians who returned from exile, settled in Lacadie, and whose descendants would eventually establish themselves in Southwestern Ontario, let us mention the Héberts, the Trahans, the Bourgeois, the Comeaus, the Breaults, and naturally the Thibodeaus.

Please note that only one Thibodeau came from France to Acadie at the beginning of the colony: it was Pierre, born in 1631 who died December 26, 1704 in Port Royal. Originally from Poitou, he arrived in Acadie in 1654 with Emmanuel Le Borgne from Belle-Isle. He was a miller by trade at Prée Ronde at the height of the Port Royal River. In 1698, he founded Chipoud:(Hopewell,N.B.)

Around 1660, Pierre married Jeanne Terriot, daughter of Jean and Perrine Bourg. They had 16 children, 8 girls and 8 boys of whom 7 pass down the Thibodeau name.

The Thibodeaus from Pain Court are descendants of the second son of the pioneer **JEAN,** born in Port Royal. He settled in Rivière-aux-Canards (there is one in Acadie), after marrying on February 17, 1703 in Port Royal, Marguerite Hébert, daughter of Emmanuel and Andrée Brun. In 1714, he moved his family to Grand Pré where his children and their families were caught in the deportation of 1755. Jean died December 9, 1746, father of 11 children at Rivière-aux-Canards. Five of his children would pass down his name.

Charles, born in 1711 in Port Royal, married Anne-Marie Melanson, widow of Charles Babin and daughter of Philippe and Marie Dugas, on February 21, 1735 in Grand Pré. This couple had a dozen children when the Acadians were sent into exile. The entire family was deported to Maryland where Mrs. Thibodeau died. In Philadelphia, on July 19, 1764, Charles remarried to Madeleine Boiron, widow of Joseph Poirier and daughter of Charles and Françoise Gaudet. He succeeded in coming back to Canada and settling in Bécancour where he died on November 28, 1779. Charles '3 sons, who survived the exile, ended up settling in Acadie and died in the vicinity. They were: Olivier, Pierre and Jean-Baptiste. Olivier is the one who will hold our attention. Born in 1753, prob- ably in Grand Pré and deceased in Lacadie on March 21, 1812 at the age of 59, Olivier married before 1778, though we do not know when or where exactly. He married Marie Cyr, daughter of Joseph and Marie-Josephte Cormier, and had 10 children. In Lacadie, Olivier Thibodeau was innkeeper. Four sons would perpetuate his name: Henri, Oliver, René and Jean-Baptiste. The first son would be of particular interest because he is the father of Hubert who came to Pain Court.

HENRI Thibodeau, deceased August 29, 1871 at St. Athanase, near St. Jean d'Iberville, at the age of 93, was therefore born in 1778. In Lacadie, August 2, 1802, he married Marie-Anne Coupal, daughter of Joseph and Marie Jourdannais and they had at least 16 children, of whom 9 survived with 5 boys to perpetuate his name: Hubert, Ambroise, Médard, Julien and Moïse.

HUBERT, Thibodeau was born in 1805 in Lacadie and died in Pain Court at the age of 55 on November 23, 1860. On January 11, 1825 in Lacadie, he married Esther Rémillard, minor daughter of Michel Rémillard and Rose Monet. After marrying, he settled in St. Cyprien de Napierville, neigh- bouring parish of Lacadie and raised his family there probably until 1834. He then emigrated to Kent County where 9 more children would see daylight. We are certain that Hubert and Esther had at least 15 children, 13 surviving to adulthood. These 3 boys and 8 girls all married and all had large families.

The following are the 15 for whom we have precise records. It is probable that other children were born before the family migrated to Ontario but these died in infancy. Hubert was born March 31 and died August 3, 1827 at St. Cyprien de Napierville; Joseph (José) born in St. Cyprien May 13, 1828, Ambroise probably born in St. Cyprien died in Pain Court October 14, 1910 at age 78; Euphanie born probably in 1830 in St. Cyprien; Rémi born about 1831; Marie born February 21, 1834 probably in St. Cyprien and died in Pain Court New Year's Day 1907; Salomé born October 16, 1835 and died September 21, 1909; Henri born in St. Pierre August 3, 1837 and died March 2, 1916 in Pain Court; Rose born June 1, 1839; Esther born April 17, 1841; William born April 21, 1843; Arcange (Cangette) born July 24, 1845 and died December 18, 1880; Juliette born July 7, 1847; Lucie-Félicité, born October 28, 1848 and died New Year's Day 1927; Philomène born August 1851 and died at age 9 months in May 1852.

Due to the fact that these 13 surviving children all married and had large families, it is not surprising that many people from Pain Court and surrounding areas have close ties since they all have the Thibodeau blood running in their veins.

Eight of the nine girls of Hubert Thibodeau and Esther Rémillard, seem to have had fairly large families, after marrying in Pain Court, except for the oldest who married at St. Pierre before Pain Court was established as a parish. **EUPHANIE** first married the widower Joseph Cheff Sr. on January 16, 1849 at St. Pierre and they had a second family of 8 children among them Hubert who married Agnès Lucier, and Adélaide who became Francis Gaudreau's wife; once a widow, Euphanie married another widower named Richard Réaume Sr., November 18, 1885 in Pain Court; **MARIE**, first married the widower Chrysanthe (Crisan) Béchard and had 8 children of whom was Crisan Jr., Joséphine, Euphrasie, Isaïe and Geneviève who survived and married; then she married Moïse Caron, twice a widower on April 20, 1870 and had 3 children: Denise who married Delphis Trahan and Salomon who married Rosanna Faubert was the father of 5 nuns and one priest, Msgr. Augustin Caron. Amongst her other descendants was also a priest and at least 6 other nuns. **SALOMÉ** married Louis Tétreault (Louison) on September 9, 1856 and lived in "Grand Bois" near Tilbury. She had several children, one of them a nun. Amongst her descendants there are also 2 priests. Father Philippe Tétreault, a Father Blanc of Africa, Father Felix Bézaire, and at least one nun, Sister Anne Bézaire, Ursuline Sister. **ROSE** (Rosalie) married Étienne Girardeau on January 7, 1856, also had several children and went to live in Kansas City and Fort Wayne, Indiana. Esther married Richard (Tatlou) Hébert on October 7, 1865 and went to live in Bay City, Michigan and in Indiana. **ARCANGE** (Cangette) married Léon Charron on February 16, 1863 and died at 35 years of age having at least 6 children of whom were: Joseph, Cyrille and Désiré who raised large families in Pain Court. **JULIENNE** married Désiré Robitaille on October 23, 1866 and lived in Windsor. **LUCIE-FÉLICITÉ** married Moïse Bourassa February 28, 1870, and had 12 children of whom one was a nun and amongst her other descendants a priest, Father Vincent Caron o.m.i. and at least 2 nuns.

As for the boys, 5 left behind a rich crop of offsprings. **JOSEPH** (José) had at least 9 children with his first wife, Adèle Bélanger, daughter of Joseph and Catherine Schmidt (first Bélanger couple in Pain Court) whom he married July 14, 1851 at St. Pierre. One of his daughters became a nun and at least four granddaughters and others also. His sons Ambroise and Cyrille made sure to not let the masculine descendants of the "Vieux José" Thibodeau die off in Pain Court and elsewhere. Ambroise married three times: first on May 23, 1854 at St. Pierre to Cézarine Laplante, daughter of Paul and Victoire Roy; they had 10 children. The second marriage on May 4, 1868 to Eugénie Pinsonneault, daughter of Jacob and Claire Tétreault first Pinsonneault in Pain Court produced 6 children. The third marriage on September 18, 1887 was to Isaac Comeau's widow, Rose Bourassa, daughter of Félix and Céleste Boutin. Of his many children, let us note that Joseph had sons that founded the Transport Company which had a great role in making known the Thibodeau name in all Southern Ontario. **ALFRED** became a prosperous broker in Detroit. Joseph was the son of his first wife, Alfred was the son of his second wife. **RÉMI** married Sara Emery and they had several children. We are not aware of what happened to this family and where are Rémi's descendants. **HENRI** married Sophie Robitaille, daughter of Michel and Henriette Roy on January 14, 1862 and they had at least 12 children of whom at least 7 died as babies. Joseph, Ambroise, and Henri Jr. married and had children assuring Henri's Sr's masculine posterity, who was the son of the pioneer Hubert. **WILLIAM**, the youngest son, had two wives. On June 23, 1863, he married Hélène Emery, daughter of Luc and Charlotte Hébert and they had at least 5 children of whom was Francis who would be known in this area as proprietor of the "moulins à battre le grain." He raised his family mostly in Chatham where he died an atrocious death, buried alive in a fire. His second wife, Lucie Hébert, daughter of Grégoire and Arcange Trudelle had 3 children. He married her December 2, 1876.

It is undeniable that Hubert Thibodeau and his sons were most prolific and consequently their descendants seem scattered to all four corners of the Peninsula of southern Ontario as well as in the United States. Considering this fact, the historian can only but see with a certain sadness the almost total disappearance of the Thibodeaus, from the scene of Pain Court. Of the 5 sons of the pioneer Hubert, only the "Old José" has descendants in the parish. Today, his sons Ambroise and Cyrille have grandsons whose responsibility is not to let the Thibodeau name die off. Bravo!

As far as the others, they went to seek their fortune elsewhere, and, in most cases, seemed to have succeeded very well.

GÉNÉALOGIST Rev. Adrien P. Roy
translated by Doreen Thibodeau

Journal Royunion '92 Back to our Roots

Patrimoine Ancestral
The Goure Family
(Gours, Goor, Gore)

Joseph Goure, the pioneer by that name in the area came from Rigaud, Québec in the early 1800's. He had married in Rigaud Véronique Guijon dit Yon.

Children:

1) **Sygfroy**   born in 1833, married Euphibé Dumas January 10, 1859

2) **Rose-Anna**   born in 1841, married George Peel March 15, 1861. George was the first Peel to come to Canada from England.

3) **Marguerite**   married Francis Dumas on January 7, 1868. He was a brother to Euphibé Dumas, Sygfroy's wife.

4) **Jean-Baptiste**   born in 1843, married Marguerite Pinsonneault, daughter of the pioneer Jacob, May 3, 1869.

5) **Mariette**   the youngest, married Isidore Lauzon on December 9, 1871.

Notes of interest

     Rose -Anna Goure and David Roy belong to the same generation of settlers in Pain Court. David married Euphémie Pinsonneault in 1858. Rose Anna married George Peel in 1861. In 1869 Jean-Baptiste Goure, brother of Rose -Anna married Marguerite Pinsonneault, daughter of Jacob and sister to Euphémie. Thus David's and Rose-Anna's families became linked forever.

     Could it be that Jacob Wilfrid Roy, son of David and Mary Ellen Peel, daughter of Rose-Anna Goure first met as children at the Pinsonneault's or/and the Goure's family reunions?

     . . . And then they grew older . . . until that magic spark lit?   . . . Could be!

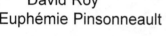

David Roy	Jean-Baptiste Goure	George Peel
Euphémie Pinsonneault	Marguerite Pinsonneault	Rose Anna Goure

Uncle and Aunt

Jacob Wilfrid Roy   to both   Mary Ellen Peel

It must also be remembered that George Peel and André Roy Sr. and sons owned farms in the very same area of Dover Township.

Jean-Baptiste Goure and Marguerite Pinsonneault had nine children, eight boys and one girl. The three older boys never married. Claire, entered the Congregation of the Sisters of the Holy Names and became known as Sister Gerard Magella. The five youngest boys married and kept alive the Goure name in the area.

Camille, his youngest son married Elizabeth Roy, daughter of Charles and Adelaide Béchard. Charles was a grand nephew of André Roy Sr. Their descendants are still numerous in the area, especially the sons and daughters of Célina (Martin) and Denis.

Jean-Baptiste Goure
Marguerite Pinsonneault

Thomas Peel and Mary Dooty's Children
all born in England

Thomas William - butcher in England

George Peel - married RoseAnna Goure in Canada.
.   Children all born in Canada

Robert - lived east of London

John - married Ann Chester, came to Dover,
     County of Kent, Ontario

Mary - Mrs. George Lister married in England. Annie - Mrs. Southwell - England
Came to Canada and lived in Clearville, Ontario

Eliza - Mrs. Carter - England

Sarah - Mrs. Scholfield - artist in England

Ellen - Mrs. Banford - teacher in England

Clara - Mrs. Rowe - England

George Peel and Roseanne Goure
Children - Canada and USA
John Walter - died at 16 months P. C. cemetery
Georgina - (Kitty) married Joseph Roy
Joseph - (Joe) married Annie Dorothy Glassford
Tom - single

John Peel - George's younger brother

John Peel - born at Snelland Lincolnshire, England - August 3, 1852
Ann Chester - born at Rose Mary Lane - January 6, 1855

They came to Canada n in 1871 - John age 19 and Ann age 16. John was given $100.00 to leave England. They lived on the Bear Line near the 5th concession with George Peel, his brother who married Rose Goure. They lived with them for 2 years. Then George bought property at the corner of the Bear Line and the river. John moved to property on the river, Lot 15, which was transferred from Miles Dolsen to John Peel in 1881 for $5000. For 50 acres. John died in 1935 on this farm.

This farm is now King Agro property and Maurice Roy lives in the new house. The log house was bought by Joe Szucs and erected beside the Hind cemetery on the sixth concession in Dover, as a museum.

Patrimoine Ancestral
Faubert

This is only one line of Faubert in Pain Court. It was my grandmother Caron, Elmire Faubert's ancestors. She was married to Médéric Caron.

Another interesting line of Faubert descendants at Pain Court is André Laprise, married to Virginie Bélanger close descendants to the Faubert's. For further references contact Marie-Anne Faubert of Chatham, Bernard Faubert of Toronto or Marie-Louise Faubert of Pain Court

Faubert - Canada

Ignace Faubert - born May 13, 1766, Lac des Deux Montagnes, married on February 20, 1792 to Marie Anne Latrémouille at St-Joachim de Châteauguay, died March 16, 1828 Ste-Martine.

Pierre Faubert - born 1810 Ste-Martine, married October 30, 1835 to Marie Touchette at Ste-Martine Québec. He was the son of Ignace Faubert and Marie-Anne Latremouille. He died December 15, 1890 in Pain Court at 80 years old. Marie Touchette born in 1811, died on December 21, 1882 in Pain Court. She was the daughter of Jean-Jacques Touchette and Suzanne D'aoust.

Antoine Faubert - born on August 8, 1839, Ste-Martine, his father Pierre Faubert and his mother Marie Touchette. He married on January 31, 1860 Marie-Olive Robert, daughter of Alexis1 Robert and Euphebée Meunier dit Lagacé, born 1844 at Pain Court, Ontario.

Alexis 1 - Father and mother of Marie-Olive Robert, married January 7, 1839 at St-Pierre, Raleigh, Euphebée Meunier dit Lagacé. He died May 21, 1901 at Pain Court. He was 96 years old. She was born 1819 at Madawaska and died in 1915 at 96 years old. Grandparents of Father H. Robert.

N.B. picture page 124   1851 - 1926
A. D Emery parish book 1851 - 1926

FAUBERT

Elmire Faubert, daughter of Antoine Faubert and Marie-Olive Robert. She married Médéric Caron, November 14, 1882. Elmire was born in 1866 and lived in the Chatham area on Highway 40 between the 4th & 5th Concession, Dover and Chatham Township. She died at Pain Court, March 17 1937, she was 71 years old.

Antoine Faubert, was born August 8, 1829 at Ste-Martine Québec, was married January 31, 1860 to Marie-Olive Robert born 1844 in Pain Court, moved to Dover Township in 1850, lived in Pain Court and then moved to Chatham a few years later.

They had 11 children:

Èlmire married Méderic Caron
Rose married Marcel Marshall, a farmer
Marguerite married Peter Yott, a farmer
David a farmer
Nelson a farmer
Louise married Philippe Lucier, Grande Pointe
Alfred married 1- Marguerite McGrail (died)
             2- Lucie Roy - May 11, 1921
Napoléon at home 1904 records
James, John and Salina all died at a young age.

Antoine Faubert was a school trustee for a number of years. He was a very prominent farmer. He died at Chatham June 28, 1907.

1 - Elmire Faubert, married Médéric Caron. They had 15 children:

Josephine married Wilfrid Béchard
Salina died at 4 years old
Dennis died at 1 year old
Rémi married 1 Régina Béchard 2 Maria Laprise
Alfred married Lucie Béchard
Marie-Louise married Ovila Cheff
Célina married _____McBride
Oliva married Alphy Roy
Alphonse married Ida Bell
Mélina married Eugene Thibodeau
Délia married Adolphe Roy
Magdelena married Paul Ouellette
Cécilia died by fire at 4 years old
Alcide married Alexina Ouellette
Joseph-Albert died at 4 years old

2 - Rose Faubert, married Marcel Marshall (Marcil)

Lisa married Crisan King (Roy)
Rosa married James B King (Roy)
Mary married John Hart
Helen married Joseph Charbonneau

Interesting to note, Crisan and James were brothers and their father was Lucien Roy (King). Another brother Josephat married Délima Laprise. Their sister Rosanna Roy married Napoleon Sterling.

Lisa married Crisan Roy, they had 4 children
Edgar, Wilfrid, Gladys, Félix.
Rosa married James Roy (King), they had 5 girls

Délima married Vital Béchard
Célina married Erminie Sterling
Madeleine married Arthur Bélanger
Clara married Raphaël Guérin
Lena married Elzear Cadotte
Helen married Joseph Charbonneau. They had 18 children.
Mary married John Hart and they had at least 8 children.
Lena married Elzéar Cadotte, she was the daughter of Rosa and James Roy (King).
(She was special as she was my babysitter.)
They had 5 children:
Francis married Rita Ann Poissant
Shirley married (1) -Yvonne DeMeyer
                           (2) - Janet Tracy
Barbara Ann married Roger Sheeler
Pierre married Camillia Miraux
Paul married Joanne Couture

3 - Marguerite Faubert married Peter Yott Their children:
Helen Yott married George Sherwood
José Yott married _____Bellamy
Olive Yott married Harry Urquart
4 - David Faubert

5 - Nelson Faubert

6 - Louise Faubert married Philippe Lucier.   Their children:
Edna married Eugène Primeau
Irene married Alphore Trahan
Marie Lucier married Esdras Malette

7 - Alfred Faubert married 1 - Marguerite McGrail
                           2 - Lucie Roy May 11, 1921
1- two children
2- no children

8 - Napoléon Faubert 1 - O'Connor - 2 children:
Richard
Margaret married Alphège Goure
2 - Suzie Laprise - 6 children

9 - James   10 - John   11 - Salina Faubert
All died very young.

*Please note that these files are incomplete.
For further references,
Biographical Records of Kent County Commemorative Book,
published in 1904, J.B. Beer & Co.
"Généalogie Tanguay"

-Caroline Roy Laprise

Faubert

ROBERT CARON de La Rochelle, France	marié le 25 octobre 1637 à Québec	MARIE CREVET fille de Pierre Crevet et Marie Lermercie
ROBERT CARON né le 10 février, 1647 à Québec, décédé le 30 avril 171	marié le 14 nov. 1674 à Château-Richer	MARGUERITE CLOUTIER fille de Jean Cloutier et Marie Martin
JOSEPH CARON né le 7 avril 1686 à Ste-Anne-de-Beaupré	marié le 27 février 1713 à Cap St-Ignace	MARIE-MADELEINE BERNIER fille de Pierre Bernier et Françoise Boulé
PIERRE NOËL CARON né le 27 décembre 1735	marié le 4 juillet 1757 à St-Thomas-de-Montmagny	MARIE-GENEVIÈVE THIBAULT veuve de Louis Lemieux fille de Jacques Thibault et Marie-Anne Proulx
CHARLES CARON né vers 1762 décédé le 6 mars 1842	marié le 24 juillet 1786 à St-Thomas-de-Montmagny	MARIE-JOSEPHTE BONNEAU fille de Zacharie Bonneau et Josette Noël
AUGUSTIN CARON né vers 1790à St-Thomas -de-Montmagny décédé le 22 janvier 1844	marié le 31 juillet 1815 à Lacadie	MARIE JOURDONNAIS fille de Pierre Jourdonnais et Marie-Françoise Rémillard
MOÏSE CARON né le 5 février 1825 à Lacadie, décédé le 23 juillet 1907 à Pain Court, Ontario	marié le 15 janvier 1849 à St-Jacques-le-Mineur	CÉLINA TETREAULT fille de Albert Tétreault et Marie-Rose Rémillard
*MÉDERIC CARON né le 4 août 1857 à St-Jacques-le-Mineur	marié le 14 novembre 1882 à Chatham (St-Joseph)	ELMIRE FAUBERT * fille de Antoine Faubert et Marie-Olive Robert
DÉLIA CARON née le 13 février 1899 à Pain Court, Ontario	mariée le 12 novembre 1918 à Pain Court, Ontario	ADOLPHE ROY fils de Thomas Roy et Charline Ouellette

Caroline Roy Laprise

À nos chers défunts

Pour le repos
de l'âme de nos
chers défunts qui
reposent dans les
cimetières des
paroisses de St-Pierre,
de Pain Court et
de Grande Pointe.
Ainsi que tous ceux
qui sont morts
à l'étranger.
Qu'ils reposent en paix.

Chapitre 3

Mariage, Famille,

Paroisse

1919 - 1938

Chapter 3

Marriage, Family,

Parish

La vie rurale

Aimez la terre
Conquête de votre travail
Fruits de vos sueurs
Gloire de vos fatigues
Aimez la terre
Richesse de notre pays
Trésors de vos familles
Nourricière de vos enfants
Respectez la terre
Source de votre bonheur
Ici-bas
Sanctuaire de nos aïeux
Endroit de votre dernier repos

Bulletin Terre de Chez-Nous, Québec

192

"Power of Words"

Words can have enormous power in our lives. They have the ability to heal us, encourage and empower us, console and comfort us. These are the words of love. Then there are words that can hurt and sadden us, make us feel low and worthless. These are words of hate and anger.

The most important thing to remember about words is that while they can have great power and influence over us, they can have that power only if we willingly assent to them. That goes for words of love and concern as well as those of hate and anger. Allow me to explain. Words, or rather the person who utters them, tends to be very controlling, depending on how much control you have chosen to give this person who uses them. Therefore, you have control over the words you hear if you have not given that control to others. When someone speaks to you with hate and anger you will only be hurt if you choose to let yourself be hurt.

Many people find this hard to believe because most of us are so used to accepting the words of others without questioning their behaviour. But it does not have to be so. Ask yourself these questions: Is the person who is using nasty words a sick person? Does that person know all the facts or is it simply an evil-minded person who enjoys hurting others? God help us! You need to ignore them and protect yourself.

On the other hand, there are the words of love, appreciation and friendship. These are very special words. Give them all the power you possibly can. You won't be sorry you listened and took them to heart.

My youngest sister, Anne-Aline Roy - Barrette, remembers her Mother, Délia, in a Mother's Day tribute, rendering a eulogy of special and heartfelt words to let shine through the heart and soul of her mother's spiritual and inspirational gift, that of a fulfilling and lasting legacy of maternal love.

Une grande vivante: Délia Caron-Roy

Née à la toute fin du dix-neuvième siècle, soit en février, 1899, à Pain Court en Ontario, fille de Méderic Caron et d'Elmire Faubert, Délia y demeurera sa vie entière jusqu'à sa mort en février, 1985, mais non pas sans y laisser sa trace. En 1918 elle épousa Adolphe Roy, "Becca" Roy.

Incontestablement, à sa tâche de fille, de soeur, de tante, d'amie, de voisine, d'épouse, de mère et de grand-maman, elle apporte le don le plus rare - le génie du coeur. Son existence même nous oblige encore aujourd'hui à nous interroger du plus intérieur de soi-même, sur le sens d'une vie guidée par l'intelligence du coeur, remplie de tendre compréhension et d'affectueuse sagesse.

Simple femme parmi tant d'autres de son époque, Délia a déployé des trésors d'énergie souriante, d'ingéniosité souvent humoristique, de créativité renversante et de grande abnégation pour que ses dix enfants (cinq garçons et cinq filles) s'épanouissent pleinement comme personnes libres et aimantes. Il est dit que la femme joue un rôle de premier plan dans l'évolution d'un peuple. Toutes ne sont pas des étoiles dans le ciel, mais toutes doivent être une lampe qui éclaire la maison, un flambeau qui éclaire le monde. Pour nombre de voisines et d'amies, ma mère a été cette lampe. Sa sagesse humaine lui permettait de saisir les enjeux de l'intérieur à partir d'une intuition pleine d'amour. De cette sagesse pratique et de cette intelligence féminine se dégageaient chez elle le goût du beau et du bon, le sens de l'être humain dans sa totalité, une impression d'optimisme contagieux, une douce transparence, une présence indéfectible et une disposition remplie de tendresse. En un mot, le courage d'être: être pour soi, être pour les autres et être pour Dieu. Pas tâche facile quand elle se mettait au service de sa famille, de ses voisins ou de sa paroisse. Elle s'attendait d'incompréhension ou d'indifférence, mais elle donnait sa mesure gratuitement. Sa vie des profondeurs pouvait nourrir la solitude extrême, mais sans la rendre amère. Au milieu des échecs comme des réussites, cette grande vivante que fut ma mère, gardait un coeur alerte, indépendant et libre. Quelle fécondité existentielle!

En dépit de tout, elle osait croire en son Créateur. Envers et contre tout, elle se savait aimée de Lui. Lorsqu'elle se présenta devant son Créateur, elle n'arrivait pas les mains vides. Son époux Becca qui la prédécéda, sûrement l'accueillait dans l'amour du Christ pour l'éternité. Veuve depuis juin 1974, la vie ne semblait pas la favoriser. Cependant, elle continuait, dans son vieil âge de porter sur son existence un sens aigu de la responsabilité vis-à-vis ses sept enfants vivants.

Pour tout dire, ce que maman nous amène à comprendre, c'est une triple vérité: qu'à la sainteté ordinaire nous y sommes tous et toutes appelés; que le génie du coeur manifesté tout au long de la vie surgit d'une conviction profonde; que nous sommes faits pour la vie et que l'attention constante aux choses et aux événements que nous vivons fait appel à cette intelligence du coeur à travers laquelle se dévoilent la volonté et le mystère de Dieu pour nous.

Le regard contemplatif, le courage d'être pleinement qui elle était, l'amour de l'autre, la foi en l'autre, la communion avec les autres de tout âge sont le fruit d'une vie axée sur l'être duquel découle tout l'agir. Comme Marie, mère de Jésus, elle "portait tout cela dans son coeur." Elle y portait le germe divin. Délia Caron-Roy n'est pas morte; son esprit demeure. Tu es bienheureuse, Maman toi qui as cru.

Anne-Aline Roy-Barrette
Ottawa, Fête des mères, 1997

Irene Perrot

It is an honour, and also rewarding to commend this renowned author, a relative, who so brilliantly communicated her talents to the world, and also to her parents who counted among the pioneers in Pain Court. The novelist's great grandfather, Thomas Blais, originally from St-Henri de Lozon, Québec, was the first pioneer of the Blais families to settle in Pain Court. He was a crown land recipient, today Lot 12 on the Creek Line Rd, West.

Irene Perrot was born in Pain Court, Ontario, on August 13, 1899. Her father, Jules Perrot, was a native of "Dijon" France and her mother, Célina Blais, was the daughter of Philippe Blais and Philomène Ravenel dit Lalime who married at Pain Court, January 22, 1884.

Furthermore, she was one of my mother's closest friends. Both were born in 1899, became friends from their very first day in school and possibly the reason why mother and I attended a ceremonial tea at the O'Hara residence on Victoria Ave for the launching of her second book "Cathedral Windows" in 1948.

Irene attended the "Pines" in Chatham but later in life made her home close to her sister's in Tecumseh. In the 1940's, Miss Perrot, a novelist, distinguished herself in the field of Roman Catholic fiction. According to Victor Lauriston, a local historian and author of Romantic Kent, "Miss Perrot's writings were in a class by themselves, stressing always the spiritual values and ancient virtues."

In addition, Miss Perrot enjoyed bridge, teas, horse racing, exotic plants, antique jewellery and her silver collection.

Her first novel "Trees Grow Tall" was published in 1946 followed by "Cathedral Windows" in 1948 then her third novel "Twin Tradition" in 1950. This third novel is a fascinating story of a man who mistakenly thought he could practice medicine and art and do both successfully. "No man can serve two masters," was the catalyst in the writing of this latter novel.

Her fifth novel "Freedom from Fear" was published by Stockwell Publishers Ltd. of England and was in circulation in Canada in 1968. This particular volume was translated into French, Flemish and Italian. I should add that Irene Perrot's qualifications are fully authenticated by a membership of the Authors' League of America, the Canadian Authors' Association and the Shakespearian Foundation.

Miss Perrot a former resident of Kent Manor, in Chatham, said she got her writing inspiration from the late Arthur Stringer, a well-known Kent author of 62 novels and a resident of Cedar Springs. Advance copies of her work went to Paul Martin, then the Canadian High Commissioner to the U.K., and also the British Museum and the Canadian Library in Rome. She added two more books to her collection.

Irene Perrot died on February 10, 1980. She was 80 years old and is buried in the Pain Court cemetery. Her two sisters, Victoria Perrot and Emma Perrot, never married. They served as receptionists at rectories, mostly in Tecumseh, for many years.

1. Lauriston, Victor, Romantic Kent,
p. 727, Copyright Canada 1952

M. Venance Sanscartier
Mon appréciation d'un grand vivant et quasi-centenaire

"Retenez bien ce qu'on vous a raconté". . . sage conseil de mes parents et qui, heureusement aujourd'hui, me facilite la tâche de vous transmettre des souvenirs éloignés mais encore bien présents de M. Venance Sanscartier, personnage façonné par le mot d'ordre: "Ma foi, ma langue, ma patrie" et qui a su laisser sa marque.

Oui, mon père parlait souvent de lui (M. Venance Sanscartier) et il l'estimait beaucoup.

Ce n'est pas par pur hasard qu'il est venu s'établir chez nous, pourrais-je dire plutôt, que ce fut providentiel. Laissez-moi raconter. . .

Pour bien situer la vie de M. Venance Sanscartier, il faut faire un retour en arrière et vous fournir un aperçu de la situation politique au Canada dès le tout début du 20e siècle. Comme c'en était le cas, le parti libéral était au pouvoir sous le leadership de Sir Wilfrid Laurier, premier ministre du Canada de 1896 à 1911, et un des plus brillants et remarquables Canadiens français de notre siècle.

C'est vers ce temps là que des Canadiens français, nos ancêtres, sous la clairvoyance de cet éminent politicien, choisissent d'émigrer du Bas Canada vers la péninsule de Kent. Ils franchissent de nouvelles frontières en voie de défrichessement et viennent implanter les racines de la langue française et la foi chrétienne dont nous sommes les fiers héritiers.

Parmi cette foule d'émigrants qui affluèrent vers cette terre promise se trouvait Venance Sanscartier, le pionnier des familles "Cartier" de nos communautés environnantes.

Il est vraisemblable que Venance s'arrêta premièrement à Pain Court pour se déplacer ensuite à Grande Pointe où il s'établit en permanence, prenant possession d'un lopin de terre situé sur la 10e concession du canton de Dover comprenant les lots 10 et 11 respectivement.

C'est le 22 novembre 1864 que Venance Nouvion dit Sanscartier, âgé de 24 ans et fils de François Nouvion dit Sanscartier et de Esther Auger, épousa une jeune demoiselle de chez-nous, Julienne Charron, âgée de 22 ans, et fille de Jean-Baptiste Charron et d'Ermine Beaugrand dit Champagne. Leurs douze enfants ont perpétué leur travail de pionniers.

Venance était un homme de principes, nourri dans la foi chrétienne et jouissant d'une solide réputation, aimé et respecté de tous ses concitoyens.

Quel cachet particulier renfermait la popularité de M. Venance? C'est qu'il était un grand ami d'enfance de Sir Wilfrid Laurier. Tous les deux sont nés à Saint-Lin, Québec en 1841. Ils étaient voisins et ont fréquenté tous les deux l'école du village, mais ce qui est encore plus remarquable c'est le fait qu'ils sont restés de très grands amis.

Même si les distances à cette époque paraissaient infranchissables, elles ne diminuaient en rien l'attachement et la solidarité qui existaient entre ces deux grands amis d'enfance. C'est à maintes reprises que Sir Wilfrid Laurier se rendait à Grande Pointe pour saluer son fidèle ami, Venance et sa belle grande famille.

La terre ancestrale, berceau de l'histoire de la descendance de M. Venance Sanscartier, passa en succession de père en fils, tous cultivateurs de trempe comme le patriarche.

Son épouse, Julienne, est décédée à Grande Pointe le 8 octobre 1926 à l'âge de 84 ans. Venance Sanscartier ayant atteint ses 99 ans, est décédé le 27 juin 1940.

Toute leur vie ce couple ont témoigné de leur attachement mutuel partageant joies et peines. Héritiers d'un riche patrimoine culturel, ils l'ont transmis fidèlement. Ils demeurent dignes de nos éloges et de notre admiration.

La famille de Venance Cartier avec leurs époux et épouses

Gracieuseté du livret souvenir "Centenaire de Grande Pointe" (1886 - 1986)

SIR WILFRID LAURIER

NOUS FAISONS UN APPEL AUX CANADIENS-FRANÇAIS DE KENT-OUEST
VOTEZ POUR A.B. McCOIG LE POPULAIRE CANDIDAT

Annonce parue dans l'hebdomadaire L'AMI DU PEUPLE
le premier octobre 1908, publié à Chatham, Ontario par J.R. Coté.

Archibald McCoig né à Tilbury le 8 avril, 1874. Ce politicien écossais siège au conseil municipal de Chatham pendant cinq ans de 1900 à 1904, puis se fait élire à l'Assemblée législative de l'Ontario en 1905. Aux élections fédérales de 1908 McCoig est sur les rangs et reçoit la confiance des électeurs. Il siège comme député fédéral de 1908 à 1922. Après plus de quinze ans de politique, il est nommé au sénat en 1922 jusqu'à 1927.

En grandissant, j'ai souvent entendu mon père parler de ces politiciens de grande renommée comme Archie McCoig et Sir Wilfrid Laurier.

" Grandeur de notre langue"

Elle n'est pas si pauvre notre langue, cette langue française faite de beauté, de clarté et d'harmonie, créée pour chanter les grandes épopées, aussi bien que pour pleurer les grand deuils, langue fine, nuancée, souple, capable de revêtir toutes les formes de la pensée.

"Langue faite avec les cris, les colères, les souffrances et les sanglots d'un peuple très intellingent, langue enfin que d'après les marins venus parmi nous ont rapporté du sol français. Langue, avec laquelle nos mères nous ont bercés sur leurs genoux aux refrains dolents des vieilles ballades normandes." " Nous constatons qu'il y a déjà douze générations au Canada qui rendent hommage à leurs ancêtres!"

Mon enfance

Je suis née le 21 mai 1919. J'ai été baptisée, Caroline Elmire Florence Roy, à Grande Pointe, par le R. P. Joseph Emery, natif, et curé de la dite paroisse. Eugène Thibodeau et Mélina Thibodeau m'ont portée au baptême.

Dans les années '20, les accouchements se faisaient à la maison. On me dit que j'ai vu le jour vers 10 heures du matin à la maison paternelle située au carrefour de la 9e concession et du Baldoon Rd. dans le canton de Dover, maison solidement bâtie et qui, aujourd'hui, lorsque je l'aperçois durant mes randonnées dans ce beau coin du pays de mon enfance, elle peut me clignoter mille et un souvenirs des cinq premières années de mon enfance où elle m'a abritée moelleusement sous son toit.

C'est en avril 1924 que mes parents, Adolphe et Délia, ont décidé de déménager à Pain Court sur la 3e concession pour prendre possession de la ferme d'Alexandre Roy habitée alors par son fils Eugène Roy et que lui, à son tour, déménagea sur le bord de la rivière Thames, là où se trouve, aujourd'hui, une concentration d'habitations modèles et imposantes connue sous le nom de "Thames Valley Estates" et développée par le feu Norman Roy, fils d'Eugène Roy.

The house where I was born on the Baldoon Rd. and built in 1871.
Photo by Chatham Daily News

My Childhood

I was born May 21, 1919 at 10 o'clock in the morning. The blessed event was at the farm homestead situated at the intersection of the Baldoon Rd and the 9th concession in Dover township, then known as the "Baldoon Settlement."

Part of the following writeup appeared in the Chatham Daily News under the heading "Built to Last," an historical excerpt of my former home and above all, an architectural and heritage landmark of Kent County now owned by Roy Anderson, also a prominent and well-known farmer of Dover Township.

"This double brick house has withstood the test of time. It was built by Alfred Yankee Williams on land originally owned by Captain Fraser of the Canadian Army, through land grants in 1834, then known as the "Baldoon Settlement." The property went from Fraser to a man named Henderson before coming into the possession of Williams. The farm and house changed hands to Williams' son, Jack, who left the house in 1904. At that time, Bill Montgomery owned the farm until it was taken over by Adolphe Roy (King) in 1918 and later by Francis Ouellette in 1924. The Ouellette's have lived there until the year 1974, when they retired. They sold the farm to Roy Anderson, keeping the house and an acre of land on which it stands. The entire house is built of hardwood, white oak, except for the doors which are pine. The house was the first on the road to have electricity. Bricks for the house were fashioned in the nearby field "brick yard".

Well, I clearly remember this brick and tile yard situated a quarter mile from my home. This light industry produced bricks to build homes in the vicinity and also tiles made available to farmers for their multiple uses such as drainage, wells, etc.

"Long lives yield many treasures, pictures, keepsakes, property or savings, the standard currencies of inheritance passed on from generation to generation. But there is another precious legacy, one that is often lost, memories, closely-held images of people, places and things that are the blueprints of a life," eighty years of blessed and cherished happenings which I want to share with you.

I was always a right-handed person, unlike some of my children who are left-handed. By the age of eight years old, I was very near sighted. My vision crossed, giving me much difficulty reading the blackboard. So I have been wearing corrective lenses ever since.

Memories of my childhood flash through my mind as I reminisce on this 1996, 40° F March morning in Port Richey, Florida. The overcast sky turned into a one inch downpour. Roses are in bloom and so are the daffodils, those refreshing harbingers of Spring. My heart feels light and happy as I fancy myself being a two year old again. One situation in particular, incidentally zooms back to our home on the Baldoon with Aunt Agnès Caron (Roy) and dear Mrs. Philomène Roy (Josephat) and her three children, Magdelena, Adelard and Armand, the whole congregation standing in the kitchen waiting merrily to ring in my third birthday. Oh! yes, indeed! May 21st was special and a party was in order with aunts, cousins and neighbours as welcomed guests.

My preschool years were quite wholesome from what I can remember.

My recollections of a gypsy community not too far from our place on the Baldoon is one of those incidents that I can recall and maybe it could bring to light memories for others who have encountered these same perplexed circumstances.

As months went by, I had friends on the porch, the gypsies, with big bags full of "I wanted to find out what?" You see, the electric train stopped three times a week at a depot in front of our house to pick up passengers on their way to Chatham and Pain Court. These people caught my eye, so to speak. I always anticipated their arrival. Their garish coloured garments, dressed up with beady ropes and shiny, shimmering pendants, along with their mannerisms, no doubt instigated my inquisitiveness.

Of course I was forbidden to talk to strangers just as it is today, but even a spanking could not deter my curiosity and perseverance to know more about these people and especially the jute bags they carried on their backs. Well, my trump card was to peek into them. What I found was a whole slew of handmade crafts and trinkets, colourful handmade straw woven baskets, strings of beads and even roots, that is, trading wares for peddling at the Chatham market in exchange for food.

Thank you Aunt Rosa

A special note of appreciation to Aunt Rosa Roy, my occasional babysitter when I was growing up, an aunt I loved dearly. Her young daughter Lena, Mrs. Elzéar Cadotte, was only five years my senior, but she was someone special, like a big sister to me. They lived next door to us on the corner of the Baldoon Road and the ninth concession in Dover, but later moved to the Chatham area closer to the other Faubert families on the south-west corner of the 5th concession and No. 40 highway. To this day, the buildings are very well kept but the old homestead was demolished some twenty five years ago.

Here is what prices were like 1920 - 1930

Five gallons of gasoline	85 cents
One gallon of kerosene for lamps	18 cents
1 qt. of oil	15 cents
A haircut	25 cents
Roll of toilet paper	25 cents
The telephone bill	$2.25
Three lbs. of rice	18 cents
Gallon of milk	12 cents
A dozen eggs	22 cents
A small apple pie	10 cents
2 lbs. of butter	25 cents

Kerosene oil was used in the lamps and also in some stoves. There was no electricity. Many people's income was a "dollar" a day. Some received $3.00 a week and board. Children were born at home. When the doctor was called, he stayed until the birth, which was quite long sometimes. The billings were generally $10.00. It's hard to believe how much things have changed.

Keep in mind this was 65 years ago, during the depth of the depression. I remember very vividly this period, the 1920s and 30s.

Did you know . . .

In 1845 matches made their first appearance on the market. They sold for 2 packages for 3 pennies.

Oil lamps made their appearance only in 1860. Only the rich people could afford the luxury of this type of lighting. At first they were very unpopular because of the explosions.

Post Cards in January 1895 became legal to send to relatives and friends in Canada. For years it cost only one penny to mail a post card. By 1914 millions were being mailed every year.

By 1895 changing times - more occupations were opened to women. At the time they were expected to stay home and look after the family. . .furthermore they did not have the right to vote.

History of Automobile Licenses and Permits in Ontario

1903 - 1904, There were 178 cars in Ontario. They carried a license which consisted of brass numbers on a leather plate.

1905 - 1910, Licenses were composed of large rubber numbered plates, white on black.

1911 - In this year licenses were made of porcelain.

1909 - Chauffeurs first licensed.

1927 - All operators were licensed.

1912 - Metal plates were introduced. For many years licenses varied in colour from year to year. Later about the years 1965 - 72 they simply alternated from white letters on blue to blue letters on white.

1973 - Beginning next year the licensing system will be substantially changed. Heavier metal in blue and white showing 3 letters followed by 3 figures. The following two years a validating sticker will be sold to affix to the 1973 plate. The process to be repeated thereafter.

Trucks - will not be included in this change. They will continue full licensing procedures with new plates each year.

Station wagons - will no longer receive a special license; they will be licensed as automobiles.

*　　*　　*

My summers were never dull. Cousins my own age came over. Sylvia Roy would spend a few days with me. Her occasional visits would always coincide with Marie May's, our cousin from Pike Creek who would come and stay with us during the summer months. I loved to play with my two close-knit cousins and enjoyed their company immensely but a remorseful incident springs to mind. That of biting my dear friends on their arms. No doubt a defensive mechanism for showing one's authority or displeasure. Although I was severely reprimanded for this unwarranted behaviour, I persisted in doing it. "Why?"

201

It was always on a Sunday morning when Dad would announce his trips to Pike Creek. Being my father's partner on these "early to rise excursions" was fun indeed, a habit reinforced through the years which transformed me into . . . a galloping grandmother of sorts if I say so myself . . . you see I love people and I love to visit . . .what else could be more pleasant and rewarding?

What is still vivid in my mind is the hand driven ferry crossing at Prairie Siding close to where the bridge now stands.   That crossing was a nightmare.   To calm me down Dad would hold me assuredly in his arms but the rest of the trip compensated for my fears.

The short journeys were not only pleasurable, they were also memorable. Dad would stop for Sunday services at St. Peter's Church. After mass the proper thing to do was to visit the cemetery where our ancestors and relatives were buried. From a very tender age dad's mastery of genealogical knowledge instilled in me a sense of appreciation and pride regarding my roots.

. .   " To know where you come from is to know who you are . . . These much anticipated " ren-dez-vous" were educational to say the least, but more importantly in all of this, is to realize the impact words can have on such a young mind and how ingrained they remain in one's subcon-scious, the living proof as I write these recollections.

The next stop was Jeannette's Creek, Mémère Carlyne's homestead, where uncle Zéphore and uncle Frank lived along with their two sisters, aunt Julienne and aunt Euphémie. Both sisters helped with the founding of "Les Soeurs Hospitalières de St-Joseph" in Windsor.

Soon after, we arrived in Pike Creek to be greeted by Aunt Rosie's smiling face and jolly dis-position, even though she was a cripple.

"She's a nurse, so why can't she do something about it?" was the question I put forth to Dad. My uncle was also in ill-health and could hardly work. I was always sad to see them in this sorrow-ful state but their cheerfulness and positive approach to life dissipated all negative thoughts as they accepted courageously what fate had given them.

Setting off on these adventuresome all day roundabouts were the highlights "de mon enfance."   Often we would stop by to greet uncle Zéphore Ouellette at his home in Windsor. He was afflicted with cancer of the throat. These visits were sad to say the least and these horrible suf-ferings not easily understood. A child's mind works very diligently but I was too young to associate death with cancer. When uncle died most of his family moved to Detroit where Hilary, his oldest son, and Carmen, the oldest daughter, lived, worked and cared for their mother and the rest of the family. We kept a close relationship with the family until their death.

However, these visits had a very pleasant aura . . . their girls had beautiful clothes and we gladly appreciated their hand-me downs. Mother being a skilful seamstress could ingeniously recy-cle these used garments into lovely clothes for me to wear.

Mother seldom accompanied us on these trips. Circumstances did not permit her to do so. Why? She was either pregnant or there were no babysitters. During the summer months, I took these trips with my Dad at least twice a month or more to "Hôtel- Dieu Hospital" to take food and clothing for the poor. At that time, the sisters cared for and alleviated the plight of the sick and the poor with donations they received.

Mother had extensive gardens and so did our many other relatives. I grew up helping her in the garden. She also collected clothing from people who gave so generously. These and the rich bounty from our gardens were distributed by the sisters to the poor and the sick of their community in Windsor. I have fond memories of the seven sisters who were there to greet us. They hugged me, loved me and thanked my father for everything. I really treasured these moments, and the attention they gave me.

In April of 1924, father decided to move back to Pain Court on the Creek Line Rd. in Dover, a farm originally owned by Alexandre Roy which Dad bought from his son, Eugène Roy. I was a mere five-year-old child. My parents were already making long range plans for their children to be educated in a bilingual environment. Also there was a congregation of Roy, all related, where Dad chose to farm and raise his family. He was surrounded by his brothers, André across the road, and Francis who lived next door where my father had spent all of his younger years, the homestead of his father, Thomas Roy.

Both my parents could speak French and English fluently, therefore my formative years being well-grounded in both languages. I managed to toss here and there a few words in Belgium and sing a few short tunes which I picked up from the Belgian workers hired to thin out sugar beets and harvest our tobacco crops.

La classe d'étudiantes et étudiants de la 9e et 10e années de l'École de Continuation de
Pain Court en1933-34, Au premier plan: Caroline Roy, étudiante en 9e année, 3e étudiante (assise).
Photo courtesy of Roland Bélanger

As an elementary student enrolled at Ste-Catherine School in Pain Court, those were eight years of camaraderie and hard work with a mixture of fun and laughter. My elementary education was fully bilingual. I attended Pain Court Continuation School where I successfully completed grades nine and ten, then transferred to the Pines, in Chatham, in 1934- 35, under the guidance of the Ursuline Sisters to resume my high school education, in English only. I was 16 years old when I finished high school. I later decided to return to Pain Court Continuation School when the school board managed to obtain a government permit to teach grades 11 and 12, thereby resuming my bilingual studies.

During this period, I worked hard but I remember well I weighed 136 pounds at 13 years old. By the time I reached 18, I was 5' 3 and weighed 110 pounds. I had bright and sharp dark brown eyes, an inquisitive mind, a thirst for knowledge and compelled to be on the up and up, business wise, that is. It baffles me somewhat that I can still remember events and episodes long past and can freely write about them.

By the way I do possess a fairly high pitched voice, depending upon the amount of stress involved. Count me out when it comes to having pets.

At a young tender age, I was driving horses in the fields with my Dad. I not only inherited the nickname "Katie," my old black mare's namesake, but I was relentlessly serenaded with the "K K K Katie" song, a familiar fun tune of the 20s which goes like this :
> K K K Katie
> Beautiful Katie
> You're the only g g g girl that I adore
> When the . . . m - moon shines
> Over the cow shed
> I'll be waitin' at the k k k kitchen door.

SIDE NOTE: Geoffrey O'Hara, teacher, writer, and music composer in the early to mid 1900's. Born in Chatham, Ontario. Pursued his music degree in the USA. He wrote KKK Katie a most popular song during the first World War.

My closest friends still call me "Katie." The nickname still stands but unfortunately, my beautiful black mare is long gone.

I'm the oldest of five girls and four boys. Interestingly enough, I remember very well when they were born; I was elated to see them but as the years went by, this took a toll on my young nervous system. Being the oldest, I had to bare the brunt of the responsibilities.

I was nineteen when I married 25 year old Trefflé Laprise, on January 18, 1938. Afternoon weddings were not the norm then. The nuptial mass was celebrated in Immaculate Conception Church at 9:30 a.m. with Rev. Father Zotique Mailloux as celebrant.

We were both elders of our respective families, both from French ancestry, Catholics and good die-hard liberals, as far as the political system is concerned. Tossed here and there were also some very good conservatives, no doubt.

Drawing to a close, the first chapter of my life, I find that it should end, more or less, on the educational side, an area where I always found strength, security and comfort to refurbish one's mind and soul. Age has no boundaries; nor learning power has no boundaries; abilities to learn are endless. With this philosophical principle in mind, I pursued my long cherished dream to return to school as an undergraduate adult student. Therefore, in 1964, I enrolled at the University of Ottawa in the Social Studies Department and later transferred to Western University in London, in 1968, to

204

complete my program. This latter venture was most interesting since I had some of my own children already on Campus. These are, more or less, my academic achievements which I learned to develop and apply to the best of my ability.

Caroline 4 yrs old, Yvonne 1 yr old

La croix du chemin -
un héritage de notre patrimoine ancestral religieux

Pour souligner l'année jubilaire de l'église en 1852, le curé Claude-Antoine Ternet voulut commémorer cet événement en organisant des processions extérieures avec l'élévation et bénédiction solennelle de trois croix de chemin: une érigée le 3 septembre 1852 à Grande Pointe, une deuxième à Pain Court le 10 septembre et le 17 septembre, une troisième à Millerode.

À travers les années, les "croix" furent remplacées et dressées aux mêmes endroits . Vers l'année 1925 la croix située sur la 3e concession au coin de la terre de M. Fred Caron, juste à l'endroit où la route fait un virage celle-là a dû être remplacée et j'ai souvenance d'être là au milieu de plusieurs paroissiens groupés autour d'elle pour la célébration de la messe.

Les paroissiens se rassemblaient souvent à cet endroit pour prier ou réciter le chapelet car les distances ne permettaient pas toujours de se rendre à l'église. J'ai souvent prié avec ma mère au pied de cette croix et presque toujours nous avions des fleurs à déposer. Par contre, beaucoup d'autres paroissiens en faisaient autant.

Dans le même temps une deuxième croix fut élevée sur la 4e concession ouest, au coin de la terre de M. Henri Bélanger.

Placés sous son patronage dès notre plus tendre enfance, ces croix du chemin étaient porteuses de valeurs humaines pour tous ceux et celles qui les approchaient. Respect, inspiration, recueillement, méditation, confiance, Rédemption: voilà ce qu'elles personnifiaient!

Tradition passée, sûrement, mais certainement pas oubliée. Aujourd'hui, elles symbolisent une continuité avec mon passé puisqu'en passant devant une église où la croix rayonne, le signe de croix effectivement, est dans l'ordre, valeur patrimoniale transmise par nos pères.

Bénédiction du Jour de l'an

Mes enfants,
Quand vous êtes venus au monde,
Votre présence a bouleversé notre vie.
Vous avez été notre joie, notre fierté, notre espérance.
Vos peines nous ont fait mal.
Vos douleurs ont été les nôtres.
Vos angoisses ont été nos angoisses.
En cette année nouvelle, nous rendons grâce au Seigneur,
Pour votre naissance, pour votre vie, pour votre présence.
Que la lumière vous inonde.
Que la joie vous accompagne
Et que le Seigneur vous bénisse
Maintenant et à jamais.

Je me rappelle bien quand mon grand-père, Thomas Roy, bénissait mon père, Adolphe.

Pendant une vingtaine d'années, environ, je suis restée fidèle à cette même tradition demandant à mon père, Adolphe, de me bénir lorsque je lui rendais visite le Jour de l'an au matin.

My neighbours, the Montgomery's

I also remember well our neighbours, "the Montgomery's" who took me under their wing when mother went off to the market on the electric train. They would babysit me. I loved them dearly and especially the girls. They were very kind, endearing and fussed over me much to my delight.

Another item of interest was the big "call bell"rigged up for the farmers of the immediate surroundings. My father rang it at 7:00 a.m. for the call to go to work. At noon, it was mother's turn to summon the men for lunch. I was so anxious to ring that bell but I was still too short and too light in weight for the task. The bell nested on the roof of the shed which was filled to the rafters with cords of wood for the winter. I finally had my wish when I turned four. Many times I managed to ring it, but once in a while the long rope would play a trick on me and pull me up from the stump which was placed there purposely for me to reach the rope. This bell served other purposes as well, like warning the community of a disaster or fire or simply a call for help.

My memories of Hôtel-Dieu

Let me elaborate on the foundation of the "Hôtel-Dieu Hospital". A handful of devoted nuns from Québec, "Les Soeurs Hospitalières de St. Joseph" came to Windsor in order to establish a place to care for the poor and the sick. Their livelihood rested on charity from the people. Sister Marie Euphanie Ouellette was the first postulant to enter the novitiate of Hôtel-Dieu. Her sister, Julienne, followed Euphanie very shortly after. Both had their work cut out, like collecting food and clothing to distribute to the poor. The other five sisters cared for the sick at no cost. Sister Euphanie was born in 1867. She died November 1, 1944 at the age of 77. Her remarkable life with the sisters lasted 54 years. Sister Julienne Ouellette did likewise. Born in 1871, she also spent 54 years with the Sisters at Hôtel-Dieu. She died after a long illness, on June 23, 1948. All sisters worked hard and diligently in cooperation with all the good hearted people who voluntarily gave food, work, money and also their support toward establishing "Hôtel-Dieu Hospital" in Windsor. Mrs. Rosie May and Brigitte Roy of Pain Court were among the first graduate nurses at the hospital. Both were my paternal aunts and also nieces of Sister Euphanie and Sister Julienne.

"All personnel involved worked together with doctors and nurses and laymen under stressful circumstances to reach their goals. By 1930 the depression years added more hardships and more demands on the growing hospital. As the 40s rolled in , the idea of caring for the elders became a further goal, which successfully led to the opening of "Villa Maria Home" on the Detroit River, close to the Ambassador Bridge. This institution is thriving today. After overcoming hardships of all descriptions, the "Sisters of St. Joseph Hospitalières" still maintain a high profile in this progressive institution." [1]

Hôtel-Dieu Hospital is now known as Hôtel-Dieu Grace Hospital of Windsor.

From these experiences, I learned to care, and it has remained a part of my life ever since. "Try to alleviate the sadness in peoples' lives" is a motto I learned on my mother's knees and I have tried since to transmit it to the best of my abilities.

1. Windsor Star

Mes Souvenirs de l'Hôtel-Dieu

Grâce à ces femmes de coeur qui ont travaillé d'arrache-pied, sans compter ni leur temps ni leur force pour la fondation de cette institution. Les paroisses environnantes de Windsor, Saint-Joachim, Belle-Rivière, Tilbury, Pain Court, Grande Pointe, Lasalle, McGregor, Comber, et Rivière-aux-Canards ont aussi contribué de diverses manières à faire grandir cette institution hospitalière et religieuse. Plusieurs jeunes filles des dites paroisses ont suivi les traces de mes deux grands-tantes, Soeur Marie Euphémie et Soeur Julienne Ouellette, comme Soeurs Hospitalières de l'Hôtel-Dieu, afin de réaliser leur vocation vis-à-vis les malades et les pauvres.

Voici ce que je retrouve dans les archives de l'Hôtel-Dieu: Soeur Marie Euphémie Ouellette (dite Soeur Marie) 1890

Tourière, première postulante au Noviciat de l'Hôtel-Dieu, aide très précieuse à nos fondatri-ces pour les quêtes des premières années, les achats, messages à faire et digne représentante de la communauté en toutes occasions. Habile au soin des malades, à l'aiguille, au pinceau, etc. Son religieux maintien reflétait avantageusement sur la communauté. Décédée le 1 novembre 1944 à l'âge de 77 et de religion 54 ans 8 mois 11jours.

Soeur Julienne Ouellette (dite Soeur Julienne) 1894

Tourière, soeur naturelle de ma Soeur Marie, fut la digne émule et compagne de sa soeur pour les oeuvres extérieures pendant plusieurs années; ensuite le bon Dieu s'en fit une victime de souffrances physiques et morales qui l'accompagnèrent jusqu'à sa mort survenue le 23 juin 1948. Elle était âgée de 77 dont 54 ans, 5 mois 11 jours de vie religieuse.

Ajoutons à leurs rangs les religieuses suivantes:

Sr. Cécile Laprise de Pain Court	Sr. Evéline Emery de Grande Pointe
Sr. Florida Cadotte de Grande Pointe	Sr. Viola Beaulieu de St-Joachim
Sr. Mae Cartier de Grande Pointe	Sr. Aurore Beaulieu de St-Joachim
Sr. Cécile Cartier de Grande Pointe	Sr. Cécile Leboeuf de St-Joachim
Sr. Flore Cazabon de Pointe-aux-Roches	Sr. Marie de Lefer de St-Joachim
Sr. Bella Goure de Pain Court	

The Electric Train And Some Other Memories

Oh! That famous electric train . . . "le p'tit char". . . as it was called locally by the French com-munity. Like any four-year-old,   I was thrilled to ride on this train. Seldom would I go to Chatham, but going to Pain Court was all an adventure. Mother would bring me along when she decided to visit her parents, the "Médéric Caron's" who lived on the fourth concession in Dover just half a mile before the end of the tracks at the "Dover Hotel," a wayside inn owned and operated by Dieudonné Gagner Sr.

I was deeply frustrated when the engineer rolled past my grandparents dwelling. I simply could not understand why it would only stop at the Dover Hotel - end of the line. Mother desperately tried to explain but her pleadings were to no avail. It was understood that we had to walk to my grandparents but I firmly stood my ground. A scene unravelled half way down the road. This certain lady shamed me as I sat in her neighbour's yard, refusing to walk any further. She, no doubt, had a magic formula that helped release my obstinate behaviour but when we reached our destination, Grandma's humiliating talking-to put an abrupt stop to her grandchild's tantrum.

My family did not own a car then. On Sunday, we attended church in Grande Pointe where I was baptized. We then proceeded to see my ailing grandfather "Caron." Being bedridden and unable to shave, father tended to his needs once a week. Travelling during the summer months was pleasant indeed, but as winter rolled around a horse drawn buggy or sleigh was a different story altogether. Saturday night we piled at least a dozen construction bricks in the oven, so they would be warm and ready to be wrapped in blankets and placed in the sleigh to keep us warm for our trip on Sunday morning.

Then came the wrapping of shawls around my face leaving two small slits. I despised that contraption which didn't go too well with my inquisitive character. I had a small seat, facing my Mother and Dad. Lastly the top coverlet was "la robe de boeuf"- a coarse, heavy blanket made with the hide of a beef cattle, cleaned, treated, and with its pieces sown together; the genuine leather blanket assured us of a comfortable and cozy journey. And naturally I always sat close to the whip, coaxing Dad to speed up the horses.

Visiting my Pépère and Mémère Caron was a joy in itself. They always greeted me with open arms. My visit with grandfather was sometimes off limits and I wanted to know why I could not see him. The answers did not satisfy my curiosity. I managed to slip away once, unnoticed. Finally, I understood the reason why the children could not go and see him. You see, Grandfather had a failing memory and sometimes his actions were unpredictable.

My grandfather Caron, Médéric, a brilliant man, led an active life. He obtained a university degree at Assumption College Windsor, taught school for two years in Mount Clemens Michigan, was ordained a deacon in the church, but made a last minute decision not to embrace the priesthood. He opted to follow in his father's footsteps and established himself on a farm one mile from his father on the fourth concession in Dover where he raised a large family of 12 children. He was appointed justice of the peace, and was clerk of Dover Township for a period of 30 years. He died May 4th, 1924, and I remember well as he was laid in the family living room. I was five years old.

Later in life, mother informed us that her father had stated that none of his children would receive an education other than a grade four or a grade five. Reading and writing sufficed. This all came to pass. None were educated like he was, but all became very honourable citizens and self-made men and women. He apparently felt that way specifically because too much responsibility rested on those that were well educated at the time.

This same year, my parents decided to move to Pain Court close to my father's relatives and close to the old homestead. At the time my father was a farmer and cattleman. He fed and wintered cattle during the winter months. I vividly remember an incident relative to father's herd; I was five years old then, dressed in a cute red winter coat and matching hat. Mother and I helped move these cattle to Pain Court via the Bear Line. About 40 to 50 cattle were driven on foot from the ninth concession in Dover. Our job was to guard all the neighbours' gates as the herd passed by, waving and clapping our hands so as to deter them from entering the neighbouring properties. I trembled, traumatized by the thundering hoof beats trampling the dusty roads for miles and miles about the countryside, an ordeal hardly conceivable for a five-year-old youngster. At the time, I begrudged my dad for his callous acts.

As I look back, it appears that much was expected of me. Furthermore, it seems that I was a busy body of sorts and was not brushed aside with simple answers.

My Mother, in her later years, recalled an incident which had humiliated and embarrassed her at a preaching mission at St-Philippe's Church in Grande Pointe. The zealous missionary had encouraged mothers to bring along the babies and children. I must have been between three and four. The baskets, with the collected offerings were placed on the communion rail, about three feet from the preacher. Well, I had noticed those baskets and, like other youngsters I roamed around. Apparently I had a special goal to accomplish, which was to get part of the offering and bring it with me. But as soon as I managed to put my hand in the basket, the missionary raised his hand to deter me. Well, apparently I took three shots at it when finally, mother had to intervene and restrain me from leaving the pew. Without a doubt there were many such blunders and embarrassments on my part.

I was named after my Grandmother Roy. I loved her dearly but she was a relentless teaser. My very first recollection of her was that I had to be her good little girl after I had cried my heart out because of her continuous pestering. The minute she saw me, she grabbed me, then she would threaten to cut up the frills on my dress. She would pinch me on and on until the tears would roll down. Then we were friends. She would play her violin for me nearly every time I went to see her. Grandpa was quiet and would smile at Grandma's tricks. He surely understood my concern because she loved to play tricks on him also.

My Grandpa Roy's birthday was on New Year's day. There was always a big celebration, with balloons all over the house and noise makers of all kinds. To add insult to injury, Uncle Frank and Uncle Leo joined in by teasing us also. Everyone had a touch of Mémère Roy's instigating ways and cooperated to make the children miserable. No wonder I loved her. She was funny and full of life. Even when bedridden, I wanted her to play her violin. I was eight years old then. She would always say; " I'm very sick but get my violin under the bed, I will try to play one more time."

Living close by and having a car for transportation, we managed to visit my Grandparents on a weekly basis until their death. Grandma Roy passed away on December 20, 1928 and Grandpa Roy died two years later.

*   *   *

Sundays were picnic days and we drove to Mitchell's Bay. There were no tables. We had to bring our own or sit on the grass. After we had spent sometime in the water, mother always had an appetizing lunch waiting for us and watermelon wedges for a special treat.

*   *   *

New Year's was the highlight of the Christmas festivities. On this day we went to our Grandparents and we received gifts. Christmas was the day to celebrate the birth of Christ. When we were old enough, "la Messe de Minuit" was on the agenda. These customs were brought from France by the ancestors. The nativity scene was the focus of the Christmas celebration. Nearly every home in the parish had one displayed on the mantel or on a table somewhere in the house for everyone to admire and meditate. The "réveillon," the grand feast of the season, was celebrated after Midnight Mass. This we observed for eleven generations in Canada. A traditional part of the Christmas meal was the "bûche de Noël," a log-shaped cake. For the main course, we feasted on turkey and dressing, the stuffed goose being reserved for New Year's along with "les tourtières" and sliders.

The Christmas season began with the liturgical celebration of the Midnight Mass. Every family of the parish was in attendance with parents and children alike, so reverently disposed, their voices striking up "Minuit Chrétien" in unison with "Marie-Thérèse" pealing out the hour of solemnity as the celebrant, in processional grandeur, advanced towards the manger with the Infant Jesus. The choir celebrated with fanfare and exuberance under Mme Marie Emery's professional expertise. The church trembled with the sounds of the violins and the men singing their hearts out beginning half and hour before mass. It was very impressive. Mr. Leopold Gagner was a main figure with his violin but there were others. Mr. Toussaint Campbell was one of the main soloist and so was uncle Jacob Roy, a gifted tenor. I wish I could remember everyone who participated.. People loved it, so did the children. The church was packed with revellers -- standing room only. Then it was family celebrations at home followed by "Le Réveillon," special goodies, and neighbours came over. New Year's was very different. It was a very happy reunion, crowded with aunts, uncles, cousins, you name it. Eat and be merry was the motto of both my paternal and maternal grandparents. I remember one New Year's day at Grandmother Caron. I was about eleven years old. Only mother and I went for dinner. Well, Mémère wanted to know where the rest of the family was. "Go back home" she said, "and bring the whole family, so that they too can be happy with the rest of us."

* * *

By this time I do have a lovely little sister, Yvonne. She was dressed like a doll. I had to share the attention with my little sister, something I resented and did not fully understand the motive. She was followed by Léontine who arrived on the scene 18 months later. Playtime was curtailed that much more because Yvonne had to be supervised and Léontine had to be rocked to sleep while mother did other household chores. My free time was spent with Martha, our hired help's daughter, and my faithful and dear companion. One day, Martha decided to teach me to sing Belgium songs. Unfortunately most have slipped from my memory but this is one I remember, more or less:

Do Do Keinaken Do,
Do and Do,
Yuskes to,
L'enfant dormira bientôt.

Both parents along with an older daughter, Maria, worked in tobacco for my father. During the winter months, Mother would go to the market in Chatham, so Martha's parents and Maria, the older sister, looked after the children. One incident springs to mind regarding Mother's habitual Saturday shopping trips. This particular Saturday, Mother's regular schedule was changed. She arrived earlier and found her daughter a little tipsy. You see, our hired help brewed their own beer, so apparently, and meaning no harm, they had given me beer to drink and the rest is history. These are only but a few pleasant memories of my childhood.

* * *

Already, I had experienced the death of my grandfather, Médéric Caron, on May 4th 1924, when I was five years old. Death was doubly traumatic because of the fact that the body was laid out for two days or so in the very house they had lived in. I must agree. It was more realistic and we would learn to cope at a much younger age.

My next encounter with death was at the age of six, with the passing of Mrs. Ladislas (Alma) Trudell Caron born September 29, 1890, married April 22, 1912 and died May 31, 1926, leaving nine children. I remember the shock we experienced as school children seeing her dear children struggling with the loss of their beloved mother. From grade one to grade eight, it was a steady solemn procession of school children walking to the house where the Caron's lived and where the deceased lay. The whole community was in mourning. To this day, it's still vivid in my mind.

* * *

At the age of five, I started school at the Town Hall on the Bear Line. This was a one room public school, and our land was assessed to that district. The teacher, Marie-Jeanne Massie, was the bilingual teacher, from Alexandria, Ontario. Later, she married Amédée Bélanger, a prominent farmer on the third concession of Dover. She was very well loved and a devoted teacher. She was teaching eight grades comprising of thirty and many times forty students or more. She was bilingual but French was restricted to one hour a day under the famous Regulation "Law 17." Officers would check at least once a month with no specific announcements. Our main language was French, so this law brought many restrictions and heartaches to French Canadian parents and ratepayers.

On a lighter note, grades seven and eight, especially the 12 to 14 year old boys, were not always exemplary models. They constantly annoyed the teacher but many were good students. The grown up boys, if I remember correctly, were the Tom Béchard's: Léo, Adélard; the Joe Robert's: Oscar, Réginald; the Eugène Caron's: Romain, Urbain, Dominique. I remember stopping after school where the Caron's lived, purposely to see Rosaire. He was one of my schoolgirl crushes and he would generally greet me at the gate. He was only four-years-old.   I would stop and play awhile but his mother would greet me and made sure I was on my way home safely.

She was a lovable person, a devoted mother working for the church and the school. More on these older boys. Mother always packed a good lunch for me, but these unruly guys always managed to have me throw my lunch in the waste paper basket then they would hand me some of their lunch. Evidently I never forgot that. Today, their schoolyard tactics are all very clear to me. My first year in school was quite an adventure but at the same time quite reassuring thanks to a few grown-up girls who cared and helped me to get to and from school. Marie-Anne Faubert, Theresa Gamble and Florine Caron, contributed to my well-being.   Their caring attention made my schooldays that much more pleasant.

The following year, my Father transferred his taxes to the separate school board. So come September, I attended school in Pain Court across from the church, better known as Bob Despin's Garage and much later as the Benoit Restaurant, "Chez Étienne." It was the second year that the Sisters of St. Joseph of London taught in Pain Court. Sister Anna-Marie was principal and taught grades six to eight. Grades one to three had Sister Hilaire and Marie-Louise Pinsonneault taught grades four and five. Next door was the public school but it eventually closed. Later it became the home of André Maure, then his son Joseph Maure and his family took over, followed by Henri Maure and his family.   Today, the property is owned by Rodolphe and Pearl Potvin.

Going to school in Pain Court is where all kinds of magical events took place. At lunch time, grades seven and eight students would toast our sandwiches on a great big pot belly stove, which kept the school comfortable, but on extremely cold days we had to keep our "over shoes" on because the floors were too cold for comfort. Unfortunately my progress was nil. Even at six years old I was still not ready to settle down, yet. I remember scribbling all over my books, until finally, mother visited the school and discussed this with the teacher. That didn't change much either so the teacher decided that I should repeat grade two. Come September, I remember being not too happy losing all my friends to grade three. A month went by, and one day Sister Hilaire came to me with a rope in her hands.

"Well," she said, "if you insist in not doing your work properly, I decided to hang you to the ceiling and let you dry up there." Oh! La! La! That was a threat which was efficient. The situation was very clear to me and right then, things changed for the better. By Christmas, I was transferred to grade three with all my friends. By the year's end, my grades were excellent and I ranked third in the class. The following year I was transferred to grade five. My parents were delighted with my progress. Dad coached me along, especially in reading and public speaking. That year at the school fair, I captured first prize in public speaking with a reassuring and well executed speech, "How I Baked My First Pie." To top this, Father Emery, our parish priest, invited me to the rectory to deliver my speech, just for him. To my surprise, he gave me a beautiful 24" doll, beautifully attired. A beauty. Thereafter, I was determined to do my very best. The following year, in grade six, I received a $5.00 gold coin for a French essay published in "Le Droit." All these incentives propelled me to greater accomplishments. In 1928, we transferred to our new school (St. Catherine) across the road. From December to June, we shared our classroom with grades nine and ten. The following September, I entered grade seven with Marie-Anne Pinsonneault, an excellent teacher. After Christmas, I followed grade eight in the same classroom. There was a great advantage to having two grades in the same room. You could do your work but listen in to the teacher teaching the other grade. By now, this was really pushing it. I had to work hard, I could not do as well as the others but I did manage to pass my written exams in Chatham. This gave me the privilege to enter high school in Pain Court the following September; I was 13 years old.

*   *   *

I do realize I need to go back a few years when I was between six and eight years old. Mother worked in the fields. The babies were left in the car, so she could supervise and attend to our needs. When I was six, every Sunday I had to attend catechism classes for my first communion. Dad sometimes would drive me there, but I had to walk the two miles back. All the kids loved to stop at the store for a pop or an ice cream cone, a box of Cracker Jack, black balls or licorice pipes. We could share a nickel treat with all our friends then. We always left for home on a happy note.

After much preparation at school and on Sundays after mass, "an all you can eat" celebration was called for on July 5, 1925 the day of my first communion.

Another traumatic experience occurred a few weeks later, July 19,1925. It was the sudden death of my 20 month old cousin, Jules Roy. He was my neighbour and I loved this little angel. At this early age, I really didn't understand this encounter with death. Everyone talked of a little angel in heaven. I was all dressed in white, my first communion attire, when I visited him at the house. He was also dressed in white, radiant and beautiful in his coffin. I loved him dearly and refused to reconcile myself to never see him again. Luckily, I had a baby sister, Léontine, to chase away the tears and recapture my childlike and carefree spirit.

On my way home from school the mayflower bushes at Mrs. Eva Trahan attracted my attention. Sure enough I just had to break a few to trim my hair and my shoes. One day I forgot to dispose of them before getting home. Mother noticed and inquired where I had picked those beautiful pink flowers. The truth had to come out.   Mother asked me to hop into the car with her and we drove to Mrs. Trahan's home much to my dismay. I was sent to the door alone to confess. I asked her to forgive me. It was very humiliating but I still loved these flowers. With this ordeal behind me, she gave me permission to take a few but not waste them. It was the principle of taking without asking. To this day, I have these flowering ornamental bushes growing at the cottage in Rondeau Park and they do blossom profusely in May and the early part of June.

*   *   *

By June 1927, Raoul, our first baby brother, appeared on the scene.   I loved him and took good care of him, but the demands on my time and recreation became very limited. Léontine was only 18 months at the time, two babies who needed much care and attention. Yvonne was growing up and could do her share of the work. All this surely was taking its toll in our lives.

*   *   *

With her gardens bearing fruits and vegetables in profusion, Mother cared for our livelihood. To elaborate somewhat, we had two acres of gardening and fruit trees. There were 15 apple trees, five apricot trees, 12 to 15 peach trees, two long rows of raspberries, a large strawberry patch, cherry trees, black currants, melon patches, cucumber patches, and large amounts of sweet corn.

Mother's garden was interlaced with a profusion of flowers. Her friends visited and solicited seeds and roots. At the farm market, she was always a first with cucumbers and melons.

Caroline Roy, Léontine Roy, Raoul Roy, Yvonne Roy
Lot 16 third concession Dover 1928

The Root Cellars

It was called a "Cache," a root cellar for storage. These were made by digging into the bank of the creek about 3 feet deep and 6 to 8 feet across. It was then covered with pieces of wood somewhat like a tent, a tepee with a roof, leaving a door for entrance. This in turn was covered with earth and straw, with an air vent left open at the top. These were carefully sealed against the cold after they had been filled with provisions such as potatoes, apples, cabbage, carrots and all kinds of vegetables. Generally they were opened by mid-March when house supplies had been exhausted. This was our yearly storage.

My interest was the muskmelon patch. Come muskmelon season, I would eye the most perfect ones and save them for the Fall county fairs. Practically every year, I hit the jackpot, with my luscious near perfect cantaloupes. A first prize ribbon attached to my dress boosted my ego, of course, and I paraded around like a proud peacock.

It was Mother's garden and she was a genius at it. May I add that her mother was also known to have special talents and beautiful gardens. Her lovely peonies adorned the outside perimeter of the garden and they were the first bloomers in the area. A master gardener she was. Grandmother's garden consisted of at least half an acre in small vegetables, another half acre in fruit trees with corn and potatoes interlaced between the rows of trees. One half acre was in potatoes for year round use. To have early potatoes, the myth was that they had to be planted on Good Friday, rain or shine or snow. I personally planted some in the furrows prepared by my father when there was two inches of snow on the ground. In those days, most of the crops were planted according to the position of the moon. I was taught, in my early years, many good points relating to the phases of the moon and frankly I still adhere to these meteorological beliefs which is part of our folklore.

Every year the depression was changing our way of life. That meant more preserves, more gardening. Mother worked diligently preserving about 300 two-quart jars of peaches, raspberries, cherries, strawberries, another 100 two-quart jars of tomatoes and some 50 jars of cooked corn. We did a lot of homemade jams, namely crab apple, grape, strawberries, currant and raspberries. Name it, we had it on the shelves in the fruit cellar neatly stored and labelled. Cucumbers were put up in five gallon crocks, a 30 gallon crock was used for dills.
In the middle 30s, we were experiencing a full-blown depression and it was not easy. In order that sufficient supplies would be available to last the winter, more and more preserves had to be stored. Raising fowls was a must for the home and also to supply customers' demands at the Chatham Market. Every year hundreds of chickens were raised, together with 50 to75 turkeys and as many ducks to supply the Christmas market.

With four cows and sometimes five, we had our milk, cream and butter. Surplus amounts were readily picked up by customers at the Chatham Market. The Market Square stood where now stands the new parking garage and Sears Mall. Since then, the Eaton's Department Store has been demolished. Across from Eaton's were five butcher shops with fresh-cut meats for your special needs. Next to Eaton's parking lot was Soutar's seed store and further down, Smith's seed store. To accommodate people with horses and buggies, there were posts at the end of the Market Square. I loved to go to the Market. It was more like a meeting place, a social gathering of sorts, as everyone knew each other. The market's interior was decorated with all kinds of fowl, very well displayed, a host of articles, crafts, flowers, homemade baked goods. If you were looking for something in the line of food, you were sure to find it at the Market. City people and country folk alike had a wide variety of things to choose from, something for everyone's taste and needs. For example, you could you could buy a five-pound yellow corn fed chicken adorned with a sprig of fresh parsley for $1.25. Real genuine golden broth for chicken soup or sliders or chicken pot pie. I call it "soul food" at its best.

If you had too many parcels to carry, young lads with wagons would help you carry all this to your car or buggy for a nickel or a dime. It made their day. It was a simple pleasure of life to go from stall to stall with a big basket on your arm admiring all the exhibits so meticulously displayed. And it had its special aroma - enticing and homy.

Everyone pitched in to try and bring home a contribution to family needs. Every nickel and dime were much appreciated by the children willing to work while helping others.

Furthermore, the Indians and gypsies also were at the entrance of the downstairs Market. They had a huge selection of woven baskets in so many attractive colours. The scent of freshly woven baskets was soothing and pleasant. Actually this market area consisted of two streets, one block long. Soutar's and Smith's seed stores also met the farmers' needs. It was a pleasure to go to the open market lined on both streets. It was fashionable and usually it was a special treat to be at a restaurant for lunch. The "Rendez-vous" was a top priority for lunch, 25¢ for a bowl of soup and crackers or a bowl of chili. Every Saturday, a beef stew special was 75¢ with coffee, a hot pork or hot beef sandwich was 85¢ with coffee included. In my teen years, I was a waitress at the "Rendez-vous" and helped Uncle Jacob Roy on weekends. A nickel tip was most welcome. Everything was cooked fresh daily. These are fond memories. Remembering Aunt Georgina and Aunt Mélina, Uncles Jacob Roy and Francis Roy; an assortment of fresh luscious pies for the restaurants, baked daily in their big kitchen in Pain Court where now stand the Central Hotel and the grocery store.

*   *   *

It is interesting to note that Grays China Hall is the only store standing and operating in the same location in Chatham today. This landmark, then, attracted customers from far and near, and today, its trademark had never lost its appeal. Browsing is a feast for the eyes and buying, a fulfilling experience of genuine salesmanship. Sixty years ago, I bought my first mantel clock and my first Wedgewood chinaware with the money from the produce and fowls sold at this same market.

It's a pleasure to dwell on these fantastic and precious memories even if it did represent hard work and patience for everyone.

"Dress Code"

With the opening of our new school at Pain Court in 1928, also came the new ruling, that everyone would wear uniforms. Even though some were dissatisfied with the ruling nothing changed. Eventually everyone complied.

I was in grade 5 and I always wore uniforms throughout grade school and through high school. Sometimes mother experienced problems with white blouses as they were easily soiled. I remember mother washing blouses at night, hang them over the stove to dry so they would be ready to wear in the morning. We only had one blouse each in depression days.

My years at the "Pines" in Chatham were no different, everyone wore uniforms in the 30s and thereafter.

Services and Utilities

"Let's reminisce on facilities and services at that time."

Bathroom facilities were outside and primitive, as I recall. Toilet paper was a luxury. Therefore old newspapers piled in one corner of the outhouse, ready to be recycled, was the norm and it served the purpose. In the winter months, we had "chamber pots" upstairs and glad to use them. Many mishaps did arise due to these fancy and not so fancy portable granite loos. Many a tale can be spun around these conversation pieces. No matter what, it was not the most agreeable of chores. You were a lucky victim if you safely discarded its contents and unlucky if you walked on shaky ground.

Most families in the country did not have running water. We were privileged to have a 500 gallon cement tank for holding the rain water to do the washing. Hand pumps were upstairs so we could bathe, wash the clothes and dishes. For drinking water, we had brick wells, one for drinking and cooking, and a second one to water the horses, the cattle, pigs and milking the cows.

Monday was generally wash day. Tide, Cheer and Wisk soaps were unknown then, but homemade soap bars were plentiful. Louella Caron and Thérèse Donlon, two venturesome ladies of the 90s, still make their own soap from time to time, for their own usage. This is how Louella Caron concocts a batch of 100% pure extract. Lard is collected in various containers, then boiled in water to extract all the salt. Then lye is sprinkled slowly over the lard, being very cautious not to burn yourself, and then mixing it well. This mixture is left to cool for a day, then it is cut up in bars. Generally, you have to let the soap cure and wait a few weeks before usage. One pouring yields two or three dozen bars. The soap was also used to whiten clothes. White linen was placed in huge copper boilers and allowed to boil on the stove for one hour. This process made for a very steamy kitchen.

Le pavage de la rue principale à Pain Court vers 1921

Ref. Pain Court et Grande Pointe,
Paul-François Sylvestre p. 41

15e Congrès Eucharistique Diocésain tenu à Pain Court le 19 août 1926

**Ecce Quam Bonum Et Quam Jucundum
Habitare Fratres In Unum**

Une des pages insérées dans le programme souvenir du 75e.

The 75th Anniversary Celebration
Of Our Parish 1926

*Char dans le défilé du jubilé de diamant célébré à Pain Court
le 5 et 6 juillet 1926. Caroline Roy (7 ans) assise, et 4 ^{e} de gauche à droite.*
Photo : Gracieuseté de Roland Bélanger

The year 1926 remains forever memorable in the history of our parish. Men, women and children put their heart and soul into this project. I was seven years old at the time.

I was on the float amongst a group of children dressed in Indian costumes. Our teacher was Clara Caron. She managed to teach us an Indian song of which I can only remember very little of its refrain:

> "C'était un p'tit sauvage, wish té,
> Tout noir tout barbouillé, wish té,
> S'en va à la rivière, wish té,
> Pour y baigner ses pieds, wish té,
> T'in a wishtin a gush kish kot."   à répéter

Everybody loves a parade and more so, children, whose only outings were either parochial or family gatherings. It was the horse and buggy era. There were sheds, two blocks long and two wide, where the parking lot now stands. The horses were tied to the posts inside these sheds, awaiting their masters who were either attending church services or had other commitments.

My uncle Jacob Roy directed the famous play "Les martyrs Canadiens." This was an evening performance of great magnitude. Witnessing grown-up men acting as missionaries being tortured and Brébeuf tied to a post and being burned had an impact beyond comprehension. To this day I can visualize these scenes. People gave their time, their talents and put their heart and soul into promoting the history of our community. Franceline Cadotte, my sweet and lovable friend, executed a special dance on stage for this event and its rerun is on the parish video 1995.

Furthermore the ladies of the parish saw to it that there was plenty of food served for two days, since hundreds came from afar to visit. I enjoy reminiscing over these memorable events which took place in our parish, historical events to love and cherish. A temporary stage was mounted in front of the rectory. My parents were very much involved in the parish activities and so were all the parishioners.
L'union fait la force!

Le Père Emery

Le Père Emery assume la tâche considérable de composer un livre sur l'histoire de Pain Court et de ses concitoyens afin de commémorer le jubilé de diamant de la paroisse. Ce livre bien illustré et documenté est de grande valeur. Une seconde édition a été publié en 1995, projet entrepris par le Club d'âge d'or, car il y avait grande demande par les jeunes familles.

1ère rangée g. à d. (en avant) - Gérard Béchard, (W. Médard), Réal Béchard, Régis Caron, Lionel Thibodeau, Roland Caron, Aurèle Roy, Adrien Caron, Elzéar Goure ?, Arsène Goudreau, Norman Bélanger, Roland Gagner.

2e rangée g. à d. - Alfred Pinsonneault, Roméo Trahan ?, Célina Goure, Dorothy Caron, Bella Goure, Géraldine Maure, Florence Béchard, Pauline Caron, Éveline Gagner, Germaine Pinsonneault, Blanche Caron, Armand Roy, Philippe Béchard.

3e rangée g. à d. - Godfrey Maure, Lena Robert, Laurentia Caron, _____, Antoinette Bourdeau, Régis Clairmant, Roméo Thibodeau, Alcide Béchard, Cécile Goure, Léona Caron, Victoria Maure.

Photo: gracieuseté de Rosita Robert Blais -
        identification des élèves-par Régis Caron.

Nouvelle École - 1928

En octobre 1928, la commission scolaire décide de bâtir une nouvelle école paroissiale car le nombre des enfants d'âge scolaire avait tellement augmenté. J'étais en 6e année, lors du déménagement dans la nouvelle école Ste-Catherine. La première directrice de la dite école séparée à Pain Court fut Soeur Anna-Marie en 1923, de la communauté des Soeurs Saint-Joseph.

Ce fut la dernière oeuvre du Père Emery car il quitte la paroisse en novembre 1928 en route pour St-Joachim. Son coeur n'avait pas oublié les enfants de Pain Court, car en juin 1929 il invite tous les enfants d'école de se rendre à St-Joachim pour une belle fête de fin d'année. Comme il n'y avait pas d'autobus, des gros camions nous ont transporté à cette belle grandiose fête remplie de charme et de souvenirs.

Ci-dessus :École Ste-Catherine érigée en 1928

À droite :   Soeur Corinne Renaud connue sous le nom de Soeur Anna-Marie.
Elle a joui d'une longue retraite bien méritée au Mont St-Joseph à London, Ont.

Blé d'Inde "Essivé"

Rassemblés autour de la grande table de cusine, chacun se sucrait le bec avec son petite bol rempli de blé d'Inde "essivé" arrosée de mélasse ou de gros sirop "Bee Hive."

Le blé d'Inde "essivé" (lessivé) est un régal du Père Boudreau et bien d'autres d'ailleurs. C'est un de ces mets du bon vieux temps apprêtés par ces femmes depuis longtemps trempées dans le métier.

Pour quelques-uns, c'est un plat spécial de leur grand-mère. Pour d'autres, si la mémoire est bonne, ce serait peut-être de la trisaïeule ou serait-ce une de ces recettes jalousement conservée d'une génération à l'autre? N'importe. Ces fruits de la terre si minutieusement mariés avec les fines herbes du potager et aromatisés de tendresse suffisaient pour apaiser tous les soucis quotidiens.

Vous voyez, toute la cuisine se faisait en concordance avec la bonne terre de chez-nous.

"Là où est le coeur est le trésor," comme le dit un vieux dicton. Oui, ces bonne-femmes avaient l'âme tellement rapprochée du sol que chaque plat confectionné avait sa saveur unique.

Eh! bien, l'apprêtage du blé d'Inde "essivé," comme le prononçait vulgairement nos ancêtres, est un de ces plats dont je me rappelle lorsque ma mère, à l'approche de l'hiver, nous donnait l'ordre d'aller cueillir de beaux épis de blé d'Inde mûrs pour la préparation du blé d'Inde essivé.

Une fois le blé d'Inde égrainé et déposé dans une cuvette remplie d'eau, on l'arrose avec un peu de lessi et on laisse le tout tremper pendant plusieurs heures pour amollir ou adoucir les grains. Puis on fait de multiples lavages à l'eau claire. Une fois bien lavé, on ajoute du bicarbonate de soude pour aider à la fermentation. Ensuite la cuvette est bien placée au froid où il y a possibilité de gel pour en assurer la conservation.

Au bout de 10 jours, le blé d'Inde lessivé est prêt à être consommé, soit rôti avec de la graisse de bacon, soit ajouté à la soupe du jour, soit encore servi comme dessert avec du gros sirop. Quel régal pour ceux qui jeûnaient durant le carême!

On conservait le blé d'Inde fermenté au gel. Il y avait toujours du blé d'Inde égrainé conservé dans un sac de coton blanc; ce sac était placé dans une pièce bien au sec.

Lorsqu'on voulait préparer une 2e ou même un 3e cuvée de blé d'Inde essivé, on n'avait qu'à piger dans le sac de coton.

Dans la même chambre, il y avait plusieurs poches de blé d'Inde à éclater de 3 à 4 variétés au moins. Dans cette même dépense on retrouvait des cordes de pommes séchées. Comme nous avions une centaine de pommiers, c'était facile d'en avoir pendues sur des cordes durant l'hiver.

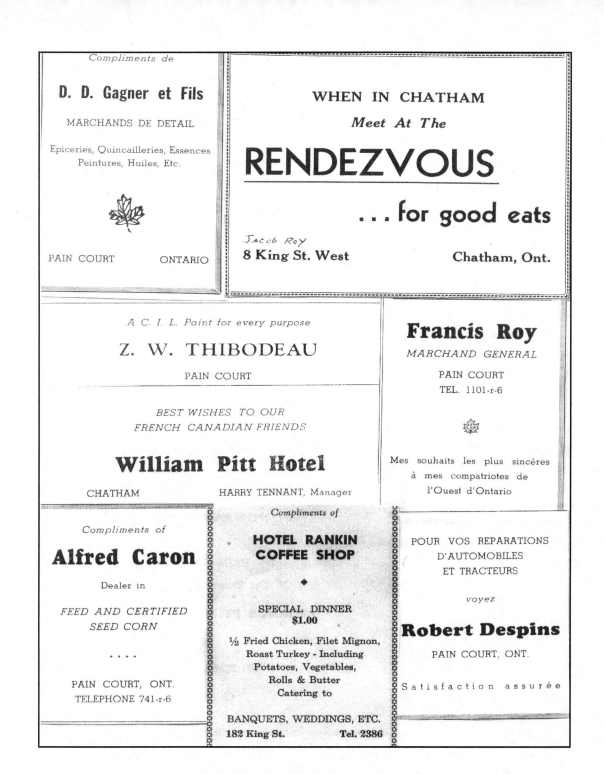
Way of life of Pioneers

Life was hard, no question about it. Neighbours helped neighbours, and entertainment was in the homes. Winters were pleasant with card playing at least once a week at different neighbours. Each neighbour took turns to celebrate "Mardi Gras," pancake turnover. This I loved to be invited to, but as I grew up, I had to babysit my brothers and sisters so my parents could participate. This was a real pleasure party. The frustration of receiving a pancake in the face was the ultimate. For revenge the pancakes flew. As weeks passed, young and old still talked about the Pancake Turnover.

PICNICS - FISH PONDS - 1926 - 1950

Picnics and fish ponds were synonymous words. Since 1926, Mrs. D.D.Gagner and Mrs. Eugène Caron were always at the fish pond booths. They cared a lot about children and they knew what made them happy. They understood children and knew that they loved to fish at the pond at all picnics.

At this time, children were very happy to have 25¢ to spend and 50¢ in some privileged instance. So you could fish a surprise bag for a nickel or a dime. Fortunately this meant we would enjoy something for our money, something to take back home. Mrs. Helena Gagner who operated a store knew what children were interested in. So did Mrs. Eugène Caron. They wrapped and wrapped gifts by the hundreds as this was always the main attraction for children. Everyone surely expressed happiness at the fish pond. By 1950, gifts for the pond had to meet much more extravagant tastes and gifts had to be more expensive, thereby bringing less profit for the annual St-Jean-Baptiste celebration, on June 24th.

Bureau de Poste

La vie continue mais nous sommes toujours en pleine dépression.   En 1936, Alphy Cheff s'occupe du bureau de poste de Pain Court. C'est alors que Francis Roy, voulant aider son beau-père commence le service de livraison du courrier dans les routes rurales. Vers 1930, il se décide de faire en même temps la livraison du pain. Les habitants sont heureux et apprécient ce service de porte en porte. On achète un pain pour 5 sous, une aubaine. Mais environ un an plus tard, le pain se vend à 7 sous.   Ma mère déclare qu'à l'avenir il faudra boulanger deux fois la semaine. Ce n'était pas facile à 12 ans de pétrir une quinzaine de pains le matin avant mon départ pour l'école . . . une distance de deux milles. C'était parfois très difficile, je vous l'assure. Ma mère besognait avec les plus petits. Plus tard, des vendeurs de viande, vendeurs de lait frappèrent à nos portes. Leurs tournées réguliaires allégeaient la tâche des cuisinières.

The Butchers

Do you recall when the butcher started his rounds, delivering fresh meat with his little truck equipped with a proper refrigeration unit? Householders were grateful to have Mr. Edmundson taking care of their needs for frozen meats. He started peddling from early spring to late fall, twice a week and covered a wide area from Chatham to Pain Court and the surrounding district. He had different cuts of beef or pork, and wieners tied together, pork sausages, cold meats, 10 to 12 lb. pieces of bologna from the processing plants. Also he would take orders for the next delivery. Meats were cut to specifications and that was another plus for this most welcome and dedicated Mr. Edmundson.

In winter, farmers had their own cattle and pigs. As the freezing season began, the wood shed, the garage, the basement entrance would serve as a freezer. Neighbours would get together and slaughter a 1000 lb. cattle and they each bought a quarter and hung it in their sheds. After ten days of freezing temperatures, they would call this period "curing" it was time to cut the roasts as required. The same applied to pigs. It was a different way of life as compared to the era of the nineties. Nonetheless it was a happy period, because people were concerned about each other.

Barn Raising Event

In 1928, disaster struck. It was a hard year, and tobacco was down to 3¢ a pound, the crash of the stock market and the grain market. Our tobacco barn burnt down, arson was suspected but never proven. This added insult to injury in these depression days. Then followed the rebuilding of a barn during the summer months.

Barn raising was a memorable event for hundreds of people. Our barn was built in 1928 by Narcisse Laprise, a renowned barn builder of the community who came to Pain Court in 1867. He had no schooling, but in his own way could figure exactly the amount of square feet of lumber he needed to build this barn. From the top of his head his quick calculations were identical to those with advanced calculating abilities.

The fir beams came directly from British Columbia, transported here by railroad cars, unloaded unto wagons, and horse drawn to the construction site on the creek road in Dover, 2 miles from the village of Pain Court.

Twelve to fourteen men were on the job every day for more than three months. These men were fed two meals a day during this whole process. I was ten years old and was mother's helper at the peak of the summer holidays. To add to all this work, mother was expecting a baby, Bernard, born October 24, 1928. Moreover, some women would give a hand from time to time but that also meant extra people to feed. Rest assured if this was today, they would have a bucket lunch. How amazing that mother managed to do all these menial tasks! She was special. In early September, the barn was ready to raise. The largest barn built in our area. One hundred men were asked to volunteer, pulling the cables to get some 24 trusses in place. With them came their wives, children and friends to witness this event. Yah! Yah!Yah! Yahu! It was an impressive and a spectacular event. After everything was said and done, men were welcome to all the beer they could handle. Many kegs. What a happy crowd helping and enjoying themselves! By 6 p.m., it was time for a wonderful lunch. Ladies had helped to make sandwiches for a full day. Others provided cakes and pies that could rival any bakery. It surely was a community spirit at its best. Since then, I cannot remember another barn raising of any size. It was the last "chef d'oeuvre" of this worthy master and ingenious carpenter, Narcisse Laprise, my husband's grandfather and great-grandfather to all our children.

Three sons, Joseph, Gilbert and Donat, worked side by side with their father Narcisse, learning to cut beams with an axe, cut wedges at certain angles to make mortise joints so the beams would fit within one another at various angles and become a very solid piece of structure finished with wooden pegs.

Les années 1925 à 1930

Voici que la construction est terminée en 1928 mais hélas, pour ma mère c'était pénible. Le 24 octobre elle donne naissance à notre cher petit frère Bernard. Elle se sent dépourvue et épuisée par le ménage de la maison et l'entretien de 4 enfants et un nouveau né, Bernard. Nous essayons d'alléger sa tâche mais c'est pas facile. Maman semble toujours aimable en dépit des soucis et laisse rarement entrevoir sa fatigue.

Vers la fin de la 2ᵉ décennie, il y avait beaucoup de changements, et bien des événements mémorables ont marqué ma vie à cette époque. Ma nouvelle demeure à Pain Court, ma première communion, la mort de petits Jules, mon séjour à l'école. En 1926, la maladie et la mort de ma grand-mère Charline que j'aimais tellement. Le son de son violon n'y sera plus, ses taquineries amusantes seront du passé, la chaleur de son amitié ne sera que des souvenirs. Hélas, le temps passe et la grande dépression éprouve notre courage et s'acharne à notre existence. Mon cher grand-père, Thomas Roy, devenu veuf, semble succomber aux forces de l'ennui et de la maladie. À peine trois ans se sont écoulés et voilà que la mort vient frapper mon grand-père Roy en avril 1930. Il avait 74 ans. Déjà pour moi, âgée de 11 ans, j'étais marqué de plusieurs deuils, car tous ces êtres étaient chers. Durant au moins trois ans je visitais avec mon père, mon arrière grand'mère Bridget Hickey, mère de mon grand-père Thomas Roy. Elle était très âgée et fut admise à l'hôpital St-Joseph, où nous la visitions. Le 6 décembre 1931, elle aussi nous laissa pour une destinée meilleure. Elle était âgée de 95 ans. La perte de ces personnes chères envahit mon existence pour un certain temps. C'est alors qu'il faut reprendre courage pour faire face à de sinistres situations causées par la dépression. En 1932, nous déménageons, cette fois-ci, sur la terre paternelle de mon ancêtre, Thomas Roy.

Sleeping Accommodations

There were many bedrooms in our house but the heating system consisted mainly of primitive wood-burning stoves. Only one or two bedrooms would be heated, one for the parents and one for the children. The conductor of heat throughout the house was a stovepipe, 6" across, connected to the stove downstairs, emerging through a hole in the ceiling, criss-crossing the rooms to be heated, and leading to another opening in the brick chimney upstairs. As the family grew, there were up to three children sleeping in one bed.

As we grew older, we went in the cornfields and filled bags and bags of corn leaves and husks to make mattresses. It sounds quite primitive, but it was more comfortable than an ordinary straw mattress.

As the years went by, we managed to have down-filled mattresses on our bed. We were raising geese and ducks, so with time, goose feather ticks adorned each bed in the house. Duck feathers were salvaged also but the quality did not match the feathery goose down.

Our nightly acrobatic feat was to toss and fluff the feather ticks as high as we could. Then one by one we'd line up, and with a good head start, we ran as fast as we could, plunging headfirst into the 18 to 20 inch pile of soft down, amidst shrieks of fun and laughter. A scurry of footsteps pitter-pattered about until a gruff voice from below sounded the alarm. Reluctantly, we turned in exhausted and ready to count sheep.

Many years elapsed before a store-bought mattress was affordable for each bed in the house, although our parents did have a quality one on their iron bed long before we did. This was logical because they worked very hard and did earn a good night's rest.

Decade of the "THIRTIES"

We are now facing the decade of the thirties. Mostly everyone felt those oppressing years. It became a matter of survival as revenues from the land were barely enough to survive. Once a month, bags of oats and wheat, at least 20 of them, were loaded onto a wagon ready for delivery the next day. For economical purposes, the neighbours would join in by adding a few bags of their own to form one big load for the chopping mill.

At daybreak, my father would hitch the team of horses to a fully loaded wagon ready to be transported to the Taylor Mill Company. Passing by way of Grand Ave. and King St., the wooden iron-rimmed wagon wheel, buckling under an excessive overload, would squeak and screech on the cobblestoned street led by a team of two horses grudgingly pulling their charge, clippety-clopping along in unison till they reached the Taylor Milling Company on William St. By 5 o'clock, they would return with multiple bags of rolled oats and flour. The oats were used for oatmeal, porridge and other baking goods. We had a special room to house the supplies for winter. I recall a stocked room with 5oo pounds of sugar, barrels of flour from the milling company, barrels of oatmeal, at least a dozen ten-pound pails of syrup for pancakes, a variety of barley and rice and two barrels of dried white beans and dried peas for garnishing different soups. So together with chicken, cows, pork and beef, everyone managed to survive. All winter long, we had a good variety of apples, bushels and bushels of them. You can add to this bounty hundreds of jars of various canned fruits. We did not have a car, then, which caused more hardships, but the same was true for many of the people around us, so together, we did strive to make life more bearable.

By 1932, the banks were closing in on many farmers as well as city people. Some lost their homes, others lost their farms. Landlords had difficulties also because people did not pay their rents or their mortgages. They had to survive first.

For our family, it meant moving to another place and financed by the government "Farm Credit" so we could buy another farm.

From 1933- 35, a 100 acre cleared farm with a house, sold for $7,500. to $8,000., bearing interest at 5%. In 1940, a partly cleared farm with a house sold for $4,000. to $5,000. for 50 acres. It was practically impossible to find any lenders. No one seemed capable of risking anything. This period surely took its toll on the welfare and morale of the people. Furthermore, there was no electricity and no natural gas lines in the rural areas, to keep us warm. It was only later that they started drilling wells for natural gas, south of the village of Pain Court.

These formative years moulded our character and surely put forward our intellectual and moral values. The decade of the nineties seems to bring forth once again these fundamental values, as people struggle once more with monies and with their way of life. It seems unthinkable in this world of affluence, that poverty is once again lurking at our doors as well as those of every country of the world.

LIFE GOES ON

My sister, Loretta, was born in 1931, the depression era. Regardless, this was a special event for a 12-year-old as I was chosen to be her godmother and Joseph Roy as the godfather, a very special first cousin of mine.

In that year, I did compile interesting facts from Loretta's files. A new car could be bought for $640.00, a new house with moderate needs, $6,796.00, a loaf of bread 8¢, a gallon of gas for 10¢, a gallon of milk for 50¢, Amaco razor blades 4 for 25¢, gold was $20.67 and ounce, Dow Jones average was 138, and life expectancy in 1931 was 59.7 years.

How did we celebrate this special event? Well my father took us to the airport, just newly opened, for our first aeroplane ride. The ride was thrilling, the scenery never to be forgotten. Witnessing a baptism and being propelled in the beautiful open skies made one's day heavy with schedules and excitement. Having a godchild added extra duties to my curriculum, you see, because I was determined to honour my commitments as best as I could . . . I was twelve and my sister Yvonne was nine. Between the two of us we managed to give mother the help that she needed with our two brothers, Raoul and Bernard.

At this stage, my homework was piling up as I was expected to complete grades seven and eight in one school year. Trying to juggle both, household chores and the double load of home-work, with good marks as an end result, proved to be a challenging school year. Nevertheless when September rolled around, I entered high school at 13.

This same year, we were making a new start on another farm and another home. Those were menial and meagre times. Saturday was washing, and scrub day on a scrub board. Many times, tears rolled down and fingers were sore. As expected, progress kicked in, somewhat, by 1933. We had a gasoline powered engine to do the washing. What a relief! It was noisy but it did alleviate blisters and sore fingers.

Mother had her hands full and really deserved this luxury, in order to overcome these hard-ships. Everyone was conscious of the circumstances and consequently we tried to care for each other. Cooking, baking, washing and caring for very young Edmond, who was only six months old, my sister Loretta barely two years old and my brother Bernard five years old, seemed like an over-whelming task for our mother. Psychologically, it was devastating as this period of the early 30s was a time of drastic changes for children, but especially for parents struggling to survive.

After working mercilessly all summer, a special day was set aside to go shopping. Generally, it was the week before the start of school year in September. We came home with a new pair of shoes, pencils, ruler, erasers, scribblers and needed books. Furthermore, we always went to Pete Karry's Restaurant once a year for a "Banana Split": three big scoops of ice cream, 2 vanilla and 1 chocolate, sliced bananas sprinkled with nuts and decorated with three maraschino cherries, for a whole quarter. An extra treat was at least 5 doz. bananas to bring home which sold for 25¢ a doz. How we appreciated everything is unbelievable!

We were also promised a whole branch of bananas from "Zakoor" market next door to C.P.R. station, in Chatham for Christmas. This was hung from the ceiling for us to eat and enjoy at Christmas time. There was also a crate of oranges to savour, but other gifts, there were none, except card games and one piece of clothing. Toys and dolls and trucks, we did not have, but nevertheless we seemed to be happy and guess what? We survived.

There was always work for everyone around the house. Everyone pitched in. Once a week the floor boards in the kitchen had to be scrubbed. After a few years, we managed to buy a linoleum. For an instant shine, we washed it with milk. For most members of the family, their task was to bring in pieces of wood but for us then, it was bushel baskets of corn cobs used to heat the house and do the cooking. We had over 100 apple trees, and as fall rolled around every Saturday was cooking time. Mother would roll the crust, and we'd peel apples to make at least 20 pies on week ends. Her pies were super scrumptious. Cakes were available but only on Sunday, a two-layered hot jelly cake. Mom's version was deliciously sweetened with brown sugar and cinnamon, sandwiched with homemade raspberry jam, and smothered in "real" thick whipped cream. For our school lunch, we seldom had dessert but we always had apples. Many kids at school never had apples, so we traded an apple for a piece of cake, an orange or a tart. This made everybody happy.

Pain Court Barber

Just across the street from the church, now an empty lot, there once stood a small white frame house which still holds a lot of memories. In the 20s and 30s Mr. and Mrs. Joseph Cadotte and their large family resided there. Their children attended school next door where now stands the "Benoit Restaurant" formerly the well-known "Robert Despins Garage" in Pain Court.

When the Cadotte family decided to move to larger quarters, Aurèle Roy rented the little back kitchen from his grandfather, Régis Trudell, and started the "Pain Court Barber Shop." It was quite an entrepreneurial feat for a 16-year-old student. And besides he had the knack to attract customers. To accommodate his young clientele he would cut hair from 4 p.m. to 6 p.m. Later he extended his hours to 10 p.m. for grownups. Because of his thriving business, he now could afford his 25¢ specials: "Two for the price of one until 6 p.m. for school children and the same for adults with the special extended till 8 p.m." A walk in service. It was first come first serve. Business tripled and he extended his hours to 10 p.m. He earned a fair income at the time and became a very special barber in the area for about 10 years.

As years went by, it became imperative for him to raise his price to $1.00. This was not particularly welcomed by some. By 1940, he retired from the barber shop and was farming full time.

At the age of 28, Aurèle, son of Léo Roy and Ursule Trudell married Laurienne Caron, daughter of Alphy Caron and Elizabeth Fisher, on December 27, 1943. They later settled on a farm in Raleigh township close to CFCO Towers. They farmed in that vicinity all their lives until Aurèle's death in 1983. Laurienne needed courage and understanding to accomplish the mission she did so well.

In addition, Aurèle had skill and successful interests as a portrait and landscape artist. As a tribute to his artistic talents, many homes in our surrounding district proudly grace their walls with Aurèle's oil paintings.

This white frame house was also occupied by the family of Philippe Blais Sr. and it served the family well. Disaster struck this home on January 20, 1948 and it was burnt to the ground, leaving them without shelter. Without any delays, the parish organized a fund for food and clothing. The men gave their time to build a house. The fine community spirit which prevailed was demonstrated with the completion in 16 days of a substantial seven room house for the Blais family who were devastated by this fire.

The Sugar Beet Era

At the time of this writing, a new spark has ignited the sugar beet industry in our area - Canada and Dominion Sugar Co. closed its doors 30 years ago, against the claim of sugar beet growers. In 1996 the swing of the pendulum is trying to bring back the sugar beet industry.

At that time, External Affairs Minister Paul Martin Sr. in an interview said the announcement came without any notice and shouldn't have been done without at least notifying us: "I, along with the Minister of Agriculture, went to great pains for this industry and I am not going to give up."

The American refineries had a pilot project to revive the industry in our area in 1996, enlisting a few farmers for their pilot research on sugar beets. Three hundred acres were harvested in 1997 with all sugar beets transported to an American Company in Michigan.

My father, Adolphe Roy, was a prominent sugar beet farmer in the thirties. He was well versed in the cultivation and harvesting of the crop. At that time, and much later, it served farmers well. It was a stable industry with guaranteed income.

As sugar beet labour was hard tedious work, immigrants from France and Belgium came to Canada and to our area to thin sugar beets. There were very few jobs available and wages were $1.00 a day but thinning the sugar beets brought $6.00 an acre, considered good money in the thirties. You were very lucky if you managed one acre a day. I myself at 13 - 14 could only do three quarters of an acre and it was very hard work. My father had 25 to 30 acres every year. Beet planting started in mid May, followed by thinning during the month of June, then once or twice more during the summer. By the end of September it was harvest time, but delaying the harvest added to sugar contents which was of utmost importance, as farmers were paid extra for sugar contents.

In 1925, electric cars had been running for many years. Unfortunately, about two miles of the tracks were removed from Pain Court. There was still a distance remaining to deliver sugar beets to Chatham. A weigh station was installed near the tracks immediately across the farm of Rosaire Sterling today on the 4th concession in Dover. Miss Valerie Sterling, then 17 - 18, was the attendant at the weigh station. I remember her as a very pleasant, beautiful and intelligent young woman. I accompanied my father to the station with every load of beets. Not for pleasure, but to work and help him. I was to empty by hand, the four corners of the wagon, so he could manage to shuffle the beets with a special fork into the box cars on the track. Nothing was easy at that time, as everything was done by hand. Later, farmers could also weigh hogs at the weigh station and load them in special box cars to be sold and delivered to distant points. As the years went by, trucks and special wagons were equipped to haul these beets directly to the factory. I remember beautiful teams of horses pulling 10 to 15 tons of beets out of the fields, to be delivered to Chatham. These hard-working men were the "Caron's": Romain, Urbain. So was Harvey Caron, another dedicated farmer's son toiling in the beet fields at harvest time, to make a few extra dollars together with the Béchard boys: Adelard, Harvey and Ernie.

Sugar beet plant

Adolphe King wears a smile when talking about his beet crop. He is seen in his 1938 beet field just after thinning. Adolphe has been very successful with sugar beets.

Ref. C&D Sugar flyer 1938

By 1930, there were rumours to close the weigh station and finally by 1932 most tracks were removed.

By 1934 and for the next 4 years, when the beet season started, we did not go to school until all the beets had been harvested. Father would uproot the beets by machine. Our job was to pull them out of the ground, shake them to loosen the soil, then throw them in piles. Then with a sickle or knife equipped with a hook, we managed to cut the leaves off, and throw them in a heaping pile for the men to load them up into a large wagon for delivery to the Chatham factory. Whatever we managed to do in a day, they tried to deliver it the following day. The manpower needed for these operations was unbelievable.

We were all involved: my seven year old brother Ralph, six year old Bernard, together with Yvonne 12 and Léontine 10. By December, we were glad to leave the beet fields to resume our school year. It seems as if nothing was very humorous then. All work and very little play. Yet Yvonne always managed to crack up some stupid jokes to make us laugh. This was the survival of the fittest in the thirties.

In 1996 mechanical innovations has made enormous strides towards harvesting sugar beets.

```
╔══════════════════════════════════════╗
║                                        ║
║   NOUS FAISONS LE COMMERCE DE          ║
║   TOUTES LES SORTES DE GRAINS          ║
║   de Semence et d'Alimentation, Pôteaux║
║   de Cêdre, Engrais Chimiques,         ║
║   Concentres "Roe"                     ║
║   N. & G. ROY                          ║
║   PAIN COURT                           ║
║   Téléphone 1113 r 13                  ║
║                                        ║
╚══════════════════════════════════════╝
```

Well, it is amazing to note that an ordinary farmer by the name of Alfred Caron, son of Médéric Caron of Pain Court decided to go into grain dealing. He had a big truck and transported grains from the farm to various points in Ontario. He had a very thriving business during the thirties and forties until he met a sudden tragic death in October 1949, while dynamiting tree stumps on his property. He was 61 years old.

At this same period, two enterprising King boys - Gérard Roy King and Napoléon Roy King, both sons of Henri Roy of Pain Court started an operation with an old Ford truck in 1930. They were delivering grains to chopping mills and to all markets available. In 1933, they upgraded their operation to a Chevrolet truck. Business was prospering in an old shed on the property where King Grain now stands. There they had a cleaning mill for the grain which made their product more saleable and enviable, thereby bringing more success to their enterprise. By 1934, they continued with a brand new Dodge truck, bigger and better to assure more progress. By this time, Gérard made most deliveries and he was making contact with many processors, making the enterprise more accessible to gain orders for future deliveries. In 1934, a new seed cleaner was installed in Pain Court to accommodate the local farmers. Their business operated under the name of N. and G. King. This operation continued successfully and in 1939, hybrid seed corn was introduced in Kent County. Napoléon King was a pioneer in the business. This simple beginning was later known as King Grain Company.

During this period, King Grain purchased "Lindsey Chopping mill" in Pain Court adjacent to the Dover Hotel parking lot today. This is where we could buy feed or bring your own to be chopped. This included chicken feed, hog feed and cattle feed. Gaspard Martin successfully operated this mill for many years. His brother, Arthur, carried on many more years. It has since been demolished and replaced by a new home in the village.

Mme Philibert Bourassa

Mme Bourassa, je désire vous remercier pour les belles heures passées auprès de vous. Oui, j'aimais bien mes grand-mères Roy et Caron. Mais, je garde de vous d'inoubliables souvenirs. Les enfants, dans leurs bas âges, aiment les caresses et l'attention. Aujourd'hui, je constate que cette bonne femme avait beaucoup de peine de voir son époux, Philibert, malade. Elle se sentait tellement impuissante vis-à-vis la situation. Il est mort le 6 avril 1925 à l'âge de 92 ans et moi, j'en avais que 6. Je constate, aujourd'hui, qu'il n'y a pas d'âge pour se rendre utile et consoler les personnes affligées ainsi que toutes autres personnes que l'on rencontre sur son chemin.

Comme je marchais tous les jours à l'école et que je passais devant sa demeure, j'étais heureuse de voir cette chaleureuse dame venir me saluer et m'apporter un petit biscuit ou autre friandise. Je me rendais compte qu'elle me choyait et que moi, en retour, je pouvais lui apporter un peu de bonheur. Elle m'invitait toujours à lui rendre visite pour quelques instants à la sortie de l'école. Comme c'était à mi-chemin de ma demeure, je m'arrêtais là, pour prendre une pause divertissante.

Mme Bourassa est née Euphémie Béchard en 1851 à Pain Court, fille de Moïse Béchard et Lina Rémillard. Elle est décédée le 23 novembre 1932 à l'âge de 81 ans. La mort lui avait arraché trois jeunes enfants. Je me rends compte, dans ma propre vieillesse, les ennuis qui auraient dû envahir son coeur et lui causer bien des soucis.

Leur garçon, Paul Bourassa, resté célibataire, se chargeait bien d'aider ses vieux parents. Homme dévoué et dans la cinquantaine, il se prêtait inlassablement aux exigences des jeunes joueurs de balle. Rempli d'enthousiasme, il dirigeait les jeunes athlètes et se chargeait de les transporter ici et là pour les parties de balle et les compétitions. C'est vrai, il y a toujours eu des personnes dévouées pour la jeunesse. De ma connaissance, il a versé de l'argent pour l'instruction des étudiants voués aux études et qui espéraient devenir enseignants dans nos écoles paroissiales.

Quel grand coeur d'homme!

Humorous Interlude

Parents and children worked as a team in order to survive. There were four cows and sometimes five to milk before going to school. Sometimes mother would give me a helping hand, but for a 12-year-old it became a bit of a chore. All this work before leaving for school in the morning besides a bonus of walking 2 miles.

One morning I was late so I hurried to milk the cows and turned the separator at full speed in order to feed the young calf.

Now, feeding young calves was a slow process and it required patience but this very morning the milkmaid deliberately let the calf drink at one go. On my return from school, bad fate awaited me. The calf had died as a result of drinking too fast. Losing a calf was a big financial loss and rest assured a hard lesson to cope with.

On a happier note, cats were always around at milking time. We had to have a bit of fun so we squirted milk to the cats. They expected a treat every morning. My four years old brother Raoul, was waiting with his cup for a treat of warm milk from the separator bowl. One gulp and the cup was empty.

With all this milk and cream it was a must to have two crocks of milk on the cupboard in order to let it sour, much like yogurt. What a morning treat with brown sugar! Dad had the first serving because he was the first one up. He would light up the stove with wood and corn cobs. Sometimes we managed to buy a ton of coal at Daniel's Coal Yard where Harvey's Restaurant now stands.

Guess it's time to fill the churn with cream in order to have butter. This task was time consuming. In winter months, Dad would help us once in a while to operate the churn. Sometimes he would get comical and show us how well he could operate it. So faster and faster he would churn until once, on account of too much pressure building in the churn, plop, off came the cover, so guess what? Butter all over the place. The ceiling was covered, the walls, the floor and anyone in close range got creamed. So what if everybody was laughing because it was Dad's fault, this time! Of course this would happen every once in a while if we were not careful how we operated this churn.

No butter for the market that week and less butter for our own consumption. There was a price tag for this. We all felt it was a very tedious task that had to be done once a week.

There was work for everyone regardless of age. The smaller kids would feed the chickens in the chicken coop, while Mother gathered the eggs. They had a little container and threw feed to the chickens, ducks and turkeys. It was fun.

People Who Immigrated to Our Area

The decade of the thirties brought an influx of immigrants searching for a better life in Canada. The Kent area was a popular destination for new Canadians. They came from various parts of Europe but especially from France, Germany, Belgium, Holland and Hungary. All were in search of work during the depression years of the thirties, especially those with agricultural backgrounds. Many settled on farms working for farmers in our district. They were perceived as being very knowledgeable workers in the area of tobacco and sugar beets. They willingly became shareholders and shared responsibilities in these areas of farming. As the years went by, many more citizens were added to the list. Many familiar reputable names became known. Szucs, Gyssels, Casier, Leclair, Delrue, Delanghe, Haelewyn, Raspburg, Mortier, Bloomers, Renders, Laevens, De Clerk, Hoekstra, Van Bastelaar, Vanden Enden, Dulisch, Classens, Van Roboys, Rozell, Roth, Blondeel, Korpan, Bossy, Stallaert, Devos, Van Damme, Debaere, Pawlak, Klein, Derbecker, Emrich, Klinard, Van Praet, Serruys, Van Couteren, Verstraete, Koekuyt and Renversez and many more whose names escape my memory. Their children were integrated in our schools and were top students in their respective grades. Most of these scholars were fluent in three languages, French, English, and their own mother tongue spoken in the homes. Amazing! They contributed much to the economic and cultural development of the immediate areas. Some became very prominent and prosperous farmers, others were active in municipal and governmental affairs.

Léon Charlebois

M. Léon Charlebois, natif de Rigaud, Québec, était gérant de la banque bilingue à Magog, Québec en 1919. Plus tard, il fut transféré à Pain Court pour ouvrir une succursale de la banque "Standard" située dans l'emplacement de l'hôtel Dover. Après un séjour comme gérant de cette banque, il retourne à Rigaud pour épouser son amie Antoinette Perron. À son retour il prend domicile à Chatham et devient entrepreneur d'un magasin de fourrure en 1925. Vers 1930, il vient s'établir à Pain Court avec sa famille afin de profiter de l'enseignement bilingue à l'école Ste-Catherine. Vu qu'il voyageait de Pain Court à Chatham tous les jours, j'ai osé lui demander de voyager avec lui pour me rendre au "Pines." Il y consentit mais sous une condition que je sois toujours ponctuelle.

Pas de problème! Cette adolescente de 16 ans qui voulait coûte que coûte finir sa 12e année n'aurait jamais osé être en retard! D'ailleurs faire la navette entre Pain Court et Chatham en compagnie de M. Léon Charlebois était vraiment un privilège.

C'était un homme généreux, d'humeur égale, actif dans les organisations paroissiales ainsi que celles de la ville de Chatham.   Il invite ses deux fils, Bernard et Jean-Maurice à se joindre au commerce.   En 1951, son fils Yvon, se joint à la famille pour continuer la tradition de leur père. C'est Jean-Maurice et Yvon qui se sont engagés à continuer l'entreprise familiale pendant bien des années. Après 66 ans dans le commerce de fourrure et ayant bien desservi leur clientèle, ils décident de prendre leur retraite, une retraite bien méritée.

À la famille Charlebois, ma reconnaissance. Merci à Léon Charlebois. Salut à sa femme, Antoinette, toujours remplie d'enthousiasme, toujours débordante d'amour envers sa famille et la société. Antoinette est décédée en 1968. Son époux Léon est décédé le 29 novembre 1972.

Butchering

In September, as fall rolled around, we generally had fattened two or three pigs during the summer for our own use. When the pigs had reached 130 to 140 lbs. they were ready to be slaughtered in November, a procedure that I dreaded. Dad needed help, and I was his helper. He would tie the pig's legs, throw it on its back and I had to sit between the legs on its belly. He would then insert the knife to cut a big artery in the neck. By this time the pulleys in the tree were ready, and the water was boiling in the large steel barrel. We would hook the pig by the hind legs and with the pulley he would dip the pig up and down in the boiling water in order to clean and scrape the pig's skin in order to remove the hair. It was left hanging in the tree for an hour to cool off, the guts were cleaned and then transferred to a big tub.

Meanwhile, the heart was washed and cleaned. The kidneys would be saved for kidney stew. The tongue was a special meal itself. The head was brought to the kitchen, cut up in fine pieces, seasoned and boiled, then pressed into a mould for "head cheese." This was eaten as a sandwich spread.

After the cooling period, Dad would lower the carcass to a wood block using pulleys. The carcass was then quartered and brought to the basement. We covered the pieces with salt and put them in large 30 gallon crocks. First came the pork tenderloins, after the fat "la panne" had been removed. "La panne" was used especially to make a special hors d'oeuvre, "des crétons ": a residue of rendered fat mixed with brown sugar. A delicacy for snacks or for breakfast with toast.

There was no refrigeration so huge crocks filled with brine were used to pickle the pieces. Special cuts of meat like the hams were smoked hanging over a barrel. An essence was brushed on the hams to be smoked. It took a few days to accomplish this process. After it was cured, it would keep without refrigeration. It surely was extra good ham. Sometimes we did not cure and smoke the hams. We would simply slice all of them and cook all these slices, layered them in four or five gallon crocks, cover them with the fat ready to be warmed up quickly for a meal with potatoes and gravy.

By spring, the same containers were refilled. The process was repeated twice a year thereafter.

Even at the close of the thirties, we still did not have refrigeration of any kind. There were enough preserves stacked and stored to ensure a generous surplus that would outlast the winter months. Throughout our freezing temperatures, we managed to have a quarter of a beef at a time, kept frozen in a cold shed. We did cut roasts of beef, had pieces for beef stew. I still know the different cuts of pork or beef available in the shops. " Well, we are now ready to spend a good winter."

Fruit farming was also part of the farm picture to be counted on for survival, either as a cash revenue or for our own consumption. Our orchard comprised 10 acres. Can you picture 100 apple trees waiting to be harvested: Greenings, Russets, Spy, Baldwin, Kings, Macintosh. In late autumn, we started selling apples that had fallen to the ground, but were still edible and in good condition. People would pick the best they could find and there was plenty. Big jute bags sold for 50¢. Come December, we had managed to salvage barrels and barrels for our winter use. We made at least 20 apple pies a week on Saturdays, baked apples, apple sauce cakes, etc. Anytime we wanted apples, they were available. We could not be choosy but we had plenty of nutritious apple deserts loaded with vitamins.

Seasonal Planting

When seasonal planting rolled around it meant the end of my school year. I was summoned to the field to work beside my Dad from May 1 to December 1, approximately. I was thirteen years old. It took many hours of hard work to plough a field with a team of horses and a two-furrow plough. Sometimes three horses were harnessed because when my father ploughed in early Spring to prepare or ready the soil for the early peas and oats, if the weather was good, I had to drive three horses hitched to the harrows to even up the soil. Then the soil had to be disked; this was done either with tractor power or horse power. To level the ground for planting you had to walk behind the drag harrows and if not levelled enough for planting you had to go over it a second time with a culti-packer pulled by three horses.

A day's work handling discs or drag harrows seemed like the ultimate of chores that I could ever accomplish. I was too exhausted and too tired to even sit at the table to eat.

With all the crops in by June, it was cultivating time, especially sugar beets, as this was a must before thinning beets. So for three or four weeks, sugar beet thinning was my assignment followed by hoeing weeds in all the crops.

By July, peas were ready for harvest. When fully ripened, the vines were cut, then raked in rows much like hay. With a team of horses and wagons outfitted with high racks, the vines were loaded by hand with pitchfork, tossing and mounting the vines up to 6' high, ready to be delivered to a pea station operated and supervised either by the Libby's or Campbell's Company. These peas were graded and processed in the Chatham plants and some were delivered to a freezer plant for packaging. Depending on the weather, a good harvest yielded many bushels and good cash money. A reward was presented by the Company to the seasonal pea grower with the highest average per acre.

In mid-July the golden wheat harvest beckoned the 12 to 15 farmers, more or less, to organize their first seasonal round robin neighbourly thrashing bee, followed by oats and barley crops.

Most farmers had a grain binder that released shocks of grain four or five at a time in a straight row. I was told that I barely had enough strength to pull the release mechanism, therefore Dad built me a square block around the device so I could reach it. As for the shocks of grain, it was the entire family who was elected to stand these shocks upright so the grain would stay dry until thrashing time.

It required many teams of horses and wagons to bring the sheaves in from the field. They would drive up close to the threshing machines and the man with the wagon would pitch the sheaves one by one until his wagon was empty, then another drove up. One man had to watch the grain coming out of the pipe at the other end of the machine and fill bushel baskets or jute bags most of the time. Others carried these to the granary and emptied them.

About the countryside, the steam powered threshing machine thrashed weeks on end relentlessly gulping batches of dried shocks and spewing out straw, forming huge golden straw stacks in the barnyards. These later served as animal bedding and also silage or as a refuge for our feathered friends during the cold winter months.

It meant hard work for everyone, but at the same time it was fun to mingle with all the neighbours, a community spirit at best. Generally, after harvest, in July, there were park outings and relatives and friends made their rounds.

Meanwhile, the ladies were preparing a good healthy meal for everyone. Generally it took a day or two to complete the job and move on to the next neighbour to thresh his wheat, his oats, or his barley. It was a pleasurable event for everyone, even if it meant hard work and long hours in the hot summer. In fact this was like going on holidays being at different households for a few weeks. Everyone seemed happy to be able to render their services, men and women alike and to celebrate, in their own way, that the crops had been saved.

Le temps des "des battages" s'annonce.

La famille Adophe Roy travaille en équipe. Il fallait bien prendre une p'tite pause pour se faire photographier. De gauche à droite: Yvonne, Léontine, Bernard, Raoul, au volant du "Ford" et Caroline assise sure le "binder." (lieuse)

Les "moissonneurs" à l'oeuvre
Une touche de Jean F. Millet, artiste reconnu pour ses tableau de scènes champêtres et du travail de la paysannerie.

Rondeau Park and Seacliff Park

During the summer months and always on a Sunday, a group of schoolmates would organize an outing to Rondeau Park and to Seacliff Park in Leamington, as well. With our driver, a packed lunch and enough money for a 25¢ banana split at the ice cream parlours and another spare quarter to rent a bathing suit to test the water, we were off for an engaging and fulfilling Sunday journey.

In 1935, Rondeau Park had a host of entertaining exhibits of birds, large peacocks, cages upon cages of different species of animals, deer that we could feed in a small enclosure, pony rides, dart games, miniature golf. It was a pleasure to be a part of the crowds at Rondeau. Seacliff Park was also a beautiful park, with its wonderful beach and flower beds which coloured the well mani-cured landscape bordering the Erie shores. But the greatest attraction was the sound of a juke box in the pavilion challenging us to dance our hearts out to the popular tunes of the day. After a week of hard work, these were rewarding outings indeed.

~ A new car ~

Approximately seven years had elapsed since our last car, and a new one put smiles on everyone's face. Nonetheless, the work situation had not changed. We had to give it our all, at all times. There are few young farmers who can actually put an exact date of the moment they began farming. Most grew up on the farm and can boastfully and truthfully say they have been farming since a very tender age. There were many tasks that could be accomplished with the help of our parents.

Tomato Harvest

We did not grow tomatoes, as such, but come August and September it was a fine opportuni-ty for me to secure a job at Libby's for the six to seven weeks of tomato harvesting. I had my first job at 15 and it continued every year, thereafter when my credit was established. I travelled with Rose Bourdeau and Orville Cheff. In order to make extra money we worked overtime, two shifts each. From 3:00 P.M. till 11:00 P.M. I peeled tomatoes and from11:00 pm. to 7:00 a.m. it was sort-ing tomatoes on the line. Rose was labelling for two shifts and Orville was a mechanic for two shifts. It was strenuous and demanding work but the money sure came in handy. I remember buy-ing a brand-new coat for the first time in my life and a beautiful dress. Mother was a talented seam-stress and managed to assemble attractive pieces of clothing for the whole family, but to go in a store and buy a piece of clothing on display with well-earned cash was a thrill in itself.

Era of Prosperity

By Christmas 1936, we had an upright console radio. Our first radio. The music, the news and Amos and Andy brought life to our household. Shortly after, there was furniture in our living room and dining room. To this day, the family still treasures this antique oak dining room set along with its 12 piece set of Limoges chinaware.

Just as we were enjoying the better things in life, we suddenly lost our grandmother Caron whom we loved and cherished. Very seldom would she miss a week without visiting us on Saturdays, together with her son, Alcide Caron, and his wife Alexina. We made it a point to babysit their three girls, Thérèse, Lucille, and Aline every week when they drove to Chatham, to fetch groceries for the coming week. This was also a welcome break for our mother, to be with her mother every week for a visit. I admired my grandmother and I visited with her after school at least once a month. Her pastime was to knit. I was eager to do likewise. She tried and tried to teach me, but in vain; it was just impossible for me to twist those needles the right way. After many botched attempts, she rightfully concluded that it was not in me to learn this skill due to my awkwardness in mastering the needles. Well, she was right, I never did.

To my eyes, Mémère Caron was a picture of loveliness. At night she would unwind her beautiful waist length grey hair, and managed to twist her long strands into a bun held securely on top of her head with long hairpins. I was simply in awe of her finesse.

It was in March of 1937, a sad period for everyone. She became very ill, apparently suffering from a cerebral haemorrhage. Her sufferings were short lived, dear soul, and she peacefully passed away to eternal rest on March 17, 1937. She was 73 years old.

A few months later it was brought to my attention that she had willed to me all that was within the walls of her personal bedroom. That was something very special, and when I married in 1938, this furniture and accessories graced the bedroom of our newlywed home.

Unruly behaviour wasn't overlooked and being deprived of a meal was acceptable as a form of disciplinary punishment. Since everyone looked after each other, one of us always managed to secretly deliver a morsel or two to whoever had broken the rules. Most of the time we were all to blame.

Already it is back to school, but only for a short three weeks until the sugar beet harvest beckoned everyone to the fields. This year it would be at the "Pines" in Chatham. This would give me an opportunity to speak English, as well as upgrading my English courses. As customary, we were fully-fledged students only after the beet harvest was done and that meant early December.

By November 3, 1936 mother needed a helping hand to greet our new baby sister Anne-Aline. This proved to be a very challenging period because of mother's convalescing as well as the welfare of the baby. When all was taken care of in the morning and dinner was cooking for the family, I toiled in the beet field until dinner time. Dad came in for lunch with the other children and later I brought dinner to Mother and made sure the baby was very comfortable. By two-thirty it was back to the field, until 4:30, at which time days seemed to be much shorter. It was understood that I had to get supper on the table for the family.

Soon mother managed to care for the baby and prepare supper for the family. This gave me more time to do more work in the sugar beets, with my brothers and sister. By December, everyone was ready for a break and, trust me, everyone was happy to return to the classroom and greet all his or her friends. Our school work demanded long hours of study in order to catch up. Everyone was very understanding and helped us continuously. Everyone cared and loved us, were even willing to sacrifice recreation time to coach us along and lending us their notes to copy. No words can fully describe our appreciation to whomever contributed to helping us in any small way at that time. May God bless you and shower upon you his gifts of Love, Peace and Health.

By the end of the 30s, most people had managed to get a firm grasp onto a better life. Like all teenagers, I was anxious to drive and Dad was willing to teach me. The bare 50 acre wheat field was the obstacle course and its one and only hurdle was a cross fence at the end of the field, which I was to avoid at all costs. With a couple of afternoons of training, I became more comfortable at the wheel. I surely was anxious to get my Dad in the car with me. Time was closing in and I was ready to quit when unexpectedly, in a split second, I crashed into the fence as I was backing up. I was emotionally crushed. Dad's new car was scratched and a fender bent. Oh! it was repairable alright but I was forbidden to touch the car again. Interesting to note also, that no one in our family ever owned a bicycle while growing up.

As the teen years came about, I made good friends and soon some of the young lads who drove a car invited the girls to join them for outings during the summer months. This was a splendid idea and fun, but by the fall of 1937 a special person started visiting more often. I worked at Libby's in Chatham during the tomato season, so there was no time for dating, just very short rendez-vous. But my friend, Trefflé, was 25, and he concluded that we knew each other well enough to get married. This actually was far from my mind because I had anticipated to become a teacher before too long. He already had a home and finally, after a very short courtship, we decided to make wedding plans. My parents were devastated and tried, in vain, to deter me from getting married. I felt I had given very much to my family over the past decade, and marriage could not possibly be worse. So the wedding was set for January 18, 1938. This event will mark the beginning of my next chapter.

We grew up in very hard times and when we were handed some small trinket, it was very much appreciated. Even though there were hardships, it has made me the person I am today and I wouldn't trade it for the world. I'm a hard worker. I'm compassionate. I know that there is a God who loves me. I am very thankful for what I have. I'm not greedy. I am content in whatever state I'm in and when I'm hit with a trial, I never give up.

Now watching my own children and grandchildren grow up, who have pride and do appreciate things, I wonder . . . will they be able to overcome the dilemma? I hope and trust that my recorded memories fulfill a twofold mission: firstly, to give the young people of today some idea how things were 75 years ago; secondly, to allow the not so young to step back in time and relive the memories of days gone by.

Club de balle-molle vers 1905

Première rangée, de gauche à droite: William Boyer, André Roy,
Amédée Béchard, Dieudonné Gagner, Edouard Béchard et Louis Béchard.
Deuxième rangée: Alphonse Ouellette, Trefflé Gagner, Félix Bourassa
et Jacques Bourdeau.   Debout: Paul Bourassa

The Crack of the Bat Is Only a Rumour.

There are many conflicting theories as to how, where or when the sport of baseball truly began.

However, in the middle 1800s when the amateur leagues were giving way to the professional direction of the game, baseball was at the helm, in the early 1900s, for regional sports enthusiasts.

Far from Cooperstown, baseball teams began to emerge and league games between various teams of the local surrounding communities of Kent County were exhibited following a regular schedule throughout the season luring die-hard fans both young and old to the baseball lots, either rooting for their home team or simply singling out a particular budding phenom with Big League potential.

Bill Blair, the pride of Pain Court in 1914

In our small towns there were such talents who excelled in baseball and whose names are still on the lips of partial "connoisseurs" recounting tales of their favourite baseball exploits.

One such athlete was the late Willie Blair (Blais) from Pain Court and I quote an excerpt from the article "Pearson the ballplayer" which appeared in the London Free Press and written by L. N. Bronson (Chatham Planet research, Weldon Library, UWO).

"Bill Bellaire (Blair) the pride of Pain Court pitching for the Bankers team in the Chatham City baseball league of 1914, faced the new second baseman of the Kent Regiment Club. It was a six inning twilight affair which ended in a 3 - 3 tie. Bellaire (his name often appeared as Blair) fanned 10 men altogether – he struck out a future prime minister of Canada and a Nobel peace prize winner three times. The Regiment's second baseman was Lester Bowles "Mike" Pearson whose father took over the pastorate of Park Street Methodist (now United) Church the first Sunday in July 1914."[1]

The very few left of Uncle Bill's generation can attest to the following anecdote laced with an explicit vernacular so typical of Pain Court's legendary, piercing blue-eyed tear jerker, the one and only Monsieur Médé (Amédée) Béchard, to his hired crew on a scorching midweek afternoon, labouring in a thistly growing crop of field corn: *"Hé les gars, les 'châdrons' peuvent 'attende'. Pendez vot' pioche. Willie Blais 'pitch apra médi'. On s'en va à ball game. Embarquez - tassez-vous. Ça s'ra pas long."*

And the much obliged rooting supporters would crowd the rumble seat of his Model T, put-putting its merry way to Chatham's Tecumseh Park baseball diamond everyone ready to marvel at the 22 year old hurler on the mound, along with Monsieur Médé, the leading spirit of the clan, all spiffed up in his long-sleeved white shirt and black pants outfitted with loose suspenders and capped off with a ruffled porkpie straw hat, while cheering him on to victory.

Hail to uncle Bill and three cheers for Monsieur Médé,
the champion spirit of the game.

Thanks for the memories!

A special tribute to my late father, Philippe Blais Sr. who lived baseball and made me love the game. He volunteered as manager of Pain Court's junior and senior teams for a number of years.

Angéline Blais Marentette

1. Copyright permission granted -
"The London Free Press" dated April 23, 1999.

The Baseball Exploits of Grande Pointe's Very Own.

Sylvio Létourneau on the left with coach Harry Bourdeau
Photo taken by Caroline Roy at a baseball game in Grande Pointe in 1937.

Another baseball figure who has made a difference in the glory days of amateur baseball is Sylvio Letourneau, a team player from Grande Pointe in and around the 30s and 40s.

According to Sylvio: "It was Archie Sterling, then Mayor of Chatham, who paved the way for baseball players to attend baseball training schools in the warmer climate of the United States."

As an adept colourful right-hand pitcher displaying outstanding baseball skills, Sylvio was scouted by a major league club and was invited to train in Orlando, Florida. It was from this schooling that he was recognized as a possible, future professional baseball player.

A following testimony to his baseball skills appeared in the Chatham Daily News:
"A resident of Grande Pointe, only a few miles from Chatham, Létourneau has been a consistent winner. The cool French Canadian tosses them right-handed and this department has yet to see him pitch a really bad game."

A further article read, " Syl was on the mound yesterday and pitched three innings. Not a man reached first base and he had four strike outs." The scouts in Orlando said that he was the best looking prospect they had seen.

Sylvio Létourneau married Blanche Lécuyer, April 2, 1945. He's the son of Sylvère Létourneau and Marie Emery. Blanche is the daughter of Adjutor Lécuyer and Léa Lebrun. They have three sons and one daughter but today only Marc farms with his father.

Sylvio and Blanche were commended for their contribution of a parcel of their land known as
"Parc de
Grande Pointe
Park."

Interesting to note that Meadowbrook Lane is the entrance road to a new subdivision built in the village of Grande Pointe. This land once owned by Adjutor Lécuyer was inherited by his daughter Blanche.

Thank you both for your insight and interest in your community.

Révérend Père Z. Mailloux

Le Révérend Père Z. Mailloux ami spécial de la jeunesse

Il s'est dévoué pour la jeunesse de notre paroisse de 1933 à 1945. Les élèves de l'école de continuation de Pain Court, c'est-à-dire ceux et celles de la neuvième et dixième année, ont bien joui des heures passées auprès du Père Mailloux. L'explication de la bible nous reste encore imprimée dans le cerveau. Nous avons apprécié le Père Mugan récemment ordonné et qui se montrait intéressé à vouloir maîtriser la langue française. Nous avons été choyés ayant deux prêtes pour desservir la paroisse.

Toutes les organisations paroissiales étaient rehaussées par leur présence et encouragement. Pour prélever des fonds, les dames s'occupaient des soupers, des pique-niques ainsi que d'autres activités. Les enfants de Marie se montraient intéressées aux engagements de leur société. Un match de tennis ou une partie de cartes, par exemple, attiraient les jeunes. Les activités organisées au sous-sol de l'église rassemblaient la jeunesse de la paroisse. En 1941, afin d'améliorer les moments de détente, les hommes lui prêtent mains fortes et deux allées de bowling sont installées au sous-sol de l'église. Jeunes et vieux, laïcs et religieux passent des heures à se divertir. Pour une quinzaine d'années environ, les deux allées font bien l'affaire pour les gens de la place mais le bowling gagne du terrain et on abandonne les allées au sous-sol pour joindre les ligues de Chatham où tout est plus moderne.

Le Père Mailloux a démontré beaucoup de courage et d'énergie lors de la construction de la nouvelle église en 1937. Il commence par inspirer ses paroissiens les exhortant d'être fiers de leur paroisse. Durant la construction de 1937, les cérémonies religieuses avaient lieu à l'école. Les salles de classe accommodaient les paroissiens pour les messes du dimanche. Durant les mois d'été la messe avait lieu en plein air, à l'entrée de l'école. Les efforts du Père Mailloux et des paroissiens ont été couronnés de succès lorsque l'église, reconstruite, ouvre ses portes pour la première messe officielle, célébrée le 8 décembre 1937, fête de l'Immaculée-Conception.

La mort inattendue du Père Mailloux en juin 1945 plonge la paroisse dans un deuil profond.

La paroisse de Pain Court doit une dette de gratitude au Père Mailloux. Ses qualités d'homme pieux et sincère lui ont mérité une place spéciale dans le coeur de ses paroissiens.

Les Enfants de Marie

Lorsque le Père Mailloux est nommé curé de Pain Court, il continua le travail d'apostolat auprès des jeunes, travail déjà bien établi par son prédécesseur, le Père A.D.Emery.

Aussitôt, il mit de l'entrain pour que les jeunes filles puissent joindre la Société des Enfants de Marie. Avant longtemps, un terrain adjoint en arrière de l'église est déjà en place pour un "tennis court." Quel beau passe-temps! Les aînées de cette période étaient Rose Bourdeau, Viola Daniel, Antoinette Caron et d'autres qui déjà n'étaient plus en classe.

Les filles, en général, étaient bien intéressées à ce beau passe-temps. Nous participions à des sessions de religion, des défilés impressionnants pour les modes. Il fallait s'abstenir d'aller aux salles de danse publique, donner le bon exemple et rendre service aux organisations paroissiales. De temps à autre, il y avait une partie de cartes pour les enfants afin de défrayer les dépenses de nos activités.

En 1937, j'ai été élue présidente de la société et j'ai occupé ce poste jusqu'à mon mariage en janvier 1938. Il y avait beaucoup de travail supplémentaire qui s'imposait vu que l'église avait été détruite par le feu. Alors le travail bénévole se faisait le dimanche. L'ouverture de la nouvelle église eut lieu en décembre 1937. Par coïncidence, je fus la première des Enfants de Marie à se marier dans la nouvelle église, le 18 janvier 1938, et ce fut la chorale de l'école secondaire qui exécuta le beau chant. Merci encore une fois chers amis.

Sur ce fait je vous laisse pour aller fêter Noël 1996 avec mes enfants, mes petits-enfants et mes arrière petits-enfants. À vous tous, un joyeux Noël! Que ce message vous apporte l'expression de mon amour! Que le ciel vous prodigue ses divines faveurs chaque jour de l'année nouvelle!

Classmates September 1936 to June 1937

Friends fill the heart with timeless treasures. I want to honour, in my own special way, my Grade 12 classmates at Pain Court Continuation School. You are all very dear to me and this I write as a special tribute to every one of you. Friends make memories, and the heart preserves them. Remembrance fills my heart with gratitude, as I gaze at this picture. Many of you have chosen to devote a lifetime of relentless work for the advancement and enjoyment of future generations. Some of you have been teachers for more than 20 years. Many have raised large families, some chose the nursing profession and practised most of your life. Others became servants of God through various religious congregations and served as teachers, as business administrators for their respective congregations, some in foreign lands, others in their own community. Some have catered to our well being as grocery clerks. Some have died at an early age leaving behind their families.

Every one of you left his or her mark on society. Everyone lead exemplary lives and have accomplished great deeds of love and charity, thereby crowning his or her lives forever. Dear friends, I hereby express my desire to project your image to the world of today. May God bless you and keep you for many more years.

J'admire votre courage, votre persévérance. À tous, je vous souhaite un accroissement de paix intérieure, de joie, de bonheur. Allez de l'avant avec ce goût de lumière et d'amour qui vous habite. Que Dieu vous comble de ses grâces et vous transforme en des êtres de paix, de bonheur, de santé, de compassion, de douceur et de tendresse. Gardez toujours votre sens d'humour, chères amies et chers amis.   Mes souvernirs restent bien vivants, souvenirs pleins de vie, de chaleur et d'amitié.

Mes amies de classe

Mes amies de classe, 12e année, École e Continuation de Pain Court, 1936 - 37.
De gauche à droite: Jeanne Gagner, Jeanne Roy, Vivienne Gagner, Sylvia Roy,
Florence Pinsonneault, Rosalie Caron, Clara Jubenville, Yvonne Gagner, Julienne Gagner.
Photograph : Caroline Roy (Laprise)

École de Continuation de Pain Court, 9e et 10e années 1934 - 35
Assises de gauche à droite: _____ , _____ , Yvonne Trudell,
Léona Bélanger, Marie-Thérèse Caron, _____ .
Première rangée, debout de gauche à droite:
Yvonne Gagner, Clara Jubenville, Viviène Gagner, Jeanne Gagner, Florence Trudell,
Mae Caron, Julienne Gagner, Marie-Anne Caron, Sylvia Roy.

Deuxième rangée, debout: Florence Pinsonneault, Rosalie Caron, Jeanne Roy.

Photographe - Caroline Laprise

MERRY CHRISTMAS AROUND THE WORLD

French..Joyeux Noël

Afrikanders...................................Een Plesierige Kerfees

Danish...Glaedelig Jul

Flemish... Hyvää Jouloua

Dutch...Vrolijk Kerstfeest Eneen Gelukkig Nieuwjaar

German..Frohliche Weihnachten

Greek...Kala Christouyenna

Indonesian.................................... Selamat Hari Natal

Irish...Nollaig Slova Dhuit

Japanese.......................................Kurisumasu Omedeto

Korean...Sung Tan Chuk Ha

Norwegian..................................... God Jul

Spanish..Feliz Navidad

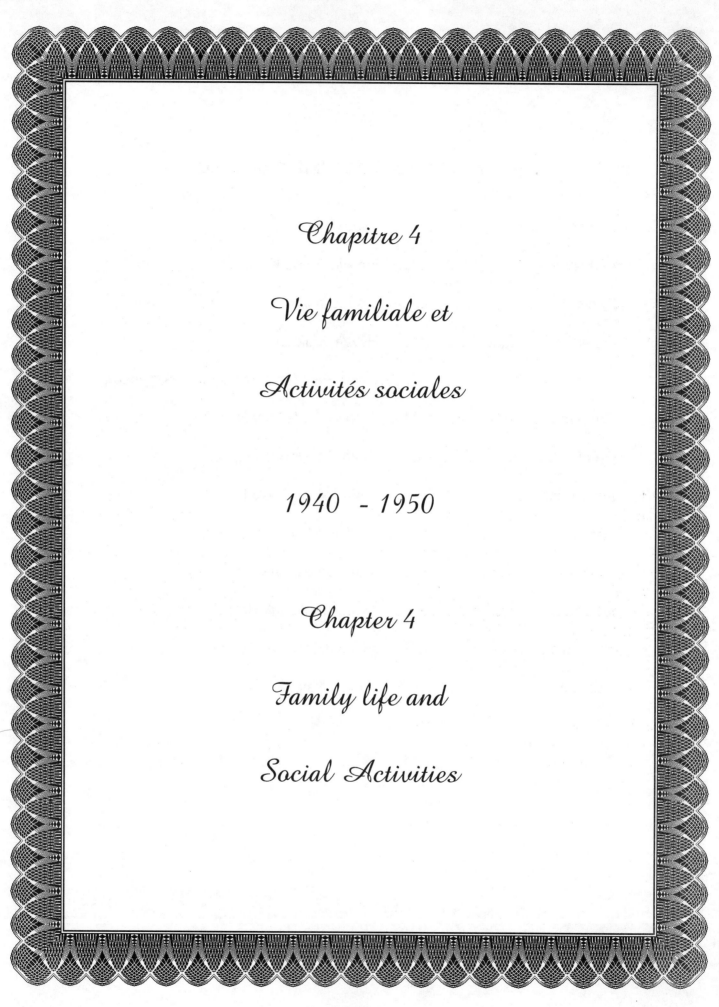

Chapitre 4

Vie familiale et

Activités sociales

1940 - 1950

Chapter 4

Family life and

Social Activities

La Joie de Servir

1940 ~ 1975

À la présidence, on applaudit:
Assises de gauche à droite: Louise Trudell, Alexina Caron, Marie-Anne Trahan, Zulma Trudell, Florence Caron, Lena Robert.
Debout de gauche à droite: Caroline Laprise, Adeline Bélanger, Eulalie Gagner, Irène Gagner, Marie-Anne Faubert, Ida Bourassa

La Société des dames de Ste-Anne honore 12 de ses membres pour environ vingt-cinq années de leadership auprès de la communauté. Comme geste d'appréciation, un banquet spécial en présence d'ami rehaussait la fête du 2 mai 1976, dans la salle paroissiale.

~   ~   ~

On May 2 1976, the "Ladies of Ste-Anne" honoured 12 of its members who served as president from 1940 to1975. In thanksgiving for a silver anniversary of devotion, self-sacrifice and leadership, a banquet in their honour was attended by parishioners, families and friends. This special banquet was organized under the leadership of Jessie Robert, president of the Ladies of Ste-Anne.

Presentations were made by Laurette Raymond.

Yvonne Bélanger

My memories of my mother, Yvonne Bélanger, are those as seen in the eyes of a child. What would my children say about me, if they only knew me for the first 10 years of their life?

The word that best describes her is "Passionate." Everything that she did or said or felt was with great emotion. She was not a shrinking violet. When she had an opinion, you knew it; when she took on a task, she gave it her all.

Prayers and reflections on love were part of our lives. It wasn't until I was in the "real world" that I realized that not every family said the rosary together at bedtime, or incorporated the practice of their faith in every day life. "Maman" loved to tell us stories and most of the time, they had a little message that was meant to affect our behaviour.

She loved to sew, not only clothes for us, but for our dolls too! She was a great cook, homemaker and teacher. She introduced me to all those skills. Where did she find all the time and energy to do it all? She and my father worked as a team. He was devoted to her and helped her as much as he could.

A few days before she died, she wrote each one of us a short note, assuring us that everything would be fine and urging us to keep praying. I recently read the autopsy report and the doctor's summary of her last days. Her death was not a peaceful one. In one sentence, the doctor remarked on her tremendous will to live.

In her short life of 36 years, she brought seven children into the world, six girls and one boy and left a lasting impression of someone with a deep unshakeable faith in God and a love for life. This is the legacy that she left us.

Claire Vickery
May 24, 1997

Roland et Yvonne avec leur nouveau-née Louise,
entourés de Jean-Charles, Claire-Marie et Denise

Un éloge à Yvonne, ma grande amie, une compagne sympathique, énergique, dévouée et sincère vis-à-vis les multiples projets que nous avons entrepris et réalisés ensemble pour le bien-être de la communauté paroissiale et celles des environs.

Yvonne, fille d'Alphonse Trudell et Maude Bourdeau, est née le 30 juillet 1923. Attirée sans doute par l'amour de l'étude que lui ont communiqué ses instituteurs et institutrices, d'abord, à l'école du rang et par la suite, à l'école de Continuation de Pain Court où elle obtient son diplôme de 12e année, Yvonne entretenait en elle le désir d'enseigner. À cette fin, elle se dirige vers l'École normale de l'Université d'Ottawa en 1939 pour un stage d'un an. Institutrice diplômée, elle se dévoue pleinement auprès des élèves de sa communauté. Yvonne est une institutrice née. Nombreux sont les élèves qui ont profité de ses qualités d'éducatrice.

Le 2 septembre 1944, elle épousa Roland Bélanger, fils de Wilfrid Bélanger et Alma Caron

Après son mariage elle continue à jouer plusieurs rôles: celui d'épouse et mère de sept enfants: Jean-Charles, Marie-Claire, Denise, Louise, Marie-Hélène, Jacqueline et Diane. Lorsque l'occasion se présente, elle offre ses services comme remplaçante dans les écoles de la communauté. Auprès des fonctions paroissiales, elle en fait autant. Femme débrouillarde, engagée et douée d'un sens de leadership, elle occupe, alternativement, le poste, soit de secrétaire ou de trésorière et même parfois s'adonne volontairement aux deux tâches en même temps. Son destin était celui de servir avec amour, le sourire aux lèvres. C'était sûrement sa mission puisqu'elle s'est orientée vers deux voies exigeant le don total de soi: celle de mère et celle d'institutrice.

Yvonne nous a quitté le 25 février 1960 dans la fleur de l'âge . . . oui, elle n'avait que 36 ans mais quel héritage elle nous a laissé. Elle est passée parmi nous en faisant du bien. Elle était toujours à la hauteur des talents qu'elle avait reçus de son Créateur.

Aujourd'hui, son esprit de bonté et de sacrifices se perpétue à travers ses enfants et petits-enfants qui, à leur tour, font honneur à une maman et une grand-maman qui a su se donner sans réserve pour sa famille, sa paroisse et toute la communauté entière.

Caroline Roy Laprise

Mme Almina Lécuyer

O Holy Spirit beloved of my soul,
I adore you. Enlighten me, guide me,
strengthen me, console me.
Tell me what I should do, Give me your orders.
I promise to submit myself to all that you
permit to happen to me.
Let me only know your will.
This submission to the Holy Ghost
is the secret of sanctity
Almina Emery
1880 - 1977

100 days Indulgence Cardinal Mercier

Mme Almina Lécuyer est la fille de Amable Lécuyer et Emélie Bourgeois. Elle épousa, le 1er mai 1900, M. François Xavier Emery, né le 17 février 1875. Il était le fils de Francis Emery et Rosalie Tétreault.

Almina avait une soeur Bessy, Mme Percy Cornfield de Chatham et un frère, M. Adjutor Lécuyer de Grande Pointe. Elle est décédée le 8 juin 1977, âgé de 97 ans.

Elle était la mère d'une fille unique, Gertrude, et de cinq garçons: Raymond, Bernard, Adrien, Léonard et Montfort.

Son époux, Francis, est décédé le 24 avril 1946, âgé de 71 ans.

Eulogy

Mrs. Elizabeth Hammar was born at Glen Allan Ontario, February 14, 1894. Baptized in St. Joseph's Church Macton with Mr. & Mrs. Bryan Thorpe as sponsors.

My childhood was spent with five brothers Jack, Roy, Jim, Alex, Tom and three very good sisters, Nell, Teresa and Gertrude. We were a lively group together with our parents who could sing, play and dance especially step dancing or minuet with the best of them.

After I graduated from high school, I entered Hamilton Normal School and graduated there. I taught in the separate school and played the organ in the church, sang for weddings and funeral masses; sometimes I had help but I was mostly alone.

As fate would have it, I attended the teacher's course at Ontario Agricultural College in Guelph for two summers. Through a fellow teacher who had been accepted by two school boards, I was asked if I would like to come to Southwestern Ontario with her. After thinking about it, I applied to the board SS No. 2 Tilbury. We were accepted and landed in Kent county September 1919.

Three years later, I married the late W. A. Trudell who died a year and half later leaving me alone to receive our son who was born the following month.

Hence I went home to my mother's and after four years I married C. Zephir Daniel of Dover where we farmed until 1956, some 25 years. During this period, I was active as president of the Ladies of Ste. Anne about 1936. Then two more terms 1943 and 1944 as president, later serving as assistant and honorary president at Pain Court. 1945

We moved to 527 Lacroix, 1956 in Chatham. Here I worked with the church, C.W. League and was active in St. Joseph Hospital Auxiliary. Doctors asked me not to accept any office work or committee work due to my health.

During my time in Kent, I have been:
1 - Promoter of the League of the Sacred Heart.
2 - Most offices on the executive of the C.W.L. wherever I happened to live.
3 - Organist and singer at masses for a number of years in the Catholic Church.
4 - Teacher in public and separate schools.
5 - Past president of United Farmers of Kent.
6 - Past president of Catholic Women's League.
7 - Past president of Liberal Club.
8 - Secretary-treasurer of Ladies Auxiliary of St. Joseph Hospital and a life member.
9 - Past president of west Kent Trustees and Ratepayers Association.
10 - Secretary-treasurer of Southwestern Ontario Liberal Women's Club.

During my time as president with the Ratepayers and Trustees Association, it was through my efforts that Kent County Health Unit came into being 1947.

March 22, 1950

Mr. and Mrs. Daniel had two boys and two girls, Billy Trudell, Maurice Daniel, Maureen and Marie Thérèse. Billy Trudell farmed with his step-father for a period of time and was known in technical engineering. Maurice completed his studies and serves as a medical doctor in the vicinity of St. Clair Beach Ontario.

. Mr. and Mrs. Daniel announce the engagement of their daughters Maureen and Marie Thérèse who were wed at a double ceremony on September 6, 1954, at Immaculate Conception Church, Pain Court.

Maureen who obtained her Bachelor of Arts degree in home economics at Brescia Hall became the bride of William Morley Myers of Dresden. Mr. Myers graduated from Osgoode Hall in 1951.

Marie-Thérèse obtained her Bachelor of Arts in general arts at Brescia Hall and her Masters degree in social work at St. Patrick's College in Ottawa. She was wed to Melbourne J. Mason of Ottawa who was a graduate of St. Patrick College with a Bachelor of Commerce degree.

Mrs. Daniel passed away August 8th, 1971 at the age of 77. Her husband died January 16th, 1977.

Maureen Myers

Les dames de Ste-Anne
À la présidence 1915 - 1940

Époux

Rose Roy . . . . André
Maria Faubert . . . . Théophile
Rosanna Caron . . . . Solomon
Annie Caron . . . . Adélard
Eva Trahan . . . . Hercule
Blanche Trudell . . . . Willie
Elizabeth Daniel . . . . Zéphir
Delphine Roy . . . . Eugène
Ida Bourassa . . . . Félix
Sophie Buck . . . . Charlie

À la présidence 1941 - 1998

1941 Eulalie Gagner . . . . Trefflé
1943 Elizabeth Daniel . . . . Zéphir
1945 Caroline Laprise . . . . Trefflé
1950 Irène Gagner . . . . Raoul
1953 Louise Trudell . . . . Hector
1954 Marie-Anne Trahan . . . . Victor
1955 Alexina Caron . . . . Alcide
1956 Zulma Trudell . . . . William
1958 Lena Robert . . . . Wilfrid
1961 Zulma Trudell . . . . William
1965 Florence Caron . . . . Gérard
1967 Adeline Bélanger . . . . Gérald
1969 Marianne Faubert . . . . Léonard
1976 Jessie Robert . . . . Gérald
1978 Thérèse Thibodeau . . . . Raymond
1979 Barbara Béchard . . . . Urbain
1980 Blanche Foy . . . . Charlie
1982 Linda Béchard . . . . Armand
1984 Mary Ann Martin . . . . Vianney
1986 Linda Béchard . . . . Armand
1987 Angela Roy . . . . Roger
1989 Linda Béchard . . . . Armand
1991 Angela Roy . . . . Roger
1993 Madeleine Pinsonneault . . . . Fernand
1995 Lucille Raymond
1997 Yvette Roy . . . . Edmond
Yvette Roy . . . . Edmond

Les chroniques des Dames de Ste-Anne

La Société des dames de Ste-Anne fut établie en 1915 par le Père A. Emery lorsqu'il ressentit le besoin d'une organisation qui lui viendrait en aide financièrement.

Il faut reconnaître les anciennes présidentes qui ont su maintenir les traditions d'une société qui continue encore de nos jours. Elles sont: Rose Roy, Maria Faubert, Eva Trahan, Rosanna Caron, Annie Caron, Blanche Trudell, Delphine Roy, Elizabeth Daniel, Sophie Buck et Ida Bourassa.
Les temps étaient difficiles mais dû à leur ténacité et à leur persévérance ces dames ont pu accomplir de beaux projets.

En 1941, Eulalie Gagner continue les événements coutumiers tels que les parties de cartes et les pique-niques annuels. Aidée de Caroline Laprise comme une vice-présidente, le dévouement envers la Société leur était primordial.

En 1943, sous l'habile direction de Elizabeth Daniel présidente, et de la vice-présidente Caroline Laprise ce fut le début des "Thés printaniers."

Durant son terme comme présidente en 1945, Caroline Laprise, introduit l'assurance coopérative d'hôpital aidée de Yvonne Bélanger, la secrétaire-trésorière. En 1948, elles ont introduit une clinique de santé pour les enfants de Pain Court et de Grande Pointe au sous-sol de l'église de Pain Court.

Irène Gagner fut la prochaine présidente en 1950. Sous sa direction, les ventes d'un sou ainsi que les banquets annuels et les parties de Noël étaient dans l'ordre des choses.

En 1953, Louise Trudell a été nommée présidente. Des ventes de pâtisserie ont été organisées pour aider les familles de la paroisse qui sont dans le besoin.

En 1954, l'année du centenaire de Pain Court, Marie-Anne Trahan est élue présidente. Au cours du terme de Marie-Anne Trahan, Mme Marie Emery a été honorée pour son grand dévouement comme organiste dans notre paroisse. Fidèle à son poste depuis plus de 50 ans, on la retrouvait chaque matin de la semaine, beau temps, mauvais temps, assise à l'orgue toujours en parfaite harmonie avec son Créateur. C'est elle qui rehaussait les célébrations liturgiques: messes du jour, funérailles, mariages, chorales à quatre voix pour le temps des fêtes et autres fêtes spéciales sans oublier la chorale du centenaire de la paroisse.

Vouloir marcher dans les traces de Mme Emery, c'est de partager ses talents pour la plus grande gloire de Dieu.

Alexina Caron a été élue présidente en 1955. Les bingos, les ventes de pâtisserie, les ventes d'un sou se sont continuées. À Noël, des paniers de nourriture ont été livrés aux familles démunies.

En 1956, c'est le tour de Zulma Trudell pour un terme de deux ans. Des fourneaux ont été achetés pour la cuisine. Cette année-là, nous avons célébré le 25e anniversaire de prêtrise du Père Euclide Chevalier et du Père Pierre Boudreau.

En 1958, Lena Robert est élue présidente pour trois ans et durant cette période les dames et les placiers ont acheté un nouvel orgue pour l'église. Les dames, en 1960, ont présenté à la famille de Joseph Robert une machine à laver pour leurs chers poupons, les p'tits Triplets: Joël, Jean et Jacques.

Zulma Trudell occupe la présidence pendant les prochains quatre ans. Elle introduit les parties de cartes à la maison ainsi que l'aide bénévole à l'hôpital de Cedar Springs.

En 1965, Florence Caron accepte un terme de deux ans. Elle nous abonne au magazine populaire catholique "La revue de Ste-Anne." Florence Caron a aussi organisé un comité en charge de visiter les malades. C'est alors que la Société a préféré être reconnue comme "Dames de Ste-Anne," plutôt que "Dames d'Autel."

En 1967, Adeline Bélanger est élue présidente pour deux ans. C'est durant sa présidence que les dames ont publié un livre de recettes intitulé "Cuisine de Chez Nous." Elle a beaucoup travaillé pour les ventes d'un sou qui ont été un grand succès et une source de revenus pour la société.

Marie-Anne Faubert occupe la présidence pendant plusieurs années. Durant son terme, plusieurs banquets et réceptions ont été organisés. Il est bon de souligner le 25e anniversaire de prêtrise du Père Léo Charron, l'ordination du Père Léo Dénommée et le départ des Soeurs Grises d'Ottawa parmi nous depuis 22 ans.

Aussi nous avons fêté la retraite de M. Edmond Chauvin pour son dévouement à l'enseignement comme professeur au secondaire. Ensuite, c'est une deuxième ordination, celle du Père Jacques Carron. En 1972, sous la direction du Père Charron, nous avons adopté une paroisse en Haïti.

Marie-Anne a rempli plusieurs rôles auprès de la Société des Dames de Ste-Anne ayant à son compte 5 décennies et plus d'affiliation, 4 décennies et plus dans l'administration et 6 années consécutives à la direction.

Imaginez-vous bien le surmenage durant son mandat. Toujours de l'avant avec ses coéquipières, elle n'a jamais fléchi sous la pression.

Femme sans pareil, son royaume était la cuisine. Son tablier de cuisinière à la portée de la main, elle avait toujours le temps d'accommoder les autres soit pour les "lunch" à l'improviste, les banquets, les dîners, etcetera.

N'est-ce pas vrai de dire que s'asseoir à la table bien garnie de Marie-Anne était une guarantie de savourer encore une fois la "bonne cuisine de chez-nous."

En 1976, pendant que Jesse Robert fut présidente, la salle paroissiale a été rénovée. C'est aussi durant sa présidence qu'un banquet spécial a été organisé pour honorer 12 anciennes présidentes des dames de Ste-Anne. Une plaque a été placée dans la salle paroissiale.

Thérèse Thibodeau a offert ses services comme présidente en 1978. Plusieurs dons ont été présentés à l'hôpital St. Joseph au cours de l'année. Un banquet a été planifié en l'honneur de M.

Amédée Emery pour ses nombreuses années de dévouement à l'enseignement.

En 1979, sous la direction de Barbara Béchard, un banquet a eu lieu à l'occasion du 50e anniversaire de Mgr. Augustin Caron.

Blanche Foy est élue présidente pour l'année 1980. Durant cette année, les dames ont aidé une famille de refugiés Vietnamiens. C'est aussi l'année que le Père Léo Charron nous quitte après16 ans de services.

Linda Béchard est choisie présidente pour l'année 1982. Durant cette année, plusieurs meubles ont été achetés pour le presbytère.

En 1984, Mary Ann Martin est devenue présidente. Nous avons célébré l'ordination du Père Eugène Roy et aussi la retraite de Angéline (Blais) Marentette en juin 1985 pour ses 35 années d'enseignement à l'école Ste-Catherine, ainsi que 35 années et plus comme directrice des chorales d'enfants et d'adultes pour les messes le dimanche, les funérailles et pour les fêtes spéciales de la paroisse.

Durant cette même année, les plans de construction pour une nouvelle entrée à l'église ont été tracés et les dames ont promis leur aide financière.

En 1986, Linda Béchard est élue présidente et un nouveau poêle est acheté pour la cuisine.

Angela Roy a accepté la présidence pour un terme en 1987. C'est l'année que les dames ont joui d'une parade de mode. Nous avons célébré ensemble l'ordination du Père Robert Couture, ainsi que le 40e anniversaire du Père Charles Sylvestre. C'est en 1987 que les Dames ont décidé de s'aventurer avec les bingos électroniques à Chatham.

En 1989 Linda Béchard offre ses services une 3e fois comme présidente. C'est une année tout à fait spéciale pour la Société des dames de Ste-Anne. L'année 1990 marque le 75e anniversaire des Dames de Ste-Anne de Pain Court. Laurette Raymond, qui à toujours travaillé pour l'avancement de la Société, s'est donnée corps et âme pour préparer le 75e, épaulée par les autres membres de la Société.

En 1991, c'est Angela Roy, qui mène à bonne fin un terme de deux ans comme présidente, suivie en 1993 par Madeleine Pinsonneault. Ils ont réussi les bingos à Chatham qui ont rapporté de bonnes sommes d'argent afin de soutenir les projets des dames.

Lucille Raymond offre ses services pour 1995 - 96.
Yvette Roy prend la relève comme présidente en 1997 - 98.
Ref - Archives des Dames de Ste-Anne.

Mariage de Caroline Roy et Trefflé Laprise
le janvier 18, 1938

Assistants des mariés

Filles d'honneur ....Maria Charron
                            Anna Laprise

Garçons d'honneur ....Gérard Caron
                               Aurèle Roy

Bouquetières ....Marie-Thérèse Caron
                            Evéline Caron
                            Laurette Roy

Our First Home
Built by Grandfather Médéric Caron in 1905

1905
1938

Je suis heureuse de vous présenter ma nouvelle famille, les "Laprise"

Première rangée de gauche à droite:
Jeanne, Trefflé, Soeur Marie, Soeur Cécile, Wilfrid et Anna.

Un engagement solennel
Mariage - 1938

Nous sommes au début de l'année 1938. Les flocons de neige voltigent. L'air froid caresse notre visage. C'est l'hiver et la date choisie pour le mariage approche. Il y a bien des préparatifs, mais ça sera très simple. Rien qui approche les cérémonies d'aujourd'hui. Chaque jour qui se déroule fait palpiter le coeur et dissiper les inquiétudes.

Le grand jour du 18 janvier est arrivé. C'est un beau matin, clair et sec. La neige brille sur toute la campagne. Sans trop de cérémonie, nous nous rendons à l'église pour 9:30. La chorale de l'école secondaire entonne un beau chant pour la marche nuptiale. Les Enfants de Marie, dont j'étais présidente, défilent en belles robes blanches avec voiles blancs suivies de deux charmantes bouquetières portant fleurs et anneaux de mariage. Ensuite, les deux filles d'honneur annoncent mon arrivée. Marchant sur le beau tapis blanc, je m'avance vers l'autel. Mon futur époux se dirige vers moi suivi de son cortège. Ce fut le premier mariage célébré depuis l'ouverture de l'église reconstruite après le feu du 2 janvier 1937.

Mes amis, la parenté, les écoliers, les enseignants, tous ont contribué à rehausser cet engagement solennel. Avec les bons souhaits échangés, nous nous sommes rendus à l'hôtel Central pour savourer un délicieux déjeuner-dîner très spécial. C'est oncle Jacob Roy qui avait fait les préparatifs, car depuis quelques temps déjà je lui prêtais main-forte à son restaurant "Le Rendez Vous" à Chatham. Je vous assure que tante Georgina et oncle Jacob savaient préparer avec délicatesse un repas par excellence et organiser les choses à la perfection. À la suite d'un toast aux nouveaux mariés, nous avons dégusté un repas copieusement garni. Suivant l'ordre du jour, c'est le rassemblement du cortège nuptial chez Wolfe's Studio à deux heures pour les photos de noces, suivi d'une réception à la salle Gagner, située à proximité de la "Dover Hotel." Après le défilé des invités, nous avons dégusté et apprécié ensemble un autre bon repas. L'orchestre Gagner nous a fourni la musique jusqu'à minuit. Cette belle journée mémorable s'est bien passée, grâce à l'aide des filles d'honneur et les garçons d'honneur. Nous avons certainement apprécié la présence des invités et les cadeaux de noce. Tous quittent la veillée le coeur content.

Les voyages de noces à cette époque étaient limités, car nous étions encore en pleine dépression. Notre propre maison suffisait et faisait notre plein bonheur. Nous étions heureux d'avoir un foyer qui nous appartenait. Ce foyer était très spécial pour moi car il avait été construit en 1904 par mon grand-père Médéric Caron aidé de son fils Rémi. C'est dans cette demeure que nos huit enfants vécurent ensemble, ont grandi et travaillé la terre des ancêtres puis d'où ils sont partis pour aller s'établir ailleurs. En 1974, c'est Jean-Marie, le plus jeune des garçons qui s'est engagé à fonder un foyer au même endroit où il a grandi et, à son tour, a vu grandir sa famille.

Je reviens à oncle Rémi, marié le 9 janvier en 1906 à Régina Béchard, fille de Théodore Béchard et de Louise Bénéteau. Issus de ce mariage sont trois fils et deux filles, Vital, Roland, Roméo, Luciana et Elsie. Le 6 novembre 1918, leur mère, Régina a succombé à la grippe espagnole lorsqu'elle attendait son 6e enfant. Luciana aujourd'hui âgée de 91 ans avait épousé Jack Briggs en 1924, et en deuxième mariage novembre 1980, elle avait épousé Armand Desmarais. Tous les membres de sa famille sont morts depuis plusieurs années déjà. Longue vie à toi, Luciana.

Les jours passent mais nous sommes jeunes, remplis d'ambition et de courage. Nous commençons à peinturer et à renover notre nouvelle demeure. Le printemps s'annonce et bientôt les champs seront prêts à recevoir la semence d'une récolte nouvelle. Il faut embellir les parterres de fleurs et faire la culture du petit jardin. J'épaule mon mari pendant les récoltes et quand vient l'hiver c'est entendu que nous faisons des couvre-pieds. J'étais enchanté d'apprendre l'art de piquer les couvre-pieds avec ma belle-mère. Elle finissait des pièces superbes. Il me reste des souvenirs bien vivants, remplis de vie, de chaleur et d'amitié vis-à-vis les rencontres de ces charmantes dames qui se joignaient à nous pour piquer des couvre-pieds.

Les hivers semblaient moins longs.
L'arrivée du printemps coïncide avec la naissance de Gérard, né le 14 mars 1939. Maintenant il faut faire des ajustements car le petit Gérard a besoin de sa place et surtout toute notre attention. C'est un petit bambin de 10 livres et 3 onces. On continue sur ce chemin qui est le nôtre et voici qu'il faut faire le jardin et faire l'élevage des poussins et des canards afin de se procurer des vivres pour l'automne. De longue main, j'avais bien appris les manières de survivre et par là combler notre bonheur. À cette époque nous avions très peu d'objets de luxe. Imaginez donc, pas de radio, pas même de courant électrique dans la maison, pas de téléphone, alors, pas d'appareils électriques et aucune fantaisie bien entendu.

Raymond-Vincent Roy   Gérard, Claude, Florent, Roger, Laprise et Anne-Aline Roy

C'était les lampes à l'huile, les poêles à bois et à charbon en hiver et des cotons de blé d'Inde en été pour faire la cuisson. Heureusement, il y avait une pompe à main dans la maison qui fournissait l'eau courante.

C'est l'été. Il y a hélas bien des soucis. Le bébé, les jardins, les repas pour les hommes qui travaillent fort. Comme le foyer est propre et bien organisé, ça va très bien. Même si le travail nous encombre, nous prenons le temps de voisiner avec la parenté et les amis.

Avec les récoltes de céréales bien à l'abri, vient ensuite le "cannages" de fruits et de végétaux, nettoyer les jardins et prêter main-forte pour la récolte du blé d'Inde qui se fait à la main avec une épluchette à la main. La méthode est longue et parfois pénible lorsque la température frise le gel.

Tandis que j'aidais mon mari avec les moissons c'était le moment idéal pour les grand-mamans de gâter leur joli petit-fils, Gérard. Heureusement que les grands-mères et les chères tantes, Anna et Jeanne, étaient là pour nous rendre service.

Cependant lorsque j'avais du temps libre, je m'empressais de visiter ma mère car elle aussi était très occupée avec son petit bébé Raymond Vincent. Sa tâche demandait de grands sacrifices, vu son âge avancé de 40 ans et voir au besoin des huit autres membres de la famille. Femme de cultivalteur, elle surveillait et apaisait adroitement le remue-ménage que pouvait entraîner l'exploitation d'une ferme.

La famille Laprise franchit une nouvelle étape en 1940. C'est le beau bébé, Roger Berchman, qui s'annonce le 13 août, jour même de la fête de mon père. Toute la famille se réjouit en ce jour providentiel.

Cette nouvelle naissance augmente le travail et les soucis envers la famille. C'est presque impossible pour moi de partager mon temps entre l'entretien du foyer et celui de la ferme. Les tâches quotidiennes sont primordiales mais il y a aussi nos deux trésors, Gérard et Roger à amuser. C'est une période bien spéciale pour le développement de l'enfant.

Le froid est rigoureux et la neige commence à "freiner" nos visites ce qui nous permet de prendre le temps de cajoler et caresser nos chers petits qui demandent plus d'attention.

L'emprise de l'hiver se fait sentir. Comme d'habitude, une des pièces de la maison est convertie en atelier d'artisanat. Des après-midi d'affilée sont consacrées à assembler et à piquer. Chacune de nos compagnes apporte son originalité, son savoir-faire et son humour anticipant d'en finir deux pièces chacune, une fois la tâche accomplie.

Le fruit de nos labeurs vaut bien la récompense de pouvoir admirer ces pièces fabriquées de nos propres mains.

Parlons aussi des couvre-pieds "d'étoffe." Nous recueillons les pièces d'étoffe. Nous les découpons de façon à ne pas avoir de perte de tissu convenable pour les couvre-lits: et lorsque toutes les pièces sont assemblées, on les transpose sur le métier. Au lieu de piquer, chacune des pièces est attachée avec de la laine de couleur aux quatre coins ainsi qu'au centre. Ça fait joli une fois assemblée. Les couvertures de lit sont essentielles pour les jours froids d'hiver.

Toutes ces pièces, esthétiquement composées de motifs originaux sont des pièces de collection recherchées par les "mordus" d'artisanat.

C'est l'automne 1941. Mon époux est embauché chez "Campbell Soup." Il fait aussi la culture de tomate pour la même compagnie. Grâce à cet emploi, nous avons pu acheter une radio à piles. Pour la première fois nous écoutons les nouvelles et de la belle musique.

Cela nous a permis aussi de nous procurer une machine à coudre neuve, un appareil domestique indispensable pour confectionner le linge de bébé, et celui de la famille, le raccommodage et les couvre-pieds. Dorénavant, je serai en mesure de tailler de beaux vêtements, un métier appris de ma mère.

L'hiver semble moins long même si l'on travaille fort. Les bûcherons sont enchantés de passer une heure pendant le dîner dans une ambiance reposante, avec musique et reportage des nouvelles du jour.

Il n'y a rien sans sacrifice. C'était pénible d'envisager la récolte des tomates. Dans un joli petit wagon neuf, je traîne Gérard et Roger au champ. Grâce à Roland Sterling et Orville Goure, deux employés fiables et avenants, tout se passe assez bien et les tomates sont transportées à la "cannerie" Campbell Soup.

Le 25 novembre 1941 nous saluons Claude Rosaire Laprise, charmant petit garçon de 8 livres et 3 onces, né à la maison paternelle. Assistant à cet évenement était la garde-malade Margaret Carron et le médecin Johnson. Parfois je me sentais un peu abattue par le travail qu'exige ces trois petits enfants. Pendant les mois d'hiver mon époux et moi-même partagions le quotidien ce qui rendait la vie plus intéressante.

Le 26 septembre 1942, lors d'une visite chez mes parents, mon petit frère, Raymond Vincent, entre à la maison en criant, "ma tête, ma tête"puis il s'évanouit à nos genoux. Ma mère et mon père, ne sachant quoi faire, le transporte à l'hôpital. Les médecins lui donnent les premiers soins, mais le 30 septembre il succombe à une hémorragie cérébrale. Les jours qui suivent furent pénibles pour la famille. Cet enfant de 4 ans était choyé de tous.

La vie continue. À chaque jour suffit sa peine. Nous avons trois enfants qui exigent beaucoup et les soucis se multiplient.

Reflections on the Outhouse - la p'tite maise
D'après le "Larousse dictionnaire de l'ancien français"
la Moyen Âge - maise: n.f. Habitation, cabane.

Plumbing on the farm always left much to be desired. Our favourite nesting place was a two "seater" situated a short distance from the house under an old shade tree. There were neat openings carved in the door with a jack knife. These half-moon or star jagged carvings served two purposes: either it allowed you to gaze out and take the time to smell the roses as the saying goes, or you were preoccupied leafing through an old discarded catalogue sorting out its dull pages. Rolled tissue was nowhere in sight, therefore if newspaper supply ran out you had no choice but to resume using the slippery old pages.

Summer visits to the outhouse usually provided a leisurely reprieve from a hectic and busy schedule. Sometimes, one would be rudely awakened to the realities of life when a rock would be hurled at the door, resounding like a mallet hitting a drum. There were occasions when the resounding bang on the door would send you scurrying to get yourself pulled together for a quick exit. Winter visits were more hasty since tracking through snowdrifts was often required. You had to whisk away the snow before mounting your chilly perch.

How thankful we were the day Dad declared the makeshift toilet would be installed in a small spare bedroom upstairs. It became known as the "bathroom" for the winter months. But there was a downside to this primitive commodity . . . whose turn was it to empty the pail? My four boys were ecstatic when one of the foursome purposely tripped with the pail, they soon realized there was a punishment for bypassing the rules. The temptation to play tricks was always there, so it happened again and again. To add "insult to injury," these slips were aggravated and funny because of the lack of electrical conveniences.

Finally, electricity was installed in 1943. What a blessing! These innovations are taken for granted today but when shortage of power occurs we think once again about our blessings. We thank God for our commodities that could have alleviated the hardships for the generations of the 20s, 30s and 40s.

In 1943, the care of three small boys growing up was not an easy task. I managed but a neighbour, Louella Blais Caron, who had just married in 1942 gave me a helping hand twice a week. At the time my frail nerves were pushed to the limit, and could have easily provoked a depression. The days she spent with me alleviated my anxieties. It was quality time and work. I'm most grateful to Louella for her encouragement, I admire her, and I know she is a strong woman.

By March 19 1943, Florent was born. The delivery was at home with Dr. Kenny in attendance and the help of Margaret Carron Jubenville, an efficient registered nurse. A beautiful 7 lbs. 12 oz.

baby with blond hair, we loved him so much. Mr. Zephir Thibodeau was building us new cupboards and finished just in time for the new baby. These same cupboards grace the kitchen walls, and are still "looking good."

With a new baby, and having to feed an extra four and sometimes five men all winter while working in the bush became overwhelming; help was a necessity. It was Thérèse Pinsonneault who gave me a helping hand three days a week for minimum wages of three dollars a day. Everyone seemed happier in those days, as they felt they were fulfilling a double mission helping others and helping themselves to obtain necessities of life. She was only 17 at the time.

By 1943, many times Thérèse was taken home with horse and sleigh by Roland Sterling as roads were impassable by car. This turned into a pleasant romantic gossip. Thérèse survived.

Primary Venture 1940

Our primary venture on the farm was buying a 50 acre farm with 33 acres of bush in 1940. Wood was plentiful then, but clearing the land for cultivation became a strenuous task. Men spent the winter in the bush, cutting down trees, pulling logs with horses, and stacking them in piles ready for the sawmills. My brother Ralph, only 16 years old, my husband and a hired man Roland Sterling, sometimes a few neighbours put in long hours. I was in the kitchen cooking hefty meals to replenish their energies.

In the spring of 1944, a young 16yr. old neighbour Orville Goure began working for us after school and on Saturdays for spending money. By 1946, he became a full time employee. For 10 years or more, he and his friend, Roland Sterling, worked side by side helping us and caring for our growing boys. When they left , in 1954, Gérard was 13, Roger was 12, Claude was 10 and Florent 9. The whole Laprise family owes a debt of gratitude to these two helpful hardworking neighbours.

By 1947, added to the crew of men was another crew, three young lads, Gérard, Roger and Claude, ranging in age from six to eight. They were summoned to the bush every Saturday morning from early spring on, and worked diligently, picking stumps strewn all over the terrain.. It took at least 10 years to clear the debris in order to cultivate this 33 acres of land. Today, it is one of the best loam available for growing excellent crops.

The Ice Box Era

A few years elapsed before Ralph Allard began delivering milk, buttermilk, butter, cream and other small commodities at our doors. This was another welcome service. Later he began buying all surplus eggs from the farms, as well as cream to make butter. Ice was as much a staple as bread and milk in the days before refrigeration. Without ice in the"Ice Box"it was hard to preserve these dairy products especially in hot weather. This ice was cut in "crystal clear" blocks from the Thames River and Lake Erie during the winter season. It was preserved in ice houses surrounded by "brin de scie," sawdust from the sawmill. It was imperative that food for babies be kept fresh.

At home we managed before the ice box period with a brick well called a "cistern" full of cold fresh water. It consisted of cross pieces at the top; from there we hung four to five pails tied with a rope and hooked on these cross pieces. We lowered the pails partly in cold water to preserve its content. Sometimes the procedure met with disaster as we either dropped the pail or overturned it. It was expected. No children were allowed in the area, as it was dangerous to fall in when planks were open. No wonder that ice delivery was a breakthrough. In very hot weather, many mornings we woke up to find the pan overflowing onto the kitchen floor. But the rewards were great. Ice cold water to drink. Ice to make our own ice cream, ice to soothe headache and other of its various uses.

This service continued for approximately 15 years. Later, cars were more plentiful, the corner store was closer, a trip to Chatham was easier. It is somewhat interesting to note that during the war, 1940-1945, manufacturing of refrigerators was fully curtailed. The impact was alarming. No refrigerators except gas refrigerators could be bought anywhere. In 1946 with four small children less than six years old and expecting Caroline Fernande, we managed to have a homemade freezer built and delivered in August. Our first refrigerator appeared in the home in June 1948. It surely was a blessing. Also, in the late thirties, there was door to door delivery of all kinds of bread, buns and cakes. We loved the brick loaves and the crust was delicious.

The Era Of The Radio

Along with all new innovations came the opening of a Central Post Office in Chatham in 1932. Already in 1927, CFCO in Chatham carried the first farm and home hour broadcast in Canada.

Mr. Beardall relinquished his amateur broadcasting licence in favour of a commercial licence in 1929. At this time, the station was located in a house but was moved downtown to operate from the Community Trust Building on King St. Later it was transferred to the William Pitt hotel on the third floor. On April 6th 1947, CFCO began to operate from a new transmitter building south on No.2 Highway in Raleigh Township. In 1927, the interest in Radio began for the pioneers. Many enjoyed the services of the radio, but as I remember it was not till the mid thirties that we had a battery radio and the same held true for many less fortunate households in the country.

Progress was the word, even though there was very little money. It was a period of rapid growth and changes, somewhat like we are experiencing at a different level today. Seemed as what we experienced at the time was practically unreal.

Snack Time

Guess what - no chips - no tacos - no corn chips - no cheesies - no onion rings, so what munchies do we have in the thirties? Upstairs we go - bring a pan of dried apples, a dozen ears of Indian popcorn - black and dried and a few ears of small white popcorn. We all pitched in to shell this popcorn by hand, two ears for each child. O K, we are now ready to pop this corn. Pop, pop it goes - and into the huge earthenware bowl decorated with fruits, a special from Wanless hardware in Chatham filled with a crumbling mound of snow-white popped kernels. Now here comes mother with the cracker jack syrup. Everyone is around the kitchen table, lips smacking and waiting to munch. This was snack time. Everyone was happy and glad. We could enjoy snack time every night, but had candied popcorn about once a week. If we lacked brown sugar, we used white sugar, syrup and red colouring to make pink popcorn. Everyone was happy with very little. In the mid thirties, we managed to get a second hand Victrola which provided some music, so we were free to jump and dance around from time to time. This was very special.

Do You Recall?

You may recall, the Japanese internment camps, also the German prisoners of war camps, located in the Chatham area during World War II. Farmers were welcomed to hire these prisoners who were under strict surveillance. Farmers were asked to provide employment for many of them at different intervals. They were excellent workers but were prisoners in our country due to the outcome of this world conflict. Personally we are very grateful to them for helping us with a fire out of control in the straw stack that would surely have destroyed all our sheds and two barns. Our four sons, Gérard 7, Roger 6, Claude 5 and Florent 4 years old were the masterminds behind this catastrophic event in 1946.

In a few weeks, everyone and everything had, more or less, returned to its normal state and the dark cloud which hovered still, was cast away by one cloud fringed with a silver lining. You see, a long-awaited miracle finally happened in our family. Our first daughter Caroline Fernande Carmel was born August 27, 1946 at St. Joseph Hospital. It was a moment of rapture and ecstasy when I first gazed at my bouncing baby. Being blessed with a beautiful baby daughter brought the male Laprise household to a level of outpouring love and admiration.

It was understood that our first daughter would be called Caroline after the maternal great grandmother Carline Roy. The baby sister had definitely cast a spell over the rough and tumble energetic foursome treading ever so carefully and reverently about whenever Caroline (nicknamed Coline) demanded their attention. But soon the novelty wore off. Their affection turned to teasing and their teasing had Coline screaming constantly, and even their dad joined in, adding fuel to the fire.

Surprise! Surprise!

In 1947 my life seemed quite hectic, when suddenly my health deteriorated and a hormone deficiency menaced my health. In order to regulate this disorder, there was no choice but to heed Dr. Samson's advice and to enter Victoria hospital in London, so that a team of specialists could monitor and evaluate the problem.

After some 50 years the condition remains but with monthly injections of hormones I enjoy a fairly healthy life.

Preparations were in order and I entered the hospital for a period of five weeks. It was not easy to leave my four young active boys and a baby girl in the care of Marie Pinsonneault, our neighbour's 18 year old daughter, even though she was pleasant, caring, and well versed in household duties as well as outgoing and vivacious. These attributes were a big plus with children. So together with my husband they managed.

After a lapse of three weeks, the whole family visited me at the hospital. My beautiful 9 month old baby girl started walking unsteadily towards me with outstretched arms, coaxed by Marie's reassuring voice. What a surprise!

In 1947, this household was really buzzing and mother had an overload, let me tell you. Once again I needed some space and this I could get, after a pleasant farmer's daughter told me she was interested in helping. She lived in Comber, and came to help me all winter through to April at which time she had to go back to the farm to help her father. This angel was Cécile Brosseau-Baillargeon. Her work was meticulous, her cooking excellent, and in her spare time she did crocheting. She taught me how to do crochet work, and she made a few nice pieces for me. I'm still proud to display them today. Cécile with her pleasant disposition surely contributed to our well being and we are grateful.

At the turn of the 50s I was very active in social affairs as well as church and school organizations.

Innovations, new ideas, new techniques at all levels of society and of farming contributed to a very prosperous and advanced way of life in the 50s.

Tobacco Field

Rev. Father Paul Milne

Front row, left to right: Florent, Claude, Roger and Gérard with Hercule Gagnon holding their sister Coline.
Back row, left to right: Halarie Rivard, Adolphe Gagnon, Emile Gagnon and my husband Trefflé.

Last load of lumber from our farm in 1948

1946

Bathing Facilities

Bathing facilities on the farm were also very primitive in the 40s. We had what they called a summer kitchen where we had the luxury of taking a bath in a large round galvanized tub. Fortunately we had soft water from a deep well for baths and for doing the laundry. It was stored in a big cistern above the first floor of the barn. It was a system installed by my grandfather Caron in the early 1900. An old-fashioned windmill would pump water into the cistern. There was a piped system to the house and with a hand pump we hauled the water into our buckets. This was a blessing. In a large boiler we would heat this water on the stove and transfer it to the tub. Who gets in first? Babies of course, as everyone was required to bathe in the same tub of water. By 1950, bathrooms with electricity and running water were readily installed.

The 50s, a new decade, a new addition to the Laprise family. Guy Vincent, our sixth child, was born on Sept. 23, 1950.

Another son appears on the scene to claim his share of the tender loving care and attention in the Laprise household. He was a darling baby full of energy who at three months could stand by himself close to the kitchen booth. Within a year he was sharing in all disturbing mischief that kids can think of.

Things were drastically different during depression years. Unlike today, we didn't have the luxury of natural gas nor propane to heat the home, so when fall came around we harvested corn, shelled it at the farm and the cobs were hauled to the basement; this was winter's supply of heating and cooking. Corn cob fires were treacherous at times when the big box stoves were filled to capacity. The stove pipes would sometimes turn red under the tremendous heat. It was quick heat but as the fire died down absolutely nothing could retain and control the heat, especially at night. We made sure to dress the babies properly, and many a night they spent cuddled in our arms for warmth.

5 iéme

EXPOSITION

Annuelle de

Blé d'Inde et de Grains

de l'Union des Cultivateurs de

Kent et d'Essex

tenue à

PAIN COURT, ONTARIO

Du 18 au 20 Janvier, 1939

Bureau de Direction
de l'Union des Cultivateurs de Kent et d'Essex

Aumônier ....M. L'Abbé Isidore Poisson, curé de Stevenson

Président Honoraire ....L'Honorable Sénateur Gustave Lacasse, Tecumseh

Vice-Présidents Honoraires –
M. Léo Sylvestre ....Windsor
M. Jérémie Ducharme ....Belle Rivière
M. Louis-Philippe Pinsonneault ....Pointe-Aux-Roches
Président ....M. Philippe Chauvin, Pointe-Aux-Roches
Vice-Président ....M. Eugène Roy, Pain Court
Secrétaire ....M. Gérard Caron, Pain Court

DIRECTEURS
Louis-Philippe Pinsonneault ....Pointe-Aux-Roches
Arthur Houle ....Grande Pointe   Réginald Caron ....Pain Court
Philias Grondin ....Pointe-Aux-Roches   John Rivait ....Staples
Eugène Levasseur ....St. Joachim   Charles Gauthier ....Belle Rivière
Laurent Lachance ....Tecumseh   Jérémie Ducharme ......Belle Rivière
Hector Bondy ....Rivière-Aux-Canards   Paul Gouin ....Tecumseh
Bernard Thibert ....Tilbury   Napoléon Roy ....Pain Court
Léo Dufour ....Sandwich Ouest

Comité d'organisation
Président ....Hercule Trahan
Vice-président ....Arthur Houle
Secrétaire ....Gérard Caron
Directeurs ....Sylvestre Caron, Willie Trudell, Idas Lebrun, Théodore Emery

Juges

Blé d'Inde ....J.A. Garner, Chatham, Frank Weaver, Turnerville
Grains ....Thomas O'Neill, Chatham, N. D. McKenzie, Chatham

CERCLE DES FERMIÈRES — COMITÉ
Présidente ....Mme Annie Caron
Vice-Présidente ....Mlle Annette Carron
Secrétaire ....Mlle Bernadette Martin
Directrices ..... Mme Délia Gagner, Mlle Léona Pinsonneault, Mlle Marie Anne Faubert

PROGRAMME L'EXPOSITION commencera par une grand-messe chantée dans
l'église de Pain Court à 9:30 a.m. le mercredi 18 janvier.
Nous présenterons un programme récréatif – les mercredi et jeudi soirs à 8 heures
précises au sous-sol de l'église. Tout le monde est invité. Des artistes de renommée
seront au programme – vues animées, etc.

LE VENDREDI – 20 janvier, journée du congrès– Plusieurs éminents orateurs seront
au programme.

LE DIMANCHE – 22 janvier – Election et banquet annuels de l'U.C.K.E.

La Société St-Jean-Baptiste de Pain Court fait honneur à la race qu'elle représente.

PAUL MARTIN, M.P.

1941

Salutations aux membres et amis de la Société St-Jean-Baptiste de Pain Court

EUGENE ROY

BIENVENU

When in Pain Court make the

DOVER HOTEL

your stopping place for

ROOMS, MEALS, BEVERAGES

VICTOR TRAHAN, Manager

Compliments de

NAPOLEON ROY

MARCHAND DE GRAINS ET PRODUCTEUR DU BLE-D'INDE

KING'S HYBRID

J. G. JOHNSTON & SON
Groceries, Provisions,
Crockery, Glassware and Hardware
PRAIRIE SIDING
1177 R 22
SUPERIOR CHAIN STORE
1939
PRAIRIE SIDING MEMORIES

As a boy, I remember vividly the local Johnston Store that sold and delivered groceries to a wide area of Raleigh and Dover townships. This store operated by J.G. Johnston and his son Walter (Soup) was a godsend to many families as it extended monthly and even longer periods of credit to many families who paid when they could.

Locals assembled on the wide store steps in nice weather to exchange news and gossip. What an exciting experience for a wide-eyed young boy. On some summer evenings, "Revivalists" preached and banged tambourines for anyone willing to listen. On cooler evenings, cards were played inside. On some weekends dancing took place on the second floor.

Along the C.N. railroad track stood a station where passengers could flag an eastbound train in the morning into Chatham and return in the evening on the "mail train" which brought bags of daily mail to the Post Office housed in the store. A large freight shed also was located along the track and travelling shows entertained us on a summer's evening with sword swallowing, knife tricks etc.

A Hiram Walker's grain elevator also completed the corners of the road crossing the rail tracks. Actually in those days of few trucks, slow cars and little cash, this community offered much to the surrounding area.

George A Bruette

Mrs. Doris Carey whose maiden name was Johnston was born in Prairie Siding in 1921. She died in 1998 at the age of 77.

Her father managed the grain elevator in Prairie Siding for years, and her uncle John Johnston owned the general store in Prairie Siding.

Doris relates: "I have beautiful memories of my childhood. My father would whittle little cars and trains for my two brothers and mother would make doll clothes for my two sisters and myself. She would also make clothes for the family. In fact my mother made all my clothes until I went to vocational school."

"My parents were just perfect" she said. We would all go out and cut down our Christmas tree and take it home to decorate it. We would make popcorn streamers along with all the other decorations.

Marion Johnston was a cousin of Doris, and so was Walter (Soup) Johnston who operated the general store in Prairie Siding after the death of his father John Johnston.   Marion married Walter Crow on March 11, 1932 at St. Peter's Tilbury East, Ontario. She was a dedicated registered nurse, and lived in Pain Court all her married life, and was our neighbour.   She was well-known and very compassionate towards everyone, especially in her nursing career. They had two children, Clayton and Marlene.

COMPLIMENTS OF

A. R. REAUME

GENERAL MERCHANT

Reaumeville

Here at the foot of the bridge crossing the Thames at that time, 1915 - 1925 on the Dover side was a small store operated by one-armed Alec Reaume. Alec also was the bridge attendant who raised the bridge whenever a large tug towing a loaded coal barge made its way eastward up the Thames to unload its cargo in Chatham.

Before the bridge Alec operated a ferry which offered crossing over the Thames. Some school children living on the Raleigh side needed this service to attend Public school #5 Dover on the Jacob Road. In Sugar beet days beets would be barged from this location to the factory in Chatham.

Today this store exists as a home and has experienced several owners over the years including one well-known resident, Mrs. Magdelena Jubenville (née Béchard), now deceased.

Many old timers can still remember Alec Reaume with his bushy moustache selling penny candy from behind the counter.

George A Bruette

L' office national du film - 1943

En 1943, c'est M. Jean Beaudoin, le directeur des programmes français à l'Office national du film, qui se fait toujours un plaisir de desservir la population du sud-ouest Ontario mettant à notre disposition des catalogues de films 16 mm. en français et en anglais pouvant servir dans les classes ainsi que pour des rencontres spéciales dans nos paroisses françaises. M. Beaudoin a toujours gardé un grand intérêt envers ses amis de Pain Court et de Grande Pointe par l'entremise des films.

Nos sincères remerciements à General Motors Product pour la version française du film "Marian Congress." Nous l'avons présenté le 27 mars 1949 à la salle paroissiale. Merci à M. Kearney du département de publicité qui s'en est chargé.

Une fois l'API établie nous sommes devenus membres du National Film Board avec l'aide de la bibliothèque publique de Chatham. Cette agence nous a rendu de multiples services. Avec notre affiliation, nous avions accès aux projecteurs sonores de la bibliothèque et aux films anglais selon nos besoins.

Pendant plusieurs années j'ai propagé et desservi des films dans les classes et dans la communauté en générale.

Avec l'évolution technologique de la télé, ce sera elle qui deviendra maîtresse dans les foyers.

Kent Cooperative Medical Services

This cooperative medical service was a mutual benefit association organized for the purpose of providing prepaid hospitalization on true cooperative principles for residents of school sections and also for members of Farm Forum, Women's Institute, church professionals, business, or fraternal groups within Kent County. The association is managed by a board of directors elected by memberships. Rates at the time, for a standard ward was $4.50 a day.

Annual Rates for family was	$17.00
Single	$ 8.50
Dependent children over 21	$ 8.50

In 1947, with Mr. Orval Hogg secretary and Arthur Wootton as director and speaker for Cooperative Medical Services, we eventually succeeded in implementing this service with our members.

Thanks to the relentless efforts and visions of Yvonne Bélanger and Caroline Laprise, this project became a rewarding and worthwhile enterprise that benefited all those who participated.

One of the most successful cooperative movement in Kent County during the forties was "Thamesville Cooperative." Through hard work, members of the co-op progressed to the point of being able to offer large groups to enroll into the Kent Cooperative Medical Services.

Factory workers and well established institutions could offer assistance in their place of employment, but for remaining segments of society there was absolutely no protection whatsoever to help meet any hospitalization expenses.

As costs rose from year to year, families became devastated, especially in catastrophic cases. It purely took weeks and months of conscientious work by devoted people to bring about this needed transition, so that all may benefit in joining   the Co-op Medical Services of Kent, thereby bringing relief from hospital bills.

The ideal way to recruit was through the Ladies Altar Society of Pain Court and Grande Pointe. Every member was entitled to be part of the Cooperative Medical Services. The society members in charge collected dues annually and delivered said dues to Thamesville Cooperative Services every year.

It was a tremendous task but after a few years the rewards were very beneficial to the families. A year later, we concentrated on establishing a Child Health Centre with the generous help of the Public Health Nurses.

Re Thamesville Co-op Medical Services - bulletin in my possession

Child Health Care Centre

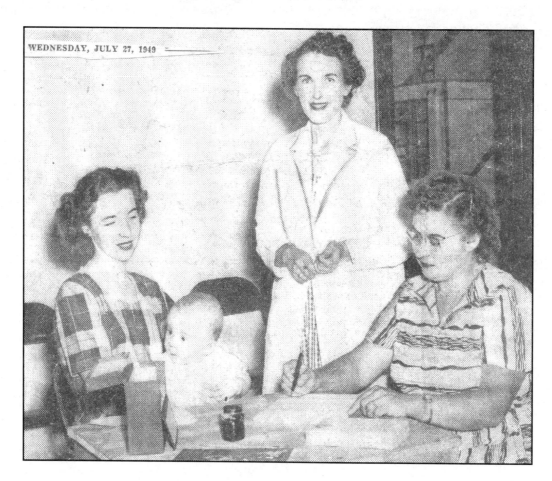

WEDNESDAY, JULY 27, 1949

Clinic Pays Visit to Pain Court
Wednesday, July 27, 1949

Mothers are taking advantage of the health service offered by the Kent County Health Unit for children. Recently, Pain Court was visited by the "Well Baby Clinic" sponsored by the Parent-Teacher Association of Pain Court and Grande Pointe. Left to right are: Mrs. Raymond Cartier of Grande Pointe with baby Rosaire Cartier, Miss Fraser and Mrs. Caroline Laprise, Clinic Chairman.

The Child Health Centre was conducted in the church basement at Pain Court. This clinic was sponsored in 1948 by the Parent-Teacher Association. (P.T.A.) All infants and children of pre-school age were welcome with their parents, every 4th Monday of each month between 2 and 4 o'clock. There was a public health nurse, a lady or a nurse assistant volunteer of the P.T.A. and children were examined thoroughly and immunization shots were given by a medical officer of health, protecting children against tetanus, diphtheria, whooping cough and smallpox. These shots were administered to each child for 3 consecutive months. This clinic brought peace of mind to families and at no cost to the families. Many times we had close to 100 children participating in this plan.

It was through the good will of all the volunteers of the parish, the cooperation of all teachers who encouraged the clinic attendance and also to the dedicated medical staff of Chatham, that this humanitarian task existed for many years.   The first clinic was held August 23 1948, in the church-basement with Mr. Watson as public health services coordinator, Mrs. Thompson as nurse supervisor and Léontine Roy as secretary. Approximately 55 to 60 pre-school children were present and registered and at least 40 mothers were briefed at a conference. Caroline Laprise and Yvonne Bélanger, the two leaders of the project, thanked Dr. H .R. Samson, the nurse and all the mothers for their support.

Baby Contests

Under the sponsorship of the Ladies Altar Society with Mrs. Elizabeth Daniel as president, we had our 1st baby show contest in 1947 at our July 1st celebration in Pain Court.

It was Dr. H. R. Samson a dedicated general practitioner who helped establish the baby clinics held monthly in the parish church basement. His assistants were Dr. C. C. White, Dr. Turner, Dr. Beattie and others who helped later.

As an incentive for mothers to bring the babies to the clinic monthly, we decided to hold baby contests. In 1947 it was held at Pain Court when 24 toddlers competed to capture honours. Drs. C. C. White and Beattie presided the show. Baby Elaine Carron, daughter of Mr. and Mrs. Herbert Carron, captured 1st prize.

Even the men contributed from time to time as their wives were busy registering or weighing babies in the contest. Others were local nurses who volunteered. A second show was held in 1948 under the sponsorship of the Parent-Teacher Association at Pain Court. In 1949, Dover Township chose the most beautiful baby in Kent County at the home of Mrs. Calixte Benoit who owned the general store. This was the third show, held by the Parent-Teachers Association of Grande Pointe and Pain Court in conjunction with the child health centre held every month in the church basement at Pain Court. There was a parade of baby buggies when 18 entries competed for the Baby Beauty Trophy. Anxious Dad pushed the empty baby buggy back and forth in front of the house as their off-spring was being weighed and examined by Dr. H. R. Samson and his assistants. Mothers waited patiently. When called, they proudly presented their "darlings" to the nurses: Mrs. Murray Cadotte and Mrs Gerald Bélanger. Babies seemed the most unconcerned of all.

The final results placed 13 month old Wayne Charron as King of the babies. He was the son of Mr. and Mrs. Oscar Charron of Grande Pointe. Four month old Claire Bélanger, daughter of Mr. and Mrs. Roland Bélanger, captured the prize for the healthiest baby under six months. Seven month old Robert Faubert won the prize as second best, and ten month old Bobby Lozon, son of Mr. and Mrs. Laurence Lozon, was third. Honourable mention went to Donna Jean daughter of Mr. and Mrs. Edas Brown, and four month old Linda Ann daughter of Mr. and Mrs. Lionel Pinsonneault. The two ladies in charge of the Baby Contest were Caroline Laprise and Yvonne Bélanger.

Les retraites fermées

Depuis 1946, je me rendais à Détroit, accompagnée de Mme Alexina Caron, pour assister à des retraites fermées au couvent des Soeurs Marie Réparatrice. En 1948, j'ai accepté, sous la recommandation du Rev. Père Meloche, directeur de la nouvelle maison de retraite fermée à Oxley (Harrow), une position sur le conseil exécutif temporaire pour les retraites fermées françaises des dames, aidée d'un chapelain. Mon travail consistait d'organiser les paroisses françaises rurales de Kent et Essex pour les retraites fermées. C'était une oeuvre à encourager de toutes nos forces surtout pour les groupes de langue française autant pour les femmes que pour les hommes. À chaque mois, "La Ligue des retraitants" avait un déjeuner à tour de rôle, dans les paroisses bilingues respectives. Leur engagement était très édifiant car de 60 à 75 se réunissent à tous les mois pour messe, déjeuner et conférence.

Ligue des Retraitants

Chaque année les fondateurs de la ligue se rendaient dans une paroisse française de Détroit pour une retraite française. Vers 1938 ils se décident d'approcher le clergé ainsi que d'autres ligues pour fournir des conférenciers au ralliement des hommes dans les paroisses françaises de Kent et Essex. C'était une oeuvre à encourager; il y avait environ 60 à 75 hommes qui se réunissaient tous les mois pour profiter d'une messe en groupe et un conférencier de choix. Cela fournissait un développement intellectuel et religieux ainsi qu'un lien formidable pour ceux qui y participaient. La Ligue des retraitants prends de l'essor sous la direction de M. George Janisse. En 1948, M. Janisse devient directeur du comité d'organisation assisté du Père G.L. Blonde pour la maison de retraite à Oxley.

Grâce au dévouement des dames, un déjeuner était servi pour recevoir la Ligue.

Lors du départ de M. Janisse en 1948 d'autres retraitants ont siégé à leur tour. Président: Edmond Chauvin remplace M. Janisse, suivi de Émile Démarais qui remplit sa tâche avec entrain pendant une dizaine d'années. Lors d'une grave maladie il cède sa place à M. Richard Drouillard qui accepte de diriger la Ligue des Retraitants.

Nombreux sont les hommes qui font des retraites de trois jours à la maison d'Oxley.

Retreat House opened by his Excellency Bishop Kidd at Oxley

The retreat house for laity will henceforth be known as Holy Family Retreat House, Oxley. It was officially opened August 1948. Rt. Rev. W. F. Langlois, D.P., V.F., and Leo Lepage were honorary chairmen of the Board of Directors of the Holy Family Retreat House. Other members of the Board included, H. E. Gignac, K.S.G., Chairman, Rev. J. A. Rooney and Col. Paul Poisson, M.O. building and property committee; organization committee, George Janisse, Rev. G. L. Blonde; Rev. W. E. Dillon D. P. and John Wall, financial committee; Rev. L. J. Poisson and George Hanrahan, publicity committee. Rev. A. L. Meloche who had been in charge of lay retreats for several years was secretary of the Board. The first retreat was scheduled for Friday July 16, 1948.

Ref. Catholic Register

Altar Society Has Big Year - 1945

It was under the diligent leadership of Elizabeth Daniel, that the ladies managed to accomplish many worthwhile projects. Father Laliberté, pastor and spiritual advisor, accepted our donation of two thousand dollars for worthy projects and improvements in the parish.

Furthermore, Christmas baskets were given to needy families and clothing was provided for the needy in the parish.

It was reported that the society had 139 members and 24 honorary members over 75 years of age.

Caroline Laprise reported on the co-op medical plan for hospital care and pointed out that 85 people had taken out memberships. Delphine Roy extended appreciation to Elizabeth Daniel and her executive for their fine achievement of the past year.

Elizabeth Daniel was a special person with the ability to achieve numerous worthwhile causes. For many years she was president of the ladies society and I was privileged to serve under her leadership for three years prior to my election as president in 1946. Honorary President was Elizabeth Daniel, Vice President, Philomène Caron, Louise Trudell Second Vice-president, Secretary Yvonne Bélanger and Treasurer Marie Anne Caron. Josephine Primeau managed the kitchen committee, Antoinette Marentette was church convener while Philomène Caron remained card party convener, and Sophie Buck and Marianne Faubert as helpers. Marie Emery our devoted organist continued her worthy cause. Délia Gagner was chairman of the social committee with Florence Caron, Pauline Gagner, Glorianna Bélanger. Henriette Maure purchased prizes during the year. Councillors for all the committees were Léa Charbonneau, Joséphine Primeau, Irène Gagner, Alma Martin.

Children of Mary Sodality

This wonderful group of young women 15 years and older had seen this society formed in the early thirties under the leadership of the parish priest Rev. Zotique Mailloux. The young girls refrained from going to dances and smoking. As the years progressed, fewer girls wanted to adhere to official rules and consequently less young girls were admitted in the Sodality.

By 1946, the Ladies Altar Society took the necessary steps to amalgamate with their group a junior branch of members called the Sodality of the Children of Mary. This group of young ladies were called upon to help the Ladies Altar Society on various projects be it religious, social or voluntary help.

(By Chatham Daily New Staff photographer) 1948

Members of the parish of the Church of the Immaculate Conception last night enjoyed an old-fashioned "Leap Year Mardi Gras" through the planning of the Ladies Altar Society. During the evening euchre, jokes, contests, folk songs, pancakes and prizes were enjoyed. Responsible for the evening's entertainment were ladies shown above. From left to right are Mrs. Bernadin Maure, Mrs. Caroline Laprise president, Mrs. Alfred Caron, Mrs. Gérald Gagner, Mrs. Eugene Caron, Mrs. Z. Gagner, Mrs. Eugene Primeau and Mrs. Norman Bélanger.

On "Shrove Tuesday 1948" one hundred or so Pain Court parishioners congregated in the church hall to join in a leap year "Mardi Gras" party convened by the Ladies Altar Society.

The guests of honour were W. Montcalm of Ottawa who gave an agricultural seminar in the parish, along with Georges Michaud, also of Ottawa, who had been touring Kent and Essex for the last two months instructing farmers on "Copératives." (Credit Unions)

Euchre and various other games were played. Then came the fun of matching Valentines followed with a presentation by the older members of the group together with the two special guests. Philippe Caron and Erminie Sterling volunteered as chorus leaders with Trefflé Laprise at the piano.

The serving of traditional Shrove Tuesday pancakes was the "clou de la soirée." Try and picture yourself in the midst of 100 or more boisterous but fun-loving people ready to party, everyone armed with pancakes dripping with golden syrup, tossing them in the air like a whirlwind of flying saucers, either dodging them as they sail by or simply being at the mercy of your opponent as he or she aims smack at your face, or arm or head, whatever, or better still, catching them in flight and plastering them wherever the whim fancies with everyone either cursing or laughing trying to beat each other at his own game.

This traditional custom has been passed on for generations, though very seldom in large groups, but more so, in neighbourly community entertainment. The evening came to a close with everyone joining in by singing our favourite folklore songs, followed with the national anthem for an evening closure of memories to cherish and remember.

La Société des Enfants de Marie

Le 16 mai 1948, les Enfants de Marie, sous l'habile direction de Alice Roy, présentent "Les Trois Enfants de Fatima" dans notre paroisse. La pièce fut merveilleusement exécutée.

Le coeur de chant, les solos de piano par Alice Roy et Vivienne Roy ont vraiment captivé l'auditoire. Diane Robert et Yvette Gagner ont ravi l'auditoire par leur chant.

La narratrice, Angéline Blais, a dépeint les sept tableaux de la pièce.

Marie-Louise Faubert accomplit à perfection le rôle de Notre-Dame de Fatima.

L'ange de Portugal	Aline Caron
Lucie de Jésus dos Santos « voyante »	Evelyn Maure?
Francisco Marto « voyant »	Thomas Blais
Jacinta Marto « voyante »	Louise Caron
Olimpia Marto . « mère »	Aline Caron
Maria-Rosa dos Santos « mère »	Rose-Marie Benoit
Caroline « soeur aînée de Lucia »	Lucille Caron
Thérèse « soeur aînée de Jacinta »	Clara Martin
Jean « frère aîné de Francisco et de Jacinta»	Francis Trudell
Marraine « directrice de l'orphelinat »	Vivienne Roy
Une petite orpheline	Claire Caron
Une garde-malade à l'hôpital	Thérèse Pinsonneault
Le Maire de la ville Ourem	Raymond Blais
Le géôlier employé du Maire	Paul Thibodeau
Trois bergers	Roméo Pinsonneault
	Edmond Lauzon
	François Caron
Deux bergères	Eléonore Martin
	Glorianna Faubert
Deux dames étrangères	Yvette Gagner
	Clara Martin

Le spectacle émouvant et grandiose fut répété à trois reprises et avec salle comble pour les trois présentations.

Chaque artiste était maître de son rôle et chacun a su captiver l'attention des spectateurs.

Il faut signaler que cette pièce fut pour les gens de notre région une révélation. En ce qui concerne les apparitions de la Vierge à Fatima, elles étaient très peu connues au début des années '40. Par après, il y eut bien des échos de Fatima: un film sonore à été réalisé, un congrès marial a eu lieu, des consécrations au Coeur Immaculée de Marie telles que demandé par la Vierge ont été accomplies. Petit à petit la dévotion à Notre-Dame de Fatima s'est répandue à travers le monde et les pèlerinages se multiplièrent.

Par pur hasard, mes amis Angéline et Gérard Marentette durant leur voyage à Fatima en mars 1986, ont eu le privilège de rencontrer Jean Marto (frère de Francisco et Jacinta) et son épouse lorsqu'ils ont visité la maison natale de Francisco et Jacinta Marto à Aljustrel-Fatima dont

Jean en est le propriétaire. De dire Angéline: "Un couple rayonnant d'humilité et de simplicité."

Une petite anecdote de la part de la cousine et voyante, de Lucie Dos Santos, affirme que la Maman Marto envoyait le grand frère Jean au pâturage avec les moutons afin de protéger les deux petits voyants des gens transportés de curiosité voulant les voir ou les interroger dû au phénomène céleste dont ils avaient été témoins.

Fondation - Club des Placiers

Depuis 1946, le Club des placiers se dévoue au service de la paroisse sous la direction de Adrien Caron et du Père Chevalier. Un groupe d'hommes s'organise pour faire la quête du dimanche et depuis ce jour, les membres ont continué de prendre les offrandes à la messe. En 1970, le club compte 35 membres actifs. Même s'il ne sont pas nombreux, ils ont pu organiser de nombreuses activités pendant plusieurs années. Avec la coopération des "Dames de Ste-Anne" ils ont pu organiser plusieurs soirées sociales. Le bien-être des jeunes est un des buts du Club. Durant les mois d'hiver ils ont construit la patinoire dans le parc et ils se sont intéressés au Club de base-ball de Pain Court. Avec la coopération des membres, ils ont développé le Parc Centenaire en 1954 et ils continuent de s'intéresser à son développement. En 1988, le Club des placiers cède sa place aux Chevaliers de Colomb.

Get Agricultural Tips

Talking over some of the finer points of farming at the farm school being held in Pain Court yesterday, today and tomorrow, are three interested parties. From left to right, they are Alfred Pinsonneault, Trefflé Laprise and Anthony Tittley, Agronomist, Field Man for Rural Families of Kent and Essex.

(Staff Photo) Chatham Daily News

L'Union des familles rurales de Kent et Essex - 1948

L'organisation est destinée à promouvoir le bien professionnel, économique et social de ses familles. Philippe Chauvin président, Roland Gagner secrétaire et propagandiste, et Georges Michaud, agronome, voient à l'efficacité du travail de préparation.

Le 21 novembre 1948, dans la salle paroissiale de Pain Court, s'est tenue une importante réunion des cultivateurs des comtés de Kent et d'Essex en vue de fonder définitivement l'union des familles rurales. La nouvelle association fut le couronnement d'un travail préparatoire d'au delà d'un an sous la direction de l'agronome Georges Michaud. Au delà de 125 cultivateurs ont décidé de procéder à la fondation et ont élu des officiers.

À la demande des gens, Georges Michaud présida aux élections. Henri Lessard du "Droit" fut prié d'agir comme secrétaire. Les directeurs siégèrent alors pour élire le bureau de direction ou comité exécutif. Philippe Chauvin président, Caroline Laprise et Mme Léo Masse vice-présidentes, Roland Gagner Secrétaire, Régis Caron trésorier, Alcide Marchand et Louis Cazabon conseiller. Il fut décidé que Roland Gagner sera le propagandiste et recruteur de l'Union. Cette dernière s'est choisie des patrons d'honneur dont Mgr. J.C. Cody, évêque du diocèse de London, l'honorable Sénateur Gustave Lacasse de Tecumseh et le Dr. Paul Poisson de Windsor.

Georges Michaud fut vivement remercié et applaudi pour ce qu'il a fait en faveur du mouvement. C'est à l'unanimité et au milieu de nouvelles acclamations qu'il a été fait président d'honneur de l'Union.

Philippe Chauvin, président, a souhaité la bienvenue aux visiteurs et aux cultivateurs présents. Il souligna qu'il faut des adhérents renseignés, convaincus et actifs. Il montra également que la coopération économique est un gage de stabilité nationale et même internationale.

Gérard Caron, président de la St. Jean-Baptiste de Kent et Essex ainsi que Henri Lessard, rédacteur au "Droit d'Ottawa" ont adressé la parole à leur tour.

L'Union des familles rurales poursuivra des réunions mensuelles afin de discuter diverses questions, par exemple la question d'affiliation avec la fédération d'agriculture de Kent.

Roland Gagner a été nommé délégué de l'Union des familles rurales à la fédération de Kent. Il a également été chargé d'en parler avec l'Union des cultivateurs français de l'Ontario. Les assemblées mensuelles ont été fixées au deuxième mardi de chaque mois dans chacune des paroisses à tour de rôle.

Antoine Titley, agronome en Ontario, continue pendant plusieurs années auprès de la population agricole canadienne française du sud-ouest Ontario.

C'est Roland Gagner, secrétaire, qui, chaque mois nous renseigne sur tous les points importants qui se déroulent dans les différentes paroisses de la région. C'est ainsi que nous pouvons porter main-forte aux organismes paroissiaux. Les rapports mensuels sont intéressants et à point. Nos sincères remerciements pour les heures de travail pour le bien-être de la population française et pour l'avenir de nos confrères.

Pèlerinage de l'Union des familles rurales

Caroline Laprise et Mme Léo Masse organisent un pèlerinage au sanctuaire de Midland à l'occasion du troisième centenaire du supplice de nos Saints Martyrs Canadiens. Accompagnés de Mgr. Langlois, 46 pèlerins de la région de Kent et Essex s'embarquent pour un pèlerinage inoubliable à Midland et Penetanguishene.

Durant tout l'été, se déroulent divers événements surtout historiques; pèlerinages afin de glorifier nos Saints Martyrs Canadiens qui ont tracé leur chemin jusqu'à Pain Court avant le début de sa fondation. Père Brébeuf a établi une petite mission dans le comté de Kent. Il lui a donné le nom de St-Joseph.

Une statue en bronze du Père Brébeuf fait partie du monument du Sacré-Coeur érigé dans la cour de l'église. Ce culte religieux commémore un fait historique et patrimonial.

En route vers Midland et Penetanguishene.
En premier plan se trouve Caronline Laprise (2e à droite), l'organisatrice du pélerinage.

Le Mouvement Coopératif

Le mouvement coopératif prend un nouvel essor chez nous. Un comité de directeurs provisoires vient d'être nommé pour faire progresser cette initiative. Voici les noms de ceux qui en font partie: Alfred Pinsonneault, président, Napoléon Roy, gérant et Roland Gagner secrétaire. Ces messieurs commenceront à faire une tournée de recrutement à travers notre paroisse.

L'union des familles rurales a encouragé plusieurs organisations favorisant les fermiers dans Kent et Essex. La coopérative "Lower Thames" de Pain Court progresse à chaque jour. Elle compte 55 membres et le recrutement se fait continuellement.

Quand à la coopérative de Pointe-aux-Roches, elle va de l'avant. Elle compte 50 membres et elle s'est procurée d'un élévateur à Haycroft sur le Canadien-Pacifique pour la livraison de blé d'Inde, des fèves soya, de blé et de d'autres céréales. Cette même coopérative a célébré son 50e anniversaire en 1998.

P. T. A. Organized - 1948

With the Canadian Martyrs as patrons and Father Laliberté our pastor and chaplain, the Parent-Teacher Association was formally organized in Pain Court March 2, 1948.

In a few well-chosen words, Father Laliberté explained the urgent and timely necessity of such an organization. Quoting Pope XI's Encyclical in 1939, he explained that Christian education is the formation of heart, character and conscience, and that the major responsibility of the child's education rested on the mother's shoulders.

I, Caroline Laprise, was chosen as the organizer. For months I had studied, read correspondence, sought advice from Hierarchy and other authorized leaders of this truly apostolic work. Programs were distributed and explained to parents and teachers. In brief, it stated the meaning of such an organization, the obligation to heed the words of the Holy Father, its aim and its benefits. Partly in questionnaire form, this launching program was interesting as well as enlightening. A nomination committee was appointed and at the following meeting on March 13 a slate of officers took charge.

President   -   Mrs. Caroline Laprise
Vice-president   -   Mrs. Yvonne Bélanger
Secretary   - Mrs. Glorianna Bélanger
Treasurer   - Mrs. Florence Caron
Councillors   - Mrs. Alma Pinsonneault
                     Mrs. Célina Martin
                     Mrs. Éva Caron

Mme Trefflé Laprise, présidente et fondatrice du Comité des Parents-Professeurs dans le diocèse de London pour les écoles bilingue.

Mother's Day Banquet

Mother's Day, the Parent-Teacher banquet was held in Pain Court May 9, 1948. A delightful banquet was served to over 300 persons in the church (basement) hall by the ladies of the parish.

His Excellency Bishop Cody, the guest speaker, emphasized the importance of Parent-Teacher Associations. "The education of the child should not be left entirely in the hands of the teachers" he said. Parents should cooperate with teachers in the process of moulding future citizens.

At the conclusion of his address, a spiritual bouquet was presented to the bishop by two little boys, Jérôme Caron and Léo Dénomé. A Mother's Day tribute in the form of a floral bouquet was presented by the bishop to the mothers of the parish for their kindness and devotion to their children. Mrs. Josephat Pinsonneault accepted gracefully the honour in the name of all mothers.

As president of the Association, I graciously thanked his Excellency for his words of encouragement and inspiration.

Following these performances, Bishop Cody then presented French oratorical awards to three winners in a recent competition, Rosita Robert, Agnes Laprise, and Yvette Gagner.

This Parent-Teacher Association was organized throughout Kent and Essex bilingual separate schools. Shortly after, Father Feeney did the same for all separate schools in the diocese of London.

Senator Gustave Lacasse of Ottawa was the special speaker. His presentation was followed by a solo from Gérard Caron. The impressive banquet came to a close with a duet sung by Roland and Thérèse Gagner, accompanied by our devoted organist Amédée Emery.

Fête des Mères

Nous ne saurions trop féliciter ceux qui eurent la première pensée de consacrer une journée par année à la glorification de la mère de famille. Cette fête que nous célébrons en ce dimanche du 9 mai 1948 revêtira un cachet tout particulier et plus solennel que d'habitude, dû à l'initiative du Comité des parents-professeurs de la paroisse de Pain Court qui a organisé une soirée spéciale à cette fin, soirée qui sera rehaussée par la présence de notre évêque Monseigneur John Cody du diocèse de London.

La femme que le Créateur donna à l'homme pour compagne mérite le respect de tout le monde, toujours et partout, mais elle le mérite davantage quand elle devient épouse. Et encore n'atteint-elle l'apogée de sa noblesse et de sa dignité que lorsque sa vie se prolonge et se perpétue dans les enfants que Dieu lui donne sous le signe du mariage chrétien? Qu'elle soit reine ou paysanne, elle a droit alors à la reconnaissance et à la vénération de tous puisque l'humanité tout entière lui doit d'une génération à l'autre, son existence.

Brief Synopsis on Sugar Beet Industry

The Canada & Dominion Sugar Co. Ltd. has its head office at Chatham sugar beet refining plant. Sugar beets are one of Southwestern Ontario's most profitable and stable crops, grown by more than 1,400 farmers in Kent, Essex, Lambton, Middlesex, Elgin, Huron and Perth counties.

Purchase of the crops brings district growers more than 2 million dollars annually.

In a sugar beet flyer dated April 8, 1943 it reported that although total acreage signed for sugar beets that season had only reached 13,500 acres, the Canada and Dominion sugar Company would operate at least one factory. A sugar company official was noted as saying that they considered 20,000 acres a minimum acreage to permit the economical operation of even one factory.

In 1944, they say that the sugar beet production was equivalent to 40,000 pounds of refined granulated sugar. The price to the growers would be $11.00 per ton of beets delivered with 16% sugar content.

Even after paying the labour, the farmer's return in 1944 was over $75 an acre. The average price for all growers was $12.52 per ton, which meant that the return per acre was $112.50 for factory delivered beets. Farmers in our area were deeply involved in this industry. In 1945 the Federal Government announced there would be prisoners of war available to provide farm labour to relieve the farmers' anxiety over possible shortage of workers.

Purchase of the crops brings district growers more than 2 million dollars annually.

The Chatham and Wallaceburg plants are able to process 45,000 acres, producing around 125,000,000 pounds of pure beet sugar. The Wallaceburg plant remained closed for the fourth consecutive year because of reduced acreage.

In 1948, total acreage was 18,400 acres.

Trefflé Laprise, a top grower among sugar beet men of Ontario, produced another high-yield crop in 1948. From his 21.42 acres he got 369 tons, or 17.2 tons to the acre. Five acres planted to tobacco in 1947 gave the heaviest yield, while the remainder was on white bean ground. Mr. Laprise plans to grow around 35 acres of Ontario's most stable crop in 1949.
Ref. Canada & Dominion Sugar Flyer - 1948

Trefflé Laprise
R R 7 Chatham, Ont.

Caisse Populaire

Opens new headquarters, after 24 years in operation since 1948.
A new office for the French community "Caisse Populaire de Pain Court Limitée" was officially opened August 14, 1972.

President of the 325 member group is Edmond Gagner with Alphonse Marentette as office manager and Rita Caron, treasurer.

The "Caisse Populaire" officers are housed in the former convent which was occupied until June by six nuns, members of the Sisters of Charity. They were transferred to other Ontario centres.

The new offices were blessed by Rev. Léo Charron prior to the open house. Other "Caisse Populaire" are located in Windsor, Belle Rivière, Pointe-aux-Roches and Tecumseh. Most are members of the Ontario Credit Union league. The "Caisse Populaire" is chartered since November 1947 to serve the community and surrounding area.

On June 30, 1982, it officially closed after 35 years of operation. The loss that our members experienced by the closure of the "Caisse" was greatly minimized by the fact that business continued to operate. The total assets of the "Caisse Populaire" were purchased by the Kent Dutch-Canadian Credit Union Limited.

Ouverture officielle de la Caisse de Pain Court

C'est le lundi le 14 août 1972 qu'avait lieu l'ouverture officielle de la Caisse Populaire de Pain Court. De droite à gauche, nous apercevons Mme Rita Caron, trésorière, le Rév. Père Léo Charron et M. Alphonse Marentette, gérant de la Caisse .

Le Rempart (Photo: John Haslip)

Caisse Populaire 1948 - 1982

En novembre 1947, une trentaine de membres se réunissent à la salle paroissiale de Pain Court sous la direction de l'agronome Michaud. Après plusieurs conférences, les membres ont signé la demande pour La Charte de la Caisse Populaire. Mme Caroline Laprise et Mme Marie-Anne Caron sont témoins et signent la charte. Le 29 avril 1948, les directeurs ont élu M. Louis-Philippe Caron gérant et Étienne Benoit, assistant de la Caisse pour l'année 1948. Le bureau temporaire est situé chez Étienne Benoit pour une période de deux ans. En 1950, M. Gérard Caron offre un local dans sa demeure.   Il y a de l'entrain et de l'avancement pendant quatre ans avec M. Louis-Joseph Richer comme gérant. C'est en 1954 que Mme Della Thibodeau offre ses services à plein temps avec un bureau aménagé à son domicile. Le conseil des directeurs est reconnaissant lorsque le bureau ouvre en 1954. Comme les officiers donnent leurs temps gratis, la collaboration est nécessaire. Des experts en ce qui concerne les Caisses visitent les écoles afin d'expliquer et faire comprendre la Caisse d'épargnes aux jeunes.

En janvier 1967, le bureau est déménagé chez Rita Caron et Alphonse Marentette devient gérant.

Enfin la caisse a pu se procurer un bureau permanent dans l'ancien couvent. L'ouverture officielle a lieu le 14 août 1972.

M. Edmond Gagner, président de la Caisse de Pain Court, a coupé le ruban d'ouverture. Révérend Père Léo Charron bénit les bureaux. Plusieurs personnalités étaient présentes, dont Louis Bezaire président de la Caisse de Windsor, et Gérard Chevalier de la Caisse de Pointe-aux-Roches qui, a tour de rôle, ont présenté leurs voeux de prospérité. Le personnel se compose de Alphonse Marentette gérant, Paul Haslip commis et Rita Caron trésorière.

C'est notre Caisse et soyons en fiers.   Le progrès qu'elle démontrera à l'avenir dépendra de l'intérêt qu'on leur prête. La Caisse de Pain Court peut devenir prospère elle aussi comme les autres institutions bancaires dans Kent et Essex.

"Depuis quelques années, la Caisse avait connu des difficultés financières. Son fonds de réserve et ses actifs ne suffisaient pas aux caprices de cette période de crise économique où les taux d'intérêts fluctuaient sans scrupules. Alors la Caisse populaire de Pain Court ferme ses portes le 30 juin 1982, après avoir desservi les résidents de Pain Court et du canton de Dover durant près de 35 années. (1948 - 1982) Il a été très difficile pour les membres d'envisager la fermeture de la Caisse. La population de Pain Court mérite des félicitations pour la confiance et l'appui qu'elle a montrés en sa propre institution financière." [1].

Nos sincères remerciements à tous ceux qui ont servi fidèlement comme directeur pendant bien années. Alphonse Marentette mérite notre reconnaissance pour avoir rempli ses engagements comme gérant de la Caisse pendant environ 20 ans.   Louis-Joseph Richer aussi mérite notre appréciation pour les heures de bénévolat vis-à-vis un travail constant de vérificateur (des comptes) de la Caisse pendant 25 ans et plus.

1. Album Pain Court 83 p. 17

Assemblée Décembre - 1948

C'est avec humilité que je m'acquitte de ma position comme présidente des Dames d'Autel pour l'année1948. Mes paroles ne suffisent pas pour exprimer la joie et le bonheur d'avoir travailler parmi vous et pour vous, pour le plus grand bien de la paroisse et de la société. C'est grâce à l'humble coopération des autres officières et l'effort de toutes les dames que je suis parvenue à remplir mes responsabilités de présidente. Sans elles mes efforts auraient étés en vain.

Mon seul but était de coopérer avec toutes les sociétés de notre paroisse pour son plus grand avancement. Merci à tous, mais un merci spécial qui vient de la profondeur de mon coeur à mon exécutif Marie-Anne Caron trésorière, Philomène Caron vice-présidente, Yvonne Bélanger secrétaire et aux conseillères Alexina Caron, Edna Primeau, Eva Charbonneau, Edna Gagner, Alma Martin et Delphine Roy.

Caroline Roy Laprise

Point de vue canadien-français - 1949

Ce sont les mères canadiennes françaises de la péninsule qui présentent aujourd'hui, au bureau de direction du quotidien le "Chatham Daily News," leurs plus sincères remerciements. C'est avec une joie inexplicable que nous lisons dans votre journal quelques lignes écrites dans notre langue maternelle. Nous constatons que ce geste saura créer des liens de bonne entente entre les deux éléments de la région.

Le Saint Père Pape Pie XI, dans son encyclique en 1939, cite que "l'éducation chrétienne c'est la formation du coeur." C'est en effet sur les épaules des mamans que repose, en majeure partie, la responsabilité de l'éducation religieuse, morale, sociale et physique des enfants. Pour accomplir le désir du Saint Père, il faut saisir tous les moyens, à côté et à l'exemple des autres qui savent bien profiter de tout.

Une oeuvre à encourager, ce sont les retraites fermées pour les groupes de langue française. Nous avons à Oxley la maison "Ste-Famille" pour les retraites fermées. Vous trouverez là un repos spirituel et corporel. Vous aurez un aperçu clair et distinct des desseins de Dieu sur votre vie, votre famille et vos affaires. Il faudra encourager votre mari, vos enfants d'y assister. Soyez apôtres. C'est cela l'Action Catholique. En 1950, il y aura six retraites fermées pour les dames de langue française.

Il me semble que chaque mère de famille de la péninsule de Kent et Essex devrait se préoccuper d'un problème aussi vital et aussi sérieux que celui des écoles. Il s'agit de l'éducation religieuse ainsi que celle au point de vue national.

Il est précieux de hâter l'avènement d'une institution comme celui d'un collège classique dans la péninsule pour la pleine formation catholique et française. Ceci contribuerait au bien-être religieux et national des nôtres.

Soyez aux aguets, mères de famille! Ne vous laissez pas leurrer par une fausse sécurité, basée sur des promesses de campagnes électorales. Que sera le rapport de la commission royale d'enquête sur l'éducation? Le temps d'attendre est passé. Unissons nos efforts pour défendre nos enfants, nos écoles. On doit se rappeler que les écoles séparées de l'Ontario font partie du système scolaire Ontarien et qu'elles sont régies par des lois du ministre de l'éducation de l'Ontario. Pourquoi alors ne partagent-elles pas également les revenus provenant des impôts payés et d'autres revenus dédiés aux écoles. De plus, si nos écoles séparées bénéficiaient de la juste répartition des taxes, nous pourrions aménager des locaux pour y recevoir nos tous petits. Alors obtenons pour nos enfants la meilleure éducation possible. Préparons la jeunesse actuelle et orientons-la vers un avenir honorable.

Le comité des Parents-Professeurs de Pain Court se dévoue entièrement à la jeunesse. Les parents des enfants qui entreront au jardin en septembre sont invités à une réunion.

Un coup d'oeil sur l'éducation physique de l'enfant vous dirigera vers la clinique des enfants, tenue régulièrement dans la salle de l'église de Pain Court le 4e lundi de chaque mois sous les hospices du comité des Parents-Professeurs. Une garde-malade et un ou deux médecins spécialisés sont à la disposition des mères et des enfants. Ces services vous sont offerts gratuitement.

Le 19 juin, Pain Court pourrait-il oublier l'ordination du Père Adrien Roy o.m.i., un enfant de la paroisse. Quelle bénédiction! Que Dieu répande d'abondantes bénédictions sur sa famille, sur ses amis et sur la paroisse entière à l'occasion de sa première messe, célébrée le 20 juin, 1949.
Pour en parler plus dignement, il faudrait tremper sa plume dans la poussière de l'arc-en-ciel. Il y aurait bien de belles choses à dire mais pour le moment, invitons tous les paroissiens à prêter mains fortes afin que cette fête soit un véritable succès.

Le comité de la Survivance Française en Amérique annuellement met de côté la semaine du 22 mai pour des manifestations patriotiques. Cette année, la fête sera consacrée aux Saints Martyrs Canadiens. Dimanche, le 22 mai, allons à Rivière-aux-Canards, allons invoquer les Saints Martyrs, Saint Jean-Baptiste et Dollard des Ormeaux, leur demandant de jeter un regard favorable sur les Canadiens-Français de la péninsule. L'autobus partira de Pain Court à 10 h.

Du 30 juillet au 1er août, un pèlerinage régional organisé par l'Union des familles rurales se rendra au sanctuaire de Midland où son Éminence le Cardinal James C. McGuigan célébrera une messe pontificale le 31 juillet. Divers autres événements se dérouleront durant le pèlerinage.

Mères de famille, éducatrices des foyers, grâce à votre zèle et à votre esprit de dévouement, il y aura prochainement, chez nous, une renaissance de foi et de patriotisme.

Mme Caroline Laprise
présidente du comité des Parents-Professeurs de
Pain Court, mai 1949
Chatham Daily News, Chatham

Benoit's General Store

In 1920, Mr. and Mrs. Arthur Houle owned and operated a store on the corner of the 10th concession and Winterline and in 1915 Mr. and Mrs. Calixte Benoit started their business on the corner of the 9th concession and Winterline. These first stores were truly supermarkets. In the beginning the Benoit's started selling only groceries but in a short time they were selling all kinds of products such as yard goods, hardware, drugs, shoes, clothing, harnesses, horseshoes, gas, oil and they even stocked car parts for the Ford car. In 1920 most of the items were sold in bulk such as in 100 lb. bags or in barrels. People often exchanged eggs and butter for the groceries. The store also offered a delivery service on Mondays and Tuesdays picked up the eggs and butter in exchange for the groceries. Other stores in the area that opened at later dates were Joe Couture and Clement Charron on the 8th concession and Trefflé Emery where St-Pierre's Garage in now located.

Le magasin de Joe Couture

Gagner Grocery Store

Mr. Dieudonné Gagner Jr. operated a general store, partly a grocery store and a hardware store sometime before 1930.

He occupied the living quarters with his family on the same property. This store was across the road from the Dover Hotel. Mr. Dieudonné Gagner Sr. owned and operated the store before his son, Dieudonné Gagner Jr. took over the business.

In 1934, D. Gagner Jr. was appointed Clerk of Dover Township and his son, Raoul W. operated his father's grocery store and raised his family there until 1954. Upon the death of his father in 1954, he, in turn, became Clerk of Dover Township, a position he kept until his retirement in 1976. During this time he sold the store and moved on the Creek Line Road, just beyond the cemetery. There, his wife Irene, operated a prosperous hair salon.

In 1956, Mr. and Mrs. Victor Trahan became owners of the Gagner store; Mrs. Trahan was the daughter of Mr. Dieudonné Gagner Sr. who owned the Dover Hotel. They operated the store about 15 years at which time they rented all the living quarters and accommodated the Canadian Imperial Bank of Commerce until it closed some 20 years later.

Upon their retirement, they acquired a new home across the road from the Immaculate Conception Church. At this time, Mr. Victor Trahan's father was well up in age, so Mr. Dolphis Trahan thrived under the tender loving care of his son Victor and his wife Marie-Anne until his death in 1972 at the ripe old age of 103 years.

Eugene Roy-King

Eugene Roy (King) was born in Pain Court, Ontario, County of Kent, Township of Dover, the 23rd day of September 1896. He was the eleventh of a family of twelve children. His parents Alexandre Roy and Marie Bélanger were descendants of two pioneer and well-known families of the district.

Baptized in Immaculate Conception Church in Pain Court September 25 1896, he remained a loyal, esteemed and devoted member of his parish.

On September 23rd 1919, he married Delphine Caron and from this union four boys and four girls were born. Delphine passed away on September 28, 1956. On May 26th 1958, Eugene married Eva Demarais, a widow.

Professional Background

His main occupation since 1912 had been mixed farming from which he retired in 1957, the owner of 650 acres of the best land in the township and leaving behind a very successful record.

Social Background

A member of "La Société St-Jean-Baptiste," he served as secretary and president of the Pain Court section for at least 5 years.

A member of the Knights of Columbus since 1927 - 1928 and 1944 until 1965 as a fourth degree member.

A member of the Kiwanis Club since 1951 and the Pain Court Ushers Club since 1931. He was elected in 1939 - Vice president of l'Union des cultivateurs de Kent et Essex. Eugene was elected to the position of Vice-President on the Kent County Historical Society executive.

Public Life

– From 1928 - 1934, he served as a member and director of the "White Bean Growers."

– In 1939, he was the organiser of the Kent County Federation of Agriculture and president in 1956.

– In 1942, he was one of the organizers of the "Ontario Sugar Beet Growers Marketing Board" and served as president until 1952. He was appointed president of the Canadian National Board in 1954, served in this capacity until 1958.

– In 1945, he was elected a director of the Ontario Burley Tobacco Marketing Association and served as president until 1952.

– He served for 8 years as a director in Corn Growers Association.

– He helped in the promotion of the Ontario Vegetable Growers' Association under the provisions of the Federal Marketing Act.

Political Background Municipal

Elected Councillor of township of Dover for the years 1935 and 1936, Deputy Reeve for the years 1937 and 1938 and Reeve of the municipality in 1939 and served in this capacity until 1942. These positions made him a member of the Kent County Council from 1937 to 1942. The proven results of his administration has shown him as a sound administrator and a good politician.

Provincial and Federal Field

1919 - interested in United Farmers of Ontario.
1930 - became an active member of the Conservative Party and was named a director of the Kent County Association.
1934 -1953 - member of the Federal and Provincial executive of Kent County.
1953 - Conservative Candidate in the federal election defeated by Blake Huffman.
1959 - He was named Sheriff of the County of Kent.

Military Background

Conscripted in May 1918.
Served in Canada until 1919.

Service in Education

- He was a school trustee for 9 years. He was one of the promoters of the bilingual system of education in the Pain Court area.
- Mr. Roy has travelled extensively and has visited practically all the provinces of Canada and many states in the USA. In southern Ontario, he was respected and was looked upon as a man who has made a success of his life. He was recognized as one of the leading citizens of the region. He died suddenly September 9, 1965 at the age of 69 years.

"Ces Dames aux Chapeaux Verts" - 1950

"Les Copains" drama group, Pain Court, is preparing its first production
for presentation April 2. Shown here at rehearsal, some members of the cast are
discussing their parts with director, David Carter. Around the table from the
left, they are, Marion Primeau, Jeanne Laprise, David Carter, Jeanne Martin,
Jeannette Blais, Amédée Emery.

Ref. Chatham Daily News

Transition of Original Pain Court Separate School

In 1928 when the new separate school board built a new school across the road from the original one, the old school was put up for sale. It was bought by the "Benoit family."

This property served the community very well. The ground floor was converted into a garage, known as "Bob Despins" garage. They serviced everything from cars, to tractors, to machinery. It became a depot for many things because Robert Despins was a first class mechanic. This school became to some extent, a technical school because men and boys loved to hang around the place to learn technical skills.

Adjacent to the house and garage was the "Stand" as it was called then, famous for its "penny candy" and Martin's ice cream - a variety store of sorts. The second floor of this huge building was converted into two apartments. On one side lived Rob Despins and his family, the other side is still occupied by Steve's family.

Mr. Despins' wife, Gertrude Deschênes, was a very talented seamstress working for Mr. Léon Charlebois who operated a "furrier" business in Chatham. She was friendly and pleasant and everyone loved her.

They had one son, Robert Despins Jr. born April 6, 1938. He died accidentally when he hit a tree on lot 16 River Rd. Raleigh. He was 34 years old. His father Robert Sr. had predeceased him by two months in 1971. His mother Gertrude died in 1946 of cancer at the very early age of 43, leaving young Robert only 8 years old. They were all sadly missed by the whole community.

The garage was then remodelled and converted into a restaurant. There, the Steve Benoit family has catered to generations of children as well as adults for half a century.

For the men, it was a meeting place for early coffee and a 7 a.m. chitchat. The restaurant "Chez Étienne" along with a gas bar is still operated by Rose Marie Benoit.

Sorrowfully missed at the counter are Steve's well-garnished genuine whoppers and his generous cups of brewed coffee, filled to the brim, sometimes overflowing like Steve's good-natured, nonchalant and carefree style. He was everybody's friend at Rosie's, especially his dear "Olive" whose friendship brought solace to her poor "George."

Steve passed away in 1990, but his unique explicit remarks and memories still remain in our heart, giving us many a silent laughter.

Le premier autobus scolaire à Grande Pointe

Dans les années 1930 - 1940, très peu d'étudiants pouvaient s'inscrire à l'école secondaire régionale à moins qu'ils se pensionnent à Pain Court parce que les moyens de transport étaient insuffisants. Plusieurs étaient pensionnaires venu de Tilbury, Pointe-aux-Roches, St. Joachim et ailleurs.

On corrigea en partie ce problème en 1945 quand Édouard Emery introduit un autobus scolaire avec le seul but de transporter les étudiants de l'école secondaire. En 1949, Édouard vendit son autobus à son frère Trefflé qui, lui, finit par augmenter le service à 7 autobus pour pouvoir fournir du transport au niveau élémentaire. En 1980 la compagnie d'autobus Emery fut vendue à la compagnie d'autobus Denure de Chatham.

Avec le temps, il y eut beaucoup de mécaniciens dont les services étaient disponibles aux résidents locaux. Parmi ceux-là se trouvaient Adrien Emery à l'angle de la 9e concession et de la Winterline, Ernest Sylvain sur la 9e concession, Tony Emery et Orville Cartier sur la 10e concession, Armand Tétreault sur la 8e concession et actuellement Vincent St. Pierre à l'angle de la 10e concession et de la Winterline et Ed Tétreault junior situé au Dover Centre. De plus, pendant plusieurs années, Clayton Myers a offert le service de débosseler ainsi que des carrosseries.

Livre Centenaire de Grande Pointe 1986

Pour Survivre

Extrait:
F.X. Chauvin, M.A., Historien.
Réunion régionale de l'Association d'Éducation de l'Ontario, tenue à Windsor 1944 à laquelle j'étais présente.

Après plus de deux siècles et demi, cette région demeure, malgré son isolement, un foyer poussant et robuste d'esprit français et de pensée chrétienne. Plus tard le Père Point écrira: "Le Canadien est encore français dans l'âme comme dans le sang, dans sa vie de famille comme dans sa vie religieuse. Plus heureux que son frère d'Europe, ses moeurs primitives n'ont pas été gâtées par l'esprit révolutionnaire du dernier siècle: franchise, droiture, simplicité, docilité, gaieté, générosité, esprit religieux, et chevaleresque. Ces mots définissent bien le caractère canadien."

Ce n'est pas tout; cette campagne est poursuivie dans le domaine de l'éducation. Dans tous les coins surgissent des écoles françaises et catholiques en dépit de la foi, car les enfants, pour les fréquenter, ne manquent pas. Treize de ces nouveaux foyers d'A.B.C. et de religion reçoivent une moyenne de quatre-vingt à cent élèves. Partout le mot d'ordre aux Canadiens est "Sauvez l'avenir."

Le Père Point nous répond lui-même: "Cétait le régime de l'incohérence. Nous vivions d'exceptions."

C'est bien cela. Le système avait donné lieu à d'intolérables abus dans l'administration. Le peuple voulait dire son mot dans les affaires publiques. C'était la rude montée vers le gouvernement responsable.

Quel est l'avenir de ce petit peuple qui a donné à l'enseignement des Soeurs zélées et des instituteurs et institutrices bien entraînés, à la terre des fermiers industrieux et progressifs, à la politique municipale, provinciale et fédérale des représentants distingués mais qui, surtout, demeure rigoureusement fidèles à ses traditions. C'est-à-dire foncièrement Canadiens-Français dans son tempérament, ses disciplines raciales et religieuses, son sens économique, ses goûts, ses rapports sociaux et sa manière de vivre en général.

C'est un fait démographique établi dans le monde qu'un peuple d'agriculteurs qui cultive lui-même sa terre et qui est groupé autour d'un centre spirituel, non seulement garde sa langue et sa foi mais conserve sa cohésion et peut subsister indéfinitivement. Il faut se rappeler que plus de deux siècles d'histoire laissent leur empreinte sur la situation actuelle. Nos compatriotes des campagnes conservent leur caractère ethnique essentiel: "Notre peuple garde ses terres, il les agrandit même, les enrichit et consolide ses positions."

"En terminant, permettez-moi de lancer à tous un avertissement. Comme peuple n'ayons pas peur d'analyser nos forces et nos faiblesses, mais ne nous laissons jamais saisir par un complexe d'infériorité. Un peuple digne n'a pas le droit de se rapetisser."

Ref - " Pour Survivre" - cours résumé présenté par F.X.Chauvin - a Windsor 1944

École Ste-Catherine - Pain Court - 6e, 7e et 8e années 1947

École de Continuation de Pain Court - 11e et 12e années 1946 - 47.
Professeur: Marie-Marthe Lapensée de Plantagenet, Ontario.

Référence Oncle Jean - 1947

Vis-à-vis le projet de la fondation d'un collège français dans la région, ce sont les femmes canadiennes françaises, les mères de famille qui devraient réclamer la fondation d'un collège. Seul ce collège vous donnera l'élite nécessaire à tous points de vue. Ça serait un collège pour refaire le français maître de tous les foyers canadiens français de la Péninsule.

Avant d'adopter ce plan, les hommes auront probablement besoin d'être éclairés, entraînés et convaincus. La femme, en matière de patriotisme, a le coeur plus éveillé. Si la femme de 1912 avait cédé, toute la famille y serait passée et quel triomphe pour les auteurs du Règlement XVII.

À la demande de l'Oncle Jean, nous nous sommes réunis autour de la nouvelle croix de Cartier sur le terrain de l'école Ste-Catherine en août 1948. Il avait la mission de propager les "croix de Cartier" dans la péninsule. L'an 1998, a marqué le 50e anniversaire de cette croix érigée sur le terrain scolaire à Pain Court.

La fête était grandiose et vivante.

La Croix de Cartier - Pain Court - 1948

Chapitre 5

Mes Souvenirs

1950 - 1960

Chapter 5

My Memories

Les 12 commandements du bonheur

1. Éviter la véritable infériorité: LA PEUR

2. Vivre la plus belle journée: AUJOURD'HUI

3. Éviter la chose la plus facile: SE TROMPER

4. Éviter la plus grande erreur: ABANDONNER

5. Se méfier de la plus grande faute: L'ÉGOÏSME

6. Pratiquer la plus grande distraction: LE TRAVAIL

7. Éviter la vraie faillite: LE DÉCOURAGEMENT

8. Écouter les meilleurs professeurs: LES ENFANTS

9. Conserver ce qui est le plus nécessaire: LE BON SENS

10. Éviter le plus bas sentiment: LA JALOUSIE

11. Pratiquer la plus belle action: LE PARDON

12. Tenir à la plus belle chose: L'AMOUR

Les Amis de la Prière
Soeur St-Joseph - Ste-Hyacinthe
Québec   J25-5T9

L'inauguration du premier banquet annuel des Dames de Ste-Anne

Les Dames de Ste-Anne donnent un nouvel élan à leur société. Une centaine de sociétaires se joignent à leur exécutif pour célébrer ensemble l'inauguration de leur premier banquet annuel.

Sponsor Pain Court Dinner

First annual dinner sponsored by Ladies of Altar Society of Immaculate Conception parish, Pain Court, was held last night at the King's Hotel. More than 100 ladies of the district attended. Executive committee members who were responsible for the successful evening are, left to right in front, Mrs. Norman Bélanger, Mrs. Félix Bourassa, Mrs. R.W. Gagner, Mrs. Régis Caron and Mrs. Léonard Faubert. Standing behind from left to right are, Mrs. Trefflé Laprise, Mrs. Frank Primeau, Mrs. Zéphyr Daniel, and Mrs. Leonard Jenner.

The Chatham Daily News (Staff Photo) March 22, 1950

Alphonsine Martin

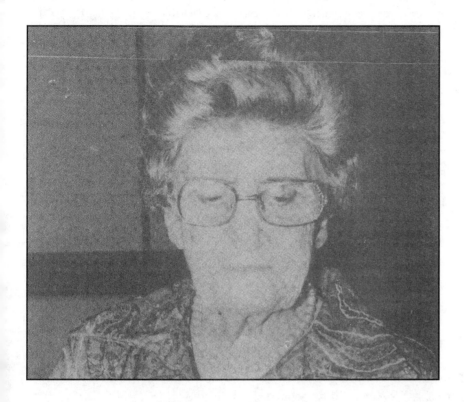

Alphonsine Martin of Thamesview Lodge celebrates her 90th birthday, Thursday in commemoration of her birth June 1, 1888.
She was born in Tecumseh and has lived in Grande Pointe and Pain Court most of her life. Among her other accomplishments, she has raised eight children. 1978

Alphonsine Lachance, fille de Xavier Lachance et Emily Brouillette, est née le 1 juin, 1888 à Tecumseh, Ontario, Canada. Dans sa jeunesse, toujours dévouée à ses parents qui se livrent à l'agriculture, elle reçut sa première éducation à l'école du village de sa paroisse.

En 1908, elle épousa Joseph L. Martin, un jeune homme qui avait déjà perdu sa première femme; laissé avec un petit garçon, Elzéar, agé 4 ans.

Ils s'établirent sur une ferme dans le canton de Dover, située sur la Winter Line et la 7e concession. De leur mariage sont nés huit enfants: Agnes (Soeur Marie Gervais), Réginald, Joseph J., Thérèse, Ulysse, Euclid, Agathe et Vianney (décédé à 4 ans). Toujours fidèle à l'esprit de la famille chrétienne, Alphonsine sème dans le coeur de ses enfants les principes religieux et les vertus de charité et de compassion.

Les années se déroulent. En 1958, Alphonsine et Joseph se retirent au village de Pain Court près de l'église.

Leur amour se manifesta par une vie en parfaite union et un respect mutuel. Le sourire constant donnait au visage d'Alphonsine sa naturelle expression de douceur et de tendresse. Joseph qui fumait la pipe assis tranquille dans le foyer. . . Oh, la scène touchante!

Joseph est décédé le 28 juillet, 1964 à l'âge de 85 ans.

Notre foi nous fait ce que nous sommes et pour Alphonsine cette foi a soutenu une inébranlable confiance en la divine providence de Dieu.

Membre active du Club d'âge d'or de Pain Court et par-dessus tout une chrétienne fervente et sincère, elle se dévoue à toutes les bonnes oeuvres de sa paroisse. Sa bonté naturelle, sa charité, sa générosité n'avaient pas de limite pour tous ses amis des environs.

En 1977, elle déménagea à la résidence Thamesview Lodge à Chatham où elle passa les dernières années de sa vie.

Elle est morte le 22 février 1990, à l'âge de 102 ans.

Alphonsine et Joseph Martin reposent dans le cimetière de la paroisse de Pain Court.

Nous nous rappelons de son humilité, sa piété, sa vie de dévouement et de bonté envers tous. Alphonsine Martin était une femme que nous ne pouvons pas oublier et qui mérite l'estime de tous.

M. Ulysse Martin et sa fille Patricia.

Mrs. Anthony Edith Bruette

One of the better known residents of Prairie Siding was Mrs. Edith Bruette, who taught school at S.S.# 5 Dover on the Jacob Road from the 1920s until shortly before she died in 1950. Many people can recall receiving their elementary and even two years of high school from Mrs. Bruette in the one room red brick building. No school buses, no calculators or computers, no modern teaching tools existed in those days. A teacher had blackboards, chalk, pupils' slates, maps and some books. With often as many as forty or more students, the strap was also a necessary tool to keep discipline with such large numbers and so many classes.

Edith, whose maiden name was Wright, was born and raised on a farm outside Guelph Ontario. After high school and teacher training, she taught among Mennonites in the Bowmanville area before coming to Kent County. Of course in those days in addition to the $200.00 to $300.00 salary, the teacher was boarded around the section, often times a month at a time with various families. She cured this situation after Anthony Bruette began courting: she married and had her own house.

Mrs. Bruette raised a couple of boys through child placement facilities before giving birth to her only child, a son George A. Bruette. She later adopted a daughter, Anita who is now deceased.

Mr. George A. Bruette

Ci-haut nous remarquons Mme Joséphine Primeau, une excellente cuisinière
et dévouée paroissienne, avec les jumelles Yvette et Annette Trahan.
Chatham Daily News Wed. Jan. 10, 1951

Pendant plusieurs années, les élèves de l'école Ste-Catherine ont pu profiter d'un bol de
bonne soupe chaude avec leur dîner, grâce à l'organisation des parents-professeurs.
Par après, un verre de lait était aussi disponible pour les élèves.

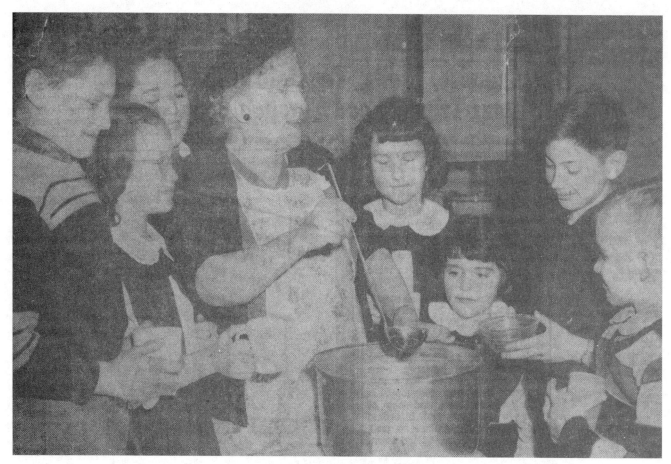

Soup's On at Pain Court

Soup's on for the children of the Pain Court primary and high school. Every day at noon, students who eat lunch at the school are provided with cups of hot soup to supply them with additional nourishment. Seen above grouped around Mrs. Eugène Caron, one of the two efficient cooks, are Urbain Béchard, Louise Caron, Gérard Laprise, Mrs. Caron, Marilyn O'Rourke, Yvette Pinsonneault, Gérald Lauzon and Guy Gagner.

Chatham Daily News Wed. Jan. 10, 1951

Père Dominat Caron

"Dominat Caron est né à Pain Court, le 12 février 1896, de Joseph Caron et de Hermine Laplante. Il fit ses études classiques au petit séminaire de Sainte-Thérèse de Blainville et au collège de Saint-Jean, sa philosophie à l'Université d'Ottawa et sa théologie au Scolasticat des Oblats. Il fut ordonné prêtre par Mgr. Emard, le 7 juin 1925, à Ottawa."

Il avait deux frères, Eugène et Hector ainsi que trois soeurs, Delphine - Mme Eugène Roy, Délima - Mme Zacharie Gagner et une demi-soeur Lucie - Mme Joseph Faubert. Le Père Dominat Caron est l'auteur d'un manuel de Chimie. Son corps repose dans le cimetière de Notre Dame de Hull.

*   *   *

Father Dominat Caron, a professor of Chemistry at the University of Ottawa for thirty years had recently been appointed head of the Chemistry Department at Pius XII University in Roma Basutoland now known as Lesotho.

Father Dominat Caron, age 60, died of a heart attack on the eve of his departure for Africa, July 11th, 1956 at the home of his friend, Dr. Ernest Beuglet where he was a guest awaiting to be escorted to a dinner and reception in honour of his new appointment.

The reception was arranged by the Windsor Essex and Kent Chapter of the University's Alumni Association. Father Caron was well-known in the scientific circles. He was the author of a book for junior college Chemistry and used by upper school classes in Ontario.

Funeral services for Rev. Dominat Caron o.m.i. were held at Immaculate Conception Church Pain Court. His body was then taken to the University of Ottawa Chapel to lie in state. Rev. Rodrique Normandin, rector of the University, officiated at a solemn requiem mass. At this University, he had obtained all his degrees, B.A., B.Sc., D.PH., D.TH. He was the cousin of Rev. Augustin Caron and uncle of Rev. Vincent Caron who officiated at his funeral together with Rev. Father Adrien Roy o.m.i. These four zealous priests recruited and encouraged students to undertake studies at the University of Ottawa.

Attend Marriage Course

Attend marriage course: A large group of young men and women from Chatham, Big Point and Pain Court have completed a course in preparation for marriage. Instruction was under the direction of Rev. Fr. Arthur, O.F.M. Cap. Gabriel Benoit, BA. of the law firm of Clunis and Kee, Dr. S. Kinney and Dr. H. G. Peco of Chatham and Colonel Dr. P. Poisson, Tecumseh, Ontario. Another course will be organized at St. Joseph's Church Chatham. Young people who took the recent course are shown above, standing from left to right: Colonel Dr. Poisson, B. Charlebois, Jeanne d'Arc Charlebois, B. St-Pierre, J. Blais, A. Caron, Evéline Roy, J. Carron, G. Plamondon, E. Caron, B. Carron, H. Lebrun, N. Roy, R. Lebrun, R. Blais, G. Pinsonneault, G. Marentette, H. Gagnon, J.L. Trahan, A. Rivard, A. Marentette, V. Caron, R. Pinsonneault, Raoul Roy, B. Trudell, M. Dozois, L. J. Richer, T. Trudell, Thérèse Roy et Père Arthur o.f.m. Seated left to right: C. Benoit, T. Caron, J. Daniel, V. Caron, Z. Martin, A. Martin, E. Toulouse, M. Brulé, F. Roy, A. Blais.

Un profil de quelques petites entreprises qui ont desservi la communauté de Pain Court et des environs.

HOMMAGES

de

GERARD S. CARON

★

ASSURANCES - IMMEUBLES

★

PAIN COURT

Meilleurs Voeux

de Succès

STEVE BENOIT

GARAGE . . RESTAURANT

Pain Court

Sincères Felicitations

de

CARROW ELECTRIC

PAIN COURT

◆

Agent de Television

"HALICRAFTERS"

1954

Félicitations de

ARTHUR HOULE

PAIN COURT

Représentant de Pioneer

Hybrid Seed Corn

BIENVENUE

à

Nos Fêtes

Centenaire

WELCOME

to

Our Centennial

Celebrations

● ● ●

Le club des placiers . . .

PAIN COURT USHERS CLUB

E. MARTIN, Président.

AVEC LES HOMMAGES
DE LA DOYENNE DES COMPAGNIES
CANADIENNES FRANÇAISES AU CANADA

La Sauvegarde

● ● ●

Réginald Caron — Représentant Régional — Pain Court

Compliments of

LEONARD FAUBERT

PLUMBING & DRILLING

Pain Court

Phone 5171J4

La paroisse de Pain Court - 1954 Synopsis

– Histoire Chronologique –

1854 – Le 31 août – la première pierre angulaire fut posée à l'Église
      Immaculée Conception.

1860 – Premier bureau de poste.

1864 – Une cloche a été ajoutée à l'Église.

1870 – Premier moulin à bois et à farine (Moulin Béchard).

1874 – Première église détruite par le feu - une autre, portant le même
      nom a pris sa place.

1910 – Un chemin de fer électrique nommé Chatham, Wallaceburg and
      Lake Erie fut construit.

1911 – Le nom de Pain Court prend naissance pour faire suite à Dover
      South - construction de l'église nouvelle - démolition de la
      vieille église.

1919 – Les conscrits, fils de Pain Court, reviennent de la guerre - Ils sont
      au nombre de 11.

1923 – Les premières religieuses - l'Ordre de St. Joseph - arrive à
      Pain Court.

1925 – L'électricité est installée dans Pain Court.

1926 – La célébration du 75e anniversaire de la Paroisse coïncide avec
      le Congrès Eucharistique Diocésain.

1928 – Construction d'une école catholique et française, résultat du
      dévouement du R.P. Point.

1937 – Église détruite par le feu. L'église présente a été construite
      immédiatement sur les ruines.

1942 – Érection de la croix de Cartier dans la cour de l'école.

1950 – Arrivée des Soeurs Grises de la Croix.

1954 – Ouverture de l'École de Continuation de H. J. Payette.

Référence - Livre du Centenaire 1954

Graduates And Their Pages -1954

The Graduates - left to right : Marie-Anne Cheff, Jerry Richie, Claire Goure, Dieudonné
Gagner, Gérald Thibodeau, Rose-Marie Martin, Gérard Couture, Lucille Trudell.
The Pages - left to right : Geneviève Pinsonneault, Wayne Cadotte, Claudette Laprise, Joseph
Caron, Claude Thibodeau, Carmelle Martin, Rosaire Martin, Rose-Marie Gagner.

Le char centenaire Laprise
Laprise Centennial Float

Parmi le défilé des chars, on remarque, de gauche à droite:
Guy, Florent, Claude, Roger, Gérard et Trefflé Laprise,
une famille à l'avant-garde dans le domaine de l'agriculture.
Aux mancheons de la charrue on remarque Gérard Couture
personnifiant le fermier dans le spectacle

" *Sous le sourire de Notre-Dame à Pain Court* "

*   *

*   *   *

Tableaux Historiques Racontant l'Histoire de Pain Court Depuis les Débuts jusqu'à Nos Jours

SOUS LA DIRECTION DES RÉVÉRANDES SOEURS GRISES DE LA CROIX ET DU COMITÉ DES PARENTS DE PAIN COURT

Prologue ....courte annonce du centenaire
Narratrice : Mlle Jeannette Blais

LE LOINTAIN PASSÉ
1er tableau : Prise de possession du Canada par Notre-Dame.
Notre-Dame : Rose-Marie Béchard.
Indiens : Thomas Blais, Vincent Maure, Gérald Lauzon,
François Caron, Roméo Pinsonneault, Jean-Paul Pinsonneault.

2e tableua: Départ des Pères de Brébeuf et Chaumonot
chassés par les Indiens.
Père de Brébeuf : Pierre-Louis Pinsonneault.
Père Chaumonot :   Yvon Pinsonneault.
3e tableau : Première semence à Pain Court.
Semeur : Gérard Couture.

LES DÉBUTS DIFFICILES
1er sketch : Visite du missionaire dans une famille
pionnière de Pain Court en 1858.
Ancien pionnier, M. Jean-Baptiste Primeau :
M. Bernadin Maure
Jeune pionnier, M. Joseph Primeau : M. Joseph Richer
Jeune pionnière, Mme Délima Primeau : Mme Régis Caron
Jean-Baptiste Primeau : 9 ans: Vincent Thibodeau.
Rosalie Primeau, 6 ans: Rosalie Faubert.
2e dketch: Une classe de temps, 1858.
Institutrice : Mlle Aline Caron.

Père Raynel: M. Edmond Chauvin.

Élèves : Vincent Thibodeau, Léo Dénommé,
Ronald Charbonneau, Bernard Caron,
Patricia Roy, Aline Marchand, Marie-Claire Gagner,
Robert Pinsonneault, Jacqueline Laprise, Claire Caron,
Jean-Maurice Lachapelle, Victor Trahan,
Jean-Paul Bélanger.

3e sketch : Une réunion des marguillers en 1855.
Marguillers: M. Joseph Roy, Bernard Trudell,
Bernard Charlebois, Roland Bélanger, Edmond Gagner.

LES FASTES DU SOUVENIR
Les fastes du souvenir représentés par les filettes du
souvenir . . . . Les dates rappellent les faits les plus saillants
des Cent Ans.
Souvenir personnifié par Mlle Jacqueline Gagner.
La Reconnaissance personnifié par Mlle Jacqueline Gagner.
Fillettes : Joanne Caron, Juliette Gagner, Rosalie Benoit,
Caroline Laprise, Yvette Roy, Hélène-Jeanne Roy, Patricia
Caron, Louise Roy, Marie-Louise Pinsonneault, Aline Martin,
Yvette Trahan, Annette Trahan, Juliette Béchard, Alma-Gay
Caron, Diane Faubert, Marguerite Bélanger, Adrienne Roy.

La chorale du centenaire est sous l'artistique direction de
M. Amédée Emery et Mlle Angéline Blais.

Pain Court Centennial Pageant
"Sous le sourire de Notre-Dame"

*Père Ulysse Lefaive
plays role in pageant*

*Left to right: Louis-J Richer
Gérard Couture
Joseph Roy*

*Left to Right: Joseph Roy, Bernard Trudell, Edmond Gagner,
Edmond Chauvin, Roland Bélanger, Bernard Charlebois.*

328

Centennial Festivities

When the parish of the Immaculate Conception in Pain Court celebrated 100 years of service on July 3, 4, 5, 1954, the story of a name's birth played an important part. "Notre pain est court, tout petit, mais nous le donnons de bon coeur." This statement was frequently repeated by hardy French Canadians who in the early part of the 19th century trekked out an existence a short distance northeast of the banks of the Thames River. This statement was also the birth of a name. The name "Pain Court" was not plucked out of thin air or from imagination. It originated from extreme hardships suffered by the ancestors of the present residents of this thriving, French Canadian settlement near Chatham.

SIGNS REGISTER AT OPENING CEREMONIES
Sister Andréa, Mr. Stanley Randall and Adrien Caron

H. J. PAYETTE

Un grand nombre de personnalités religieuses et civiles ont assisté à l'inauguration de la nouvelle école secondaire H. J. Payette de Pain Court en 1954. Pour l'occasion, M. Stanley Randall, assistant-surintendent d'éducation en Ontario, coupe le ruban qui marque l'ouverture.

Soeur Marie-Andréa, principale de l'école, M. Randall et Adrien Caron, président de la commission scolaire, sont les premiers à signer le registre de la nouvelle école. Mgr. Bourdeau de Pain

Court et Père Chevalier de Grande Pointe sont les invités d'honneur pour l'ouverture.

Son excellence Mgr. Cody préside à la bénédiction de la pierre angulaire de l'école de continuation, H. J. Payette au début de l'an 1954.

La nouvelle école marque sa première graduation pour les finissants de l'école H. J. Payette. Les premiers finissants sont Rose-Marie Martin, Claire Goure, Marie-Anne Cheff, Lucille Trudell, Dieudonné Gagner Jr., Gérald Thibodeau, Gérard Couture, et Jerry Richer.

Les discours d'adieu furent prononcés en français par Gérald Thibodeau et en anglais par Lucille Trudell. L'inspecteur Payette insista sur l'importance des études secondaires.

Cette imposante cérémonie fut terminée avec un délicieux goûter suivi d'une soirée dansante à la salle St-Philippe de Grande Pointe.

Réunion de classe
1954 - 1984
De gauche à droite: **Rose-Marie Martin (Daniel), Gérard Couture, Lucille Trudell (Kerr), Marie-Anne Cheff(Brown), Jerry Richie, Dieudonné Gagner, Gérard Thibodeau, Claire Goure (Dufault), M. le professeur Edmond Chauvin.**

En mai 1984, huit anciens camarades de l'école secondaire de Pain Court, son réunis pour commémorer un événement important dans leur vie sont les premiers gradués de l'école neuve, Filles; Lucille Trudell (Kerr), Claire Goure (Dufault), Rose-Marie Martin (Daniel) et Marie-Anne Cheff (Brown). Gars: Dieudonné Gagner, Jerry Richie, Gérald Thibodeau et Gérard Couture.

.

Inutile de dire que ce fut une rencontre des plus agréables, où les souvenirs d'autrefois, mêlés aux expériences de la vie ont procuré de longues heures de plaisir et de joie. Ensemble, avec leur ancien professeur, M. Edmond Chauvin, ils ont assisté à la messe communautaire et ont présenté les offrandes au moment de l'offertoire.

Devout Group

On a warm sunny summer day in 1854, a devout group of Pain Court settlers gathered in front of a wooden church and took part in a memorable ceremony. The building was their first church, situated on the site of what is now the church cemetery. Through their minds flashed memories of earlier years, when only the family kitchens were places of worship and how they had to journey on foot, five miles east to what is now St. Peter's Church located in Tilbury East and erected 50 years earlier.

These vignettes from our past played a large part in the church's three day centennial celebrations where 4,000 visitors or more descended upon the small settlement for the festivities.

An outdoor historical pageant depicted several scenes from Pain Court's history dating back to the time between November 2, 1640 and March 1641 when Father Brébeuf, travelling upstream on the Thames, passed through Kent county. He was on his way to the mission of Ste-Marie located at Huronia in the Georgian Bay Area, now known as Midland where a basilica and fort honouring the Canadian Martyrs attract thousands of tourists yearly.

Other scenes of the past depicted how pioneers went about the labourious tasks of seeding the soil and thrashing the wheat. The pageant showed the visit of the missionary into a pioneer home and also the life and times of a school teacher and her pupils. All the "tableaux" attempted to transport the audience to pioneer days in 1854.

However, Pain Court's real history began much earlier. At the beginning of the last century, the settlement's pioneers were very poor, due to lean wheat harvests. The closest flour mill was situated 50 miles away at Detroit and travellers and settlers had no other means of transportation to the mill except by canoe in the summer and by foot and sleighs over the frozen Thames River in the winter.

Another tableau of the pageant dealt with the arrival of a zealous priest, from France, Father Pierre Point. His first destination was Toronto, on July 5th, 1843. Shortly after, he embarked for Sandwich where he established headquarters for his future worthwhile mission. Between 1842 and 1846, the tireless father Point founded thirteen bilingual schools in Essex and Kent. One of these was erected in the parish of Pain Court.

The third church built in a gothic structure in 1911 perished in flames in 1937. It was completely rebuilt and once again, an imposing church, a pastor's rectory , a convent and other church property, have been the heart of the settlement, which takes pride in its history.

Parishioners, comprising of men, women and children, took part in the interesting portrayal of the settlement's earlier days. For all those who attended, this was unforgettable. A great deal of effort had gone in the three day celebration. Two enterprising individuals of the project were Father Ulysse Lefaive, the young and energetic assistant pastor, along with Sister Charles-Auguste s.g.c., the gifted and devout principal of Ste-Catherine School. She summoned up one of the renowned authors of her religious order to write the pageant script, a "chef-d'oeuvre," a highlight of the three day centennial celebration, a piece of literature that should remain in the archives of the parish.

At the helm, were two hard working men, Edgar Martin and Raymond Gagner. They formed various committees and together had given much time and energy to present a bang-up centennial. The parade committee consisted of Chairman Edgar Martin, Eugene King, Louis-Philippe Caron, Joseph Roy, Willie Trudell, Edmond Gagner, Ulysse Marentette and Sister Charles-Auguste s.g.c.

Visitors included priests and nuns from various orders throughout Ontario and Québec and various parts of Canada.

Closing Session of the Centennial under the
Chairmanship of Mr. Edgar Martin

Most Rev. J.C. Cody, bishop of London, celebrated a solemn pontifical mass.

Mr. Alcide Côté, the Minister of Postal Services, introduced by Mr. Blake Huffman M.P. and thanked by Edmond Chauvin, enhanced the closing of the celebration followed by Hon. Louis Cécile, the Minister of Travel and Publicity, who extended his congratulations and urged the village to mark its location with road signs and to promote its cultural developments. He was introduced by Eugene Roy and thanked by Louis-Philippe Caron.

Mr. George Parry M.P.P. for West Kent brought provincial congratulations to all the constituents of the community.

Éphémérides – L'année centenaire
1854 - 1954

Pariossiens qui ont servi sur le conseil municipal:
Parishioners who have served on the Municipal Council

Béchard, Narcisse	Boyer, William
Bourdeau, Tom	Blair, Willie
Carron, Théodore (préfet)	Caron, Adélard
Caron, Louis-Philippe	Gagner, Dieudonné
Gervais, Delore	Martin, Henri
Martin, Edgar (préfet)	Roy, Tom (préfet)
Roy, Eugène (préfet)	Rose, Joseph
St.Pierre, James	Trudell, Regis
Trudell, Willie	

Plusieurs événements importants se sont déroulés durant l'année centenaire dans la petite municipalité de Pain Court et des environs.

M. Dieudonné Gagner, greffier de la municipalité de Dover pendant 20 ans, a été fêté par un groupe d'amis à l'occasion de sa démission.

M. Edgar Martin est élu président du Club des placiers. M. Delore Gervais et M. Louis-Philippe Caron sont élus respectivement sous-préfet et conseiller de la municipalité de Dover.

La Caisse populaire ouvre ses portes chez Mme Z. Thibodeau.

La Révérende Soeur Charles-Auguste, directrice de l'école Ste-Catherine, est décorée du mérite scolaire.

Son Exc. Mgr. Cody préside à la bénédiction de la pierre angulaire de l'école de continuation H.J. Payette de Pain Court au début de 1954.

M. Harry Goudreau, et M. Gordon Blair, membres des forces armées du Canada, reviennent de la Corée.

Père Augustin Caron, curé de St. Joachim, célèbre une messe solennelle en l'église de Pain Court, sa paroisse natale, à l'occasion de son 25e anniversaire de vie sacerdotale.

M. Raoul Gagner est nommé greffier de la municipalité de Dover.

Mgr. Bourdeau P.D. curé de la paroisse Saint Joseph de Zurich, est nommé curé de la paroisse de Pain Court.

M. Wilfrid Laprise succède à M. Adrien Caron comme président de la commission scolaire.

Le Père Ducharme curé de Pain Court, hospitalisé à London, succombe à la maladie. Le vicaire, Ulysse Lefaive prend charge de la paroisse. Avant le départ de ce dernier, une bourse de $600.00 lui fut présentée par M. Edgar Martin et M. Philippe Caron trésorier du Club des Placiers, au nom de tous les paroissiens.

Nous apprenons avec regret la mort accidentelle du jeune Yvon Thibodeau heurté par un camion qui sortait de reculons de la cours de ses parents, M. et Mme Raymond Thibodeau.

Nous offrons également nos sympathies à M. et Mme George Klein nos voisins dans la région du Townline et sixième rang de Dover qui ont perdu leur enfant unique de trois ans lorsqu'elle est tombée dans le fossé à proximité de leur demeure.

M. Maurice Daniel, étudiant en médecine à l'Université d'Ottawa, est rentré chez ses parents, M. et Mme Zéphir Daniel pour un mois de vacances.

Le 13 mai 1954 nous avons été privilégiés d'accueillir et d'honorer la statue miraculeuse de Notre-Dame du Cap. Cette statue originaire du sanctuaire national du Cap-de-la-Madeleine, a fait le tour du monde pour propager la dévotion mariale et celle du chapelet.

M. et Mme Joseph Robert nous présentent le 8 avril 1960, trois petits garçons à l'hôpital St. Joseph de Chatham. Les trois petits garçons pesaient au moins quatre livres chacun. Déjà ils ont une grande famille, car Maurice a deux ans et demi et Deborah est âgée d'un an. Les jeunes parents auront besoin d'aide et de courage pour pourvoir aux besoins de leur belle famille. Nous souhaitons bonne chance à tous, et paix, bonheur, santé aux trois jolis bambins, Joël, Jacques et Jean.

Les travailleurs du Québec et du Nouveau Brunswick sont arrivés dans notre milieu pour travailler sur les fermes de la région.

Un comité de parents-instituteurs est formé à l'école de Continuation H.J.Payette.

De grandes manifestations populaires et religieuses marquent le centenaire 1854 - 1954 de la fondation de la paroisse.

Pain Court, Ontario

Standing left to right: Jacob Bourdeau, Joseph Roy, Léopold Bourdeau, Orville Pinsonneault, Harry Lewis, Hervé Caron, Arsène Myers, Walter Crow. Seated : Raymond Gagner, Bernadin Maure, Bob Isaac, John Lachapelle, Armand Roy, Charlie Foy, Philippe Blais Sr.

Assemblée de l'A.P.I. février - 1959 Grande Pointe

Adresse de remerciements à Mère Eulalie, supérieure, pour sa causerie "La télévision en éducation."

Mme Caroline Laprise se dit heureuse et très honorée de se faire le porte-parole des parents pour vous remercier et vous exprimer notre appréciation et notre reconnaissance pour la préparation approfondie d'un sujet aussi délicat que "la télévision en éducation." Soyez remerciée, Mère, et soyez assurée que votre exposé sur les vérités des enfants vis-à-vis la télévision nous aidera à mieux comprendre.

Soixante-quinze pour cent (75%) des éducateurs ont constaté une diminution de travail à cause de la fatigue physique chez l'enfant. Ils ont de la difficulté à se concentrer. En plus, la télévision ne cultive pas l'habitude de réfléchir et de concentrer. Les images passent trop rapidement à l'écran pour saisir et retenir la pleine valeur des programmes télévisés tandis que les mots font une impression imprimée dans l'esprit. Les réflexions basées sur l'essai de la télévision dans les écoles seront intéressantes à suivre.

La télévision est une aide audio-visuelle mais ne remplace pas les éducateurs. Soyez assurés que vos connaissances acquises comme éducatrices ont aidé à rendre votre exposé clair et à point en face d'un bienfait technologique mais en même temps, un bienfait qui peut créer des problèmes. Vous avez clairement signalé que la télévision est entrée dans le monde de l'enfant et c'est évident que ses programmes seront pour eux favorables ou néfastes dépendant de la manière dont les éducateurs y feront face. La télévision ne doit pas envahir toute une vie. L'idéal est de trouver sa juste place selon les besoins personnels des individus soit éducatifs ou récréatifs.

Vos conseils, vos paroles fortifiantes et inspirées nous aideront à envisager avec courage nos devoirs comme parents chrétiens en collaboration avec les enseignantes et enseignants pour l'oeuvre de l'éducation de notre jeunesse grandissante.

Veuillez accepter nos plus sincères remerciements, Mère Eulalie.

Recommandations du comité du jardin d'enfants

Les parents-professeurs lancent au printemps de 1958, la fondation d'un jardin d'enfants, sous la direction de Robert Gauthier qui siège au Ministère de l'éducation à Toronto. C'est un projet pilote introduit dans le système scolaire bilingue.

L'inscription eut lieu le 1er avril pour l'entrée du jardin d'enfants en septembre 1958. Le comité du jardin d'enfants accepte avec plaisir les recommandations de la commission scolaire. Mère Charles-Auguste, principale, M. Adrien Caron et Mme Caroline Laprise font partie du comité. Ce comité se charge d'esquisser un plan qui s'appliquerait aux deux sections de l'école séparée: celle de Pain Court et celle de Grande Pointe.

Le plan acceptable est souscription au lieu de taxation, c'est à dire $5.00 par mois pour chaque élève enregistré. Un montant de $5.00 comme taux d'inscription sans exception est payable à la commission scolaire mais disponible à un comité du jardin pour ameublement et amélioration durant l'année scolaire. En plus, $10.00 à l'entrée en septembre est payable sans exception à la commission scolaire par l'intermédiaire du personnel du jardin d'enfants.

La comité déclare qu'au jardin aussi bien qu'en première année, aucun billet devrait être distribué dans les classes. Le personnel enseignant se rendra responsable pour les cotisations chaque mois. Celles-ci doivent être remises au trésorier des deux Comités parents-professeurs, qui, en retour, remboursera la commission scolaire le 30 novembre, le 31 mars et le 30 juin.

Les enfants du jardin recevront gratuitement une tasse de soupe lorsqu'elle sera disponible. Hommage à Mlle Carmelle Desgroseillers qui a géré habilement et avec finesse le début des jardins d'enfants de notre région.

Grâce aux parents et aux professeurs intéressés, nous jouissons encore aujourd'hui en 1998 de l'implantation des jardins d'enfants dans notre région. Grâce à la clairvoyance aussi de notre commission scolaire, qui après plusieurs années de souscription, a pu intégrer le jardin d'enfants dans le système scolaire de Pain Court et de Grande Pointe. En 1997, je remarque avec fierté le personnel enseignant de nos écoles. Plusieurs d'entre eux sont passés par les premiers jardins d'enfants de la région. Nous avons un film des enfants du premier jardin de Pain Court établi en 1958.

En septembre 1960 nous comptons 32 élèves au jardin sous la tutelle de Mme Thérèse Brown. Pour une deuxième année, les parents des élèves défrayent les dépenses en versant leur cotisation à chaque mois à l'association parents-instituteurs.

Élèves en 1960 - 61; Michelle Lacroix, Marcelle Roy, Annette Carron, Denise Pinsonneault, Micheline Lozon, Michelle Blais, Gisèle Pinsonneault, Marla Zimmer, Françine Legrand, Annette Sterling, Jocelyn Chauvin, Colette Laprise, Jacqueline Bélanger, Michelle Trudell, Michelle Ann King, Paula O'Neil, William Smulders, Marc Haslip, David Robert, Marc Richer, Gérald Thibodeau, Guy Rivard, Paul R. Béchard, Yvon Carron, Dennis Thibodeau, Gerrie Classens, Wayne Couture, Vincent Roy, Raymond Lachapelle, Roland Béchard, Pierre Martin, Raymond Faubert.

Millie's Antique Shop

History does make life interesting so it seems for Ernest Béchard, son of Mr. Willie Béchard on the Given Road. It started when Ernest bought a piece of land exactly where Victor's House of Blinds now stands.

Shortly after, he moved a frame house on the same property probably around May 1946. There was an old garage on the property which he converted into a welding shop and also as a temporary repair shop.

As pure luck would have it, the economy at the time was picking up so in June of 1954, he built a brand new repair shop. Business was good and progress was in the making. His neighbour across the street, Mr. Jenner wanted to sell his home and lot and since it was a fairly modern home, he decided to buy it and moved in during the early fifties.

Ernest Béchard was interested in progress.

As time passed, he heard that the Pain Court Dance Hall on the Dover Hotel property was up for grabs. This Gagner Hall was a landmark. It was rented frequently for weddings, parties and meetings. Every Friday night there was dancing or other entertainment in this building. Well, Ernest bought it, moved it on his property, repaired it and converted it in a two storey "Antique Shop." By 1966, business was thriving and it kept Millie rummaging the countryside to find antiques for her shop which she operated with her husband until 1974.

Their son, Eugene, now lives on the property. Millie has a new home next door on the property once owned by Ovila Martin which Ernest had bought in 1970.

Charlie Buck

Next door to Ernie resided Mr. Charlie Buck married to Sophie Béchard in 1928, both already in their mid-thirties. He was a very pleasant man and a skilled carpenter. He could replace any broken piece of furniture. He had precision tools and lathes that accompanied his talents and workmanship.

Their only son, Maurice, a graduate from the University of Ottawa, became a competent high school teacher and resides with his family in Port Colborne, Ontario.

L'avenir est à ceux qui luttent

C'est un vieux dicton celui-là; il n'est pas pour cela moins vrai. À l'occasion de la clôture du centenaire paroissial il est bon de se rappeler que les ancêtres ont bâti de peine et de misère ce que nous avons aujourd'hui.

Si Pain Court est le village à l'aspect canadien dont nous sommes les témoins, ce n'est pas parce que nos ancêtres étaient endormis et recherchaient la paix à tout prix. Ils ont su garder le foyer français, il se sont dévoués pour conserver une école où le "Français" est à l'honneur, et tout cela s'est fusionné pour bâtir une belle paroisse "Canadienne Française." Pour ceci, ils n'ont fait que suivre les conseils des bonnes religieuses qui nous ont enseigné que la religion catholique commande aux Canadiens français de garder leur héritage national parce que c'est un droit naturel, une vertu.

Canadiens français de Pain Court et d'ailleurs, sommes-nous de dignes fils de nos pères? Gardons notre foyer "Français." Conservons le français à l'école et de cette façon nous continuerons l'oeuvre commencée par nos ancêtres.

Un paroissien de Pain Court - 1954

Some Highlights of the P.T.A. Association
1950 - 1960

1 - January 1948, students visited Dominion Glass Co. plant in Wallaceburg. Parents did likewise at a later date.

2 - Scotchlite tape was bought and applied to bicycles.

3 - Many scholarships were awarded to contestants taking part in contests with different area schools.

4 - Parents agreed to help with expenses re: film board, projector etc.

5 - We financed different guest speakers for the parents.

6 - In April 1949, Mr. Phil Dagneau, county prosecutor animated a discussion on court procedures which was informative and interesting.

7 - Many outside speakers visited.

8 - We formed numerous study committees in order to advance curriculum development.

9 - November 27, 1959, Mr. Laing, inspector, addressed the meeting regarding options to the curriculum.

10 - Other inspectors who addressed our meetings were Mr. Lemieux, Mr. L. Lacroix, Mr. R. Gauthier.

11 -   We visited with other school principals and trustees, Mr. Wright principal of Merlin, Mr. W. A. Allen of Wallaceburg.

12 -   In 1959, Parent-Teacher association organised to serve soup during the winter months. Mothers took turns to help Mrs. Philomène Caron and Mrs. Joséphine Primeau who prepared the huge kettles of homemade soup.

Many pupils boarded buses at 7:30 in the morning and did not return home before 5:30 p.m. By 1960, busing became more efficient thus relaxing the special needs of children.

Barbershop Grande Pointe

In 1957, Joseph W. Benoit opened his barbershop in the office of Lionel Benoit's Service Station. In 1959, he moved his business to a new building adjacent to the service station and added a billiard room to complement his barbershop. June of 1964 saw the closing of the billiard room to make way for the opening of the Grande Pointe post office in its place. In 1974, both enterprises were sold to Leonard L. Emery.

Electrical Contractors

Adrien Emery and his brother Bernard of Grande Pointe started an electrical business in the early 30s. They wired many of the local homes including St. Peter's Church. Bernard and Adrien moved away in the early 40s, while another brother, Montfort began the business once again. In fact they wired our home in 1945. Leonard took over the business and then his sons picked up the challenge. Other area electricians were Real Charron and Al VanDenEnden of Grande Pointe.

Esdras Malette, électricien

Esdras Malette était un des premiers électriciens de Grande Pointe. En 1929, Hydro Ontario étendit sa ligne primaire au village de Mitchell's Bay. Cela fournit beaucoup de travail aux électriciens locaux. Esdras Malette commença par l'installation électrique dans sa propre maison et magasin puis il aida bien d'autres gens. L'entreprise comptait finalement parmi les siens, Ernest Labadie et Victor Malette qui installaient l'électricité dans les environs de Mitchell's Bay, Grande Pointe, Pain Court et Prairie Siding. Victor travaille encore dans les environs bien qu'il soit plutôt associé avec l'industrie privée. Ron Malette continue la tradition de la famille dans la région.

The Grande Pointe Welding Shop was established in 1947. It was owned and operated by Arthur Daniel who did general repairs to farm equipment, constructed small metal boats and crop sprayers, and during slow periods he would install drainage tile in the farms. In addition, he sold merchandise such as chains, nuts and bolts, oxygen and acetylene tanks, as well as chemicals for spraying. Mr. Daniel closed shop when he retired in 1973.

Grande Pointe
St. Philippe's Church - 1949

When the church was demolished
From left to right: Gérard Emery, Harry Bourdeau,
Orville Cheff, Sylvio Létourneau and Otto Myers.

The larger timbers in the church had been made by hand from tree trunks when the church was built 67 years ago. Many of the beams that supported the building retained their bark through the years. Shown above is a group of volunteer workers who helped with the demolishing of the church.

Martin's Popcorn

La famille Homer Martin établit en 1934 une entreprise de pop-corn. Au tout début, deux arpents étaient consacrés à la récolte du maïs, mais chaque année la superficie d'hectares augmentait.. En 1943, l'entreprise exploitait 250 hectares dès 1945, elle en contrôlait 450. Avant la guerre, le pop-corn était un commerce prospère et on le transportait partout au Canada.

La famille Henry Couture établit en 1943 l'entreprise "Atomic Popcorn."
En l'espace d'un an, les hectares ont augmenté de 21/2 arpents au début de l'année `43 pour aboutir à 250 en 1944 avec l'entreprise faisant son propre emballage de maïs soufflés.

Cependant en 1947, les Martin et Couture ne pouvaient plus cultiver le pop-corn du tout car les États-Unis faisaient du "dumping" de pop-corn moitié prix.

Les cultivateurs étaient payés $0.06 la livre pour le maïs séché et on le vendait à $0.04 la livre après le nettoyage et l'emballage.

En 1961 lorsque le marché s'améliora un peu, Roméo Martin acheta l'entreprise après le décès de son père. En 1962, il s'empara de la compagnie "Atomic Popcorn Co." et combina les deux opérations. Il géra Martin's Happy Hour Popcorn jusqu'en 1978 quand il vendit le commerce à Gérard Laprise.

Il est bon de souligner que "Martin Happy Hour Popcorn" était une petite industrie recherche. Ses produits garnissaient bien les étagères des grosses chaînes d'épicerie et pouvaient tenir tête aux autres entreprises rivales.

En 1990, l'organisme "Kent Agricultural Hall of Fame" a choisi de reconnaître Mme Maria A. Martin comme une de leur membre, elle qui a prêté main-forte pour aider son mari, Omer, à bâtir l'industrie du pop-corn dans le comté de Kent durant les années `30 et `40.

L'Honorable Jean Lesage

Rencontre des Canadiens français de la péninsule. Le banquet fut présidé par le Dr. Rosaire Lanoue et organisé par Léo Sylvestre, le 13 mai 1954.

Le ministre du Nord Canadien et des ressources naturelles, M. Jean Lesage, est en visite officielle à Windsor. Il adressa la parole à un groupe imposant de Canadiens français représentatifs de la région de Kent et Essex au Club Shawnee de Tecumseh.

M. Lesage se dit enchanté de rencontrer le groupe de langue française du sud de l'Ontario. "Partout, lorsque j'en ai l'occasion, je prêche et j'encourage les voyages de liaison française d'un océan à l'autre et je ne cesserai d'affirmer que les Canadiens sont chez eux partout où ils se trouvent. En vous connaissant mieux, les compatriotes de Québec trouveront le dévouement qu'ils pourront dispenser pour vous aider." M. Lesage fut remercié par Mgr. Gilbert Pitre de Tecumseh.
À l'occasion de cette fête nous rencontrons M. Philippe Contave, ambassadeur de Haïti au Canada. Il nous a rendu visite à Pain Court afin de visiter la ferme.

Le Premier Ministre Trudeau

En Septembre 1969 déclarait le premier ministre Pierre Elliot Trudeau.
"Comme francophones nous possédons l'un des héritages les plus riches du monde en matière de progrès et de liberté. La tradition française a toujours marqué un courant très fort de résistance à la tyrannie d'accueil aux idées nouvelles et d'ouverture sur l'avenir. Être français c'est refuser les idées toutes faites, c'est battre la marche, c'est risquer quand l'entourage hésite, c'est foncer vers le lendemain."

Special Tribute to Dr. Samson

In 1951, during the winter things around the home were very hectic. All the children were very sick, first it was chicken pox, followed by an epidemic of the "mumps." The situation was practically unbearable and many families were afflicted. Dr. H. R. Samson a family physician paid home visits to help the families. He also had four boys and was most understanding of the situation. These episodes were further aggravated when Gérard, then twelve years old, developed mastoids. He was admitted to the hospital for a week, contracted mumps, was discharged and returned home. The situation with Gérard became horribly critical as he developed "encephalitis," inflammation of the brain.

Dr. Samson made a desperate attempt to save his life. With a registered nurse, Jeanne Laprise, he spent the whole night administering medications intravenously while Gérard laid listless and motionless. The child was dying! Throughout the night he observed and treated him to the best of his ability. Because of prayer and Dr. Samson's superb effort, we saw a glimpse of life by morning. Recovery was a very slow process, days, weeks went by, while we all worked diligently to help him regain his strength and his memory.   He was able to return to school three months later.

Encephalitis is a crippling disease and often fatal. Another family in Chatham, not so fortunate lost their 9 year-old son.

It was a very trying experience, but thanks to Dr. Samson we all recovered. He was well known for his relentless efforts, his caring and understanding, as well as his medical research. His prestige as a family doctor was well recognized in our community. He served well at organizing the "Child Health Centre" in 1948. It was held in the Parish Hall of Immaculate Conception church in Pain Court, for all the surrounding areas.

The community was sorry to hear that he was leaving this area.

Concours d'orthographe 1950
De gauche à droite; Délima Lozon 8e année, Victor Trahan 7e année,
Louise Caron 7e année, Jérôme Béchard 8e année.

Family Highlights of the 50s - 60s

The Laprise family now stands at four boys and one girl. Frankly, exhaustion had seeped in. It was a full time job trying to meet everyone's needs. The responsibilities were overwhelming. Bookkeeping had to be done along with providing meals for three men working in the field, together with the responsibilities of the children and household chores.

At this time, I had help from my sister Yvonne Lucier who relieved me once a week from household duties. It became much harder to find help with a large family. In the spring it was gardening, raising chickens and ducks; lawns had to be cut.

During this period I was very active with community life also; activities were multiplying, the community was prosperous, and people were cooperative and happy. As president of the Ladies of Ste-Anne we initiated Co-op Medical Services and money raising projects. In 1948 I initiated, with much success, the Parent-Teacher Association for the elementary school.

342

In 1947, through child placement facilities, Mrs. Guyitt, the social worker for Children's Aid Society asked us to consider taking an 11 yr. old girl in our care. It was not an easy decision but it was worthwhile. Our foster child was Délima Lozon born August 25, 1936, in Pain Court, daughter of Antoine Lozon and Éloise Turner. There were six children in the family.

It was somewhat hard for her to adjust to a different life style with four boys and one girl. But it was not long before we were a large happy family. She was an excellent companion for my one year old daughter, Coline. Délima became a credit for our family. She was a very good student and a polite, pleasant and conscientious worker.

On September 23, 1950, Guy Vincent Laprise appeared on the scene to claim his share of care and attention in the Laprise household. He was a darling baby who at 3 months could stand by himself on the kitchen booth. Within a year he was sharing in all the disturbing mischief that kids can think of.

By the late 40s and into the 50s, we had help coming from different parts of the country. In the spring it was thinning sugar beets, in the fall it was harvesting. We had prepared accommodations to receive our helpers. It was not easy to meet some of their demands. By 1949 we decided to accept farm workers who came from Québec; they were living on our farms to fulfill our demands in the sugar beet industry. This was a much better arrangement. A polite group of young men from Stratford Centre in Québec took up residence in our shack in the fall of 1949. We reminded everyone to behave well and not fight with each other or they would be immediately laid off. In this pleasant group there were Halarie Rivard, Hercule Gagnon, Adolphe Gagnon, Paul-Emile Gagnon. Jean-Marie Rivard, and Gérard Gagnon returned the following year. Many came early in the summer to take jobs with other farmers before the beet harvest season. That same year Halarie Rivard consented to work for us till mid-December and later took up employment with his buddies at King Grain Ltd. for the winter months.

They were all good workers, reliable and respected in our community. They migrated here in southwestern Ontario from their birthplace, in the province of Québec, much like the first pioneers of our village but under much more favourable circumstances.

In July 1950 we had a welcoming party for Halarie Rivard and his bride Françoise Gagnon as well as for Hercule Gagnon and his wife Jeannine Gagnon, a distant relative, and all their friends and relatives who accompanied them. Halarie took up residence in our rented house for many years. We did spend many pleasant evenings, singing and dancing with my husband at the piano or with the guitar. We enjoyed their company. Mr. Rivard continued to work for us during the summer months. In 1954, he became a full time employee with King Grain and remained with them for 35 years. He was always reliable and trustworthy.

Halarie remained in this area while Hercule Gagnon, after five years, chose to return to Sherbrooke, Québec with his pleasant wife and his two children only to return for holidays and so did Paul-Emile Gagnon, Jean-Marie Rivard and Adolphe Gagnon.

Joseph Halarie Rivard manoeuvring one of the detasseling machines
for King Grain Ltd. while Napoleon Roy (King)and Ray Bourassa look on.

By the fall of 1953 it was urgent that I get a helping hand. Rita Roy came to my rescue. She married Joseph Demars on June 6, 1953 and decided to lend me a hand at least once a week until May 1954. It was a pleasure to be with her and take a break from the stressful situation as I was expecting another child. Her companionship along with her help gave me so much relief.

For the last 6 years it was a blessing in disguise to have, by my side, Délima, now 18 in 1954. She was in grade XII her last year of high school. This was somewhat stressful for her also, on account of her studies and graduation that year.

After graduation Délima chose to live with her sister Thérèse Lozon married to Léon Lozon the 9th of February 1948 at Grande Pointe. On October 11th 1954, Délima married Gilbert Duquette at St. Philippe's church in Grande Pointe. They bought a farm close to Thamesville Ontario. They had a son Gary and a daughter Angela.

Our boys were growing up also, but their father had work cut out for them, either in the field or in the shed.

In 1955, Valier Voyer, an agricultural school graduate from Québec, filled the vacancy for several years but also worked for King Grain during the winter months. After two years he opted to work full time for that company and within two years, became full time manager of "Semence Champs Pleins" at Ste. Rosalie, Québec, owned by King Grain of Pain Court.

By this time our boys were growing up and Gérard, the oldest, started operating machinery with his father, followed by Roger and Claude. As there was no work in late fall and winter, they decided one by one to enter the Agricultural College of Ste Martine, Québec, south of Montréal for further studies in farming, livestock, horticulture and woodworking. All managed to build their own bedroom suite and a secretary (desk), before leaving this college. Other school friends from Pain Court and Pointe-aux-Roches also attended the Agricultural College south of Montréal. Among them were, Jean-Paul Pinsonneault, Roméo Pinsonneault, and Robert Chauvin, all graduates of the College, in the same period.

Gérard graduated in 1957, but Roger left in his second year to join "Les Frères des Saints Apôtres" with Father Ménard, as superior, in Montréal. There he laboured and catered to the poor, helping to better themselves in various ways. After 4 years, he left the order and returned home in the fall of 1960 to become a full-fledged farmer.

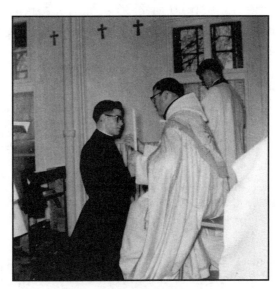
Roger

Claude also attended the College for two years but decided to spend one more year at Ridgetown College of Agriculture in 1959 to further enhance his farming knowledge. Florent was the first member of our family to graduate from this College in 1962, and taking his first assignment as field-man for Campbell Soup Company of Chatham.

* * *

By June 1951, Roland Sterling who had worked for us over twelve years, decided to leave our employment to start farming on his own. He was married June 7, 1951. He made a success of his enterprise as he was well versed in farming. His son, Carl, took up residency on his grandfather's farm in Pain Court and today is recognized as a good precision mechanic. He is well established here and serves many farmers' needs in this area.

During the 50s, life was very hectic, so it seems. Everyone seemed to grow up and project their own image. Everyone had heart to accomplish many projects. Gérard was busy strummin' his Hawaiian guitar, Roger was making good progress with his accordion while Claude was blowing the trumpet quite well, and Florent played accordion and piano. "Oh, my nerves!" My nerves were going to the dogs. Beckoning was either a music lesson, or a hockey practice with various school activities besides.

In 1949, Edward Emery sold his school bus business to his brother, Trefflé. He eventually expanded the service to seven buses to include busing at the elementary level. By 1950, bus service added benefits but also confusion. Every morning at 7:30 sharp, the startling and sounding alert of "le bus! le bus!" had everyone scurrying about, grabbing a last morsel of breakfast with the school bag in one hand and the lunch box in the other, hurriedly and anxiously going out the door for fear that the bus would leave them behind. Some mornings it was survival of the fittest, especially when trying to use the bathroom when ten people were in need to get ready. These "early to rise" bus skirmishes, engaging the whole family in a frenzy, could fill a few chapters.

Ongoing for five years, this hectic rigamarole which caused unnecessary confusion had to stop. A petition was circled around to bring some fairness to pupils strapped in this bus route. For some, departure meant leaving the household at 7:30 a.m. and returning 5:30 p.m., a much too stressful schedule for young children which meant foregoing playing time and dismantling the family spirit.

With June just around the corner, we started planning the beach outings for the summer. It was fun to pack up and go to Mitchell's Bay for a ride ever so often. The five younger children ranging from 3 years to 10 years loved that outing. By 1949 we would rent a cabin at the Bay, for a week, the same row of cabins standing alongside the baseball diamond and the picnic area today.

These cabins were the property of Léo Pinsonneault who then owned Mitchell's Bay Inn. Helen, his only daughter and married to Raymond Cartier, diligently went about cleaning all the vacated cabins. Everyone was excited. How pleasant it was to see the radiant faces!

My mother would also have a rental and did her share of supervising. Trefflé would join us after working hours. This outing was a yearly project. Playing in the water to their heart's content, and inviting friends was a big plus. For a change of scenery and also to compensate for the age difference and interests of our children we rented a small cabin trailer at Arsene Emery's beach park in Emeryville and thereafter rented a small cottage at Erie Beach in 1954. After a frightening incident with one of the children we soon learned that the waters were too dangerous in that area, so we came back to Mitchell's Bay. It was much closer and they could entertain their friends as well. It was a pleasant time wherever we went because in the early 50s there were very few swimming pools except in the Chatham parks. In fact, we never had a pool but continued to rent accommodations at different intervals during the summer. In fact, when Jean-Marie was born June 21, 1954 we were at a cottage. Later we purchased a cabin at Rondeau Park.

When the formal dates for the coming holidays were finalized, everyone was doing his share of the preparations and everyone fulfilled his daily task to perfection as the anticipation of the summer holidays was mounting.

By September of 1949 the four boys were in school. So more work was cut out while preparing to meet demands of the family in transition. We managed for a while but soon help in the home was needed enabling me to give a helping hand with the school work. We were privileged to welcome Evelyn Bagnell in our midst. She had experience in the home as well as on the farm. Her mother, Vélina Béchard, a first cousin of mine, had trained her daughter for household duties of all description: cooking, washing and ironing etc.

Evelyn's smiling face and humorous disposition helped to relieve my emotional stress and encouraged everyone to contribute in his own way in doing household chores and outside maintenance. I was thankful for her help. Evelyn left us in the fall to help her parents. She married Charles Montpetit in June 1954 and has been residing in Tilbury ever since.

Camping at Rondeau Park with Guy, Jean-Marie and Colette

La Feuille d'érable, une page d'histoire

Cinquante ans passés bourgeonnait "La Feuille d'érable," journal patriotique du sud-ouest ontarien publié pendant plus de vingt-cinq ans. À l'occasion de la Semaine française de Windsor, notre collaborateur a prononcé une causerie sur les débuts de cet hebdomadaire franco-ontarien à l'intention des membres du Club Richelieu de Windsor. Nous en reproduisons ci-après de larges extraits.

"La Feuille d'érable" au cours de sa première décennie illustre néanmoins une page d'histoire au pays des Grands Lacs, une véritable fresque locale, vis-à-vis les Canadiens français.

Le premier numéro paraît le 29 janvier 1931 et son parrain est le Sénateur Gustave Lacasse. Quant aux objectifs qu'il entend poursuivre, ce n'est pas trop clair car c'est alors que nous entrons en communication avec une des voix les plus éloquentes du fait français au Sud-Ouest Ontarien. Voici que nous prenons contact avec un vigoureux et redoutable défenseur des droits de la minorité franco-ontarienne.

Si on peut qualifier "La Feuille d'érable" de journal patriotique, de véritable chien de garde des intérêts de la population francophone, c'est en grande partie dû à l'orientation donnée par le fondateur à cet organe d'information. Le Sénateur Gustave Lacasse explique au point de départ que le journal entend servir les Franco-Ontariens, ceux de la région de Kent et Essex. Le Sénateur écrit: La Feuille d'érable a un programme bien défini et s'efforce de le mettre à exécution. A noter que "La Feuille d'érable" courageusement débordera souvent son cadre régional pour épouser des causes provinciales ou nationales, pour appuyer des communautés francophones d'ailleurs par exemple Welland, Port Colborne, Sudbury.

La Feuille d'érable demeure toujours un organe d'information essentiellement respectueux de la diversité du milieu dans lequel elle se baigne. "Dans la rédaction de ses textes, le Sénateur Lacasse, surnommé le "Lion de la péninsule," adopte un ton de prédicateur. Il sera souvent surpris d'ailleurs à livrer un sermon."

Médecin, homme politique, père d'une nombreuse famille, âme dirigeante de plusieurs entreprises, M. Lacasse épouse toutes les causes méritoires et chaque fois dévoile une facette différente d'une personnalité riche et dynamique, presque écrasante parfois.

"La Feuille d'érable annonce régulièrement la création de nouveaux organismes patriotiques, religieux ou culturels et encourage ses lecteurs à appuyer la grande famille francophone du Sud-ouest Ontarien, telle que l'Association des dames Canadiennes-françaises fondée en 1957-58 à Windsor, Pain Court, St-Joachim, Pointe-aux-Roches. Le journal fait écho aux nombreuses activités d'autres groupes: le Club LaSalle qui offre des bourses d'étude pour l'Académie Ste-Marie; la ligue des retraitants dont les activités sont plus souvent décrites en première page du journal; la Société de la Ligue des Nations dont Paul Martin se fait le plus éloquent porte-parole: les sociétés du Saint Nom du Sacré Coeur de Jésus, de même que la Société Médicale d'Essex au sein de laquelle le Sénateur oeuvre activement.

Mais c'est la société St. Jean-Baptiste de l'Ouest de l'Ontario qui reçoit l'appui le plus inconditionnel de la "Feuille d'érable." Les fêtes nationales du 24 juin et du 1er juillet sont organisées sous l'égide de cette association qui veille activement au développement et à la promotion de la langue française dans la péninsule des Grands Lacs.

Parmi les activités auxquelles l'hebdomadaire accorde une importance calculée, on compte le concours provincial de Français. Il s'agit d'une initiative lancée par Robert Gauthier, autrefois inspecteur des écoles bilingues de la région. Il y a aussi les activités de l'église et les personnalités religieuses dont les photos ornent presque chaque semaine les pages du journal.

Cet hebdomadaire cessa de paraître en 1958, après avoir suivi les francophones pendant 27 années. Nous accueillons avec enthousiasme le "Rempart" quelques années plus tard.

Paul-François Sylvestre

Fédération des femmes canadiennes-françaises

C'est depuis 1958 que la Fédération s'est créé une nouvelle cellule à Pain Court. Lors de sa fondation durant la Première grande guerre mondiale son but principal était de secourir les combattants et leurs familles. Les temps ont changé. Aujourd'hui, elles se dévouent plutôt à promouvoir la conservation de la foi et de la langue.

Voici comment nous cheminons vers ce but: d'abord, c'est l'organisation des bingos pour les jeunes, des offrandes de cadeaux pour le curé et pour les occasions spéciales qui se présentent, des prix de français pour les finissants des deux écoles (élémentaire et secondaire), des ventes de pâtisserie ainsi que l'adoption d'un séminariste indigène afin de défrayer le coût de son instruction.

C'est ainsi, qu'à notre façon, nous essayons de mettre en pratique la devise de notre fédération . . . "Pour nos Foyers."

Laprise Family Photo at Jean-Marie's Baptism

Ma Famille

La vie continue et prends encore plus d'entrain vers les années '54 et '55. Les aventures humaines qui créent la fraternité se multiplient. Les travaux des champs, les soucis de la maison, le soin des enfants, la bonne entente conduisent les êtres humains au bonheur.

En février 1954, Mlle Suzanne Laporte se joint à nous et s'occupe des besoins primaires des petits enfants à la maison, tout en accomplissant les travaux ménagers. Lorsque nos adolescents rentrent à la maison elle prend sa place parmi eux, et se réjouit avec eux. Ils s'entretiennent de musique, d'histoire, de délibération et Suzanne finit les activités avec des petites délicatesses, ce qui plaît aux enfants. Nous gardons des souvenirs tangibles de son dévouement. En hommage d'appréciation, que Dieu lui accorde joie, force et sérénité!

Être mère, c'est avoir vécu pour les autres et non pour soi. C'est à recommencer tous les jours de sa vie pendant qu'on élève sa famille en gâtant un peu ses petits enfants et en se souciant de leur moindre tracas. Être mère c'est se réjouir d'un premier sourire, c'est guider un premier pas chancelant, s'émerveiller devant un premier balbutiement. C'est être tout cela en plus c'est être l'épouse du père de ses enfants. C'est ainsi que nous aidons des êtres à vivre en plénitude.

En juin 1954, nous sommes heureux d'accueillir un nouveau membre dans la famille Laprise. C'est Jean-Marie. Charmant et souriant, il arrive pour prendre sa place comme le bébé du centenaire, c'est-à-dire qu'il fait parti des cérémonials du centenaire.

Coline, Guy and Jean-Marie

Le film du centenaire nous laisse entrevoir notre enfant être déposé sur l'autel de la Sainte Vierge par le célébrant du baptême Mgr. Augustin Caron, assisté par le Père Vincent Caron, entouré de la famille et des amis.

C'est un moment privilégié pour l'enfant lorsque le célébrant le consacre à la Vierge Marie.

*   *   *

Au mois d'août 1954, nous sommes enchantés de recevoir Joanne Lebrun à notre service. Sa belle humeur, son beau sourire et son habileté comme femme de ménage met de l'entrain dans le domaine Laprise. Joanne a su partager les ennuis et les joies familiales des parents car elle aussi faisait partie d'une grande famille, celle d'Ovila Lebrun et Edna Lozon, ses parents.

Cinq garçons à surveiller, ce n'était pas un cadeau. Ils sont remplis d'entrain. Ils travaillent bien et ils ont beaucoup d'amis qui viennent les visiter.

Le 22 août, 1955 nous accueillons une charmante petite fille, Colette Nicole. Nous l'aimons, nous la chérissons.

Partout ça bouge: sur la ferme, dans le foyer, dans les écoles, dans la paroisse.

C'est devenu impossible d'obtenir de l'aide pour les mamans à la maison. Ce sont les amis qui partagent la tâche d'aider les mamans qui attendent un nouveau-né. En 1955, c'est Alice et Gérard Roy qui prennent soin de Jean-Marie pour deux semaines lorsque je passe un stage à l'hôpital pour accueillir notre deuxième petite fille, Colette. Ils en ont fait autant pour Mme Gertrude Carron.

C'est à mon tour de garder, le petit Jacques Carron, âgé de 3 ans, lors d'un accouchement de sa mère en 1950. Plusieurs familles en ont fait autant. Déjà en 1955 il y avait une pénurie d'aide pour les mamans. L'éducation était devenu l'ordre primaire pour les jeunes filles de 14 à 18 ans.

Les progrès scientifiques et technologiques nous ont apporté des meilleurs récoltes, des meilleurs prix, et donc une meilleure vie. Les mouvements Coopératifs s'établissaient, les caisses populaires faisaient de grands progrès et contribuaient à une vie florissante.   Par contre, cette vie achalandée et accélérée pouvait causer un excès de "stress" pour les gens consciencieux.

Les grandparents Josephat et Délia Laprise

Le 25 mars 1959, nous avons été très heureux de participer aux agapes organisées par la St-Jean-Baptiste du Sud-Ouest afin de rendre un vibrant hommage à M. Josephat Laprise de Pain Court avec vingt-cinq autres compatriotes pour services rendus à la cause française catholique dans la péninsule de Kent et Essex. Le certificat de mérite patriotique fut présenté par "Juge Legris" ce jour même à Windsor. M. Alfred Cartier de Grande Pointe reçut le même mérite et certificat.

Le 8 octobre 1959, la famille Laprise a subi une grande perte, celle de la mort d'une chère maman, Délia Laprise. Les petits-enfants ont exprimé aussi leur peine de perdre leur grand-mamans qui les a beaucoup choyés. Elle était âgée de 57 ans, née à Grande Pointe le 19 février 1892, fille de Théodore Charron et Phébée Hébert.

Nous l'avons aimée durant sa vie et nous l'aimons encore. Sa personnalité sereine dévoilait sa bonté, son dévouement inlassable et son grand coeur de maman. Merci Maman.

Temps des Vacances 1956

Nous acquiesçons à l'invitation d'un séjour de vacances pour deux semaines avec le Père Chevalier accompagné du Père Louis Rivard et du Père Paul Bénéteau au chalet sur une île de la baie Géorgienne. Philippe Cartier et sa femme Marie Jeanne, Alcide Marchand et sa femme Cécile, Roland Griffore et son épouse Jeanne se joignent au groupe. La journée débute par la messe, suivi du déjeuner. Quelle aventure! Nous étions tellement heureux. Chacun se laisse vivre à sa guise. C'est une course à la pêche tous les jours et vers 7 heures le soir une autre sortie pour la pêche. Nous revenons avec du poisson pour le lendemain. Ça c'est des vacances. Tous partagent les soucis. Une vraie famille.

Malheureusement après une semaine de plaisir, un message nous arrive que le Père Dominat Caron est mort subitement, ce qui oblige les Pères Bénéteau et Rivard à revenir car c'est le Père Caron qui remplaçait le Père Bénéteau dans la paroisse. Alors le lendemain à 7 heures on s'embarque Trefflé et moi-même avec les Pères pour revenir chez-soi pour les funérailles. C'était la pluie battante pour 33 milles sur la Baie Géorgienne en fureur dans le petit bateau de seize pieds du Père Rivard. Dieu nous a bien préservé mais nous étions parfois saisis de frayeur. Après un voyage inoubliable, nous arrivons à la maison à cinq heures du matin afin de nous préparer pour les funérailles.

Pendant notre absence les anges du foyer étaient Gérard et Angéline Marentette. Ils avaient bien du courage de nous rendre une telle faveur avec une grande famille de 8 enfants à surveiller. Ce n'était pas un cadeau pour des nouveaux mariés, malgré qu'Angéline nous prêtait main-forte à maintes reprises pour la fin de semaine. Pour les deux semaines passées en vacances les enfants avaient besoin d'une figure de père dans la maison. Chacun avait sa tâche à remplir.

À notre arrivée, les enfants avaient subi une grande perte: leur petit "pony" s'était assommé sur la fondation de l'écurie. Rien ne pouvait assouvir leur grande douleur, car le "pony" faisait partie de leur vie de tous les jours.

L'entrée des classes 1956

Les vacances sont finies; c'est septembre 1956, c'est le temps de faire les valises pour les jeunes qui se préparent à faire leurs entrées pour les études à l'étranger.

Chacun aide à remplir sa propre valise avec le nécessaire pour l'année scolaire. Nous en avions trois à préparer, une pour Gérard et une pour Roger qui entrent au collège d'Agriculture de Ste-Martine au sud de Montréal et une pour Florent qui entre au Juniorat des Pères Oblats de l'Université d'Ottawa.

En 1957, voici que Claude se prépare lui aussi à s'inscrire au collège d'Agriculture de Ste-Martine avec ses frères.

La brave petite Coline, âgée de 12 ans, s'inscrit à l'Institut familial Notre-Dame des Victoires, sous la direction des Soeurs du Bon Pasteur. Dans notre foyer c'était chose ordinaire de préparer des valises pour les étudiants qui s'engageaient à faire des études à l'étranger. Mais pour Coline ainsi que pour la famille, c'était un peu plus pénible à cause de son bas âge.

Heureusement, elle avait une compagne de classe, Lucille Roy, fille de M. et Mme Napoléon Roy. Les deux ont joui de leur séjour à l'Institut familial. Les Soeurs du "Bon Pasteur" ont su comprendre les soucis et les anxiétés de ces deux jeunes filles loin de leur famille.

En plus de leur études académiques elles jouissaient des cours d'arts ménagers: la couture, le tricot, la préparation de la table et des mets délicieux, la peinture, et le dessin. Tous les cours étaient enseignés par les Soeurs du Bon Pasteur. Coline profite encore aujourd'hui de ses études supplémentaires et fabrique de très belles pièces de tricot et prépare une belle table spéciale qui ravit les invités.

Aujourd'hui en 1996, cet Institut Notre-Dame des Victoires, rue St-André à Ottawa, est l'Ambassade japonaise au Canada!

N.B. Lucille a continué ses études et est devenue garde-malade diplômée.

De gauche à droite : Louis-Paul Caron, Bernard Caron, Jean-Paul Cartier, et Florent Laprise.

Jean-Marie et Colette

Le 8 août 1954, nous avons failli perdre un de nos bons citoyens, M. Hercule Trahan, lorsque son tracteur a renversé dans un grand fossé rempli d'eau sur le 5ᵉ rang est de la Winterline.

Grâce à M. Trefflé Laprise, un des premiers sur la scène, il a pu transmettre des appels d'urgence à la commission des policiers, afin de sauver Hercule Trahan qui était coincé sous le tracteur dans le fossé.

Avec l'aide de "Rural Hydro" M. Trahan s'en est échappé sain et sauf.

Pain Court Baseball Team

The last organized senior baseball team in Pain Court - 1950s

Standing : Ivan Béchard, Raymond Thibodeau (pitcher
Philippe Blais Sr.(manager), Raoul Bélanger.
Middle : Vincent Goudreau, Donald Provost, Vincent Caron,
Gérard Marentette, Raymond Blais.
Front : Reginald Blair, Bob Provost (pitcher).

Holiday Gifts

This rich guy gave three nuns $100 a piece to donate to their favourite charity or person for the holiday season.

The first nun immediately took her $100 to the Salvation Army with the request it be used for food for the poor.

The second nun donated her $100 to the Cancer Society.

The third nun who worked in the slum area, scouted the district till she found this old dishevelled gentleman, who looked like he could use a suit of clothes and a good meal.   She walked up to him - handed him the $100 and said "God-Speed."

Several days later the old gentleman rushed up to the nun and handed her $500

Nun: Old gentleman "What's this for?"
Old gentleman: Sister, "God-Speed" won at 5 to 1 odds.

Pain Court Arrange TB Survey - 1951

Shown at the meeting are left to right, Mrs. Robert Bradley, Mrs. Robert Parry, Mrs. Leonard Jenner, Mrs. Bruce Bradley, committee cairman and Rt. Rev.W. Bourdeau.

Mrs. Leonard Jenner of Pain Court was very active in the ladies organizations at the time. The clinic in the basement of the church served this enthusiastic group of ladies very well for the mass TB Xray survey for the population of Dover township. Right Rev. W. Bourdeau was parish priest at this time.

Because of the enthusiastic support being given the survey in that area, the clinic hours have been extended both afternoon and evening.
Photo Star Kent Bureau

New Addition to École Ste-Catherine

In 1958, the new two room addition to Ste-Catherine School in Pain Court was officially opened. Mr. Wilfrid Laprise, president of the School Trustees Association, was present at the ribbon cutting ceremony with Rev. Father Chevalier, the parish priest, along with Edmond Gagner representing the Parent-Teacher Association.

Mgr. W. Bourdeau was on hand for the opening together with hundreds of parishioners in attendance.

As a whole it seems that much progress had been achieved in our schools and our society during the decade of the 50s.

Rest assured, where there's a will there's a way. A new gymnasium was a first for Ste-Catherine's elementary.

La Banque de Montréal

En avril 1961, la Banque de Montréal décide, pour une deuxième fois, d'ouvrir une succursale à Pain Court afin de desservir la communauté environnante.

Au début du siècle, c'est-à-dire vers 1910, ce même édifice avait été construit en vue d'ouvrir une banque à Pain Court.

En 1983, après 22 années de services fort appréciés, elle ferme ses portes. Nous remercions tous les employés qui y sont passés au cours des années, en particulier Barbara Regon et Aileen Reid.

Entre temps, Arthur Houle est devenu propriétaire de cet édifice. Au cours des années le rez-de-chaussée du building servit, vers la fin des années trente, premièrement, comme logis, ensuite comme salle de classe pour une dizaine d'années environ, faute de manque d'espace à l'école Ste-Catherine; au premier étage se trouvaient deux logis confortables à louer.

Par après, ce même rez-de-chausée servit comme boutique de coiffeur à Charles Lachance, habile coiffeur, bijoutier et pouvant même réparer les montres. Cette petite entreprise était bien reconnue et Charles, toujours prêt à rendre service, jouissait d'une clientèle florissante.

L'édifice imposant, au carrefour ouest de Creek Line et de Winter Line, rappelle bien des souvenirs à tous ceux et celles qui l'ont fréquenté, soit par affaire ou comme locataire, soit comme élève ou enseignante, soit comme client pour obtenir une coupe de cheveu ou bien pour acheter une bague de fiançailles ou autre bijou, ou simplement pour jaser chaleureusement avec Charles et Cécile dans leur boutique bien achalandée.

Chronicles – Chroniques

"Nun from Pain Court goes to Basutoland mission." Sister Jean-Victor Trahan, daughter of M. Victor Trahan and Sister of Holy Names of Jesus and Mary Order, is leaving shortly with Sister Ernest Armand of Windsor for the Roman Catholic mission fields of Basutoland, Africa, where she will remain for 10 years.

1960 Jaycees

Officials of the 1960 Jaycee Fair Board signed contracts with the amusement company Thomas Green. John Haslip, Pain Court resident, is Jaycee president. He will attend the fall Ontario presidents' conference in Toronto, accompanied by Archie Dick, vice-president, and Les Pont second vice-president. John Haslip leaves November 12 to attend the World Jaycee International Convention in Rio de Janeiro to continue his participation in the final portion of the film. John L. Gordon, producer of Movietown News declared at a National Convention in Hamilton that the sequence taken in Chatham is an outstanding Jaycee unit in Canada. Chatham placed second in the world competition in 1959 at Minneapolis.

The Board of Directors believe the film will give "tremendous" publicity to the city of Chatham.

Hommage à 25 valeureux franco-ontariens

Le 25 mars 1959, la population française du sud-ouest de l'Ontario a rendu un vibrant hommage à un groupe de 25 compatriotes dont on a reconnu publiquement leurs grands services pour la cause française et catholique. Les agapes furent organisées par la Société St-Jean-Baptiste du sud-ouest de l'Ontario.

L'honorable Louis Cécile, ministre du bien-être social siégeant dans le Cabinet Frost, était le conférencier d'honneur. Le Rev. Père Lanoue présenta à ses deux paroissiens, M. et Mme Édouard Lanoue, les hommages de toute l'assistance. Ils sont les heureux parents de quatre prêtres et deux séminaristes.

C'est le juge Legris qui distribua les certificats de mérite patriotique.

Les récipiendaires étaient:
M. John Girard, Belle Rivière.
M. Albert Mercier, à London depuis 11 ans.
M. Ferdinand Parent, Tecumseh.
M. John Rivest, Staples, 11 enfants.
M. Philippe Chauvin, Pointe-aux-Roches, membre de la commission scolaire pendant 23 ans, fondateur de la Caisse-populaire de Pointe-aux-Roches.
M. John D. Renaud, Belle Rivière, membre depuis 1907.
M. Josephat Laprise, Pain Court, 6 enfants, 2 religieuses.
M. Alfred Cartier, Grande Pointe, 15 enfants, 2 religieuses.
M. Ferdinand Chaput, 16 enfants.
Notaire Georges Sylvestre de St. Joachim, 11 enfants.
M. Armand Bénéteau, 11 enfants, un prêtre, Rivière-aux-Canards.
M. Jean-François Gagnon, McGregor, 16 enfants, 7 instituteurs.
Dr. Paul Poisson, Riverside, 9 enfants, membre actif de la ligue des retraitants depuis 25 ans, l'un des responsables de la fondation de la maison de retraites à Oxley.
M. Ernest Lajoie, Sarnia, 11 enfants, surnommé Père de la paroisse St. Thomas d'Aquin.
Rev. Soeur François-Xavier, SSJ Windsor, 39 ans de vie religieuse et 40 années d'enseigne ment dans les classes bilingues.
Rev. Soeur Élénore, Ursuline de Windsor, née à Rivière-aux-Canards, 38 ans de vie religieuse et 40 ans d'enseignement dans les classes bilingues.
Rev. Soeur Louise-Virginie, SNJM née Corinne Lajeunesse, compte 38 ans d'enseignement..
M. Théophile Bélanger de Sarnia, originaire de Pain Court, fondateur de la Société St-Jean-Baptiste de l'ouest Ontarien en 1926.

Study Committee October 1959

The executive committee of the P.T.A. appointed Caroline Laprise as president of a study committee, and Alexina Caron, as its secretary along with two other members, Raoul Gagner, Trefflé Emery to study possibilities of adding options to the school curriculum for H.J.Payette Continuation School.

The following is a report of the study committee dated January 27, 1960. As president of this study group, I hereby present this report. Most of you have attended our committee meetings of curriculum development. I feel much information has been transmitted especially by our inspector, Mr. Laing.

Roland Bélanger, chairman of the school board, presented Mr. Laing to approximately 45 parents and teachers. The inspector proceeded to give us an insight into different possibilities and aspects of the school curriculum.

Please note the differences between a high school curriculum and a bilingual high school curriculum. His first approach was to add grade XIII, not an option but a grade which undoubtedly would improve our academic status.

In regards to night courses, Mr. Laing made it clear that we needed at least 15 students for a special class in Chatham and our investigation made it clear it was practically impossible.

I now refer you to commercial options. There are three types of commercial options: commercial option, commercial department (economics), and special commercial. Finally, commercial option was recommended by Mr. Laing. He made it clear we needed a competent teacher and the school board would be able to carry the expenses.

Music as an option would certainly develop artistic talents and appreciation for worthwhile music. It could be taught if a competent teacher were available. Mr. Laing suggested that a music teacher in elementary school could serve for the high school as well.

Questions relative to domestic science for girls and industrial arts for boys were clearly answered. It is understood that special rooms would be made available before we could consider these options, probably in four to five years.

Since the agricultural science program requires specialized teachers, Mr. Laing suggested that these elaborate courses should be left to special agricultural schools, such as Ridgetown and Guelph.

Referring to arts and craft shops, he suggested that we visit the Dresden High School. This would include painting as an art, wood carving, working with leather, pieces of iron and wood, bearing in mind that a qualified teacher is available and the classes not overcrowded.

Geography was recommended highly as an important subject and should be taken into consideration especially in our changing times.

Finally, he said that the final decisions rests largely on the commitments the school board could permit themselves to undertake.

Bear in mind that this school was primarily established to prepare students for normal school and provide teachers to teach our children with the best academic course possible. Twenty years later, we recognize that changes have occurred and there seems to exist a great diversity in students abilities some not really academically but rather technically inclined. Therefore, there is a growing need to develop more options so that we may better serve our students.

As president of this committee, I have served to the best of my ability and in the best interest of all citizens of our prosperous community. It was agreed upon that together we would strive to have options available by September 1960, providing that the school board would undertake the financial commitment for:

1 - Grade XIII   2 - Commercial option
3 - Geography   4 - Music
5 - Arts and crafts

President of Committee
Caroline Laprise

Québec Students discover Pain Court is "Like Home"

On July 19, 1959 thirty-five teenagers chatted happily together yesterday while women hustled about the basement of Pain Court's Immaculate Conception, preparing breakfast for them.

"I'll bet that's the most talking they've done all week," said John Haslip, Chatham Junior Chamber of Commerce president, whose idea this was.

Eleven of the boys and girls were French-speaking Québec students on an exchange visit to Kent county. In Pain Court they had found a bit of home away from home, a place where language created no barrier. And many of them were surprised to find that practically everyone there could speak French.

Women of the church's Altar Society prepared and served the breakfast.

Jaycee President Haslip who arranged yesterday's church gathering, said that while more might have been done in the way of scheduling special events in which they could take part, he thought the guests were having a good time.

They were formally welcomed on their arrival here July 17 by Chatham Mayor Garnet Newkirk and Dr. H.A. Tanser, the city's director of education. Later they toured the Libby, McNeill and Libby plant and attended a dinner given by the Jaycees.

On Wednesday they will be treated to a swimming party at Chatham's new Memorial Pool and will then be driven, with members of city council as chauffeurs, to Mayor Newkirk's country home for an outdoor supper. Some of the teenagers feel they had more than they had expected in the way of entertainment.

La vie agricole et l'éducation

Voici un extrait du discours de M. Rémi Lalonde de l'école secondaire de Cornwall au banquet qui clôturait le congrès de l'Union des Cultivateurs franco-ontariens à l'arena de Casselman en 1960.

"Je ne suis pas un expert comme a pu laisser entendre votre secrétaire. Il a été bien aimable et bien indulgent dans sa présentation. Sachez dès ici, Mesdames, Messieurs que je suis fils de cultivateur qui a toujours conservé un attachement filial pour la terre, et une grande admiration pour votre métier.

Disons que j'ai continué ma vocation agricole dans la profession de l'enseignement. Puisque que nous traitons aujourd'hui du problème rural, j'affirme que le problème de l'éducation et de l'instruction chez les nôtres est d'importance primordiale.

Mais nous avons un devoir en tant que parents de voir à l'éducation de nos enfants. Sans doute, il ne seront pas tous des cultivateurs, des religieux, des instituteurs, des avocats, des médecins. L'agriculture est une des occupations qui date de l'antiquité. Cette occupation a toujours été l'une des plus importantes. Il y a deux raisons pour cette importance. L'une d'elle c'est qu'environ la moitié de tous les travailleurs du monde entier sont employés à l'agriculture.

L'autre raison, c'est que nous dépendons directement des agriculteurs pour la production de la plupart de nos aliments et de nos produits bruts pour nous vêtir. Il y a une foule d'occupations et de professions agricoles, entre autres nommons le vétérinaire, le cultivateur spécialiste dans les engrais chimique, le technicien agricole, le technicien d'insémination artificielle, le gérant de coopérative d'horticulteur, l'architecte, le paysagiste, le gérant de Caisse populaire, l'agronome et toute la gamme d'occupations comprises dans le mot 'cultivateur.' Celui-là aujourd'hui doit réunir dans un cerveau tous ces métiers et bien d'autres. La ferme est devenue une importante industrie mécanisée exigeant un patron instruit et alimenté d'un jugement sain et pourvu d'un sens de comptabilité agricole nécessaire s'il veut survivre.

Il nous faut une instruction plus élevée mais mieux orientée vers les besoins ruraux. Il importe de traiter et de connaître le développement, le goût et la compréhension de l'agriculture par l'enseignement agricole au niveau primaire. Malheureusement la province ne répartit pas encore équitablement ses octrois entre l'école publique et l'école séparée Catholique et bilingue. On doit répondre à tous nos besoins franco-ontariens.

Réf. Le Droit, Ottawa

Interesting Historical Data on
"Education" in our Schools

In 1900, what was then a public school is today known as "Chez Étienne Restaurant and gas bar." Mr. Potvin's house on the left was known as a Separate Catholic School dating back to 1875. The public school became a separate school in 1923 and the public school building was sold to Joseph Goure. Some years later it was sold to Joseph Maure who lived there with his family, until his son, Henri Maure, became the owner and also raised his family there after his father's death. Pupils who attended both schools at different intervals were: Hercule Trahan, Sophie Béchard, Paul Bourassa, Délima Emery, Jules Perrot, Délia Caron (my mother), Irene Perrot, Zacharie Gagner, Philomène Caron and many others.

In 1987, Rodolphe Potvin, a local carpenter bought this house and remodelled it to its present stage.

In 1879 salaries for elementary school teachers were: $ 410.04 and females received $ 303.05. By 1935, according to Blanche St-Pierre's diary, salaries were $ 600. for teaching grades 1 - 4 at S S # 4 public school in Dover.

About the same period grades 5 - 8 were taught by Miss Higginson who was principal, followed by Mrs. Sylvester Carron for one year and later by Miss Blanche St. Pierre who taught at this school until 1958 when it was amalgamated to form the new St. Philippe Catholic School in Grande Pointe. Other teachers who taught there were Blanche Foy, Lena Robert, Jeannette Blais, etc.

At S S # 13, a public school, was tutored by Marie-Jeanne Massie who taught eight grades in a one room school. Teaching was mainly in English with only 20 minutes a day of "French" until 1927 when the famous law "Règlement 17" was abolished. She married Amédée Bélanger in 1933. This school served many years as an extra classroom in the Separate School system of Pain Court.

At S S # 7 Pain Court, a separate school, Alexina Ouellette taught classes for over 10 years including all grades 1 - 8 ,in French for only 20 minutes a day, as the famous law only permitted limited time. She married Alcide Caron in 1930 and continued teaching some 3 years, part time. At this period when enrollment grew by leaps and bounds more children were admitted to the classroom and an improvised classroom was arranged by dividing the big one room school into two classrooms.

Other teachers there included Pierre Gouin, Annette Carron, Blanche Foy, Marie-Louise Carron, Vincent Caron for 5 years followed by Marie-Jeanne Sterling for 5 years until S S # 7 was amalgamated with École Ste-Catherine, Marie-Jeanne remained with the teaching staff in Pain Court for 2 more years, until 1950.

At S S # 5 Dover a public one room institution was tutored by Edith Wright later known as Mrs. Anthony Bruette. She pursued her teaching career until shortly before she died in 1950. As of 1998, this school is still standing idle on the Jacob Road in Dover township with its barricaded windows and a "No Trespassing" sign nailed to its door engaging passers-by to reminisce about the good old school days.

At Grande Pointe S S # 9 a separate school was open about 1912 replacing a primitive school in order to accommodate a growing population. Some of the teachers who taught in this era, at a two room school were Helen Trudell, Ida Rouillé of St-Joachim who married Félix Bourassa, Eva Faubert who later joined St. Joseph Sisters in London. Later other familiar names were: Léopoldine Houle, Zulma Martin, Blanche Caron Foy, Maurice Bélanger, Blanche St-Pierre, Pierre Gouin. This school became part of the amalgamation system in 1958.

S S # 14 also became part of the new system in 1958; it was known as St. Philippe school of Grande Pointe. In 1948 and later, Amedée Emery, Florence Roy and Marguerite Pinsonneault were teachers at this school. Prior to this period, I can remember Mrs. Pattenaude, Laurier Brisson, Glorianna Gagner.

Finally by June 1958 the school board built a new school in the village of Grande Pointe adjacent to St. Philippe church. They amalgamated S S # 4, S S # 9, S S # 14. During the construction period Grades 5 and 6 pupils of S S # 9 and S S # 14 attended classes in the parish hall with Amedée Emery and grades 7 and 8 pupils with George Gagnon as principal. Grades 1 to 4 remained at their respective schools.

The teaching staff for the new centralized school consisted of Jeannette Emery, Florine Grifford, Amédée Emery and George Gagnon. A kindergarten class was added in September 1958 with Eileen Labadie as teacher.

At the time of the official opening in 1958, board trustees responsible for the changes were: Donald Cadotte, Wilfrid Laprise, Gérald Gagner, Oscar Robert and Léonard Emery.

S S #4 corner of the 7th concession

S S # 9 (1912) Dover

École St-Philippe June 12,1958
Centennaire 1886 - 1986

S S # 7 - 4ᵉ concession 1930 à 1940

Gauche à droite :

1ᵉʳᵉ rangée: - Halarie Gysels, Harry Sterling, Junior Delore Gervais, Garnet Pelkey, Raymond Thibodeau, Bernard Trudell, Raymond Couture, Raoul Bélanger, Raymond (Willie) Béchard.

2ᵉ rangée: - Edward Lobestal, Léonard Goudreau, Lionel Pinsonneault, Joseph Gervais, Hubert Caron, Stanley Laevens, (avec Ardoise), Gérard Pinsonneault (Denis), Cyril Crevits, Marcel Crevits.

3ᵉ rangée: - Yvonne Crevits, Jeannie Gyesels, Jeannette Carron, Thérèse Trahan, Evéline Bourassa, Thérèse Roy, Alma Caron, Lucille Roy.

4ᵉ rangée: - Florence Trahan, Blanche Giroux, Laurette Thibodeau, Yvonne Trudell, Rita (Alphy) Roy, Hélène Pinsonneault, Annette (Jim)Béchard, Bernadette Pinsonneault, Rita Bélanger.

5ᵉ rangée: - Rita Carron, Florence Trudell, Rose Charron, Elsie Crevits, Mary Gervais, Pauline Roy, Rita (Amédée) Pinsonneault, Béatrice Pinsonneault, Mae Béchard, Sylvius Trahan, Lawrence Gervais, Roland Roy, Roland Thibodeau, Frank Gervais.
Demeure à gauche - Alphonse Pinsonneault Noms: Gracieuseté de M. et Mme Régis Caron

École S. S. #13 Dover School - 1933
(l'école du Town Hall)

Photo: Gracieuseté de Marie-Anne (Béchard) Faubert

À genoux : Bill King, _____ , Lionel Caron, Jérôme Faubert, Laurent Caron, Bernard Faubert, Marie-Anna Caron, Gérald Béchard, Raymond Béchard Raoul Béchard, _____ , Joseph Caron.

2e rangée : Simone Monstrey, Evangéline Roy, Marie Béchard, Lucienne Caron, Evéline Therrien, Yvonne Therrien, Bernadette Faubert, Rita Faubert, Marie-Jeanne Robert, Rita Robert, Lionel Béchard.

3e rangée : Mlle Julianna Caron (institutrice), Marie-Anne Béchard, Clara Béchard, Laurienne Caron, Madeleine Verplanche, Marie King, Blanche Béchard, Madeleine Béchard, Béatrice Robert, Yvonne Béchard, Gertrude Caron, Jean-Baptiste Roy, Romain Béchard, Léonard Faubert, Jacques Caron, Roger Kettle, Rosaire Caron.

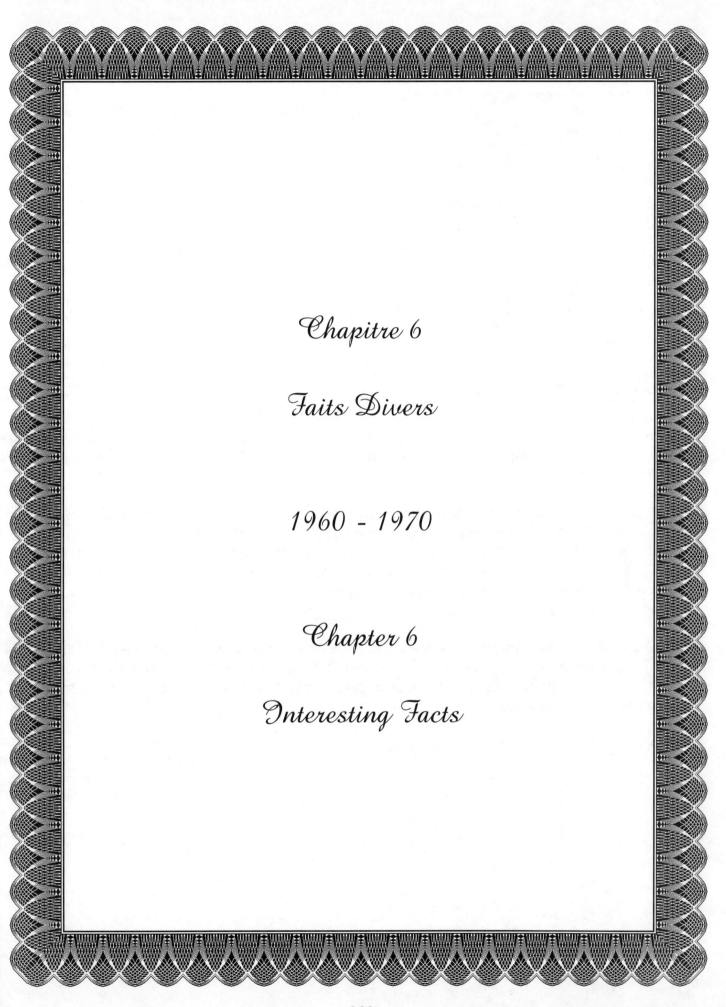

Chapitre 6

Faits Divers

1960 - 1970

Chapter 6

Interesting Facts

Si tu crois en moi tu vivras éternellement

L'esprit d'Alma Richer sera très longtemps parmi nous . . . même si, physiquement, elle nous a quittés. La maladie l'a emportée le 15 mars, 1975; elle l'avait combattue jusqu'à la fin avec le courage et la sérénité qui ont toujours caractérisé ses actions. Elle est née à Pain Court en 1926 d'Alma Trudelle et de Ladislas Caron. En 1950, elle a épousé Louis-Joseph Richer; ils ont eu dix enfants: Jean, Claude, Marc, Paul, Joseph, Marie-Ange, Pierrette, Marguerite, Thérèse et Lyse.

C'est à cette famille ainsi qu'à sa communauté qu'elle a prodigué un dévouement inlassable et qu'elle a manifesté un exemple inoubliable de foi, d'espérance et de charité chrétienne. "On allait la visiter malade, et c'est nous qui en revenions ressourcé," a déclaré le curé Léo Charron à ses obsèques. Témoignage éloquent . . .et typique, car tous ceux et celles qui ont eu le bonheur de la connaître ont été marqués par cette femme profondément humaine, universellement sympathique et rayonnante d'optimisme chrétien.

Parmi toutes ses préoccupations, trois oeuvres lui étaient particulièrement chères: les Dames de Ste-Anne, la Fédération des Femmes Canadiennes-françaises dont elle fut plusieurs fois présidente de section et dont les Conseils régionals et nationals reconnurent publiquement son mérite par des décorations au cours de l'an dernier et le centre culturel Brébeuf qui vient d'être établi à Pain Court. Les membres de ces mouvements ont perdu une collaboratrice précieuse dont l'exemple continuera sûrement à porter fruit.

À sa famille, à ses frères et à ses soeurs, nous offrons nos plus sincères condoléances. Avec eux nous remercions la Providence du privilège très spécial d'avoir pu connaître un être si pénétré de l'esprit et de l'Évangile, si riche de qualités, dont le souvenir sera longtemps, longtemps une inspiration très salutaire.

Jean Mongenais
Le Rempart - 15 mars, 1975

Mrs. Sylvester Carron

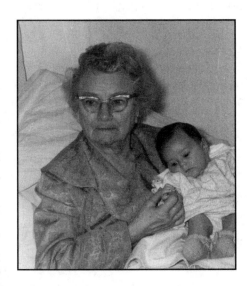

Mildred Jones was born in 1889 in Point Edward. She is the daughter of John William Jones and Mary Moran.

On October 31, 1918 she was married to Sylvester Carron son of Theodore Carron and Maria Charlton. Theodore served as warden of the county about that period.

Mildred Jones started her teaching career in Huron county. Later she taught at St. Patrick School in Merlin and boarded at Joseph Hickey's residence. Mr. Hickey kind of loved to play jokes on her. On a special occasion he asked if she loved crow meat. More or less stunned she accepted the challenge. It turned out to be a joke - because really it was a pigeon casserole.

After teaching ten years she was married in 1918. They had a family of three girls: Margaret, Mary and Annette. Edward and Theodore were their two boys. Mrs. Carron continued teaching for a number of years while her family was growing up. She taught at SS #4 public school in Dover in the 30s with Miss Higginson as principal, and teaching grades 5 to 8. After two years she replaced Miss Higginson as principal and taught grades 5 to 8, while Blanche St-Pierre was teaching grades 1 to 4. After a few years Blanche became principal.

In the early 40s she took a position at St. Joseph's School in Chatham and ended her teaching career in 1946. She was 57 years old. Her teaching carried over a period of some 38 years. She died March 1976, at a ripe old age of 88.

Mildred deserves much credit for her contribution to education. She was an example of courage, devotion, perseverance and loyalty, serving her husband, her family as well as students wherever she was teaching.

Family synopsis of Mildred and Sylvester Carron:

1. Edward, M.M.C.D the oldest son served overseas in 1939 with Royal Canadian Regiment. He returned to regimental duty and was promoted to Major. He continued to serve his country at different levels until late 1960 about 25 years.

2. Margaret, registered nurse - married Lawrence Jubenville who served at different levels of Dover township council. A son Michael is a graduate of Guelph Agricultural College and carries with the family farm. Mary Ellen married Leonard Caron.

3. Mary, registered nurse, married a Robertson. They have 2 boys and 5 girls: Roberta, Mary Beth, Sally, Margaret all are RNA's; Jane is a real estate agent; Robert is a paramedic and a mechanic; Peter is teaching fire protection in the Canadian Air Force.

4. Annette, registered nurse married Romain Delanghe. They have 5 boys and 4 girls. In 1973 she obtained a degree in Social Work at the University of Regina. She retired in 1985. Mary her daughter, obtained her Master in Psychology and is instructor at the University of Regina, Kate, Bachelors degree in Psychology, University of Regina. Program manager for the government of Saskatchewan. Peg, program manager, Royal Museum of Regina. Patti, bilingual degree in education and teaches in Ottawa.   Ted a graduate of RMC Kingston, Ontario Agricultural pilot - winter - Video Commercial producer. George, Registered nurse, Prince George General Hospital in B. C., owner of George Music Internet Music Supply. Roger, graduate of RMC Kingston, Ont. Flight instructor - aero space, Saudi Arabia. Eddie, family lawyer, Edmonton Alberta. Frank, graduate RMC Kingston, Ont. Captain Armed Forces in Ottawa, Ont.

5 Ted, married Alice Jubenville. They raised six girls and 3 boys, Joe - mechanic, Steve - welder, Ben - welder, Ann - business management at Western University, Jackie - University of Guelph - Hotel management, Laurie - Quality Control, Suzanne - registered nurse, Rosalie - registered nurse.

Mrs. Mildred Caron, we do recognize you for your accomplishments, for your dedication toward mankind. Your spirit will live on and your children's children will continue in your footsteps and honour you for generations to come.

Caroline Roy Laprise
Ref. Margaret Jubenville Carron

Dora Couture

Dora is the daughter of Délia Demers and Jean-Baptiste Couture. She has four sisters, Florence who married Hector Ouellette, Loretta who married Eddy Damphousse, Dorothy who married Rene Sauve and Annette who married Don Howe. She also has six brothers, Omer who died as a child. Adelard who married Aldea Barrette, Herman who married Madeleine Caron, Ernest who married Elmire Caron, Arsene who married Rita Lucier and Gerard who married Godeleive Bossy.

Dora married Harvey Couture July 29, 1946. They have three daughters, Joanne who married Paul Cadotte, Angela who married Helmut Pawlak and Diana who married Ronald Sterling. They now have six grandchildren, Chantal, Kevin, David, Shawn, Daniel and Christopher.

Dora has worked very hard. Throughout the years, she has always helped her husband on the farm. She is a member of Les Dames de Ste-Anne and has helped them with their events. In July 1996, Dora and Harvey celebrated their 50th anniversary at the Countryview Golf Course. Afterwards, the guests gathered at their home in Grande Pointe. It was a very memorable day!

My mother has always been there for her husband, her children, her grandchildren and everyone else who knows her. We all know we can always count on her. She is the best mother anyone could ever wish for and I love her very much.

Mrs. Angela Pawlak

Une femme perspicace

Lors de mon passage à Ottawa alors que mes enfants fréquentaient les écoles de la Capitale, j'ai fait bien des connais sances et j'ai gardé beaucoup de souvenirs qui sont restés bien vivants, des souvenirs pleins de vie, de chaleur et d'amitié. Cependant une entrevue qui est passée à la télé en 1968 avec Dame Ethel Breton m'a piqué la curiosité et m'a incité à vouloir la rencontrer.

Elle a passé son enfance à Cabano dans le comté de Temiscouta. C'est à l'âge de 6 ans et demie que, pour la première fois, elle a démontré son talent. Debout sur la table pour mieux voir par la fenêtre elle attire l'attention de sa mère:
"Remarque bien cette maison maman, car dans deux jours tu ne la verras plus," déclare-t-elle à sa mère.

En effet, deux jours plus tard sa mère a été témoin de cette maison détruite par l'incendie.

Mariée très jeune à Gérard Breton de Cabano, Ethel a eu 11 enfants dont neuf bien vivants. Elle ne sait d'où lui vient certains pouvoirs. Ayant quitté l'école à l'âge de 10 ans elle souligne qu'elle n'a certainement pas étudié son art mais que son aptitude lui est venue naturellement.

Mme Breton de Hull révèle les secrets du tempérament grâce à la télépathie et à l'étude de la physionomie. Elle se croit dans l'obligation de partager son "don" et refuse rarement à ceux qui recherchent son aide. Elle est douée d'une grande intuition, d'un talent pour la télépathie, d'une imagination vive et d'un tempérament chaleureux. À maintes reprises, j'ai pu lui rendre service surtout lorsqu'elle traversait des moments difficiles. Elle est âgée de 85 ans.

Mardi, 27 mars 1962

ANNIVERSAIRE FFCF ÀWINDSOR -- Plus de 150 personnes ont assisté au banquet qui a marqué le 5e anniversaire de fondation de la Fédération des femmes canadiennes-françaises à Windsor. Parmi les personnalités qui ont pris part à cette fête on retrouve, de gauche à droite: Mme T. A. Laprise, présidente de la section de Pain Court, Mgr. J-Wilfrid Langlois, v.f., curé de la paroisse Notre-Dame-du-Rosaire, Mme Benjamin Michaud, présidente régionale de Toronto, conférencière invitée, l'honorable Paul Martin, et Mme Louis Bézaire, présidente de Windsor.

Photo DNC par Roland Dagenais

FFCF 5e anniversaire dans la région

À l'occasion du 5e anniversaire de la fondation de la FFCF, région de Windsor métropolitain, plus de 150 personnes ont assisté à un banquet au Centre canadien français sous la présidence de Mme Louis Bézaire, présidente régionale.

Visiteurs distingués sont venus de Toronto et d'Ottawa. Membres des gouvernements provinciaux et du fédéral, personnalités laïques et religieuses ont applaudi la conférence de Mme Benjamin Michaud, marraine du groupe de Windsor et représentante provinciale.

Mme Michaud avait choisi comme thème "La valeur de la femme canadienne-française," comparant la femme canadienne à la Bienheureuse Marguerite d'Youville. La conférencière invita toutes les femmes à conserver intactes les vertus illustrant nos mères d'autrefois.

"Demeurez dans votre rôle de femme canadienne française" a-t-elle dit. "La cause ne sera jamais perdue s'il reste encore une femme de chez nous pour la défendre."

Mme Michaud a rendu hommage à toutes les femmes fortes de chez-nous qui ont élevé de grandes familles et qui se sont montrées dignes de leurs ancêtres dans leur dévouement pour le foyer, l'école et l'église.

M. Benjamin Michaud, surintendant-adjoint de l'enseignement primaire en Ontario, a transmis des souhaits du Ministère de l'Éducation et a donné des statistiques révélatrices sur les écoles bilingues de l'Ontario. Il a rendu hommages aux femmes qui contribuent au succès des écoles bilingues.

L'honorable Paul Martin, député fédéral d'Essex, a encouragé nos associations patriotiques à "continuer leurs demandes" dans la revendication des droits et privilèges des Canadiens français.

"Nos sociétés St-Jean-Baptiste, nos clubs Richelieu, tout comme nos sections des Femmes Canadiennes-françaises sont des moyens efficaces pour faire pression auprès du gouvernement en vue de reconnaître notre droit d'existence au pays," a-t-il dit.

Mardi, 27 mars 1962 Le Droit

Fédération des femmes canadiennes-françaises à Pain Court

Le 15 novembre 1958, Pain Court devient la plus jeune section de la Fédération des femmes canadiennes-françaises de l'Ontario. Un groupe de dames se réunissent dans une des classes de l'École Secondaire de Pain Court pour entendre Mme Benjamin Michaud, présidente de la section de Toronto, leur expliquer les buts de l'organisme.

Le but de cette réunion était d'établir une section locale. Voici l'exécutif de la nouvelle section:
L'abbé Euclide Chevalier, aumônier
Mme Alexina Caron, présidente
Mme Caroline Laprise, vice-présidente
Mme Florence Caron, 2e vice-présidente
Mme Marguerite Roy, secrétaire
Mme Albertine Chauvin, trésorière
Mme Carmel Laprise, Mme Bertha Pinsonneault, Mme Marguerite Gagnier, Mme Marcelle Roy et Mme Armand Béchard, conseillères.

Pendant le thé qui a suivi la réunion, nous avons décidé d'organiser une soirée publique afin de faire mieux connaître la FFCF dans la paroisse.

Père Euclide Chevalier, aumônier, a félicité les dames de leur initiative et les a encouragées à organiser des soirées récréatives pour les jeunes de l'école secondaire au gymnase de l'école. Il suggère que les parents participent à ces soirées afin qu'ils soient plus près de leurs enfants et qu'ils puissent ainsi gagner leur confiance. Le Père a ensuite annoncé qu'il donnerait des cours d'orientation aux jeunes afin qu'ils soient plus au courant des diverses vocations qui existent et qu'ils sachent choisir judicieusement.

Toutes les membres de la FFCF sont invitées d'assister au congrès provincial à Ottawa.

En 1959, la section de Pain Court fut nommée Section Marguerite d'Youville à l'occasion de la Béatification de Marie-Marguerite Dufrost de Lajemmerais, en religion Mère d'Youville, le 3 mai 1959. Elle est la fondatrice des Soeurs de la Charité (Soeurs Grises) de Montréal. Son Éminence Paul Émile Léger assista à la cérémonie dans la basilique St. Pierre de Rome en compagnie de 24 archevêques et évêques canadiens.

Bel accueil des sections de la Fédération des femmes canadiennes-françaises (FFCF)

La rencontre a eu lieu en avril 1961, au Centre canadien français sous la présidence de Mme Aline Bézaire présidente de la section de Windsor. Les trois sections de la FFCF dans le sud de l'Ontario ont offert un chaleureux accueil à la présidente nationale du mouvement, Mme Rose-Alma Sauvé-Boult, à l'aûmonier général Mgr. Napoléon Gélineau et à l'abbé J.E. Martin, tous les trois d'Ottawa.

Elles saluent également les présidentes régionales: de Toronto Mme Benjamin Michaud, de Sturgeon Falls Mme Edmond Allard. On remarque aussi la présence de Mme Jean-Louis Pelletier, secrétaire-archiviste nationale de la Fédération ainsi que Mme Élie Sylvestre, présidente de St-Joachim et Mme Caroline Laprise présidente de Pain Court.

Dans son allocution, Mme Sauvé-Boult a félicité les femmes canadiennes- françaises de la région du Sud de l'Ontario pour leur beau travail et a fait l'éloge de l'aumônier général dont la haute culture n'a d'égale que sa modestie. Elle a aussi rendu hommage à tous les aumôniers locaux: Mgr. Augustin Caron de St- Joachim, Père Euclide Chevalier de Pain Court, et le Père Léo Charron de St- Jérôme dont leur présence aide à resserrer les liens qui unissent les membres de la Fédération avec l'Église.

Au nom des sections du Sud de l'Ontario, Mme Caroline Laprise a remis à Mme Rose-Alma Sauvé-Boult un cadeau-souvenir.

En ce qui concerne la revue des modes de chapeaux printaniers, c'est Mme Paul Quenneville, de la Fédération de Windsor, qui a lu les textes de références pour la présentation.

Père Oscar Martin, curé de la paroisse de Rivière-aux-Canards, assistait à titre d'aumônier régional de Windsor métropolitain de l'ACFEO.

The 1960's marked the end of an era

Growing up on a farm during the 60s was an interesting time to witness the transitions which agriculture and rural living confronted.   Pain Court and Grande Pointe, two of Kent County's progressing communities, entered the past decades with conventional one room schools, church, community hall, small stores, a site for delivering grain to the railroad siding, welding shops, sawmills and feed mills. By the end of the 60s, most of these rural foundations were gone. My father and mother, born at the end of the nineteenth century, had witnessed all these changes and I doubt if any of them met with their approval. Such was an era of "progress." Out with the old, in with the new. New had to mean better, of course.

Survey by York University

In 1964 - 65 York University conducted a survey in the area of Pain Court and Grande Pointe. I was personally interviewed in my home at two different intervals by different teams of research analysts. This coincided with the period my sons and others, were reaching out for a more technical education at the Agricultural College of Ste-Martine, south of Montreal.

I did complete an extensive questionnaire at the time, followed by another questionnaire sometime later. Pain Court, being a very efficient community in agriculture, additional research was in order by the educational system. Much interest was generated at the time in our culture and our practices.

Laprise Family Photo - 1960

Trefflé et Caroline entourés de leurs huit enfants en 1960
Debout de g. à d. : Jean-Marie, Trefflé, Caroline, Colette
Au premier plan de g. à d. : Coline, Claude, Gérard, Roger, Florent et Guy

*More and more farm power is needed today by Trefflé Laprise, as by most other farmers.
Here he is seated on his latest acquisition, a diesel that will handle five furrows.
Farmer's Advocate, December 14-28, 1963*

French traditions came to stay in Ontario
from 1670 - 1963

Jean Daniau dit Laprise left the province of Poitou, France, in 1670, to settle on the Île d'Orléans, opposite Québec City in the Gulf of St. Lawrence. Eleven generations later his descendants are cash-crop farmers in prosperous Kent County, near Chatham, Ontario.

"At one time," says Trefflé Laprise, "we, French Canadians of Ontario felt very isolated in our little villages. We did not know you, the English Canadians. We did not understand your way of living."

But that is all changed. Since the coming of good roads, and automobiles, we have come to know and respect our English neighbours. I think the separatists in Québec are as we were 20 years ago.

Pain Court, Ontario, a ten minutes drive from Chatham, is one of the most complete French settlements in Southern Ontario. A bilingual sign welcomes the visitor, stamps are bought at the Bureau de Poste and money banked at the Caisse Populaire. Both public and high schools in Pain Court are bilingual and have courses designed for French-speaking students. Children from English-speaking backgrounds learn their French in kindergarten, and last year's winner of the French composition prize was a child whose family background was not French.

Sunday supper in the farm kitchen - Trefflé Laprise talks to five of his six sons.
Farmer's Advocate December 1963

Cash Crop Farmer

Most people are engaged directly or indirectly in cash-crop farming in this rich, fertile area. The Laprise's have 425 acres, and have already set up their two elder sons, Gérard and Roger, on 50 acre farms of their own. The other sons, Claude, Florent, Guy-Vincent, (13) and Jean-Marie (9) will have their own farms later. There are also two daughters, Caroline and the family's youngest child, eight-year-old Colette.

As on most family farms, the father and sons work together, hiring help only occasionally at specially busy times. Equipment is shared, and Roger and Gérard are paying for their tractors and a beet harvester by operating them on neighbouring farms.

"But," says Mr. Laprise, "land around here is expensive. I have six sons, and cannot give them more than 50 acres each. That is not enough land for economic farming, and they must take other jobs."

Gérard works with an anhydrous ammonia fertilizer plant, while Roger and his wife, Rosemarie, together operated a canning and labelling machine this summer. Claude hauled sugar beets, while 20 year-old Florent has a summer-long job as crop supervisor for a soup company.

"I got the job because I am French," he admits, frankly. "I was only in the middle of my class at Ridgetown Agricultural School, and I never thought I would be appointed. But the company knows that twenty-five per cent of local farmers are French-speaking and so they chose me."

Florent is the first member of his family to go to Ridgetown. His elder brothers studied agriculture at Ste. Martine, Beauharnois, near Montréal, where, in addition to farming courses, all became highly skilled in woodwork. Gérard, married with two children, Jean-Marc and Jeannine, made most of his own furniture, and Roger and Claude have followed suit.

The boys treasure a woodsman's axe which belonged to their great-grandfather, Narcisse Laprise, who was brought to Ontario as a 9 year-old boy. Narcisse was famous as a pioneer and barn-builder, and it was at this time that the family name changed from Daniau to "Laprise," which means "strong grip" in French.

Ontario Is Home
Farmer's Advocate December 1963

The entire family agreed that for them, Ontario was "home." They do not feel their French background cuts them off from the life of the English-speaking farming community around them, and neighbourhood relations are good.

"I even think we have the advantage," says Madame Laprise. "We have two languages, and two ways of living, to choose from. It was not always like this, but it is so now." wives

Florent and Caroline Laprise check over the marriage contract of a Québec ancestor. The bride's father agreed to provide the wedding dress, a heavy bed cover, and a cow in milk with her calf - all to be delivered on the eve of the marriage.

The older boys, who spent years in Québec at agricultural school, would love to return there with their wives to live but, they say: "The land here is richer, more fertile. Farmers make a better living in Ontario."

The name Pain Court, means in French "small loaf" or " le pain est court" meaning "we are short of bread" and the village was so named because bread, in the early days, was such a prized delicacy. The nearest flour mill was 50 miles away in Detroit.

Family History

Tracing the family history has been the hobby of Trefflé and his wife. They have made three holiday trips to Québec City in order to consult old records at the Palais de Justice. They traced their complete family genealogy through eleven generations from the recorded marriage in Québec City in 1670 of their first ancestor Jean Daniau of Poitou, France. Five generations of the family were settled in Montmagny, north of Québec City along the gulf of the St. Lawrence, where many cousins are now living. Four generations of Laprises have been established in Ontario. - 1963

Trefflé's father, Josephat, is still living (and recently re-married, with a big family celebration at the family's Rondeau Park cottage). Trefflé has vivid memories of his pioneer grandfather, Narcisse, who was often a dinner guest after Trefflé's own marriage.

A future project for the Laprises is to visit France, to see how much further they can trace their family history. But Madame Laprise this summer spent six weeks in the Orient, visiting friends and relatives in religious orders in Japan, Hong Kong and the Philippines – "so," she says, " it is my husband's turn to go to Europe, if we cannot both go."

Madame Laprise has been active in local educational circles and has helped in the development of French schools. She feels that now the academic education of French-speaking pupils has been secured, the next goal is more technical and trade schools.

French Cooking

Many French traditions are observed in the family's home cooking. Madame Laprise still makes " pâtes" sliders the way her mother and grandmother taught her. However, Christmas meals would not be complete without the "tourtière."   Christmas Day itself is kept mainly for the children, and the big family gathering takes place on Le Jour de l'An, or New Year's Day, just as in Québec.

Grandmother's Tourtière
Tourtières – chicken or turkey pies – are a Christmas tradition in French Canada, and would be welcomed by any family tired of turkey left-overs. This is my mother-in-law's recipe, inherited from her mother.

Simmer the following in a little water for 50 minutes:
2 cups ground pork   1 cup chicken, turkey or beef
2 medium onions   2 sticks chopped celery
Then add:
1 cup raw diced potatoes, pinch of salt, pepper, sage, parsley and flour.
Thicken mixture with 1/4 cup of water mixed with 1 tablespoon of flour. Let cool, and bake in semi-rich pie crusts. May be kept in freezer un-baked.

Flaky semi-rich pie pastry
3 cups flour   1 cup shortening
3/4 cup water   2/3 teaspoon salt   ½ teaspoon baking powder
Mix flour, salt and baking powder. Add chilled shortening, mix until well blended. Add water and mix well, gradually adding more flour until when lightly stirred it will come easily from bowl. Chill and roll. Glaze pie top with milk before baking.

Prosperous Decade

Mr. and Mrs. Harry Backus

The year 1960 marked the beginning of a prosperous era. It was a most interesting period for those growing up on the farm as well as operating one. Great technical and industrial advances in farming communities of Pain Court and Grande Pointe marked an era of prosperity.

Life on the farm was progressing favourably. Scientific and technological development accounted for better yields, better prices, thereby contributing to a better living on the farm.

By this time, Cooperative Movements and Credit Unions were established. They contributed to progress and a better life for all. With the pace of life accelerating, excessive stress shifted towards the farming communities.

One by one our sons cautiously ventured into this new generation of farmers. In 1960, we accepted a new challenge and bought 50 acres of land on the river front concession in Raleigh with reserved rights to 75 more acres within the same year; this was known as the "Backus" farm. Milton Backus was born in Morpeth, Kent County in 1859. He owned 125 acres on the river front, Raleigh. In 1960 we became owners of this tract of land lot 16 and part of lot 17 river front Raleigh from Harry Backus, with the Percy Huff farm to the west and the Cecil Huff farm to the east.

"Neighbours since 1960"

In 1813 this Huff farm west of us was known as the Thomas McCrae farm. "Following the defeat of the British at the Battle of the Thames in Oct. 1813, American forces controlled the Thames Valley west of Moraviantown. In early December three officers and 36 men of the 26th American regiment established a post near here at the Thomas McCrae home.

Before daybreak December 15, 1813, they were surprised by Lieutenant Henry Metcalfe and 32 members of the Norfolk and Middlesex Militia the Kent Volunteers and the Provincial Dragoons. After a brief resistance the Americans surrendered and were taken prisoner. Today the monument stands next to the Thomas McCrae Home." [1].

1. Ref. Monument Plaque

Summer retreat Rondeau Park

In 1960 we also tended to our recreational activities when we purchased a cabin, in the cabin section of the Park. We were greeted by our neighbours Dr. Hipkins of Ridgetown and Tassie Baxter of Chatham, Real Estate. Many pleasant hours were spent there during the next four years, with our children and their friends. December 31, 1964 this cabin had to be removed, according to government law. There were two bedrooms, one with double bunks. It was apparent that as the children grew up, an extra cabin was needed in order to accommodate my children and their friends.

By 1962 our next venture was to buy a larger cottage on the lake front at Rondeau Park. This resort served us very well for the last 38 years. It still is my home in 1999. It has served my parents, my brothers and sisters, my own children, my grandchildren and great grand children. A prized possession. One can ponder the delightful parties, the bonfires, the swimming, the friends, the camping parties, the open pit barbecues for young and old, the year by year movies of related events at the cottage.

Added to this was the schedule of swimming lessons 5 days a week, during the summer holidays. Colette graduated as a swimming instructor in 1971 from the Rondeau Yacht Club.

There was a time to play hard but also a time to work hard at the Laprise household.

Célébration du premier mariage dans notre famille

Le 9 juillet 1960, Gérard Laprise, fils aîné de la famille Laprise, prend pour épouse Aline Cartier, fille aînée de Philippe Cartier et Marie-Jeanne Houle de Grande Pointe.

L'habitude des gens était d'assister à la célébration nuptiale suivie d'un rendez-vous à la maison afin de déguster un régal préparé par les dames. Pour cette occasion, Mlle Rose-Marie Benoit s'était chargée du festin car elle s'y connaissait dans ce domaine.

La température était idéale et l'après-midi des plus divertissante. Les gens retournent enchantés tandis que les nouveaux mariés, comblés de bonheur, étaient sur le départ d'un voyage de noces.

Trefflé et Caroline Laprise au mariage de leurs quatrième fils, Florent Laprise

The 60s moved ahead at a tremendous pace. New Years Day 1963, our second son, Roger, announced his wedding date for February 23. A gracious new bride became a member of our loving family. We greeted Rose-Marie Houle of Pointe-aux-Roches, daughter of Raymond Houle and Orélie Giroux. Her smiling face was a nice omen around us.

At this time Roger and Rose-Marie took up residence on the river front of Dover, a 50 acre farm owned by his great grandfather Thomas Roy in 1904. It was then known as the "Foote Farm."

In 1964, our fourth son, Florent, after his graduation in April, 1963 from Ridgetown College of Agriculture, decided he would marry on April 4, 1964. We welcomed a beautiful bride in our family, Bernadette Pinsonneault, daughter of Charles Pinsonneault and Irène Lafrenière. They took up residence on 50 acres, river front Dover, part of the land also owned by his great grandfather in 1904.

Les grands-parents

Left to right - Joseph Laprise, Laura Corriveau Laprise, Albéric Pinsonneault,
Yvonne Lafrenière, Florent and Bernadette Laprise, Délia Roy, Adolphe Roy.

On July 31, 1968 Claude, our third son, married Marie-Reine Masse, daughter of Léo Masse and Émérentienne Caza. Their lovely wedding took place at St. Francis Church in Tilbury.

Our family grew by leaps and bounds in a few years and we enjoyed all of them. All the boys had access to the machinery we owned so they could operate their farms efficiently. It was a hectic time to say the least, especially during farming season.

Our eldest daughter, Caroline, managed to become part of the roller coaster ride by announcing her wedding date for June 29, 1968. A graduate in computer technology in 1964 from Ottawa, she opted to enter the registered nurses aid course at Cedar Springs Hospital School, now known as Southwestern Regional Centre. This profession she exercised until retirement.

After graduating she was married to David Trudell of Thamesville at a beautiful summer wedding ceremony in Pain Court. He was the son of Robert and Ann Trudell of Thamesville. Unfortunately, he had lost his mother years prior and cared for his Aunt Mabel Trudell. Tragically, he also lost his only brother Robert (Bobby) two months after the wedding. David was welcomed in our family and became part of it.

Rest assured the decade of the 60s was somewhat hectic and exhausting. Consequently much self control was the order of the day.

Sad but true, at the close of this decade we experienced a wrenching situation, as my husband Trefflé had some difficulty adjusting and coping with exhausting situations of the sixties. Family pressures, economic pressures and farming pressures, all contributed to stressful situations.

It did not constitute the quiet era of the depression years of the 30s nor the progressive years of the 40s and 50s.

With the end of this period came retirement for my husband. The boys were now taking an increasing interest in new initiatives on the farm. They were progressing very favourably. Trefflé took up residency at our river front home in Raleigh in 1970 somewhat away from the hustle and bustle of multiple farm operations.

Time is of the essence as we grow older and try to sort out our own priorities. This period of tranquillity would now permit him to fulfill some of his own ideals, like visiting the sick, and helping the St. Vincent de Paul Society.

Another project dear to his heart was his interests in foreign missions, especially those in South America in the area of Peru which he visited several times.

A mission well done.

A stroke of luck - A trip abroad 1963

Leaps and bounds really describes the decade of the 60s. Economic stability, a growing family, technological advances, all contributed in some way to our progress.

Mid January 1963. It was a challenge for me to walk into the stock market exchange in Chatham and invest a few dollars in the commodity market. No more no less than what I felt I could risk to lose. This was a serious period for growth.

After a few weeks those few dollars had doubled even tripled my original investment. It was a very stressful but a rewarding experience nonetheless. January 18, 1963 was our 25th anniversary; I encouraged my husband to join me for a few hours at the stock market. I was hoping for some gains so we could escape to Hawaii for our first trip after 25 years of hard work. We were elated with the returns but those plans did not mature.

By March I had accumulated a very comfortable sum of money, so it was time again to make further plans for travel, to visit friends who awaited me in the oriental countries. I visited Bob and Janet Forsyth who had already made several successful trips to Hawaii, Japan, and Hong Kong at this time. They were most informative, showed me slides of their trips. This information was most valuable; I proceeded to formulate a schedule for travel to Japan, Hong Kong, Hawaii, the Philippines and the Pacific Coast of the United States. In those years you bought travelling miles and not simply a ticket to one destination. The more miles, the cheaper the travel. They were meticulous in preparing the most minor details. Everything was to the point and without a hitch.

By March 12th, I was boarding a flight to Japan via Anchorage Alaska. After refuelling and visiting the immediate area of Anchorage we boarded for Japan. It was amazing to behold the land of the midnight sun, the dazzling Aurora Borealis playing in the skies during our flight in the Northern Hemisphere. For a few hours the turbulence was chaotic as many passengers experienced air sickness. We arrived at our destination in Japan somewhat late but safe and sound. After clearing customs, within minutes I was greeted by a travel agent Bob Forsyth, who approached me with identification and message to pick me up.

The airport was almost an hour's drive from downtown Tokyo within a few blocks of Imperial Hotel where dignitaries are received and welcomed.

Soeur Anna-Marie (Jeanne Roy)

After a good rest, Sister Anna-Marie (Jeanne Roy), sister superior of the Sisters of the Immaculate Conception convent in Tokyo, called and picked me up later that day. She was my very special schoolmate in Pain Court during our high school years. Sister had been a missionary sister in Japan for a few years then. She was very fluent in many languages, as well as Japanese. She was well-known in the Japanese circles. As Mother Superior, she had built an orphanage in Koryama, a few years before I visited. In 1963 she was in the process of remodelling a large school in Wakamatsu which I also visited with her for an impressive graduation at the school with dignitaries attending. This area is in Northern Japan.

After luncheon we were privileged to be the guest of the Mayor of Wakamatsu for the day. Nothing was spared for our well being. We visited shrines, the ski slopes, the landmarks in North Japan, arts and crafts of all descriptions as well as the city's Mayoralty offices.

The next day Sister Anna-Marie inspected the school buildings in preparation for renovations and an addition to this existing school at Wakamatsu. Sister held an architectural diploma at the time.

Since most travel in Japan is by train, the next morning we boarded the train for Tokyo. Strange but true there was a few stops in order to accommodate the necessities of life. I had to comply to common bathrooms, somewhat of a shock and so were common baths.

After these travels and especially on weekends, Mr. and Mrs. Fernand Gervais treated me to all kinds of surprises. They lived on the US Naval base just outside of Fuchu where he had been stationed for the last 3 years. He was from Madawaska Maine, lost his father at 3 years old, joined the Naval Armed Forces at 16 and at 20 he married Juanita McClean who was from New Brunswick, adjacent to Madawaska. Juanita had come to our area to be with her sister Irene Maillet. They lived in our rented home in Pain Court and Alfred Maillet was a skilled mechanic for King Grain Ltd.

I was privileged to be able to enjoy remote and historical places in Japan by train, by bus or by car. I enjoyed theatres as impressive as Radio City Music Hall, the shrines, places of worship, Universities, hot springs, especially in Nikko where we travelled with the mayor of Fuchu and his wife. At the impressive hotels there are strict rules of attire. Firstly, you leave your shoes at the door. Then, you receive a basket containing a kimono and retire to an area in order to change your attire. This attire, you must wear at all times while staying at the Hotel. The futons, the rice pillows, the Geisha Girls, the sit down meals on the floor for six different courses, the common baths in the Hot Springs under the hotels and last but not least, the ricksha rides so different and unforgettable.

These were humourous interludes sometimes but the poor old souls laughed along with us. We visited the City of Kamakura - one of the most impressive shrines and largest place of worship for Tokyo with Mount Fuji in the horizon. A wonderful spectacle. We boarded a ricksha for a tour of the city. Guess what? The driver had problems getting up the hills and over the tracks; at one point he tried three times on main street to pull us over the tracks. Merchants were lined along the street laughing to their hearts content. But the driver persisted, hoping to accommodate his tourists. Finally, Fernand jumped off and I was taken over the tracks and up the hill. The problem? I was too heavy. It was hilarious and made everyone's day.

How could I ever thank the responsible people who cared for me so well. I still hope to have more opportunity to express my gratitude.

Father Angelus Haruyama

While visiting this country I agreed to sponsor a Japanese postulant who wanted to become a sister of the Order of which Sister Anna-Marie was superior. A few weeks later a Franciscan seminarian visited me. He had lost his mother at 6 years old and was cared for by the Franciscan Monks. At this time he anticipated attending the seminary for four years, in order to enter the priesthood. So I agreed to pay a tuition for him for 4 years. He was thankful and delighted, so was I. Father Angelus Haruyama was ordained in March 1968 and was stationed at St. Joseph Friary in Tokyo. In 1972 he was in charge of new Franciscan candidates at Rhoppongi close to the University of Tokyo.

For a month I was privileged to visit interesting places with Sister Anna-Marie, Juanita and Fernand Gervais. To relate more would require an extra chapter. By the last week I was confident enough to travel from one place to the other by train around Tokyo. A million persons a day pass through Tokyo station. Young people 10 - 12 years old were pleased to help you in your travels. These memories will last me a lifetime. My emotional stability has been enhanced by these experiences so no price tag could scrape the surface to pay for this wonderful visit, an unforgettable experience.

With tears in my eyes I left reluctantly for Hong Kong. More awaited me there. I brought parcels and messages to the Sisters of Hong Kong. They were in the process of building a larger school on the side of the mountain close to the main city. Everyday the Sisters served soup at the school for all the mountain people who came. They lived mostly with roots of every kind. A few boards provided their shelter on the mountain side.

I managed to learn and experience living with boat people for a few days. Their boat is their home. From birth they live and die on these boats. It's impossible to understand this life unless you share it with them. The contrasts has to be seen in order to understand.

I left the port of Hong Kong on a huge ship with some 200 passengers on the tourist deck and 2000 Chinese people on the underdeck to travel to the Spanish island of Macau. Next morning we had a one day pass from sunrise to sundown; we could cross into China at only one point, to visit the graves of their beloved, buried on the Slopes of mountains in China. This was super impressive, as that night, everyone was running to have a space to lie down for the night.

My special travel agent was super knowledgeable. He had a crippled wife so a visitor was most welcome especially for his bedridden wife. She was so pleasant and I made an extra effort to make her happy.

When I returned to Hong Kong I boarded a Japanese airline for the Philippines. It was 106° when the plane landed. As usual planning was perfect. There, I met with the Billy Graham troops, stationed at the same hotel in Manila. I had a special package to deliver to the Missionary Sisters of Immaculate-Conception there in Manila, got acquainted and returned later. The heat, the mosquitos made you very uncomfortable. We slept in beds surrounded by mosquito nets. If that was not enough the sisters advised me to strip all polyester clothing and not to wear any hose while in the Philippines.

It was Easter Week, and my mission there was to visit Sister Dolores, a sister to Mrs. Adrien Caron of Pain Court. She was a missionary Sister at Loretto Academy in Manila. She was due to arrive the following week from a mission in the northern territory. There was no time lost; the sisters invited me to spend three days in retreat with a special preacher from France. He was a French general, a doctor and an ordained priest. Never did any preacher impress me so much. This simple preacher, in three days, covered so many angles: religious, economic, social and especially family life. I left rejuvenated and hoping I would meet Sister Jane Dolores.

On Easter Sunday, we were briefed. The Japanese airlines were on strike leaving us stranded there for at least one more week until the Billy Graham troops would return from their mission in the islands of the Philippines. Many travellers did not take chances and departed on an ocean liner docked at the time.

In the meantime I visited with the missionary Sisters of the Immaculate Conception. Good Friday we visited the area where any person can carry their own wooden crosses, large or small in an area some thirty kilometres from Manila. Some thirty-five persons were carrying a cross close to a parish church. It was laymen who organized this event and no priest was present in that area. To my surprise the church statues are fully dressed as we are.

The beautiful carvings of these talented people are impressive and displayed in shop after shop. Their outdoor markets on the outskirts are fabulous. The day before I left, Sister Dolores visited with me. What a pleasant visit. She did accompany me to the airport the next day.

During this delay period I also met with Brothers of the Sacred Heart who published the Catholic Register, a Philippino version. They were from Holy Cross College Digos, province of Davao, about 600 miles from Manila. The superior boarded the same plane as the Billy Graham troops and detoured as I did to Japan; he was seated directly behind me. The Artificial Flower Magnate of the Philippines was sitting with me. He was travelling to Japan for the international convention for production of artificial flowers. We all benefited from an interesting dialogue.

A Swiss airline picked us up at Manila but I had to fly to Japan with the Billy Graham troops to their destination. Fortunately they had provided another airline to take me to Hawaii. I transferred and we landed at the airport in Honolulu just after a devastating storm which had wreaked havoc on all the islands. Part of my schedule to the islands had been cancelled due to flooding.

I spent a week at the Sunset Hotel where the South Pacific movie had been filmed. I visited all I could possibly see on tours and otherwise. Amazing beauty but not as impressive as the heart wrenching poverty of the other countries.

I spent five days on the island of Hawaii. I enjoyed the erupting volcano, the lava fields running to the ocean to form acres of land close to shore. There were the large cattle ranches, the thousands of acres of agricultural land, the waterfalls, the sulphur fields smoking, the Hawaiian Luaus, the sumptuous hotels with open air restaurants by the ocean, the gathering of natives from all the islands who also performed at an outdoor theatre by the ocean. It was somewhat of a dream, an ecstasy. How can one area hold so many natural phenomena.

It was time to fly from Hawaii to Los Angeles. I packed all my belongings. As we landed in Los Angeles it was bitter cold, 41° the first week of May. Somewhat cold for summer attire. Everyone scrambled through their luggage for warmer clothing. There I remained for four days. Visited with Anita Gagner from Pain Court who had taken a position as a nurse there. Thérèse Roy of Pain Court picked me up and brought me to visit her sister, Vivienne Roy and Jerome Faubert, my neighbours in Pain Court. They had 3 children at the time and a thriving business. It was pleasant to visit with relatives. We visited the Movie Star district graced with beautiful mansions, the Movie Hall of Fame and the M.G.M. Studio.

As I boarded the plane for Seattle, there was a stopover at San Francisco. I had time to glance at the skyline, the ocean resorts, hundreds of acres of fruit groves and vegetable fields in the valley.

My relatives, the McBrides, greeted me at the Seattle airport. For another week I visited all my relatives the McBride's. My mother's sister Célina Caron married a McBride. She had four boys and one girl. They are still today in that area. Ralph, Leslie, Frederick and Edward as well as their sister Marie are still in the area of Seattle.

Seattle is most picturesque with its beautiful lakes, parks and the mountains surrounding it. Furthermore, I arrived just three days after the closing of the world fair. It was amazing to have a glance at the world fair phenomenons. Then I toured the Boeing 727 plant where Frederick was an engineer. I could not forget the wonderful ocean restaurant that we visited with Edward. Leslie took the responsibility of caring for me at his beautiful home on the hillside facing the lake. A post card setting. Ralph we visited some 20 miles outside Seattle nestled in the Valley, between mountains. Marie lived somewhat close to the University of Seattle and greeted us.

After all this excitement, I was thankful to board for the last leg of my journey; my husband waited patiently for me at the Detroit Metro Airport. With all these travels, I had learned to be somewhat patient. People in these oriental countries never seem to be in a hurry. They never complain how time consuming travel might be.

For those fluent in French, you might find my philosophy thesis interesting at the end of this chapter.

Everyone at home survived without mother, but all were glad to greet me home. No money can buy the memories, the knowledge, the quest for more education which I acquired in the years that followed. I completed my social sciences studies at the University of Ottawa while my children were attending University and grade school. At this time, I had a position for accounts receivable at Hôpital St-Louis de Montfort. Afternoons and weekends provided ample time for household duties and night courses.

Technical Advances

In January 1964, the Department of Agricultural Economics in Guelph, with Darrel Plaunt, Associate Professor, a group of Cooperators in the EL Farm Project were organised by this department together with Mr. John Wallace of Ridgetown and agricultural representative of Kent County, Mr. D. M. Rutherford. Cooperators in EL Farm Accounting Project were as follows:

Evan Arnold, R. R. # 1 Chatham
Paul Dilliott, R. R. # 1 Ridgetown
Frank Dobbelaar, Port Lambton
Max Forsyth, Dresden
Robert C. Huff, Merlin
Norman King, Pain Court
Robert G. Parry, Pain Court
Louis Schneider, R. R. # 5 Chatham
William Shanks, R. R. # 1 Wheatley
Stanley Wonnacott, R. R. # 2 Fletcher
Albert Collard, R. R. # 3 Shedden
Trefflé Laprise, Pain Court
Carl Faubert, R. R. #2 Tilbury

These cooperators specialized in different branches of farming. Dr. Plaunt spent some time with each cooperator discussing their coding system. At the meeting Dr. Plaunt explained the changes that were going to be made in 1965 to the Mail in Farm Account Project.   These changes were namely a speed up of the analysis by using hired computers rather than data processing system at the College of Agriculture and also a change in coding reports by the cooperators themselves.

The department was quite pleased with the new method of processing data as it allows checking the accuracy of each record quite closely as well as producing your reports quickly and cheaply. The new method of processing in 1965 has allowed the department to proceed with the developing of an electronic inventory and analysis. We feel work is progressing favourably. Similar programs today, 30 years later, have progressed through innovation of the computer era.

Re - Dr. Plaunt, Professor at Agricultural College in Guelph
Department of Agricultural Economics August 1964

Cadets à Pain Court 1969

L'un des événements culminants et des plus impressionnants de l'année scolaire est nul autre que la démonstration annuelle de la revue des cadets.

Ce corps de cent vingt-cinq cadets, comprenant garçons et filles, vient de Pain Court et Grande Pointe.

Sous la direction du Major Edmond Chauvin et des instructeurs, lieutenants Stanley Bénéteau et Jacques Caron, ce corps de cadet se distingue surtout en étant le seul dans la région du sud-ouest de l'Ontario qui exécute les commandements en français.

Le lieutenant John Moad de London accompagné du Major Ralph West font l'inspection et adressent des félicitations aux jeunes et à leurs instructeurs. Ils commentent sur la précision de la marche, la dextérité dans la manoeuvre des fusils, l'administration des premiers soins aux blessés, et l'habilité des jeunes dans la culture physique.

Une mention spéciale est adressée au corps de cadet féminin. En plus du corps de tambours, les jeunes filles se distinguent dans la marche de précision et dans la danse du Highland Fling. Mlle Christine Foy se mérite des compliments pour la danse écossaise aux sabres.

Le Major Ralph West a présenté l'honneur du cadet le plus méritant à Henry Mielczarek et l'honneur du commandant en charge du corps à Stephan Podleski.

C'est peut-être le plus petit corps de cadet dans la province mais il est certainement le plus enthousiaste. C'est M. Edmond Chauvin surtout qui est responsable de leur succès.

Les parents et les élèves désirent le remercier pour son intérêt et son dévouement.

Pendant l'été, en août, six de nos jeunes cadets font une belle expérience au camp Ipperwash. Gérard Thibodeau et Laurent Cartier ont fait un stage de deux semaines, Paul Pinsonneault, Jean-Marie Laprise, Marc Haslip et Marc Richer font un stage de six semaines. Ceux-ci ont été parmi les cadets chanceux qui ont fait un échange avec ceux du Québec et qui ont eu l'occasion de faire le voyage par avion au Camp Val Cartier pour deux semaines. Ils sont revenus enchantés de leur expérience.

Highland Fling -1969

Cadets à Pain Court - 1969

L'un des évènementsw culminants et des plus impressionnants de l'année scolaire est nul autre que la démonstration annuelle de la revie des cadets.

Ce corps de cent vingt-cinq cadets, comprenant garçons et filles, vient de Pain Court et Grande Pointe.

Sous la direction du Major Edmond Chauvin et des instucteurs, lieutenants Stanley Bénéteau et Jacques Caron, ce corps de cadet se distingue surtout en étant le seul dans la région du sud-ouest de l'Ontario qui exécute les commandements en français.

Une mention spéciale est adressée au corps de cadet féminin. En plus du corps de tambours, les jeunes filles se distinguent dans la marche de précission et dans la sanse du Highland Fling. Mlle Christine Foy se mérite des compliments pour la danse écossaise aux sabres.

Le Major Ralph West a présenté l'honneur du cadet le plus méritant à Henry Mielczarek et l'honneur du commandant en charge du corps à Stephan Podleski.

C'est peut-être le plus petit corps de cadet dans la province mais il est certainement le plus enthousiaste. C'est M. Edmond Chauvin surtout qui est responsable de leur succès.

Les parents et les élèves désirent le remercier pour son intérêt et son dévouement.

Pendant l'été, en août, six de nos jeunes cadets font une belle expérience au camp Ipperwash. Gérard Thibodeau et Laurent Cartier ont fait un stage de deux semaines, Paul Pinsonneault, Jean-Marie Laprise, Marc Haslip et Marc Richer font un stage de six semaines. Ceux-ci ont été parmi les cadets chanceux qui ont fait un échange avec ceux du Québec et qui ont eu l'occasion de faire le voyage par avion au Camp Val Cartier pour deux semaines. Ils ont revenus enchantés de leur expérience.

Pain Court Trustees Pledge to Keep Bilingual School

Free Press Chatham Bureau

Pain Court Trustees are determined to keep the H. J. Payette Continuation School operating as long as ratepayers can afford it, an annual meeting of secondary school ratepayer was told last night.

Roland Bélanger, 1966 board chairman, said board members have heard persistent rumours that the school, Kent County's only completely bilingual secondary school, will close.

But trustees have decided the four grade secondary school has an important place in the community life, because of the special French instruction it offers in a bilingual township.

Mr. Bélanger said inspectors have reported the school's academic standards are high, and students who have transferred to other English or French-speaking schools for advanced instruction have had excellent records.

The board's chairman told ratepayers that the school fills an important function because the bilingual school system in Dover Township is training French teachers in great demand for other schools across the province.

At present, the school has an enrolment of 115 and the board is buying specialized technical and vocational training for 33 pupils at Chatham secondary schools, and seven advanced academic students at Chatham Collegiate Institute.

Treasurer Raymond Bourassa said the Pain Court school - described as "unique in the province" - has fully qualified staff members.

R. W. Gagner urged the board to make a long-term study of all future alternatives for the Dover secondary school in order to protect ratepayers' interests.

He pointed out that the Robart's plan, with wider educational choices for secondary schools, has already reduced the Pain Court enrolment, and further cuts could jeopardize the school's operation.

Les Dames de Ste-Anne - 1966

The Ladies of Sainte-Anne have been active in the parish for more than 35 years at which time they were known as the Ladies Altar Society.

It has 159 subscribed members and twenty honorary members in 1966. It was decided to affiliate the Society of the Arch-Confraternity of the Congregation of Sainte-Anne-de-Beaupré in order to benefit from privileges and merits enjoyed by members, hence the change of name.

The society was founded in 1930 with Father Zotique Mailloux as pastor. At this time, they took care of the linens for the altar, the flowers, the candlesticks and any related business for the care of the sanctuary. After 35 years, the nuns started catering to the needs of the church.

In 1966, there was a name change but the society is still very active in the parish. Catering to banquets is in order. Luncheons after the funeral masses of beloved members of the parish help alleviate the worries of the bereaved. Members gather at 3 p.m. at the funeral home to offer prayers for the deceased member. At the funeral, an honour guard is formed. A mass is also offered for the deceased souls.

Elections take place in November. For 1970, Mrs. Léonard Faubert was elected president by acclamation and again for 1971.

Glorianna Bélanger
Secretary

Pupils bid farewell to Mère Jeanne-Marie – 1964

More than 200 misty eyed students chanted "aurevoir Mère Jeanne-Marie" as she solemnly walked away. The last 11 years of Sister's thirty-one years of teaching have been spent in Pain Court instructing grade one pupils, and this will probably be the last time she will see most of them. Mère Jeanne-Marie was a teacher of numerous talents - a gifted teacher. "These have been the best years of my life, she said. In all, I've taught more than 350 students at Ste-Catherine School."

She was born in Hull, Québec, and the oldest of seven children. Sister Jeanne-Marie joined the Order of the Grey Nuns in Ottawa in 1930 but before committing herself to convent life she travelled to Montréal to see Frère André for consultation about her chronic asthmatic condition from which she suffered since early childhood and also to tell him about her aspirations for the future.

"Go, you will persevere," he said to her in a curtly tone of voice.

She pursued her chosen vocation and never looked back. She wasn't cured of asthma but her long-suffering bouts were much alleviated and kept under control with the supervision of Dr. Blake Barlow, her physician and specialist for respiratory ailments whom by chance she met when she came to our area. To her, Dr. Blake Barlow was a godsend, and she kept repeating and reminding us of her good fortune.

Unfortunately, she left us in July for Sudbury Ontario. In 1963, she was awarded l'Ordre du mérite scolaire for her long service in the French teaching profession. In addition to teaching, she was the sacristan for the parish. She will also be sadly missed by everyone who crossed her path.

NB. A reminder to her former pupils.
As you can recall, Mère Jeanne-Marie was a mimic and as far as acting goes she was a natural. Her family name was "Charland" and when summoning her pupils that it was time to leave, her famous saying was: *"V'nez-vous en mes p'tits Charlands."* Or to bring back order and quiet among her thirty some pupils she would blurt out in a serious tone of voice: *"J'vais sortir mes dents d'caoutchouc."*
And with Mme Marentette's permission, a colleague and a very good friend of Soeur Jeanne-Marie, that is where "les dents de rubber" originated from and is still, to this very day I am told, strongly embedded in the mind of the very young at heart.

Farewell to Sister François-Rachel – 1958 - 1963

Sister Françoise-Rachel, a dearly beloved teacher on the staff of École Ste-Catherine for five years, was reluctantly bid adieu by her former Grade VIII pupils, parents and teachers.

She is now instructing a group of Indian boys and girls at Albany, James Bay. Her pupils are eager to learn of their "big country" and already know of the riches of farms in the southern part of Ontario. I trust you will continue on with your mission.

May God bless you and transform you into a peaceful being full of happiness, compassion, tenderness and love.

La Société de St-Vincent de Paul

La Société de St-Vincent de Paul a pour but de venir en aide aux besoins spirituels et temporels des nécessiteux et des abandonnés sans tenir compte de leur nationalité, de leur croyance ni de leur passé. Les paroissiens passent les premiers mais les activités ne sont pas limitées aux confins de la paroisse. Les membres travaillent bénévolement dans l'ombre sans chercher d'autre récompense que celle d'avoir servi le Bon Dieu et d'avoir aidé le prochain. La discrétion est à la base de la Société.

Officiellement, la Société a fait ses débuts dans notre paroisse en 1964. Les membres fondateurs sont le curé Léo Charron, Trefflé Laprise, Bernard Charlebois, Réginald Martin, Wilfrid Pinsonneault et Gérard Caron.

Plusieurs se sont associés à la Société à travers les années. En plus d'être membres actifs, la Société de St-Vincent de Paul accepte des membres honoraires. Ces membres font une contribution à la société et jouissent des bénéfices des membres actifs. Quelques paroissiens furent associés comme membres honoraires par le passé. Vous êtes tous bienvenus d'en faire partie.

Gisèle Caron 1961 - 1962

School days in Pain Court were fun for a young Toronto girl in 1961.

This Kent county village's nine room separate school had something to offer that even Metropolitan Toronto's highly touted educational system doesn't provide: a complete elementary education taught in French.

That was the attraction that brought Gisèle Caron, a petite, brown-haired, brown-eyed Torontonian to live and attend school in Pain Court. While still a grade 1 student at Ste-Catherine School, she hopes to someday become a kindergarten teacher. Gisèle is the daughter of Mr. & Mrs. Rosaire Caron, a Toronto Real Estate salesman born and raised in Pain Court. The parents decided they wanted Gisèle to hang on to her French ancestry through language and tradition. Their next step was to find a family with whom Gisèle could stay for the school year. Their choice was the Benoit family who operates a restaurant directly across the street from the school and most importantly immediate relatives to Gisèle.

Gisèle loves to go to school and especially favours her teacher, Mother Jeanne-Marie who has been a grade school teacher for 28 years of which eleven have been in Pain Court. Last month she was asked to present a farewell gift to the principal of the school who was leaving. She represented the whole student body when she was asked because of her excellent French pronunciation and well mastered accent.

Thanks to Aunt Cia, and cousins Rose-Marie, Bernadette and Rosalie who spent one hour each night helping her with studies. Gisèle is fully bilingual and also mastered Italian and speaks it fluently. She is presently a very prosperous real estate broker in Toronto, married to an Italian builder and has two children. She has a brother Marc working for the James Bay Hydro development project.

King Grain   1942 - 1965

1942 - A new seed corn dryer is built.

1944 - A new elevator is put up to meet growing demands.

1946 - Corn dryer built in 1942 is not large enough; a larger capacity dryer is put up.

1947 - A fire destroys the dryer; a new warehouse and new elevator are built in October.

1948 - In March, we are ready to take deliveries. A new warehouse is purchased at CNR tracks in Chatham and an office opened.

1949 - An elevator is constructed in Chatham to handle cash crop grains.

1950 - Pride corn distributorship was taken on for Canada and Northern States of the USA.

1953 - Export market is developed for Ontario grown seed wheat for shipment to Ohio, Michigan and New York State.

1956 - A large warehouse is built in Pain Court.

1956 - King Grain decided to move into Québec. Mr. Voyer sells "Gold Seal Seeds" in St. Hyacinthe area.

1957 - Sales are good in Québec, a warehouse and a cleaning plant is constructed at Ste-Rosalie, Québec.

1958 - Our seed plant in Pain Court handles a greater volume of seed grains. New silos and a new elevator are built.

1960 - Mr. King and associates purchase a lease of 2,600 acres on Walpole Island under Romol Corporation Ltd. It was taken over in order to carry on research work for the development and testing Pride Hybrids as well as conducting trials on new varieties of cereal grains and clovers.

1960 - To meet demands in Québec, a warehouse is purchased in St. Polycarpe for a second distribution point in Québec.

1961 - Business in Québec has become large enough that a new business is incorporated under the name "Semence Champs Pleins Seeds."

1961 - A 50 ft. - 50 ton automatic truck scale is installed at our Chatham plant.

1962 - A new year! Pride sales are increasing, Pride 63 becomes very popular and Québec farmers now are planting a larger acreage of corn. Plans have been laid for production of over 2,000 acres of grain corn this year, a new experience for Québec farmers.

At this time, Bill Mosey was seed grains expert.
Joseph Richer - He gives the best deal for feed grains.
Paul King - Fertilizer specialist for lower prices.

Raymond Bourassa - Shipping and receiving at Chatham.
Paul Raymond - Shipping and receiving in Pain Court.
Napoléon King.- Top Brass

On February 25 - 1965, Reeve Bert Dunlop of Dover Township officially opened the new addition to the Pain Court plant of King Grain & Seed Co. Ltd. This $80,000 expansion comprises one of the most modern and up to date seed corn processing plants in Canada, a new general office for the company, a retail store and a 20,000 square feet warehouse.

M. Napoléon Roy, président de la compagnie King Grain and Seed ainsi que Pride Hybrid Seed, fut le récipiendaire d'un certificat de mérite décerné spécialement en remerciement pour ses multiples contributions aux besoins agricoles ici en Ontario ainsi qu'au Québec.

On lui accorde cet l'honneur lors d'un banquet à l'Université de Guelph. Nous lui offrons nos félicitations à l'occasion de ce digne hommage.

Cannerie "King Canning"

En septembre 1969, nous remarquons une activité toujours grandissante à la cannerie King Canning gérée par M. Gérald Roy (King) depuis 25 années. La cannerie opère deux lignes de mise en conserve, une pour les tomates, l'autre pour le blé d'inde sucré. Plusieurs femmes de la région lui ont prêté main-forte pendant bien des années. En 1995, l'entreprise a un nouvel entrepreneur, M. John Lawrence, homme d'affaires de Chatham.

Golden Future Predicted 1968

In March 1968, Stanley J. Randall, P.C. of Ontario and Minister of Economics and development addressed the Chamber of Commerce in Chatham. He declared that farms in the St. Clair Region of Kent, Essex and Lambton counties were the most intensively mechanized in Ontario. He predicted "steadily rising agricultural productivity for the area." Farmers should be prepared for such advances and urban growth, setting aside land for recreational purposes, all of which will affect agriculture in the future.

This region's potential, said Mr. Randall, is its close proximity to the US, its ready access to the raw material sources and its need for technical skills. These attributes will all help provide Ontario's exploding labour force with many new jobs to propel our economy towards a bright future.

It is amazing that 30 years later this same pattern is emerging again, after a booming three decades of progress. Progress however is like a wheelbarrow, it stands still unless we push it, the minister had noted. However "you people know all about pushing" he declared to the Chamber of Commerce. "It was your energetic pushing to get ahead that attracted a large complex of automotive and transportation equipment" and industries ranging from machinery, building materials and glass products to furniture and clothing. I'm positive that by the year two thousand "we will be pushing with a purpose once again" as Mr. Randall exhorted us to do in 1968. This was the era of Garnet Newirk as Mayor of Chatham and Darcy McKeough as P.C. Minister of Municipal Affairs.

Cultivateur Cléophas Lozon - 1970

Cléophas Lozon de Grande Pointe est un des cultivateurs le plus remarquable de la région. Il va certainement se mériter le titre de champion parmi les cultivateurs de blé d'Inde. Jugez d'après ce que les gens nous rapportent vis-à-vis son compte.

La récolte de Cléophas pour l'année 1970 n'est par encore vendue mais s'évalue à 200,000 minots environ. Ce qui est encore plus remarquable concernant cette récolte exceptionnelle c'est qu'elle est déjà prête pour le marché pour la simple raison que M. Lozon est propriétaire de son propre séchoir.

Bravo Cléophas pour tes innovations ingénieuses. Au point de vue de la nouvelle technologie, cela en dit beaucoup à propos de ton esprit d'entrepreneur. Ta femme Marguerite, toujours à tes côtés pour t'appuyer et t'encourager, mérite elle aussi d'être reconnue et félicitée. Je veux saluer ta belle famille, c'est à dire tes trois fils: Raymond et son épouse Agnès Béchard, Robert et son épouse Linda-Diane St-Pierre et Ronald et son épouse Lorraine St-Pierre ainsi que ta fille Rosalie, épouse de Wilson Bradley Scott.

Norman Bélanger

Kent County agriculture suffered one of its severest upsets in 1962 with the death of 46 year old Norman Bélanger. He was considered a leading agricultural official not only in his county but throughout Ontario. People were shocked to hear about his death in the capital city of Ottawa while doing the type of work he had done for at least 13 years. He died suddenly October 24, 1962.

As second vice-president of the Sugar beet growers Marketing Board, he was one of the main beet board officials in Ottawa. He was to present a brief, urging the federal government to strengthen its National Sugar policy.

All lines of Agriculture were important to Bélanger. His help was valuable and his cool and collected manner always beamed a ray of hope and confidence, that somehow the industry would not die. He was a dedicated man both to his work and his family. He was a leader not only in his home community but in provincial agricultural affairs and also in the Kent Federation of Agriculture.

At the time of his death, he was doing the work he liked best. He was well-educated, and fluent in French and English. He and his wife Glorianna Gagner, a former school teacher, received their education at Ste-Catherine elementary school in Pain Court and their secondary education at Pain Court Continuation School.

It was an enormous task and responsibility for her to raise their family of nine children. She was a dedicated woman with courage and tenacity to fulfill whatever duties she had towards the family as well as towards society. Norman was inducted November 25, 1997 in Kent County Agricultural Hall of Fame. Mrs. Bélanger accepted the honour on behalf of her late husband, Norman.

Nomination de M. Léopold Lacroix 1966

Le Droit 14 septembre, 1966

Le ministère d'éducation de l'Ontario vient de désigner officiellement un cinquième fonction-naire supérieur au sein de son ministère. Il s'agit de M. Léopold Lacroix, inspecteur de l'arrondisse-ment de Plantagenet, au poste de surintendant-adjoint à la division de l'avancement professionnel et de la formation des instituteurs.

Les quatres autres fonctionnaires franco-ontariens attachés au ministère de l'Éducation à Toronto sont Roland Bérieault, Benjamin Michaud, Hervy Cyr et Jean-Marc Tessier.

M. Lacroix occupe ses nouvelles fonctions à Toronto depuis le premier septembre. Son tra-vail le retiendra tout particulièrement dans le domaine relatif aux cours de spécialisation profession-nelle pour les professeurs des écoles franco-ontariennes bilingues en Ontario.

Après ses études primaires à Haweskbury et ses études secondaires à l'académie de La Salle à Ottawa et à De La Salle à Toronto, il décrochait un baccalauréat des Arts de l'Université de Toronto.

Diplômé de l'École Normale de l'Université d'Ottawa, M. Lacroix a enseigné dans les écoles primaires d'Ottawa, Sturgeon Falls. Par la suite, il a obtenu le diplôme de "High School Assistant" du collège de Toronto.

Nommé inspecteur d'école en septembre 1959, il débuta dans le district de Chatham. Il fut inspecteur fondateur du district d'inspection de Belle Rivière pour les comtés de Kent et Essex. Trois ans plus tard, il fut assigné à l'arrondissement de Plantagenet où il réalisa en deux ans les nombreux projets de centralisation d'écoles régionales.

M. Lacroix fut aussi directeur du premier cours offert par le ministère d'Éducation à l'Université Queen's de Kingston, à l'intention des candidats à la direction des écoles primaires.

En avril 1966, il accédait à la présidence de l'association des inspecteurs d'écoles en Ontario lors du congrès annuel de l'organisme tenu à Toronto.

M. Lacroix, père de cinq enfants est installé à Toronto avec sa famille.

Le concours de français fête son 25e

À l'école Ste-Catherine de Pain Court, la section juvénile a présenté sa grande soirée pour commémorer le 25e anniversaire du concours de français dans nos écoles bilingues. Cette soirée était rehaussée par la présence du Rev. Père E. Chevalier, du Rev. Père Pierre Boudreau vicaire de la paroisse et de l'inspecteur de nos écoles M. Léopold Lacroix et Mme Lacroix, M. Delore Gervais préfet du comté accompagné de Mme Gervais, tous les parents et les amis.

Après la proclamation des lauréats l'inspecteur Lacroix félicita et encouragea chacun à se montrer fier de ses succès et à continuer de toujours perfectionner notre belle langue française. Il souligna que "nous avons un avantage, vivant dans un milieu anglophone de pouvoir apprendre facilement la langue anglaise." La secrétaire Mlle Rose-Marie Gagner a donné un rapport à l'Oncle Jean d'Ottawa qui les a félicités d'avoir fêté le 25e anniversaire du concours de français.

U. S. Students try French on teenagers at Pain Court
April 23, 1961 week-end

Sandusky's Community school superintendent Rex Milligan said "He firmly believed that if they were going to study French they must be able to use it." Students from Sandusky Ohio had an opportunity to practice their French with students from Pain Court District High School while enjoying dancing as well. They were guests of honour at a dance for teenagers organized by the "Femmes canadiennes-françaises" of Pain Court. They toured the French school and watched lessons in progress. Today they are continuing their practical lessons with Sr. Marie de la Providence. The group of six girls and two boys returned home with pleasant memories of their brief stay. Receiving student committee were Rose-Marie Caron, Madeleine Couture, Robert Dénommé and Ronald Béchard. Mr. Léonard Faubert Sr. was the man the principal had met at the grocery store.

Une de mes amies de classe, Claudia Gagner -
60 ans de vie religieuse

En juin 1962, les paroissiens de l'API St-Pie X d'Ottawa ont offert leurs hommages à la Révérende Soeur Marie-Gérald s.g.c. née Claudia Gagner, directrice de l'école paroissiale, à l'occasion de son 25e anniversaire de vie religieuse. Soeur Marie-Gérald, fille de M. et Mme Zacharie Gagner, est originaire de Pain Court. Elle a fait ses études primaires et secondaires à Pain Court.

La petite France Ménard lui a présenté une gerbe de roses tandis que le petit Louis Letellier lui a offert des livres de méditations.

En 1997, Soeur Marie-Gérald a célébré son 60e anniversaire de vie religieuse. Les paroissiens de Pain Court et tes ami(e)s de classe désirent se joindre à toi pour t'offrir leurs hommages les plus sincères en ce grand jour d'anniversaire. Que la divine Providence t'accorde santé, paix et beaucoup de bonheur.

Les centres d'animation "Pep Jeunesse"

En 1971, les centres d'animation "Pep Jeunesse" sont à la recherche d'étudiants francophones qui travailleront pendant l'été avec des groupes de jeunes franco-ontariens du sud Ontario. Les étudiants formeront une équipe d'animation embauchée par le ministère d'Éducation de l'Ontario. Salaire approximatif de $1,000.00 - $1,500.00 pour l'été, selon la période de travail et l'expérience.

C'est alors que trois jeunes filles ont profité de former des classes pour jeunes enfants pendant les mois d'été. Elles ont réussi très bien dans leur entreprise. De plus, elles ont rendu d'immenses services aux mamans de la région.

Chroniques

La température du mois de janvier a presque battu tous les records. Ici beaucoup ont fait des investissements pour l'achat de motoneige. Ils constatent qu'en janvier 1970, ils en ont eu usage pour leur argent.

M. Lionel Martin

Nous sommes heureux d'apprendre que M. Lionel Martin vient de faire l'achat du magasin de Ben the Tailor sur la rue King à Chatham. Nous te souhaitons bonne chance, Lionel. Que les anciens clients te restent fidèles et pour ceux qui ne sont pas encore entrés chez toi qu'ils deviennent, à leur tour, de fidèles clients.

M. Martin, homme très aimable et consciencieux, avait déjà travaillé avec M. Ben the Tailor dans son commerce pendant 10 ans. Les canadiens français étaient fiers de faire leurs achats chez un commerçant qui parlait français. Nous sommes fiers de te saluer Lionel pour ton bon travail et ta ténacité pour au-delà de 40 années. Tu as aimablement bien servi ta clientèle chez Ben the Tailor pendant 20 ans. Maintenant tu es propriétaire de l'entreprise florissante *"Lionel's Men's Wear,"* 210 rue King ouest.

Félicitations, tu fais la joie des citoyens de Pain Court, de Grande Pointe et de tous ceux des environs.

1970

Toujours avec un esprit d'apostolat, les dames de Pain Court se donnent rendez-vous à l'hôpital de Cedar Springs pour donner un coup de main à ceux et à celles qui se dévouent auprès des malades. Elles ont constaté combien ils ont besoin d'aide bénévole et combien cette aide est appréciée. Toutes personnes dévouées qui seraient d'humeur à porter secours aux malades de Cedar Springs, sachez à l'avance que vos services sont appréciés.

Le 27 février 1972, M. et Mme Jean-Paul Caron se préparent à célébrer leur 25e anniversaire de mariage dans l'intimité de leur belle famille. Félicitations!

Il faut féliciter le comité sportif du Club des Placiers qui, depuis quelques années, fournit l'aménagement d'une patinoire au parc centenaire. Les patineurs en jouissent beaucoup.

Le 21 janvier 1970, M. Joseph Laprise a célébré avec sa famille son 80e anniversaire de naissance. Le matin, ils ont assisté à une messe d'action de grâce ensuite ils se sont rendus au Holiday Inn à Chatham pour un déjeuner intime avec sa 2e femme Laura Corriveau et ses enfants.

Nos sociétés paroissiales choisissent leur exécutif pour l'année 1970.

Placiers - Rosaire Sterling sortant de charge
Nouveau président - Paul Roy
Vice-président   - Norman Roy
2e Vice-président   - Jean-Charles Bélanger
Secrétaire   - Raoul Bélanger
Trésorier   - Paul Raymond

Les Dames de Ste-Anne
Présidente   - Marie-Anne Faubert
Vice-présidente   - Rosalie Lapointe
2e Vice-présidente - Cécile Roy

Secrétaire	- Glorianna Bélanger
Trésorière	- Florence Caron

Fédération des femmes canadiennes-françaises
Présidente sortant de charge Alma Richer

Présidente	- Margo Roy
Vice-présidente	- Carmel Pinsonneault
Secrétaire	- Rose-Marie Roy
Trésorière	- Laurette Raymond

Succès dans les entreprises

Nos félicitations à M. Louis-Joseph Richer qui, le 21 janvier 1970, est élu président de l'Association Saint-Jean-Baptiste de l'ouest de l'Ontario. Nous sommes fiers de lui et nous lui souhaitons bonne chance dans sa nouvelle fonction.

Autres membres de son exécutif:

Mgr. Augustin Caron	- aumônier
Vice-président	- Paul Leboeuf, Pointe-aux-Roches
Trésorier	- Marcel Goupil
Secrétaire	- Louis Blais, Pain Court
2e vice-président	- François Caron, Pointe-aux-Roches
3e vice-président	- Paul Bonenfant, Windsor

Mot du président,

L'année 1970 qui commence s'annonce pleine de promesse et d'espoir. Tous nous vivons d'espérance que demain sera meilleur et que l'année qui s'ouvre devant nous apportera la réalisation de nos rêves.

Ouverture du poste CBEF 540 - 1970 le 18 mai

L'ouverture du poste Radio-Canada français de Windsor apporte la joie, la consolation et l'espérance dans les coeurs de la population canadienne française des comtés Kent, Essex et Lambton. Nous avons notre réponse à une prière persévérante.

On ne pourra jamais trop remercier M. Omer Parent et Compagnie, M. le sénateur Paul Martin, M. Eugene Whelan pour la réalisation d'un projet que l'on rêvait depuis 1949. Je pense que la radio française est encore plus appréciée par les plus âgés qu'elle ne l'est par n'importe quel groupe. Félicitations à Radio-Canada pour avoir nommé comme directeur de notre poste français un homme aussi capable et gentil que M. Forestier.

Hommage au Père Léo Charron

Dimanche le 31 mai 1970 avait lieu en l'église Immaculée Conception de Pain Court une fête en l'honneur du Rev. Père Léo Charron, curé de la paroisse, à l'occasion de son jubilé d'argent d'ordination sacerdotale. Rev. Père Léo Charron est fils aîné de M. et Mme Henri Charron de Belle Rivière. Il a poursuivi ses études au collège du Sacré Coeur à Sudbury et par la suite au Séminaire St. Pierre de London.

La fête débuta par une messe d'action de grâces. Ce fut une messe concélébrée. Il y avait au moins une trentaine de prêtres qui se sont réunis pour assister à la célébration du 25e anniversaire de leur confrère.

Les dames de Ste-Anne ont préparé un superbe banquet à l'occasion de la fête grandiose. La réception au presbytère fut suivie d'un grand banquet paroissial. M. Chauvin, professeur de l'école secondaire Payette, se fit l'interprète et présenta les bons voeux et les félicitations. Les paroissiens lui présentèrent une bourse. Il est reconnu, en particulier, comme curé fondateur de la paroisse St. Jérôme à Windsor.

Tous ceux et celles qui l'on connu se sont empressés de lui offrir des voeux sincères de paix, de joie et de santé.

M. Richard Drouillard - 1970

Richard Drouillard, professeur de français au Tilbury High School prend sa retraite. Il s'est dévoué pendant 32 années à l'enseignement, débutant à Smooth Rock Falls où il a enseigné sept années. Il fut directeur de l'école secondaire à Pain Court, ensuite professeur d'orientation à Chatham pendant 10 ans. Il fut louangé pour son travail et son dévouement. Un banquet fut offert par la commission scolaire de Kent à l'hôtel William Pitt. Durant plusieurs années, il s'est dévoué pour l'Association Saint-Jean-Baptiste de Kent et Essex. Il a prêté main-forte auprès de la Ligue des Retraitants dans les paroisses bilingues de Kent et Essex.

Groupe de visiteurs - 1970

Les élèves de la douzième année de l'école secondaire Payette reçurent au mois d'avril des visiteurs de Michigan. C'était une visite surprise.

Des demoiselles qui suivent des cours de français au Michigan étaient anxieuses de voir comment elles se tireraient d'affaire pendant une fin de semaine au milieu d'un groupe francophone. Le mot d'ordre était de parler français. Après avoir visité quelques endroits dans Chatham et des environs qui pouvaient les intéresser, elles ont visité les entrepôts de King Grain. Samedi soir, une veillée dansante leur a permis de se réjouir en français avec les jeunes de la place. Elles retournèrent enchantées de leur visite.

À différentes reprises durant l'année, des rencontres avec des jeunes du Québec furent aussi organisées.

Rev. Père Léo Dénommé
Juillet 1970

Léo, fils de M. et Mme Télesphore Dénommé de Pain Court, a été ordonné prêtre dans sa propre paroisse en juillet 1970 par Mgr. Jules Leguerrier o.m.i. évêque de Moosenee. Il est missionnaire dans la congrégation des Oblats de Marie Immaculée. (o.m.i.)

Il est assigné à la paroisse de l'Assomption, Maniwaki, Québec. Un superbe banquet fut servi pour la famille et tous les invités dans la salle paroissiale de Pain Court.

Le bureau de poste Benoit

Le premier bureau de poste fut ouvert à Grande Pointe en 1882. Le premier receveur était Francis Charron, de 1882 à 1883, suivi par Joseph Cheff, de 1893 à 1915. Le bureau de poste de Grande Pointe fut fermé en 1915 et la région fut desservie par le bureau de poste de Bear Line. Les adresses devinrent R R 2, Bear Line.

Le 17 juin, 1964, le bureau de poste de Grande Pointe fut réouvert avec Joseph W. Benoit comme Receveur de 1964 à 1975, quand il le vendit à Léonard L. Emery, qui fut receveur de 1975 jusqu'au présent.

Le magasin du village était le lieu de rencontre le plus populaire pour les adultes et pour les enfants. Un des premiers magasins fut établi par M. et Mme Zéphir Cheff. On y achetait ses provisions, réclamait son courrier et même on faisait couper ses cheveux.

En 1957 Joseph Benoit a ouvert un salon de coiffeur dans le bureau de la station-service de Lionel Benoit. En 1959, il déménagea son commerce à un nouveau bâtiment adjacent à la station-service. Il ajouta une salle à billards pour compléter l'ensemble de son salon de coiffeur. En juin1964, il annonça la fermeture de la salle à billard et l'ouverture du bureau de poste de Grande Pointe à sa place. En 1974, on vendit les deux commerces à Léonard L. Emery qui continue à les gérer de nos jours.

The Grande Pointe Welding Shop was established in 1947. It was owned and operated by Arthur Daniel who did general repairs to farm equipment, constructed small metal boats and crop sprayers, and during slow periods he would install drainage tile in the farms. In addition, he sold merchandise such as chains, nuts and bolts, oxygen and acetylene tanks, as well as chemicals for spraying. Mr. Daniel closed shop when he retired in 1973.

Livre Centenaire
Grande Pointe 1986

Pain Court Post Office

The village post office was officially taken over in 1949 by Johnny Lachapelle after postal services were suspended briefly to allow for the change over.

Mr. John Lachapelle was already operating a successful business as garage operator next door to Roszell Cold Storage. We are grateful to Mr. and Mrs. John Lachapelle for their fine services while serving the community for 22 years.

By the end of the year 1969 he effectively took his retirement and moved to his new home in Pain Court. On January 8, 1971 the village post office has been relocated in Lachance Jewellery shop and Barber shop.

In 1974 the government transferred the Post Office to a new quarter in the same building as "La caisse populaire de Pain Court." Mr. Edmond Chauvin became the new postmaster with additional help from Mrs. Laurette Raymond, and Mrs. Jeanne Haslip.

By 1982, September 24 saw the dawning of a new era for the Pain Court post office. A brand new structure was built on a property formerly owned by the Roman Catholic School Board, and adjacent to what was known as the convent.

It was officially opened on September 24, 1982 and is presently operating in the same building in 1998. Mrs. Patricia Caron Rush became the first postmaster at the new post office. She was transferred by government officials to be in charge of the Amherstburg Post Office. At the present time, Mary King Bowman and Suzanne Martin are operating the Post Office.

From 1930 to 1950, mail was faithfully delivered in our area by Francis and Jacob Roy, followed by their sons Thomas, Joseph and Robert Roy until 1970. By 1972, Leonard Emery took over the delivery of mail in our area.

Delore Gervais   1972

Mr. Delore Gervais passed away March 3, 1972 in St. Joseph Hospital Chatham at 77 years. He was the son of Stanislaus Gervais and Mary Peltier, and he lived in Pain Court all his life. He farmed all his life and retired in 1947. Since then, he was very active in Dover township politics serving as assessor, in 1924 to 1953 then he was elected councillor and deputy reeve in 1954. In 1955, he became reeve and served as reeve for 7 years until 1963 when he retired. He was the first Dover representative to the Lower Thames Valley Conservation Authority from 1961 - 1962.

Notable Changes 1965 - 1970

There were notable changes in Chatham, North of Pain Court. In 1965, a spokesman for Brad-Lea Meadows Ltd. expressed that over 300 homes had been built, another thirty will be built North of McNaughton and East of Tecumseh Secondary School.

The fantastic growth in Northwest Chatham first began in 1964 with the construction of "Thames Lea Plaza" and its 14 specialty stores.

In 1965, Holiday Inn was opened on the North bank of the Thames River. It was over a million dollar investment.

In 1965, the modern new Dover township building was opened on Grand Ave. just East of the new plaza.

A colourful ceremony in June 1966 marked the official opening of Union Gas Company of Canada Ltd. head office on Keil Drive.

During the centennial year, the new home for Chatham Motors Ltd. at Grand Ave. and Keil was opened.

Then we were treated to a new headquarter for C.F.C.O. on Keil Drive.

In 1968, a new wing was added to Holiday Inn. This same year "Thames Towers" was officially opened at a cost of 1.3 million.

Also opened in 1968 was the new "Thamesview Lodge" on Grand Ave.

In early January 1969, the new John Uyen Separate School in Brad-Lea Meadows subdivision was opened to students.

All the projects have been built on what was formerly farm land in Dover township. Land values since 1964 have moved upwards. A home lot that sold for $3,500 in 1965 in Brad-Lea Meadows today in 1969 is costing $5000.

The rapid development of these areas was attributed to the construction of the city's pollution control plant at the westerly outskirts, which has permitted the former farm property around the Parry Bridge to be immediately available for development.

All these recent developments permitted more growth along the River Road and the village of Pain Court.

Mr. and Mrs. Vernon Jubenville of R. R. # 1 Pain Court have returned from a trip to Toronto. The couple made the trip in the quest of purchasing clocks to add to Mr. Jubenville's antique collection.

November 1970 saw the return of many hunters from a hunting trip in Georgian Bay area at the St. Philippe Club.

Bernard Gagnier of Pain Court was the star hunter with three moose to his credit. One deer was shot by Robert Levesque of Stoney Point. Father Roger Bénéteau was another proud hunter with a deer to his credit. Their hunting partners were Alcide Marchand, Roland Griffore, Norman L'Écuyer, Father Chevalier, all of Grande Pointe.

Foy's Century Farm which features a 1860 sign lies between the Winter Line and Bear Line on concession 7 in Dover, has been in the family more than 100 years. Today in 1970, a descendant representing the family's five generations owns this 100 acre farm. His wife, Blanche Caron was a grade 2 teacher at St. Philippe School in Grande Pointe. The couple have six children, George, Russell, Clara, Christine, Joseph, Robert. The Foy farm is devoted to production of crops such as corn, wheat, oats, hay and soybeans. During the winter months, they maintain a herd of feeder cattle. The family home was constructed by Mr. Foy's grandfather, George Foy.

Walpole Island Ferry

December 1st 1969

The opening of the million dollar bridge joining the Canadian mainland with Walpole Island across the Snye River was officially opened on December 1, 1969.

A three car ferry, adjacent to the bridge, has always been the island's sole link with the mainland. Farmers working land on the island called it a blessing since crossing big truck loads   of corn and soybeans proved to be very treacherous and many mishaps already had happened. It was an important improvement to the island's population.

Conseil paroissial 1970

Depuis deux ans, des laïcs et une religieuse travaillent en collaboration avec notre curé, pour former le conseil paroissial. Ce groupe est composé d'un président, vice-président, secrétaire et huit directeurs, une religieuse et deux représentants de la jeunesse. Notre but est de seconder le curé dans l'administration des affaires de la paroisse. En agissant ainsi, nous permettons à notre pasteur de mettre plus de temps à la disposition des paroissiens pour le bien spirituel et l'exercice des cérémonies religieuses.

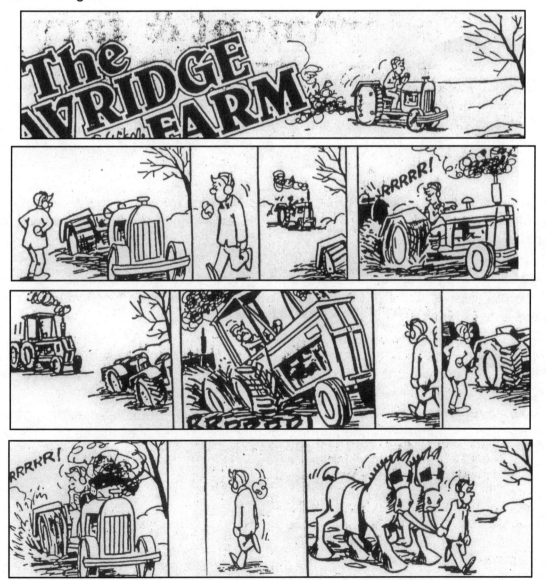

Monseigneur Caron's dream

Mgr. Caron
Ordained May 25, 1929

It was in and out of the hospitals in 1965 and 1966 and he was paralysed for four months during the period. A promise made while he was paralysed in a hospital bed was that if he ever got back on his feet he would build a small chapel. Monseigneur Caron retired in early September to the farm where he was born and immediately set about building the chapel and a home in which to live. It was a miniature chapel 18 feet wide and 30 feet long. It featured enough seating space for 18 people, the number in his family and will open to anyone of either Roman Catholic or non Roman Catholic who may wish to stop in.

His dream chapel was opened Thanksgiving Day 1969. Present for the occasion were his five sisters, all of whom are nuns with the Holy Name of Jesus and Mary Order along with his three brothers and other relatives.

Monseigneur Caron was ordained 40 years ago. He first served as administrator at Stoney Point, spent 17 years at River Canard, 11 years at St. Joachim and 5 years at McGregor. He retired at 65 and started to fulfill his dream.

Mr. Léopold St. Pierre of Pain Court nailed the cross to the chapel exterior. He paid strict attention to details of interior work of the chapel which demanded utmost care especially the altar.

Monseigneur's retirement was blessed and he devoted much of his time helping other priests in their parish. Many parishioners attended church at this fine chapel over the years. He passed away March 8, 1983 at 80 years old.

Dover Farmers Assist Neighbour

In October 1968, a group of Dover township farmers congregated for an old-fashioned working bee, while one of their neighbours Ernest Couture is recuperating at Public General Hospital. Four large combines and 15 wagons were used by the farmers to harvest the 40 acres of soybeans. "He'll sure be surprised when he hears his soybean crop has been harvested," said his wife Elmire.

Taking part in the outpouring were Alphonse Caron, Orville Couture, Octave Benoit, Ovila Couture, Herman Couture, Harvey Couture, Sylva Laprise, Fréderick Caron and Arsène Couture. The Couture farm is located on concession 5 Dover, approximately 3 miles from Pain Court.

Tragedy casts shadow on Oxfam march

Ben Bruisma as he passed our farm (in the background)

The death of a district pioneer of the Pain Court area is mourned by many friends today May 3, 1969. Oxfam officials of Kent said that the 4,081 walkers taking part in the 30 mile event received pledges for seventy thousand four hundred and thirty six dollars for a day's work, that's $70,436. dollars. Approximately 70% of the participants completed the route.

Mr. Bradley died of a heart attack along the Oxfam route earlier that day but his grandson, Stephen Bradley, 14 years old of Pain Court completed the route. Ben Bruisma, then 79 years old, was a known friend of Mr. Bradley. He was among those who completed the route and collected over a thousand dollars from his sponsors. Mr. Bruisma was well known around Pain Court also, as he was seen and interviewed by many of the residents on his bicycle trip though the area. A photo of him when he paused for a break at our place. It was a pleasure talking to him and serving him refreshments.

This special walk was well organized with St. John Ambulance attendants who were in force along the 30 mile route. They treated walkers with sore feet and even bee stings. More than 200 were treated at the Pain Court stop. Enthusiasm ran high, people of all ages from all over the county participated in this second annual event. Success was huge. Mr. Bill Scholtens jogged all the way to the finish line in four hours forty five minutes and Mr. John Visser was just a few minutes behind him. Among those taking part in the walk were Garnet Newkirk, mayor of Chatham, and Oxfam representative Otto Seeger.

Mr. Bradley, a native of Ohio and a dedicated humanitarian was 78 years old and one of Canada's greatest conservationists on his farm near the mouth of the Thames River, which served as a resting ground for millions of migrating ducks and geese. Manley and Jasper Miner welcomed Mr. Bradley frequently to their bird sanctuary in Kingsville. Their tribute to Mr. Bradley: "We bow our heads in sorrow because he was not only our friend but a friend to all mankind."

According to William Gray, Bruce Bradley was "a pioneer of the finest stock." Mr. Bradley was a great farmer and a great citizen in our area. He settled in our area and took waste land which previous owners could not make produce and turned it into a fertile meadow. Fifty years ago, I remember well, he offered work to school children when pennies were scarce . Everyone was welcomed as long as they were willing to work. Come springtime, he would pick up the children after school with his truck. They would do two hours of weeding in onion fields and carrot fields then, he would drive them back by 7 o'clock. On Saturday, it was a full day's work.

It was Miss Lucy Goudreau who always helped Mrs. Bradley with the after school snacks. Mrs. Bradley always had a big basket of sandwiches ready to pass on to all the working children. Sometimes it was a peanut butter sandwich, sometimes peanut butter and jam. The famished children appreciated these treats while sitting on a spacious verandah of the Bradley home. Mrs. Bradley also accompanied the workers from time to time to the fields. Children were paid every day after they had laboured in the field. I can remember parents talking about their children who loved to jingle quarters and dimes in their pockets. It was hard work but that's the secret of being happy, enjoying the fruits of your own labour. They also expressed their confidence to struggle ahead in these less fortunate years of the depression. "I can be somebody." Well these are in many instances today's prosperous farmers and housewives of Pain Court, Grande Pointe and Prairie Siding who at one time or another did work for pennies and dimes at the Bruce Bradley Farms. My boys were part of this working force.

A special treat for those who attended church was a trip to Pete Karry, the restaurant at the foot of the Fifth Street Bridge. Every one could order a treat of their choice with Mr. Bradley always picking up the tab. This was exciting in 1950.

Mrs. Lucy Duphette remembers well, she was 15 years old, when she enjoyed a special trip to Ottawa and New York with Mr. and Mrs. Bradley and their three sons, Robert, David and John. Mrs. McCubbin, Austrian - born and school teacher at the Bradley compound, also accompanied them on many other trips. To this special family, we offer our deep felt sorrow. Behind this fine idealistic man, rest assured there was an inspiring soul, Mrs. Bradley.

To their three sons, Robert, David and John Bradley, take special pride in your parents and may your children, your grandchildren and future generations be blessed with the spirit of love and charity of your father and mother. Mr. Bradley was taken as he lived: walking for charity.

La jeunesse, où s'en va-t-elle? 1969

On entend souvent ces paroles aujourd'hui "La jeunesse où s'en va-t-elle?" "Que font les jeunes?" Si vous aviez été témoins du grand spectacle de la journée du 3 mai 1969, la marche "Oxfam," vous auriez été surpris et étonnés du bel esprit de cette jeunesse en marche. Par centaines, ils défilaient. Chaque pas de marche pour les défavorisés, les sans-abri, les mal-aimés voulait dire "je fais ma petite part afin de venir en aide à ceux qui sont moins fortunés que moi. "Quelle noble cause!"

Certainement tous ceux qui y ont participé, jeunes et vieux, méritent notre plus grande estime. Leurs sacrifices, leurs fatigues et même leurs ampoules n'iront pas sans porter fruits. Pour eux surtout, les souvenirs seront mémorables. Connaissant leur enthousiasme, ils seront là encore si l'occasion se répète. À tous les commanditaires, un gros merci; votre récompense sera fructueuse. L'École H.J. Payette de Pain Court a rapporté un trophée dénotant 45% des 99 étudiants ont parcouru les 30 milles. D'après les classifications, ils sont arrivés les premiers, comptant environ 10 écoles secondaires de la région. Bravo les jeunes, vous avez raison d'être fiers.

Un gros merci est dû aussi aux bonnes dames qui sont venues les encourager en leur servant "sandwiches et liqueurs."

Un grand humaniste, Bruce Bradley, avait commencé la marche avec cette jeunesse qu'il aimait tant, mais il a succombé à une attaque de coeur après avoir parcouru à peine deux milles. On aurait dit qu'il avait fait la demande de mourir avec ceux auprès desquels il dénotait un zèle et un dévouement sans réserve. Depuis plusieurs années déjà il se dévouait à fonder un groupe de "Up with People." Son rêve s'est réalisé puisque présentement on compte environ une centaine de garçons et filles qui font retentir leurs voix harmonieuses à travers la région.

Le Rempart
Mme Paul Raymond 1969

Mes éloges chère Laurette car tu as laissé des souvenirs qui restent bien tangibles et remplis d'affection et de bonne volonté envers les causes communautaires.

Caroline Roy Laprise

On parle d'eux . . . d'elles   mai 1970

Les édudiants Jérome Caron, Michael Jubenville et Maurice Caron rentrent dans leur famille: Jérome de l'Université Kitchener-Waterloo, Michael de l'Ontario Agricultural School Guelph et Maurice du Collège de l'Agriculture de Ridgetown.

On nous annonce que l'hôtel Central a un nouveau propriétaire, Bob Lamarsh qui depuis longtemps demeure sur le chemin de la rivière. Il fera son entrée le premier avril 1971. Le nouveau propriétaire se dit très heureux de son marché et compte garder la bonne réputation dont joui l'hôtel Central. L'ancien propriétaire, Harry Vanderkroft et sa dame, prennent leur retraite et vont s'établir à Chatham. Ils étaient hautement appréciés par leur clientèle.

En décembre 1969, M. Gordon Blair sera très heureux de vous recevoir à son nouveau poste d'essence B.P. Un mécanicien licencié prendra charge de tous les réparages.

M. Rodolphe Potvin, menuisier reconnu, vient d'ouvrir une boutique de meubles chez nous.

Les nombreux clients de Denise Caron, coiffeuse, se réjouissent d'apprendre que l'ouverture prochaine de son salon de coiffure lui permettra de les servir à plein temps.

Lionel Faubert, un de nos cultivateurs progressifs, vient de faire l'achat d'un séchoir pour le maïs. Il se compte très satisfait des résultats. Plusieurs cultivateurs découvrent les avantages d'avoir leur propre séchoir.

Ginette Reno, le 18 mai 1970, la célèbre vedette canadienne française, s'est créée un nouveau groupe d'admirateurs lors de son grand récital à l'inauguration du nouveau poste de la chaîne française de Radio-Canada CBEF, 540 à Windsor. Née à Montréal, elle a été élue Miss Radio-Télévision en 1968. Ginette Reno a commencé sa carrière à 14 ans dans des concours d'amateurs. Sa voix riche et pleine a su exprimer ses nombreux succès et ses nouvelles créations. Elle a captivé des auditoires de choix dans plusieurs pays d'Europe. Ici à Windsor les gens lui ont accordé des ovations.

Mai 1970, Gérard Caron fils de M. et Mme Adrian Caron est diplômé du Collège d'agriculture et de technologie de Rigdetown.

Éphémerides 1970

M. Roger Roy, fils de M. et Mme Aurèle Roy a obtenu de l'Université de l'Acadie en Nouvelle-Écosse un Baccalauréat en Science Biologique.

Mlle Rachel Chauvin, graduée de l'école Normale d'Ottawa, enseignera pour la commission scolaire des Écoles Séparées bilingues de la ville de Toronto.

M. Clément Demers a obtenu un Baccalauréat de l'Université de Windsor.

M. Rosaire Roy a obtenu de l'Université Laval de Québec une maîtrise en Linguistique.

Parmi les nouveaux citoyens du village nous remarquons la famille Francis Trudell qui tout récemment prenait possession de l'ancienne demeure de M. et Mme Ovide Poissant.

M. et Mme Halarie Rivard achetaient récemment une demeure sur la rue Bernadette, voisin de M. et Mme Jim Blair.

M. et Mme Paul Roy ont fait l'achat d'une des plus belles fermes de Pain Court. En plus, l'emplacement de l'ancienne ferme est l'une des plus anciennes, établie vers 1790 par Dame Sarah Ainse.

Nous voulons offrir également des félicitations à Mlle Rose-Marie Gagner, fille de M. et Mme Edmond Gagner qui a reçu son diplôme de garde-malade de l'hôpital St. Joseph de Chatham.

Bonne chance à nos jeunes filles qui viennent de graduer de la treizième année et qui continuent leurs études. Louise Emery et Elaine Demers se dirigent vers l'Université d'Ottawa. Germaine Martin et Carmelle Cartier se rendent à l'Université de Toronto.

French Heritage Prized - 1968

This bilingual community about five miles from Chatham could become a centre for bilingual academic secondary education in Kent County if the ratepayers have their wish.

The threat of the school closing in 1968 existed because of financial reasons. This did not sit well with ratepayers. They drafted a resolution which they presented to the county's advisory committee. Pain Court was considered ideal as a county centre for bilingual education. Students seeking bilingual education would be sent to Pain Court, just as rural students were bused to Chatham for technical courses.

A favourable announcement came from the department of Education of Ontario in 1968 advising that they could make the Pain Court School a vital part of Kent County's education system. It was Mr. Roland Bélanger who headed this venture as chairman of the school board.

The bulwark of French culture in Dover has been its three bilingual schools and two elementary schools at Grande Pointe and Pain Court, including the Pain Court Continuation School. In order to preserve our culture, we must maintain our schools no matter what the cost might be.

Mr. Edmond Chauvin of Pain Court Continuation School, a member of the special sub-commission of the Synod, claims there are indications of a resurgence of interest in the French language and culture.
Father Charron declares that, according to statistics 1968, there are 40,371 French speaking people in the Catholic diocese of London, which represents 16.6% of the total population of Catholics.

According to Louis-Joseph Richer of Pain Court, a businessman and an elected parish representative to the Synod, claims it is up to Canadians of French descent to maintain and bolster their identity.
"It is now up to Canadians of French descent to pick up the challenge and retain their French status, primarily in the homes and in the schools" said Mr. Richer.
In doing so , we would continue to develop primary school teachers who will specialize in French and thereby continue the tradition.

Mr. Napoleon Roy (King) of Pain Court and president of the Chatham Chamber of Commerce emphasized that he was opposed to separatism in Canada. Mr. Roy agreed with Father Charron that a French radio and television station is urgently needed in Southwestern Ontario.
Joseph Foy, a 14 year old a grade 10 student of Pain Court Continuation School said he is of the firm opinion there are definite advantages in knowing two languages. "I'm sure this will help me in later life." My mother is French and my father is Irish and we all speak English as well as French in our family.

Premier Robarts has openly declared "he is in favour of bilingualism and would do everything in his power to maintain a bilingual atmosphere in the province of Ontario."

"Noces d'or de mes parents"

Au mois d'août 1968, c'est avec grand plaisir que les enfants et les petits- enfants s'intéressent à préparer et à célébrer le jubilé d'or de M. et Mme Adolphe Roy. Tous ont fait leur part pour rehausser le 50ᵉ anniversaire.

Les petits-enfants s'organisent pour avoir une parade typique du vieux temps. Au volant d'une auto fantaisie Ford se trouve notre fils Roger choisi pour conduire le défilé, suivi de Denise et Mariette Roy paradant leur bébé, Simone Roy, dans un carosse en jonc remontant aux 1800. Chaque famille est représentée ce qui rend le spectacle attirant et excitant pour ceux et celles qui sont de la fête.

À 14 heures, c'est la messe en plein air sur le parterre de leur demeure, célébrée par le Père Vincent Caron o.m.i., cousin de ma mère. Au moins 200 personnes faisaient partie des agapes grandioses. Une journée mémorable en compagnie de la proche parenté et celle venue de loin ainsi qu'une foule d'amis des environs.

Pour l'occasion, un souper préparé avec soin, a été servi en plein air. Une température idéale a su combler notre bonheur et celui des jubilaires.

Le jubilaires de M. et Mme Adolphe Roy

Couple Honoured on 50th Wedding Anniversary

Mr. and Mrs. Adolphe Roy of Pain Court celebrated their 50th wedding anniversary in August 1968. The couple were married in 1918 at Pain Court and Rev. Alfred Emery officiated.

They had eight children, 23 grandchildren and seven great grandchildren.

During the afternoon an open air mass was celebrated at 2 p.m. with Rev. Vincent Caron, a close relative, officiating. Friends and relatives joined the celebrants for a brunch in the afternoon. This was followed by a sumptuous supper in the Marina Room of the William Pitt Hotel in Chatham, followed by music and dancing.

Pain Court Cadets 1970

May 8 1970, was the Inspection of the Continuation School Cadet Corps of Pain Court. Its annual inspection came through, once more with flying colours. It continues to maintain its reputation as Canada's best.

The colourful presentation of military and civilian skills drew an appreciative audience of parents, neighbours and youngsters in almost perfect weather. The event was bilingual.

The corps, associated with Kent-Essex Scottish Regiment, has scored high in the past, in competition with similar organizations from across Canada. How Pain Court scored this year will not be known for some time.

Bernadette Bélanger and Robert Gagner were named outstanding female and male cadets during the inspection.

Raymond Marentette received an award as the best marksman and the corps commanding officer. Cadet major Paul Haslip was presented an award by Lt. Col. Paul Tuz, officer commanding the Kent-Essex Scottish Regiment. Cadet Capt. Thomas O'Rourke is second in command.

Lt. Col. Tuz commended the corps in both French and English for an "excellent" parade. He said he was not prepared to argue with those that claim the corps is Canada's best.

The program included both boys and girls precision drills, a rifles demonstration tumbling, hunter safety and first aid in which a simulated explosion was staged, and Highland dancing.

Capt. Philip Ash of London, area cadet officer and Lloyd Crewson, Kent area school superintendent were among those who attended.

The corps, although one of the smallest in the province, is regarded by cadet movement officials as one of the most enthusiastic. It has won the coveted Lord Strathcona Award for all efficiency twice in the past and most recently in 1967.

**Artistes qui participèrent à la soirée de talents
le 28 février 1969 à Pointe-aux-Roches**

M. Roland Lozon -
Pain Court

Linda Couture -
Pain Court

Danny St-Pierre, Larry St-Pierre,
Ronald Demers - Grande Pointe

Jean-Marie Laprise -
Pain Court

Philosophie

Éthique Générale

1964

Mme Caroline Laprise

Morale

C'est avec hésitation, que j'ose présenter ce travail, car une trentaine d'années se sont déjà écoulées depuis mes dernières classes. Puisque mon but n'est pas d'obtenir un baccalauréat mais plutôt d'enrichir ma pauvreté d'esprit, je désire rendre au plus précis de mes connaissances, un essai sur "La Morale dans le confort face à la morale dans l'indigence."

Je tiendrai particulièrement compte des besoins essentiels de l'homme: connaître, aimer et être aimé, et réaliser ses possibilités comme être humain.

Fille d'humble cultivateur, ma vie a été enrichie par un noble cultivateur ainsi que huit enfants aux yeux pétillants, dont quatre déjà, embrassent avec fierté la carrière de leurs parents. Oui, cette profession a subi une évolution scientifique et économique rapide. Il faut nécessairement adhérer à cette évolution si on veut survivre comme cultivateurs compétents. Il s'agit donc, pour nous, de garder l'esprit ouvert, confiant et courageux de nos ancêtres défricheurs plutôt que de tenir les bras aux mancheons d'une charrue.

Trop souvent, si j'ose le dire, des éducateurs, des revues, et même des bons livres, laissent entendre que le cultivateur se classe presqu'au dernier échelon de la société. Je me demande si nos collets blancs et nos collets bleus, par désintéressement, ont involontairement failli dans l'établissement de leur échelle des valeurs.

Assurément des cultivateurs avec un investissement de $50,000. à $100,000. et des transactions commerciales de $30,000. à $60,000. par année méritent plus d'intérêt qu'il ne leur est accordé. Il va sans dire que l'électronique entre déjà dans leurs méthodes de travail. Si le cultivateur ne veut pas faire banqueroute il doit bâtir sur de solides fondements académiques et techniques, aussi doit-il avoir une très grande flexibilité devant le pouvoir d'adaptation pour les méthodes modernes, afin d'obtenir un rendement maximum. Il me semble qu'il doit à la fois être comptable, industrialiste, mécanicien, architecte et cultivateur. D'un autre côté j'aimerais signaler que s'il cultive des qualités d'esprit fondamentales, telles que l'humilité et la confiance en même temps que ses récoltes, il ne tombera pas dans la grande déviation économique et technique. Pour lui sa réussite repose directement sur le plan de Dieu qui lui fournit les températures favorables et variées, telles que la chaleur, le froid, l'humidité, la pluie et le beau temps. Ces facteurs déterminants et essentiels sont requis pour les cultivateurs du monde entier, tandis que l'industriel, le professionnel et les employés se rendent à leur travail plus ou moins inconscients des vues de Dieu, ne tenant compte que des malaises qu'ils éprouvent et du parapluie qu'il faut apporter. Ces pensées semblent salutaires et nous ne pouvons guère les laisser s'échapper des valeurs matérielles mises à la disposition de l'homme. Espérons que cette évolution dans le confort soulagera progressivement la misère des peuples et saura combler le besoin vital du monde presqu'entier, la faim, si bien exposée dans quelques essais.

Ce fut au retour d'un voyage dans les pays d'Orient, que j'ai éprouvé un bouleversement moral qui a semblé faire ébranler mon échelle des valeurs. Ceci m'amène à vouloir connaître davantage, car les opinions et les jugements valent ce que vaut le savoir.

Aujourd'hui, nos communications actuelles quasi rapides comme l'éclair ont raccourci à presque rien, le temps entre l'acte humain et ses conséquences dans le monde. Aujourd'hui, il y a donc danger d'affirmer l'identité des hommes sans tenir compte, ou en comprenant mal, leur individualité. Pour chaque individu, il lui faut combler ses besoins-là dans le pays où il se trouve. Trop souvent nos dirigeants s'élèvent pour regarder le monde en général, étudier les phénomènes sociaux des masses, mais oublient les facteurs qui déterminent la vie particulière de chaque homme. Sartre, dans son refus du prix Nobel l'exprime en disant: "Par liberté j'entends une liberté plus concrète qui consiste d'avoir plus d'une paire de chaussures et de manger à sa faim," et j'ajoute, en oubliant que l'homme crève de faim parce qu'il n'a pas de chaussures pour se rendre au travail et s'aggrave par le manque d'un toit pour s'abriter. Il y a aussi la femme qui va se vendre pour l'argent parce qu'elle ne peut se donner qu'à un homme pour être aimée; en d'autres circonstances c'est la faim qui détermine ses actes. Voyez ensuite l'homme de réputation pris par une crise cardiaque plongé dans la mélancolie et le désespoir. Ce ne sont que quelques exemples pour faire voir combien on est porté à généraliser tout et à oublier les facteurs déterminants et renverser les échelles de valeurs pour satisfaire nos besoins fondamentaux.

Qu'elle est la fin dernière de l'homme? La recherche du bien. La vie vaut la peine d'être vécue lorsqu'on peut puiser en soi la capacité d'augmenter dans la société le capital de bien. Par bien, j'entends l'ordre dans sa propre vie et dans la société. L'ordre tient justement compte de l'hiérarchie des valeurs, les valeurs matérielles étant mises au service des valeurs spirituelles; c'est en vue de ces valeurs qu'il faut chercher à diminuer les souffrances de l'homme sur terre et le rendre heureux. La morale a donc pour rôle de montrer où est le bien et non faire converger notre attention sur le bonheur personnel ou l'intérêt égoïste. Ceci m'amène au point ou je me transporte vers l'Orient pour étudier avec vous la morale dans le confort et dans l'indigence au point de vue économique, politique, social, religieux et éducatif, tenant compte de quelques scènes, non lues, mais vues et vécues.

Dans le confort nous sommes préoccupés à nous dépasser continuellement dans le domaine économique. Il faut nécessairement avec notre premier mille dollars viser au deuxième, et toujours plus, car les exigences de la vie et les obligations sociales et économiques du pays sont continuellement à la hausse. Parfois nous sommes inclinés à penser que la science de la production semble mieux équilibrée que celle de la consommation des richesses. Face à ceci dans les pays sous-développés, l'économie consiste à viser le besoin essentiel de la vie, manger. D'abord ces pays possèdent à peu près aucune méthode scientifique ou technique de production pour l'agriculture qui est la base de l'alimentation. D'autre part beaucoup de terrain ne se prête pas à produire, ou le climat n'est pas favorable à la culture.

Dans le domaine industriel il manque les matières premières pour mettre en marche le progrès. Nous sommes appelés à créer des marchés afin que les industries puissent fabriquer et disposer de leurs produits. Par ceci, l'indigent réaliserait ses possibilités comme individu selon les besoins dans son pays.

C'est en parcourant les campagnes pour plusieurs jours que j'observe les cultivateurs qui tournent à la main des acres de terre avec une simple bêche, ou à d'autres endroits ils font usage des boeufs sauvages; comme au Japon il y a quelques machines qui facilitent la cultivation du sol. J'assiste aussi aux procédés de fertilisation. Le sol est enrichi avec les déchets humains préservés dans des endroits propices, transportés ensuite sur les fermes et déposés dans des locaux pour être appliqués à la récolte en majeure partie par le sexe féminin. Quel spectacle! Mais pour eux ça sera l'espoir de mieux produire pour mieux manger. Pourquoi pas la mécanisation? Je demande? Ils répondent: "Ceci enlèverait le travail à la population et par conséquent leur pain quotidien." Déjà plusieurs organismes ont été formés et entrent en fonction, pour tâcher d'y apporter une meilleure éducation et une amélioration nécessaire à une survivance plus saine. Avec une évolution plus concrète, par des méthodes scientifiques et techniques, et l'indispensable coopération de dirigeants compétents, espérons que nous constaterons une transformation très rapide.

Regardons maintenant l'aspect religieux. Le Concile nous dit que les statistiques parlent. Aujourd'hui, 1900 ans après avoir reçu le message du Christ et le mandat d'annoncer l'Évangile à tous les peuples, l'Église se retrouve devant un monde encore non chrétien au moins pour les deux tiers. Nous constatons avec joie les bienfaits retentissants des rencontres de Jean XXIII et de Paul VI avec plusieurs chefs religieux de diverses dénominations ainsi que la simplicité de ces visites libres parmi les peuples Chrétiens et non Chrétiens. Serait-ce des traits d'union durables qui s'établissent entre l'Orient et l'Occident? Le Christianisme voit très clairement qu'il doit devenir plus "catholique" et de plus en plus universel pour atteindre tous les peuples, dialoguer avec chacun d'eux et ainsi être en mesure de s'adapter à tous. Examinons, si c'est bien là notre mentalité?

Ce qui compte chez le missionnaire de 1964, c'est cette capacité de respecter cette variété entre les groupes humains. L'Église, devenue beaucoup plus présente et active, semble préciser une nouvelle vision du vrai sens des missions plus conforme à la réalité.

Le point essentiel de départ, pour mériter le nom de Chrétien, c'est d'être missionnaire. Être missionnaire c'est être universel, c'est vouloir servir le Christ, plutôt que sa propre culture. C'est renoncer à confondre sa manière propre d'être Catholique avec le catholicisme. C'est accepter qu'il y ait d'autres styles de vie et de pensées chrétiennes.

Chez certains peuples, comme par exemple au Japon, on constate beaucoup de ferveur, de révérence envers leur être Suprême le "Bouddha." Leurs sanctuaires Bouddhiste et Shinto sont profondément imprégnés et débordant de respect pour les sept dieux: le Dieu d'amour, sous forme apparente d'une statue féminine, le Dieu de Miséricorde, le Dieu de Musique et d'autres encore. Ces sanctuaires sont fréquentés continuellement comme le sont nos sanctuaires, Notre Dame du Cap, l'Oratoire St-Joseph, Ste-Anne de Beaupré et quelques-unes de nos églises. Il va sans dire que nous admirons cette attitude de profond respect, chez un peuple en majorité païen. Un autre détail: leur culte ne permet pas l'entrée au temple avec des chaussures. Ils présentent des offrandes d'argent ou les produits des champs à ce Dieu qu'ils visitent. Toujours ils se recommandent à ce Dieu et demandent ses bienfaits par l'élévation de l'esprit et du coeur.

Aux Philippines, le drame prend un autre caractère. Beaucoup se disent Chrétien, mais leur christianisme est spécialement démonstratif. Voici l'exemple des "Flagellantes." Le Vendredi Saint à midi, plusieurs personnes se rendent à une montagne rappelant le Calvaire, la gravissent en portant une croix proportionnée à la grandeur du Sacrifice qu'ils veulent offrir. A ceci s'ajoutent "les Flagellants" qui exécutent leur tâche de flageller les sacrifiants chacun selon sa propre recommandation. Après le cérémonial qui dure 3 heures, ils procèdent au découvrement de Jésus crucifié. Le peuple défile pendant des heures pour embrasser les pieds du Seigneur. Ensuite le crucifix de bois mesurant au moins six pieds est transporté dans tous les coins de la paroisse pour enfin être déposé dans le tombeau. Cérémonie très émouvante, mais qui porte à presque oublier le vrai sens de la Rédemption. Pour ajouter au spectacle, toutes les statues sont revêtues comme les personnes du temps. À une époque où l'on manquait de prêtres, des cérémonials avaient lieu. Des laïcs les organisaient et ils étaient centrés selon les écrits du Nouveau Testament.

Plusieurs missionnaires disent bien que le dévouement inlassable et courageux ne suffit pas.

Il faut premièrement répondre aux besoins essentiels de ces gens avant de leur présenter l'Évangile. Ils nous faut des laïcs bien renseignés et convaincus pour réaliser certains projets où il s'agit de mieux comprendre les besoins des gens en vivant avec eux et comme eux. Nous en avons des preuves tangibles et vécues chez les Baptistes qui dépassent de loin les Catholiques dans l'évangélisation de certains pays d'Orient. Pourquoi? Cette conquête est due aux forces laïques, comme par exemple "Billy Graham Troops" qui parcourent différents pays. Comme j'ai voyagé un peu avec eux, j'ai reconnu leur capacité de professionnels compétents qui se dévouent et qui s'engagent à passer leurs vacances en missions étrangères. Nous rencontrons aussi des laïcs qui se donnent pendant certain nombre d'années à cette oeuvre, et ainsi préparent le terrain d'action. Chez les Catholiques il existe aussi un organisme semblable "Cursillo," qui a été fondé récemment en Espagne. Les membres ne sont pas encore trop actifs en mission. Le progrès missionnaire est retardé par l'apathie et le désintéressement de la presque totalité du monde vivant dans le confort.

Ceci nous amène à la politique qui joue elle aussi un rôle primordial dans nos pays démocratiques. Malheureusement, il y a de graves lacunes causées par les abus d'une société égoïste qui cherche parfois à dominer par ses actes et ses connaissances plutôt que de tenir compte des besoins de l'homme. Il est dit qu'un peuple a le gouvernement qu'il mérite. Si ce principe est vrai et l'histoire semble souvent le prouver dans les pays démocratiques, alors quoi penser de ces pays où le mode de vie leur est dicté.

Nous sommes tous convaincus que les gouvernements du monde entier jouent et joueront dans l'avenir le rôle primordial dans l'avancement et le développement de leur pays. Toutes les valeurs naturelles peuvent être mises à la disposition des êtres humains afin qu'ils puissent vivre dans une saine liberté d'esprit. C'est ainsi que nous, les hommes, pourrions satisfaire leurs besoins fondamentaux.

De plus en plus dans tous les pays, on s'aperçoit que des pays reconnus autrefois comme sous-développés attachent aujourd'hui une grande importance à l'éducation. Les gouvernements se chargent dans la mesure du possible de financer, étudier et appuyer tous changements nécessaires à l'évolution de leurs peuples.

Par exemple, au Japon on y attache une importance sans pareil. Les enfants, dès l'âge de 4 ans entrent en classe. Là, des psychologues compétents examinent et étudient les possibilités et les comportements de chaque enfant qui se présente. Chacun est dirigé selon ses aptitudes. En deuxième année, on enseigne les sciences. Les sciences de laboratoire des écoles primaires rivalisent assez facilement avec bien de nos écoles secondaires. J'en suis restée bouche-bée. J'ai assisté aux fêtes grandioses d'une collation des grades. Je dirais que le gouvernement apporte son entière collaboration dans l'éducation. Il crée et met gratuitement à la disposition de tous, des écoles et l'équipement nécessaire à leur évolution. Malheureusement, il y a exception. Les écoles privées ordinairement construites et retenues par les missionnaires ne jouissent pas de ses avantages. Devant une évolution aussi rapide elles manquent le capital nécessaire.

En Chine et chez les réfugiés de ce pays, l'éducation se place à un niveau alarmant. Des milliers d'enfants ne fréquentent aucune école durant toute leur vie. Ensuite nous nous posons la question: pourquoi y a-t-il tant d'illettrés? Heureusement qu'il y en a des plus privilégiés qui se placent avec un peu d'argent dans les écoles clairsemées ou dans les institutions. La classe, dans bien des endroits, se fait trois fois par jour afin d'accommoder trois groupes différents. Dans cette nation nous constatons une pénurie de personnel enseignant, d'écoles et de matériaux nécessaires à l'évolution normale de l'éducation. C'est à notre monde de confort d'aider à combler ses lacunes si un juste équilibre doit être maintenu entre ces pays sous-développés et les pays libres.

La situation aux Philippines est un peu semblable, quoique depuis leur indépendance, ils ont fait des progrès considérables. Il y a de fabuleux avancements instigués par des âmes dévouées tant laïques que missionnaires, qui mettent leurs connaissances à la disposition de ce peuple malheureux. Ce qui nous intéresse aussi et qui rend la tâche d'éduquer quasi impossible sont les dialectes. Par là, j'entends qu'il y en a soixante-douze.

Que dire des universités, des églises et d'autres établissements encore en ruines depuis la guerre et dont les piliers s'élèvent dans les airs, et démoralise l'esprit de ses habitants. Des années s'écouleront avant qu'ils puissent faire disparaître les souvenirs néfastes d'une telle catastrophe. Le progrès en général est retardé dans le domaine de l'éducation.

J'ai eu le bonheur de rencontrer les pères Carmélites qui rédigent le Catholic Digest pour l'Orient. Le supérieur annonce son départ pour les États-Unis dans le même avion que moi, et j'ai pu lire son récit dans notre Catholic Digest du mois de novembre dernier. Il me laisse entendre que depuis des années ils travaillent à établir leur collège. Ce fut une tâche énorme mais ils sont parvenus. Maintenant nous ne possédons aucune imprimerie si vital au développement et l'avancement religieux et économique de ces peuples. D'autre part, il y a aussi des religieuses que j'ai bien connues de notre pays qui, après les classes, s'engagent aux besoins matériels des familles. Nous les voyons aider à construire des maisons qui abriteront quelques malheureux.

Ceci me rapproche du point de vue final, le social. Dans divers pays j'ai eu le bonheur de connaître un peu ce point de vue qui, comme les autres m'ont assurément fait réaliser pourquoi j'étais choyée et privilégiée dans mon pays. Il me semble inutile d'élaborer sur ce point, le confort qui est le nôtre. Je reconnais qu'il y a de l'indigence dans notre société mais il faut voir pire pour réaliser comme ils sont incapables de soulager leur propre sort tandis qu'ici les manques peuvent être remédiés.

Examinons le sort des 5 millions de réfugiés chinois à Hong Kong, Kowloon et Macao. Avec une centaine de touristes, je voyage par bateau à Macao, île portugaise. Environ 2,500 chinois nous accompagnent. C'est sur l'Île de Macao que se trouve la grande barrière communiste de la Chine. Il y a trois ans, c'est à cet endroit que la révolution éclata. La population est 2% portugaise, 1% de nationalités diverses et 95% Chinois réfugiés. Les Chinois voyagent avec tout ce qu'il possèdent, linge, couvertures et plats. C'est le 6 avril, 1963. C'est jour libre, jour pour commémorer les morts. Les barrières sont ouvertes à partir du lever du soleil jusqu'au soleil couchant. Ceci permet aux parents et amis de traverser en Chine Communiste pour visiter leurs parents défunts. Leur tradition en ce jour sacré leur permet de gratter les os des parents décédés et enterrés dans des bocaux sur la montagne.

C'est le débarquement. Nos émotions se confondent. Les gens descendent chargés de bagages. Ils se jettent partout sur les gazons des parcs et le long des rues. C'est une course affolée pour se rendre dans un endroit où il pourront dormir jusqu'au lever de soleil. Leur coeur déborde de joie, mais c'est la tristesse qui s'imprime sur leur figure.

Le gouvernement britannique vient en aide en construisant une centaine de maisons appartements. Chacun consiste d'environ 250 chambres et abrite à peu près 2,000 personnes. Ce milieu est très rapproché de l'aéroport à Hong Tai Gin, Kowloon. Aimeriez-vous vivre dix par chambre et coucher par terre? Aimeriez-vous manger un bol de riz par jour et être heureux avec un bon verre d'eau? Pensez-y? Pour eux c'est un peu de bonheur, car ils sont restés sur la montagne avec peu d'abris pendant 6 mois, 1 an, ou plus, avant de jouir de ce nouveau local, à l'épreuve des typhons, de la pluie et du froid. Au centre nous y trouvons un hôpital de 30 lits qui voit aux soins des malades. En 1963, le gouvernement Américain verse une somme de 7 millions en médicament pour les refugiés. J'ai rencontré à cet endroit, quatre soeurs Maryknoll du sud de l'Ontario. Les malades assistent aux cliniques et retournent chez eux.

Lorsqu'il y a des typhons, ceux qui habitent la montagne convergent dans les institutions rapprochées. Nos soeurs missionnaires et autres les reçoivent par mille dans les écoles. Ils y demeurent quelques jours et leur nourriture consiste de trois bols de soupe par jour. Ensuite, ils regagnent la montagne pour amasser les débris et s'y rétablir.

J'ai vécu une journée dans un "San Pan" avec une famille de trois enfants. Beaucoup naissent, vivent et meurent dans ce bateau. Ils font la pêche et vendent les surplus afin de suppléer au nécessaire. "Aberdeen," place reconnue pour les marchés de poisson, nous enlève l'appétit pour les mets les plus soigneusement préparés. C'est au marché de Hong Kong que nous voyons une cinquantaine de bateaux russes apporter les vivres des paysans de la Chine Communiste. Ici à l'arrivée des bateaux les chinois refugiés et d'autres achètent ces vivres, les empaquettent séparément, les remettant sur le bateau avec l'espoir que leurs parents subsisteront. Ceci je l'ai vécu; ce drame nous arrache les larmes et déchire le coeur. Pensez-vous qu'ils s'occupent de la société? Non. Ils se comptent heureux de vivre en pays libre et trouvent le bonheur en aidant leurs proches à vivre.

Le théâtre chinois est beau, artistique et démonstratif, mais des séances durent de 30 à 45 minutes. Vous pouvez constater que le chinois possède beaucoup d'habilité et de délicatesse dans les arts, par les marchandises qui nous viennent de Hong Kong. Par conséquent, il est très ouvert à l'évolution.

Aux Philippines, c'est un peu semblable, le manque de nourriture influence le mode de vie. D'autre part l'art de la sculpture est remarquable et fantastique. La femme est très artistique et transforme habilement les matières premières de linge. Ici nous voyons bien des abris pauvres. Aimeriez-vous demeurer dans une ou deux pièces de grandeur 10' x 14' et manger des bananes et du riz de jour après jour? Seriez-vous vraiment heureux?

Au Japon une évolution rapide a transformé ce pays. Il y a la construction d'appartements modernes et de plus en plus les gens laissent leur foyer construit souvent de paille et de boue pour élire domicile dans les appartements. Beaucoup de capital étranger améliore leur façon de vivre. Le Kimono est surtout réservé pour les fêtes spéciales et la génération d'aujourd'hui se rapproche de la vie occidentale et parfois l'influence. La culture de ce peuple possède des véritables qualités de patience et de politesse.

Ils possèdent aussi des fameux théâtres où se déroulent des représentations célèbres et artistiques d'art dramatique. Les sciences de ce peuple sont très avancées, et ceci leur permet de mettre sur le marché mondial des produits à prix modique; en plus, la main d'oeuvre n'est pas trop dispendieuse.

Les Japonais restent vivement attachés à leurs traditions. Dans bien des foyers on remarque l'évolution moderne. Ils possèdent une télévision, un radio. Une partie de la maison est de style Américain tandis que l'autre, strictement Japonais. Ici on remarque une plaque ou fac-similé d'autel en marbre ou autre pierre où sont préservées les cendres de leurs parents défunts. Ceci est chose sacrée et commande une grande révérence.

C'est au retour de ce voyage et après des réflexions sérieuses qu'il me paraît nécessaire de réviser mon échelle des valeurs qui semble s'ébranler et s'écrouler sous le poids des forces extérieures qui la menace.

Je reste confuse, car notre vingtième siècle a plongé le monde dans un climat de crise, de conflit; le vent souffle présentement aux quatre coins du monde. L'Amérique et la Russie s'engagent dans une course affolée pour maintenir le pouvoir des armes nucléaires. À toute reprise des fusées se placent en orbite et d'autres pays se préparent pour s'y joindre. C'est la famine aux Indes et partout. Ce sont les guérillas qui s'engagent dans une lutte acharnée en Asie du Sud. C'est le tonnerre qui gronde dans l'Afrique et les drapeaux de révolution qui s'élèvent dans les capitales de l'Amérique du Sud. Il y a des rencontres sanguinaires sur le sable de l'Afrique et de l'Europe qui ne demande pas plus qu'une survivance économique dans ses conflits. La Chine déchaîne des problèmes universels en restant enchaînée à une philosophie Marxiste, tandis qu'elle a des billions qui ont faim. Leur mauvaise entente avec la Russie présente une atmosphère au point de rupture. Aux États-Unis, il y a aussi le problème des droits civils et au Canada se sont les politiciens qui poursuivent opiniâtrement la question du drapeau et les termes de la Confédération tandis que les peuples sont plongés dans l'anxiété. Partout l'homme prend conscience de lui-même comme être, et réclame son identité et s'efforce d'affirmer ses droits et de se projeter dans l'avenir par ce progrès.

Face à ce dilemme, espérons voir l'être libre dans le confort effectuer un dépassement de soi pour voir, comprendre, aimer et par là aider ceux qui visent à leur identité. Nous diminuerons ainsi les souffrances de l'homme sur terre, nous contribuerons à notre propre bonheur et à celui du moins privilégié et nous maintiendrons l'ordre dans l'observation de la hiérarchie des valeurs matérielles mises au service des valeurs spirituelles pour la plus grande gloire de Dieu.

le 18 novembre 1964
Caroline Laprise

Ref. FAA
UNESCO
Colombo Plan

Chapitre 7

Pot-pourri

d'actualités

1970 - 1980

Chapter 7

Potpourri of

Current Events

Tu en fais tant pour les autres

Seigneur bénis les gens
qui consacrent leur vie
au bien-être d'autrui.

Bénis les gens
qui n'hésitent jamais à
tendre la main à ceux
qui en ont besoin et
qui offrent avec générosité
leur temps et leur amitié.

Seigneur bénis les gens
qui, par leur sourire et leur
bonne humeur,
savent apporter au coeur
un peu de chaleur.

Bénis les gens qui ont
une telle confiance en la vie
qu'ils deviennent
une véritable source d'inspiration
pour toutes celles et tous ceux qui
gravitent autour d'eux.

Amanda Bradley

Congregation Honours Organist

Mrs. Marie Emery, organist at the Immaculate Conception church at Pain Court for the past 50 years was honoured at a testimonial dinner staged in the church banquet hall last night. Above, Mrs. Emery is seen with a group of the church officials who assisted in the organization of the banquet and the presentation of gifts. Left to right are: Monseigneur W. Bourdeau, Mrs. Emery, Gérard Caron of the church choir, Mrs. Edward O'Neil, who played the church organ previous to Mrs. Emery, Edgar Martin, president of the Ushers Club and Mrs. Victor Trahan, president of the Ladies Altar Society.

(Staff)   1954 Chatham Daily News

Hommage à Madame Marie Emery

L'héritage musical qu'elle nous a légué a
influencé et inspiré plusieurs générations de sa communauté.

La paroisse de l'Immaculée Conception de Pain Court a perdu au cours de l'année qui s'écoule, une paroissienne de grande valeur, en la personne de Madame Marie Emery. Voici une personne qui a vraiment aimé sa paroisse.

Pendant 57 ans, elle fut notre organiste. En plus, de 1911 à 1928, c'était encore elle, qui assumait la tâche onéreuse de la préparation du chant pour les grandes soirées paroissiales. Celles-ci se succédaient en moyenne de cinq à six par année. Sa patience et son dévouement, surtout envers les plus jeunes, étaient remarquables et celui qui écrit ces lignes en connaît quelque chose.

Madame Emery était toujours disponible, toujours prête à rendre service. C'est ce qui explique peut-être le fait qu'elle n'avait que des amis et n'a jamais connu ce que c'est qu'un ennemi. Son coeur généreux ne pouvait rien refuser à qui que ce soit. Elle était très compétente et cependant elle est toujours demeurée bien humble, simple et très sincère.

La Providence l'avait dotée d'une belle voix et d'un remarquable talent pour la musique. C'est avec cet amour du beau qu'elle a mis sa belle voix d'abord au service de son Église. On pourrait dire que pendant une quarantaine d'années elle était la grande responsable de la chorale paroissiale. Au début d'août 1971, Madame Emery nous quittait pour un monde meilleur. Coïncidence extraordinairement remarquable pour celle qui, pendant des années et des années avait chanté les louanges de la Vierge et du Sacré-Coeur. Voici que le Seigneur la rappelle à lui le premier vendredi du mois, le jour dédié au Sacré-Coeur. Ce jour même elle avait reçu, comme à l'accoutumée, la Sainte Communion et le soir de ce même jour, elle s'éteignait dans la paix serrant dans sa main son chapelet, son inséparable compagnon depuis des années. Honneur à vous les paroissiens de Pain Court, Madame Emery a eu des funérailles dignes de l'artiste très chrétienne que nous avons connue.

Ses fils, Amédée, Alphy et Mozart qui pleurent encore leur mère, ont vu, dans la piété et le recueillement de la part de ceux qui assistaient à la touchante cérémonie d'adieux pour leur brave mère et notre ancienne organiste, le plus beau témoignage de notre estime et notre appréciation pour services rendus.

À notre bon ami, M. Amédée Emery, notre organiste actuel dont nous admirons l'art et le dévouement, nous disons: " Vous êtes le digne fils d'une digne mère et nous apprécions hautement vos services et tous vos co-paroissiens sont fiers de vous."

À notre paroisse, je souhaite que nous trouvions d'autres types du même genre afin qu'à leur tour ils nous aident à progresser et à grandir davantage dans l'amour du beau et de tout ce qui peut élever l'âme à Dieu.

Une paroisse peut grandir et progresser spirituellement à condition que les individus qui la composent, à l'exemple de celle qui nous a quittés, doivent plus qu'ils en reçoivent.

-Augustin Caron, ptre.

Alexina Caron (Ouellette)

Née à Alexandria, Ontario le 17 octobre, 1900 et décédée à Windsor le 24 juin, 1991.

C'est peut-être des traits communs, enfant d'une grande famille agricole canadienne-française catholique, qui a attiré l'attention d'Alcide à Alexina, une nouvelle arrivée à Pain Court. Cette "maîtresse d'école" s'est devouée pendant huit ans à l'enseignement des élèves de la première à la huitième année dans la petite école rurale séparée SS # 4 sur la quatrième concession de Dover. Selon la tradition de l'époque, Alexina a dû abandonner son emploi lors de son mariage.

Monsieur Alcide Caron épouse Alexina Ouellette le 2 janvier 1930 à Pain Court. Les nouveaux-mariés se sont établis sur la ferme Caron à Pain Court. Pendant trois ans elle continue l'enseignement à temps partiel dans la région.

Dans la vie de maman, c'est l'éducation des cinq filles qui était une préoccupation dominante. Cet intérêt important a été bien communiqué à ses enfants qui sont devenues enseignantes impliquées dans l'éducation du français, chacune à sa façon. Maman elle-même a toujours poursuivi son éducation en assistant à des cours, soit de peinture, d'expression dramatique, d'art culinaire, d'éducation religieuse, et cela même à un âge avancé. Ses goûts du beau, de curiosité intellectuelle, du développement de la personne a été communiqué à ses enfants qui cherchent à élaborer leurs connaissances en suivant des cours dans différents domaines. Elle a vu à ce que ses enfants enrichissent leurs connaissances musicales en insistant qu'elles prennent des leçons de piano, de chant, de violon, expérience qui lui a toujours manquée.

L'aspect religieux était d'une grande importance pour maman. La messe de presque tous les jours, le chapelet quotidien, des retraites annuelles, des neuvaines, des offrandes missionnaires, le support financier de "son prêtre" africain, voilà différentes façons d'exprimer sa religion. Dans le sens pratique, elle offrait un tour de voiture à ceux qui ne conduisaient pas - voisins, religieuses, amis. Sa charité ne permettait pas qu'on critique qui que ce soit en sa présence, surtout jamais un prêtre. "On ne sait jamais toutes les circonstances" disait-elle. Comme elle aurait été heureuse de voir treize prêtres à ses funérailles.

Maman insistait sur l'importance de la paix dans le monde, en commençant d'abord par la paix dans la famille. Grandissant avec douze enfants, elle a connu très jeune les bienfaits de l'amour et du support mutuel. Cette expérience se renouvelait chaque année dans les rencontres de famille à la ferme paternelle. Malgré les distances qui séparaient ses frères et soeurs, personne ne voulait manquer ces fêtes où l'on se rassemblait autour de la grande table pour s'amuser, revivre le passé et rire de bon coeur. Elle tenait à ce que sa descendance jouisse de la même expérience. En effet elle serait heureuse de voir que cette bonne entente existe. Il ne faudrait qu'assister à des rencontres familiales des sept enfants d'Aline pour en être témoin.

Maman a beaucoup joui de la vie. Elle adorait voyager. En plus de ses retours annuels à sa famille à Alexandria, elle a eu l'occasion d'explorer en Californie avec papa, visiter plusieurs pays d'Europe, faire la traversée transatlantique en S. S. France et participer à un pèlerinage en Israël. Ce goût d'aventure, elle a bel et bien transmis à sa descendance.

Et le grand voyage vers l'éternité s'est effectué le jour de la Saint Jean-Baptiste, très paisiblement en présence de ses quatre filles: Aline Bondy, Rivière-aux-Canards, mère de sept enfants et grand-maman de dix petits enfants; Lucile Caron, Windsor, enseignante retraitée; Louise Olsen, Northville, Michigan, enseignante retraitée travaillant à United Airlines; Anne-Marie Caron-Réaume Toronto, agente d'éducation en langue française à Queen's Park. L'attendant là-haut à bras ouvert, Marie-Thérèse Caron, professeur de français à l'université de Windsor, décédée en 1988.

Aline Bondy
Lucile Caron

Un mémorial à ma soeur, Jeannette Blais Howard,
décédée le 22 avril 1979, à l'âge de 49 ans.

La mémoire du coeur m'inspire à reconnaître une grande éducatrice, une de ces êtres chers placés expressément dans le plan de la création pour accomplir une mission spéciale: celle d'éduquer et d'instruire.

Jeannette Blais Howard est née à Rivière Rouge, Michigan, le 9 septembre 1929, du mariage de Philippe Blais et d'Anna Béchard. Elle était l'aînée d'une famille de huit enfants. Après avoir fréquentée l'école Ste-Catherine et l'école secondaire de Pain Court, elle s'est dirigée vers l'École normale de l'Université d'Ottawa où elle a obtenu un brevet d'enseignement, une profession qu'elle a exercée pendant une trentaine d'années dans les écoles catholiques françaises et anglaises du comté de Kent ainsi qu'un stage de trois ans à l'École Secondaire de Pain Court.

Le 29 décembre 1956, elle a épousé Henry Howard. Elle est la mère de trois enfants: Révérend Père Dennis Howard, Marc Howard, diplômé de l'Université de Carleton et Docteur Jeffrey Howard, biologiste.

En 1976, Jeannette a obtenu son diplôme de l'Université de Windsor.

Douée d'une personalité forte et d'une intelligence supérieure, elle a partagé ses talents d'organisatrice auprès de nombreux organismes scolaires et communautaires. Elle s'est dépensée pendant plusieurs années auprès des membres de sa profession. Elle a été présidente et secrétaire de l'association des Enseignantes et Enseignants Franco-Ontariens. Elle a été active quand elle a enseigné le "French" dans les écoles anglaises catholiques de Chatham offrant gratuitement de son temps et de son expertise pour mettre sur pied un programme de dépistage pour l'enseignement du français langue seconde. Elle s'est dépensée en servant sur le comité de négociations afin que les professeurs aient de meilleures conditions de travail.

Sa volonté de servir sa communauté l'a amenée à se dévouer comme membre et présidente de la société "Marian Auxiliary" de l'hôpital St-Joseph de Chatham.

Jeannette avait cette passion d'aller plus loin, d'accepter des défis qu'elle exécutait toujours avec sagesse et amour.

En 1976, elle est retournée à son alma mater pour se dévouer auprès des enfants de la paroisse où elle a grandi. Depuis deux ans sa santé dépérissait car Jeannette souffrait de cancer. Ceci ne l'empêchait pas de continuer son travail. Tous ceux qui l'entouraient admiraient son courage et sa détermination de servir malgré la souffrance et l'épuisement.

Pour résumer ce mémorial, laissez-moi vous citer les paroles d'un grand éducateur et formateur d'âmes, le Rév. Père René Lamoureux, o.m.i. principal de l'École normale de l'Université d'Ottawa.

"Le monde pour se bien porter," dit-il, "a besoin de savants, d'artistes et de saints. Quand il va mal, c'est qu'il lui en manque. C'est aux éducateurs, avec l'aide de Dieu, d'en produire. Il vous suffira de mettre tout ce que Dieu vous a donné de coeur et d'intelligence dans l'accomplissement de chacune des tâches dont se compose la longue journée d'un éducateur."

Ces paroles éloquentes du Père Lamoureux décrivent parfaitement l'âme ardente qui était Jeannette. C'est ainsi que l'oeuvre de sa vie s'est manifestée dans le plan divin professant jusqu'au bout une foi vivante et un coeur sincère.

Angéline Blais Marentette

A Life Lived For God And For Others

It has been 19 years now since my mother died, and each day I sense her presence and influence in my life. I recall a woman of deep faith, of strong determination and a woman of divers gifts which she willingly shared with others.

Jeannette Anna Blais Howard's life is a testimony of the goodness which God has placed within each human being. What is necessary is for us to respond to the potential that the Creator has put within all of us. My mother's life is a witness to someone who despite great personal suffering and many challenges has given her all to her God and fellow man.

Part of my mother's legacy is her three sons, Mark, Jeff and Dennis. My brothers have been both very much influenced by my mother's life. My brother Mark is living in Ottawa. Much of his career has been spent working with troubled young people who are transitioning through the legal system. A very challenging profession. Presently, he is changing careers and has resumed his studies at the University.

439

My brother Jeff has just recently graduated with a Ph.D. in biology, and has been doing cancer research in Toronto over the past number of years. I often think of my mother's death as a result of cancer like many other members of our family. It must have somehow played a part in inspiring Jeff to this choice of profession. I am very grateful that my brother is a part of the great crusade to defeat this terrible scourge which has brought such great suffering and loss to so many families.

I, Fr. Dennis Howard, am very honoured to write this testimony about my mother. Presently, I am living and ministering in the United States as a pastor of a community whose vision is to building up Catholic family life, to evangelize and to show hospitality to all. I was ordained on April 28, 1990. Over the past 8 years I have served in the parishes of St. Francis Xavier in Tilbury, St. Vincent de Paul in Windsor, St. Anne's in Tecumseh and am presently pastor of Mt. Zion Catholic Pastoral Centre in Montrose Michigan.

Our father, Henry Albert Howard, a chronic diabetic, presently resides at Copper Terrace in Chatham, Ontario.

I know that my mother had a profound influence on my vocation to the priesthood. I remember at the time of her death those who came to the funeral home and payed homage to this woman who was my mother. Myriads of individuals came forth and thanked us for her life and the influence she had had on their lives. It was a time I will never forget. Shortly afterward, I was faced with the need to make a decision about where my life would lead me. I remember thinking, and believe that the Lord spoke to me asking me, "What kind of legacy will you leave behind when you have left this world?" I thought of my mother and her life. It was then that I realized that I had to say yes to God and do what he was asking of me so that my life would have an effect on others.

Jeannette Anna Blais Howard's life could hardly be characterized as a selfish one. Her life was generously poured out for others. This is what I hope my life will be characterized by. I hope that people will remember me and experience in my life what I and so many others have experienced in the life of Jeannette Howard. A life lived for God and for others.

Father Dennis Howard

Testimonial Dinner Honours Past Presidents of Church

Mrs. Felix Bourassa, Mrs. Gérald Robert, Mrs. Raoul Gagner, Mrs. Victor Trahan
. . . During honorary banquet for Ladies of Pain Court Church

PAIN COURT (Staff) - A testimonial banquet was held at Pain Court's l'Immaculée Conception church Sunday honouring the 12 past presidents of the Ladies of St. Anne.

A plaque bearing the names of the women was also unveiled by church pastor Rev. Léo Charron. Acting president of the club, Mrs. Gérald Robert, assisted in the ceremonies.

Women honoured were: Mrs. Charles Buck, Mrs. Trefflé Gagner, Mrs. Trefflé Laprise, Mrs. Raoul Gagner, Mrs. Hector Trudell, Mrs. Victor Trahan, Mrs. Alcide Caron, Mrs. Wilfrid Robert, Mrs. Gérard Caron, Mrs. William Trudell, Mrs. Gérald Bélanger and Mrs. Léonard Faubert Sr.

Each received a commemorative certificate for her service. Mrs. Gérald Robert was assisted by Mrs. Laurette Raymond for the presentation.

Mrs. Buck, who is convalescing in the Canadianna nursing home, was unable to attend but her husband, Charles, 94, joined the festivities.

Mrs. Felix Bourassa was also honoured for 48 years she has dedicated to the Ladies of St. Anne.

Chatham News 1976

Noces d'or à Pain Court
Golden Anniversaries in Pain Court

60 ans - anniversaire - 60 years

M. et Mme Laurent Maillet	25 février	1995
M. et Mme Henri Béchard	24 novembre	1984
M. et Mme Alfred Jubenville	6 juillet	1980
M. et Mme Francis Couture	22 août	1976
M. et Mme Wilfrid Pinsonneault	16 février	1987

55 ans - anniversaire - 55 years

M. et Mme Henry Cadotte	4 juin	1954
M. et Mme Ulysse Marentette	25 mai	1974
M. et Mme Réginald Martin	20 octobre	1988
M. et Mme Gérard Roy	16 avril	1995
M. et Mme Adolphe Roy	11 novembre	1973
M. et Mme Oscar Robert	18 juillet	1974
M. et Mme Ovila Couture	7 février	1994

50 ans - anniversaire - 50 years

M. et Mme Félix Bourassa	20 mai	1970
M. et Mme Léo Béchard	24 novembre	1965
M. et Mme Urbain Cadotte	19 novembre	1990
M. et Mme Donald Beausoleil	27 août	1996
M. et Mme Hector Béchard	30 octobre	1975
M. et Mme Edmond Béchard	16 juillet	1999
M. et Mme Lawrence Béchard	14 octobre	1991
M. et Mme Wilfrid Bélanger	23 septembre	1963
M. et Mme Raymond Bourassa	26 octobre	1991
M. et Mme Edmond Chauvin	5 août	1991
M. et Mme Réal Caron	24 février	1976
M. et Mme Vital Caron	7 février	1976
M. et Mme Régis Caron	4 novembre	1994
M. et Mme Jean-Paul Caron	27 janvier	1997
M. et Mme Ovila Couture	7 février	1989
M. et Mme Wilfrid Couture	1 décembre	1974
M. et Mme Alphonse Faubert	23 août	1997
M. et Mme James Feenan	26 novembre	1988
M. et Mme Raymond Gagner	20 avril	1990
M. et Mme Gérald Gagner	2 décembre	1989
M. et Mme Edmond Gagner	26 avril	1997
M. et Mme Augustin Laprise	24 avril	1995
M. et Mme Arthème Laprise	3 avril	1998
M. et Mme Lester Lauzon	17 avril	1995

M. et Mme Félix Lucier	26 septembre	1992
M. et Mme Gilbert Laprise	11 février	1968
M. et Mme Wilfrid Laprise	24 septembre	1995
M. et Mme Euclide Martin	28 avril	1992
M. et Mme Joseph Martin	25 janvier	1986
M. et Mme Joseph (Lévis) Martin	28 octobre	1958
M. et Mme Ulysse Martin	29 décembre	1992
M. et Mme Roméo Marentette	24 juin	1998
M. et Mme Bernadin Maure	21 avril	1986
M. et Mme Émile Pinsonneault	16 octobre	1949
M. et Mme Orville Pinsonneault	18 novembre	1991
M. et Mme Gérald Pinsonneault	5 octobre	1996
M. et Mme Josephat Roy	24 novembre	1965
M. et Mme Erminie Sterling	3 février	1970
M. et Mme Joe Scuzs sr.	11 novembre	1980
M. et Mme Victor Trahan	23 juillet	1973
M. et Mme Raymond Thibodeau	23 octobre	1998
M. et Mme Alex Trahan	21 novembre	1980
M. et Mme George Serruys	18 mai	1996
M. et Mme Armand Béchard	12 novembre	1984
M. et Mme Jean-M. Charlebois	1 mai	1998
M. et Mme Robert Crow	26 février	1999
M. et Mme Omer Rossignol	14 février	1999
M. et Mme Frank Gervais	30 avril	1999

45 ans - anniversaire - 45 years

M. et Mme Raymond Béchard	23 juin	1996
M. et Mme Donald Cadotte	19 février	1994
M. et Mme Léonard Faubert	20 novembre	1991
M. et Mme Roland Gagner	5 août	1989
M. et Mme Alphonse Marentette	20 juin	1998
M. et Mme Lawrence Jubenville	15 septembre	1993
M. et Mme Urbain Cadotte	19 novembre	1985
M. et Mme Percy Nugent	22 août	1995
M. et Mme Halarie Rivard	8 juillet	1995
M. et Mme Alphy Robert	7 janvier	1969
M. et Mme Réginald Robert	10 août	1976
M. et Mme Wilfrid Robert	22 avril	1980
M. et Mme Ernest Roy	18 novembre	1989
M. et Mme Francis Roy	10 septembre	1962
M. et Mme Napoléon Roy	28 août	1996
M. et Mme Roland Roy	4 octobre	1986
M. et Mme Bernard Trudell	7 juin	1996
M. et Mme Alfred Pinsonneault	1 juillet	1998
M. et Mme Joseph M. Scuzs	17 mai	1997
M. et Mme Rosaire Sterling	août	1997

40 ans - anniversaire - 40 years

M. et Mme Gérard Béchard	21 novembre	1984
M. et Mme Jim Blair	17 mai	1998
M. et Mme Philippe Blais jr.	4 novembre	1995
M. et Mme Ernest Bondy	2 octobre	1994
M. et Mme Gérard Couture	13 avril	1995
M. et Mme Armand Couture	30 novembre	1979
M. et Mme George Devos	5 octobre	1994
M. et Mme Gérard Marentette	2 avril	1996
M. et Mme Alvin Griffore	28 août	1994
M. et Mme Alphonse Pinsonneault	20 novembre	1973
M. et Mme Lionel Roy	29 juin	1983
M. et Mme Paul Raymond	28 juillet	1988
M. et Mme Réal Martin	2 mars	1983
M. et Mme Hercule Trahan	18 octobre	1955
M. et Mme Réal Charron	2 mars	1983
M. et Mme Orville Goure	2 octobre	1994
M. et Mme Ronald Pinsonneault	23 novembre	1994
M. et Mme Bernard Sterling	30 août	1992
M. et Mme Philippe Blais sr.	27 novembre	1968

Noces d'or et plus - Grande Pointe
Golden Anniversaries and more - Grande Pointe

Josephine Griffore	- 1922 -	Léo Pinsonneault
Grace Létourneau	- 1933 -	Clifford Griffore
Florine Caron	- 1935 -	Trefflé Grifford
Éveline Tétreault	- 1933 -	Réginald Charron
Cécile Grifford	- 1935 -	Alcide Marchand
Amanda Pinsonneault	- 1923 -	Norman Benoit
Beulah Griffore	- 1934 -	Wilfrid Benoit
Edna Delanghe	- 1934 -	Léo Leclair
Céleste Demers	- 1930 -	Eddie Tétreault
Mabel St.Pierre	- 1934 -	Harvey Ouellette
Florence Couture	- 1943 -	Hector Ouellette
Rita Lucier	- 1945 -	Arsène Couture
Stella Lucier	- 1936 -	Armand Lozon
Irène Lozon	- 1931 -	Victor Demars
Valcia Labadie	- 1930 -	Edouard Emery
Alfrida Lauzon	- 1931 -	Hector Lozon
Vélina Béchard	- 1933 -	Horace Bagnell
Bergère Marchand	- 1927 -	George Lauzon
Martha Campbell	- 1924 -	Harvey St.Pierre
Yvonne Roy	- 1942 -	Félix Lucier
Gloria Demers	- 1947 -	Frédérick Caron
Blanche L'Écuyer	- 1945 -	Sylvio Létourneau
Mae Demers	- 1940 -	Rex Cheff

Marguerite Bélisle	- 1941 -	Cléophas Lozon
Joséphine Richer	- 1931 -	Alcide Authier
Jeanne Authier	- 1940 -	Roland Grifford
Loretta Lozon	- 1937 -	Amédée Authier
Marie-Jeanne Benoit	- 1946 -	Aurèle Béchard
Rita Charron	- 1938 -	Clifford Cadotte
Marie-Jeanne Houle	- 1938 -	Philippe Cartier
Aurore Charron	- 1942 -	Raymond Cartier
Doria Lucier	- 1934 -	Hector Tétreault
Dora-Marie Couture	- 1946 -	Harvey Couture
Aldéa Barrette	- 1938 -	Adélard Couture
Constance Bélisle	- 1935 -	Laurent Maillet
Florence Lauzon	- 1928 -	Harvey Lucier
Géraldine Houle	- 1944 -	Harvey Richer
Marion Couture	- 1938 -	Sylva Létourneau
Clarence Belleville	- 1926 -	Vital Caron
Laurentia Barrette	- 1923 -	Evariste Perreault
Laura Lozon	- 1942 -	Aurèle Ouellette
Irène Sinneuve	- 1948 -	Roméo Martin
Maria Létourneau	- 1948 -	Roméo Marentette
Orvella Tétreault	- 1929 -	Dan Lucier
Claire Caron	- 1943 -	Norman L'Écuyer
Marie-Anne Richer	- 1938 -	Elzéar Goure
Léona Fleury	- 1932 -	Mansinie Lozon
Valcia Cartier	- 1934 -	Almo Labadie
Hermine Lozon	- 1934 -	Alfred Tétreault

La Ligue du Sacré-Coeur et ses ambassadrices
Hommage et bénédiction aux zélatrices du Sacré-Coeur de Jésus

Hommage et bénédiction,
Marie-Anne,
pour ton jubilé d'apostolat.

Lors d'une retraite paroissiale le 11 mars 1948, le prédicateur nous invite à fonder "La ligue du Sacré-Coeur" dans la région ainsi que "L'apostolat à la prière" deux organismes de paire.

C'est alors qu'un groupe de paroissiennes se sont embarquées dans le mouvement comme "zélatrices du Sacré-Coeur" sous ma présidence, Caroline Laprise, surveillante de l'agenda mensuel pour une durée de 22 ans, aidée de mes fidèles ambassadrices de livraison.

Nous, les zélatrices, avons été les ambassadrices de bon augure livrant chaque mois le "Messager" de porte en porte, d'une concession à l'autre de la paroisse. On pourrait dire que nous avons à notre compte deux décennies et plus de bénéfices et tout cela pour l'amour du Sacré-Coeur de Jésus.

Affiliés au "Messager du Sacré-Coeur" depuis 22 ans, les autorités nous laissent entendre que la publication sera discontinuée. Eh bien! On ne laisse pas tomber une telle affiliation sans faire du recrutement.

Viens au tour de Marie-Anne Caron de prendre la relève. Occupant le poste de secrétaire-trésorière de notre affiliation depuis sa fondation, elle décide de continuer à propager la dévotion déjà bien établie dans la paroisse par l'entremise d'une vente annuelle de calendriers du Sacré-Coeur. L'année 1998 a marqué le jubilé d'or de son apostolat.

De la part des paroissiens et paroissiennes de Pain Court, je vous remercie pour votre attachement filial au culte divin du Sacré-Coeur de Jésus, un héritage religieux implanté par les bâtisseurs de notre paroisse et à conserver, je l'espère, pour toutes les générations à venir.

Neuvaine perpétuelle au Sacré-Coeur

Coeur de Jésus, nous souvenant de tes nombreuses promesses de bonheur, en particulier dans les Béatitudes, nous nous rappelons avec confiance celles que tu nous as faites par Sainte Marguerite-Marie.

- Je vous donnerai toutes les grâces nécessaires à votre état.
- Je mettrai la paix dans vos familles.
- Je vous consolerai dans vos peines.
- Je serai votre refuge assuré pendant la vie et surtout à l'heure de la mort.
- Je répandrai d'abondantes bénédiction sur toutes vos entreprises.
- Je serai pour les pécheurs un océan de miséricorde.
- Les âmes tièdes deviendront ferventes.
- Les âmes ferventes s'élèveront à une grande perfection.
- Je bénirai les maisons où mon image sera exposée et honorée.
- Je donnerai à mes apôtres le talent de toucher les coeurs les plus endurcis.
- Je graverai en mon Coeur à jamais le nom de ceux et celles qui propageront cette dévotion.
- Je donnerai à ceux et celles qui communieront sans interruption neuf premiers vendredis, la grâce de la pénitence finale et la réception des Sacrements.

Seigneur, nous voulons entrer dans l'esprit d'amour et de liberté que tu manifestes dans ces promesses. Aide-nous à mieux comprendre les pauvres et les opprimés. Fais que nous te reconnaissions dans les membres souffrants de l'humanité. Toi qui vis et règnes pour les siècles des siècles. Amen.

Coeur Sacré de Jésus, j'ai confiance en toi.
Fête du Sacré-Coeur le 19 juin.

Napoléon Emery

He was born in Pain Court, May 10, 1873. He married Léona Létourneau on July 6, 1903. They celebrated their fiftieth wedding anniversary July 6, 1953 at Grande Pointe. Mr. Emery died on June 11, 1976. He was 103 years old.

His wife Léona Létourneau was born September 13, 1884. She was the daughter of Ferdinand Létourneau and Justine Giroux who married in Pain Court, on February 2, 1882. Léona died at Grande Pointe July 14, 1955. She was 71 years old.

From this marriage, were 7 girls and 3 boys. Three died in infancy.

Marie-Anne	married	Paul Lozon	April 24, 1925
Ovéline	married	Joseph Demers	January 15, 1929
Alda	married	Donné Lozon	July 22, 1932
Florida	married	Eddie Lozon	December 27, 1938

Léon-Pierre died July 20, 1934, at 9 years old.

Armand	married	Bertha Lauzon	April 28, 1932
Orville	married	Beulah Labadie	February 2, 1939

Napoléon was the son of Alex Emery and Catherine Réaume who were married in Pain Court February 9, 1858. Napoléon's brothers and sisters were;

Léon	died at	10 months old	April 17, 1861
Edesse	died at	3 1/2 years old	February 18, 1870
Alex	died at	16 years old	February 17, 1870
Joseph	married	Marie Ducèdre	April 28, 1879
François	married	Mary Simard	November 22, 1887
Napoléon	married	Léona Létourneau	July 6, 1903
Henri ?			
Marie ?			

At his death, Napoléon Emery had 35 grandchildren, 25 great-grandchildren, and 2 great-great-grandchildren.

Alex Emery - Napoléon's father

Alex Emery, was the son of Luc Emery and Charlotte Hébert who were married at St. Pierre, lived in Pain Court and later moved to Grande Pointe.

The records show that Luc and Charlotte had 7 sons and 3 daughters.

Charles Emery	married	Catherine Primeau	May 29, 1860
François	married	Rosalie Tétreault	September 10, 1861
Joseph	married	1. Julie Léquille	February 25, 1868
		2. Sophie Primeau	November 27, 1871
Antoine	married	Mathilde Lauzon	February 7, 1875
Jacques-James	married	Henriette Faubert	January 25, 1870
John	married	Philomène Tétreault	May 13, 1862
Alex	married	Catherine Réaume	February 9, 1858
Elizabeth	married	André Riché	November 6, 1884
Edesse	married	David Houle	January 21, 1884
Hélène	married	William Thibodeau	June 23, 1863

Alex Emery died February 17, 1873 at the age of 38 being married 15 years.   Alex and Catherine had 8 children. (See above)

Catherine Réaume - Napoléon's mother
Catherine was the daughter of Paul Réaume (Hippolitte) and Agathe Faubert. Paul Réaume was born at St. Pierre December 3, 1804. Agathe Faubert was the daughter of Jean-Baptiste Faubert and Suzanne Peltier. Her parents were married at l'Assomption in Windsor.

Paul Réaume and Agathe Faubert married at St. Paul's Anglican Church on December 13, 1831 and were reinstated at St. Peter's Church Tilbury January 12, 1833. They had at least two children:

Isidore Rhéaume	married	Hélène Cyr	February 11, 1867
Catherine Rhéaume	married	Alex Emery	February 9, 1858

Catherine became a widow in 1873. On July 22, 1874 she married Jules Tétreault at St. Joseph Church in Chatham. From this union were born 4 daughters, half-sisters to all the Emery family:

Valerie Tétreault	married	Frank Cartier	October 29, 1901
Claire Tétreault	married	Albert Toulouse	November 18, 1901
Rosée Tétreault	1. married	John Toulouse	May 4, 1897
	2. married	Zénophile Lucier	October 27, 1909
Natalie Tétreault	married	James Lozon	November 28, 1893

N.B.   John Toulouse died at 24 years old, the same year he was married to Rosée Tétreault.

Catherine Tétreault widow of Alex Emery died at a ripe old age of 67 after raising two   families.

Much more time is needed, to clarify this history but what I wish to do is to honour the efforts and sacrifices of all members of this honourable family. Léona Létourneau was a special and dedicated woman, who has worked very hard. I remember her going to the market every week in Chatham. Her humorous nature was unique and captivating.

On fête un ancien professeur - 1972

M. Jacques Carron, aux études au séminaire de London, passait des vacances à Pain Court chez ses parents M. et Mme Alphonse Carron. Les élèves du secondaire ont saisi l'occasion d'honorer leur ancien professeur, Jacques Carron, en l'invitant à un banquet préparé pour tous les professeurs de l'école secondaire. M. Jacques Carron avait enseigné jusqu'en juin 1971 à l'école secondaire de Pain Court.

Jacques, nous sommes fiers de toi et nous te sommes redevables pour ta contribution à l'éducation ainsi que pour ta direction auprès de nos jeunes comme chef d'activités du Club de Pain Court. Merci et que Dieu te bénisse et te donne la grâce de persévérance dans ton choix de vocation.

Samedi le 11 juin, 1974, Jacques Carron a reçu le diaconat à la cathédrale St. Pierre de London de Son Excellence, Mgr. E. Carter. Le 10 mai 1975, Rev. Père Jacques Carron fut ordonné prêtre à London. Sa première messe fut célébrée à Pain Court le 11 mai 1975 suivie d'une réception pour tous les paroissiens et les amis et d'un banquet servi en son honneur pour tous ses invités.

Les paroissiens lui offrent leurs félicitations et demandent à Dieu de lui accorder de grandes grâces.

Éphémérides   1970 - 1972

1) Bonne chance à nos jeunes filles qui viennent de graduer de la 13e année et qui continuent leurs études. Louise Emery et Elaine Demers se dirigent vers l'université d'Ottawa. Germaine Martin et Carmelle Cartier s'inscrivent à l'université de Toronto.

2) M. Jean Cartier, fils de Clara Cartier retourne à la base navale de Halifax après un court séjour à Grande Pointe.

3) M. C. Roszell, propriétaire de "Roszell Cold Storage" prend sa retraite après avoir servi la communauté de Pain Court et des environs pendant plus de trente ans. Nous souhaitons bonne chance à M. et Mme Roszell qui ont élu domicile à Chatham. Au nouveau propriétaire, Robert McCormack, nous lui souhaitons la bienvenue.

4) Les parents et amis de Jacques Cartier se rendirent au Collège d'agriculture et de technologie à Ridgetown pour la journée de revue des gradués. Il nous fait honneur en remportant le premier prix pour sa belle maison d'oiseaux qu'il avait construite, le cinquième prix pour son projet de soudage abstrait, le troisième prix pour son mouton qu'il a dressé et il a remporté aussi le trophée présenté par Funks Seed & Company pour son exhibition de blé d'Inde.

5) Seize des élèves de l'école St-Philippe et membres du corps de cadet ont fait un voyage à Pont Rouge Québec.

Plusieurs élèves des 7e et 8e années faisaient partie du groupe de jeunes qui se sont envolés vers le Québec pendant le congé de mars.

Club 4 H 1971

Dernièrement, deux groupes de jeunes filles Club 4 H ont été fondés et parrainés par les Femmes canadiennes-françaises. Des cours seront offerts pendant les mois de janvier, février et mars.

Les Dames de Ste-Anne et la FFCF prendront part à deux journées d'étude et de conférence préparées par le ministère du Commerce et de Développement. Le but de ces deux rencontres est d'étudier pour mieux comprendre l'importance du rôle de la femme dans la préparation du budget familial, apprendre à faire des achats ainsi que l'importance du rôle qu'elle peut jouer dans l'économie. Alma Richer et Caroline Laprise s'engagent comme monitrices en y mettant de l'entrain pour la réussite du Club 4 H.

Le 2 décembre, Mlle Susan Gordon de Chatham présente les certificats et donne les commentaires.

Les jeunes filles qui font partie du Club 4 H ont présenté une soirée spéciale pour leur mère, fin avril 1971.

Les jeunes filles qui font partie du club ont passé une journée intéressante au Tecumseh High School de Chatham récemment. Elles ont présenté une saynète intitulé "First Aid In The Home." Mlle Yvette Couture, journaliste de presse pour le groupe, donnait une courte causerie en français et en anglais au poste (de radio) CFCO. M. Harold Smith l'a félicitée pour son habileté de s'exprimer dans les deux langues officielles du pays.

Club 4 H 1972

Sous la direction d'Alma Richer et de Thérèse Thibodeau, le club 4 H s'adonne aux cours de couture et d'art ménager. Comme fruit de leurs efforts, elles ont tenu un défilé de mode pour les mères. Elles sont entrées en compétition avec d'autres clubs de la région et elles ont rapporté plusieurs prix.

Les dirigeantes ont reçu un vase de cristal comme cadeau d'appréciation.

Sociétés paroissiales de Grande Pointe

Les officiers pour l'année 1971 sont déjà choisis. Ils tracent leurs plans pour l'année en cours.

Club des placiers:
   M. Alvin Griffore, président
   M. Arsène Debaere, vice-président
   M. Omer Benoit, secrétaire-trésorier.

Dames de Ste-Anne:
   Mme Joanne Miller, présidente
   Mme Yollande Griffore, vice-présidente
   Mme Mary Debaere, vice-présidente
   Mme Jeanne Quenneville, trésorière
   Mme Marie-Anne Lebrun, secrétaire

Conseillères:
   Mme Anna Benoit
   Mme Jeannette Benoit
   Mme Clara Cartier
   Mme Rita Demers
   Mme Jeannette Cartier

Chez les dames ça bougent toujours. Le 19 mars 1972, elle ont organisé un souper. Ce fut un véritable succès. Les gens sont venus de près et de loin pour faire honneur à la bonne cuisine.

Pour la Saint-Patrice 1971, les dames invitent leurs amies des paroisses voisines à leur partie de cartes et à leur vente de pâtisseries.

School launch paper drive

Do you know them?

Lower Thames Valley

On se réjouit à la nouvelle que "Lower Thames Valley Conservation Authority" vient d'annoncer que les plans de développement et l'embellissement de tout ce terrain en bordure de Mitchell's Bay à l'étude depuis plusieurs mois seront mis à exécution dès ce printemps 1972. Ce projet nécessitera une dépense qui dépassera $500,000. Les plans prévoient la construction d'une grande marina qui fera l'envie des navigateurs. Malheureusement la pollution des eaux du lac Ste-Claire et de la rivière Ste-Claire s'étend jusqu'à Mitchell's Bay. Cet endroit depuis longtemps déjà est reconnu comme le paradis des amateurs de pêche et de chasse.

October 11, 1974 was the official opening of this 1.5 million dollar Mitchell's Bay Marine Park, a new facility owned and operated by St. Clair Parkway Authority. It was symbolically opened in August by the officials of the Province. However, high water levels in adjacent Lake St. Clair prevented an opening until October. The Park will operate year round.

Future uncertain at Pain Court and Grande Pointe   1972

Graduates and present-day students at Pain Court secondary school were urged last night to do their part to assure the continued existence of the school.

The plea was made during last night's commencement exercises by Dover township clerk Raoul Gagner. The students and parents were reminded of the personal sacrifices made by hundreds of ratepayers over the years to help provide bilingual education in the community.
"No one here can say what the future will be," he said.

In his speech, given in both French and English, Mr. Gagner reminded his audience that in 1910, the Ontario legislature passed Regulation 17 which limited the teaching of French in all Ontario schools to one hour a week.

"After years of bickering, attitudes changed and in 1926 the ruling was changed."
He said the University of Ottawa Normal School was then established to prepare teachers for the bilingual schools in the province.

Congratulatory remarks to the graduates were later offered by Rev. Léo Charron, Rev. Charles Lanoue and Dr. J.R. Button of the Kent Board of Education.

Angela Couture received the general proficiency award and Donna Bourgeois received top honours in "Français." The graduates were introduced by Amédée Emery.
Chatham Daily News

Angela Couture, Donna Bourgeois and Amédée Emery

The graduates were:

Louise-Anne Bélanger	Marie-Hélène Bélanger
Ronald Blair	Donna Bourgeois
Romain Caron	Marie-Claire Carron
Annie Classens	Angela Couture
Linda Couture	Charles Gagner
Jeannine Lachance	Jean-Marie Laprise
Bernice Lozon	Denise Marentette
Edmond Marentette	Jeanne Poissant
Marie-Ange Richer	Denise Roy
Lucille Sterling	Rose-Marie Sterling

Pierre Calvé

At Pain Court Continuation School about 400 of Kent County Secondary school students enjoyed a 90 minute concert program by Pierre Calvé, popular Montréal born singer.

The young singer described as the French Canadian equivalent to Gordon Lightfoot was sponsored by l'association de la jeunesse Franco-ontarienne (AJFO) in cooperation with the Ontario Department of Education and the Québec Minister of Cultural Affairs.

Pierre Calvé made his debut in 1961. After 6 years in the Merchant Marine's he decides to launch his first record "Chansons de ports et de haute mer." From then on he travelled extensively throughout Canada.

Students represented both the French speaking schools of the county and the French language classes in other secondary schools.

Pierre Calvé en tournée

En collaboration avec le:
Ministère des affaires culturelles de Québec
Ministère de l'éducation du gouvernement de l'Ontario
Secrétariat d'état du gouvernement canadien.

Pierre Calvé est en tournée à travers les régions du nord de l'Ontario, le sud-ouest, la vallée de l'Outaouais en 1970 - 1971.

Aventurier avant tout, il abandonne la marine marchande pour la chanson. Mais on n'abandonne pas une vie pour une autre sans en garder de merveilleux souvenirs. Dans ses chansons il prolonge cette aventure en racontant la mer, les marins, les ports, et les pays de soleil qu'il a bien connus. Il émane de lui une fraîcheur et une sincérité qui lui attirent l'amour de tous.

Il est d'origine montréalaise. Il abandonne ses études à l'âge de 16 ans et s'engage dans la marine marchande et navigue pendant 6 ans. Au printemps 1961, il débute à "La Piouke" boîte à chansons située sur la plage Bonaventure en Gaspésie.

À l'automne de la même année il lance son premier microsillon "Chansons de ports et haute mer." Le succès de ce premier disque détermine sa carrière. Pierre Calvé va voyager par la chanson.

D'autres voix se sont ajoutées au répertoire de Pierre Calvé outre Monique Leyrac et Pauline Julien.

Adieu M. le professeur Edmond Chauvin

Banquet testimonial en l'honneur de M. Edmond Chauvin le 19 mai 1974, au sous-sol de l'église Immaculée Conception. Accompagné de son épouse Albertine, environ 250 personnes sont venues lui rendre hommage.

M. Edmond Chauvin prend sa retraite après 23 années d'enseignement à l'école secondaire de Pain Court. C'est en reconnaissance pour ses longues années de dévouement que sa famille, ses anciens élèves et ses amis ont su démontrer leur appréciation.

Homme dévoué à la tâche en tout temps, dédié à sa carrière sans oublier ses devoirs comme époux et père de 8 enfants, il a su gagner l'admiration et le respect de tous. Enseignant, sa spécialité était l'histoire et la géographie. Il ne faut pas oublier non plus les groupes de cadets qu'ils a entraînés tout en leur inculquant la fierté de la Patrie.

Le banquet fut présidé par M. Louis-Joseph Richer. Le Père Léo Charron souhaite la bienvenue à tous. Pour l'occasion, c'est M. Amédée Emery qui prononce les éloges. À la table d'honneur nous remarquons M. Raymond Thibodeau président du conseil paroissial et M. Roland Bélanger représentant et président de la commission scolaire de l'école secondaire de Pain Court. Les chants ont été exécutés par la chorale de l'école Ste-Catherine sous la direction de Mme Angéline Marentette.

C'est avec regret que nous le voyons partir mais il va sans dire que nous lui souhaitons de grandes joies et espérons de tout coeur qu'il jouira de ses années de retraite en se récréant auprès de sa belle famille et saura jouir d'un repos bien mérité.

Père Charles Lanoue - 1971

Ne demandez pas aux citoyens de Grande Pointe ce qui se passe. Ils sont trop occupés.

Nous nous arrêtons un instant pour vous dire que nous sommes très heureux de vous annoncer que le Rev. Père Charles Lanoue, est de retour parmi nous après un voyage en Europe où il a eu le grand plaisir d'assister à la grande réprésentation de la Passion à Oberromergau, un spectacle inoubliable. Durant les 22 jours, il visita l'Allemangne, la Belgique, l'Italie, la France et l'Angleterre.

Under the capable leadership of Father Lanoue, parish priest at St. Philippe's Church in Grande Pointe, the tour travellers returned from a pilgrimage to Rome and the Holy Land. The group spent 3 days in Rome which included an audience with His Holiness Pope Paul VI.

A flight to Tel Aviv took them to the Holy Land. Points of interest visited during their stay included: The Mount of Olives, Place of the Ascension, a view of Palm Sunday Road and a solemn entry to the Holy Sepulchre. Those who accompanied Father Lanoue on this biblical journey were: Marguerite Caron, Sister Rosina, Lila Chauvin, Emma Duplessis, Bernard Goure, Rev. E.H. Robert, Marie-Alice Peltier, Elsie VanOverbeke, Lorraine Laprise, Mary-Alice O'Neil and Eva Tremblay. The trip was most successful and thoroughly enjoyed by all.

Un merci à Mgr. A. Caron qui a eu la bonté de desservir la paroisse pendant l'absence du curé.

Carnet de chez nous . . .
1970 - 1975

These buildings were built in 1907 - 08. The house was built in 1905
and the garage was built around 1945. It burned down in the fall of 1972.

En septembre1972, hélas, c'est le feu qui vient ravager le garage à la maison paternelle Laprise. C'est dans ce bâtiment que les garçons exécutent les réparations d'équipement aratoires, les tracteurs et les camions. Heureusement que Jean-Marie s'en est échappé, sauf pour quelques brûlures, lorsque le feu envahit tout le bâtiment. Les pompiers de la région, connus pour leur efficacité et leur promptitude, ont fini par protéger la maison du dégât. Ceci cause une suite d'inconvénients vue les récoltes pressantes d'automne.

Au printemps, 1973, nous nous préparons à reconstruire le bâtiment détruit par le feu. C'est d'une importance primaire de réaménager tout ce que le feu avait ravagé afin que les opérations sur la ferme se continuent.

Comme toujours cette décennie a été marquée par la mort de plusieurs de mes proches à Pain Court. En juillet 1973, ma soeur Léontine, atteinte du cancer du sein et souffrante depuis 5 ans, nous laisse, à 47 ans, pour recevoir sa récompense éternelle. Elle a enseigné à Pain Court, Welland et London les cours de français.

En juin 1974, mon père Adolphe Roy meurt subitement à Chatham à l'âge de 79 ans, lorsqu'il s'occupait du nettoyage automatique de son tracteur. À ce moment j'étais à Hamilton pour le concours de Français des écoles secondaires du Sud-Ouest. Marie-Ange Richer et Colette Laprise, deux étudiantes de l'école secondaire de Pain Court, nous représentaient ce jour-là. J'étais accompagnée d'Alma et de Joseph Richer. Pour moi ce fut une grande perte lorsque j'ai eu à envisager la mort subite de mon père.

Beaucoup de peine a envahi mon coeur encore une fois en 1975 lorsque Alma Richer nous a laissés, à 47 ans, pour recevoir sa récompense. Elle aussi à été une victime du cancer du sein.

Hélas, quelques temps plus tard nous envisagions la mort de Yvette, fille de Raoul et Theresa Roy, garde-malade à la salle d'urgence de l'hôpital St-Joseph de Chatham, le 14 septembre 1977, dans la fleur de l'âge. Elle avait 25 ans.

Beaucoup d'angoisse a envahi mon coeur pendant ces années chargées d'épreuves. Cependant, la vie doit continuer même si c'est pénible. En février 1972, j'étais gravement malade et j'ai dû subir à Ottawa, une opération pour vésicule biliaire. Durant deux mois de convalescence j'ai demeuré avec des amies, Yvette et Suzanne Duval, et mes soeurs, Loretta Roy et Anne Aline Barrette.

Il faut reprendre courage à deux mains car plusieurs transitions sont d'une importance supérieure.

. En avril 1974 nous sommes heureux d'accueillir dans notre grande famille Lucille Benoit, fille de Wilfrid Benoit et Beulah Griffore. Elle devient l'épouse de notre fils Jean-Marie. Ils s'établissent dans la maison paternelle. C'est alors que je déménage à notre chalet au Parc Rondeau.

La vie continue parsemée de joies et de peines. Après la mort de mon père en juin 1974, voici que Dieu laisse tomber une rose sur mon chemin.

Le premier "Bal des Roses," organisé par Mme Louis Bezaire présidente régionale de la FFCF à Windsor, a eu lieu à la fin juin 1974. C'était à l'occasion du 15e anniversaire de la FFCF dans la région du Sud-Ouest Ontarien. C'est à ce gala que l'on choisit de décorer plusieurs dames des sections de "l'Ordre du mérite" pour leur dévouement inlassable envers les causes franco-ontariennes. À cet effet, ces dames de Pain Court furent décorées: Alma Richer, Caroline Laprise et Albertine Chauvin.

Beaucoup de peine et d'angoisse habitent chez moi durant ces années. Ce n'est pas toujours facile de faire face aux épreuves et de continuer sur le chemin qui est le nôtre.

Raoul Roy King

I anticipate sharing with you a short episode of my life on the farm in Pain Court. I lived at the old homestead of my grandfather Thomas Roy where my father Adolphe was born and lived most of his life.

When I was young, going to school, I always dreamed of going to other countries and help them to farm in a really efficient way. My mind kept wondering all over the world trying to determine where to go first. Had no idea until one day Napoléon King asked me casually if I would go to Hawaii for Pride Hybrid Canada and Pride USA to put up a dryer for corn and Sorghum. He emphasized that I was a guy for the job and I would get along well with the people of that country.

By January 6 1971, my cousin Jos King died suddenly and I had signed as his backer for mail delivery for R.R.7 Chatham. At the time this position had to be filled but fortunately after a short period there was a new government assignment to the job of mailman. This made way for me to leave for Hawaii along with Roland Bélanger, Rosaire Pinsonneault and Napoléon King. Blake Snoblen who sold the dryers to Metcalfe Farms Hawaii Inc., arrived at the Laui Airport Kelawea, Kauai to greet us with the manager Bob Nui. We were escorted to the living quarters. "The Plantation Mansion" a super luxury place operated by a young couple from Los Angeles, Mike and Charlene Dyer.

This 4000 acre sugar plantation which went bankrupt was leased to Pride Co. for seed corn and sorghum. Seed corn was shipped by air cargo from "Laui Airport" to Detroit for planting here in Canada about May 1st. Sorghum was grown for cattle feed in conjunction with Parker Ranch which was the largest cattle ranch in the world 300,000 acres and 250,000 heads of cattle, all whitehead Herefords. As the crop of sorghum matured, millions of birds conglomerated on the crop and ruined it. A few late varieties were harvested.

Overall, the farm workers would come to me with the problems, no matter what, we had fun but it was gratifying to help them out. If I was stuck, I would improvise some way. I finally completed the erection of the dryer complex. It was getting close to May, my departure date. The foreman begged me to go home to do my farm work and return after but this was out of the question.

Hawaii is such a beautiful place to live. Volcanos do erupt now and then, he Himea Canyon which they call the grand canyon of the Pacific, they have more sunshine days per year than any other place with 75° to 85° daily temperatures. You smell year round, the bougainvillea, the orchids and the bird of paradise.

The island of Maui is known for a Leper colony.

Toward the last days, I was getting sad because the Hawaiians are loving and kind, that's the way they live their lives. There was a farewell "Luau" party. I commended them on their way of life and promised I would return sooner or later. I returned 12 times conducting tours on the islands as a tour guide. It was the most heartwarming and gratifying moments of my life.

Aloha! Aloha Nui.

Alexander Baldwin was the consulting firm for Metcalfe Farms Hawaii Inc. On my arrival to Africa in 1975, I was amazed as Alexander Baldwin was the consulting firm there also.

Raoul Roy (King)

"Pain Court Kings"

Le Club des placiers organisa un "Steak Barbecue" le 26 avril 1974 en l'honneur des "Pain Court Kings." Plusieurs sont venus se récréer. Après le souper préparé par les dames, il y eut présentation de trophée aux joueurs.

M. Paul Bélanger à titre de capitaine de l'équipe introduit les joueurs et le nouvel instructeur M. Norbert Béchard qui viendra donner main-forte à l'équipe et au gérant Marc Chauvin. Il remercia tous les bienfaiteurs et le Club des placiers qui leur donnent l'appui qui semblent les encourager. Les méritants des trophées étaient Charles Gagner, Brian Pickering, Gregg Cadotte, Len Lucier, Gary Roy, Jean-Paul Raymond et Rick Béchard. Félicitations.

Départ des Soeurs Grises de la Croix en 1972

Le 4 août 1950 la paroisse de Pain Court accueille l'arrivée des Soeurs Grises de la Croix d'Ottawa et le 21 mai 1972 c'est à regret que les paroissiens envisagent leur départ après vingt-deux ans de service et de dévouement auprès de la jeunesse étudiante de la région.

La réalité est peut-être un peu dure. Les Soeurs Grises de la Croix d'Ottawa doivent nous quitter pour les mêmes raisons que les Soeurs St-Joseph l'ont fait en 1949. La communauté ne peut nous fournir des remplaçantes pour celles qui nous quittent. Ceci nous amène à la fête d'aujourd'hui.

Plusieurs anciennes religieuses se sont jointes aux religieuses de Pain Court, St-Joachim et Windsor.

Au cours d'une messe concélébrée par le Père Léo Charron, Mgr. Augustin Caron et le Père Oscar Martin, des adresses ont été lues au nom des paroissiens par M. Edmond Chauvin, Mme Marie-Anne Faubert, M. Jean-Marie Laprise, Mlle Marie-Ange Richer, Mlle Claudette Bélanger et Mlle Kathy Letts.

M. Louis-Joseph Richer présidait l'assemblée. André Roy et Jacinthe Marentette ont présenté le "bouquet spirituel" aux religieuses. Soeur Yvonne Charbonneau se fit l'interprète pour la Mère Provinciale et sa communauté.

La chorale des étudiants des écoles primaire et secondaire sous l'habile direction de Mme Angéline Marentette et de l'organiste, M. Amédée Emery, ont fait entendre des chants très émouvants.

Suite à la célébration liturgique, une réception et un souper préparé par les dames de Ste-Anne attendaient tous ceux et celles qui s'étaient rendus pour exprimer ouvertement leur reconnaissance.

La salle parossiale émanait un air de fête. Le décor convergeait vers une grande table recouverte d'une nappe blanche et couronnée d'un baldaquin confectionné en papier crépon bleu et blanc. Le tout faisait contraste avec un menu de plats et de plateaux variés propice à renouer les connaissances du passé entre religieuses et anciens élèves ou encore entre religieuses, parents et amis, ou simplement pour récupérer les souvenirs des religieuses qui sont passées chez-nous.

Soeur Marie-Gisèle a été la première supérieure du couvent et à juste titre la pionnière dans la paroisse. Les chevilles ouvrières qui lui ont succédée sont Mère Agnès de Jésus, très sympathique et gentille, Mère Marie-Eulalie, très aimée et qui a su comprendre le milieu; les enseignantes telles que Mère Marie-Andréa, sympathique et compréhensive suivie de Mère Antoine de Padoue, Mère Émmanuel, Mère Marie de la Providence, Mère Jeanne d'Arc, Mère Aimée du Sauveur, chacune compétente dans leur domaine; Mère Charles-Auguste, 7 ans directrice à l'école Ste-Catherine, a laissé sa marque de professionnalisme dans tous les paliers éducatifs; Mère Jean du Sacré-Coeur, Mère Jean-Marc, Mère Béatrix d'Assise, missionnaire au Basutoland (Lesotho) pendant une trentaine d'années environ et Mère Bruyère l'ont suivie à titre de directrice; Mère Jeanne-Marie 11 ans en 1ère année, suivie de Mère Thérèse Laramée; Mère Françoise-Rachel 8e année, et plusieurs autres d'entre elles qui se sont dévouées sans compter au service éducationnel dans notre paroisse.

Vers les six heures et demie des tablées de convives se sont rassemblés pour un souper d'adieu préparé soigneusement par les Dames ce qui terminait une journée mémorable dans l'histoire de la paroisse.

Le Rempart juin 1972
(en partie)

De gauche à droite : Soeur Yvonne Charbonneau, Amédée Emery,
Mère Charle-Auguste, Andréa Courtemanche, Mère Claire-Aline.

Adieu à l'école Ste-Catherine

L'école primaire Ste-Catherine de Pain Court disparaît pour faire place à une nouvelle école au caractère moderne qui deviendra le siège d'éducation de nos jeunes.

C'est toujours avec une certaine tristesse que nous voyons disparaître un bâtiment qui contient, pour plusieurs d'entre nous, des souvenirs d'enfance qui nous sont très chers. Depuis près de 45 ans, l'école Ste-Catherine recevait les jeunes de la paroisse pour les éduquer et les diriger vers des études supérieures.

Seul le souvenir demeurera dans la mémoire de ceux qui l'ont fréquentée, mais la génération qui vient ne connaîtra qu'une école plus moderne pour satisfaire à des besoins éducatifs différents.

Les travaux de construction progressent à grands pas et nous sommes assurés que l'école nouvelle sera terminée en septembre 1972.

Hommage à Soeur Marie du Calvaire et Soeur Adèle

Nous les contribuables et la gente scolaire sommes redevables pour l'enseignement fructueux reçu des religieuses de la communauté des Soeurs Saint-Joseph de London.

Soeur Marie du Calvaire, née Marie Parent, était directrice de la nouvelle école Ste-Catherine à Pain Court en 1929 - 30. À cette même école j'ai eu le privilège de recevoir en 9e et 10e années une instruction bilingue, sous la direction et l'enseignement de Soeur Marie du Calvaire. En 1932 Soeur Adèle accepte une position au niveau secondaire 9e et 10e.
.

Soeur Marie Parent est décédée le 9 avril 1978 au Mont St. Joseph, London maison mère des Soeurs St-Joseph. Pendant plus de 40 ans, elle s'est dévouée à l'enseignement bilingue dans les écoles de Belle-Rivière, Windsor, Sarnia et Pain Court.

Soeur Marie du Calvaire

Soeur Marie-Adèle

Soeur Marie-Adèle, née Joséphine Réaume, est originaire de la région de Windsor.

Éducatrice de grande renommée, elle réside présentement au Mont Saint-Joseph de London. Jeune de 95 ans elle jouit d'une retraite bien méritée.

De temps en temps, j'ai eu le bonheur de la revoir à des fonctions paroissiales. Son visage souriant et ses yeux pétillants ramènent les meilleurs souvenirs du temps où j'étais sous sa tutelle à l'école de Continuation de Pain Court.

Femmes éducatrices, femmes remplies de persévérance et d'amour, vous portez haut le flambeau de votre courage afin d'éclairer les générations de l'avenir

Mes salutations à toutes les religieuses qui sont passées à Pain Court

Soeurs de St. Joseph de London - 1923 - 1950

Sr. Anna-Marie, première directrice en 1923; Sr. Hilaire, directrice- adjointe: Sr. Scolastique, supérieure; Sr. Laurentia, Sr. Hélèna, Sr. Marie du Calvaire, Sr. Ste-Croix, Sr Marie-Antoinette, Sr. Adèle, Sr. François-Xavier, Sr. Cécile, Sr. Béatrice, Sr. Médard, Sr. Ernestine, Sr. Marie des Anges, Sr. Marie du Perpétuel Secours, Sr. Marie-Patrice, Sr. Jean-Marie, Sr. Urbain, Sr. Annette, Sr. Ferdinand, musicienne.

Soeurs Grises de la Croix d'Ottawa

Au Secondaire - 1950 - 1972
Mère Gisèle, enseignante et 1ère supérieure, Mère Andréa, Mère Lionel, Mère Aimée du Sauveur, Mère Antoine de Padoue, Mère Marie de la Providence, Mère Emmanuel, Mère Marie-Eulalie supérieure.

Directrices au primaire:
Mère Charles-Auguste, directrice, Mère Jean du Sacré-Coeur,
Mère Jean-Marc, Mère Elisabeth Bruyère, Mère Béatrix d'Assise.

Autres passées à Pain Court:
Mère Jeanne-Marie, Mère Evangéline, Mère Françoise-Rachel, Mère Germaine Gingras, Mère Marie-des-Buisonnets, Mère Elzéar,
Mère Bernadette-de-Jésus, Mère St. Albert, Mère Gilles-Bernard, Mère Ste-Brigitte, Mère Thérèse du Roasaire.

Ref. - Chroniques École de Ste-Catherine

Junior Sculptor

Doing his part to help dress up the library at École Ste-Catherine in Pain Court is 11-year-old Jean-Marc Laprise, son of Mr. and Mrs. Gérard Laprise, who made several plasticine animals in the past week. Here Jean-Marc shows some of his work to school principal Antonio Guénette.

Chatham Daily New 1972

Mr. A. Guénette became the new principal at St. Catherine school after the departure of our beloved "Soeurs Grises de la Croix d'Ottawa."

Club d'âge d'or à Pain Court
Gardons notre héritage de " vivre en grande famille"

Voici une occasion de détente bien méritée pour les fidèles pionniers qui se sont dévoués inlassablement auprès des organisations communautaires et paroissiales. Ici et là commencent à apparaître des clubs d'âge d'or dans nos communautés francophones. À Pain Court, c'est M. Edmond Chauvin qui s'occupe des démarches à suivre pour établir un tel club, aidé d'un exécutif élu parmi les aînés intéressés.

C'est le 15 janvier 1975 que le premier club d'amitié fait son début. Les aînés se sont rassemblés pour se divertir avec une partie de cartes, un passe-temps qui leur sera favorable durant les mois d'hiver.

Un goûter fut servi à la clôture de l'après-midi. On a dégusté du bon fromage, avec un choix de vin et une sélection de pâtisseries soigneusement préparées par les membres. Nous vous souhaitons bon succès dans vos futures entreprises.

Soyez conscients que ce centre d'activités et de projets est l'unique lieu qui saura manifester le besoin de rencontres intimes et la réalisation d'aide mutuelle envers un idéal "Celui de vivre en grande famille." Souvent on cherche ce que l'on peut donner à un autre . . . mais le plus beau cadeau qu'on puisse faire à quelqu'un c'est de donner son temps: visiter un vieillard isolé; se rendre utile envers ceux qui cherchent de l'aide car donner de son temps c'est donner de soi-même.

L'Archevêque Duguay disait "Que la vie passe vite," je n'ai pas le temps de tout faire ce que je voudrais. " La vie ne se mesure pas par sa durée dans le temps mais par son intensité et par sa qualité d'amour." En autre mot, est-ce que j'ai fait tout le bien que j'aurais pu faire aujourd'hui ou est-ce que je me suis laissé prendre par toutes sortes d'excuses.

Missions d'Haïti

Les élèves de Pain Court font un don par l'entremise de leur président M. Charles Gagner. Ils présentaient au Rev. Père Charron, curé de la paroisse, une bourse au montant de $150.00 à être remise aux missions d'Haïti. Cet argent était le résultat d'une campagne que les élèves de l'école avaient entrepris pour amasser des bouteilles vides dans le canton de Dover.

La coopération des élèves et la générosité des citoyens donnèrent le résultat ci-dessus. Bravo!!

Soeur Marguerite Roy m.i.c.
Son désir de servir apporte un p'tit coin de soleil en terre haïtienne

Nous étions heureux de recevoir une des nôtres, Sr. Marguerite Roy m.i.c., soeur de Mme Marie-Anne Caron, Gérard Roy, et Napoléon Roy de Pain Court.

Elle profitait d'une dernière visite avec ses parents et ses amis avant son départ pour "Des Chapelles," petite mission en Haïti. Ceux qui ont eu le bonheur de jaser avec elle se sont rendus compte de sa grande joie de pouvoir servir et alléger le sort de ces pauvres et défavorisés.

D'avance, nous sommes assurés qu'elle se dévouera sans réserve auprès de ces humains et nous lui souhaitons le plus grand succès dans sa tâche difficile mais édifiante.

Soeur Marguerite, fille de Henri Roy et d'Anna Pinsonneault, est née le 27 novembre 1927 à Pain Court. Elle fit son entrée au couvent des Soeurs Missionnaires de l'Immaculée Conception à Montréal le 1er février 1948 à l'âge de 20 ans. Depuis quelques années déjà, elle se prépare pour les missions étrangères.

En avril 1975, elle s'embarque pour la mission "Des Chapelles" et au "Dispensaire de Charpentier" pour cinq ans d'apostolat. En 1980, elle revient au Canada pour un bref repos et s'embarque une deuxième fois pour Haïti où elle continue son travail parmi les plus démunis. Cette fois-ci une maladie très grave l'empêche de compléter son engagement. C'est à regret qui'elle doit quitter ses chers protégés.

Pendant dix ans environ, Soeur Marguerite a laissé une bonne part d'elle-même dans son champ d'apostolat missionnaire ouvrant sur son passage un p'tit coin de soleil en terre haïtienne.

L'amour mène loin . . .Cet amour a germé dans le coeur généreux de Soeur Marguerite et en retour ses chers haïtiens lui ont donné un surcroît d'amour.

Our Relationship to Haiti

Since 1972 our parish of Pain Court has supported and helped to develop the parish of "Ste-Claire de Dessalines" in Haïti. Father Pierre Alix manages one of the poorest parishes of the diocese. He has been in Haïti the last 25 years and 20 years in our adopted parish. He has 4 chapels in the area and tries to serve about 60,000 souls, far too much for one devoted priest. Furthermore, he oversees some of the construction work with very little resources.

In 1971, the parish council in Pain Court were searching to adopt a parish in a developing country and to provide direct aid to some missionary work. It was through the diligent interview of the Sister Germaine Gingras of Pain Court and Sister Christine Cyr of Haïti, both from the order of Sisters of Charity, that Father Alix accepted our donations from year to year to build schools and provide necessary equipment to these schools.

In 1977, Roland Bélanger and Napoléon Roy planned a trip to Haïti to visit the development of our new parish in Haïti. They also visited Sister Marguerite Roy, Napoléon Roy's sister, doing missionary work there at the Charpentier Clinic near Les Cayes, bringing with them an extra gift for her mission.

In 1974 Marie-Ange Richer won a trip to Haïti for being runner up in the "Mlle Sud-Ouest Ontario" contest. She insisted that it was not a beauty contest but a speaking contest to promote the French Culture in Ontario.

She gave the highlights of her trip while working with children at "Pep73" recreation program in her home community of Pain Court.

"We were there to promote tourism in Haïti," said Marie-Ange. Haïti is still a dictatorship under Jean-Claude Duvalier, but is opening up more to the rest of the world. While there we had a very tight schedule and we really never had a chance to do any sightseeing. "We were closely guarded by police because they didn't want anything bad to happen to any of us."

During the tour, Marie-Ange and other girls met with dictator Jean-Claude Duvalier but the conversations were strictly on a formal basis. Marie-Ange Richer of Pain Court was chosen along with 60 other girls to be guests of the Haïtian government.

Ralph's Mission to Haïti

In November 1978, I, Ralph B. King (Roy), Agro specialist and machinery technician, was asked by Napoléon King (King Grain) to consider going to Haïti as a French interpreter and a worker with Chapman's men to put up a million bushel storage silos, 10 of them at 10,000 bushels each at Port-au-Prince, 20 miles outside the port.

I had just returned from a 6 week stay in Africa but accepted the offer for further experience and sincerely hoped it would not be as challenging as Africa. Took a flight from Detroit to Port-au-Prince where I was met by co-workers already there and settled at a luxury hotel on the mountain overlooking the harbour. Hotel EBO -LILI was chic with red tablecloths.

I surely did not appreciate my first night there. Dogs fighting, roosters crowing, saxophones playing, Samba, Rhumba beats at 2-3 o'clock in the morning; people on drugs as you know go on all night. After a hectic night the workers were up at 5a.m., breakfast at 6 a.m. and to the working site by 7a.m. A dozen men from Chatham all worked as a team. I fulfilled my work as interpreter, hired and fired the native help. After a few days of work, they asked to be paid but they never returned to work. We had a minibus driver on duty 24 hours a day as he had sleeping accommodations within the bus. We needed transportation to pick up materials and find what was highly needed.

Fortunately, we had two Ford pick-ups shipped from Chatham for our use. They had government plates on them. As we travelled the highway, the locals would move off the road to let us by. Everyone in Port-au-Prince knew we were Canadians building the "Minoterie" Flour Mill. It operated 24 hours a day, 7 days a week because of the humid climate. The plant was operated by Canadian Millers, as wheat is supplied by Canada through the world bank, free of charge, for 50 years. Otherwise the country would starve.

After a month on site, I decided to go visit Sister Marguerite Roy, at a mission in "Les Cayes" south-west of Haïti. I had managed to bring her 4 lbs. of Happy Hour Popcorn. The locals had never heard of popcorn and had never eaten any popcorn. Sister Marguerite was overwhelmed to see I could take time to go visit her and she cried. When I handed her a gift for the mission in US money, she cried again. Then I sat down with all the nuns at the mission for a delicious meal and made them laugh. They were so happy to see someone from home. I commended them for their mission of love and compassion. They were operating a medical clinic 2 km. away from Les Cayes. People came for various treatment as well as food. As I left the mission I promised I would send money every 4 months for beans and rice.

Sister Marguerite returned to Canada after a 1st five year term and happily went back again to Haïti to continue caring for the many sick. However, in 1985, she became too sick and had to leave Haïti, the mission of her dreams. "Great men or women are not judged by what they do for themselves, but rather what they do for others."

Back to the hotel, back to work. As of today, Haïti is still one of the poorest countries in the western hemisphere. In 1947, the US and Canada made agreements to help this country out of starvation. US donated 12, V12 diesel catt generators to power the plants. Canada gave wheat, built and operated the flour mills for 50 years. The US have maintained the generators, Canada is running the Mills and they are still starving; it seems so tragic. "We are God's chosen people."

Ralph King
Pain Court, Ontario

Inauguration du Centre culturel Brébeuf

Le 26 janvier 1975 - Dr. Robert Holmes M.P. coupe le ruban et Mme Alma Richer contemple avec fierté l'ouverture du Centre. Chez nous, nos organismes canadiens-français se dévouent tous à l'épanouissement de la culture française. C'est après maintes rencontres et discussions que des gens doués d'initiative et d'imagination ont pu, en ce 26 janvier prendre part avec fierté à l'ouverture du Centre Jean de Brébeuf de Pain Court. Mme Alma Richer, coordinatrice dévouée, grâce à sa persévérance et à sa ténacité, a obtenu une subvention du gouvernement avec l'aide de Guy Chevrette et du Dr. Holmes député de Lambton Kent et de Jean-Marie Comeau de Sudbury. Dr. Holmes s'est dit heureux de participer à une activité qui, d'après lui, sert à développer l'unité Canadienne. Mme Ursule Leboeuf de Pointe-aux-Roches présente, au nom des gens, une gerbe de fleurs à la présidente Mme Richer. C'est la réalisation d'un rêve. C'est avec la coopération de chacun que l'oeuvre se continuera. Le chanteur Robert Potvin de Sarnia a su tenir les spectateurs en suspens jusqu'à la fin de la soirée.

Congrès National de FFCF à Ottawa
mai 1974

Parmi les décorées spéciales à l'occasion du soixantième anniversaire de la Fédération figuraient deux membres de notre région, Mme Thérèse Hamel de Windsor et Mme Alma Richer de Pain Court.

Chaleureuses félicitations à ces deux dames dévouées. Toutes les dames se quittèrent le coeur rempli de la joie de ces belles agapes et avec un renouvellement d'ardeur pour notre Fédération.

Il faut assister à un congrès pour en reconnaître la grandeur, jouir d'une telle ambiance et constater la fraternité qui existe entre toute et chacune des membres de notre Fédération d'un coin du pays à l'autre. Un congrès national, c'est beau, c'est grand, c'est instructif, c'est émouvant. Il faut le voir pour le savoir.

La Fédération des femmes canadiennes-françaises - 1976

Le projet "Programme service communautaire pour étudiants" a démarré le 3 juin 1976 à la suite d'une subvention obtenue récemment par la FFCF.

Le projet PSCE vise à l'initiation et à la participation de la jeunesse en ce qui a trait à la culture, aux arts, enfin à tout ce qui est disponible durant les mois de juin, juillet et août. Il y aura exposition des travaux accomplis au début septembre. L'enthousiasme règne actuellement parmi les jeunes désireux de poursuivre ces cours où ils pourront développer leurs talents tout en se récréant dans un local favorable sous la surveillance des dames de la FFCF qui se dévouent au bien-être de la jeunesse.

Mention spéciale dédiée à Mme Laurette Raymond.

St. Clair College Campus

According to an article written by Win Miller September 1974, Thames Campus of St. Clair College has completed the purchase of 110 acres in the city and neighbouring Dover township as a site for permanent college buildings.

C. W. Case, chairman of the Kent advisory Committee told city council Monday acquisition of the property on the River Road Dover Township took effect Sept 3, 1974. He thanked council for its cooperation in planning for the permanent college facilities.

The college has picked up the option on an additional 60 acres, most of it in Dover township, at the northwest corner of the Bearline and River Road, the Civalier farm.

Sid Keen, the campus director, said no decision has been made on the start of construction. He said enrolment has exceeded forecasts.

The college under agreement will provide approved drainage for the campus property. The three way pact stipulates the college will not oppose applications for installation of municipal services under the local improvement act.

This new campus will prove to be a much needed improvement to our community as it will provide a learning faculty for graduating students wishing to complete or further their education, be it academic, scientific, technical or commercial.

Tiers ordre à Pain Court - 1948

Rev. Père Bernard Robert capucin
Rev. Père Francis   capucin
Rev. Père Arthur   o.f.m. cap.

À la demande des Pères Capucins de Blenheim, un groupe imposant de paroissiens se sont réunis à l'église de Pain Court pour former un noyau local composé de Tertiaires voués à l'esprit de Saint François et d'adhérents zélés du Tiers Ordre de Saint François.

Le 26 mai 1950, nous comptons une vingtaine de membres qui se sont engagés à propager et à étudier attentivement la Règle et les dévotions franciscaines, le cérémonial, le catalogue des indulgences afin de pouvoir découvrir et imiter le véritable esprit de Saint François, patron de l'action catholique..

La fraternité du Tiers Ordre est une famille où tous les frères et soeurs se connaissent, se soutiennent, rayonnent de piété et se dévouent aux bonnes oeuvres. Plusieurs membres se sont engagés, soit comme membres actifs de la Société de Saint-Vincent de Paul ou comme personnes qui ont déjà oeuvré au sein de cet organisme providentiel.

Les membres associés qui ont fait profession

1ère rangée - g. à d. Père Bernard Robert, Antoinette Dénommé, Cécile Béchard, Rose-Anna Caron, Bella Thibodeau, Délina Houle, Bella Martin, Zulma Trudell, Père Ulysse Lefaive.

2e rangée - g. à d. Élizabeth Daniel, Eva Trahan, Blanche St-Pierre, Albertine Chauvin, Alma Richer, Aline Caron, Evéline Bourassa.

3e rangée - g. à d. Célina Pinsonneault, Alexina Caron, Alma Pinsonneault, Thérèse Charlebois, Hélène St-Pierre, Ida Bourassa, Anna St-Pierre.

4e rangée - g. à d. Armand Béchard, Trefflé Laprise, Alphonse Marentette, Gérard Caron, Bernard Charlebois, Louis-Joseph Richer, Adrien Caron, Edmond Chauvin, Arthur Houle, Télesphore Dénommé.

Caroline Laprise - Aide au photographe

Rev. Père Bernard Robert o.f.m

"A mesure que le grand doigt inexorable du temps tourne les pages du grand livre de la vie, on réalise combien l'homme est éphémère! Un cri, on entre et c'est la vie, un cri, on sort et c'est la mort."

Rev. Bernard Robert 1976 o.f.m.

Hommage et reconnaissance au Révérend Père Bernard Robert, pour son dévouement spécial envers les tertiaires de notre paroisse au nombre de la quarantaine. Le Tiers Ordre fut fondé à Pain Court par Rev. Père Arthur o.f.m. de Blenheim.

Father Robert died September 20, 1996. He was born in Manitoba December 26, 1923. His funeral mass was celebrated September 24, 1996 at St. Francis Xavier parish in Tilbury where he served from 1976 - 1989 as pastor.

He joined the Franciscan order and was ordained to the priesthood on Aug. 26, 1950. In 1957 Father Anselm o.f.m. capuchin provincial of the Capuchin Fathers announced the nomination of Father Bernard o.f.m. as pastor of St. Mary's parish in Blenheim together with the two missions St. Anne, Erieau and St. Isodore, Cedar Springs.

In 1950 he became professor and later director at the Franciscan Minor Seminary. He worked as prefect and director of vocations at the Seminary. In 1957 he took over his parish duty at St. Mary's, Blenheim and was responsible for the building of the new St. Mary's church in Blenheim.

In 1969 he joined the diocese of London and served as pastor of St. Matthew in Alvinston, and Our Lady of Help of Christians, in Watford 1968 - 73, Sacred Heart in Langton 1973 - 76, St. Francis Xavier, Tilbury 1976 - 89, Holy Family, Wallaceburg 1989 - 93 and then, retired .

Father Robert was well-known in many communities. He spoke six languages fluently.

"Who ever has a heart full of love always has something to give."

Father Bernard

Chronicles - 1970 and later

Miss Carmel Cartier now enrolled in a pharmacy course at the University of Toronto was an honour student and among the school's Ontario scholar list.

Glen Wallace, principal of CKSS informed the audience at the commencement exercises that Miss Cartier had obtained the highest passing average of 93 percent, and had been named recipient of the grade 13 student assistance foundation award, valued at $450.00

Miss Cartier won the Clarence Moulthrop Trophy and medal for Mathematics, and the Laurence B. Vince Memorial trophy and medal for Science.
Complementing the graduates Mr. Wallace said "The quality of the school appears in the quality of the graduates."

Citrus Crop Shrivels

Citrus crop shrivels as winter storms hit Florida Jan. 18, 1977. At 4 pm Monday, thermometer readings;

At 4 pm	45°
At 6 pm	35°
At 8 pm	32°
At 12:00 am	28
At 4 am	21
At 6 am	20

Damages unknown but extensive.
I was in Florida during this winter.

Veteran Teachers Retire

Students of St-Philippe School in Grande Pointe honoured two retiring teachers after the last day of school in June 1972. Miss Blanche St-Pierre who has been a teacher for 38 years accepts a plaque from grade 8 student Janine Griffore, as Father Lanoue of St. Philippe parish and Georges Gagnon, principal of the school look on. Mr. Gagnon was also presented with a plaque from the students. He retires after 37 years of teaching.
Chatham Daily News   June 1972

Miss St-Pierre, a native of Pain Court who had been teaching for 38 years, received a certificate in Windsor for her contributions to education.   She also received recognition during an afternoon program at Ste-Catherine School where she was teaching in 1963. Miss St-Pierre began her teaching career at S.S. # 9 Grande Pointe and later taught at S.S. # 4 Winterline, as well as in Windsor and Pain Court.

À la fin de l'année scolaire 1971 - 72 deux enseignants bien connus, Mlle Blanche St-Pierre et M. Georges Gagnon ont pris leur retraite. Toute la population de Grande Pointe et Pain Court peut attester que Mlle St-Pierre et M. Gagnon avaient le don d'éduquer et d'instruire.

Chers amis,

S'être consacrés pour tant d'années à la cause de l'éducation:

Mlle Blanche St-Pierre - 38 ans

M. Georges Gagnon - 37 ans

C'est tout un exploit.

Pour Mlle St-Pierre, un simple calcul de 30 élèves par années, cela fait environ 1200 élèves qui sont passés sous sa tutelle. En plus, elle a été directrice pour une dizaine d'années à l'école SS # 4 Dover jusqu'en 1971.

Il en est de même pour M. Gagnon. Il était directeur à l'école SS # 9 Dover ensuite à St-Philippe de Grande Pointe. Quand on y pense, ça en fait du monde à la messe. C'est toute une réalisation!

Pour une carrière aussi prodigieuse, il me fait plaisir de vous offrir nos hommages les plus sincères. Pendant toute votre carrière vous avez été pour vos élèves, des citoyens exemplaires et des personnes consciencieuses.

Mlle Blanche St-Pierre, après sa retraite, se charge de voir au besoin de sa mère déjà âgée de 98 ans.

Que le ciel vous prodigue ses divines faveurs.

M. Joseph Brisette, de Pointe-aux-Roches, a passé 42 ans dans les écoles de d'Essex et de Kent, dont 14 ans comme responsable du secteur français à l'école St-Joseph de Tilbury et pour finir à l'école Ste-Catherine de Pain Court où il a été fêté en présence de ses confrères, des élèves et de nombreux amis. Il a également été l'objet d'un témoignage spécial du conseil scolaire de Kent.

Quelques enseignants qui ont enseigné à l'école St-Philippe de Grande Pointe pendant plusieurs années sont:

Amédée Emery	
Blanche Foy -	née Caron
Thérèse Gagnon -	née Moison
Pat Gehl -	née Roy
Florine Grifford -	née Caron
Joanne Griffore -	née Martin
Diana Martin -	née Marchand
Jacqueline Lebrun -	née Dresser
Yvonne Roy -	née Caron
Barbara Scheeler -	née Cadotte
Louella Toth -	née Demers
Madeleine Tétreault -	née Lebrun
Blanche St-Pierre	
Lucille DeSmit -	née Martin
Marguerite Gagnier-	née Pinsonneault

Référence: Album Souvenir - Centemaire de Grande Pointe -p. 40

Éphémérides 1970 - 1975

- Le banquet annuel des Dames de Ste-Anne de Pain Court eut lieu à la salle St-Philippe de Grande Pointe. La préparation chaleureuse des dames a fait preuve de leur talent culinaire en servant un délicieux repas aux invités. Le Père Charron se dit fier de ses "bonnes dames" qui se dévouent pour le bien-être de chacun et qui contribuent au soutien de la paroisse.

- Nos félicitations à M. et Mme Edmond Chauvin pour le témoignage qui leur à été accordé au banquet de "La St-Jean-Baptiste" à Belle Rivière le 21 avril 1974. Nous savons que M. Chauvin s'est dévoué corps et âme à la cause française au cours des années et le mérite qui lui a été confié n'est qu'une marque tangible de reconnaissance.

- En septembre 1974 nous accueillons, tous les étudiants et les enseignants de l'école Ste-Catherine: A. Guénette principal, Gérald Alexandre 8e année, Mme Claire Brophy 7e année, Mme Angéline Marentette 6e année, Mme Marie Faubert 5e année, Mme Lena Robert 4e année, Mme Carmen Caron 3e année, Mme Madeleine Pinsonneault 2e année, Mme Anne-Marie Thibodeau 1ère année, Mme Marguerite Schinkelshock jardin, et Mme Marguerite Gagnier la maternelle.

Nous saluons aussi bien, les élèves et les professeurs de l'école secondaire:
M. Amédée Emery - principal
M. Raymond Chartrand
M. Raymond Simard
M. Marcel Goulet
M. André Den Tandt
Mlle Cathy Biesenthol
- Un grand merci est offert à Mme Thérèse Gagnon et à Marie Cadotte pour avoir organisé un choeur de chant avec les élèves de l'école St-Philippe. Les belles voix ont rehaussé la messe de minuit.

- Les Dames de Ste-Anne de Pain Court ont su se récréer lors de leur fête de Noël. Les nouvelles officières pour 1975:
Présidente: Mme Marie-Anne Faubert
Vice-présidente: Mme Dora Sterling et Mme Bernice Couture
Secrétaire: Mme Jesse Robert
Trésorière: Mme Joan Pelletier
Félicitations à ces dames courageuses. Nous leur souhaitons une année fructueuse.

Éphémérides

La fédération des femmes canadiennes-françaises célèbre le 60e anniversaire.
Mme Richer reçut la médaille "Mérite 60" avec trente-six femmes au grand banquet national le 6 mai en reconnaissance de son inlassable dévouement pour la fédération et pour la communauté. M. Louis-Joseph Richer et sa fille Marie-Ange étaient présent pour honorer Alma très méritante de ce digne hommage.

Anne Dresser étudiante en 13e année nous est revenue enchantée de son voyage à Rome en 1971. Elle avait bien des choses à nous transmettre.

Le personnel enseignant à l'école St-Philippe de Grande Pointe pour l'année scolaire 1970 - 71 est le suivant:

M. George Gagnon, directeur, Mlle Blanche St-Pierre, Mme Louella Toth, Mme Blanche Foy, Mme Jacqueline Lebrun, Mme Joanne Griffore, Mme Florine Grifford et Mme Thérèse Gagnon.

L'exécutif de la section du FFCF de Pain Court pour l'année 1971 est le suivant: Présidente: Mme Marguerite Roy

Vice-présidente:	Mme Carmelle Pinsonneault
Secrétaire:	Mme Rose-Marie Roy
Trésorière:	Mme Laurette Raymond
Conseillères:	Mme Evéline Marentette,
	Mme Marguerite Gagnier, Mme Marcelle Roy.

Pour l'année 1971 la section de Pain Court compte 31 membres.

Chancelier bilingue.

À l'Université de Windsor en 1972 lors de la collation des grades, M. Lucien Lamoureux, désigné chancelier, a été installé.

Lorsqu'une institution du calibre de l'Université de Windsor invite à sa tête un Canadien-français, c'est un tournant de l'histoire qu'il faut noter. L'honneur qui est fait à M. Lamoureux reflète non seulement sur sa personne, mais sur nous tous, les francophones de la région. Bienvenue dans la région, M. Lamoureux.

Joseph Roy, postier

C'est avec grande peine que nous apprenons la mort subite de Joseph Roy, le 24 décembre 1971 à l'âge de 52 ans. Sa soeur jumelle, Marie, est religieuse chez les Soeurs de l'Immaculée Conception à Joliette, Québec. Depuis une quinzaine d'années il était postier de Pain Court. Il fut aussi propriétaire et gérant de l'hôtel Central à Pain Court au-delà de vingt ans.

En plus, il était un athlète accompli et rendait service aux jeunes de la paroisse dans les diverses organisations sportives.

Les jeunes patineurs à roulettes ont su à maintes reprises jouir des soirées de plaisir au sous-sol de l'église. De généreux volontaires surveillent ces jeunes, tout en admirant leur souplesse et leur énergie. Les profits de ces loisirs vont aux besoins de la paroisse et à notre mission d'Haïti en 1974 -75.

Les chasseurs des environs de Grande Pointe attendent l'ouverture de la saison des canards sauvages. Mitchell's Bay et les environs, reconnus comme le paradis de la chasse, se trouve tout près de chez-nous.

Carmel Cartier étudiante à Toronto - Donna Bourgeois et Anne Dresser étudiantes à Ottawa sont venues se rejoindre à leur famille pour les fêtes 1972- 73.

À l'occasion de leur grande soirée annuelle, les dames de Ste-Anne ont suivi leur tradition en reconnaissant les années de service et de dévouement de leurs anciennes membres. À l'honneur pour l'année 1974, on remarquait Mme Ida Bourassa, Mme Eulalie Gagner et Mme Alice Sterling. Félicitations aux honoraires de l'année 1974.

Une maison au cachet ancestral. . .

Photo : Paroisse de Pain Court 1985

Sans se douter, cette maison vieille d'un siècle environ pourrait nous raconter bien de ses joies, de ses peines si elle pouvait parler; mais heureusement, certaines gens qui en ont fait l'expérience et pour d'autres qu'elle a accueillis ou hébergés il y a quelques décennies déjà, peuvent nous en faire connaître davantage.

Selon Mme Louise Trudell, cette maison charpentée en "logues" du pays fut, au tout début de son exis tence, la demeure de son grand-père, M. John Goodreau (Jean-Baptiste Goudreau).

"Je me souviens, " dit-elle, "j'avais à peine cinq ans, d'être allée là souvent avec mes parents visiter Mémère. Il y avait toujours un baril rempli de bonnes petites galettes. On aimait ça manger les "cookies à Mémère Goudreau."

Par la suite, la famille Théodore Ouellette prit possession de ce domaine. Et M. Francis Ouellette, son fils, nous révèle quelques souvenirs . . .

"C'n'est pas d'hier ce que tu me d'mandes là," dit-il. "Rendu à mon âge - c'est pas possible, j'ai déjà quatre-vingt-un ans - on oublie bien d'ces choses-là. En tous les cas, je me rappelle d'avoir vécu là bien des années. Oui, ma pauvre mère est morte dans cette maison."

En 1943, le diocèse de London acquiesça à la demande des paroissiens et a consenti d'acheter cette propriété avoisinante du cimetière qui pourrait servir de logement au futur bedeau.

C'est le 10 août 1944, que M. Télesphore Dénommé et sa famille quittent leur paroisse natale de St-Joseph, Ontario et viennent s'établir à Pain Court. M. Dénommé fut aussitôt engagé comme bedeau de la paroisse de l'Immaculée Conception.

Avec Antoinette, son épouse, et leurs dix enfants, Joseph, Charles, Marguerite, Monique, Cyrille, Léo o.m.i., Robert, Marie-Thérèse, Claire et Cécile, il exerça fidèlement dans l'ombre le métier de bedeau pendant trente-deux ans consécutifs.

La paroisse de Pain Court doit une dette de reconnaissance à la famille Dénommé pour de nombreux services rendus à la communauté.

Malheureusement, la maison qui fut le doux refuge de "M. Télès" et sa famille pendant quarante et un ans sera bientôt démolie et avec elle disparaîtra un p'tit coin de chez nous, une partie de notre patrimoine transmis par nos ancêtres, un témoignage de patience et d'amour de la part des bâtisseurs.

NB: Mémère (Marguerite) Goudreau, fille de Thomas Blais, le pionnier des familles Blais de Pain Court.

Angéline Blais Marentette

M. Télès Dénommé à la retraite

Le 7 juin 1976, une soirée récréative a eu lieu dans la salle paroissiale de Pain Court pour honorer M. Télesphore Dénommé à l'occasion de sa retraite comme concierge de la paroisse depuis 32 ans environ. Les hommes de la paroisse et des amis des environs profitèrent de l'occasion pour offrir à M. Dénommé leurs souhaits.

Depuis le 1er juin il jouit d'une liberté toute spéciale qui lui permet de faire à sa guise. Un goûter copieusement apprêté par les hommes de la paroisse a clôturé une veillée des plus agréables.

SEPARATE SCHOOL ''C'' CHAMPIONS

St. Philippe Separate School of Grande Pointe won the Kent County Separate School ''C'' Division girls basketball title this season. Members of the team are, front row from left, Michelle Cadotte, Catherine Cadotte, Cheryl Bishop, Lou Ann Martin and Phyllis Emery. Back row, Alice Emery, Suzanne Bagnelle, Jacqueline Caron, Kim Martin and coach Paul Bélanger. (April, 1975).

Félicitations aux filles de l'école St-Philippe, gagnantes du tournoi de basket-ball à Chatham et aussi a leur dévoué entraîneur, M. Paul Bélanger.

Album Souvenir - Centenaire Grande Pointe -. 59

Fire fighters

Pompiers du canton de Dover

1ère rangée: Léo Benoit, Joseph Benoit, Lionel Benoit, Larry (Red) St-Pierre

2e rangée: Gary Cummings, Erwin Pavliscak, Jim Brown, Jerome Brown, Jerome Martin, Raymond Trahan, Vincent St-Pierre, Sylva Laprise, Larry St-Pierre, (absent) Tim Benoit, (au coin du photo).

Album Souvenir - Centenaire Grande Pointe p. 70

Le 19 mars 1976, l'Association des pompiers de Kent a eu son banquet annuel à Chatham. Grande Pointe a été représentée par:

M. & Mme Donald Benoit

M. & Mme Joseph Benoit

M. & Mme Lionel Benoit

M. & Mme Dorey Bourdeau

M. & Mme Clément Brown

M. & Mme Léonard Brown

M. & Mme Joseph Demers

M. & Mme Omer King

M. & Mme Trefflé Odette

M. & Mme Sylvius Trahan

M. & Mme Réginald Charron

Félicitations à M. Lionel Benoit qui a été nommé le nouveau président pour l'année 1976.

Ancient Art - A New Era

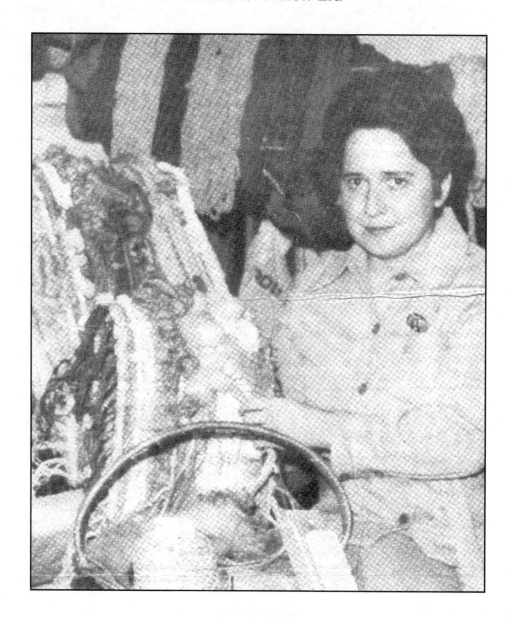

June 21, 1975
My sister, Anne-Aline Barrette with one of her woven tapestries.
Mrs. Barrette is the founder-president of the association of tapestry
artists which includes members from as far away as Montréal.

A painter with textile art experience Anne-Aline Barrette is founding president of Association of Tapestry Artisans of Ottawa. The organization which is less than a year old has an active membership of 108.

Mrs. Barrette says the organization is primarily interested in promoting the textile arts mainly in the form of hooked and knitted tapestries. The principal aim is to develop this form of artistic expression.

The use and research of other tapestry techniques is also given emphasis.
These include stitchery, weaving, macrame, wrapping, coiling, needle weaving and dyeing of yarns.

Anne-Aline Barrette, my youngest sister, who is the wife of Ottawa lawyer Roger A. Barrette was born in Pain Court Ontario and attended Ste-Catherine school. They have two sons, Roch and Paul, who attended La Vérendrye Separate School in Benson Hills, Ottawa.

Mrs. Barrette obtained a Bachelor of Arts degree and Bachelor of Commerce at the University of Ottawa. She is a graduate of Ottawa Teacher's College and the Ontario College of Education. She taught at regional High Schools for 11 years including a five year stint at André Laurendeau High School in Vanier.

Some of her excellent woven tapestries adorn the 6' x 12' walls of the main entrance of the telephone building in Ottawa, a stone's throw from the Parliament Buildings. The members have two major yearly exhibits, one at City Hall one at the National Museum of Man. The members are totally bilingual and all conversations between members are both in French and English.

Mrs. Barrette is an executive member of the Outaouais Weavers Guild and a past treasurer of the Bytown Artisans Guild. She has memberships in Canadian Guild of Crafts, Ontario Crafts Foundation, Eastern Ontario Craft Council and Ottawa Valley Weaver's Guild.

She is a proud grandmother of 4 grandchildren: Amélia, Samuel, Thalie and Colin. Both her husband and son Paul are lawyers, so Anne-Aline fulfills secretarial duties in their business office. Roch works at the main office of "La Caisse Populaire Ste-Anne" in downtown Ottawa.

TEACHER HONOURED ON RETIREMENT

There was hardly a dry eye in the house at St-Philippe school, Grande Pointe, Monday morning as Mrs. Blanche Foy was honoured at a special assembly on her retirement from 29 years in the teaching profession, 16 of those years at St-Philippe where she had recently been teaching children from Grades 2 and 3. Many parents were in attendance as flowers and gifts were presented. From left, Lynn Pinsonneault, Michel Tétreault and Denise Koekuyt are shown with Mrs. Foy.

Congrès Semaine Française
Deux nouveaux surintendants francophones

M. Vincent Caron,
surindentant des écoles françaises.

En 1974, le ministère de l'Éducation de l'Ontario vient d'embaucher deux nouveaux surintendants francophones pour les différentes régions scolaires du sud et du sud-ouest de la province.

Il s'agit de M. Vincent Caron originaire de Pain Court et de M.Germain Bourgeois originaire de_____ , qui seront tous les deux responsables des secteurs desservis respectivement par les bureaux régionaux de London et de Toronto.

Leurs nominations portent à trois le nombre des surintendants d'écoles francophones dans cette partie de la province.

M. Jean Mongenais, Président des
"Publications des Grands Lacs"

La télévision 1976

Le 17 juillet 1976 sera une date mémorable dans l'histoire des franco-ontariens de la région du sud-ouest. Pour les téléspectateurs cette date marquera la fin d'une lutte acharnée, d'une bataille pénible parce que le long du chemin nous avons perdu des joueurs qui, fatigués de se battre en vain pour la cause française, se sont noyés dans cette mer anglophone.

Si on relit les premiers numéros du "Rempart" en 1966 on verra qu'une équipe luttait déjà pour obtenir la radio et la télévision française dans notre région. C'est donc dire que ça été un travail de longue haleine, de persévérance pour aboutir enfin à une victoire. Mais attention, la lutte n'est pas finie. C'est sûr que nous, les francophones "pure laine" qui regardons la télévision française nous allons en jouir et en bénéficier. Mais nos enfants?

CBEFT

Le poste télévision CBEFT , UHF 78, est inauguré avec faste le 8 octobre 1976.

Les francophones du sud-ouest de l'Ontario ont attendu longtemps la télévision française! Le 8 octobre ils ont marqué son avènement avec joie manifestement débordante. Ils étaient près de 400 qui ont accepté l'invitation de Radio Canada à sa fête d'inauguration du poste CBEFT au salon du Holiday Inn de Windsor. Les dirigeants du poste et du réseau qui ont adressé la parole ont été chaleureusement applaudis.

"Nous sommes aussi heureux que vous, que notre programmation vous soit maintenant accessible," a déclaré M. Jacques Landry directeur général adjoint de la Radio-Télévision française de Radio Canada. En Ontario, Toronto est un centre de production de plus en plus important de sorte que notre réseau dans cette province devient une image de plus en plus fidèle de la réalité franco-ontarienne.

M. Hackney directeur de CBEFT et CBET a exprimé ses voeux et M. Aurèle Bénéteau, superviseur de la mise en ondes, a invité la population française à profiter au maximum du nouveau service de la société d'État. L'animatrice de la soirée était Louise Séguin, responsable des relations publiques à CBEFT. On a ensuite dégusté hors d'oeuvres et vin pendant qu'un orchestre de marque entraînait les invités à la danse.

Nous saluons également quelques dignitaires présents à cette fête:
Jean-Marie Dugas directeur de la télévision française.
Jean-Louis Tanguay à la direction des relations publiques.
Aline Harrison, présidente de l'action télévision française.
Le maire de Windsor, A.Weeks; le ministre Eugene Whelan et le député Robert Daudlin.

Le Rempart 1976

Students starve for United Way

A group of 50 students at Pain Court secondary school won't be eating breakfast, lunch or dinner for the next two days, all in the name of United Way, 1976 -77.

The students are staging a starve-in which began Wednesday at 7pm and will continue until 7pm Friday. With financial sponsorship, the students plan to raise a sizeable amount for United Way. The event will be held in the school's gymnasium under the direction of the teachers for the first 24 hours and parents during the remaining time. Students were searched for food or snacks. This proved to be an outstanding success.

The students are busy working on another worthwhile project the Chocolate Bar Drive. Proceeds of the sale will go towards student activities and equipment at Pain Court Secondary school. Michael King of grade 12 and Joël Robert, grade 11, are hard working salesmen in this chocolate bar drive.

L'école secondaire de Pain Court se prépare depuis l'ouverture des classes pour la décoration de leur "char allégorique" qui comptera parmi le défilé dans la parade annuelle "Red Feather." Thérèse Richer est couronnée reine de l'école. Elle représentera l'école en 1976 - 77 et on lui souhaite succès et on la félicite pour l'honneur reçu. Bonne chance à tous.

Father Louis Rivard

The new pastor of Grande Pointe considers himself at home. Being named pastor of St. Philippe's Church in Grande Pointe is like a homecoming in September 1977.

Not because I was born in Stevenson which is a small hamlet near Wheatley, but because I am now the pastor of the church which Father Euclide Chevalier helped build as pastor in 1950. You see Father Chevalier was my guide when I was a boy in Stevenson. He was the pastor there at that time.

If there was anyone who influenced my choice of vocation, it was Father Chevalier. However, Father Rivard is not the first person in his family to become a priest. He has two uncles who are priests. Father Edgar Robert pastor of the 175 year old St. Peter's church in Tilbury East, and Alphonse Robert now in Québec. Yes, my uncles had some influence on me and that is why it seemed natural for me to become a priest.

"I'm looking forward to stay at St-Philippe. I enjoy being a pastor in a farming community. My father was a farmer. We grew tobacco, soybeans and corn. When I was home for the summer my father insisted I work in the open air. He taught me everything; I'm sure I'm a doer and a hobbyist because of my father. I've built three boats. In emergencies, I'm a plumber and a carpenter. I even know how to operate a back hoe. When I talk to some of my parishioners, I can help them with some of their problems."

Father is building a cottage at the mouth of the Thames River with Father Chevalier and Father Laurent Poisson now at Ste-Anne, in Tecumseh. We call it CPR after the initials in our last names. Father Chevalier wanted to call the cottage "Mon Repos." I disagreed. Every time I go there I work like crazy. . . some resting place!

Grande Pointe Staff

Well, Father did spend seventeen years motivating the people of this fine community. He was a man small in stature but very big in ambition. He was responsible for the completion of the parish hall renovations. He re-initiated the parish picnics, spruced up the cemetery, as well as repainted the interior of the church and its statues.

With his parishioners, he inaugurated the centennial celebrations in 1986. "They know him as a man of deep faith. He took a firm stand on religious principles and his goal is to always unite his parishioners as a family. He has helped many find peace with themselves in troubled times."

Centennial Album of Grande Pointe p. 21

KNIGHTS OF COLUMBUS LEAD PROCESSION INTO CHURCH 1979
Pain Court Catholic Church Celebrates 125th Anniversary

PAIN COURT (Staff) - With much pomp and ceremony, the congregation of Immaculate Conception Roman Catholic Church celebrated its 125th anniversary Sunday. A Mass was celebrated at 3p.m. in thanksgiving, with former priests of the parish taking part. Included in the ceremony were Father Euclide Chevalier, now retired, Monsignor William Bourdeau, retired, Monsignor Augustin Caron, retired and Father Léo Dénommé o.m.i., now a pastor in Maniwaki, Québec. The Mass was officiated by Monsignor Jean Noël of Windsor, the Vicar General representing Bishop John Sherlock.

A social gathering at 5 p.m. in the basement of the church preceded a dinner with 300 people present at 6 p.m. Father Dénommé was the after-dinner speaker. Father Léo Charron, present parish priest, said a number of other activities during the year also helped celebrate the church's 125th anniversary.

Two weeks ago, Monsignor Caron visited the church, celebrating his 50th year in the priesthood.

Last Sunday, representatives of Pain Court secondary school visited the church to celebrate the school's 25th anniversary.

Father Charron informed us that the parish is also considering the publishing of an updated version of the parish's history. Amédée Emery, retired principal of Pain Court secondary school, has started work on the book with the aim of having it published by the end of the year. The new book would update a previous history written by Mr. Emery's uncle, the late Father A. D. Emery, who was parish priest.   The 304-page illustrated history book was published on the 75th anniversary of the parish. Three hundred copies were reprinted this year, and already all 300 have been sold for $20.00 each.

The parish is hoping to receive a Wintario grant to assist with the publishing costs of the new history book. Interest in the history books has been high because the congregation is so interested in its roots.

The parish library will also receive a much -more modern version of the parish's 125th anniversary.   John Haslip, a member of the congregation and local newsman, will shoot about 1,800 feet of film on the anniversary celebrations.

The film will include quite a bit about the parish people, their way of life as well as the anniversary events, Father Charron said.

Chatham Daily News

Pain Court 125e anniversaire - Messe d'action de grâces

Dimanche, le 10 juin 1979, jour de fête pour les paroissiens de l'Immaculée Conception de Pain Court.

Au centre Mgr. Jean Noël vicaire général et curé de la paroisse St. Jérôme de Windsor durant la consécration, assité à sa droite par Mgr. William Bourdeau et à sa gauche par Mgr. Augustin Caron tous deux anciens curés de Pain Court. On peut voir en partant de l'extrême gauche, le Père Louis Rivard curé de Grande Pointe, le Père Ulysse Lefaive ancien curé de Pain Court, et le Père Léo Charron curé de Pain Court.   À l'extrême droite, le Père Euclide Chevalier, ancien curé de Pain Court et à ses côtés le Père Léo Dénommé o.m.i. curé de Maniwaki Québec et enfant de la paroisse, ainsi que deux séminaristes Tom O'Rourke et Eugene Roy.

Plusieurs anciens paroissiens et amis se sont joints aux paroissiens de Pain Court pour rendre grâce au Seigneur dans une messe d'action de grâce à 15h00.   Au-délà de 300 convives s'assemblèrent au sous-sol pour le banquet. Plusieurs souvenirs ont été revécus en fraternisant et en examinant de vieilles photos qui étaient exposées ici et là dans la salle. Après le souper le film du centenaire de la paroisse fut visionné par les paroissiens.

Aux Sociétaires

La Caisse Populaire de Pain Court Limitée 1978

Une autre année très fructueuse s'est déjà écoulée au bureau de notre Caisse.

En 1978 nous avons atteint un actif de $1,475,346.00 Cela représente une augmentation de $315,476.00 ou 27%. Je suis très heureux de voir cette grande confiance démontrée par vous, les sociétaires, au cours de l'année.

Nous sommes très fiers de notre régime de pension enregistré qui avait en dépôt à la fin de l'année $466,821.00 ce qui représente une augmentation de $144,887.00.

Je tiens à remercier notre gérant M. Ron Lozon, et ses assistantes pour leur dévouement et leur persévérance au cours de cette année qui inclut trois auditions qui sont souvent très ennuyeuses et difficiles pour le personnel même si cela est nécessaire. Je veux aussi remercier le bureau de direction, le comité de crédit et nos vérificateurs pour leur excellent travail durant l'année.

Je suis très convaincu que notre Caisse continuera à avancer.

Jean M. Laprise,
Président

On parle d'eux . . . d'elles

Les paroissiens bougent - 1975

Les membres de la FFCF et leur époux ont joui d'un délicieux repas au poisson et au poulet dimanche le 5 mars. L'aumônier de notre section était des nôtres. C'est dans l'intimité qu'on a jasé de tout en satisfaisant notre appétit au cours d'une soirée très agréable.

Notre présidente dévouée, Mme Françoise Rivest, a profité de l'occasion pour souligner les buts de la Fédération, nos objectifs pour l'année, ainsi qu'un bref résumé de nos activités des années précédentes.

Mlle Thérèse Richer, présidente du Club d'activités des jeunes, a témoigné sa reconnaissance au nom des jeunes pour l'aide reçu de la Fédération. "C'est grâce a vous," dit-elle "que nous avons pu suivre des cours intéressants et éducatifs."

M. Edmond Chauvin, président du Club d'âge d'or, a donné un aperçu des activités du club et de son fonctionnement.

M. Louis-Joseph Richer, président du Centre Culturel Brébeuf, a élaboré brièvement sur les projets d'avenir. Il souligna les buts du centre: conserver intact les traditions de nos ancêtres, préserver notre culture française, travailler au bien-être d'une communauté catholique et française.

Nicole Pinsonneault, l'espoir du club
"Figure Skating" 1975

Nous voulons féliciter une petite patineuse dans notre coin du pays qui, un jour pourrait devenir une autre "Barbara Scott." Nicole, âgée de 9 ans, fille de M. et Mme Roméo Pinsonneault, fait partie du club "Figure Skaters" de Chatham depuis son bas âge. Tout récemment Nicole participait au festival des patineurs de fantaisie au "London Gardens" à London. Elle exécuta avec grande souplesse un spectacle qui lui a rapporté un deuxième prix, et une quatrième place en finale. C'est donc dire que sa persévérance et ses talents méritent nos félicitations.

Barbara Ann Scott won Canada's first Olympic gold medal in figure skating in 1948.

L'Academie Ste-Marie   1928 - 1977

Semble qu'il faut faire place pour les développements communautaires au niveau régional, provincial, et national.

En 1977 l'Académie Ste-Marie semble obliger de céder sa place et être démoli afin d'améliorer les voix de communications de la ville de Windsor. Peu après nous verrons surgir les édifices modernes de St. Clair College.

Nous constatons avec grande peine la démolition de l'Académie Ste-Marie qui, pendant des années, a vu au besoin de la population française de Kent et Essex au niveau secondaire. Les talents supérieurs déployés et cultivés au sein de l'Académie Ste-Marie ont vraiment rendu honneur à cette institution florissante.

L'Académie ont pris leurs places dans l'enseignement bilingue de la province au niveau universitaire, secondaire et primaire.

De la paroisse de Pain Court nous remarquons spécialement des apôtres reconnus de la francophonie ontarienne.   Religieuses de la communauté des Soeurs des Saints Noms de Jésus et de Marie, institutrices bilingues:

Sr Gérard de Marie	Edna Caron
Sr Claire-Thérèse	Anna Caron
Sr Clara	Clara Caron
Sr Léona	Léona Caron
Sr Marie-Thérèse	Marie-Thérèse Caron
Sr Marie-Romuald	Marie Demers
Sr Antoinette de Marie	Elmire Thibodeau
Sr Marie-Zacharie	Pamela Gauthier
Sr Gérard-Majella	Claire Goure
Sr Cécile-Antoinette	Césarine Thibodeau
Sr Blanche-Alma	Marie-Louise Carron
Sr Ubaldine (supérieure)	Annette Caron
Sr Anna-Eva	Marie-Louise Béchard
Sr Lucie	Anna Daniel
Sr Rita du Crucifix	Edna Daniel
Sr Marie Jean-Victor	Pauline Trahan
Sr Marie du Crucifix	Marie-Thérèse Caron
Sr Lucile	Lucile Caron

Hommage à nos éducatrices régionales.

Congrès provincial à l'occasion de la semaine française de l'Association d'éducation canadienne-française de l'Ontario (AEFO) le 2 au 9 avril, 1961.

"Nos écoles sont avant tout catholiques, exprime l'abbé Clifford Girard curé de la paroisse Ste-Agnès de Chatham qui a prononcé le sermon à la messe qui a marqué le début des séances du 22e Congrès de l'AEFO à l'académie Ste-Marie en 1961. Toute histoire, tant païenne que chrétienne acclame la grandeur et la beauté de la profession de l'éducation. L'éducateur chrétien, c'est l'ouvrier de Dieu. Il travaille d'abord sur les âmes qui ont devant elles une destinée humaine. Voilà donc ce qui donne à nos écoles leur première grande responsabilité," nous déclare l'abbé Girard.

S'adressant directement aux instituteurs et institutrices des classes bilingues: "Vous avez compris que la patrie ce n'est pas seulement la terre que nous habitons; ce sont aussi les ancêtres, les traditions, les institutions, la langue et la culture. Vous travaillez sans cesse au triomphe des droits les plus sacrés des nôtres et des usages les plus chers. Toujours poussés vers le progrès grâce à l'esprit d'entraide, puissions nous redire aujourd'hui les paroles de Notre Seigneur: Moi je t'ai glorifié sur la terre en menant à bonne fin l'oeuvre que tu m'avais donnée à faire."

Père Girard, éducateur et enseignant au séminaire à London a su captiver et encourager les congressistes du jour.

Après la messe, Mlle Marie Duhaine de Timmins, présidente de l'Association de l'enseignement français de l'Ontario a ouvert le congrès à l'Académie Ste-Marie de Windsor. Près de 350 membres de l'association, organisme qui compte 3000 membres, prendront part à ce mémorable congrès tenu à Windsor pour la première fois, en 1961.

"L'enseignement doit bannir une fois pour toute la pensée que nos enfants ont moins de chance de réussir du fait qu'ils sont catholiques et canadiens- français. Nos écoles doivent nous donner des chefs dont la formation chrétienne et bilingue exercera une bienfaisante influence dans tous les milieux de la société" déclare Mlle Duhaine, présidente.

Nomination

Nomination de M. Léopold Lacroix, ancien inspecteur dans les classes bilingues de Kent et Essex, à un organisme International en 1977.

M. Lacroix directeur général de la division française de TV Ontario a été élu président de "Production Harmonisée," un consortium international de télévisions éducatives regroupées au sein de l'Agence de coopération culturelle et technique des pays totalement ou partiellement de langue française.

Cet organisme réunit douze chaînes de télévision de onze pays francophones: la Belgique, le Cameroun, le Canada, la Côte d'Ivoire, la France, l'Île Maurice, le Mali, la Tunisie, le Sénégal, l'Algérie, la Mauritanie, le Maroc. La "Production Harmonisée" a pour but de favoriser les échanges de connaissances techniques et de mettre sur pied des coproductions d'émissions télévisées.

D'autre part, les organismes participant à la "Production Harmonisée" élaborent en 1977 un projet d'échange de personnel entre les différentes télévisions éducatives de langue française.

Hommage à Amédée Emery 1978

Pour rendre hommage à M. Amédée Emery à l'occasion de sa retraite comme enseignant et directeur de l'école secondaire de Pain Court, paroissiens, parents et amis se sont réunis pour un grand banquet dans la salle paroissiale de l'église Immaculée Conception. Les convives ont souligné, par leurs présence, l'estime et l'admiration pour un grand éducateur.

Ils sont venus en grand nombre: prêtres et religieuses, anciens élèves et professeurs, représentants de toutes les sociétés de Pain Court et de Grande Pointe, administrateurs des deux commissions scolaires de Kent: le Kent County Board of Education et la Commission scolaire des écoles catholiques du comté de Kent.

L'agent du ministère d'Éducation, M. Vincent Caron, fit l'éloge du décoré. Deux cent quatre-vingt convives environ s'unissaient pour célébrer et honorer un des nôtres qui, au cours de 35 ans, s'est dévoué inlassablement auprès de notre jeunesse.

À tour de rôle, les invités ont offert leurs voeux de reconnaissance et de remerciement auprès d'un éducateur et ami, à "cet homme de foi" a t-on dit, qui a su imprégner en notre jeunesse des convictions et des principes de vie qui sauront les conduire au bonheur.

Père Jacques Carron, à titre d'ancien élève et ancien membre du corps professoral au Secondaire sous la direction de M. Emery, a affirmé ses sentiments de joie du fait qu'on a su reconnaître tout ce que M. Emery a donné à la jeunesse, à l'Église et à la communauté entière.

"C'est à notre tour," dit-il "de vous parler d'amour. On a besoin de grandir dans la foi et Amédée s'est permis de faire transparaître un peu de sa vie en nous."

Dans son éloge, le Père Léo Charron a fait ressentir une reconnaissance toute spéciale pour les nombreux services bénévoles offerts par Amédée pour la plus grande gloire de Dieu auprès de son église.

M. Edmond Chauvin cite le fait de "vieillir c'est de s'enrichir" et c'est avec grande conviction et assurance que nous pouvons dire que M. Emery, tout en jouissant de sa retraite bien méritée, saura s'enrichir d'autant plus en se perfectionnant personnellement dans les travaux ou loisirs de son choix.

Un autoportrait à l'huile signé par Michel Binette, un artiste de rénommée, lui a été présenté par M. Louis-Joseph Richer au nom de tous ceux présents et de la paroisse entière.

On te salue Amédée, nous qui t'avons connu et estimé. Que Dieu t'accorde sa juste récompense pour une carrière bien remplie.

Le Rempart (en partie.)

Ladies Group Tries Out New Equipment

Ab Poonawalla, left, director of physiotherapy at St. Joseph's Hospital, demonstrates a mechanical percussor on Thérèse Thibodeau, past president of the Ladies of St. Anne's Church Group, while president Barbara Béchard and Rita Caron watch. The group raised $500 to purchase the percussor, used on patients with breathing problems.

This consisted of a special project to commemorate the 125th anniversary of the parish. It was a gift of love to St. Joseph Hospital and to their fellow men.

Chatham Daily News 1979

Inondations 1938 - 1979

Le 14 mars au soir 1979, c'est-à-dire 6 jours après les inondations de la rivière Thames qui ensevelissait une étendue de 7000 à 10,000 acres dans le canton de Dover et forçait 37 familles à évacuer les lieux, M. Thomas Wells, ministre des affaires intergouvernementales, annonçait que le canton de Dover venait d'être désigné "Région sinistrée." Après quelques jours chacun rentrait chez lui, déballant les débris et tentant d'évaluer le montant des pertes encourues.

Plus de la moitié des familles sont d'origine canadienne française. Selon M. Wilfrid Roy, les plus gros dégâts sont les sous-sols, les centaines de roues d'équipement de semeuses, wagons etc. que possède chaque fermier, les chemins, les clôtures sans compter les pertes de grain en entrepôts, telles que la fève soya et le blé d'Inde.

Le drainage qui se fait ordinairement de façon automatique, grâce à une cinquantaine de pompes électriques installées un peu partout, s'avéra un problème monumental à cause des débris.

Il y a eu aussi la perte de plusieurs milliers de dollars pour M. Bradley propriétaire d'un "feed-lot operations," le seul de ce genre dans le canton où se fait l'élevage du bétail. Sur un total d'environ 1000 têtes, il en aurait perdu au delà de 70 et il est fort possible qu'il en perdra encore plusieurs à cause de pneumonie ou autres complications.

Une barricade au coin des chemins Jacob et de Grande River Line a interdit la route aux automobilistes et camionneurs pour plusieurs semaines. Une centaine de prisonniers, dont une vingtaine de la prison de Windsor, ont fait le déblayage des routes et des fossés.

En mars 1938 les mêmes terrains avaient subi une semblable inondation causée par la glace accumulée à l'embouchure de la rivière Thames et du lac Ste-Claire.

Mitchell's Bay Flood
March 23, 1955

Mr. Leo Pinsonneault's house was completely isolated by the floodwaters. The 300 acre farm of Mr. Pinsonneault which borders on the Mitchell's Bay Shoreline was completely inundated.

Top photo - Homestead of Léo Pinsonneault.

The Anchor Inn at Mitchell's Bay, shown above was the first building in the area to feel the effects of the flood water. Located near the shore, it was cut off within a few minutes after the strong winds whipped the Bay waters into huge waves.

Star Kent Bureau photos

"Drama of Inches"

Drama of inches on flood scene increases on February 3, 1968. Levels were believed to be receding but the danger of very heavy flooding was not dismissed. Residents of Dover, Tilbury and Jeannette's Creek regions breathed easier when the Lower Thames Valley Conservation Authority announced that dynamiting was carried out at the Lake St. Clair mouth yesterday afternoon. It was holding back flood waters. Spokesman for the Authority said the area which sustained heavy damage from high waters two years ago in 1966, now appears to be out of danger.

Floods of March 14, 1979

Ken Jubenville was one of several volunteers who carried cases of dynamite to the Lake St. Clair ice via swamp or by propeller driven boats from Mitchell's Bay. Only a few cases were used but all remaining explosive had to be carried back and returned to Norm Leach Explosives of Chatham. Thirteen holes were drilled about 25 feet apart and 20 sticks of dynamite placed in each hole. The resulting simultaneous explosions ripped a channel about 125 feet long in the two to three feet thick ice. It was to make sure there was a place for the river ice to go into Lake St. Clair. This venture helped alleviate some of the disastrous flood in Dover township at the time.

In 1979, massive Thames river flooding west of Chatham in Dover township has inundated homes and farm buildings and aroused concern for the welfare of livestock exposed to cold water and without food.

From the air it was difficult to tell the depth of water. Depths seemed to vary between two to seven or eight feet. The tally March 10, 1979 was 8000 to 10,000 acres of prime farm land under water, mostly valued at over $4000. an acre.

Farmers fear crop damage after this massive flooding, especially to acres of wheat under water said Rosaire Pinsonneault. Rising Thames River waters have punched holes in Dover township dikes, causing excessive flooding near Lake St. Clair.

Throughout the ordeal, it was the tale of neighbours helping neighbours sometimes at the expense of their own home property that kept residents going. MPP Andy Watson said he believes spring crops will suffer little damage because water will have drained off by planting time. Watson was past Kent County Agricultural representative at the time.

This last devastating flood brings back memories of a few previous floods to hit all surrounding areas and Chatham. Thamesville and area was completely flooded in April 1947. Dresden's main street during peak of 1947 flood reached a depth of eight feet in town. Also cattle and pigs huddled around haystack island at Howard township farms April 8, 1947. Youngsters enjoy 1947 truck rides on Thames Street, present-day Bowman Funeral home area in Chatham. Thames St. north of Fifth St. bridge, the river stood at 19 feet, 10 inches above normal on April 7, 1947. Five feet of water on highway #2, kept trucks busy pulling cars to safety.

Over the years, floods have caused untold damages and unforgettable memories of devastation throughout the county.

In past decades I remember hearing so much of high waters and low water levels. I wish some of our ancestors could bring more light today on this particular issue. It is interesting to note that, according to our forefathers, we now entered (in 1997) a period of 7 years of higher water, as the last seven years have been remarkably lower levels on the lake. Based on Lake Erie observations, the water levels have greatly increased in the last year. So goes the anecdote of the pioneers: 7 years of High water and 7 years of Low water levels.

Reconstruction of Famous Home
by Joseph and Lea Szucs and Joseph M. Jr. and Mary Elizabeth Szucs.

In 1980 - 81 the Szucs families conceived a worthwhile project of demolishing and reconstructing an old log home probably built around the end of the eighteenth century 1780 - 90 and owned by Paul King (Roy) lot 15 Front Concession in Dover. This really was an historical log home apparently built by Sally Ainse's slave. She was living on Ainse land described as a home in the Upper half of lot 10, first township of East Dover. Her improvements extended to include lot 11, a fenced in plain and an orchard.

The government ordered a survey of the land and sent Patrick McNiff to divide it up into 200 acre lots. He found twenty-eight homes already built along the river. In 1780, Ainse entered into a transaction that brought her into Kent County history and made her one of the largest landowners on the Detroit frontier. Ainse developed the ability to base her trading operations in lucrative areas. In 1767, she moved north to the mouth of Lake Huron. After the American Revolution the centre of trade shifted to Pont Chartrain - Detroit - and she moved with it. Census records of the day show she was a wealthy woman. She owned a house, two lots and one male and two female slaves. She had four horses and extensive stores of grain flour and corn.

By 1780, her business records show her ordering two 'bateaux' loads of trade goods and received payment of more than 3000 British Pounds, an extremely large amount at the time.

Sally Ainse also known as Sarah was a full blooded Oneida Indian who was born around 1728 in what is now Pennsylvania. She learned to live and thrive in both the Indian and White worlds and became a wealthy women. At 17 she married Andrew Montour, the son of a French woman captured as a child and raised among the Oneida.

Montour was an agent and interpreter for the British Crown. He was instrumental in many government negotiations with the First Nations living in Pennsylvania and Ohio. Andrew left Sally and dissolved the marriage. Shortly before the birth of their fourth child Sally set out to succeed on her own. Ainse moved to the Thames and settled on land several miles west from the Fork, now Chatham.

This centennial log home, skilfully dismantled and reinstated to its original status by "the Szucs Families," has now become a centre of attraction at lot 18 at the Jack Hill cemetery site on the 6th concession in Dover township.
The upkeep is magnificent. Flowers adorn the property and evergreens give it an air of elegance attracting hundreds of tourists.
As declared by Mrs. Mary E. Szucs, various functions such as picnics for seniors, wedding celebrations etc. take place during the summer months only.

Nos décorés 1971

L'association Saint-Jean-Baptiste remet 18 diplômes de patriotisme à leur banquet annuel au Centre canadien-français à Windsor en présence de 400 convives. La population française du sud-ouest de l'Ontario a rendu un vibrant hommage à un groupe de compatriotes dont on a reconnu publiquement les grands services rendus à la cause française et catholique.

Des diplômes de mérite patriotique ont été remis par M. Jean Noël. Des amis sont venus des quatres coins de la péninsule saluer ces hardis travailleurs qui ont oeuvré la plupart du temps dans l'ombre sans reconnaissance ni remerciement. De Pain Court nous remarquons M. et Mme Alphonse Trudell; M. et Mme Alfred Pinsonneault; L'abbé Léo Charron; Soeur Clara Caron de la communauté des Soeurs des Saints Noms de Jésus et de Marie de Windsor; Soeur Yvonne s.s.j. née Viola Gagner de la communauté des Soeurs Saint-Joseph de London et Mme Clara Cartier de Grande Pointe.

Area Cadets win trophy for third time -1971

Pain Court High School Cadets were awarded the Strathcova Shield for the third consecutive year as the most proficient cadet corps in Western Ontario at a ceremony in the school.

Captain Phil Ash, district Cadet officer of London, presented the Shield to Cadet Mayor Tom O'Rourke, commanding officer of the corps.

Antonio Guénette principal of the Ste-Catherine School was presented with a certificate by Captain Ash making him a second Lieutenant in the Canadian Armed Forces.

The Pain Court corps is made up of all 74 boys in the school plus grade 8 classes of the Ste-Catherine and St-Philippe Separate Schools in Kent. More than 200 students and parents attended.

Les cadets de Pain Court sont à l'honneur - 1971

Lundi le 14 février 1972 lors d'une soirée sociale organisée par les élèves de l'école secondaire, une présentation honorable fut faite au Corps de Cadet.

Le Capitaine, Phil Ash de London, officier du district pour les cadets, présente à Cadet Major Thomas O'Rourke, commandant du Corps, le "Strathcona Shield" pour le meilleur corps du sud-ouest Ontario. En 1971. Ce fut la troisième année consécutive que l'école fut honorée ainsi en 1971. Il se sont mérités cette plaque honorifique cinq années sur neuf.

Le corps se distingue aussi en étant le seul dans l'Ontario qui donne son entraînement et ses commandement dans la langue française.

Aux cadets, filles et garçons, aux officiers responsables Major Edmond Chauvin, Lt. Stanley Bénéteau, Lt. Gérald Alexandre, Lt. Philippe Blais et Lt. Antonio Guénette, à tous, bravo!

Pain Court Cadet Corps Commended At Inspection 1972

A grade 10 student of Pain Court Secondary School walked off with three top awards during Friday's annual inspection of No. 2621 cadet corps.

Cadet Lieut. Robert Blais, son of Mr. and Mrs. Philippe Blais, Pain Court, received awards as master cadet and best shot of the school.

The awards were presented by Col. J. A. Baxter, C.D., commander of the Windsor militia district, who served as reviewing officer for the colourful inspection.

The cadet of the year award was presented to Cadet Commanding Officer Jean-Marie Laprise, 17, a Grade 12 student, who has enrolled in the two-year program at Ridgetown College of Agricultural Technology. The teenager is the son of Mr. and Mrs. Trefflé Laprise.

The top girl cadet award was presented to Cadet Sgt. Louise-Anne Bélanger, 18, daughter of Mr. and Mrs. Ralph Bélanger of R. R. # 1 Pain Court. A grade 12 student, she plans to enroll in the fall in Grade 13 of Chatham-Kent Secondary School in Chatham.

Col. Baxter told the 115 member corps it put on one of the finest inspections he has ever witnessed. "I know you are striving to win the Strathcova trophy for the fourth straight year. I hope you are successful."

Col. Baxter urged the students never to let the cadet movement fail.
"With young people like you I have no fear about the future of Canada." he said.

Rev. Léo Charron of Immaculate Conception Church in Pain Court told the cadets: "We are very proud of you."

Accompanying Col. Baxter was Captain Philip Ash, C.D., district cadet officer of London, who served as inspecting officer.

The program, dedicated to Stanley Bénéteau, a teacher in the high school who is leaving at the end of the month, featured tumbling demonstrations, a dance hunter safety and first aid and a rope bridge walking exhibition.

Départ

Les paroissiens de Pain Court regrettent de voir partir de leur communauté M. et Mme Stanley Bénéteau et leur famille pour aller s'établir à Ottawa.

On n'oubliera jamais Claire et Stan qui se sont dévoués pour les jeunes de la paroisse. M. Bénéteau enseignait les sciences à l'école Secondaire depuis 16 ans. Il s'est distingué également en qualité de capitaine du corps de cadet. En plus de ces nombreuses activités, il dirigeait le hockey chez les jeunes.

Claire, avec sa bonne humeur et son sourire expansif, a su se mériter l'affection de tous les petits du jardin d'enfants.

Avant leur départ pour Ottawa, une soirée de reconnaissance fut organisée par le Club des placiers. M. Bénéteau est embauché comme chef du département des sciences, à la nouvelle école polyvalente Garneau, dans la région d'Ottawa.

Parents, élèves, amis, voisins, tous ont profité de la bonté et la gentillesse de ce jeune couple, des paroissiens modèles.

À M. et Mme Bénéteau et à leur petite famille, les paroissiens de Pain Court vous offrent leurs voeux de reconnaissance et leurs souhaits de bonheur et de succès.

Unveiling the Plaque

Unveiling the Plaque - a plaque commemorating Pain Court's 125th Anniversary was unveiled on Sunday, October 5, 1980. Unveiling the plaque are from left: Amedee Emery, genealogist of Pain Court; L. J. Richer, president of the Centre cultural Brebeuf; and Prof. Gaetan Gervais, director of the Ontario Heritage Foundation.

Chatham Daily news

The Children are Moving On

With the dawning of the 70s came more responsibilities and I felt close to an emotional over-load. Everyone was striving to find their "niche" in life and anticipating a prosperous future.

By 1971, Guy was in his 4th year of University and took up a position in the accounting department of M. J. Smith Seed Company in Chatham. Jean-Marie graduated from high school in 1972 and entered Agricultural College in Ridgetown in September of the same year. Colette graduated from Pain Court high school in 1973. She in turn, registered at the Agricultural College to specialize as an agricultural lab technician in September 1973.

Looking into the crystal ball we see Guy announcing his marriage to a devoted nurse, Penelope McDonald, who graduated from St. Joseph's School of Nursing in London. The wedding took place June 26, 1972. An elaborate reception took place at the home of her parents, Mr. and Mrs. Jack McDonald née Mabel Burke.

A very pleasant event. The happy couple were treated to an old-fashioned buggy ride around the back yard of their home. After a pleasant rendez-vous the bride and groom left for a honey-moon.

During that summer, Jean-Marie was very busy working on the farm and especially on Walpole Island with his older brother Gérard, while Colette was a life guard at Thamesville swimming pool in the park.

Travelling to Europe 1972

As everyone was busy doing his or her own thing, I decided to rent the cottage for part of the summer, and fly to Europe to be with my sister Loretta who was then studying in France for the last year. It was a special opportunity. I boarded a chartered Dutch Airline filled to capacity for Amsterdam. All people on board were from the Chatham and Wallaceburg area. It was a super flight as I was seated with the plane's captain and crew next to the cockpit. I was fully briefed by this knowledgeable crew to visit the most scenic and historical places in Holland, France and Germany.

I realized later it was impossible to even imagine the beauties to be admired in different countries unless you are there in person. My quest for knowledge was fulfilled as I roamed these European countries.

On July 12, 1972 I landed in Amsterdam at 9 a.m., where I had hotel reservations on arrival. The hotel was adjacent to the train station as requested. It surely was convenient, as most accommodations are close to the train stations in Europe. This trip would last seven weeks and I would return to Amsterdam Aug. 29, 1972 to board a flight back home. People were friendly, the welcome was most impressive. I most enjoyed the wine and cheese party on the memorable scenic boat ride through the canals of Amsterdam, the picturesque surrounding of the historical tour of the large Seaport of Rotterdam, the Flower stock exchange market, the seawalls, the dykes protecting the fertile lands of the countryside, acres upon acres of flowers. All was viewed with respect.

Vellinga's Travel agency advised me to buy a Eurail Pass for the entire duration of my trip as an economy measure. For three hundred and twenty-five dollars I travelled by rail from east to west and north to south for seven weeks, through France, Belgium, Germany, Switzerland, Austria, Italy and Spain. What a bargain!

Travel was exceptional at that time. Rates for good hotels were $8.00 to $10.00 a night with a continental breakfast. Europa Hotels were $12.00 but not always available. This was for double occupancy as I travelled with my sister for three weeks. Students had accommodations at Y.M.C.A. for a dollar a night. Timing was perfect, considering the money in my pocket book.

I'm on my way to Paris, France to greet my sister on my Eurail Pass which was first class. On my way through northern France I passed by the land of my ancestors, the fertile farmlands of the province of Normandy where my ancestors the "Roy" lived before migrating to Canada. In Paris, I was greeted at the station by my sister and I stayed with her at the convent of "Les Soeurs de la Sagesse." For a week we travelled around Paris, and its famous "banlieues", to the Palais de Versailles, the museums, the art galleries, the Eiffel Tower, the shopping areas all by express train around Paris.

By regular train we travelled south along the east coast of France, through the Plains of France known as the prairies up to the province of Poitou, France and visited the area of Niort, from which my husband's ancestors "The Laprise's" migrated to Canada in 1680. From there we travelled east towards the Atlantic passing "Auvergne et La Rochelle," areas from where my ancestors the "Caron" migrated to Canada in 1636.

Travelling by train gave us the opportunity to admire the vineyards of France - the scenic beauty - the villages and the countryside unfolding before our very eyes. We are now hugging the northern seashore up to Nantes where we rested for two days at Lauretta's Motherhouse Convent.

We travelled back to Paris on the last leg of this journey. We were tired but captivated by all the beauty and the knowledge acquired. We relaxed for two days in Paris, and embarked for a trip to Bruxelles - capital of Belgium. It was an overnight stop. Our convenient Euro pass let us board the train whenever we were ready. It was 7a.m. as we headed for the Federal Republic of Germany.

Our stop in Cologne was pleasant, as we admired old historical landmarks especially the Cathedral of Cologne. Then we travelled south to Bonn and overnight in Koblenz. Next morning we headed for Frankfurt and covered a tour of this historical city followed by two days in Munich, Germany. I plainly fell in love with Munich: the museums, time square, the clock , the chimes, the endless memories and thousands of people, mingled with tourists catching a glimpse of this beautiful city.

Next day we rolled into the unforgettable sportsmen resort of Innsbruck, Austria for a comfortable stay at Europa Hotel. It was a day to visit the resort area and a walk about the city square in the evening. At the hotel we had guest tickets for a wine and cheese party with entertainment to follow. A real treat for tourists for $2.00.

We were entertained by the same group of entertainers who travel to Kitchener, Ontario for the Oktoberfest Gala every year. We left very happy and relaxed for our next stop in Zurich, 9 p.m. to 12 p.m. with free entertainment and a champagne party at a posh hotel. The following morning the wake-up call was at 5 a.m.; Loretta resented getting up and disapproved of our schedule. This trip to Geneva, required boarding at 6a.m. Heading south, the scenic beauty of the Rhine was captivating with a brief stop in Bern and the picturesque scenery of Lausanne, an unforgettable beauty.

Geneva was our last stop of this memorable two week journey. Loretta had spent a year furthering her education at the University a year prior, so our visit was most enlightening and educational. We spent some time at the United Nation Headquarters in Geneva, visited the marina, the hundreds of shops displaying watches and jewellery at bargain prices.

After two days we boarded for Lyons France. This is where we parted as Loretta had to enroll at the University Campus for another semester. I continued to Toulouse France without a hitch in travelling plans to Barcelona and the Spanish Riviera.

Within a day I was in Barcelona at 7 p.m. Nobody is in a hurry in Spain. Hundreds of taxis are running in Barcelona but it took 2 hours before I could find transportation to my hotel: Spanish people first!

Next morning took me on a tour of the city, an afternoon tour took me to visit museum and churches which was super interesting. Evening stroll was on the Spanish Riviera. Following afternoon I boarded the train for Marseilles, France on the Mediterranean Coastline, and overnight in Nice. I enjoyed the Mediterranean breeze, the wonderful castles on the Mountain side, at trip to the beaches and extra trip to Monaco and the Casino, the plush mountain side Castles and Marinas.

No rest in sight yet, as I board the following day for Vicenza, Italy. Already three weeks of my trip had elapsed. It's like a dream, as time eludes me. Soon I'm in Northern Italy, to be greeted by my old friends Fernand and Juanita Gervais and their four sons, Ken, Steven, Billy and Carl.

Emotions ran high, four years had elapsed since our last rendez-vous at Rondeau Park. It was a dream come true. What a surprise. The children were growing by leaps and bounds. Baby Carl, was 6 years old, beautiful and a real conniver. I just loved him. It was pleasant and heart-warming to reminisce with everyone.

Well guess what? I lost a day in my travel, so consequently I arrived a day late in Vicenza! This did not go well with an officer in the Navy. Well it was not easy, so while we washed and dried my clothes we talked to our hearts content till 2 p.m. Juanita and I had been warned we were leaving at 7 a.m. Little rest but bubbling over with happiness we were on our way as scheduled for a maximum of 10 days. In the military you do report on time for work at the base. A post Commander from Germany volunteered to replace Mr. Gervais while he was on holidays.

On this trip we travelled hundreds of miles south from Vicenza to Rome and the Vatican City. On our way south we visited the leaning Tower of Pisa, the fabulous markets and enjoyed the gorgeous scenery. There seemed to be no end to the statues, the marble fountains lining every waterway.

With Mr. Gervais in the US Armed Forces, special passes were issued for them and their family to travel and visit the country. We did spend 4 days in the area surrounding the Vatican. We took long walks in order to visit the Rotunda, the Ruins, the open markets and the deli stands all along the city streets.

We boarded a special bus to visit the Pope's summer residence at Castel Gandolfo. We were privileged since our hotel accommodations were within two blocks of the Vatican Cathedral where thousands of people gathered for daily services.

Every day I counted my blessings as I felt extra special with the Gervais'. Within the Vatican Cathedral, church services are going on all day. As pilgrims visit they can attend mass and spend the whole day admiring the wonders of this holy place. Tours are conducted throughout the day by informed personnel who describe all areas, and explain the different quarters of the Vatican.

At night we enjoyed the cool summer breezes and walked miles admiring the landscape, the fountains, the statues, the Spanish Steps where we can rest and savour a pop, a pizza or ice cream.

The following day we're on a tour to Castel Gandolfo. There we attended a special service with the Pope speaking Spanish, Italian and French. It was very pleasant in a smaller church with the pope greeting us and within a few feet, as he walked down the aisles to bless us. This was a very serene day as we felt blessed.

Leaving this city was not easy as there was so many places to visit and enjoy. It's time to resume our journey north. Sometimes directions took us to the wrong places, a few times in the middle of nowhere or in a vineyard. All was not lost as it provided additional knowledge of grape cultivation for Italy's wine industry.

As we travelled north we visited the scenic city of Florence, graced with seven outstanding bridges in the city core, dividing the area into two districts, one on either side of the river. It was very amusing to sit alongside the river at open cafes admiring the scenic mountain views graced with myriads of statues, shops on both sides of the river, open air markets with purses, belts, sculptured leather; marble statues and artifacts. Everywhere there is gold jewellery. It sure was interesting to barter with the vendors for better prices. This country holds the beauty of an older era, the roman era, with treasures unlimited.

As we arrived in Vicenza we were greeted once again and well-served and loved by the housekeeper and her four boys. An extra surprise was the greetings of the commander at the post who replaced Mr. Gervais briefing him on important issues as he was departing early next day to resume his duty in Germany.

Tired and exhausted, Juanita and I enjoyed the children for a few days and planned a few outings with them. They were special and two of them already in their teens. On weekends Fernand would take over and take us to historical sights around the area and places of interest for his sons to enjoy.

I considered myself very lucky to be honoured with such warm hospitality and be chosen as a substitute grandmother to the four boys, since both their grandmothers had died before they could know them.

With the children back in school Juanita and I took the train to Venice. The train was crowded with passengers standing all over and crowded for 100 miles. Something special amazed me: Sisters (nuns) had to scramble just as anyone else for a space with no special privileges. It was awkward with their long religious habits.   Everyone fended for himself or herself, rest assured.

As we arrived in Venice we boarded a railway car to take us to the streets of Venice by gondolas. It is amazing to see but I had no desire to live on the canals of Venice. After a day of touring the Cathedral square and viewing the crowds and the army of pigeons, it was time to return and cope with the hassles of the train going home to Vicenza. We arrived at 9 p.m. happy and exhausted.

Soon it is time to leave, and I was briefed by Fernand on how to travel north to Amsterdam and avoid mishaps while travelling through different countries in a very short period of time. Once again it was good-bye and the emotional and caring Juanita generally avoided good-byes.   Fernand tossed me twenty American one dollar bills saying this would buy a sandwich and a drink for my ride to Amsterdam eliminating the hassle of exchanging money along the way.

The first day I arrived in Milano, I stayed overnight and visited all day: the Art galleries, the churches, the museum, the markets, bringing home tapestries as souvenirs.

Next morning I boarded for a nonstop train to Amsterdam, picking up a sandwich and a drink at train stops where they cater to tourists through an open "guichet." Once again I passed through Germany, north to Bonn and Cologne and across to Dusseldorf and Duisburg arriving in Amsterdam at 11 p.m., an hour before my Eurail pass expired. I retired to my hotel across the street and boarded my flight the next morning at 8 a.m., greeting all the same friends who were returning on the same chartered flight to Toronto, Canada where buses were waiting our arrival to take us to our destination, Chatham Ontario. I was tired yet happy, my mind overflowing with unforgettable memories provoking an euphoric "détente" of satisfaction and "fait accompli."

Upon arrival there was a countless drawback offset by a great blessing . . . I had less than $20. in my billfold but the whole world was spinning in my hands.

I realized then, how important it is to have special friends.

My special friends, the Gervais Family

Remembered with Joy

Front left to right : Carl, Juanita, Steve, Fern, Billy.
Back left to right : Ken, Denise.

Denise : Passed away in 1968, she was eleven years old.

Juanita : Beloved wife of Joseph Fernand, born July 17, 1934
        died December 27, 1998.

If you have Class
Ann Landers

If you have class you've got it made. If you don't have class, no matter what else you have, it won't make up for it.

Class - never runs scared. It is sure-footed and confident and it can handle whatever comes along.

Class - has sense of humour. It knows that a good laugh is the best lubricant for oiling machinery of human relations.

Class - never makes excuses. It takes its lumps and learns from past mistakes.

Class - knows that good manners are nothing more than a series of small sacrifices and minor inconveniences.

Class - bespeaks an aristocracy unrelated to ancestors or money. Some extremely wealthy people have no class at all, while others who are struggling to make ends meet are loaded with it.

Class - is real. You can't fake it.

Class - is comfortable in its own skin. It never puts on airs.

Class - never tries to build itself up by tearing others down.

Class - is already up and need not attempt to look better by making others look worse.

Class - walks with kings and keeps its virtue and talks with crowds and keeps its common touch. Everyone is comfortable with the person who has class because he is comfort able with himself.

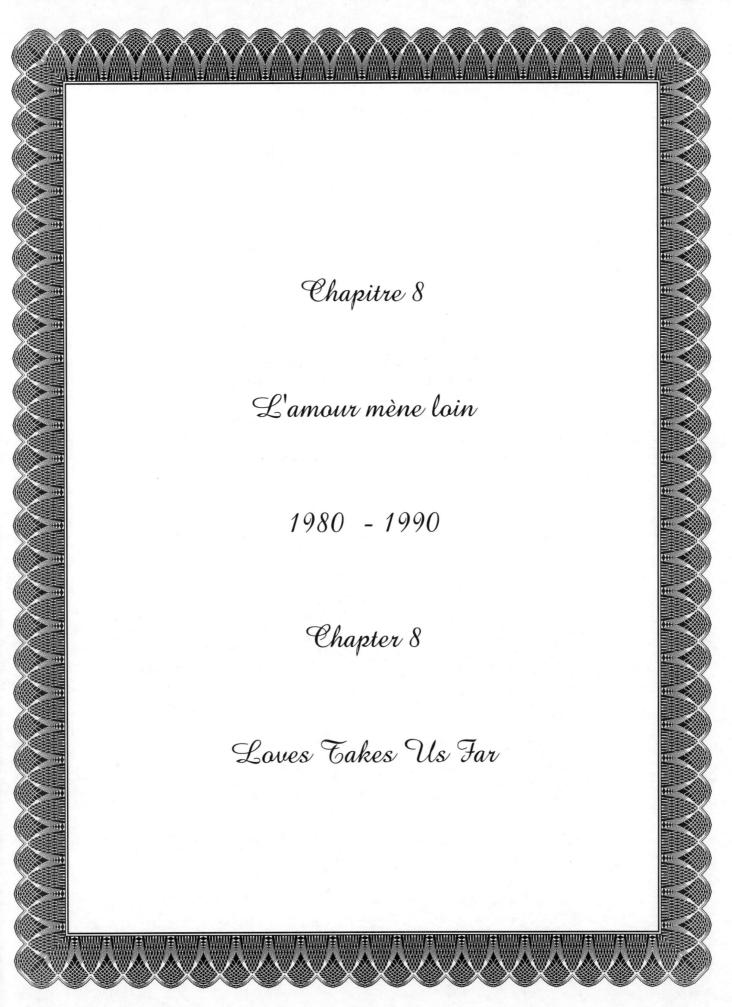

Chapitre 8

L'amour mène loin

1980 - 1990

Chapter 8

Loves Takes Us Far

Thoughts that inspire

Love - But nothing can take the place of love.
Love is the measure of life:
only so far as we love
do we really live.

John Buroughs

Love - Nothing is sweeter then love
Nothing stronger, nothing higher
Nothing wider, nothing more pleasant
Nothing fuller or better in heaven or in
earth; for love is born of God and cannot
rest but in God, above all created things.

Thomas A. Kempis

DÉLIA TÉTREAULT
MÈRE MARIE DU SAINT-ESPRIT

– née à Marieville le 4 février 1865 d'Alexis Tétreault et de Célina Ponton
– entrée chez les soeurs de la Charité de Saint-Hyacinthe en 1883
– entrée à « Béthanie », maison de bonnes oeuvres, en 1891
– approbation du projet d'une École Apostolique en 1901
– fonde l'institut des Soeurs Missionnaires de l'Immaculée Conception en 1902
– fait profession perpétuelle sous le nom de Soeur Marie du Saint-Esprit en 1905
– départ des premières missionnaires pour la Chine en 1909
– lancement d'une revue missionnaire « Le Précurseur » en 1920
– fondation du séminaire des Prêtres des missions étrangères en 1921
– approbation par Rome de la Règle de vie des Soeurs Missionnaires de l'Immaculée Conception en 1933
– est gravement malade en 1933
– meurt le 1er octobre 1941 à Montréal

CAUSE DE BÉATIFICATION

1958 – Premières démarches entreprises en vue de la Cause de béatification
1982 – Approbation par l'archevêque de Montréal des démarches en vue de l'introduction de la Cause à Rome.
1985 -- Commencement des démarchent canoniques
1987 – Clôture canonique du procès diocésain. Dossier transmis à Rome
1997 – Documents reçus de Rome le 18 décembre 1997, déclarant Mère Délia Tétreault "Vénérable."

Nous vivons aujourd'hui une grande joie – Délia Tétreault, fondatrice de notre communauté, les Soeurs Missionnaires de l'Immaculée Conception, vient d'être officiellement proclamée "Vénérable" par le Pape Jean-Paul II, le 18 décembre 1997. Une première étape est franchie dans la démarche de béatification de cette grande Misssionnaire. La beauté de sa vie éclate au grand jour. L'Église reconnaît le don particulier que Délia a reçu pour le monde d'aujourd'hui et les vertus qu'elle a prodiguées de façon intense et héroïque.

C'est avec Marie, dans l'Action de grâces, que Délia Tétreault a vécu sa vocation mission- naire sachant que l'amour mène loin.

Référence "Le Précurseur"   mai - juin 1998

Un héritage à partager

Le processus de canonisation est long et exigeant. Il fallait une femme comme Pauline Longtin m.i.c., pour diriger durant plus de 16 ans ces importants projets et y réussir. Notre bien de famille était entre bonnes mains et, aujourd'hui encore, Sr Pauline continue de le mettre en valeur.

– Cueillir dans les lettres et les souvenirs de Délia Tétreault l'héritage qui fait vivre notre communauté.
– Interviewer les personnes qui l'ont connue.
– Écrire et faire écrire sur Délia.
– Mettre en lumière sa spiritualité.
– Relever le défi de présenter à Rome la demande de canonisation de Délia et vivre le long processus de sa reconnaissance officielle comme Vénérable.

Les filles Roy de Pain Court

Trois jeunes filles de la paroisse de Pain Court s'engagent dans la Congrégation des Soeurs Missionnaires de l'Immaculée Conception de Montréal. Elles sont Soeur Marie Roy et Soeur Jeanne Roy, deux compagnes de classe, et Soeur Marguerite Roy, soeur de Soeur Jeanne Roy.

Soeur Marie Roy, musicienne de profession, s'est dévouée pendant plusieurs années pour la diffusion de la revue missionnaire "Le Précurseur." Par la suite, elle est nommée pour la mission de Joliette et accepte d'être organiste de la paroisse St-Pierre de la même ville.

Soeur Jeanne Roy a passé une bonne partie de sa vie missionnaire au Japon, environ 25 ans dont quelques années comme supérieure.

Soeur Marguerite Roy, institutrice et infirmière, s'est dévouée auprès des plus démunis d'Haïti, environ dix ans.

Revue "Le Précurseur" C.P. 157, Succ. Laval-des-Rapides, Laval, Québec. Canada H7N 4Z4

Forerunner in the Church

Délia Tétreault foundress of the Institute of the Missionary Sister of the Immaculate Conception 1865 - 1941.

In Marieville, Québec, February 4, 1865 the home of Alexis Tétreault and Célina Ponton was enriched by the addition of two new members, twins, a boy robust and apparently intent on living, and a girl, sickly and unlikely to survive. God's ways are not our ways and the predictions were not fulfilled; the boy died when only a few months old while little Délia who needed continuous care clung to life. Two years later, her dying mother entrusted Délia to her godfather Mr. Jean Alix whose wife, aunt Julie, was Mrs. Tétreault's sister. Both acted as her parents from then on.

While still a child she was impressed by the missionary stories which she craved to read in the annals of the Propagation of the Faith and the Holy Childhood stored in the attic of her father's house.

From her own declaration in 1922, Délia was struck by this dream, and she understood something.

"I was kneeling by my bed when, all of a sudden, I saw a ripe field of wheat extending as far as the eye could see. At a given moment, all the ears of wheat changed into heads of children. I was struck by this dream and I understood that they represented the souls of pagan children. God is at work in every human life. He manifests His presence at all stages."

As a teenager she was attracted to the religious life and gifted with great graces of prayerful recollection. Délia applied for admission to the Carmelite monastery; doubtless she was not accepted, because of her frail health. However on October 23, 1883 when 18 years of age she was admitted as a postulant by the Grey Nuns of Saint-Hyacinthe. Fifty years later she confided to Canon Avila Roch, Superior general of the Foreign Missions Society of Québec, a significant event which happened during her time of postulancy.

Year 1891 marked the entrance of Délia Tétreault at "Bethany."(a house of good works)

1901 - Approval of the project for an apostolic School.
1902 - Foundation of the Institute of the Missionary Sisters of the Immaculate Conception
1905 - Perpetual commitment of Sister Marie du Saint-Esprit
1910 - Departure of the first missionaries for China
1920 - Launching of a missionary review, "Le Précurseur"
1921 - Foundation of the Foreign Missions Seminary
1933 - Approval by Rome of the Rule of Life of the m.i.c. Sisters
1933 - Serious illness of the Foundress
1941 - Death of Mother Marie du Saint-Esprit in Montréal, on October 1st
1958 - First steps toward procedures for the cause of beatification of Délia Tétreault
1982 - Approval by the archbishop of Montréal of stages in view of the introduction of the cause in Rome
1985 - Beginning of the canonicle inquiry for the cause of beatification.
1987 - Canonical closure of the Diocesan procedures, Dossier sent to Rome

1997 - December 18, the Foundress of the Missionary Sisters of Immaculate Conception was proclaimed, "Venerable", by Pope John-Paul II.

Women of various backgrounds and nationalities, the missionary Sisters of the Immaculate Conception are united by a common mission which they strive to live out in countries of Latin America, to those of the Far East, including those of Africa and North America. They are eager to serve among the poorest of the poor and there are and will always be poor people to whom the Good News is still to be proclaimed.

Ref. English translation Antoinette Kimlough- Bureau de la Cause Délia Tétreault Laval p.2

Dora Vander Pryt Sterling

Caroline and Angéline sharing their thoughts on Bernard and Dora,
a couple who has made a difference through their manifestation
and willingness to serve for the love of their fellow man.

Dora immigrated from Holland after World War II, with her parents and family, Joseph and Marie Vander Pryt. They arrived in September 1950 and took up residence on the farm of Alcide Caron in Pain Court.

Dora was 17 years old and the only girl in the family. She had five brothers: Théodore 18, the oldest, John 16, then Cornelius, Francis and Joseph.

They served the farmers very well harvesting the fall crops. As winter rolled around, Dora performed housework duties. She was happy to help with my small family. Her work was meticulous and she was very efficient with the children. Soon word got around how proficient a housekeeper she was and in no time her work schedule kept her busy all winter. Mrs. Célina Pinsonneault and Mrs. Josephine Martin were delighted to have someone helping them in their advanced years. As time went on she accomplished household duties in many homes in our area: Gérard Caron, Réginald Caron, Adrien Caron, Melvin Primeau, Antoinette Emery.

Before long, Bernard Sterling, a neighbour, became fascinated by this young vivacious, hard working girl.

After a two year courtship Bernard and Dora were married at St. Francis Xavier Church, in Tilbury, August 30, 1952. The Vander Pryt had bought a farm on the outskirts of Tilbury, remodelled the home and lived there with their family.

522

Bernard and Dora had seven children, two boys and five girls. Ronald married Diana Couture, Rose-Marie married Brian Bernier, Diane married Laurent D. St-Pierre, Gisèle married Mike Johnston, Anita, Louise, and David are single.

This family is a credit to our community and you feel a better person for having known Dora. God had given her special talents and the grace to execute them for the love of her family and her community. For some 30 years she worked tirelessly with the Ladies of Ste-Anne in our parish serving those early to rise business breakfasts, funeral luncheons, ladies' teas, wedding feasts, banquets, picnic suppers, you name it; she was there when needed, so was Bernard her helper. She worked faithfully alongside Marie-Anne Faubert and Cécile King, "the kitchen ladies," a compatible threesome preparing sumptuous meals year after year, attracting crowds far and wide because of the "soul food" they served so amiably well, a time consuming job, and all "gratis" for the upkeep of their parish.

When a huge crowd or a special occasion warranted extra help, Adeline Bélanger, Marie-Louise Martin, Thérèse Sterling, Jesse Robert, Pat Schumacher and Mary Lozon obligingly and regularly came to the rescue.

As years progressed the Vander Pryt family flourished and during the winter months Dora's father would spend some of his free time building "Mission Chapels" in the district of Panama. Being a skilful construction worker, he also devoted his moments of leisure doing missionary work in Central America easing the burden of the poor so that they too could share a morsel of God's bounty.

Dora's reputation as an artist, a gardener, a bird enthusiast was well-known, but above all she remained "une femme du terroir" embracing life in all its splendour. Her rapport with Mother Nature was nurtured at a very tender age while tending the "tulpen velden" with her beloved "Vader" in Heemstede, in the Netherlands, a gift she lovingly passed on to all her children.

Her moments of "détente" were right at her back door. An informal tree grove, fenced-in by cedars and spruces, with long-standing hardwoods growing sparsely in the wood-lot, intermingling with flowering shrubs and wildflowers well-suited to birds and butterflies, was Dora's sheltered haven. It was highlighted by a "menagerie" of small animals, pets and caged-in birds including a couple of cooing lovebirds so befitting of Dora's attachment to her close-knit family and love of nature. A winding path led you to a creek bordering the northeast side of the property where wild ducks waded among the bulrush while nearby, a pair held fort close to their nesting ground. Close-by, a wooden bench, slightly hidden in a shady nook, coaxed one to relaxation and contemplation.

Dora's penchant for art surfaced when the mural adorning the sanctuary dome in her parish was in the process of being repainted. She had travelled to Lourdes and felt a special calling to help with the project. This is how she met Father B. Johnson while touring various churches in the area in search of decorative ideas.

This tireless priest, besides attending to his own flock, reaches out to another continent bringing solace and evangelization to the poor in the missions of Columbia South America. This encounter with Father Johnson was in God's plan. Dora never did partake in the finished mural as such, but prior to her death, she and her daughter, Louise, travelled with Father Johnson to visit the

Columbian missions. Dora had witnessed suffering during the war years in Europe, therefore she understood their poverty and misery. She was willing and ready to share with the less fortunate, having been blest with so much here in Canada.

Dora was a special Mom working faithfully and peacefully raising her family and attending to activities close to her heart. She was a humble, courageous and down to earth person worthy of our admiration. After a severe bout of cancer she passed away September 17, 1995. We loved her dearly and she will be remembered always in our prayers.

There was a time

A devoted and committed young woman, following in the footsteps of "Florence Nightingale," graduated from St Joseph's Hospital in Chatham in 1931. She was Ida Poissant, a caring and compassionate woman of her generation.

Ida, born April 4, 1910, was raised in Pain Court and later moved to Grande Pointe. She was the daughter of Ovide Poissant, son of Eusèbe Poissant and Mérence Lefort. Ovide was married January 30, 1906 to Marie Martin daughter of Lévi Martin and Caroline Faubert, pioneers. They had 14 children, twins who died in infancy. Ernest, Zélia, Ida, Ovila, Oscar, Antoinette, Edna, Felix, Louis, Léo, Jeanne, and Gérard. A distinguished family of the community.

In their younger years they farmed in Pain Court next to Joseph Poissant, Ovide's brother. They learned to care for their ailing uncle who had lost his wife, Léna Bourassa, in 1945. They had not been blessed with children.

Ida entered St. Joseph's nursing school in 1928, graduated in 1931 and continued her mission of mercy for many years at the hospital. Later, it was at Thamesview Lodge that she carried on her duties as a nurse. Everyone cherished her. She loved the elderly and consequently she worked at the Lodge for a long time.

What made Ida unique? She was always available either for advice or counselling or simply lending a helping hand to anyone in need. Mothers knew her well at the hospital since she was often at their bedside with their babies, or whatever else ailed them or their friends.

My mother acknowledged her gentle smiling face and loving care. So did I, especially at my bedside at the hospital. Her compassion, her tender care and that beautiful smile that cures all ills represented an angel of mercy towards the sick. She was a dedicated soul.

On November 25, 1941 at 34 years old, she married Wilfrid Mulhern, son of James Mulhern who operated a Sports Complex at the corner of King and Third St. from 1948 to 1987 about 40 years with other members of the Mulhern family. Ida and Wilfrid raised 5 children, Mary Ellen, Patsy, Elaine, Bernie and Paul.

She continued in nursing all her life. Ida cared for her ailing parents also, and continued to care and help the needy. A dedicated model of unselfish love, Ida died March 10, 1981 after a few years of illness. She was 71 years old.

Caroline Roy Laprise

The Mulhern "Sport Shop"

An empty corner lot was purchased by William Baby's, a broker, in 1902 from Victoria Eberts whose father was a prominent early settler in Chatham.[1]

W. Baby built the store, at a cost of $7000.00. It was originally a grocery store operated by Baby's two sons William Jr. and Frank. These pioneers were renowned, respected business citizens who forged ahead in the 20th century in the area of Pain Court and vicinity.

William, son of Edmond Baby and Françoise Urquhart, was born in 1844, was married at Pain Court on July 1862 to Edesse Maillet who died in 1875. Her mother was Agathe Lozon and her father was J.B. Maillet. William remarried to Mathilde Dichon whose parents were Mathildée Bourassa and Denis Dichon.

Another brother Honoré, was married to Bella Labadie daughter of Damase Labadie and Françoise Rhéaume, November 5, 1867 at Pain Court. He died in 1871 at the age of 24.

In 1908, the business portion was sold and operated by Bradley and Sons grocers. The street numbers of the property were changed by the city from 190 - 192 to 268 - 270 King St. In this same year the business was taken back by the Baby Family and was run until 1916 as the William Baby Pool room and Tobacco Shop. This building had numerous businesses operating out of it. If only the walls could talk.

1918 - 20	Labombard's Barber Shop and grocer
1920 - 22	Lewis McIntyre Real Estate and Nukol Fuel Co.
1923 - 24	G. Povrsookas Grocery
1925 - 29	Grocery Store and Scotty the Cleaner
1930 - 37	Povrsookas with a Snack bar and Rossini Wines of Windsor
1938 - 40	Grocery Store and Young's Auto Supply
1941 - 45	There was a dairy bar
1946 - 48	There was James Byrne News Agency, "Border City Star"
1948 - 88	[2] The Baby Family estate sold the property to L.J. Mulhern and Co. who officially opened the store September 12, 1948. They operated this famous store for approximately 40 years as a Sport Complex. Their inventory was amazing and the Mulhern's were efficient and pleasant.

It was then sold to Eddie Mariconda who owns a thriving Men's Wear Store in Chatham.

1 Ref. Belden publisher
2 Ref Chatham News

Éloge à André Pellerin

André Pellerin, âgé de 83 ans est décédé le 6 février 1992. Il était père bien-aimé de huit enfants dont Gustave, Gilles, Darcy, Robert, Claude et André, Lorraine et Carole. À sa mort, il comptait 21 petits-enfants et 5 arrière-petits-enfants. En première noce, il épousa Irène Lapointe et en deuxième noce, Domitilde Soucie en 1983.

Il était père, artiste, poète, athlète, homme rempli d'humour et de jovialité. André était tout cela. Il avait un coeur d'or. Il était un homme courageux et dévoué auprès des siens. Il était membre à vie du Club Richelieu d'Ottawa et a été décoré par le Club pour son travail auprès des Caisses populaires régionales, auprès du clergé français et pour son travail afin d'établir la première paroisse française à Pembroke, la paroisse Saint Jean-Baptiste.

Ses loisirs, il les passaient auprès du Club d'âge d'or, au terrain de tennis, ou en rendant service aux nécessiteux.   À la maison, c'était le travail quotidien, le dessin et la poésie.

En 1985, il visite son oncle Aimé Guay après le décès de son épouse. Par hasard je rencontre André à ma demeure lors d'une soirée récréative d'amis en Floride. Lors de ma sortie de l'hôpital, en novembre 1985, il m'offre ses services gratuitement pendant quatre mois. Il est chauffeur, cuisinier, garde-malade pour pansement à mes pieds. Son dévouement et son esprit charitable restera imprimé chez moi pour toujours.

Caroline Roy Laprise

L'Anneau Vide

Vieil anneau qu'un prêtre bénit pour elle.
Et que pieusement je glisse dans son doigt.
Tu restes le symbole et le témoin fidèle.
De sa tendresse et de ma foi.

Dans cet anneau vide, c'est elle que je vois.
Et crois même entendre.Peut-être miracle d'amour.
Le souffle de sa voix lointaine.
Mais toujours persuasive et tendre.
Qui me parle comme autrefois.

André Pellerin
Pembroke, 1988.

BRASS BELL BEARING DATE OF 1864

. . . used for more than church

Age takes bell's toll
by JIM POTTER
News Staff Reporter

PAIN COURT (Staff) – The last time Marie-Thérèse came down to earth was in 1937, when she fell over 60 feet from the burning spire of Immaculate Conception Church in Pain Court.

But Friday, the 650-pound brass bell made a gentler descent, leaving its spot in the belfry for the last time.

Sporting a large crack from the fall 44 years ago and crusted with dirt, the bell was plucked out of the tower by a crane during routine maintenance work on the spire.

According to Father C.H. Sylvester, Marie-Thérèse may undergo restoration by the church's men's group next year.

After the fire of 1937, which levelled most of the 27-year-old church, Marie-Thérèse was never the same. "It sounded like hell." Father Sylvester said, and was replaced by electronic chimes in 1968.

The bell, which measures about three feet in diameter at its base, was installed in 1911. According to an inscription under the crack at the top, it was blessed and dubbed "Marie-Thérèse" by Monseigneur P.A. Pinsonneault.

One Pain Court resident said the town "used to depend on the bell to wake up in the morning and for meal time."

The bell was used for church services, when someone was born in the town and when someone died.

She said during the 1940's and 50's, the bell was used to warn of fire.

She said although as a child she would often play in the steeple, she only had one opportunity to ring the bell, during a baptism.

"My uncle said 'go ring the bell', we were all excited. . . and you could see all the old people come out of the house to see where the fire was."

Marie-Thérèse could be heard for several miles.

Mgr. Augustin Caron préside à l'inauguration du monument
historique, le 29 août 1982, en présence de nombreux paroissiens.
Photo-gracieuseté de Alphy Emery - 1982

Bien à l'abri sous un comble de clocher, "Marie-Thérèse," à travers un siècle et plus d'existence, est la grande survivante de la communauté qu'elle a servie et à qui elle a toujours appartenue.

Depuis 1968, son timbre éclatant et cuivré de jadis s'est assourdi. C'est donc en 1982 que la paroisse Immaculée Conception lui a redonné un élan de survie. Dès lors, la cloche "Marie-Thérèse" se trouve à la hauteur de la situation. Juste en face de l'église, un monument modeste et rustique a été construit en briques surmonté d'un encadrement à jour où est conservée en permanence "Marie-Thérèse" immobilisée dans le temps, baignant dans la lumière et humant l'odeur suave de son paysage rural. Sa marque de fidélité lui a valu une plaque d'identité. Cette plaque porte l'inscription vouée à son culte, la déesse de notre patrimoine historique.

L'ensemble du monument a été conçu ingénieusement par un groupe de paroissiens dont certains parmi eux ont grandi et d'autres ont vécu à l'ombre de son clocher. Ce fut un projet d'équipe composé de Napoléon Roy, Amédée Emery, Raymond Gagner, Matthew Classens, Rodolphe Potvin, Halarie Rivard, James Blair, Wayne St-Pierre, Roméo Pinsonneault, Marion Crow et Blanche Foy.

Veilleuse et vigilante en son temps, la cloche "Marie-Thérèse," aujourd'hui statuaire et silencieuse, se laisse vivre au gré des jours pour contempler en plénitude sa progéniture. Elle allie le passé avec le présent commandant, à chacun qui l'approche, le respect et la fierté d'un héritage culturel et religieux à conserver.

Angéline Blais Marentette

531

La cloche "Marie-Thérèse"
Un retentissement patrimonial à travers l'espace du temps . . .

Oui, c'est bien elle, "Marie-Thérèse," qui savait nous communiquer les moments précieux de la vie: l'appel de l'Angelus, c'était sa façon de nous porter au recueillement; la cloche du mariage signifiait pour elle le pommier fleuri qui allait multiplier ses fruits de progéniture; la cloche du baptême, c'était encore elle qui comptait une âme de plus à l'arbre de vie; le glas des enterrements, c'était pour "Marie-Thérèse" une feuille qui se détachait malgré elle de l'arbre pour aller échoir à la poussière du sol et renaître à l'espérance de la vie éternelle. Il ne faut pas oublier, non plus, les courses des jeunes curieux s'aventurant jusqu'à son clocher pour y explorer ses remparts. Eh bien! voila toute une répercussion de souvenirs que l'écho de "Marie-Thérèse" a fait retentir du campanile antique, au fin clocher de 1854, pour être immortalisée, en 1982, à un rôle figuratif dans l'histoire de notre culture religieuse.

En souvenir de mon père, Philippe Blais, ainsi que tous les autres bedeaux qui ont été fidèles à sonner les rites du culte quotidien: M. Toussaint Campbell, M. Joseph (Jos.) Maure, M. Isidore Lauzon et son fils Léopold, M. Napoléon Tanguay et M. Télesphore Dénommé.

Angéline Blais Marentette

À la douce mémoire de Trefflé - 1980

Une vie prend sa réelle dimension par ses actes ici-bas et par là, elle découvre le seul chemin à la vie de résurrection. Trefflé savait répandre parmi les moins favorisés le sourire et le réconfort.

Il est décédé subitement à sa demeure le 20 mars 1980, après une soirée pénible de souffrance et après deux visites ce même soir à l'hôpital accompagné de son fils Florent. Il était âgé de 66 ans 10 mois.

Sa mort subite a causé de vifs regrets auprès de sa famille et pour tout ceux qui l'ont connu intimement. Encore aujourd'hui, la famille désire remercier tous ceux qui sont venus lui témoigner leur reconnaissance.

Family
Hobbies and Business

Kenex LTD hemp

Industrial Hemp Production and Processing

Jean M. Laprise
President

R. R. #1 Pain Court
Ontario, Canada N0P 1Z0
Email: kenex@kent.net

Phone: 519-351-9922
Fax: 519-352-6667
Web: www.kenex.org

LAPRISE FARMS LTD.

R.R. #1, PAINCOURT, ONTARIO N0P 1Z0

JEAN M. LAPRISE

| OFFICE | (519) 351-6633 | CELL | (519) 436-8025 |
| FAX | (519) 352-6667 | HOME | (519) 352-2968 |

EMAIL: laprise@kent.net

Government of Canada
Canadian Food Inspection
Agency

Gouvernement du Canada
Agence canadienne d'inspection
des aliments

Colette N. Laprise

Retail Food Officer   Agente des aliments au détail

Canada

Historique familial vis-à-vis
les 20 petits-enfants de ma famille

Nous sommes une génération en voie de transformation, une génération de changements de réalités et de valeurs.

Alors, il nous faut des principes de valeurs supérieures. Par là, j'entends, de ne pas rejeter nos responsabilités sur le prochain. Donc, il faut être responsable de nos propres actions. Cet engagement comprend le respect des droits fondamentaux de la personne. Avoir le courage de tout faire au meilleur de nos connaissances. Ça demande du travail bien fait, d'être honnête avec soi-même et d'avoir de bons principes de valeurs humaines.

Nos parents, même si parfois ils étaient rigides, ont certainement inculqué chez nous des valeurs primaires fondamentales face à la réalité d'aujourd'hui.

The Kent County separate school track and field championships were held Thursday at Ursuline College in Chatham. André Laprise of Ste-Catherine in Pain Court shows his winning form in the Intermediate boys shot-put event.
Photo   Mike Bennett

I'm proud to introduce all my grandchildren

Name - Jean-Marc Laprise
Date and place of birth - April 11, 1961, Chatham, Ontario
Father - Gérard Laprise   Mother - Aline Cartier
Education - Graduate of École Secondaire de Pain Court, Majored in Science at Guelph Agricultural College.

Name - Jeannine Laprise
Date and place of birth - July 6, 1962, Chatham, Ontario
Father - Gérard Laprise   Mother - Aline Cartier
Education - Graduate of École Secondaire de Pain Court, Fanshaw College.

Name - Richard Laprise
Date and place of birth - May 5, 1965, Chatham, Ontario
Father - Roger Laprise
Mother - Rose-Marie Houle
Spouse - Bonnie Sheets
Daughter of - Blake Sheets and Frances Morgan
Education - Graduate of École Secondaire de Pain Court, received the "Kinsmen Award," graduate of Ridgetown Agricultural School, received a Horticulture degree.

Farming experience - Approx. 16 yrs. I own and work my farms in Dover Township growing various crops including, Tomatoes, Seed corn, Hemp, Broccoli, Brussel Sprouts, Soybeans, Peas and Corn.

Work experience - Tax preparer for H&R Block, 1986 to 1988, Supervisor for H&R Block in 1989, Office Manager for H&R Block for 1990 -91. Taught income tax classes for H&R Block employees for 21/2 yrs. Have a small computer services company called "The Computer Phoenix." The name comes from the two Phoenix's on the Laprise coat of arms. I service all computer hardware and software for Jim Langdon's "H&R Block" Franchisees, the largest in Canada. I service the computers for Kenex & Laprise Farms Ltd.   I also assembled and serviced the computer this book was typed on.

Name - Lucien Rosaire Laprise
Date and place of birth - February 9, 1967, Chatham, Ontario
Father - Roger Laprise
Mother - Rose-Marie Houle
Spouse - April Lyn Boivin
Education - École Secondaire de Pain Court, St. Clair College, courses
include: Electronics, Hydraulics, Welding, General machining. I hold a
Millwright certificate after a 3 yr. course at St. Clair College.

Farming - Began farming in 1984, purchased my first farm in 1985.
Purchased a second farm in 1996. I grow crops such as, Corn, Soya beans, Seed corn,
Peas, Broccoli, Brussel sprouts and Tomatoes.

Work experience - Campbell Soup, Family traditions (pod stripper mechanic),
                Currently working at Kenex in the Grain division; I took part in engineering and
                constructing the grain division at Kenex.

Name - Phyllis Laprise, darling infant daughter of Florent Laprise and Bernadette Pinsonneault. She survived only 8 days and passed away November 27, 1965. She died in St. Joseph's Hospital in Chatham.

Name - Maurice Albert Laprise
Date and place of birth - May 16, 1967, Chatham, Ontario
Father - Florent Laprise
 Mother - Bernadette Pinsonneault
Spouse - Yvette Cartier
Daughter of - Robert Cartier and Norma Charron
 Education - École Secondaire de Pain Court, graduate.

Graduate School - Ridgetown Agricultural College, part-time studies
Work experience - 5 years Laprise Farms Ltd. Research on
Computerized sprayer.
Farming - 11 years on my own farm
Trades - Research in Agriculture - 10 years, Welding and Fabrication
Repair Technician.

Name - André Laprise
Date and place of birth - March 3, 1969 Chatham, Ontario
Father - Florent Laprise
Mother - Bernadette Pinsonneault
Spouse - Laurie Moore
Daughter of - Clarke Moore and Shirley Gerard

Education - École Secondaire de Pain Court
Farming - Started at 5 yrs old with father

Work experience - Eaton-Yale 3 yrs., Bouncer Jr's 1 yr., Bouncer Dr.
Feelgood's, Copperfields, Mainstreet, 3 yrs. Campbell Soup's
2 seasons, Pickle Station 1 yr. Detasselling King Grain, 3 yrs.

Name - Jamie Robert Trudell
Date and place of birth - May 17, 1970, Chatham, Ontario
Father -David Trudell
Mother - Caroline Laprise
Spouse - Nicole Burn
Education- Ursuline College graduate, Chatham, Ontario

Graduate Schools-   Kwantlen College Surrey British Columbia
Farming - helper, 4 yrs. - Chatham Ontario
Trades- Millwright/Welder 9 yrs.   - British Columbia

Work experiences - EWOS Canada millwright's helper 1 yr.
Millwright's Union Local 2736 Served apprenticeship +
experience 6 yrs. (too many places to list here; worked all over
the province in the Paper Making, Grain, and production type of
processes such as NABOB coffee.) Newstech Recycling
(de-inking plant) 2 yrs.
Sterling Pulp Chemicals, Almost 2 years til present
Hired as Millwright/ Welder and soon to be getting into   Instrumentation

Name: Christie Anne Trudell
Date and place of birth - June 2, 1972 Chatham, Ontario
Marital status - Single
Father -David Trudell
Mother - Caroline Laprise

Education- Graduate of Ursuline College, Chatham, Ontario

Graduate Schools- - Developmental Services Worker Diploma
from St. Clair College

Work experience - Chatham and District Association for Community Living
 Residential Support Worker 6yrs.

Name - Madeleine Renée Laprise
Date and place of birth - June 24, 1969, Chatham, Ontario
Father - Claude Laprise
Mother - Marie-Reine Masse
Spouse - Brian Sharp
Son of - Donald Sharp and Bernadette Scarani Mahfood
Education - Holy Family Secondary, Wallaceburg, Ontario

Graduate Schools- University of Toronto (Erindale Campus), Sheradon
College (Oakville), Ontario College of Arts, Toronto. Received BA.
Honours, BFA., and Multimedia Certificate. (AOCA)
Work experience - Own Mugisha Productions, and work for Cuppa
Coffee Animation Productions in Toronto. (Producer of Animation films)

Name - Nicole Margaret Laprise
Date and place of birth - May 29, 1971, Chatham, Ontario
Father - Claude Laprise
Mother - Marie-Reine Masse
Spouse - Steven Brown
Son of - John Wilfred Brown and Audrey Seaward

Education - Holy Family Secondary School, Wallaceburg, Ontario
Graduate School - Sheradon College, Oakville, Ontario

Work experience - Print journalism and photography.   Reporter for
Wallaceburg News and the Chatham Daily News. Reporter for
Wallaceburg News 2 yrs. Reporter for Petrolia Topic, 3yrs.

Name - Vincent Laprise
Date and place of birth - February 11, 1972
Father - Guy Laprise
Mother - Penny McDonald
Education - Graduate of Ursuline College
Graduate school - Wilfrid Laurier University, Studied Music
Work experience - Started at Canadian Tire at 15 years old and am now
Parts Manager in Chatham. Was assistant Service manager at the
Waterloo store for 21/2 yrs.
Been through one store expansion, played major role in the building of
two new stores.

Hobbies - Sing at St. Agnes Church, was Cantor for 6 yrs. at Our Lady
of Lourdes in Waterloo. Play guitar, avid reader of Church History and
have amassed a large collection of books on the subject.

Name - Jason Laprise
Date and place of birth - Sept. 10, 1975, Chatham, Ontario
Father - Guy Laprise
Mother - Penny McDonald
Education - Ursuline College, Chatham, Ontario. Graduated as a Canada Scholar,
Honoured with OAC Chemistry Award
Graduate Schools- University of Guelph:- Honours Bachelor of Science in Computing
and Information, Science, Dean's Scholarship Recipient.

Work experience - IBM Canada, Toronto, Ontario, present position: Software Developer
for net.commerce group design/implement/test software. May 98, University of Guelph:
Undergraduate research assistant, implemented a system to enter architecture informa
tion of DSP's via a graphical interface. January 98, University of Guelph: Teaching
assistant for a discrete mathematics course. April 97, Ontario Wheat Board, Chatham:
Programmer. Aug. 91, Canadian Tire, Chatham- Automotive parts sales clerk approx. 5
years.

Name - Jeremey Laprise
Date and place of birth - January 2, 1979, Chatham, Ontario
Father - Guy Laprise
Mother - Penny McDonald
Education - Ursuline College Chatham, graduate achieving the Ontario scholar's award.
University of Waterloo, Ontario, currently enrolled in the Faculty of Mathematics, candi
date for the four-year computer science honours degree. Current overall average 86.
Farm experience - worked for Florent Laprise, working on various farm equipment, farm
labour, tomato harvesting and hoeing. Pioneer Ltd., corn detasselling , Brady Farms
Ltd., corn detasselling.

Work experience - Pizza Hut Canada 4 yrs. Catholic Board of Education, instructed teachers on using several software
packages. Instructed children's camps which involved supervision, teaching software, cleaned and upgraded
computers.
Volunteer experience - Arthritis Society, yearly canvassing. Fundraising for Youth groups and several other charities.

Name - Julie Simpson
Date and place of birth - December 31, 1974, Chatham, Ontario
Spouse - Robert Simpson
Son of - Peter Simpson and Joyce Hodgson
Father - Jean-Marie Laprise
Mother - Lucille Marie Benoit

Education - Graduate of École Secondaire de Pain Court, Ontario
Secondary School Diploma OSSD/DESO, Ontario Academic Credit
OAC/CPO.

Graduate School - St. Clair College, Chatham, Nursing 2 yrs.
Work Experience - Seasonal farm work 12 yrs., Chiropractic Assistant
3.5 yrs.

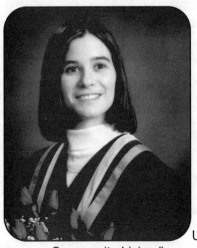

Name - Chantal Nicole Laprise
Date and place of birth - December 31, 1974, Chatham, Ontario
Father - Jean-Marie Laprise
Mother - Lucille Marie Benoit

Education - Graduate of École Secondaire de Pain Court, Ontario,
Graduate School - Laurentian University, graduated with an Honours BA. in
psychology and a BA. in Women's Studies.   Currently working on her Master's
in Social Work.

Work experience - Volunteered for the "Children's Aid Society", "Laurentian
University Women's Centre" and the "Chatham and District Association for
Community Living."

Name - Joël Marcel Laprise
Date and place of birth - December 28, 1978, Chatham, Ontario
Father - Jean-Marie Laprise
Mother - Lucille Laprise
Spouse - Anne Marie Renaud
Daughter of - Robert Renaud and Adriana Wysman
Education - Graduate of École Secondaire de Pain Court.

Work experience - Drummer for "Whaling Band" Chatham, Ontario.
Operated pea combines for Family Tradition and Omstead Foods for 3
years.

Seasonal farm work. Is presently working with Laprise Farms Ltd. in
both greenhouse and field operations.

Name - Mélanie Lucette Laprise
Date and place of birth - March 26, 1981, Chatham, Ontario
Father - Jean-Marie Laprise
Mother - Lucille Nicole Benoit
Education - Graduate of École Secondaire de Pain Court, in 1999

Work experience - Seed corn detasselling, child care, seasonal farm
work and other part-time employment

Name - Robert Crow
Date and place of birth - August 4, 1978, Halifax, Nova Scotia
Father - Malcolm Crow
Mother - Colette Laprise

Education - Hants West Rural High School, Halifax, Nova Scotia

Work experience - C & R Sterling Farms 5 yrs part-time, Eric Cochrane-chain saw operator, 4 months, Oak Grove Farms 4 months, O'Quinns Roofing 3 months, Briarwood Stables-stable hand 6 months, Joan of Arc Ranch, Alberta, Ranch Foreman (cattle ranch/grain farm) 3 yrs.

Name - Joseph (Joey) Crow
Date and place of birth - April 22, 1980, Halifax, Nova Scotia
Father - Malcolm Crow
Mother - Colette Laprise

Education - Hants West Rural High School, Halifax, Nova Scotia

Work Experience - Briarwood Stables, Stable hand, 6 months, Dexter Construction Co. Ltd. 3yrs. Some experience in Roofing, Carpentry, Cement, Automotive, Large machinery and Woodsman.

May, June and July Birthdays
Richard, Caroline, Nicole, Maurice, Jamie, Christie, Jean-Marie, Bonnie

MATURITY

~ Maturity is the ability to do a job whether you are supervised or not, finish a job once it is started; carry money without spending it, and be able to bear an injustice without wanting to get even.

~ Maturity is the ability to control anger and settle differences without violence.

~ Maturity is patience. It is the willingness to postpone immediate gratification in favour of the long-term gain.

~ Maturity is perseverance, the ability to sweat out a project or a situation in spite of heavy opposition and discouraging setbacks.

~ Maturity is the capacity to face unpleasantness and frustration, discomfort and defeat without complaint or collapse.

~ Maturity is humility. It is being big enough to say "I was wrong" and , when right the mature person need not experience the satisfaction of saying,
"I told you so."

~ Maturity is the ability to make a decision and stand by it. The immature spend their lives exploring endless possibilities; then they do nothing.

~ Maturity means dependability, keeping one's word, coming through in a crisis. The immature are masters of the alibi. They are confused and disorganized. Their lives are a maze of broken promises, former friends, unfinished business and good intentions that somehow never materialized.

~ Maturity is the art of living in peace with what we cannot change, the courage to change what can be changed and the wisdom to know the difference.

~ Nieces and Nephews ~

You are part of our heritage, preserve it well for future generations.

- Robert Lucier, Rosaire Lucier, Claudette Lucier, Marc Lucier.

- Yvette Roy, Mariette Roy, Denise Roy, Simone Roy. (King)

- Becky Roy, Germaine Roy, Kathy Roy. (King)

- Vincent Roy, Raymond Roy, Colette Roy. (King)

- Paul Barrette, Roch Barrette.

- Jacqueline Laprise, Claudette Laprise, Gisèle Laprise, Janice Laprise, Michel Laprise.

- Jean-Bernard Trahan, Alex Trahan, Yvette Trahan, Annette Trahan, Louise Trahan.

- Paul Haslip, Marc Haslip, John Haslip.

I love you
Tante Caroline

Exécutif du Club d'âge d'or

Grande Pointe 1986

1ère rangée: Florence Ouellette, Antoinette Tétreault, Laura Ouellette, Irene Martin.
2e rangée: Irene Demers, Dora Couture, Cécile Marchand.
3e rangée: Victor Demers, Harvey Couture, Armand Tétreault et Roméo Martin.

Référence - Album Souvenir Grande Pointe -
Centenaire 1886 - 1986 p. 68

Unveiling of 125th Anniversary Plaque

Maurice Bossy M.P. for Kent represented the federal government at the unveiling of the plaque celebrating the 125th anniversary of Pain Court on October 5, 1980. Mr. Gaetan Gervais assisted as director of the Ontario Heritage Foundation.

"The English inscription of this Plaque"

Settlement of this region began in the 1780's when English and French speaking squatters from the Detroit area moved on the Indians lands along the lower Thames Valley. By the 1820's in the nearby "Pain Court Block" one of the earliest French speaking communities in Southern Ontario had developed. Named "Pain Court" by Catholic Missionaries in reference to the small loaves of bread which was all the impoverished parishioners could offer, the settlement was surveyed in 1829.

In 1852 a Chapel was built and two years later construction of a church commenced. It quickly became the cultural and educational centre of French speaking Catholics in the area. By 1866 when a post office was established a small village had developed.

Our Member of Parliament
"MAURICE BOSSY"

In February 1980 Maurice Bossy was elected M. P. for Kent.   He has worked diligently for the betterment of the community and surrounding area. In March 1981 he announced publicly that a new Post Office was to be built in Pain Court, and he attended the official opening in September 1982.

During his term, he was instrumental in obtaining a provincial grant of 25 thousand dollars for the Usher's Club of Pain Court under the presidency of Edmond Gagner, to be used for renovations to the church in order to accommodate the disabled and the older generation.

Maurice Bossy, natif de Pain Court, nous affirme toujours sa fierté et sa joie d'être un des nôtres. Il se dit très reconnaissant pour l'éducation catholique et bilingue qu'il a reçu dans nos écoles. Sa mère, Zulma, ses deux soeurs Godlieve Couture et Georgette Devos, ainsi que ses deux frères, Cyriel et René, ont raison d'être fiers. Les paroissiens de Pain Court le remercient pour un travail bien accompli. Maurice et son épouse Margaret sont les parents de sept enfants et les fiers grands-parents de plusieurs petits enfants.

Les paroissiens de Grande Pointe sont également très reconnaissants pour l'attention qu'ils ont reçue de leur représentant, Maurice Bossy.

Référence - Pain Court 1983

"Les oiseaux de l'Enfant Jésus"
le 12 avril 1981
un succès théâtral éclatant

Sous l'habile direction de Mme Angéline Marentette, les professeurs, les élèves et quelques parents de l'école Ste-Catherine de Pain Court en collaboration avec le centre culturel Brébeuf, la Fédération des femmes canadiennes-françaises et le Secrétariat d'État, ont présenté une opérette qui a fait salle comble au Chatham Art Centre.

La jeune pianiste, Maria Guénette, malgré ses 11 ans, a démontré une virtuosité remarquable. M. Amédé Emery l'accompagnait à l'orgue. La vedette du spectacle fut incontestablement Eric Ouellette dans le rôle du lépreux. Son chant expressif et le rôle qu'il a si bien ressenti lui ont valu une pluie d'applaudissements par l'auditoire ému. Martin Paiement, interprétant Judas, a charmé la foule par sa voix juste et douce, par la simplicité et le naturel de son jeu dramatique. Marc Hamann, personnifiant Jésus, conduisit son auditoire au recueillement par le calme de son interprétation en transmettant son message d'amour et de compassion. Avec les décors appropriés de la place du marché à Jérusalem, la musique pertinente et le jeu admirable de tous les comédiens, le spectacle fut grandiose!

La reponsable de cette réalisation, Mme Angéline Marentette, a déclaré: "C'était un rêve que j'entretenais depuis longtemps."

Album Souvenir: Paroisse de Pain Court - 1983

20e anniversaire de la FFCF à St-Joachim

Le Père Roger Bénéteau, curé de la paroisse, se prépare de longue main pour la célébration du Centenaire en 1982, ainsi que pour le 20e anniversaire de la FFCF fondée en 1959. Les dames préparent un banquet pour l'occasion qui aura lieu le 24 mars 1979.

Les régions de Windsor, Pain Court, St-Joachim et Pointe-aux-Roches étaient au rendez-vous.

La présidente Madeleine Leal a souhaité la bienvenue à tous et a fait l'éloge de beaucoup de ses consoeurs de la fédération, en particulier Marguerite Sylvestre qui, par deux fois, a été décorée de l'ordre du Mérite. Elle a souligné de façon toute spéciale l'apport constant et sans limite de Cécile Sylvestre qui oeuvre au sein de l'exécutif depuis les tout débuts en 1959, comme secrétaire, présidente, trésorière, et encore comme secrétaire en 1979.

Mme Leal aremercié les présidentes de 1959-79
> Mme Marguerite Sylvestre   (2 reprises)
> Mme Cécile Sylvestre
> Mme Madeleine Barrette
> Mme Jeannette Lafrenière
> Mme Doris Morneau

548

Mrs. Loretta Roy (King)   1984

Mrs. Loretta Roy (King) age 66, widow of Armand Roy(King) who predeceased her in 1966 was the victim of a tragic car accident on July 17, 1984. Luckily, four grandchildren who were passengers in the same car, Chantelle and Darcey King, Kimberley and Jason Gale, escaped serious injury.

Loretta served as housekeeper to our parish priests for the last fifteen years and she will be remembered for her warmth as a truly beautiful human being and also for her lovely smile. To her children, Elizabeth, Thérèse, Diane, Robert, Marie-Agnes, Suzanne and Juliette we offer our sincere condolences.

Album Souvenir: Pain Court 1984 - 85

"Glory Days Of Old Thamesville Hotel"

According to Mr. McDermott Coutts, the hotel's glory days were between 1899 - 1919. In the early days, the hotel was frequented by many travellers and traders who displayed their goods in special rooms. Mr. Coutts, a retired lawyer, estimated the hotel has had 10-12 owners from 1934 - 1980. In May 1981 the hotel got new owners - Melvin Pinsonneault and his wife Sandra of Pain Court.

They are looking forward to cleaning up and remodelling it. Hopefully this renewal will bring forth its warmth and gracefulness of yesteryears.

Pinsonneault, who owns a general construction company, has completed sandblasting to expose the natural brick of the century old Tecumseh Hotel of Thamesville.

Many delighted customers travel miles to enjoy the delicious "cuisine" for Sunday brunch. Melvin and Sandra welcome tourists and will continue to please and captivate their new clientele for years to come.

Le pont de Prairie Siding – Bridge 1984

L'ouverture du pont de Prairie Siding eut lieu le 29 août 1984 par les dignitaires des comtés et de la province. Il remplace le vieux pont étroit bâti en 1924 - 25 qui donne accès aux voyageurs et camionneurs qui ont à traverser la rivière Thames.

En 1925 j'avais 5 ans lorsque je fus témoin de la construction du premier pont. Quel bonheur, car j'avais une peur presque phobique de prendre le bac qui servait à traverser la rivière "La Tranche" pour se rendre à l'église St-Pierre et visiter en même temps notre parenté à Jeannettes Creek.

A new swing bridge officially opened on August 29, 1984 with a ribbon-cutting ceremony attended by dignitaries from the surrounding areas and the province. It replaces the long standing narrow bridge built in 1924 - 25 and was most welcome by farmers, truckers and the general public who have to travel across the Thames River.

Welding Shop

- 1988 -

In 1974 Roger Roy was married to Angela Waddick. On March 6, 1974 they took over the old homestead of Mr. and Mrs. Gérard Roy. Roger then built and operated a welding shop on his farm. As business was very promising he decided to expand by building in Pain Court opposite King Grain Ltd. and King canning. On Nov. 1st 1987 he purchased a piece of property from Mr. Ernest Roy(King) and proceeded with building his new enterprise.

On June 11 1988, he had an open house celebration at his new plant and proceeded in commercial welding and power cleaning specialties. This plant became part of an industrialized technological pursuit in our prosperous community.

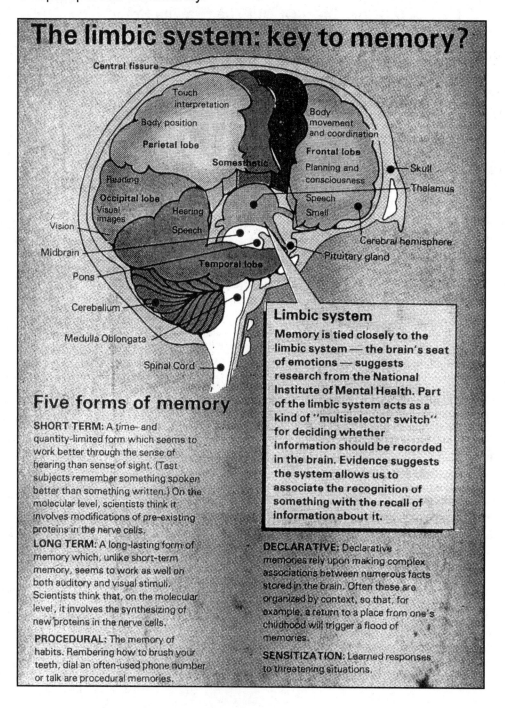

The limbic system: key to memory?

Limbic system

Memory is tied closely to the limbic system — the brain's seat of emotions — suggests research from the National Institute of Mental Health. Part of the limbic system acts as a kind of "multiselector switch" for deciding whether information should be recorded in the brain. Evidence suggests the system allows us to associate the recognition of something with the recall of information about it.

Five forms of memory

SHORT TERM: A time- and quantity-limited form which seems to work better through the sense of hearing than sense of sight. (Test subjects remember something spoken better than something written.) On the molecular level, scientists think it involves modifications of pre-existing proteins in the nerve cells.

LONG TERM: A long-lasting form of memory which, unlike short-term memory, seems to work as well on both auditory and visual stimuli. Scientists think that, on the molecular level, it involves the synthesizing of new proteins in the nerve cells.

PROCEDURAL: The memory of habits. Remembering how to brush your teeth, dial an often-used phone number or talk are procedural memories.

DECLARATIVE: Declarative memories rely upon making complex associations between numerous facts stored in the brain. Often these are organized by context, so that, for example, a return to a place from one's childhood will trigger a flood of memories.

SENSITIZATION: Learned responses to threatening situations.

Le congrès régional des femmes canadiennes-françaises

FFCF-Section Marguerite d'Youville
1959 - 1984

Le symbolisme du nom de Pain Court a servi comme thème du décor lors du congrès de la Fédération des femmes canadiennes-françaises qui a eu lieu à Pain Court. Le cachet de la réception fut la distribution de "petits pains" pour commémorer l'origine de la paroisse et le souvenir de nos aïeux.

Liste des présidentes 1959 - 1984

1959 - Mme Alexina Caron
1960 - Mme Caroline Laprise
1962 - Mme Marcelle Roy
1965 - Mme Laurette Raymond
1968 - Mme Alma Richer
1970 - Mme Marguerite Roy
1972 - Mme Albertine Chauvin
1975 - Mme Françoise Rivest
1980 - Mme Marie-Ange Richer
1982 - Mme Madeleine Pinsonneault
1984 - Mme Madeleine Paiement

Un quart de siècle d'activités constantes à Pain Court

On peut se demander si le petit groupe des femmes qui s'était réuni en 1959, sous la présidence de Mme Alexina Caron pour fonder une section de la Fédération des femmes canadiennes-françaises à Pain Court savaient qu'elles établissaient la base d'une longue tradition de service.

La détermination dont elles faisaient preuve laisse soupçonner que oui . . . De toute façon, sous la direction et l'avis des présidentes dévouées qui se sont succédées à la tête de la section, ce dévouement s'est poursuivi sans trêve. Et c'est avec une fierté fortement justifiée que les membres actuelles et leurs amies fêteront samedi le 25e anniversaire de la fondation de la section.

Dès le début, le service aux jeunes est un point-fixe des efforts des dames: organisation d'amusements ou de retraites spirituelles, attributions de prix, achats de livres français et d'équipement divers pour les écoles locales. On se dévoue non seulement à promouvoir le développement des jeunes, mais à stimuler leur fierté nationale et à préparer des chefs.

Dans le domaine culturel, on parraine seules, ou en conjonction avec d'autres groupes, des concerts par la Manécanterie Meilleure et les Petits Chanteurs de Montréal. On participe à diverses soirées de talents. On fait des visites à la bibliothèque. On présente des candidates au "Bal des Roses" et aux concours "Mlle Sud-ouest." On vend des assiettes-souvenir à l'occasion de l'anniversaire de la paroisse. On prépare costumes et décors pour la pièce "Les Oiseaux de l'Enfant Jésus" et on présente des défilés de mode.

Le rayonnement de l'action des membres dépasse la région de Pain Court: appui au "White Cross Centre", visites aux vieillards et aux malades, éducation d'un séminariste en mission, envois d'effets aux Indes, don pour défrayer les dépenses pour envoyer un jeune en stage au centre Terry Fox à Ottawa. Ce sont des activités qui ressortent parmi la multiplicité de dons à des organisations de charité diverses ainsi qu'à des familles dans le besoin.

En s'occupant tellement des autres, a-t-on le temps de s'occuper aussi de soi? Pour la section de Pain Court, oui! Conformément aux autres objectifs de leur association, les membres mettent sur pied diverses activités de formation: cours d'art culinaire, de tricot, de confection de décorations de Noël, d'exercices de badminton; ateliers concernant l'art de faire des bouquets, sur l'entretien des plantes, cours sur la ressuscitation cardiopulmonaire; conférences sur les missions, sur les problèmes de l'adolescence.

D'autre part, la section appuie divers groupes qui s'occupent de projets particuliers, entre autre l'obtention de la radio française et la promotion du journal français.

En somme, les membres de la section de Pain Court se méritent les plus hautes notes dans tous les domaines d'action qui visent aux objectifs de la Fédération.

Madeleine Paiement
le 13 juin 1984

Trip Out West - 1984

At 65, I realize that I'm a grown up child, a child who has worked very well on a project then wishes to be rewarded. That is how I felt. I wanted to grant myself a favour, to travel and explore the beauties of my own country, the wonders of the western provinces. In my early 50s I did travel to the eastern provinces but not to western Canada.

The pay off was my first two social security checks which permitted me to do so. Taking a few months to outline my trip, I boarded Canada Air Travel in Windsor on July 11,1984 for a flight to Calgary, Alberta for the Calgary Stampede.

I spent 4 days at the Calgary Stampede enjoying every minute. I attended the bucking bronco session, the horse and chariot rides, the whole panorama. I would enjoy revisiting it today at 80. It was super impressive.

By the weekend I boarded a bus for Edmonton. I visited the huge mall complex, acres and acres under cover. It's hard to believe unless you have really seen it. On my way there, I observed the huge cattle ranches, thousands of acres of golden yellow canola fields, the grain harvest.

I love nature, the mountains, the valleys, the crops.

After 3 days we boarded the bus on our way to the Columbian Glaciers. Our motel was nestled between mountains. This area was buzzing with tourists. Buses and trains brought eager tourists to visit. There we enjoyed side trips also, and a special day at the Columbian Glaciers.

As we boarded the bus one more time it was to visit beautiful Lake Louise for a day and retire at our hotel in Banff. Everyone seemed to marvel at the beauty of the snow- peaked mountains and the wild life roaming near the lakes. The scenery was endless. While on tour you could appreciate furthermore the beauty of nature, endless streets of motels and hotels, meeting university students from all over Canada working as waiters and waitresses, catering in the different languages of our Country.

By 3 p.m. it was time to board the train for Vancouver. This is my way of travelling, meeting friends from different areas of our country and from all over the world. By daylight we were in Vancouver. The next day I was somewhat tired even if I had a berth. Age is not a factor. The different time zones had caught up with me and I was exhausted.

In Vancouver I stayed at the Sylvia Hotel across the street from the Bay shore. What a picturesque scenery: people swimming, hundreds of sail boats and motor boats roaming aimlessly on the quiet waters. I enjoyed this waterfront haven. Around 10 o'clock I boarded a tour bus and returned by 4 p.m.. Beautiful Parks, the University Campus, prominent factories, the landscapes, the parks, the government buildings and places of interest too numerous to mention.

Next was the trip by boat to Victoria Island and an opportunity to view breathtaking Buchhart Gardens. You felt you were in another world strolling among the profusion of floral displays and landscapes of greenery and waterfalls. After a few days browsing and enjoying the spacious hotels and the large marinas it was time again to board the bus one more time for Port Perry. This trip took me to the northern tip of the island.

On my way I did spend 3 days with Mr. and Mrs. Philippe Cartier and members of their family who are originally from our area of Grande Pointe. It surely was very pleasant to see them, discuss past memories and their future plans. Once more I left by bus for Port Perry.

It was there I boarded a 700 passenger ocean liner, for a four day cruise in order to reach Prince Rupert, Prince George and Skagway. This ocean liner also carried trucks and vehicles bound for Alaska somewhere between 200 and 225 vehicles. On board were 2 full dining rooms and large lounging areas.

This was an exotic, satisfying trip with breathtaking sceneries, coupled with very pleasant sunny skies. I marvelled at the beautiful malls, the grain depot, modern facilities like all the large cities anywhere in Canada.

My fantasy journey came to an end when I returned to Port Perry on the same Cruise line. It was like a dream you wish would not end. From there I boarded a plane for Vancouver airport in order to fly back to Windsor, my last leg of this journey. This was a memorable, educational and satisfying trip to western Canada.

Première messe du Père Eugène Roy

La communauté de Pain Court se rassemble pour assister à la première messe
du R. Père Eugène Roy, le 6 mai 1984. Quel honneur pour notre paroisse!
Nos félicitations à Eugène et à ses parents, Norman et Helen.

Dear Parishioners,

I thank Christ Jesus our Lord who judged me faithful enough to call me into His service - Timothy 1:12, saying "Yes" to the Lord's invitation to the priesthood was not a lonely process, but one filled with many encouraging and loving people. I have over the last 26 years been especially blessed by the faith display of the parish of the Immaculate Conception. The priests, the teachers, the parishioners, my friends, and above all, my family were shining lights to me leading me eventually to consider the call to the priesthood.

As I live out my priestly ministry I acknowledge the gift that my native parish has been in my life. As a priest forever, I strive to pass on all the love I have received, the healing love that offers hope and urges me on, to serve with joy.

Thanking you all for your kindness and co-operation in the past and through the intercession of Mary our Mother, through her Immaculate Conception, asking God's blessings for the future I remain with profound gratitude to all .

Devotedly yours in Christ,
Father Eugene Roy

Album Souvenir: Pain Court 1984 - 85

Father Chevalier's Golden Jubilee
– 1982 –

Mrs. Mae Chevalier's, thinks it is fitting that a story be written about her brother-in-law, Father Euclide Chevalier. It is not every day a man celebrates 50 years in the priesthood. It's not everyday 500 people will show up at Annunciation Church in the village of his birth to help Father Chevalier celebrate.

Father was ordained May 22, 1932 at Annunciation Church in Pointe-aux-Roches. He was the first priest ordained outside St. Peter's Seminary in London. The following day he celebrated his first mass.

The next seven years he was at Our Lady of the Rosary in East Windsor, the following two at St. Theresa's in Sandwich East and the next five years at St. François Xavier in Tilbury until 1944, when he was sent to Stevenson, south of Tilbury where he erected a rectory. He hired the contractor but in his fashion showed up in work pants and boots to help get the work done. "He slept through all this in a little room in the church." Word of his skills as a builder soon spread.

The Bishop who needed not only a rectory but a church built in the parish of Grande Pointe near Mitchell's Bay did not have to look far for the man who could do it.

So it was Father Chevalier went to Grande Pointe in 1949 to build a church, St-Philippe. He loved Grande Pointe and he often said that when he left Grande Pointe he left his heart behind.

Although he left the parish he did not leave his people. He and nine local men built a cottage near Killarney on the north shore of Georgian Bay. He holidayed there every summer.

In 1955 he resumed his active priestly duties in Pain Court until 1964 with Father Boudreau as his assistant.

His following assignment in 1964 was at Rivière-aux-Canards followed by his retirement in 1968. Since then he has spent much of his time fishing and hunting, and filling in at parishes where priests are ill or on holidays. By 1982, his 50th anniversary, a big celebration was in order.

Mrs. Chevalier pointed out that he was reluctant to be interviewed but admitted he would submit. "People all over know him, people all over love him." But first there is the matter of fishing, and tossing the last of the guts into the river. The turtles will eat it. Nothing is wasted. He picks up the basin of cleaned pickerel and leads the way into the house which he and two other priests, Father Louis Rivard and Laurent Poisson, built themselves six years ago in 1975-76.

He spends the next few minutes outlining where he had worked, and as might be expected, spends a little more time talking about life in Grande Pointe.
"We were very close. You get that way when you work with people," proudly admits Father Chevalier.

He credits his health at 78 - "I've never been sick" - to a lifetime of hard work and time spent outdoors.

He talks a little about the changes he has seen in his Church. Some changes were necessary. The Church was static, but it's like that with all things. You open the gates and away they go. But the pendulums have a habit of swinging two ways.

He thinks parents who have allowed their children total license and removed from them any responsibilities are seeing there are errors in such ways. And he thinks that people who left the church now also see certain errors in those ways.

"On every highway there are signs, you need them. The Church is like the sign beside the highway, you need it too."

He talks about the most distant past, the years when Pointe-aux-Roches was known as the village of Chevalier, when his grandfather used to paddle by canoe to go to church up river; the days when children were expected to take their turn in the fields. "I picked tomatoes when I was nine years old" on his father's farm.

He talks about his father with whom he travelled in the later years. "I really miss the old gentleman." He talks of his life's calling and work "I loved this work, not that I was perfect at it." And then before we can get around to Sunday's celebration, "Father walks you to the door," as promised.

Père Euclide Chevalier

Il est né à Pointe-aux-Roches le 24 septembre 1903 du mariage de Pierre Chevalier et Aimée Lefaive. Il fit ses études primaires à l'école de son village et ses études secondaires et universitaires à l'Université d'Ottawa de 1919 à 1926 où il obtint un Baccalauréat des Arts. Ensuite, il poursuivit ses études au Séminaire St. Peter de London.

Il eut le bonheur d'être ordonné prêtre le 22 mai 1932 en l'église de l'Annonciation de sa paroisse natale par son Excellence Mgr. J.T. Kidd D.D. et aussi d'y célébrer sa première messe solennelle.

Père Chevalier a servi dans plusieurs paroisses. Il a construit le nouveau presbytère de Stevenson en 1944. Vu ses talents dans la construction, il fut transféré à Grande Pointe en1949 afin de construire la nouvelle église de cette paroisse. Il s'est vêtu de salopettes et avec son énergie et son savoir-faire, a travaillé avec ses paroissiens. La pierre angulaire de l'église fut bénite par Mgr. Cody évêque coadjuteur de London, le 27 novembre 1949. La construction du presbytère a commencé au même temps et a été complétée en mars 1950. La paroisse St-Philippe doit beaucoup de gratitude au Père Chevalier. Ses qualités d'homme sincère, de travailleur infatigable lui ont mérité une place dans le coeur des paroissiens.

En 1955, le père Ducharme, le curé de Pain Court, était en convalescence et son jeune vicaire, le Père Ulysse Lefaive fut transféré à Windsor.   C'est alors que la paroisse de Pain Court reçoit à bras ouvert le Père Euclide Chevalier.

De 1955 à 1964, il s'est distingué à Pain Court, dans tous les aspects de la société. Il s'est dévoué pour les écoles primaires et secondaire vis-à-vis l'aspect religieux et a participé aux innovations dans l'église. Il tient à son patrimoine de propager la foi et la culture de ses ancêtres. De 1964-1968 il fait un stage à Rivière-aux-Canards s'intéressant toujours aux activités paroissiales telles que pique-niques, bazaars, etc. initiant ses paroissiens aux changements liturgiques formulés par Vatican II.

Il prend sa retraite bien méritée en 1968 et et retourne chez lui, à Pointe-aux-Roches pour vivre paisiblement à l'ombre de son clocher natal s'adonnant à ses loisirs préférés.

 Cher Père, vous nous avez inspirés comme un bon père inspire et guide ses propres enfants et c'est nous qui en sommes les héritiers.

Un témoignage d'amour
Je l'ai reçu en héritage et je l'ai transmis avec amour

L'enseignement est une vocation d'amour. Moi-même élève, cet amour d'apprendre et de chanter, je l'ai reçu en héritage et je l'ai transmis, dans la mesure du possible, aux mille élèves et plus que j'ai eu le bonheur d'éduquer et d'instruire pendant 35 années à l'école Ste-Catherine de Pain Court.

C'est au jubé de l'église Immaculée Conception de Pain Court que j'ai passé une bonne partie de ma vie, comme élève et par la suite, comme enseignante, à chanter et à faire chanter des louanges au Seigneur.

Sculpture sur bois par
Pierre Cloutier (Clout') - 1985
St-Jean-Port-Joli

The thoughtfulness of my community's generosity expressed in the form of this unique wood sculpture! I shall treasure this gift as a constant reminder of your appreciation.

An excerpt from a short speech pronounced by Louis-Joseph Richer, a parent and representative of the Parish Council, at Angéline Marentette's testimonial banquet on June 23, 1985.

"We should not try too hard to make education easy. There are difficult things that must be done, whether we like it or not. Education should prepare us to face difficulties courageously, to persevere and to work constructively. Last but not least of the requirements of good education is discipline."

L'éducation . . . une aventure qui dure toute une vie

Quelques-uns de mes petits rayons de soleil de l'école Ste-Catherine.

Angéline Blais Marentette, diplômée de l'Université de Windsor, 14 octobre 1995.

POLITICAL LEADERS A CENTURY AGO
Reeves of Dover and Wardens
1850 - 1881

Information from illustrated Atlas of Dominion of Canada published in 1881 by H. Belden and Co. in Toronto.

George Wade Foote - re Belden 1881 – He was a farmer who resided on lot 16 River Front, East Dover. He has lived in the county since 1836. He was born in County Cork in Ireland in 1802. His post office was Chatham.

Mr. Foote was reeve of the township of Dover in 1859 – 1870 with 1867 exempt and served as warden of the county in 1869.

1850 - 51	Robert Mitchell
1852 -	John M. Dolson
1853 -	André Pelletier
1854 - 55 - 58	Robert Mitchell
1856 -	Thomas Shaw
1857 -	Thomas Crow
1858 -	George Wade Foote
1860 - 61 - 62 - 63 - 64 - 65 - 66 - 68 - 69 - 70	
1869 -	Warden - George Wade Foote
1867 -	Robert Steen

1st year elected by direct vote

1871 - 72 - 73	Richard Brayne
1874 -	George Peel
1875 -	Frank Baby (Bowbee)
1876 - 77 -78	Pierre Robert
1879 -	James McFarlane
1880 -	Wm. Stephenson
1881 -	John Wright

W. Clements - Came to this county of Kent, in 1852, he was born in England 1828 and resided on Lot 13 River Road - Front concession east Dover and he owned 370 acres.

T. W. Smith - In 1848 - 1st reeve of Dover and also Clerk.
William Gordon, collector, John Crow W. A. Crow and Robert Crow assessors
Thomas Crow - treasurer.
Dover Township officers:
Reeve – John Wright, Deputy Reeve - Cornelius Purser.
Councillors - Philippe Blais, Henri Thibodeau, Thomas Bourdeau.
J.W. Walsh - Dover South Clerk 1848, Joseph Béchard as treasurer.

Mr. and Mrs. Thomas Rankin born in Chatham 1838 came to Dover with Mr. Rankin his father two years later. The township at that time was a dense unbroken wilderness. Mrs. Rankin may be said to have been connected with every stage of development from the primaeval state of nature to its present prosperous and wealthy condition in 1881.

Mr. Joseph Béchard was raised in Pain Court and operated in 1844 a lumber mill just behind the Central Hotel. He was the owner. In 1848 he was treasurer of Dover South.

Joseph Montgomery - Lot 19 con 9 Dover East, came to Canada in 1860 from Ireland. He owned 320 acres in Baldoon Settlement.

Ref. - Belden Co. published 1881   pg . 911-71

Raoul Roy King

Raoul and Teresa

I anticipate sharing with you a short episode of my life on the farm in Pain Court. I lived at the old homestead of my grand father Thomas Roy where my father Adolphe was born and lived most of his life.

When I was young, going to school, I always dreamed of going to other Countries and help them to farm in a really efficient way. My mind kept wandering all over the world trying to deter mine where to go first. I had no idea until one day Napoleon King asked me casually if I would go to Hawaii for Pride Hybrid Canada and Pride USA to put up a dryer for corn and Sorghum. He emphasized that I was a guy for the job and I would get along well with the people of that Country.

By January 6, 1971. My cousin Jos King died suddenly and I had signed as his backer for mail delivery for R. R. 7 Chatham. At the time this position had to be filled but fortunately after a short period there was a new government assignment to the job of mail-man. This made way for me to leave for Hawaii along with Roland Bélanger, Rosaire Pinsonneault and Napoleon King. Blake Snoblen who sold the dryers to Metcalfe Farms Hawaii Inc., arrived at the Laui Airport Kelawea, Kauai to greet us with the manager Bob Nui. We were escorted to the living quarters of "The Plantation Mansion," a super luxury place operated by a young couple from Los Angeles, Mike and Charlene Dyer.

This 4000 acre sugar plantation which went bankrupt was leased to Pride Co. for seed corn and Sorghum. Seed corn was shipped by air Cargo from "Maui Airport" to Detroit for planting here in Canada about May 1st. Sorghum was grown for cattle feed in conjunction with Parker Ranch which was the largest cattle ranch in the world, 300,000 acres and 250,000 heads of cattle, all whitehead Herford. As the crop of Sorghum matured, millions of birds conglomerated on the crop and ruined it. A few late varieties were harvested.

Overall, the farm workers would come to me with problems, no matter what; we had fun but it was gratifying to help them out. If I was stuck, I would improvise some way. I finally completed the erection of the dryer complex. It was getting close to May, my departure date. The foreman begged me to go home to do my farm work and return after but this was out of the question.

Hawaii is such a beautiful place to live. Their volcanos do erupt now and then, the Himea Canyon is called the grand canyon of the Pacific, they have more sunshine days per year than any other place, in the world, with 750 to 850 daily temperatures. You smell year round, the bougainvillea, the orchids, the Bird of Paradise flowers and a profusion of other flowers.

The island of Maui is also known for its Leper Colony.

Toward the last days, I was getting sad because the Hawaiians are loving and kind. That's the way they live their lives. There was a farewell "Luau" party, I commended them on their way of life and promised I would return sooner than later. I returned 12 times conducting tours on the islands as a tour guide. It was the most heartwarming and gratifying moments of my life.

Aloha! Aloha Nui.

Alexander Baldwin was the consulting firm for Metcalfe Farms Hawaii Inc. On my arrival to Africa in 1975. I was amazed as Alexander Baldwin was the consulting Firm there also.

Raoul Roy (King)

Martin's "Happy Hour" Popcorn in 1961 has reopened for business under the ownership of Roméo Martin. Only the choicest golden kernels are marketed under the Company's label and it has been that way since 1935 when Omer Martin established the popcorn company.

Martin's popcorn has had a reputation for old-fashioned goodness and tenderness as it grew from its original local markets unto national and international prominence. This product of prime corn kernels noted for its expansion capability, its flavour and texture, has made Martin's "Happy Hour" Popcorn one of the country's leading snack foods.

It was one of Romeo Martin's neighbours, Gérard Laprise who accurately sensed the potential of the rich and fertile soil of Kent County area of Ontario to grow volume production of top of the line all Canadian popcorn, that would soon challenge the best of the North American Markets. Martin's is the only large commercial popcorn producing Company in Canada. It's located in the only part of Canada where the climate allows the crop to be grown to maturity.

Since Kent County farmer Gérard Laprise bought the business in 1976 from the founding Martin Family, it has been transferred from a small prosperous operation into a large modern one. Convinced of the expanding future, Laprise set about the development of more ambitious markets for the product. Backed by his own expertise Laprise sought to add new marketing direction to the Company. New hybrid varieties were imported and tested in a detailed plot management program to determine the most suitable and productive varieties for Kent County conditions. Many progressive and leading corn growers in the area responded to the challenge to grow the new fully tested hybrid seeds for popcorn production. Because of texture, high fertility levels and excellent drainage that provides optimum growing conditions, these soils are particularly suited to high yield production. This, coupled with a climate that gives plentiful rains when the corn most needs it and adequate sunshine spurs corn growth through mid and late summer.

By the early nineties the market was influenced once again, as in 1987, because the United States was dumping popcorn into Canada at the rate of commercial corn, thus bringing to a halt, progress in the popcorn industry.

In 1997 the original popcorn facility was restored and new buildings were erected. This facility is now known as the "Kenex" industrial hemp processing plant. This plant was set up in order to adequately process the 1998 industrial hemp crop, which was the first crop grown in Canada in over 60 years. This industry is operated under regulations set out by Health Canada.

Brand new technologies are currently being introduced under the leadership of Jean-Marie Laprise and a team of workers.

"FRONTIER CHURCHES"

The frontier of Grande Pointe, Pain Court and Prairie Siding are graced by impressive church communities such as St. Thomas Anglican Church, River Road Dover, St. Stephen's Church, Mitchell's Bay, St. Andrew Presbyterian Church at the crossroad of Baldoon Rd and Sixth concession, Dover Centre's Presbyterian Church and Grace Christian Church Bear Line, close to the twelfth concession in Dover.

These communities have progressed, developed, and forged ahead remarkably. They are our friends, our neighbours who worked diligently for the last century to enhance their respective communities.

"St. Thomas Church Dover 1875 - 2000 the millennium will mark the 125th anniversary of this prosperous church congregation.

Lost in the midst of time is the history of early tribes that settled in this section of what is now known as the Lake Erie district in southern Ontario. About 1640, two Jesuit missionaries from Huronia travelled through this area.

Sarah Ainse, an Indian women married to Andrew Montour, played a considerable part in the early history of the Lower Thames.

In the Spring of 1875 a little band of church people met under a shady tree on the north bank of the River Thames in Dover with Rev. F. U. Sandy, rector of Christ Church Chatham to organize a new parish and make plans for the building of a new church on the lands. Lot 12 front concession Dover of which Anne Smith of Chatham had deeded to the Bishop of Toronto, June 2, 1847 as a site for a church.
Re - Historical data of St. Thomas Church 1975

Over the decades since 1875 it is noteworthy that generation after generation the same names appear and reappear as leaders of this congregation namely St. Thomas Church: Smith, Peel, Clements, Parry, Johnston, Rankin, Newkirk, Bennett, Dolsen, Bradley, Reaume, Guyitt, Boley, Wannacott, Meritt, Brown and others.

New St. Andrew Presbyterian Church

This congregation, established their church in Dover at the crossroads of the Baldoon Road and Kent Road # 35 in the year 1903. Familiar names are Hind, Parry, Jacks, Smith and many others.

A community hall was built to accommodate different social activities within the area and dedicated women organized suppers and teas for social gatherings there, as a service for their community.

Dover Presbyterian Church

This church was built in 1913 AD. It lies at the crossroads of Baldoon Rd and the eleventh concession in Dover, somewhat of a monument for the old Baldoon Settlement known before the turn of the century. I was born there and lived five years within a few miles of this prestigious congregational church. Members devoted much time and energy on behalf of this community.

The ladies throughout the years have maintained interests in organizing social activities. It is always a pleasure to be one of the many taking part in their elaborate harvest suppers.

Familiar names of this community were, Henderson , Dunlop, Bedell, Anderson, Rankin, Ouellette, O'Neil, McPhail, McKenzie, Montgomery, Kearns.   Bedell's Frozen foods seems to be synonymous with this area.

Dover Centre memorial Park was dedicated to the heroes of this community who lost their lives in the World War II (1939 - 45).

N.B.   Alvin Graham - Navy
              Michael O'Neil - Army
              James Lunday - Air Force

Grace Congregational Christian Church

Established towards the last decade of the nineteenth century. The minister's headquarters were built in 1903 adjacent to the church. Services are held Sundays at 10 a.m. and so is the Sunday School. Members are dedicated to the welfare of the community which lies on Bear Line Rd., past Marsh Line Rd in Dover. The church hall has been renovated lately. Familiar names in the area are Devolder, Owens, Poolman, Graham. Of late, it is Minister P. Schinkelshoek who leads the congregation.

St. Stephen's Church

This congregational church stands at the entrance of Mitchell's Bay on Main Street. This area is a recreational haven for boaters, fishermen and hunters. Members of this church have been well-known and appreciated for their annual fish extravaganza and dinners for many decades. Service is held regularly on Sunday at 10:00 a.m. So is the Sunday School.

How to tell you are getting old

Everything hurts and what doesn't hurt doesn't work.
You feel like the morning after when you haven't been anywhere.
You get winded playing chess.
Your children begin to look middle-aged.
You turn out the lights for economic rather than romantic reasons.
You sit in a rocking chair but can't get it going.
Your knees buckle but your belt won't.
You're 17 around the neck, 42 around the waist and 96 around the golf course (9 holes).
You just can't stand people who are intolerant.
You burn the midnight oil until 9 pm.
Your back goes out more than you do.
Your pacemaker raises the garage door when a pretty girl goes by.
The little gray-haired lady you help across the street is your wife.
You get your exercise acting as pallbearer for friends who exercise.
You have too much room in the house and not enough in the medicine cabinet.

Our Student from Mexico

In July 1972, a student program from the University of Mexico was invited to the Chatham area. The group consisted of twelve students who were anxious to learn about our country, Canada. They also anticipated to develop, communication skills with English speaking families. This was a super opportunity for Colette, who was trying at the time to master a third language, Spanish.

We were privileged to receive, at the cottage for one month, a knowledgeable Mexican girl, Citallali Verduzcos, well-versed in Spanish. She was entering the University of Mexico, in September of 1972.

Her father was a retiree of the federal government of Mexico, and was now blind. Her mother was still working and she had one brother, Ramon.

She remained with us at the cottage, enjoying swimming, dancing and outings in Chatham with Colette. She was trying hard to master her English while Colette also enjoyed conversing in Spanish. All students were welcomed by Mayor Garnet Newkirk of Chatham. They were all entertained at various functions in the area.

A month past and they boarded for a visit to Ottawa to witness our parliament in session. After site seeing tours and being entertained in that area, they flew home to Mexico City.

It was an experience to have welcomed Citallali into our home and to learn about her culture and country. This encounter served me well for a future trip to Mexico.

A Trip To Arizona

It's 1973, it's winter, and I felt like spreading my wings and travel. It was a busy year of hard work and responsibilities. The remainder of the children at home seemed to have a firm grasp on their destiny as they had entered college.

After the Christmas celebrations, I boarded a Greyhound Bus in Chatham, travelled to Detroit and boarded the American bus line to Arizona for New Years. There I was greeted by my long time friends "The Gervais family" in Sierra Vista within twenty miles of the Mexican border at Nogales.

I enjoyed the winter scenery through Michigan via Chicago, travelled across Illinois, Missouri, Kansas and Northern Mexico to Flagstaff Arizona. I spent the next day, touring the Grand Canyon National Park and the museum. The next day I boarded for the last leg of the trip for Flagstaff to the bus depot in Sierra Vista. There was a blanket of snow as we left Flagstaff. En route, there were interesting places to note, like Havasu with the reassembled London Bridge, Montezuma Castle National Monument, with a stop at the Petrified Forest National Park. As we travelled through Phoenix, the valleys and Tucson, the 70^0 weather was a plus and well appreciated in contrast with the cold north.

I was impressed and privileged to be able to enjoy the superb viewing of the different phenomena of this famous state of Arizona.

What a pleasure it was to be reunited once more with this close family at Fort Huachuca. Everyone was growing up and it was interesting to listen to all their new experiences, their new home their new school on the army base of Fort Huachuca.

It was pleasant, at New Years being greeted by all their friends from different countries of the world. These two months passed like a flash with so many places to visit and so many new experiences in a different country.

There were many trips with Juanita to Nogales at the Mexican border. We enjoyed the luncheons in Nogales, Tombstone, and Bishee. Everywhere shopping was captivating, so were the bargains. Arizona offers much to enjoy but due to the altitude varying between 3300 and 3500 feet in many areas, I experienced difficulty breathing especially at night as this area is surrounded with mountains.

To mention a few of the very interesting areas to visit, the dog races, the horse stampedes, the Malachite mines as well as the morning town of Tombstone, the rich mines of turquoise, the health resorts for retired seniors, the Bird Cage Theatre, and the resting place of famous people. Of great interest are the Underground Caves, the mission of San Xavier del Bac near Tucson, the Historical Society Museum and nearby Kett Peak National Observatory known as the highest peak in Arizona. Lest I forget, make sure to visit "Old Tucson," Arizona Territory where the filming of western movies take place. It's March 1974, time to return home, but with a special invitation to return for Christmas 1974. I boarded the train to return home via the southern route, to El Paso, Texas, Jackson, Louisiana and Nashville Tennessee where I saw live, the last performance before the closing of the Grand Old Opera House. The New Opera house of today opened shortly after. The following day I took a tour of Nashville, visited the "Hall of Fame", the "Homes of the Famous" and boarded the bus for Detroit and then Chatham. Hours and days did pass quickly, but happy memories live on forever.

"Years come and go"
but my quest for knowledge is relentless

A very busy year was ahead. Jean-Marie was a graduate in April 1974 at the Ridgetown Agricultural College, but he also opted to be married on April 22, 1974. Colette entered her last year at the same college majoring in laboratory sciences, she entered the work force upon graduating in 1975. She worked for the Federal Department of Agriculture in Ottawa.

We all worked on the farm and as responsibilities diminished towards the family I entered the seasonal work force at Campbell's tomato processing plant every year.

With Christmas just around the corner, I left for Arizona as planned. I also anticipated an extended trip to Mexico. At that time, Snowbirds who travelled to Mexico found it was affordable, as good hotels could be booked at $10.00 US. Resort areas were slightly higher.

I enjoyed travelling by bus. This gave me special opportunities to view the countryside. This time it was through central United States and stop-overs at night, travelling via Indiana, Kentucky, Missouri, Tennessee, Arkansas, Oklahoma, an early stop in Amarillo Texas, because of heavy snow. The next day travelling through New Mexico and south to my destination in the sun.

Once again I'm greeted by the same faithful family, the Gervais, my adopted family.
What a pleasant time to visit during the Christmas holidays. At least I felt I was of some help, that I could do something for the coming festivities. The gifts, the holiday treats, the visitors, even Santa Claus visited the children. Surprise! It was Mr. Gervais in person. He played host to many families and veterans on the military base of Fort Huachuca. Holiday outings were numerous and pleasant.

It's back to school and back to work for everyone after New Years. I started booking reservations for my trip throughout Mexico. With Juanita, an expert in travel, and Fernand who was knowledgeable travelling even in Mexico, we scheduled a wonderful trip for a month. Travelling then was much safer than today, and I made this journey without a hitch.

Trip to Mexico - 1975

Kindly note before departing on this journey with me, that this has taken place twenty-five years ago and possibly many things I related may have changed, with all the progress and innovations of today's world.

Unfortunately I did not take time for a diary only a camera and an itinerary for the trip. It's the first week of February 1975. The train pulls in at the station in Nogales Mexico at 6:15 am. We boarded the train and we are on the first leg of our journey. I am accompanied by Mr. Gervais and Carl who had just turned 8 years old on January 21st. All he wanted for a gift was to accompany me on this trip.

We are off to Mazatalan some five hundred miles form the border. We arrived at an exceptional resort which provides a glimpse of all walks of life, a bit of the old culture mixed with a bit of modern cultural changes in Mexico.

Travelling by train to Mazatalan provided early morning scenes of peasants lighting their fires early in the morning. As in some remote areas, their home consisted of a few boards for shelter. Somewhat heart wrenching as the weather was very cool 40° to 50°. Some were already cooking breakfast on outside accommodations while others were sitting by the bonfire.

We arrived at Mazatalan by 3 pm overwhelmed by the picturesque surroundings and scenery by the ocean. We visited many nightclubs, and they are plentiful. We had tour guides to learn about historical sights, the square, the extravagant markets, the old part and the newer districts of Mazatalan. Our rooms were right by the ocean and the temperatures were in the 70° to 85° midday. I enjoyed this exotic resort as much as any other in Mexico.

On the sixth day at 4 pm I departed on the ocean liner "Le Paz" and sailed on the Bay of California on our way to Le Paz. My friends departed for Nogales after bidding me farewell. The next morning at 9:30 am we docked at the port and boarded a bus to Le Paz. After two days, I returned to Mazatalan on the same ocean liner in order to proceed with my schedule to board the bus en route to Tepica along the Pacific coast.

A brief stop for lunch and we were on our way to Puerto Vallarta for three nights at Ocean Hotel where the Lighthouse signal the ocean sailors.

My first night at this beautiful hotel was really cold. Unusual weather. Everyone coming to the cafeteria cried "Frio! Frio!" Everyone needed a coffee to warm up after a cold night. Kindly note that hotel rooms had windows with no glass, shutters only. Otherwise a fabulous resort. I was trans-ferred to a sheltered room where the ocean winds are more moderate. Famous actors such as Elizabeth Taylor have their resort home close to the ocean on the mountain side here. Many movie sequences are taken in this area some three kilometres south of the city square and close to Camino Réal Hotel, Puerto Vallarta. We could shop everywhere around Cathedral Square, while close by, locals are washing their clothes in the river.

We are now boarding the bus for Manzanillo. This was the home of the silver magnate of the world, 25 years ago. He owned an island close to the mainland in Manzanillo. In 1975, the tourists were almost all Mexican, which forced me to practice some Spanish, but I managed nicely with my dictionary. Coconuts were all over the place, as they export their crops. An apartment rented there for $160.00 a month. What a bargain, even in those years.

Travelling by bus was treacherous as we drove up and down those mountains. There were many precipices, some 300 to 400 feet deep. Fear was starting to take it's toll on my nerves.

We are now heading towards Guadalajara, famous worldwide. The country side is very picturesque with flower-walled villas. It is western Mexico the biggest city with a strong presence of Canadians. This resort is impressive with luxurious hotels everywhere with outside restaurants and entertainment. Well, for quick lunches during the day I learned to eat tacos without hot sauce when possible. Gourmet food was everywhere. I visited the University Campus, the Cathedral plaza at Guadalajara Square, the large international market with an extra tour of the city. I'm not very fond of large cities so this would explain a short three day stay at Camino Réal hotel. I almost left there with a bad experience, as I was jolted by the hotel asking me to pay for my stay while all my hotels were paid for in advance. This was the first time I encountered any problem. A firm no to pay again profited me by an invitation to stay another day at this hotel, gratis.

My next stop was Lake Chapala cradled in the valley, very rich for the production of vegetables and acres upon acres of tomatoes for consumption, as well as export.

Many Canadians and Americans reside there year round as this area had activities like tennis, golf clubs and good restaurants. After a day, I was off to Mexico City. There I was greeted by our sweet Mexican student of 1972, Citallali Verduzcos. At her home, I met her parents. We visited later with Ramon her brother who took us all over this huge metropolis.

For six days I was privileged to be with this special family. They had a wonderful maid, 19 years old who came from the mountains, in the vicinity of Pueblo.

We travelled everyday to visit different areas. Of much interest was; the Palace in Mexico City, the church at Polaza del Las Très Culturas, the parliament buildings, the University of Mexico campus which was huge and very modern in 1975. We watched an Aztec and Spaniards parade and a church of the 16th century, very interesting and historical.

Her relatives gathered for a trip to the museum of Arts and to travel some 40 miles outside Mexico City to Tecktiocan which was very intriguing. At night, people gathered with me and sang, played guitar and other types of music which has slipped my mind. After six days, I departed for Acapulco and thanked everyone for their generosity and hospitality.

In Acapulco the ocean front was lined with elaborate hotels. The beach was peppered with vendors, practically anything could be purchased at the beach.

This place is alright for some, but I was not impressed with it. My heart ached for all the people in dire poverty lining the main street as I gazed on the mountain side opposite my hotel.

Leaving Acapulco we travelled north east to Pueblo, home of some special pottery and china factories. Then north to Padua and overnight in Querétoro. There was much to fascinate me in that area: the beautiful square, the above ground Aqueduct, the Maximilian Chapel, the execution place and the statue of Benito Square. Querétoro is known for its wealth of beautiful "opals." The following day would be a stop overnight at San Miguel Allende. I fell in love with this quaint little place. It's the home of the University of San Miguel, adjacent to the market square is the church of San Miguel de Allende where many known treasures are stored. Then San Miguel Cathedral with all its spires projecting toward the sky. This area is a mountain valley town three hours northwest of Mexico City. Hundreds of Canadians and Americans dominate life downtown and every second building is restaurant, boutique or an art gallery.

In order to travel to Guanajuato it was a matter of boarding local bus services to travel a distance of some twenty miles. This was very special. Workers were boarding at any point along the route by waving the bus over. It was an old jalopy, but full to capacity as some boarded for only a few miles, many were riding on the steps, many boarded with live chickens, and the children accompanied their parents to the bus with practically no clothes. I enjoyed travelling this area and relish the real culture of peasants in Mexico.

I retired at Guanajuato, visiting in the evening the museum with an array of "mummies" displayed and preserved over a period of many years. The next morning I went to the market square. These markets are captivating as you see the displays of marble, precious stones, silver, crafts and innovative ideas of every description.

The following afternoon I travelled to Leon in order to resume my trip towards Nogales. Interesting but true, I arrived at 3 o'clock hoping to travel at 4 pm on the bus to Mazatalan. By that time they announced the bus was cancelled until 6:30 pm. because of a lack of passengers.

Well, that was 25 years ago. This allowed me some time to visit the square where people meet, talk, grab something to eat. Squares in Mexico generally provide live music for our entertainment. It's a real meeting place for young and old allowing one to gossip and catch up on the news.

After boarding, it was all night travel to Mazatalan with stops for coffee and nourishment. We arrived at 9 am and on my last leg of the journey by 1 pm to Nogales. We had an hour lunch stop at Los Mochis which is a beautiful area on the ocean and especially known for its fabulous seafood restaurants being a fishing port. Famous seafood places in Canada do not overshadow this area.

We are now on our way to Guaymas a reasonable driving distance from Nogales famous for American tourists and retirement villas on the ocean. By dawn we are in Hermossillo where the great plains of Mexico seem to consist of tens of thousands of acres, under the management of the federal government. There were some thousand acres of marigold flowers in bloom. What a spectacle! Other crops seem bountiful, miles and miles under cultivation.

My heart is now focussed towards the Mexican border. Alleluia! By 9 am we arrived at the American customs in Nogales. What a sigh of relief after a long night. It was my stomach which was now growling.

I barely could wait to be served a delicious plate of bacon and eggs, coffee and muffin with an order of toast American style. Really the idea had never occurred to me how we can miss certain foods. After a month of travelling this was a very special breakfast. Today might be different. I did learn to appreciate my way of life as well as all my special friends.

As usual the Gervais's were there to greet me one more time. Resting for a week, gossiping and relating experiences it was time to resume my travel to Canada, and perform my duties on the farm.

Caroline Roy Laprise   -Retired-

Le Paz boat - Carl Gervais is with me

Puerta Vallarta Lighthouse hotel

Quératoro Water System

Manzenillo - Island of Silver Magnate

Mexico City Parliament Bldgs.

San Miguel Allande Square and University Square

A Tribute To Farm Women
Excerpts from Country Guide February 1994
By David Irvine

A farm wife is expected;
- to be a wife, mother, farmer, veterinarian, housekeeper, barn keeper, peacemaker, mechanic, and all-round goffer.
- to be gourmet cook, bag lunch cook, carry-out cook, garden preserver, and Pillsbury baker.
- to be strong enough to jump over, crawl under, guard, and fix fences.
- to have a resourceful mind to deal with all farm emergencies, no matter what the condition.
- to have the ability to drive a tractor, lawn mower, 3-ton combine, and pick-up, and to herd cattle and pull calves.
- to have wisdom, common sense and a healthy sense of humour to deal with farm pressures, children, husband, house, and community responsibilities.
- to have a good memory so she can recite, on demand, farm market reports, rainfall, and farm records.
- to have top-notch communication skills to talk intelligently with bankers, sales reps., accountants, lawyers, vets, parts suppliers, and of course, her husband.
- to have patience beyond measure to handle farm stress and personal disappointments due
- to sick livestock, hailstorms, machinery breakdowns, scours in new calves, crops yet to harvest, and falling grain and hay prices.
- to be totally committed to the farm, right along with her husband.

I hope to leave with you 2 important thoughts:

1) We need to be aware of the inhuman rules about what is expected of women. My hope is that we will all be a little kinder to ourselves. We need to be patient and realized we are all in the process of learning. We all make mistakes, our children, our spouses, our loved one. And we do learn.

2) Perhaps men need to show appreciation in a more direct way for the major contributions women make everyday. Perhaps a simple card with sentimental verses, or a dinner out or an unexpected bouquet of flowers, even a thank you will go a long way to demonstrate we care.

Salut Maman

Mamam est décédée le 18 février 1985.
La Providence a choisi que ma mère nous quitte
d'une façon la plus paisible après seulement trois
jour à l'hôpital. C'est triste de perdre sa mère
même à l'âge avancée de 86 ans.

Maman s'était dévouée inlassablement pour ses
enfants, pour sa paroisse et pour ses compatriotes.
À titre d'aînée de la famille, je pourrais énumérer
mille et une chose pour lesquelles nous lui devons
notre pleine reconnaissance. Son exemple
inébranlable de dévouement était remarquable. Elle
n'était pas simplement dévouée, elle s'est donnée
entièrement et religieusement.

Merci Maman, car l'humanité entière restera
enrichie sans limite par l'entremise de vos enfants.

SOCIOLOGIE - II

UNIVERSITÉ D'OTTAWA

Le 28 février, 1967

"Les institutions"

Professeur - L. Langlois

Présenter par -   Caroline Roy Laprise

Sociologie

L'homme d'aujourd'hui est surpris par la bourrasque des tourbillons internationaux, il est bafoué par les idéologies matérialistes, il est écrasé sous le joug cruel d'exigences financières, il est menacé par le spectacle des armes nucléaires, il est hanté par la grimace douloureuse du chômage, tourmenté par le génie scientifique, bouleversé par l'apparence du moins de manque d'idéal des plus jeunes; l'homme aujourd'hui se pose mille et une questions.

Il se demande pourquoi nous nous haïssons les uns les autres. Il se demande ce que nous les humains faisons sur la terre. Il se demande comment il trouvera sa place dans la société, quelles sont les lignes de départ et pourquoi ça se passe ainsi. L'homme de notre siècle se demande pourquoi il faut aimer Dieu et comment, et pourquoi il faut donner l'exemple à nos enfants.

Tout homme se demande une foule de choses et se pose un tas de questions: l'homme qui dirige les nations, l'homme au fond de sa hutte indigène, l'homme devant sa classe, l'homme à la tête d'une paroisse d'âmes, l'homme devant le patient à l'hôpital, l'homme à l'usine, l'homme qui chante, qui prie ou qui pleure, l'homme qui élève une famille, pour tous ces hommes, les questions qu'ils se posent sont une recherche du bien, du bon, du vrai. C'est la recherche et l'analyse du contrôle institutionnel qui est l'influence effective du milieu culturel schématisé telle qu'elle se manifeste par la réponse subconsciente des gens, du groupe ou de la société. Les schèmes et institutions culturels ne nous montrent pas seulement ce que font les gens mais aussi ce que l'on s'attend des voir faire.

Dans le langage sociologique, une institution n'est pas une personne ou un groupe, mais une partie de la culture, c'est un segment schématisé du genre de vie d'un peuple. Une institution est une combinaison ou une configuration de modèles de comportements partagés par la majorité et centrés sur la satisfaction d'un besoin fondamental de groupe. Ce que fait la personne ou que font les gens qui se distinguent de ce qu'est le groupe. Les modèles de comportement, le processus, les rôles sont institutionnalisés mais les personnes et les groupes ne le sont pas. Le groupe est une pluralité de personnes qui mettent des institutions en actes.

Selon Fichtère, nous verrons les caractéristiques essentielles de l'institution.

A)   Les institutions sont intentionnelles en ce sens que chacun se propose comme but ou comme objectif la satisfaction d'un besoin social.

B)   Elles sont relativement permanentes dans leur contenu. Les schèmes, rôles et relations que les gens réalisent dans une culture particulière deviennent traditionnels et durables.

C)   L'institution est structure! Les éléments qui la composent tendent à se tenir ensemble et à se renforcer les uns les autres.

D)   Chaque institution est une structure unifiée, elle fonctionne comme une unité. Aucune institution ne peut être complètement séparée les autres institutions, mais elle fonctionne comme une série identifiable dans le comportement humain.

E)   L'institution est nécessairement chargée de valeur en ce sens que ses uniformités répétées deviennent des codes de conduite.

Alors voici une définition plus complète. Une institution est une structure permanente de modèles sociaux de rôles et de relations réalisées par des gens de certaines façons, sanctionnées et unifiées afin de satisfaire des besoins sociaux de base.

À côté des fonctions positives des institutions, il faut considérer certains aspects négatifs. Aucune culture opère dans tous les éléments pour le meilleur profit de tous. Il faut s'attendre à certaines difficultés. La principale fonction négative est la façon dont quelquefois elles font obstacle au progrès social.

1) L'institution conserve parfois des modèles de conduite alors même que les valeurs représentées par ce comportement sont désuètes. Parfois elle conserve aussi des valeurs sociales qui ne concordent plus avec la conduite externe des gens.

2) De même, les institutions aboutissent parfois à frustrer la personnalité individuelle. Les gens ne s'adaptent pas à la culture et celui qui tente de résister au contrôle des institutions est considéré comme étrange. Ils peuvent être inadaptés parce qu'ils ne veulent pas permettre aux institutions de dominer de façon rigide.

3) Une autre fonction négative est la baisse du sens de responsabilité sociale, personne n'ose prendre la responsabilité de réforme. Alors une institution peut réaliser l'injustice mais le fait qu'elle est établie depuis longtemps lui confère une sanction.

Nous savons qu'il y a nombreuses manières de classifier les groupes sociaux parce qu'il y a beaucoup de point de vue de départ pour étudier les groupes. Pour la clarté, la classification générale la plus utile des institutions est la division à deux branches, institutions majeures et subsidiaires. Nous allons en donner une brève description des institutions majeures avec quelques indications sur des institutions subsidiaires. Aucun groupe social ne peut accomplir purement et exclusivement les modèles d'une seule institution. Aucune institution sociale ne peut exister par elle même. Chacune influence à divers dégrés les autres. Le contrôle le plus serré sur les membres d'un groupe est exercé dans les groupes familiaux et éducatifs, les relations sociales sont très intimes et les valeurs en cause sont élevées et la conformité aux normes est une intention délibérée du groupe. Nous reconnaissions l'institution familiale et éducative sous ce système. Les groupes politiques et économiques viennent ensuite pour la force du contrôle social suivi des groupes récréatifs et religieux qui exercent le moins de contrôle sur leurs membres. Cet échelonnement de contrôle social peut varier selon les sociétés ou encore d'une époque à l'autre.

Chaque culture contient une institution axiale reconnaissable qui demande plus de conformité et qui exerce plus d'influence qu'aucune autre institution. Des exemples peuvent être tirés des diverses cultures pour montrer que l'institution économique est dominante et que dans d'autres cas ça serait l'institution religieuse, éducative, politique ou familiale. Nous pouvons constater que par exemple dans l'Amérique du Nord, c'est bien l'institution économique qui est l'institution axiale tandis qu'en Chine c'est bien la famille qui influence toutes les autres.

Examinons les six systèmes qui influencent toute la société.
1) L'institution familiale règle, stabilise et standardise les relations sexuelles et la reproduction humaine. Sa forme la plus répandue est l'union monogame de l'homme et de la femme vivant avec leurs enfants. Les sous institutions, les fiançailles, le mariage, le soin des enfants, les relations d'alliance, tous font partie de cette institution.

2) L'institution éducative est fondamentalement le processus systématisé de socialisation qui se développe de façon non formelle au foyer paternel et dans le milieu culturel général. Dans les cadres de ce système, on retrouve les épreuves, les titres, les

degrés, les diplômes, le travail à la maison et le système des honneurs et des récompenses.

3) L'institution politique fonctionne en vue de satisfaire le besoin d'administration générale et d'ordre public dans la société. Elle comprend beaucoup de sens, les institutions comme la police, l'armée, les élections aux emplois publics et les relations diplomatiques avec les pays étrangers.

4) L'institution religieuse satisfait le besoin social fondamental de l'homme, d'être en relation avec Dieu. En fait de relations subsidaires, il y a les relations entre clergé et laïcs, les systèmes de prière, le dispositif du Sacrifice Divin et par endroits les pratiques des magies et des superstitions.

5) Le besoin social de détente physique et mentale est satisfait par l'institution récréative. Elle comprend des institutions subsidiaires comme les jeux, le sport, la danse ainsi que les systèmes esthétiques de l'art, la musique, la peinture et le théâtre.

6) L'institution économique qui figure comme à peu près la plus importante en Amérique du Nord est la configuration des modèles schématisés auxquels la société est pourvue de biens matériels et de services. Nous examinerons plus longuement la production, la distribution, l'échange et la consommation des produits en tenant compte des nombreuses institutions subsidiaires telles que le crédit, la banque, la tenue des livres, la publicité, le marché collectif.

C'est bien de l'institution économique que j'aimerais parler davantage. Alors pourquoi l'économie est-elle considérée par la société?

Les économistes étudient le patron des réactions économiques et des compétitions car celles-ci influencent gravement les modèles de comportement de la société. Dans la société en général, les personnes sont rationnelles mais en pratique l'homme ne se conforme pas toujours, c'est à dire qu'en économie ceci n'applique pas toujours. De nos jours, il y a les associations et les syndicats qui intercèdent auprès des employeurs. Alors ici, il y a les grèves qui sont d'actualité. Ce que l'employé demande paraît rationnel mais l'employeur est pris par la peur de perdre ses employés qui lui sont vitals, alors il cédera, mais ce n'est pas toujours rationnel car souvent il affirme que ses employés ne sont pas justes dans leurs demandes.

Le consommateur lui, est souvent influencé par la publicité et non pas par la raison. Aujourd'hui le pensionné, l'assisté social, le gagne petit, le collet blanc, le collet bleu, sans oublier l'agriculteur se font égorger quotidiennement sans qu'aucun corps intermédiaire se préoccupe d'eux. Du côté consommateur, il est important que l'on trouve au plus vite le moyen de corriger diverses situations dans le domaine de l'économie et du crédit. J'ose présenter l'importance de ce point vital exprimé par M. René Hould dans son résumé des conférences fédérales, provinciales sur les institutions financières dans Le Droit du 14 février.

L'agriculteur ressent fortement cette crise économique car ce n'est qu'un faible pourcentage qui peut survivre comme entreprise économique et pourtant l'agriculture est bien l'entreprise qui saura soulager progressivement les misères des peuples et combler le besoin vital du monde presqu'entier, la faim. Selon le bulletin Banque Canadienne Nationale février 1967, la grande affaire de l'époque contemporaine est de savoir si la terre, cette terre "porteuses de récoltes et de bêtes, mère des substances cardinales" pourra dans trente ans nourrir les siens. L'humanité toute entière, sous une forme ou sous une autre, sévit les conséquences de la famine ou de la disette. Il est temps que cette "bataille contre la faim" entreprise par les pays industrialisés soit gagnée. La paix du monde en est l'enjeu. La production par habitant, n'accuse de réels progrès que dans les pays industrialisés; ailleurs elle est stationnaire ou décroît dangereusement, au moins 16% (-16) en huit ans dans certains pays d'Asie. Le Canadien disons-nous, semble l'homme le mieux nourri du monde, alors il nous importe, et ceci présuppose un gigantesque effort de coopération pour réussir l'amélioration de l'utilisation des terroirs, l'orientation des cultures, l'aide à la production et à l'exportation et l'organisation de la conservation des produits. Nous constatons le noeud du problème, il s'agit de changer la politique agricole en donnant à la profession les moyens de survivre et de conquérir la pauvreté. Ceci pourrait se faire en démontrant comment le système d'enseignement agricole doit s'intégrer à l'ensemble du système d'éducation générale.

Afin d'examiner la distribution, il y a aussi certaines tendances qui influencent les normes de comportements.

1)   La compétition est de première importance. Il y a des acheteurs et des vendeurs mais il semble toujours avoir une main invisible qui influence les prix. Il y a encore les hauts et les bas de demande. Mais de nos jours, les grandes corporations sont une influence marquée.

2)   Grâces à des limitations à la compétition, il y a certaines lois qui régissent. De nos jours, nous parlons énormément d'organisations   massives. Lorsque les organisa tions deviennent trop grandes, celles-ci sont divisées en "Partnership" afin de promouvoir et d'améliorer davantage le capital. Les corporations systèmes d'aujourd'hui pour avoir du capital mettent à la disposition des employés des "Shares" ou "Stocks". J'ose constater que ces corporations ont évoluées jusqu'aux groupes tertiaires de la société, c'est-à-dire au troisième rang, au rang des professionnels comme docteurs, avocats. Examinons plus loin les systèmes et modèles de com portements. Quand il y a a conflit entre les travailleurs et l'industrie nous rencontrons le gouvernement qui agit comme intermédiaire. Il y a aussi les fameux groupes primaires qui portent une influence inconcevable sur la production de l'industrie.

L'individu d'aujourd'hui met beaucoup d'importance à obtenir une position quelconque. Beaucoup moins de personnes aiment travailler pour rien, ou par charité. Il y a aussi les conditions imposées de se retirer à 65 ans qui apportent toujours de nouveaux problèmes d'ajustement. Ceci demande des spécialistes afin de préparer l'individu à s'adapter dans la société. Toujours la pression d'avoir un métier et d'être éduqué raisonnablement. Ajoutons à ceci la pression de notre façon de vivre, l'obligation de vivre selon notre statut dans la société, en plus de la pression des vendeurs d'acheter soit par fraude, soit par crédit. Ses multiples tendances et lacunes influencent de nos jours l'individu dans sa course affolée. Il se sent frustré par certaines lacunes du système économique. Il va sans dire que souvent l'institution politique joue un rôle primaire. Par exemple, considérons les dégâts des banqueroutes, les crédits qui portent des taux d'intérêts incontrôlables et indéterminés. Il y a aussi les fraudeurs contre lesquels le public ne semble avoir aucune protection. Ce sont ces multiples tendances et lacunes qui influencent l'individu dans ses modèles de comportements.

En terminant, il faut parler des idéologies et les philosophies qui servent à influencer l'institution économique. Il y a les systèmes capitalistes, socialistes, fascistes, communistes et de coopératives. Tous contribuent soit à l'avancement, soit au recul du système économique. Le capitalisme parfois rencontre des limites imposées par le socialisme. C'est un système pur de compétitions. Aujourd'hui, ils ont perdu le contrôle total des propriétés, surtout la construction. Ils exercent des contrôles assez considérables des propriétés et des utilités publiques. Maintenant c'est bien l'état qui stabilise le capitalisme mais parfois nous recherchons ces contrôles même si nous les détestons. Il ne faut pas confondre certains aspects économiques du système socialiste avec le communisme car le gouvernement ne contrôle pas tout. Par exemple, en Angleterre si une industrie opère avec des déficits, mais que les produits sont essentiels au pays, dans ces circonstances le gouvernement prendra contrôle.

Le système faciste prend plein contrôle des industries et des entreprises importantes et force les propriétaires de faire des contributions au bien-être social. Nous retrouvons très peu d'entreprises privées dans ce système.

Dans le système communiste, c'est l'état par contre qui exerce un contrôle total des propriétés privées. Cette façon s'est prouvée déficiente. Ce système intéresse au bien-être des personnes et concentre ses efforts sur l'énergie atomique.

En dernier lieu nous pouvons apprécier le système de coopérative qui se retrouve au sein des environnements moins fortunés. Il y a la coopérative des banques mieux connues comme Caisse Populaire. Il y a les coopératives agricoles de crédit, de production et de consommation.

Afin d'obtenir le meilleurs résultats, l'activité économique doit relever d'un système organisé et systématique. Les efforts des millions de personnes devront être effectivement coordonnés afin qu'ils puissent produire au maximum. Au dire des économistes des solutions s'imposent d'elles-mêmes.

Il s'agit de doter tous les pays d'une économie de marché en harmonisant les rapports production et consommation, réorganiser les transports partout où la vie des collectivités locales est concentrationnaire, créer des chaînes d'entrepôts et de magasins, transformer les systèmes alimentaires et bien d'autres encore. Le monde est divisé, hélas! Dans cette "compétition pacifique" qui est en fin de compte, la bataille contre la faim, deux grands systèmes économiques et sociaux s'affrontent. Le temps n'est plus où des empires pouvaient coexister sans même se connaître de nom. Le vingtième siècle a plongé le monde dans un climat de crise, de conflit que le vent souffle aux quatre coins du monde. L'Amérique et la Russie s'engagent dans une course affolée pour maintenir le pouvoir des armes nucléaires. À toute reprise, des fusées se placent en orbite et d'autres pays se préparent pour s'y joindre. Ce sont les guerilleros qui s'engagent dans une lutte acharnée en Asie du Sud. C'est le tonnerre qui gronde dans l'Afrique et les drapeaux de révolution qui s'élèvent dans les capitales de l'Amérique du Sud. Il y a des rencontres sanguinaires un peu partout et l'Europe ne demande pas plus qu'une survivance économique dans ses conflits. La Chine déchaîne des problèmes universels en restant enchaînée à une philosophie marxiste tandis qu'elle a des billions de personnes qui ont faim. Leur mauvaise entente avec les pays présente une atmosphère au point de rupture. Aux États-Unis, il y a aussi le problème des droits civils et au Canada se sont les politiciens qui poursuivent opiniâtrement les termes de la Confédération tandis que les peuples sont plongés dans l'anxiété. Ces images font naître peut-être de part et d'autre, plus d'envie, de jalousie, de pitié, de compassion que d'amour. C'est ainsi que les économistes déterminent les modèles de comportement qui influencent l'institution économique.

C'est la paix en effet qui est au bout de la bataille contre la faim.

Mme Caroline Laprise
Février 1967

Référence - Fichtère - Sociologie
Référence - Maintenant - février 1967
Référence - Banque Canadienne Nationale - février 1967
Référence - Economics - R. C. Bellan

Chapitre 9

Nouvelle génération

1990 - 1998

Chapter 9

The New Generation

1990

Assises de gauche à droite - Thérèse Thibodeau, Barbara Béchard, Jessie Robert, Linda Béchard, Irène Gagner, Rose-Anna Martin?
Debout de gauche à droite - Eulalie Gagner, Caroline Laprise, Marie-Anne Faubert, Adeline Bélanger, Lena Robert, Anne-Marie Martin, Angela Roy, Père Gilbert Simard.

Dames de Ste-Anne 75e anniversaire

– Femmes héroïques

– Femmes éducatrices

– Femmes remplies d'amour fraternel, portez haut le flambeau de votre courage et votre persévérance afin d'éclairer les générations de l'avenir.

Caroline Roy Laprise

Éloges
Mme Mae Chevalier

Gérard Chevalier

Marie-Mae Chevalier

..... "Le défi je l'ai connu jeune, j'ai choisi de lui faire face et dans le procès j'ai découvert l'élan de ma vie".....

Marie-Mae Béchard Chevalier est née à Pain Court le 14 mai 1919, dans la maison familiale de Willie Béchard et Élizabeth Pelletier Béchard. Les premiers sons de sa bouche ont captivité l'attention de ses deux grands frères, Laurent et Ernest, de sa grand-mère Angèle Faubert Béchard, de ses parents ainsi que tout le voisinage entre la 5e et 6e concession du canton de Dover dans le comté de Kent. Elle serait suivie cinq ans plus tard par un troisième frère, Raymond.

Son statut de fille unique dans une famille d'hommes a peut-être été le facteur prophétique dans l'épanouissement de sa personnalité. Malgré les efforts protecteurs de sa mère, Marie-Mae a dû se forger une place auprès de ses paires masculins pendant toute son enfance. À l'âge de 10 ans ses frères et leurs amis l'ont incitée à sauter de la "tâsserie" dans une meule de foins frais de 12 pieds de hauteur. Les aventures semblables de jeunesse furent nombreuses et ayant été sauvegardée dès le début par son père, elle a su faire face à tous les défis de la vie qui ont suivi.

Comme plusieurs de sa génération, elle marchait près de quatre kilomètres pour se rendre à l'école No. 7 sur la quatrième concession. Le chemin de terre battue était essentiellement de la boue six mois sur douze et plus souvent que pas, elle marchait à pieds nus dans un fossé pour préserver ses souliers et aussi pour ne pas s'effondre jusqu'aux genoux dans la boue. Ses études ont souvent été compromises par ces conditions routières, les maux d'oreilles pour lesquels les antibiotiques n'existaient pas et les intempéries hivernales qui paralysaient le transport à cheval et en traîneau. Sa scolarité fut donc sporadique - en moyenne deux ou trois jours par semaine, ce qui rend les accomplissements de sa vie d'autant plus étonnants. Il faut imaginer ce petit bout de femme avec ses souliers à lacets autour du cou et les orteils pleines de boue. Lorsque l'on compare cette image à celui de la femme qui est devenue cantatrice, coiffeuse, maman, sage-femme, femme agricole, fondatrice d'une Caisse Populaire et leader communautaire, nous pouvons constater l'envergure des défis auxquels elle a fait face.

Marie-Mae rencontra son futur époux Gérard Chevalier à un concert musical qu'elle avait l'habitude d'organiser dans les villages avoisinants de Pain Court. Elle avait vingt ans. Ils se sont mariés le 28 mai 1941. Au retour de leur petit voyage de noces aux chutes Niagara, Marie-Mae et Gérard déposèrent leur fortune de $10,00 sur la table de cuisine et se disaient heureux de leur fortune.

Leur premier ménage fut à Windsor dans un quartier industriel. Pendant cette période de la guerre, les fermes ne soutenaient pas très bien les familles et Gérard devait travailler dans une industrie d'automobiles. Marie-Mae s'occupait du bon fonctionnement de l'immeuble de rapport qui appartenait à sa grand'mère. Les chambreurs étaient surtout des immigrants venus avant la guerre qui eux étaient employés à la compagnie d'automobiles.

Leur premier enfant, Blanche Elizabeth-Aimée, est née en 1942 et fut nommée d'après la soeur de Gérard, Soeur Lucille, religieuse Ursuline, ainsi que d'après ses deux grands-mères, Élizabeth Pelletier Béchard et Aimée Lefaive Chevalier.

En 1943, pendant une mini-épidémie d'un genre de choléra, Marie-Mae, en dépit des meilleurs efforts d'un pédiatre, réussit à guérir sa fille de cette maladie ravageuse en la traitant à la farine brunie. Cette expérience forgea sa confiance dans ses intuitions pour la guérison. Peu après, Gérard et Marie-Mae ont déménagé à la ferme Chevalier à Pointe-aux-Roches aussitôt la guerre terminée. Cultivateurs à coeur, ils demeurèrent chez les parents de Gérard et partagèrent les soins d'Aimée Chevalier qui avait subi une thrombose cérébrale quelques années auparavant.

Leur second enfant, un fils, est né en 1944 et on le baptisa Euclide Pierre d'après son oncle Euclide Joseph Chevalier, curé séculier, ainsi que d'après son grand-père paternel Pierre Chevalier. En 1946, une deuxième petite fille, Yvette Lorette, est née. Celle-ci demeurera à jamais le bébé de la famille et jouit toujours du sobriquet "la p'tite" dans les discussions familiales intimes.

La culture de 80 âcres de terre arable supportait à peine la famille à cette époque et malgré une économie améliorée l'après-guerre exigeait toujours des économies. Marie-Mae ajouta ses énergies à celles de son époux et beau-père pour assurer la rentabilité de la ferme et le revenu familial global. C'est aussi à cette époque qu'elle débuta sa carrière de coiffeuse/barbier. Par la lecture et l'observations, elle avait maîtrisé ce métier et pendant l'hiver la grande cuisine et le perron de derrière devenaient le salon de coiffure pendant trois et quatre jours par semaine. Les trois enfants se tenaient à sa jupe pendant qu'elle gagnait quelques sous supplémentaires et de temps à autre Euclide s'endormait à ses pieds pour sa sieste de l'après-midi. L'été, son commerce augmenté par les touristes américains, son salon de coiffure était déménagé sur le perron de devant.

Ses routines étaient épuisantes. En fin d'après-midi elle se rendait à la grange pour traire les vaches et écrémer le lait pendant que les hommes travaillaient à la dernière lumière dans les champs. Les enfants couchés, elle préparait le repas pour les hommes qui revenaient des champs et pendant qu'ils mangeaient, elle conservait fruits, légumes et viandes pour l'hiver.

En 1944, Marie-Mae et Gérard, inspirés des nouvelles connaissances acquises par Philippe Chauvin, un cultivateur autodidacte de Pointe-aux-Roches, fondent avec lui et quelques penseurs de la communauté, la caisse populaire de Pointe-aux-Roches. Convaincus que le mouvement coopératif apporterait la stabilité économique aux résidents de leur communauté, ils ont fait le porte à porte dans les environs pour bien expliquer aux gens le concept d'une caisse populaire et du mouvement coopératif. Un début humble mais solide a caractérisé la petite "Caisse". Les banques commerciales qui ne jouissaient pas de réputation favorable depuis la dépression, n'étaient pas très achalandées des cultivateurs. Les cultivateurs avaient surtout tendance de "déposer" leurs petites économies dans des pots de conserve ou leurs matelas ou encore dans des petits coffres-forts. La confiance des gens et les bonnes intentions des multiples partisans communautaires de ce mouvement était à la base du succès de l'entreprise. Lors des visites à domicile, Marie-Mae ou Gérard recevaient l'engagement du sociétaire en ouvrant leur compte au capital social. Leur perron de devant ainsi que la table de salle à manger étaient en somme la caisse populaire. Au début, les maigres épargnes des cultivateurs de la région n'étaient pas facile à déloger, mais l'entreprise était gérée sans frais et donc, il suffisait d'attendre que les gens étaient suffisamment confiants que cette "Caisse" leur appartenait réellement pour qu'ils puissent l'utiliser comme un outil d'épanouissement communautaire. Pendant 20 ans, côte à côte Gérard et Marie-Mae recrutèrent des membres pour la caisse et cela sans salaire. Ils ont aussi développé l'esprit de l'économie chez les jeunes, leurs futurs sociétaires, en se rendant à l'école régulièrement pour recueillir les dépôts pour la caisse scolaire. Ces dépôts de petits cinq et dix sous ayant tout à fait autant de valeur que les cinq ou dix milles des sociétaires adultes. Aujourd'hui, ce sont ces mêmes jeunes qui sont les sociétaires les plus actifs et qui donnent le succès à la "Caisse." Ce ne sont plus des transactions de cinq et dix sous.

Éventuellement, Gérard devint gérant de la "Caisse" et Marie-Mae la préposée aux services aux clients et agents de prêts. Leur apprentissage de la comptabilité et de la gérance se fit avec l'appui des inspecteurs de la Fédération des caisses populaires, les nombreux membres des comités et de leur expérience toujours grandissante au service de leur clients et concitoyens. On leur a souvent demandé dans les années qui suivirent comment ils expliquaient le succès de cette caisse lorsque grand nombre de ces établissements, munis d'un personnel professionnel bien formé dans la comptabilité, n'avaient pas réussi. Leur réponse était simple, du travail ardu, l'honnêteté, l'appui et la confiance de la communauté francophone et un conviction que l'autonomie économique était nécessaire au bien-être de leur communauté. En 1961, la "Caisse" avait suffisamment d'actif pour payer un petit salaire à ses deux bénévoles de 20 ans. La "Caisse" déménagea à la salle St-Jean-Baptiste, un bâtiment peu utilisé situé de l'autre côté de la rue de la résidence Chevalier. Marie-Mae et Gérard ont traversé la rue pendant un autre vingt ans. Marie-Mae avoue que ses années les plus heureuses ont été celles passées au service des clients de la Caisse populaire. Son rôle de conseillère financière était mis en valeur pour les clients qui valorisaient ses bons conseils comme ceux de Gérard. Le grand tableau d'ardoise dans le bureau de Gérard était utilisé non seulement pour des réunions mais pour aider le client à bien visualiser sa situation financière et les répercussions à court et long terme de ses décisions. Une des premières femmes dans le milieu banquier de l'époque, Marie-Mae a su apporter une dimension emphatique féminine envers ses clients. Nombreux sont ceux qui gardent bon souvenir de cette femme d'affaire.

Pendant les années avant leur travail à temps plein à la Caisse Populaire, Marie-Mae et Gérard ont toujours étudié et trouvé un moyen de transformer leurs talents en revenu pour augmenter celui de la ferme. Marie-Mae fabriquait des porte-monnaie en cuir, des chapeaux de plumes de présent, des plantes en plastique coulé, ou encore, elle rénovait ses meubles et les rembourrait. S'il existait un cours pour adultes à l'école secondaire voisinante Marie-Mae s'y inscrivait. Il y avait toujours un nouveau défi auquel elle avait à faire face et de nouvelles habilités à acquérir. La maîtrise d'un nouvel art était l'objet primaire, et ce en continuant à perfectionner ses connaissances déjà acquises. Elle ne réussissait pas toujours à convaincre Gérard qu'un cours artisanal en particulier lui serait utile mais il l'accompagnait parfois, surtout pour les cours qui demandaient un travail à deux. La fierté de son époux pour ses oeuvres créatrices alimentait sa soif de nouvelles expériences. Lorsqu'elle se lança dans la peinture des tableaux artistiques, Gérard était épaté et ne cessait de faire voir à tous et chacun ses chefs-d'oeuvre. Il lui a même construit un chevalet. Ce chevalet est maintenant utilisé par leur petite-fille qui paraît avoir hérité ce talent artistique qui a été transmis d'Élizabeth Pelletier à sa fille Marie-Mae et ensuite à la quatrième génération. Gérard pour sa part, avait étudié à son propre compte et était qualifié pour la vente d'assurance. Ce métier il l'exerça pendant de nombreuses années avant d'accepter le travail rémunéré à la "Caisse."

À une époque où les soins médicaux n'étaient pas un droit universel et les médecins n'étaient pas nombreux en campagne, les cultivateurs ne recevaient pas souvent des soins adéquats. Le médecin du village voisinant de Pointe-aux-Roches avait un large territoire à desservir et il avait souvent recours à l'assistance de Marie-Mae dans la communauté. Elle était parfois la seule sur les lieux pour assister une femme à accoucher ou pour aider les malades. Toujours d'une générosité sans bornes elle possédait un bon sang-froid et une empathie remarquable. Marie-Mae et sa mère Élizabeth, trouvaient toujours le temps de rendre service à leurs voisins dans leurs communautés respectives. Les deux femmes partageaient un désir de jeunesse de devenir infirmières. Les souvenirs d'enfance de Blanche, la fille aînée de Marie-Mae, sont parsemés de visites chez les voisins des deux femmes pour changer des pansements, apporter de la nourriture ou pour visiter les mourants. Avant la venue des antibiotiques, plusieurs membres des familles campagnardes souf- fraient d'infectionssystématiques telles que les furoncles ou les clous. Élizabeth et Marie-Mae fabriquaient leurs propres pansements de vieux draps propres qu'elles stérilisaient au four. Les vieux pansements étaient reportés pour être brûlés par leurs époux dans un baril à l'extérieur. Il n'est pas surprenant que Blanche ait choisi de devenir infirmière et cela, au grand plaisir des deux femmes qui lui avaient transmis leurs rêves.

Leur famille grandissant dans les années cinquante, Marie-Mae et Gérard avaient décidé que leurs enfants poursuivraient leurs études au secondaire en français, ce qui nécessitait de les envoyer aux pensionnats dans les régions soit d'Ottawa, Sudbury ou Cornwall. Les enfants, pour leur part, connaissaient depuis longtemps cette décision et eux aussi étaient engagés au travail collaboratif de la ferme. La culture des tomates les occupait tous pendant l'été et les revenus étaient désignés pour le pensionnat de Blanche, la première à se diriger vers Ottawa. Pendant les hivers, Marie-Mae décida de faire l'élevage de cochons, qui, elle le savait bien, payerait ses études. Marie-Mae et Gérard ont ainsi assuré l'instruction en français au niveau secondaire de leurs enfants. Lorsque la "petite Yvette" devait partir pour Ottawa, Marie-Mae et Gérard se voyaient seuls. Ils ont opté d'envoyer la "petite" vivre chez ses grands-parents Béchard d'où elle pouvait assister à la nouvelle école secondaire de Pain Court et revenir chez elle les fins de semaine. Chaque enfant est reconnaissant pour les sacrifices et la détermination de leurs parents.

Lorsque leurs enfants ont quitté le foyer, Marie-Mae et Gérard ont beaucoup voyagé seul ou avec leurs enfants ou accompagné d'amis. Elle se dit heureuse d'avoir mis le pied sur chaque continent du monde et d'avoir visité plusieurs des merveilles du monde.

Marie-Mae s'est méritée le respect de ses collègues dans le mouvement des Caisses Populaires de tous les coins de la province. Elle a reçu maintes accolades de ces mêmes collègues, le plus récent de ceux-ci de la part de la Fédération des caisses populaires de l'Ontario. Elle fut la première femme employée dans une caisse populaire en Ontario.

Les défis depuis sa retraite de la "Caisse" sont nombreux. Toujours femme d'affaires elle s'est dévouée auprès de nombreuses associations féminines dans la région du sud-ouest et elle accepta de demeurer active sur des comités à la "Caisse" pour plusieurs années après sa retraite.

Elle est très active auprès de ses contemporains aînés et ceux-ci jouissent de ses multiples talents d'organisation. Du début décembre au début avril elle fait la migration comme les autres oiseaux de neige vers la Floride où elle connaît une réjuvération tant physique qu'émotive qui lui permet de reprendre ses nombreuses activités familiales et communautaires dans la région. Elle exerce toujours ses aptitudes pour l'artisanat et rapporte souvent de nouvelles acquisitions de la Floride pour ensuite les partager avec le groupe de l'Âge d'or.

Marie-Mae se compte parmi les heureux parents qui jouisse du fait que leur enfants demeurent dans leurs environs. Elle est choyée de huit petits-enfants et trois arrière petits-enfants. À date, ces derniers demeurent tous en Ontario et elle se fait un plaisir de constater pour elle-même qu'ils sont tous sains et saufs. De toutes les accolades qu'on puisse lui remettre, peu de celles-ci lui valent le titre de "mémé." Elle participe activement dans la vie de chaque membre de sa famille et ses conseils sont recherchés par chacun.

Marie-Mae jouit d'une excellente santé et d'une force d'esprit qu'elle ne prend pas pour acquis. Elle se stimule intellectuellement, physiquement et quotidiennement en entreprenant des projets qui sont d'une envergure entreprise par les plus jeunes. Le travail et le défi ont tellement été une partie intégrale de son quotidien qu'elle ne peut imaginer sa vie sans l'un ou l'autre. Lorsqu'elle a été éprouvée par les moments douloureux de la vie, elle a surmonté ces épreuves en se relançant dans le travail. Malgré le fait que nous reconnaissons tous l'importance de ces aspects de sa vie, ses proches lui souhaitent un âge d'or avec un peu moins de défis pour qu'elle puisse jouir d'une période tranquille et paisible bien méritée.

..... L'histoire familiale saura garder en mémoire votre dévouement et votre courage maman. Vous êtes une source d'inspiration pour tous ceux qui ont eu le privilège de vous connaître et de recevoir votre affection et votre amour.......

Blanche Bénéteau

Acknowledging a Courageous Woman

Mrs. Luciana Caron Briggs Démarais is celebrating with us today her 90th birthday. She was born January 26, 1908, daughter of Rémi Caron and Régina Béchard.

Rémi was the son of Médéric Caron and Elmire Faubert , who had 15 children. According to J. B. Beers Commemorative Biographical Records published in 1904, "Médéric Caron was a graduate of Sandwich College in 1878 and returned to farm in Pain Court, with his father Moïse Caron. In 1880, he was professor at Mt. Clemens, Michigan for two years. In 1882, he returned to the farm and married.

He took an intelligent interest in public affairs and has been honoured by election to a number of local offices. He was appointed Justice of the Peace. He proved himself an efficient and acceptable public servant. He served as treasurer of Dover township for a period of 30 years 1888 - 1918. His life has been an exemplary one and no man in the community was more highly esteemed.

In 1905, he built on a farm he had cleared, a brick home for his son Rémi on lot 15, concession 5, Dover. Rémi married Régina Béchard on January 9, 1906, daughter of Théodore Béchard and Louise Bénéteau. They had five children, Vital the oldest, Luciana whom we are honouring today, Elsie, Roland and Romeo, all have now passed away.

This is the very same house where Luciana was born. At the very tender age of ten, she lost her mother, November 6, 1918, a very traumatic experience but with the help of grandmothers, aunts, neighbours, and her own father, she overcame many difficulties and hardships.

Her father Rémi remarried in 1920 to Maria Laprise and eventually a second family was raised in this same old house. There were seven children, Agnes, Clare, Ernest, Victoria, Eva, Anna and Jérome. After 31 years, Rémi decided to move onto a larger farm and sold to his neighbour and brother-in-law, Josephat Laprise in 1937. Rémi died January 1961.

On January 18, 1938 Josephat's son, Trefflé Laprise married Caroline Roy, daughter of

Adolphe Roy and Délia Caron. So it was very fortunate that she lived in the same old house her grandfather had built in 1905. Here they raised a family of six boys and two girls: Gérard, Roger, Claude, Florent, Caroline, Guy, Jean-Marie and Colette. In 1974 after 36 years, Caroline moved to make room for Jean-Marie, the youngest son, who married Lucille Benoit, April 19, 1974. In this same house built by his great-grandfather, they raised a family of four children, three girls and one boy: Julie, Chantal, Mélanie and Joël. Lucille also attended the celebration. They have now moved to a beautiful new home.

After 60 years, Caroline is returning to this old house with great pride. Boxing Day 1997 was an open house for her children, grandchildren and great grandchildren.

Today we are honouring Luciana. She has weathered many storms and hardships, and has matured to the fullest of her ability. She portrays a very strong, soft-spoken person, patient and gifted with compassion for her fellow man. She is surrounded by an aura of serenity, of peace, of love and tenderness.

Even though she is now blind, she has a heart full of love. She always has something to give. At seventeen, one of her best friends Dorothée Caron, lost her mother also, so she volunteered to give her a helping hand to care in some measure to the welfare of the family. This was the "Ladislas Caron family."

Her second marriage was November 9, 1980 to Armand Demarais who died December 16, 1993. During these better years she was happy to travel to Florida, Arizona and parts of Canada.

Her life's occupation seemed to focus on washing and ironing, day after day, providing a decent living for her family, catering mostly to professional families.

We surely admire her, love her and she reigns as a matriarchal queen of courage and fortitude.

Caroline Roy Laprise

Thank God for folks like you

Luciana

In this troubled world, it's refreshing to find
someone who still has the time to be kind.
Someone who still has the faith to believe
that the more you give the more your receive.
Someone who's ready by thought, word or deed,
to reach out a hand in the hour of need.
This little prayer is a way of saying that I'm thankful everyday,
that life is blest and brighter too, by folks who are as nice as you.

Caroline Roy Laprise

Eulogy
Mrs. Virginia Jenner

Virginia Jenner was the daughter of Julius Moeyeart and Caroline Broadbend born June 16, 1920, lived in Wallaceburg and married Leonard Jenner September 17, 1939. Leonard was the son of Stella Jenner, a widow who married Henri Béchard of Pain Court. Henri was the son of Alexis Béchard and Adèle Faubert. Mrs. Stella Jenner, had five children: Clarissa, Monica, Leonard, Alfred, and Harry. Mr. Henri Béchard and his second wife Stella Jenner married June 1931 and they had three boys: Ross, Don and Jenner. They all resided in the dwelling now owned by Ernest Béchard and son. Their neighbours were Charlie Buck and Albert Peck followed by Ovila Martin.

Léonard and Virginia lived in Pain Court after they married and shared living quarters with the Béchard family. They raised four boys: Leonard Jr. now retired from Navistar, Dwaine, parts manager Riverview Motors, Brian, executive for Québec Air and Gary who works for the town of Dresden: All were educated in the Pain Court schools. Virginia only had praise for her mother- in-law and mentioned: "We had quality time and enjoyed each other as everyone shared in a household of ten."

As the children grew up, Virginia eventually started to work in the fields and became involved with social work. She was area foreman for DeKalb's detasseling crews for nineteen years. By 1948, she became very active in church organizations, helped with picnics and served many years with Marie-Anne Faubert on the dining room committee for picnics and banquets.

Virginia Jenner was a very talented and reliable worker who served under my presidency and that of Irene Gagner and others until 1961 when she moved with her husband and family in anticipation of working a much larger farm in Chatham Township. She gave her wholehearted best for bingos, banquets, penny sales, card parties and teas. Under Mrs. Irene Gagner's leadership, together with Adeline Bélanger and Rita Caron, they gave it their all for the penny sale in the fall to ring in a superb success, year after year. Virginia reminisced about the quilting bees at the church under Marie-Anne Trahan's presidency. These hand-stitched quilts always boosted the tremendous success of the annual penny sales.

In 1951 she headed the community T.B. Xray Clinic in this area. She was instrumental in the organization process for the township of Dover together with Mrs. Bruce Bradley, Mrs. Robert Bradley and Mrs. Robert Parry.

It is interesting to note that Virginia worked as a cook at both the Central Hotel and the Dover Hotel in Pain Court. She indeed had a versatile personality which enabled her to master whatever duties confronted her.

With an amazing grace, Virginia always gave a helping hand to women who were sick or had extra household duties to perform on a day to day basis. She gave me a helping hand twice a week in the year 1959 and 1960 in a household of ten. I have never forgotten her first honest comment as she came to work the first day.

"Caroline, I have known you for many years, but people have informed me that you were a very hard person to work for, that you were somewhat of a perfectionist."
Well, it sure was a pleasure to work with such an industrious, talented and respectable woman as Virginia.

On June 8, 1960, after serious reflection and consideration, Virginia embarked on a new career at the Kent County Jail and Courthouse. First, she was hired as a part-time jail guard to watch female prisoners along with court duties, and from 1980 as a full-time court services officer and manager until her retirement on June 26, 1995.
.

Although reluctant at first, Virginia remained at her job, 35 constructive years.
"I've enjoyed it all" she said "along with the challenges and the people I've worked with."

In her years of service she was the first woman promoted to "Deputy Sheriff," security of the court and staffing of the court. She worked with four consecutive sheriffs namely Eugene King 4 years, Bill Craven 2 years, Ross Cushman 10 years and George Sulman 17 years.

"In the courtroom, Virginia maintained order and decorum and cut an imposing figure. She was a fixture in the Courthouse and made a lasting impression on lawyers, jurors and people who found themselves before the Courts."1 She projected a stern image but underneath that facade was a kind, loyal and a very sweet lady that really had class.

Upon retiring June 26, 1995, Virginia expressed she would welcome one change – a new courthouse.

As part of new guidelines established by the provincial government, Virginia was forced to retire at 75 and sad to leave the job she formerly refused three times before accepting the sheriff of the day's offer. She admitted that it was time to move on.

Society as a whole was privileged and blessed to have had this remarkable, gracious and charming person to fulfill tasks of all dimensions with finesse and perseverance. To her husband, Leonard, we thank you. We appreciate the sacrifices you must have made in order that your wife could serve mankind in such an extraordinary way.

Caroline Roy Laprise

1. Ref: Chatham This Week - Wed. July 5, 1995.

Virginia's Detasseling Crew - 1944

Pictured above is one of Virginia's detasseling crews, all Pain Court
locals who worked so diligently for their foreman.

Front row, left to right : Grace Thibodeau, Angéline Blais, Gloria Vollans, Ruth Peltier,
Jeannette Blais, Alice Jubenville, Bernice Jubenville, Louella Charbonneau.

Back row, left to right : Eleonor Carter, Cécile Primeau, Edna Peltier, Madeleine Couture,
Antoinette Maure, Agathe Primeau, Jeanne Primeau, Marie Jubenville, Annette Carron,
Godleive Bossy, Georgette Bossy.

Mitchell's Bay Inn

Léopold Pinsonneault and his wife Josephine Grifford celebrated their 76th wedding anniversary on November 14, 1998. He is 95 years old and she is 93 yearsold.

Léopold Pinsonneault is the son of Alfred Pinsonneault and Hélène Daniel, daughter of Pierre Daniel and Archange Tétreault. Pierre Daniel and Archange Tétreault had 3 children. Hélène Daniel married Alfred Pinsonneault, Anna Daniel married Dominat Pinsonneault and Marie Daniel married Josephat Pinsonneault.

This was presented by Hélène Cartier, wife of Raymond Cartier,
and only daughter of Mr.and Mrs. Léo Pinsonneault

The last living member of Alfred Pinsonneault is Léopold, now 95 years old. He married Josephine Griffore now 94 years old in the year 1922 on November 14. She was the daughter of Joseph Griffore and Louise Foster who lived on the 10th concession in Grande Pointe. Leo and his wife lived between the 6th concession in Dover and the 7th concession, then known as "Pointe aux Chiens." Later, they moved to Pain Court on the 4th concession. They lived there a number of years and had a daughter Hélène who attended the small separate school - S S # 7 - on the 4th concession in Dover, then attended the High School in the village of Pain Court.

When Hélène was sixteen, Leopold, (her dad) bought acres of land around Mitchell's Bay. There was not much development then in the area, but soon Leopold and Josephine and Hélène worked very hard at this place making land workable by dredging ditches for drainage, and fixing and cleaning their modest living quarters. It was a great enterprise when you think about it especially when you are involved. Soon the land was productive, and cabins were moved in for hunters and fishermen.

Shortly after, Leopold sold a piece of land for a park now known as Mitchell's Bay Park of today where thousands of people enjoy themselves every year. Then with the help of St.Clair Gordon and Paul Martin Sr. M.P. and others he established Mitchell's Bay Inn. That was the beginning of a remarkable era in his life. They had rooms and meals for anyone across the country especially from Detroit and Ohio. It kept the Pinsonneault's very busy.

In 1947 Hélène was married to Raymond Cartier, son of Alfred Cartier and Anna McLennon. They lived there with her parents and helped with the work, till they moved on the 11th concession in Dover, not too far away. They had a son Rosaire in 1948 and another son Marc in 1954. Rosaire married Debbie Lannso and had one daughter Danielle, Marc married Jamie Oosterling and they have two daughter's Sarah and Lindsey. They are all attending École Secondaire de Pain Court.

Léopold and Joséphine are very proud of their family. They sold the Mitchell's Bay Hotel in the 70s and established themselves in a brand-new home close to the flourishing "Thames Lea Plaza." He kept on farming for a period of time. In the meantime they bought the Recess Hotel in Tilbury and the Dover Hotel in Pain Court. Afterward, he sold them also.

They are now retired in Chatham and so are Hélène and Raymond. They live close to each other in their respective homes. But Hélène and Raymond attend to the needs of Léo and Joséphine, i.e. groceries, doctor appointments and whatever else they require. They also benefit from the help of grandchildren and their wives when Hélène and Raymond are unable to attend.

Last year was a special year for Léopold and Joséphine as they celebrated their 75th wedding anniversary November 14, 1997, with their family. That same day, Hélène and Raymond also celebrated their 50th wedding anniversary and their youngest sons, Marc and Jamie, celebrated their 15th wedding anniversary. They renewed their wedding vows all together at St-Philippe's Church in Grande Pointe. It was a big celebration and a very unusual one. In 1996, Rosaire and Debbie celebrated their 15th wedding anniversary.

This couple, Léo and Joséphine Pinsonneault, should be honoured for all they have accomplished to develop Mitchell's Bay as a thriving community. It has developed tremendously since and is still in the process of future developments.

It is safe to say: "Hard work never killed anyone." We are proud to have them still with us as parents, grandparents and great grandparents. They deserve "recognition" on the occasion of the publishing of this book of memories. They are pleased to be part of everyone involved in this "Great-Project."

May God send to everyone His special blessings,
from the Léopold Pinsonneault family.

Celebrating Five Anniversaries

HAPPY 85TH
BIRTHDAY
OMER (April 6th)
&
CLARA (Provost)
(March 8th)
CHARRON 19

Fred Charron born in 1885 and
Oliva (Sterling) born in 1887.

**Happy
65th
Anniversary
Clifford &
Grace
Griffore**

January 26, 1998

With all our love from
your family & children

Also
**Happy
Birthday**

Mom - Dec. 24, 1997
(88 yrs old)
Dad Feb. 19, 1998
(88 yrs old)

RECEIVE PAPAL BLESSING 1949

The 50th wedding day of Mr. and Mrs. Emile Pinsonneault, well known Dover township couple began with a high mass which the celebrants attended in Immaculate Conception church, Pain Court on October 16th. | Following the mass the coupl had conferred upon them by th pastor the blessing of the Hol Father. On Sunday friends an relatives from distant and nea by points greeted Mr. and Mrs Pinsonneault at the home of the son Joseph at Big Point.

**HAPPY 65TH
WEDDING
ANNIVERSARY
REG
&
EVELYN
CHARRON**

January 16th, 1933-1998

*How wonderful you both look
And how fortunate we all are!*

My Great-grandchildren

Chad Laprise

André James Laprise

Amanda Laprise

Rebecca Laprise

Mattieu Laprise

Dominique Laprise

Kira Brown

Ian Brown

Melanie

Madison Laprise

Matthew Trudell

Joshua Trudell

Natasha Trudell

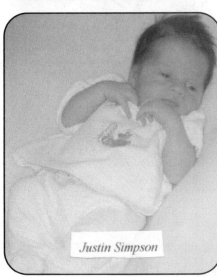

Justin Simpson

601

"Mes réflexions"

Face à la violence causée par le racisme, la pauvreté, les guerres, les déportations massives, les famines, les désastres écologiques et les misères moins spectaculaires hypothèquent le bonheur de bien des gens. Les malheurs de l'humanité remplissent les journaux et les écrans de nos téléviseurs.

Il serait facile d'allonger la liste des calamités qui écrasent notre planète. Les humains désirent beaucoup plus que survivre. Ils veulent sauver la vie, assurer à leur descendance un héritage de qualité, autant sur le plan personnel et communautaire que celui de l'environnement mental.

Pour réaliser ce projet social nous devons donner un sens à l'existence, proposer des modèles qui créent la fraternité, doter et encourager les aventures humaines qui conduisent au bonheur, à la plénitude de la vie. À l'aube du millénaire je souhaite que le Ciel nous prodigue ses divines faveurs.

Mon atelier - Maison paternel

FIVE GENERATIONS

FIVE GENERATIONS – A former Pain Court woman celebrated her 95th birthday with a visit from her family. They marked the occasion with a picture of the five generations of her family. Florida Jubenville turned 95, she met with her family at Thamesview Lodge on Sunday afternoon. Florida Jubenville, seated, is surrounded by her daughter Clara Martin and grandson Robert Martin, of Inwood; her great granddaughter Yvette Kewley of Petrolia, and her great-great-grandson Benjamin Kewley who is eight months old.   Mrs. Florida Sterling Jubenville was married to Alfred Jubenville July 16, 1920. They celebrated their 70th anniversary July 16th 1990.   Mrs. Jubenville was 97 years old May 30,1999.

Record of Events

DID YOU KNOW . . .

The first Canadian inducted into the baseball Hall of Fame was Ferguson (Fergie) Jenkins, who was born and raised in Chatham. Later, after high professional achievements, he built a home within a few miles from Blenheim.

OTHER NEWS . . .

– CHATHAM KENT –
TOURING KENT COUNTY
PAIN COURT – WATER LOVERS

LIGHTHOUSE IS 170 YEARS OLD –

The Thames River Lighthouse is acknowledged as the second oldest lighthouse in the province of Ontario. It was built in 1818 as a result of the War of 1812 between Canada and the United States. Only the lighthouse at Old Fort York in Toronto is older. When this lighthouse was tended by men, the "Cartier Family" tended the light for more than 137 years. About 1970, it became apparent that the Lighthouse was in need of serious repair. The foundation was sinking and the structure had developed severe cracks.

James L. Cooke was instrumental in getting the federal government to turn the control of the "Lighthouse" to the Lower Thames River Conservation Authority. Under "Mike Wilson's" chairmanship the L.T.V.C.A. arranged a grant from the province of Ontario.

The lighthouse was carefully dismantled and all parts catalogued, steel was driven more than 100 feet into the ground to support the new base. The Lighthouse was carefully rebuilt with the original brick, centre spar, steps etc.

The Canadian Coast Guard now looks after maintenance of the structure and the light to this day guides boaters in to the mouth of the Thames River.

Ref. "Touring Kent County" p. 24

– WATER LOVERS FIND HAVEN HERE –

All around us our well-known community of Mitchell's Bay, on Lake St. Clair, is well-known and was recognized as an ideal boating and docking facility. The hunting and fishing are great and guided boats can be arranged. Bring the whole family and join in the fun.

The French cultural flavour of the area can be experienced in Pain Court, Grande Pointe and Jeannette's Creek. The pocket of soil found here makes it ideal for production of vegetables, like celery, onions, potatoes, tomatoes, peas, sweet corn, cucumber, etc.

The St. Clair National Wildlife area in Grande Pointe, Pain Court and surrounding areas is used by thousands of ducks, geese, and swans during their migration. Many other types of wetland wildlife make this marsh their home.

Sparkling blue waters, whether you want to be in it . . . on it . . . or by it . . .this part of the country was made for water lovers. Lakes St. clair and Erie border the county with the Thames and Sydenham Rivers flowing through the area. Water is everywhere here. Enjoy refreshing boating, fishing, canoeing, wind surfing, skiing and tanning.

St. Clair Parkway has matured into a chain of a well maintained recreational area. Pull off the road, put your feet up and enjoy a picnic lunch at any of the 19 shoreline Parks. There's also Marine Bay Park at Mitchell's Bay, Uncle Tom's Cabin in Dresden and Dover Beach Park.

Wallaceburg is a charming yet bustling industrial town with picturesque waterways and quaint streets. Local attractions include the Wallaceburg and district Museum and Libbey Glass factory, outlet and a Golf Course. They also hold a yearly Antique Motor and Boat show in July. Showcasing more than 200 antique boats, autos, fire trucks and motorcycles.

Surrounding our area to the south is Tilbury and Jeannette's Creek where most of our ancestors have lived and prospered. They maintain a warm and friendly atmosphere. It includes attractions such as 175 year old historic clock, historic dash wheel over 70 years old and the Odette Memorial Library. In the same area on the shores of Thames River stands the first mission Chapel of "St. Peter's" of Raleigh built and blessed July 1802 by Father J. P. Marchand known to be a sub-mission of Assumption Parish in Windsor, a Huron Mission built in 1728 by the Jesuits, Father Armand de la Richardie 1728 - 46 and Pierre Poitier 1746 - 81.

Ref. Chatham Kent "Touring Kent County" June 1997

George A. Bruette

George A. Bruette followed in his mother's footsteps by graduating from London Normal School in 1944 as a school teacher. George received his elementary education at S. S. # 5 Dover, part of his high school education at Pain Court High School and graduated from Assumption High School in Windsor.

While teaching, George achieved his B.A. from Western and Assumption University. Later on George spent three years acquiring a Specialist Certificate in Special Education in Toronto. During this time George taught half of his forty-one year career n Chatham elementary schools and the last half at John McGregor Secondary School where he also established an enviable record as a football coach until he retired.

George was always keenly interested in sports. Not only was he known as a fastball pitcher for many years, but he acted as president of Kent County Fastball leagues until 1996. He was also a convenor and an executive member of the Ontario Amateur Softball Association in this part of Southwestern Ontario for many years.

This year 1997 George and his wife Doris celebrated their 50th wedding anniversary with their family of five children and nine grandchildren.

George Bruette

Reunion

July 27, 1997. It is interesting to note that all students who attended S. S. # 5 school in Dover Township with Mrs. Edith Bruette as teacher for over 25 years, were invited to a reunion at Mitchell's Bay. It was headed by Joe Barnier, a former pupil, who requested that old photos be brought and exchanged as souvenirs. This special event was free to all interested classmates.

Landmarks and Special Interests
Water Towers 1995 – 1996
Pain Court - Mitchell's Bay

It's amazing what progress brings to the life of a community. It's mid August 1995; to many anxious residents it's a pleasure to run the city water in their home for the first time. The impressive water tower dominates the thriving community of Pain Court. By 1996, residents of Grande Pointe are just as anxious to welcome the new water system to their homes. By the end of that year a high rising tower also dominates the prosperous and developing community of Mitchell's Bay.

Front yards were messy and muddy but within a short time, people on the installation crew and the residents worked diligently to restore everything in shipshape order.

This project has benefited all these communities, but as always, it comes with a price tag.

"I remember"
Lawrence Kerr

I was born in 1906 and the first thing I can remember is Halley's Comet 1910. It was over the neighbour's wood lot and I can still see grandmother's deeply concerned face, as she declared: "It's a sign of war." The world has been basically free of war for 45 years as Halley's Comet made its appearance once again in March 1997.

When the Titanic sank April 15, 1912 father brought home the London Free Press.

It was the first daily paper that grandfather, grandmother and I had ever seen. We lived in a divided house which was quite common at the time. Grandparents lived with their children.

Mr. Kerr, I appreciate your comments and highly congratulate you for the appearance of your regular column, in the Chatham Daily News.

Ref - Chatham Daily News 1997

A rare heart operation, the procedure known as (TMR), gave 64 year-old Philippe Blais a second chance at life. His wife, Rosita Robert Blais said "Philippe had a life-saving operation. He has life in his eyes. He had death before. This is a miracle." They don't know what the future holds, they just live every day thankful that Philippe has been given a second chance and is able to tend his garden once again, after a rare operation. He once again walks every day, just one of the many things he loved to do but couldn't after suffering two heart attacks.

Ref. Chatham Daily News - 10.08.98

20th Century Brings Change For Women

It's hard to imagine that only 67 years ago women gained legal recognition as "persons". The 20th century has been one of change for Canadian women. We can look to the past as a springboard to shape the stature of women in the future. The Government of Canada bowed to the significant pressures and announces changes to the taxation of child support payment to be effective May 1st 1997.

Sexual harassment, violence and discrimination and many inadequacies still exist in 1998. Women have challenged the law and earned their respective places in society. The turn of the century will bring about many changes as we grow and become a better informed public.

Through education, the next generation and the one after, will hopefully see a climate of peace and understanding that no one generation has ever seen.

- Many major changes -

"Forty-three years in Business"

Kent Refrigeration and furniture on Queen Street south, closed its door forever in April 1997. Some fifty years ago it was a very popular business known and patronized by the farming community. The firm was originally established by Bruce and Don McKay on King St. East at the old Market Square. Gord Moss joined the firm as salesman. He died in 1995. He had purchased the business years ago. His wife Madeleine Moss, now the store owner, has announced the closing based on liquidation of inventory.

*　　　*　　　*

The Kent County Agricultural Hall of Fame inducted three Kent County residents on October 29,1997. They were Lee Montgomery, Kate Glendening, and Norman Bélanger. Mrs. Gloriana Bélanger accepted the honour on behalf of her late husband Norman.

Mr. Kent County Agriculture

That's what the thousands of people who know Frank Parry called the man who turned 100 Friday May 13,1994.

Mr. Parry was born on the River Road in Dover Township and farmed many years on the Baldoon Road. His older brother George, served as MP for Chatham more than 12 years.

Parry's contribution to the betterment of Agriculture in Kent County as well as Ontario, has been described as outstanding. On his 100 year milestone more than 100 close friends turned out at the Chatham Retirement Resort to wish him well. His wife, Grace Fleming, died in 1985. Mr. and Mrs. Parry had two children, as well as seven grandchildren and 11 great-grandchildren.

Kent Federation of Agriculture and Chatham and District Chamber of Commerce have honoured him in the past as well as the Ontario Vegetable Growers Marketing Board and Canadian Society of Horticultural Science.

"Ontario needs to reinvest"

Mr. Ed Segsworth president of the Ontario Federation of Agriculture made this comment in Dover March 24, 1998: "Ontario needs to reinvest 160 million into agriculture. It's only fair that public money be spent on research and development since all of society benefits from improved genetics, more efficient chemicals and advanced biotechnology."

O.F.A. president who is from the Milton area was visiting the Dover farm of Rosaire Lucier, a cash crop farmer and active member of the Kent Federation of Agriculture.

A kitchen meeting at Lucier's farm in Dover attracted the executive committee of the Kent Federation and later the Chatham-Kent's new Agri-Business advisory committee. Mr. Segsworth was accompanied by OFA vice-president, Sharon Rounds of Oxford County. Both are representing the Farmers of Ontario, a coalition of 37 Ontario farm groups who are calling on the government to rebuild and restore the agricultural budget to "its deserved stature."

WAR HEROES

"Lest we forget "

Bid farewell to eleven soldiers - 1916

Congregation of Pain Court shows esteem in which the young men are held. A meeting which shall not soon be forgotten was held in Pain Court Church basement after the celebration of mass. It was a farewell to eleven young men of the parish who will shortly be leaving to join the colours. The basement of the church was crowded with relatives and friends of the young men as a mark of esteem in which they are held by the people of the entire community. Those young men were Gilbert Maure, Eugène Roy, Hervé Pinsonneault, Joseph Cacheté, Amedée Bélanger, Clifford Faubert, Ovila Charron, Joseph Peltier, Thomas Gamble, Gilbert Laprise and Hector Charbonneau. A number of addresses were given, and each of the young men responded briefly.

There was no mistaking the interest of the people, because tears flowed freely. The scene was one which will long be remembered.

"The Planet"   May 1916

World War II veteran

John Haslip

John was born in Sarnia Ontario on May 9th 1926. He is the second son of Harold and Mary Magdelene (Dennis) Haslip. He attended Our Lady of Mercy separate school and St. Patrick's High School in Sarnia. In 1944 John joined the Royal Canadian Navy. He did his basic training at HMCS Prevost in London Ontario. From there he was drafted to Navy headquarters in Sydney Nova Scotia. Following three months of duty there he was drafted to HMCS Collingwood. The ship was assigned to convoy work escorting oil tankers and freighters from eastern American ports to convoy assembly points in Halifax and other east coast ports. The European war ended on May 8th 1945. John volunteered for duty in the Pacific war.

Following a month's leave, he returned to his ship and from there transferred to Halifax for a Torpedo man's course. This branch served as ship's electricians as very few ships carried torpedoes. While at HMCS Stadacona in Halifax he was promoted to AB. (able bodied seaman) one rank higher than an ordinary seaman. In August of 1945 the Pacific war ended and John was assigned to the Torpedo School general office while waiting for his demobilization or discharge. In March of 1946 he was assigned to the Canadian frigate HMCS Charlottetown II. He was to be part of the crew that delivered the ship to the West Coast. The trip took one month from the time the ship left Halifax to Esquimalt B.C.

The ship's company received two days leave in Panama before going through the Panama Canal. Refuelling in San Pedro California allowed the crew another two days leave in the Los

Angeles and Hollywood areas. After arriving in HMCS Esquimalt, the crew spent one week in Victoria B.C. before boarding a train in Vancouver for Toronto Ontario and home. John received his release from the Navy at HMCS York in Toronto and returned home. As his father, an employee of the Pere Marquette railway, he was transferred to Chatham Ontario. During the war, John decided not to return to Sarnia and moved to Chatham in the Spring of 1946.

John took up the trade of sign painting and operated his own business until 1960. He moved into sales and at the same time took up the hobby of photography. In the early 1960's he began working weekends for the London Free Press. In the late 60's television was becoming more popular so John moved into that field also on a part-time basis. In 1975 he was offered the job as New Bureau chief for CKCO-TV. He covered the news happening in the Chatham , Windsor and Sarnia area starting with a windup 16MM movie camera and a tape recorder. Technology kept changing in the news gathering business. From film, the equipment changed to video cameras, microwave transmission of sight and sound and lap top computers.

John retired in June of 1990 but returned following a month's holiday to work part-time until November 11th 1990. The Chatham Remembrance Day service was the lack of any recognition of the efforts and the nearly 2,000 Naval personnel who lost their lives during the nearly six year war. With his friend and fellow shipmate Jack Mitchinson, they formed the Chatham and Area Royal Canadian Naval Association. The group has approximately 90 members and now are a participating group honouring their fallen shipmates at the November 11th services as well as conducting a Battle of the Atlantic service on the first Sunday of May. John served as President of the RCNA in 1997 - 98.

The only other service organization John joined was the Junior Chamber of Commerce or better known as the Jaycees. He joined in late 1946 and served on the executive for several years. He was elected President for 1959 -60. John attended several conventions including the JCI Congress held in Rio de Janeiro in November 1959 and appeared in a movie featuring the Jaycee world wide organization "CREED IN ACTION." He was made a Senator of the JCI in 1960 for his service to the local organization. John is married to Jeanne (Laprise) and they have three sons, Paul Joseph, Jean Marc and John Michel. They have lived in Pain Court Ontario since the late 1950's.

Major Ed F. Carron

Major Ed F. Carron – mm. Cd.
Son of Sylvester Francis Carron, his
mother was Mildred Jones Carron.

Major E. F. Carron married Frances
Jubenville on November 28, 1939.

They had three children;
John Michael B.A.S.C. (Analogs test engineering)
Theodore B.A.S.C.
Nicole Janine Humphrey.

Mr. Carron was born August 9, 1919 in Seaforth Ontario. Educated in Seaforth and Chatham, Ontario, graduating from Chatham Collegiate in 1936. He lived in Pain Court across from Ste-Catherine School in the former Émile Pinsonneault home.

He joined CA. (AF) enlisting in the R.C.R. October 6, 1939 as a Pte. Soldier, went overseas with the Royal Canadian Regiment in 1939. He served with them in France 1940, landed in Sicily in 1943, was taken prisoner in the last engagement the Regiment fought in Sicily (Regalbuto), escaped in Italy and made his way across France joining up again with allied forces in October 1944. Major Carron was awarded the Military Medal for destroying German aircraft while an escape prisoner of war.

He was commissioned in 1945 on secondment, served with 205 Base Wksp RCEME as a Regimental Officer, served at the CJATC Rivers as a parachute instructor and in other appointments. In 1954 he served in the Far East, including Japan. On return he was appointed Training Officer at Fort Churchill where he was directly concerned with Arctic Training for the Canadian Force.

Leaving Fort Churchill in 1958 he returned to regimental duty and was promoted Major with RCR. Later in 1960, he was posted to Newfoundland as Ranger Liaison Officer, Eastern Command. In 1964, he was seconded to External Affairs and posted to the United Nations Truce Supervision Organisation as a military Observer in Palestine.

Frequently he served as Staff Officer Logistics and administration, Northern Group Militia. This was his last posting, and he expects shortly to retire to Chatham where he will take over operation of his farms and more, get acquainted with his family.

WORLD WAR II VETERANS

Pte. Romeo Trahan was the son of Hercule Trahan and Eva Yott, of Pain Court. He has served with the Royal Canadian Regiment in England, has been overseas for three years having been a member of the first contingent to go to England. He also served in Italy and France. He was married to Yvonne Caron, July 23, 1939. After his return from the war, they adopted two boys Vincent and Dominique. He died May 5, 1967.

Pte. Leo Corriveau was the son of Mr. and Mrs Ernest J. Corriveau of Chatham. He enlisted with the Medical Corps in August 1942. Mr. Corriveau was stationed in England, France, Holland, Belgium. He was stationed in Paris, after the war for one year. Corriveau played with the CYO Championship baseball team of Chatham. He was also a member of the Arcadias while at Basic Training Centre. His mother, Laura Corriveau, was married to Josephat Laprise and lived in Pain Court village 16 years. Leo married Audrey Taylor , January 20 1948, and died August 4th 1995.

Gunner Gérald Caron son of Mr. and Mrs. Alfred Caron of Pain Court arrived overseas in 1942. He enlisted in September 1941 in the Royal Canadian Artillery. After arriving overseas he joined the infantry in France, Belgium and Italy. He later spent one year in Labrador and received his training in Chatham, Woodstock and Petawawa. We salute your bravery. He married Agathe Martin on August 30, 1947 and died February 22 1997 at 77 years of age.

Pte Gérald Gagner, was the son of Mr. and Mrs. Zacharie Gagner of Pain Court. He was married to Pauline Roy December 2, 1939 daughter of Mr. and Mrs. Alphy Roy. Gerald served with the regiment "Stormont, Dundas and Glengarry Highlanders." He was in Europe for the duration of the war. He saw action in England, France, Belgium, Holland and Germany.

During that time in the war-torn Europe, Gerald served nine to ten months on the front-line as an infantryman. This duty took its toll on Gerald's war- torn nervous system to the point of breakdown and serious wound in the upper part of his back. At a point near the end of the war Gerald was back in the thick of things in Germany. Soon after came the end of the war.

All this time his wife Pauline was home with three young boys, not knowing his whereabouts. Finally, he came home on a hospital ship because of complications to his nervous system but otherwise he was fit as a fiddle. "I am glad that I had a distinguished career while helping to defend our way of life" said Gérald, a spry octogenarian. Gérald Gagner retired from the Armed Forces, September 1945, as a private.

Mr. Leonard Emery served with the Royal Canadian Regiment overseas in the war of 1940 - 1945. He is the son of Francis Emery and Almina L'Écuyer. He married Lucie- Anna Emery daughter of George Emery and Ida Laprise of Wallaceburg.

Mr. Raymond L'Écuyer son of Mr and Mrs Rodolphe L'Écuyer was called to serve his country in 1940. So his brother Norman operated the garage until he returned from duty in the early 1950's.

On his return he decided to add a restaurant to the business. This was operated by his wife Jeannette. Later in 1961 the restaurant and garage were sold to Polydore Quenneville who operated it until he sold it to Jerry Tremblay who now operates it as J. T'S Restaurant.

Raymond was drafted, and joined the regular army. He served most of his army career with a reserve from Windsor. He was stationed during and after the war in Jamaica and served there as a guard for "German prisoners of war."

The farm at this time was taken over by his brothers Homer, Joshua, Jerry and Norman sharing equally.

Mr. Clifford Lebrun joined the reserves and married Nilla Rankin. Clifford served overseas.

Mr. Orville Marchand joined the reserves, later he served overseas, in England, in France, Belgium and Italy. He was married in England in the early forties.

Mr. Ernest Béchard est fils de Thomas Béchard et de Rose-Anna Bélisle et marié à Irene Chaplin de Verdun, Québec. Il est journalier à l'usine de Ford à Windsor, Ontario lorsqu'il est conscrit, en 1942, pour servir son pays durant la Deuxième Querre Mondiale. Comme soldat du détachement "Brockville Rifles," il est affecté à Jamaïque pour servir de garde et de cuisinier dans les camps de prisonniers. Après la guerre il prend domicile à Toronto où il a vécu confortablement avec sa femme et ses deux fils jusqu'à sa mort à l'âge de 60 ans.

Mr. Romain Béchard 18 year old son of Thomas Béchard and Rose-Anna Bélisle, enlisted in 1940. He was part of the "17th Royal Canadian Field Artillery Regiment - 1st division." He was stationed at Brantford for basic training and then at Camp Borden for advanced training. In 1940, he embarked for Europe and was on active duty from 1941 to 1945. From Ipswich England he marched across Northern Italy on to France, then to Belgium and finally was wounded at Otterlo, in the Netherlands in 1945 where the Allied and German forces were engaged in battle. It is fair to say that Romain was part of the Canadian contingent fighting for the liberation of Holland. After the war he established himself in Brantford with his family. He died of "ALS" (Lou Gehrig's disease) on December 18, 1986 and is buried in the veteran's section of the Paris Cemetery in Paris Ontario, a military tribute to a hero who fought so gallantly for his country.

Mr. Raymond Béchard son of Thomas Béchard and Rose-Anna Belisle, experienced early military training in the cadet corps associated with the "2nd Kent Regiment of the Chatham Armoury Reserve." As an adventurous young man of 16, he worked for the Great Lakes Pulp and Paper Co. in the Fort William and Thunder Bay area. His willingness to serve lured him on to enlist in 1943 at Port Arthur Ontario and was part of the "Lake Superior Regiment Light-Armoured Division." From there, his detachment was assigned to various depots across the western provinces. A significant move to Brandon Manitoba, where his experience as a trainee with the detachment of the "Woodstock Motor Transport" helped forge his future trade as a reputable transport driver. However, it was during his posting at the Ottawa Connaught Ranges where his unit counted in the "Pacific Force Echelon's" contingent that he was ready and waiting to join the American Allies in the Pacific, if need be. The call never did come since the atomic bomb put an end to the war. Raymond returned to the London Ontario Army Base for his official discharge, April 18, 1946.

Mr. Harry Goudreau , son of Siméon (Sam) Goudreau and Roseanna Charron was 22 when he enlisted voluntarily during the armed forces' recruitment of capable young men while foreseeing an eminent Korean conflict that was brewing between the divided Korea in 1950.

Harry joined as a young recruit in 1951 at Woolsly Barrick in London Ont. and was part of the 2nd Royal Canadian Horse Artillery (R.C.H.A.) Regiment and later trained at various army bases across the country.

In 1952, he patriotically volunteered to be counted among the UN Canadian Brigade, and one of the 13 UN member contingents joining the American and South Korean allied troops in combat on Korean soil.

From Seattle USA, Harry's supporting unit embarked on the A.T. Collin in 1953, en route to Okayama Japan, then by train to Port Ube, Japan and again by boat heading towards the seaport of Pusan and from Pusan to active duty in Seoul, 40 miles from the active Horseshoe Front where he was stationed during the duration of the war. This boundary line still makes news today.

For 13 agonizing months, Harry saw active duty in this remote area of the Republic working with ground troops of engineers setting up communication lines.

In 1953, a truce was agreed upon with regulations strictly enforced.

"One single shot fired could have triggered the end of the cease-fire," declared Harry.

For the withdrawal of troops, according to Harry, landing barges carrying ground troops were anchored in the Inch'on Harbour operating in a tandem fashion, that is two barges carrying an identical number of troops, one on the way in and one on the way out, until all soldiers had been deployed according to the agreement.

Harry's landing barge transported his unit to the "S.S. Marine Linx" for the return journey to America.

Harry was honourably released in Kingston Ontario on September 10th 1954.

Mr. Gordon Blair son of Willie Blais (Blair) and Fébronie Maillet joined the army at Woolsly Barrick, London Ontario, in 1951, as a recruit during the Korean conflict. He trained at Camp Borden with the Royal Canadian Service Corps. His unit was deployed to Germany and he remained there for one year. He was discharged in 1953.

Gordon Blair was married to Elizabeth Kilber. He died December 12, 1979 and is buried in the Pain Court Cemetery.

Mr. Murray Tuck was stationed at "Sioux Look Out Camp" in Northern Ontario as a guard for German prisoners of war. He was with the Royal Canadian Electrical engineering division of the Reserve Army. Years later from 1962 to 1969 he was manager of the Warwick lumber yard in Grande Pointe. He later became court bailiff until 1983. From 1983 to 1993 he was appointed Justice of the Peace.

Mr. Réginald Charron passed away at his residence April 21, 1998 at 82 years. Born in 1915 son of Fred Charron and the former Oliva Sterling, he married Evelyn Tétreault January 16, 1933. He was a member of the Branch 28 of the Royal Canadian Legion and was buried with full military honours. Sergeant at Arms John Grosvenor was presiding.

Mr. Léo Poissant son of Mr. and Mrs. Ovide Poissant was born on June 16, 1918 and died March 17, 1999. He joined the Army Reserves but never went overseas. He married Viola Labadie and resided in Grande Pointe all his life.

"Our Dedicated American Neighbour"
Fernand Gervais

US Air Force for 15 years (1951 - 1966), US Army for 11 years (1966 - 1977)
US Navy for 6 years (1985 - 1991), US Civil Service in Japan, as a civilian.

1896 -1996

These 10 postage stamps, issued to mark the first 100 years of cinema in Canada, feature miniature scenes from films destined to become major classics.

Les 10 timbres-poste émis à l'occasion du centenaire du cinéma au Canada reproduisent en miniature des scènes tirées de films appelés à devenir de grands classiques.

ST. JOSEPH'S HOSPITAL
1890 to 1998

As the 21st century looms on the horizon, 1998 is the end of an era for the St. Joseph's Hospital we have known, a turning point nonetheless, as it embarks on the restructuring process. St. Joseph's Hospital served our community for over a century. We certainly owe a debt of gratitude to all the Sisters of St. Joseph who served diligently.

To all the nurses who trained, educated and served our community so well, we owe you a debt of gratitude.

Rex Crawford - back in politics

The former Kent M.P. Rex Crawford is back in politics. Crawford now 64, said he did some soul-searching after leaving federal office in June and decided to get back in the political game and won one of two seats in the North Kent Ward of the municipal government for Chatham-Kent. "I worry about the old riding of Kent and the City of Chatham." The run for office is a return to local politics:

He was elected to Dover Township Council in 1977. He became deputy Reeve in 1979 and then reeve in 1981. Crawford was elected to the county warden's post in 1987. He switched to federal politics in 1988 and became the Kent M.P. under the banner of the Liberal Party. He stayed in federal politics until stepping in the run-up to this year's federal election.

Mr. and Mrs. Crawford celebrated their 50th wedding anniversary, June 16,1996. Rex Crawford the grand-old man of Kent County politics who lives on a farm near Wallaceburg, was honoured for 20 consecutive years of elected politics at the Dresden Rotary Club's rural urban-dinner on November 17,1997. John Phair, representing the "Farm Market," reports that Crawford rose through the ranks as municipal councillor deputy reeve, reeve, warden of Kent County and elected M.P. for the Kent riding in1988. Rex's motto was "all politics is local." Rosemary Ur says Crawford is the true "embodiment" of public service. Finance Minister Paul Martin was unable to attend but instead sent a video in which he wished Crawford was still in parliament. "Rex always made me hold the line on budgets" says Martin.

Joining Crawford at the rural urban dinner was guest speaker Jean-Marie Laprise, a Dover Township farmer, who is a pioneer in the production of industrial hemp.

Soeur Marie-Anne Caron

Je suis heureuse de vous présenter une chère amie de classe, Marie-Anne Caron, fille de d'Adélard Caron et d'Annie Gamble et soeur de Mae, Napoléon, Patrick, Bernadette, Jim et Sr. Viviènne o.s.u.

Elle a été nommée au service des cours bilingues par correspondance au ministère de l'Institution publique de l'Ontario. Par la suite, elle fait son entrée chez les soeurs de Loretto Abbey à Toronto.

I visited with her several times in Guelph where she taught French as a second language at different levels in the secondary schools.

Around 1979, she retired from the teaching profession and spent much time with her ailing father, Adelard Caron, in Windsor, where I paid occasional visits. He died February 18, 1981. After devoting her elderly years tending to members of her community, she passed away on April 5, 1988. Her mother, Annie Gamble, will be forever remembered for the wonderful amateur theatricals she directed in Pain Court in the 20s and 30s assisted by Marie Charbonneau Tanguay and Jacob Roy, two local talents "*de grande renommée*," Marie, for her musical talents be it singing, piano or step-dancing and Jacob for his gifted voice and a "natural" when it came to directing or performing on stage.

Caroline Roy Laprise

Hommage à Dame Madeleine Leal

Madeleine est née à New York en 1927, mais a grandi en Ontario. Après avoir terminé ses études à Hawkesbury et à Ottawa, elle enseigne ici et là dans la province et aboutit à Windsor en 1948. Elle épouse Wilfrid Leal en 1953 et de cette union naissent quatre enfants: Richard, Paul, Louise et Julie. En 1962, la famille vient s'établir dans un petite ferme à Ruscom, près de St-Joachim où se trouve une école de langue française.

Au cours de ses trente-deux années dévouées à l'enseignement, elle prend une part active dans l'association des enseignants tant au niveau local que provincial. Elle consacre aussi plusieurs années de service à la Féderation des femmes canandiennes-françaises en qualité de présidente locale et régionale.

Elle est élue présidente du comité du centenaire de St-Joachim en 1979 et s'occupe de la rédaction du livre souvenir avec l'aide indispensable de Paul Trépanier et d'Elmira Sylvestre. Elle dirige toutes les célébrations qui ont lieu en 1982, l'année du centenaire.

Elle aide à l'établissement de l'école secondaire l'Essor en siégeant au comité consultatif pour une durée de huit années.

Elle prête main-forte à sa paroisse comme lectrice aux messes et ministre eucharistique pendant plusieurs années. Aussi elle n'oublie pas les jeunes de sa région; elle dirige des cours récréatifs d'été et entraîne des équipes de balle.

Elle est honorée à maintes reprises pour son bénévolat dans la communauté et pour son dévouement envers la préservation de la langue et de la culture française.

Madeleine garde un souvenir très doux de Pain Court car elle se rappelle les beaux séjours chez M. et Mme Henri Roy, à l'invitation de Thérèse, leur fille, et de leur bru, Margot, deux grandes amies de sa jeunesse.

Le Centre Culturel "Tournesol"

Windsor, Essex, Kent a dévoilé récemment le nom de six personnes qui verront leur nom ajouté au Temple de la Renommée francophone du sud-ouest pour 1997.

L'investiture se fit lors d'une cérémonie le 30 novembre 1997 au Salon Richelieu de la Place Concorde. Un concert présenté par le Père Eugène Roy au piano clôture la soirée. Deux femmes ont été choisies: Madeleine Leal de Ruscom et Thérèse Hamel de Rivière-aux-Canards. Les quatre hommes sont Léon D'Aoust de Windsor, Phil McGraw, autrefois de l'Acadie, Lorenzo Lanthier d'Amherstburg et Marcel Bourassa de Sarnia.

Centre Communautaire

Il me fait plaisir de vous présenter le Centre Communautaire "La Girouette" de Chatham Kent. Le bulletin d'information "Le Flambeau" vous présente "mot du président" Roger Lozon.

La saison agricole de 1997, tire à sa fin et l'automne se défile en douceur pour faire place à l'hiver et à ses plaisirs. À "La Girouette" les choses reprennent peu à peu leur rythme habituel. Nous continuons à amasser des fonds pour pouvoir ajouter nos services à la communauté francophone. Vous êtes, bien sûr, toujours invités à faire partie de notre équipe dynamique.

L'école St-Philippe fête cette année son 40e anniversaire 1958 - 1998. Pour souligner l'occasion, La Girouette en partenaire avec l'école invite le groupe "A W I " en spectacle à une soirée portes ouvertes. Ce fut un succès. Bravo "A W I," Joseph et Denise Benoit!!

En terminant un merci spécial à Jeannine Lachance pour le travail colossal qu'elle a fait pour "La Girouette." Grâce à elle, nous sommes maintenant une organisation en marche. À la prochaine et souvenez-vous que "La Girouette," c'est votre centre communautaire.

Mot du président Roger Lozon

Thomas Blais

Données personnelles

- Originaire de Pain Court (Ontario)
- Marié à Gabrielle Tissot
- Père de François et de Christine
- Sociétaire (Cyrville) depuis 1963
- Fonctionnaire, Revenu Canada, Impôt
- Gradué de l'Université d'Ottawa

Compétence

- Directeur adjoint au secondaire
- Chef de planification des ressources humaines
- Vérificateur interne, Impôt
- Chargé de projets spéciaux, Impôt
- Coordonnateur régional de programmes, Impôt
- Membre du comité de finances et des ressources humaines, Fédération
- Membre du comté de ressources humaines, produits/systèmes et Fédération
- Membre du comté d'immeuble, Fédération
- Thomas Blais oeuvre dans le domaine des Caisses populaires depuis 35 ans.

Expérience

- 16 années dans le domaine de l'éducation
- 18 années à Revenu Canada, Impôt
- 16 années au Conseil d'administration des caisses Cyrville et Cyrville-Rockland
- Président caisse Cyrville et Cyrville-Rockland
- 8 années à la Fédération des caisses populaires de l'Ontario
- 6 années au Conseil de la Coopération de l'Ontario
- Représentant de la Fédération des caisses au Conseil provincial de l'ACFO
- Nouveau président de la Fédération des Caisses populaires de l'Ontario en 1998.

Thomas Edmond Blais, fils de Philippe Blais et Anna Béchard, est originaire de Pain Court Ontario et citoyen de la Cité Clarence-Rockland, à l'est d'Ottawa.

Il porte le nom du pionnier Thomas Blais arrivé à Pain Court en 1844 avec sa femme Marguerite Tanguay et ses enfants: Philippe, Jean-Baptiste, Marguerite, Emérentia et Louise.

Thomas est marié à Gabrielle Tissot d'Ottawa, une enseignante. Il est le père de François, un officier de la Gendarmerie royale du Canada, et de Christine Blais Sander, ingénieure chimiste chez Dupont Canada. Il est grand-père de quatre petits-enfants: Thomas et David Blais; Annalise et Jenna Gabrielle Sander.

Diplômé de l'Université d'Ottawa, Thomas a servi 16 ans comme enseignant dans les écoles d'Ottawa et 22 ans au ministère fédéral du Revenu, à Ottawa.

À sa retraite depuis 1995, il est élu président de la Fédération des caisses populaires de l'Ontario en 1998 ayant à son acquis 35 ans de bénévolat dans ce domaine. C'est par l'entremise de son beau-père, Edgar Tissot, que Thomas a su puiser le goût de se perfectionner davantage auprès de la collectivité administrative des caisses populaires.

Homme d'une envergure dynamique, tant culturelle que sociale, Thomas est doué, en plus, d'un savoir du bon et du grand. À cet effet, son attitude positive et philosophique de la vie l'a toujours favorisé.

Angéline Blais Marentette

Marie-Thérèse Caron   1930 - 1988

Marie-Thérèse Caron, fille aînée d'Alcide et Alexina Caron, a poursuivi son éducation à Pain Court, a complété sa treiz ième année à l'Académie Sainte Marie à Windsor, puis s'est dirigée vers   l'École Normale de l'université d'Ottawa pour obtenir son diplôme d'enseignement. Elle s'est dévouée pendant deux années dans les classes élémentaires à Grande Pointe sous la direction de George Gagnon. Puis sans doute, sous l'influence de trois tantes religieuses Soeurs Jésus-Marie, elle est entrée dans cette commu- nauté, cherchant à réaliser son idéalisme religieux.

Tout en continuant sa carrière d'enseignante dans les écoles secondaires séparées de Windsor, elle a suivi des cours d'été, des cours du soir, et a réussi à obtenir son baccalauréat de l'université d'Ottawa, et sa maîtrise de l'université Laval. Éventuelle- ment, elle a obtenu son doctorat de l'université du Wisconsin. De 1963 jusqu'à son décès, elle était professeure respectée dans le département de français de l'université de Windsor. Le souci du per- fectionnement de la langue et des méthodes d'apprentissage la poussaient à continuer à suivre ses cours à la Sorbonne en France et de participer dans de nombreux colloques.

Un accident vasculaire en 1983 a laissé ses marques sur Marie-Thérèse. En juin 1988, une hémorragie cérébrale massive l'a emportée à l'âge de cinquante-huit ans.

Une collègue de l'université, la docteure Fournier, a bien résumé la pensée de nombreuses personnes en faisant l'éloge de Marie-Thérèse à ses funérailles. "La fidélité pour sa tâche, son sérieux, ses vertus de chrétienne, qui garde sans bruit, sa foi, son espérance et sa charité, faisait d'elle une collègue modèle dont la modestie voulait faire oublier l'action qu'elle remplissait avec compétence et efficacité."

La famille Caron a établi une bourse à la mémoire de la professeure Marie-Thérèse Caron. Cette bourse est décernée annuellement à un (e) étudiant (e) de la deuxième année d'université qui poursuit ses études de français. Ceux et celles qui veulent faire un don sont invités à contribuer au Dr. Marie Memorial Scholarship (compte #77054.04) et le faire parvenir à l'adresse suivante:
Le Président de Assumption University
400 chemin Huron Church
Windsor, Ontario
N9C 2J9

On vous remet un reçu pour fin d'impôt.

TEEN-AGE PAINTER AT CO-SPONSORED CLASS - 1968

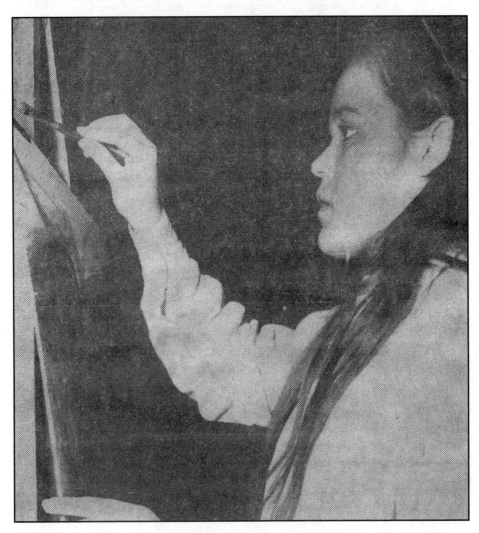

Colette Laprise, Pain Court, one of the students in the teen-age oil painting class sponsored by St. Clair College in conjunction with the Thames Theatre Artists Work Shop, gives full attention to her artistic endeavour. Registration for the next class, held in the Thames Theatre art room, will take place early in January 1969.

Colette est originaire de Pain Court. Elle a fréquentée l'école primaire et secondaire de Pain Court. Elle est diplomée du Collège d'Agriculture de Ridgetown avec specialité en "Laboratoire Agricole" en 1975. Elle a maîtrisé trois langues: le français, l'anglais et l'espagnol. En juin 1975, Colette a obtenu une position au ministère de l'Agriculture à Ottawa. Depuis 20 ans environ, elle occupe le même poste au ministère de l'Agriculture de la Nouvelle-Écosse.

La Vieille Maison

La vieille maison de campagne était presque vivante,
Comblée de respires et de petits sourires.
Sous une couverture maternelle toujours accueillante,
C'était le temps de grandir, de découvrir.

Elle nous offrait un abri des mauvaises tempêtes;
Un endroit à partager nos idées et nos rêves...
Toujours imprimés dans la clarté de ses fenêtres,
Où les visions commencent et s'achèvent.

Quelles joies, quelles peines, quelles émotions se sont
Exprimées, parce qu'ici, une famille a vécu et une
Entreprise a prospéré.

Pendant des années d'aventures, une histoire se déroulait
Et dans ces briques, un ensemble d'événements s'est inscrit.
Enfin une grand-mère complète un autre chapitre du trajet,
Enfin une mère mérite d'acquérir une tranquillité d'esprit...

Maintenant, c'est l'heure de passer les cannettes remplies
De bonbons, parler un peu, et se souvenir de l'énergie qui
Nous entoure; car enfin, une jeune femme d'autrefois
Retourne parmi les doux soupirs de sa vieille maison

Noël 1997   Colette N. Laprise

Tomato Industry

Harvesting of the 1983 processing tomato crop is in full swing in Kent County this week and quality of the fruit is reported to be excellent. Showing off a freshly-picked basket of the red, ripe fruit is Mariette Faubert of RR 1 Pain Court. Hundreds of acres of land in Kent County are devoted to tomato production. Chatham News

Since 1983 processing plants for tomatoes have closed across the country. Farmers have sustained losses over the years as contracts were lost. Interest in the tomato production was dealt a severe blow with the closing of operations at Campbell Soup of Chatham as tomatoes was a successful operation in our area.

Owner of King Canning in Pain Court followed suit and closed its door in 1997, to the great disappointment of many hard working, conscientious farmers of this community.

A ray of hope was shed when the sugar beet industry was revived in this area in 1997. Farmers sustained a lapse of 30 years, since the last operation of the sugar beet industry in Chatham. Canada and Dominion sugar Company closed its operation forever in 1967.

Joseph Caron

Joseph Caron, devant l'Ambassade du Canada au Japon où il a servi.

Joseph Caron est originaire de Pain Court et fils adoptif de Régis Caron et Marie-Anne Roy. Il a fréquenté les écoles primaire et secondaire de Pain Court et par la suite, Joseph s'est dirigé vers la Capitale afin de poursuivre ses études supérieures.

Joseph est fonctionnaire au Ministère des Affaires étrangères et du Commerce international où il sert comme sous-ministre adjoint Asie - Pacifique et Afrique.

Nous te saluons avec fierté Joseph, ton épouse Kumra et tes trois enfants Jules, André et Jasemin.

PEOPLE IN THE NEWS

Sim Caron age 35, sign-writer, the son of Ernest Caron and Phyllis Martin of Grande Pointe, has left his creative mark in the community. This creative work makes him happy. As merchants continue to improve the downtown core, some have chosen to hang Caron's unique signs. In today's age of computer, lettering is in vogue but he prefers to make signs the old-fashioned way – by hand. His signs are hard to miss as they are made of Cedar and their painted finishes conjure up images of a time long ago when craftsmanship was sought and appreciated.   He took sign-writing courses at George Brown College in 1981. Lately he has discovered tombstone etching. Caron has found an outlet for his creativity that he thoroughly enjoys. He's also interested in stained glass designing. He has also done pin-striping on cars and a variety of other works. He works in an old barn on the family farm. He admires the work of others and considers himself more of a craftsman than a sign-painter.

A SURPRISE

In November1996, while visiting with two close friends, Séville Béchard and his wife Joanne prior to their departure for Florida, a fine gentleman which I did not recognize came up to me and introduced himself. It was so heartwarming when he brought to my attention the good deeds he had experienced through my generosity some 50 years ago. Good deeds are never forgotten and a thank you is so nice to receive. He was Roger Marchand son of Joseph and Aurore Authier Marchand, our close neighbour then, Roger was only seven years old. He came to the house regularly to play with the boys. He humbly pointed out "how happy he was to visit my home as he was very well greeted with cheese and crackers, which they seldom had." There were unlimited apples and popcorn treats whenever the boys had friends over. He quoted: "Mrs. Laprise, I will never forget you."

What a wonderful feeling to hear and feel so much gratitude from a man now 58 years old. Unfortunately, his father-in-law died two weeks later of a heart attack. "Do good deeds while you still can!" A tip for all generations.

Chatham-Kent
Farm Fest Days

Chatham Daily News Sept 23,1998

FREE NET: École Secondaire de Pain Court, Vice-Principal Guy Mayer hopes the community will take advantage of the free access to the Internet. Regular free Internet access is available most days and two evenings a week in the school library as part of a new community program. Trained students will be on hand to help instruct those just starting out. An open house is scheduled for Thursday night, starting at 7 p.m. Plans are also in works to develop training partnerships with community groups and businesses to help fund the program.

On August 15-16-17, 1997 we celebrated Farm Fest Days at Centennial Park in Pain Court with Larry Cadotte in charge of arrangements. There were multiple exhibits of farm machinery - new inventions, and new technological displays for harvesting hemp as well as brussel sprouts. Car and truck dealerships - farm machinery dealerships, seed companies - test plots - food booth vendors - carnival and midway, indoor exhibits at the school gym, crafts, archery demos, refreshment tents, no till crops, electronics, fertilizer companies, a draw for a children's playhouse plus live entertainment. Something for the whole family. We trust people will have the opportunity to enjoy more of these displays in coming years

PAIN COURT STUDENTS
CONSTRUCTING MINI-HOUSE

By BOB COATSWORTH
For the Chatham Daily News

PAIN COURT — Technology students from École Secondaire in Pain Court are working together on the design and construction of a mini-house.

Students from several classes are working together on the project. Students from the construction class have been doing the work on the exterior of the 8'x12' house, and have been following standard building codes.

After three weeks of work the exterior is nearing completion. Manufacturing teacher, Guy Mayer said that a porch will still be added and the trim still needs to be put on along the roof lines.

The design class is working on the interior design, and it will appear exactly like a real house when it's finished. There is some insulating and dry walling to do yet. Even curtains will be hung and cabinets installed inside.

The house is not just a school project, but a community effort as well. A number of residents, local companies, and builders have donated materials for the house. A few people from the community are making crafts to decorate the interior.

"Building the house gives the kids a sense of pride, Mayer said. "We wanted to do something that was real. The school janitor Ludger Michaud came up with the idea, along with help from the community. It helps the students learn about building something practical, a real structure, not just from textbooks."

The house will be raffled off in August as a part of Pain Court's Farm Festival. A few of the computer programming students are designing and printing 5,000 tickets for the raffle. Tickets will be sold for $2 to help raise money for new equipment. The school will also be donating a $500 cash prize. Two small picnic tables made by students and bicycles will be given away as well at the August festival.

Armand King shows picture of his old school and his fellow students in 1938.

**I dedicate this article to Armand King and his sister
Magdelena, my playmates of the 1920s on the Baldoon Road.**

Teacher Never Forgets His Kids

If there was a prize for a teacher's dedication, Myles Leckie would receive it without a question.

Leckie was the teacher at the one room schoolhouse S.S.#12 Dover, Bearline from 1934 to 1938. To celebrate the 60th anniversary of his last year teaching in 1938, he has given his former students one last assignment. Leckie who is 83 in 1998 assigned his former students from grade 1 to grade 8 the task of preparing a story on their lives, what they have achieved since those days.

There were 40 students in the school and 22 of the remaining 28 living sent their biographies. Armand King was a student in Leckie's class, and remembers his teacher like it was yesterday. King said the school students have kept in touch over the years. They had a 35th anniversary get together and a 50th and now a 60th in a different way.

Leckie took the information and made a booklet which he mailed to all his former students. The students' school picture and a current one was included in the book.

King said Leckie has kept in contact with his former pupils all these years. Doing this has kept us all in contact with each other as well. I fondly remember the baseball games Leckie took his students too . . . He had a Model T, but he'd pull a wagon to carry more kids along.

Leckie decided to do the booklet for this 60th anniversary as an alternative to having a get together. Armand said he's never heard of a teacher who has been so interested in former students for so long.

He left teaching in 1938 to begin a career in Market research in Toronto with Canadian Facts Ltd. He then joined Elliot Hayes Ltd. and retired as the president in 1974 and started building and managing golf courses.

He learned to fly over the years and even come down to meet his students and take them for plane rides.

Leckie said it was the Depression, when he graduated at 1934. The only teaching job was in Dover. He spent four years and got to know the kids and their families. In the days he taught we could pat a student on the shoulder. You're not allowed to do things like that these days. "I'd also give the strap like a parent. They respected me like a parent. That was a great feeling."

Armand, his wife and family lived and operated a successful farming operation in Pain Court. Furthermore, he owned a thriving plumbing operation in Wallaceburg in the early 50s - 60s.

1. Ref- Chatham Kent Citizen by Randy Coate.

Bio Career Summary of Jacques T. Bélanger

Jacques (Jake) was born and raised in Dover Township, a farming community on the outskirts of Pain Court, near Chatham, Ontario. After completing High School, he began his working career with the Royal Bank where he attained the position of accountant.

After two years, he left the bank and went to work at Rockwell International, an auto parts manufacturing company in Chatham. He subsequently worked at Rockwell for twenty-five years, first as a labourer and then in various Supervisory and Management functions.

During this time he completed various engineering courses and received certification by the Society of Manufacturing Engineers. Prior to leaving Rockwell he held the position of Plant Engineer.

He accepted the position of Manager of Engineering and Operations at Chatham Hydro in 1989. He was appointed General Manager in 1991 and served in that capacity until 1998 when the Public Utilities were amalgamated in the corporation of Chatham Kent. He also was President of Municipal Electric Association District Eight and Chairman of the Lambton Kent Utilities Cooperative.

In addition to Mr. Jacques (Jake) Bélanger bio career summary presented to me in 1997, I'm privileged to acknowledge his appointment to the Board of Governors for St. Clair College in Chatham. The college is extremely fortunate to have such qualified individuals toiling to serve on its board: Jacques Bélanger of Pain Court, manager of manufacturing engineering of Meritor Automotive Suspensions Systems Company of Chatham; Lynn Mc Geachy Schultz of Chatham, senior Kinesiologist Robert Feldmann of LaSalle, general manager of western region for Union Gas Ltd.

Bélanger will provide representation on the board for the region's important manufacturing sector. From 1991 to 1998 he was general manager of Chatham Hydro. Prior to that he worked for Rockwell International in Chatham for 25 years. Fluent in French and English and a certified manufacturing engineer he has completed numerous management developments and industry related programs.

Ref. Chatham Daily News

M. Jacques Bélanger, né le 29 octobre 1944, fils de M. Norman Bélanger et de Glorianna Gagner, a épousé Mlle Patricia Martin, fille de Ulysse Martin et Kathleen Béchard le 12 septembre 1964. Ils ont trois filles, Nicole, Mary Lou et Monique. M. Bélanger, son épouse Patricia sont diplômés de l'École secondaire de Pain Court ainsi que leurs trois filles.

Harold Smith   1989

Harold who has lived all his life, within a mile of our farm in Dover, became a well-known farm news commentator to the agricultural community.

Dennis Guy, a fifth generation hobby farmer, took over as farm director of CFCO in 1989 from long time host Harold Smith, a farmer in Dover. Smith had done farm news at CFCO since 1962, twenty seven years of well-received farm news for a prosperous farming community. In the nineties, the amount of agricultural news was somewhat cut back at the radio station. The new owners of CFCO made it clear they wanted control. Eventually, we experienced shorter versions of Woodland Forum that we were accustomed to receiving during the Harold Smith period. It was a job well-done Mr. Smith.

The Dover man received his first exposure to radio 20 years before his well-known program started in 1962, Smith announced. He did Sunday Church programs live from CFCO's studio at the former William Pitt Hotel in Chatham - But that came to an end when CFCO founder and owner Jack Beardall came in and told Smith: "You're on the farm and it is war time and I can't pay you anything." The door opened again for Smith when Beardall was selling the Station. Beardall said he had believed for 25 years the CFCO was short on agriculture broadcasts, so Smith approached the new management with a proposal. "It was exactly what they wanted done and should be done," he says. Harold was told he would get $40.00 a week to start and if he was good he'd get a raise later. "I thought $40.00 was better than nothing so that it was." [1].

By 1997 in July, CFCO 6.30 AM Agri-news, programming with Andy Watson as Farm Director, became No. 1 in Kent, Essex and Lambton counties especially the farming Community.

We are pleased with the research, the information and the progress that Andy Watson and staff have brought about. He relates very well to his agricultural audience. I'm positive that the popularity of his program has increased considerably in the last year.

CFCO Radio Station was sold March 6, 1997. It will join with CKSY FM. .95 and bring a coordination of programs to the area. CKSY FM .95 opened in 1986 and brought informative programs during the last decade.

1. Ref. Ellwood Shreve, Farm Market

Andy Watson

Nestled on the bank of the river Thames very close to Pain Court stands a quaint picturesque home surrounded by acres of beautiful pines designed for the Christmas Market. Andy served as Kent's agricultural representative from 1968 to 1978. Interesting to note that his interests in "Hobby Farming" encouraged him, as well as his children, in providing and experimenting in varieties of grapes and raspberries for the purpose of marketing as a hobby. People of the surrounding district enjoyed taking this opportunity to pick these crops so close to home.

Andy Watson was born April 1, 1937. He completed his studies at Ontario's Agricultural College and served as agricultural representative in the counties of Waterloo 1959 - 1962, Northumberland 1962 - 1968, Kent 1968 - 1978.

In 1978 D'Arcy McKeough decided to resign from the Ontario Cabinet and from politics, so two months later Mr. Watson won McKeough's seat in the Ontario Legislature in a by-election.

In October 1978 he left his ministry as Kent agricultural representative to become an Ontario Member of Parliament. Mr. Watson succeeded Mr. Don Rutheford as agricultural representative in 1968 and remained our representative until 1978 when he left and became our member of parliament until 1985.

His successor as agricultural representative was Barry Fraser in 1978. Many years have elapsed but it is interesting to note that on the banks of this historic Thames River, within a mile stretch of each other, lie the roots and mansions of three famous and recognized Members of Parliament: Mr. Eugene Roy (King), Mr. George Parry and Mr. Andy Watson. Furthermore, within this same mile, lies a prestigious subdivision of beautiful homes, housing many more famous people, as well as the centennial St. Andrews Anglican Church. For decades the western end of Mr. Watson's small farm was used by barges carrying sand and gravel while the eastern tip at the end of the Winter Line was where barges were loading sugar beets to be taken to Canada and Dominion Sugar factory in Chatham.

Our Loonie   1998

The world currency markets kicked sand in the Canadian Dollar's face for the third straight day closing January 28, 1998 at 68.25 as the weakling dollar stumbled to its latest all time low. The languishing loonie skidded to an historic close, as analysts watched their dollar disintegrate in recent days.

No one can say for sure where and when the loonie's crash landing is finally going to end. A technical analyst Katherine Beattie at Standard and Poor's MMS international, said "It is interesting trying to pick resistance levels.

A closer look at the Dow Jones industrial quotations Jan 30, 1998 indicates it is at 7973.02. It posted gains in February up to 8457.70 by February 26 and continued upwards to 8904.40 by March 24, 1998. The Dow now on a roll posted gains April 3 - 14 - 16 to finish at 9162.27. By May 1st it closed at 9192.66 posting further gains.

On June 16, however it was a grim scene at the stock market as investors eagerly took profits, driving the Dow down 207.01 to 8627.93, and the dollar down to 67.63. On September 25 the loonie closed at 66.13 US as currency traders placed their bets on speculation about a possible decline in US interest rates. After months of being battered back and forth it posted its biggest one day gain more than a cent on October 7, 1998.

The Canadian dollar rallied December 24, 1998 and posted its biggest daily gain since early October propelled by traders' belief that a weaker American dollar on the world markets could help the loonie.

The Canadian currency ended the year 1998 at 65.22 cents US up 0.66 of a cent on that day December 24, but still below the 69.91 cents US level it started the year at.

This same day, traders had become optimistic about the prospects of the Canadian economy. The market was also influenced by currency developments in Europe.

December 24, 1998 eleven European countries stretched from the Arctic Circle to the shores of the Mediterranean adopted the same currency. Stocks and bonds will be quoted in "Euros." The Euro will increasingly be used for bank transactions business deals and public finances in years to come.

Personal references

`97 Market events

Chronology of the major events that moved the stock market in 1997:

Jan. 13:   Spectacular drill results in Indonesia push Bre-X stock higher.

Feb. 6:   Dean Witter and Morgan Stanley merge, forming world's largest securities firm.

Feb 26:   US Federal Reserve Board chairman Alan Greenspan warns of excessive optimism and inflationary pressures in the US market.

Feb 27:   Eaton's seeks bankruptcy protection.

March 21:   Rumours surface about exaggerated Bre-X claims.

May 5:   Independent audit confirms Bre-X's Busang discovery is a hoax.

June 24:   Scotiabank bids $1.25 billion for National Trustco.

June 27:   Royal Bank bids $2.4 billion for London Insurance Group.

July 1:   Britain hands over control of Hong Kong to China.

Aug. 19:   Great West Life bids $2.9 billion for London Insurance Group, topping Royal's bid.

Sept. 8:   Eaton's gets last-minute restructuring deal to avoid bankruptcy.

Sept. 18:   Accounting firms Price Waterhouse and Coopers and Lybrand merge. Rivals KPMG and Ernst and Young soon follow suit.

Oct 27:   Markets panic as stock losses mount in Asia. Dow closes down 7.2 percent while TSE 300 loses 6.2 per cent.

Nov. 14:   Price of gold drops below $300 US an ounce for the first time since 1988.

Dec. 12:   Bank of Canada raises interest rates half a point to bolster the falling dollar, the biggest bank rate increase in more than two years.

Dec. 19:   Canadian dollar trades below 70 cents US for the first time in almost 12 years.

Shae-Lynn Bourne

GOLDEN BLADES – Chatham's Shae-Lynn Bourne and partner Victor Kraatz of Vancouver, display their gold medals from last November's shooting for their sixth consecutive Canadian Senior ice dance championship this weekend at the site of their very first title in 1993, Hamilton's Copps Coliseum.

Once, twice, three times Bronze – for the third year in a row Chatham native Shae-Lynn Bourne, and her partner Victor Kraatz have finished third in ice dancing at the World Figure Skating Championships in Japan 1997.

Chatham Daily News

COUNTRY MUSIC STAR

"Bob Lucier" of Toronto, son of Mr. and Mrs. Félix Lucier of Grande Pointe, has released a record in 1997 at the "Caribou Club." Bob features country music and plays with his band at the Club in Toronto. The French Canadian artist appears in several scenes in the movie "Road to Nashville." He is shown as a member of "Bill Anderson's" Po. Boys.

The 26 year-old artist actually attended the 1966 and 1968 National Country Music Convention in Nashville.

Before the "Caribou Club" engagement, Robert Lucier did personal appearances with Tommy Hunter. He went on tour across Canada with him and recorded with Sound Canada. He toured the United States as a member of the Bill Anderson Show. He is well-known in Country Western Circles in Toronto, Newfoundland, Nashville and Western Ontario.

When in Toronto, interesting to note that for many years he taught lessons on Hawaiian Steel Guitar and regular guitars to students in his area. At this time he opened a Music Store "Southdown Music Enterprise" at Southdown Shopping Centre along with Music lover's Cliff Short and Mel au Coin.

Bob Lucier has appeared regularly on the Tommy Hunter, CBC television Show at 10:00 p.m. Fridays, as an outstanding steel guitarist until Tommy Hunter retired from the TV show in 1993 after 25 years of performance. The guitarist appeared at many night clubs including "Edison Drake," "Silver Dollar," "The Cloverleaf" and the "Horseshoe." Mr. Lucier regularly performed on Hamilton television with the "Caribou Show Band."

He received his bilingual education at Grande Pointe and at Pain Court Secondary High School, where he graduated in 1960.

Two of his 1997 releases are "Sail Along" with Shot Jackson and Bob Lucier, 20 old time songs of the 50s, available from Heritage Music, 41 Antrim Crescent, #311 Scarborough, Ontario MIP 4TI and a second release in 1997, with Todd Nolan, Bob Lucier, Mel au Coin and Doug Deveaux.

Sideman Studio, Raglow, Ontario.

Lionel Ouellette (right), owner and president of Can-Tech Quality Ltd., shows off the company's new CNC machine. With him is CNC operator Steve Ouellette.   Photo by Peter Epp April 1, 1998

CAN-TECH QUALITY HONOURED
BY CHAMBER OF COMMERCE

The Chatham and District Chamber of Commerce honoured their industry of the month of March 24, 1998.

Can-Tech Quality Limited is a tool and die operation that provides sheet metal tooling for the automotive industry, manufacturing products for Tier 2 customers in Southwestern Ontario as well in the American Midwest. Owner and president Lionel Ouellette started the company in 1984 on Leeson drive in Chatham, and has experienced continued growth in both customers and products.

A 15,000 square foot expansion was built about two years ago, and plans are in place right now to install an engineering room. Can-tech Quality has 20 employees.

Ouellette explains that the company has a variety of machinery in place, including CNC machining for both cutter paths and production machining and prototyping, as well as tryout presses and production presses. The new CNC (computer numerical controlled) machine was installed about three months ago.

Peter Epp
Chatham This Week

Mr. & Mrs. Hector Ouellette née Florence Couture are the proud parents of Lionel Ouellette and the grandparents of Steve Ouellette, the son of Lionel Ouellette owner and manger of Can-Tech Quality Limited. People in the vicinity of Grande Pointe and Pain Court are honoured and wish you the best in all your endeavours. As we enter the millennium, I trust you will be a guiding light for others with your knowledge and expertise.

Montfort et Lucille Emery

Nous sommes heureux de saluer spécialement Montfort et Lucille Emery pour leur dévouement sincère envers la caisse populaire de Tecumseh. Montfort Emery est originaire de Grande Pointe, fils de François Xavier Emery et Almina Lécuyer. Il fit ses études primaires à Grande Pointe et le secondaire à l'école de Continuation de Pain Court. Sous l'égide de ses frères Léonard et Adrian, il réussit le début de ses études en électricité en 1940. Il exerce avec son frère Léonard le "brochage" de ma propre maison et bien d'autres.

Les frères Emery sont devenus des experts de renommée dans le domaine du filage industriel et j'entends que leurs descendants s'engagent dans ce métier aussi. Montfort est décédé en 1990. Il laisse dans le deuil sa femme Lucille Poulin et six enfants; Julien, Louis, Françine, Thérèse, Pauline et Marie.

Lorsque la caisse populaire de Tecumseh ouvre ses portes en 1958 ce fut sous les soins de Montfort et Lucille Emery. Ils l'ont nourrie, soignée avec dévotion pendant plus d'une quinzaine d'années. C'est d'ailleurs dans leur salon, que les sociétaires venaient faire affaires souvent en dehors des heures d'ouverture.

Pour cela, ce couple recevait le salaire d'un dollar par année mais ce sont justement ces soins, pour lesquels la communauté francophone de Tecumseh et les membres actuels de l'institution seront toujours redevables car la caisse a grandi en une institution vigoureuse.

Au milieu des années '60 on construit un bureau soit une pièce adjointe à la maison des Emery qui eux continuaient à se dévouer pour l'organisme. L'actif de la caisse a atteint en 1988, 13 millions de dollars.

Grâce aux initiatives des administrateurs qui ont axé leurs efforts d'une part vers la formation du personnel et d'autre part vers l'augmentation des services auprès de ses membres, ils ont réussi un actif de plus de 19.5 million lors de leur célébration du '40 anniversaire de service en 1998.

La caisse a été et est encore une institution financière importante dans cette communauté où les francophones de la région peuvent faire affaires en français.

En 1997, M. Jean-Paul Fortier est nommé nouveau directeur général. Il oeuvre à la caisse depuis 1994 ayant plus de 25 ans d'expérience auprès des caisses Desjardins.

Quarante ans de services à la communauté, ça se fête!

(PR)C'est devant plusieurs sociétaires et leurs invités, sans oublier les membres du conseil d'administration, présents et passés, en plus des employés, que la caisse populaire de Técumseh célébrait ses quarante ans d'existence le 18 octobre 1998

Parmi les nombreuses présentations, le président de la Fédération des caisses de l'Ontario, Thomas Blais, un tableau d'un artiste natif de Windsor, Bernard Poulin, au président du Conseil d'administration de la caisse populaire de Técumseh, Paul Lachance.

M. Blais a tenu à souligner que la soirée était «une célébration par excellence du passé et de l'avenir» d'une caisse qui fait partie de «la principale institution financière en Ontario français, regroupant plus de 200,000 sociétaires avec un actif de 1,8 milliards de dollars». La caisse, à travers les années, a attiré plus de onze mille sociétaires et les six personnes qui étaient membres au tout début le sont encore, dont le Dr. Paul Quenneville.

On parle d'eux et d'elles

M. Maurice Lacasse, natif de Tecumseh Ontario et vivant à Hull depuis plusieurs années avec son épouse Angéla Dionne et leurs deux enfants, nous laisse pour une destinée meilleure en avril 1996. Maurice laisse dans le deuil son épouse Angela, Martha et son époux Michel Séguin et Gaston, son fils. Il est le frère de Hélène, Georgette, Annette, Jean-Louis, aussi que de feu Fernand, Hector, Hubert, Aline, Yvon et Lucien.

Nous gardons des souvenirs tangibles de son dévouement inlassables lorsqu'il était professeur à l'école secondaire de Pain Court. Les parents et les élèves ont été témoins de son enthousiasme, son patriotisme, et de sa clairvoyance au niveau éducatif et social.

Il quitte l'enseignement et se lance dans les cadres de la Radio comme annonceur au poste d'Edmunston, Nouveau-Brunswick. Par la suite, Maurice travaille comme fonctionnaire au gouvernement fédéral.

"Mistenflûte" le 2e ouvrage d'histoire de M. Lacasse fut officiellement lancé sur le marché le 23 mars 1980 dans les salons de l'institut Canadien-Français à Ottawa.

"Mistenflûte" souvenirs de l'auteur, couvre une période de près d'un demi siècle de vie de la famille Gustave Lacasse de Tecumseh.

*   *   *

C'est avec regret que nous apprenons la mort de Jérôme Faubert, le 5 avril 1997 à l'âge de 71 ans. Pendant sa jeunesse Jérôme et ses frères Bernard, Patrick et Oliver étaient nos premiers voisins et chaque jour ils nous rendaient visite. Ils ont su rendre la vie un peu misérable pour leur petite soeur unique Marie-Louise Faubert-Martin. Il laisse dans le deuil sa femme Vivienne Roy et cinq enfants. Jérôme et Vivienne, natif de Pain Court, ont élu domicile en Californie. À la famille j'offre mes sympathies et un merci spécial pour la belle réception recue lors de mon passage en 1963.

*   *   *

Robert Chauvin de Pointe-aux-Roches vient d'être élu administrateur auprès de l'union des Cultivateurs Franco-Ontariens (U F C O) lors de l'assemblée annuelle qui a eu lieu à Caledonia dans l'est de l'Ontario. L'UCFO est un organisme, comme le nom l'indique, qui représente les intérêts de la communauté agricole de l'Ontario Français. M. Chauvin est diplômé de l'école d'Agriculture de Ste Martine, Québec. Il est également impliqué dans le conseil communautaire du Collège d'Alfred (CCCA) Robert Chauvin est membre du comité fondateur provisoire qui s'est penché sur la planification à long terme du Collège. Son épouse, Hélène Caron, est originaire de Pain Court.

*   *   *

C'est avec grand plaisir que nous constatons la mission que Claude Roy accomplit au Mexique, depuis quelques années comme "Director of Financial Planning for Moore Latin America" ainsi que son frère André Roy rempli une tâche pour Volvo à Singapore pour une période de 3 ans. Danielle travaille comme physiothérapeute à Ottawa. Claude, André et Danielle sont les enfants de Paul Roy et Rose-Marie Caron Roy de Pain Court.

Did you know . . .

Farming in Kent – 180 years ago a statistical survey in 1817 revealed the state of the agricultural economy in Kent County. Cheese and butter could be had for 18¢ a pound - wool between 30 and 45¢ a pound. A four-year-old work horse could be purchased for between $33 and $38.00. A cow from anywhere from $12 to $15.00 and a good ox for $25.00, a sheep was bought for $2.50 or less.
Ref. Farm Business Guide 1998

Soybeans Galore –
The first year that Ontario's soybeans were recorded in 1942 – only 41,000 acres were harvested. Average yields were 21 bushels to the acre. But in 1996 – 269,000 acres of soybeans were harvested in Lambton alone, while in Kent a total of 239,000 acres were harvested. Average yields were 39 bushels an acre, in Kent. Average price was $10.02 a bushel.

Did you know . . .

The first European to gaze upon the waters of Lake Erie was French explorer Étienne Brulé in the mid-1600s and Brulé saw Lake Erie for the first time from the shores of what would later become Chatham-Kent at present day Rondeau Park.
By the way, Rondeau Provincial Park is Ontario's second oldest provincial park having just recently celebrated its 100th birthday in 1996. Algonquin Provincial Park was established a few years earlier.
Chatham This Week '98

644

Did you know . . .

Ontario's Oldest Century Farm - The Pajot farm at La Salle is the oldest century farm in Ontario. The farm has been worked by members of the Pajot Family since 1749 after Thomas Pajot crossed the river from Detroit and settled in Sandwich East Township in the tiny community of Petite Côte.   Oswald Pajot is the seventh generation descendant to work the original 34-acre Pajot Farm, located at 671 Martin Lane, La Salle.

Ref. Livre paroissiale de la paroisse St-Joseph de Rivière-aux-Canards, 125e anniversaire 1864 - 1989

Did you know . . .

In 1991, Louis-Joseph Richer was recently inducted into the Kent County Agricultural Hall of Fame by being the recipient of the Chatham and District Chamber of Commerce, Agriculturalist of the year award. He was born in Plantagenet, near Ottawa and received his early education there. He had his first exposure to Kent County farms when he came as a student to detassel corn on the King and Edgar Martin farms. Joe Richer has used his natural aptitudes and education in finance and farming to help promote the sale of Kent County and Ontario products around the world. As grain trader and accountant and later vice-president of King Grain Ltd. he worked to develop markets for special quality soy beans in the Pacific Rim Countries.

POPE   JOHN PAUL II

Cubans' flock ready to greet the Pope today, January 21, 1998. Motorists drive past a billboard welcoming Pope John Paul II in Havana Cuba. Cubans are prepared for the arrival of the Pope today for a Historic five-day visit.

Mexicans are preparing to greet Pope John Paul II, January 22, 1999. It will probably be his last visit to Mexico as he is weak and his health has been failing.

New resident in Grande Pointe

In January 1998 Lucien Laprise his wife April Boivin and baby Madison, took up residency in a remodelled home built a century ago, in 1903, by François Labadie.

Originally it was built to accommodate a religious teaching order in the parish. Its proximity to the church and rectory was ideal but it was unfortunate that at the time the project fell through. Mr. François Labadie did take residency there for a few years.   Later it was transferred to Alphy Ouellette and his wife Louise Béchard.

You probably know the rest of the story!

Walter Percy Chrysler

Did you know, that W. Percy Chrysler's roots were here, in Kent?

Walter Percy Chrysler whose company still carries his name was born in Kansas, but his grandparents lived many years ago in the Chatham area. Their log cabin is said to have been built on the south bank of the Thames river near modern day St. Clair Street.

William Chrysler in 1820 harvested about 2000 pounds of tobacco, making him among the biggest tobacco farmers in this part of Ontario.

Ref - Farmers Business Guide 1998

Once in a Blue Moon

Two blue moons in the same year only happens about every 34 years. The first blue moon occurred on January 2, 1999 and the second blue moon will occur on March 31, 1999.

He grew hemp and flax

Hemp will be making a comeback to Kent, Lambton and Essex Counties but among the largest hemp and flax producers in Ontario during the 1930's was a Forest area farmer, Howard Farleigh who was a conservative M.P.

Ref. Farmer's Business

ECHINACEA

Did you know that millions of "Echinacea" seedlings are grown in Greenhouses in Pain Court and shipped across the country to be grown especially for medicinal purposes?

ASK THE PHARMACIST: TAMMY MAURE

Question: Tammy, I have heard a lot of talk about using "Echinacea" to cure colds. Is this true?

Answer: The use of Echinacea dates back to the early 1700's when it was used to treat saddle sores on horses. The portions of the plant used then and still used today for medicinal purposes include the aerial portion, the whole plant including the root and the root itself. Echinacea appears to work by stimulating the immune system. To fully appreciate Echinacea's effect, it is important to understand some aspects of the immune system.

Lisa Martin

Douze nouvelles enseignantes reçoivent leur brevet

(PR) Lors d'une cérémonie à la Place Concorde le 19 juin et devant le directeur de la formation à l'enseignement de l'Université d'Ottawa, le docteur Raynald Lacasse, douze finissantes recevaient leur baccalauréat en Éducation. L'une d'entre elles s'est particulièrement distinguée, soit Lisa Martin de Pain Court, co-récipiendaire de la médaille d'argent (2e plus haute moyenne) des trois campus de l'Université d'Ottawa. Les autres diplômées sont: Annie Bordeleau, Danielle Demers, Christine Drouillard, Rochelle Drouillard, Jill Lauzon, Jacqueline Leardi, Yvette Lepage, Monica Martin, Jennifer McKinnon, Kelly-Anne Triolet et Christina Truant. Dans la photo, il y a, de gauche à droite, le Dr. Lacasse, Lisa Martin et Jacqueline Lalonde, la coordinatrice et professeure conseillère.

Ref. Le Rempart

"A Life of Dance"

Gloria Bondy – 50 years of teaching dance was celebrated June 13, 1998. Bondy's illustrious career began early at the age of three in Windsor where she was born. As a tiny three year old she was contracted by CKLW Radio in Detroit to perform a song and dance routine on a weekly show, for several years. She established her first dance studio in Chatham in 1948 and in 1975 the Bondy family operated Canada's largest chain of performing arts studios with branches in Chatham, Windsor, London, Sarnia, Leamington and Tilbury.

Chatham Cultural Centre was rocking June 13, 1998 with the dancing feet of more than 200 Chatham Kent residents taking part in the golden gala – a three hour long dance-musical, that will honour Bondy still an active dance teacher in Canada.

She holds the highest degree that can be achieved in dance – "Dame des Danseurs." The achievement consisting of examinations in all form of dance, theory, mime, practical teaching and choreography, was presented to her in 1980.

I personally enjoy the gracious art of dancing and many of her students over this period have been honoured and won dozens of first place trophies throughout Canada.

"TEAM EFFORT" – Ethanol Plant

Area dignitaries gather as the first load of corn is delivered to the Commercial alcohol's brand new plant in Chatham on November 11, 1997. Larry Janssens and Al Kerkhof both of R.R. # 5 Wallaceburg were on hand to watch 40 tons of their corn harvest delivered to the new ethanol plant at Chatham. Brian Crow and Ken Robert employees of Commercial Alcohols Inc. take samples of delivered corn and grade and weigh the product.

A supplier for the ethanol plant W.G. Thompson's, Wes Thompson, tells farm Market that his company has already established a strong working relationship with commercial alcohol, having been a supplier of corn for the Company's Tilverton ethanol facility.

Jim Hazzard, St. Clair Agri Services general manager says commercial alcohols will be a major buyer of corn for the area making the local market far more competitive.

Cargill will be another major supplier of corn for the new Chatham Plant. Brian Crow of Pain Court says samples are taken outside and transported via a vacuum tube to the grading station which is located above the unloading dock. When the plant does reach full capacity it will be processing 1100 tonnes of corn daily or about 15 million bushels of corn annually.

The plant will operate around the clock 365 days a year. This operation will produce 150 million litres of fuel ethanol and industrial alcohol each year.

Re Kent Market News
Peter Epp

Jean Chrétien inaugure l'usine
d'éthanol à Chatham le 23 octobre, 1998

October 23, 1998
CP File Photo

(PR) Plus d'un millier de personnes s'étaient déplacées pour entendre le premier-ministre du Canada, Jean Chrétien, lors des festivités d'inauguration de la nouvelle usine d'éthanol de la compagnie Commercial Alcohols à Chatham. Beaucoup d'enfants étaient de la fête. Mme Denise Benoit de Grande Pointe y était avec deux de ses enfants car « c'est une journée spéciale pour Simon et Sophie. Ce n'est pas à tous les jours qu'ils peuvent voir et entendre le premier-ministre ». M. Chrétien a prédit que plusieurs autres usines de ce genre seraient construites ailleurs au pays et a ajouté qu'il « faudrait en construire une dans ma circonscription ».

L'éthanol est produit à partir du maïs de la région. Malgré que l'usine de Chatham n'est en opération que depuis un an, elle n'opère pas à pleine capacité. Éventuellement l'usine utilisera 385 mille tonnes de maïs, (15 millions de boisseaux) par année. Il faudra 130 mille acres en culture pour suffir à la tâche.

Parmi les nombreux invités de marque présents à l'inauguration, il y avait le ministre fédéral de l'agriculture Lyle Vancleif, et Noble Villeneuve, le ministre provincial.

Ref - Le Rempart

Une compagnie de Pain Court encourage la culture du chanvre

*Jean-Marie Laprise, Noble Villeneuve ministre de l'Agriculture
en Ontario, à Pain Court le 7 août, 1997.*

(PR) Santé Canada rendait publique dernièrement un projet de loi pour réglementer et autoriser la culture du chanvre industriel. La loi doit être approuvée à temps pour les semences du printemps 1998.

Au bureau d'Essex du Ministère de l'agriculture de l'Ontario on prévoit qu'une douzaine d'agriculteurs d'ici seront parmi les premiers à choisir de faire pousser cette plante. C'est la compagnie Kenex Limited, à Pain Court, qui importera les premiers grains de semence, en provenance de l'Europe. Kenex est une compagnie privée qui a déjà investi des millions de dollars afin de connaître les meilleures méthodes de culture et de transformation du chanvre et espère même que son usine sera prête ce printemps. La personne derrière cette opération, Jean-Marie Laprise, participait, le 30 janvier, à un symposium au Palais des Congrès à Montréal. En novembre, à St-Louis au Missouri, Monsieur Laprise s'est rendu à la réunion annuelle de la «North American Industrial Hemp Council». «J'y ai trouvé le talent, l'argent et l'intérêt nécessaire à faire de l'industrie du chanvre une partie importante de l'économie de l'Amérique du Nord dans le prochain millénaire, si on nous donne la chance,» dit-il.

Des réunions pour intéresser les agriculteurs sont prévues, dans la région, en février et en mars.

Le chanvre n'est pas une nouvelle plante mais sa culture a été interdite depuis plusieurs années en raison de sa proximité génétique au cannabis ou marijuana. Depuis quelque temps, tout un mouvement s'est formé au Canada afin de dé-régulariser sa culture, étant donné ses nombreuses utilisations. Cette plante a aussi été suggérée comme culture de remplacement du tabac. Certaines personnes se souviendront que le chanvre a longtemps été utilisé dans la fabrication de la toile, du canevas, de tissus et de cordage. La plante aurait, en plus, des utilisations commerciales dans l'industrie automobile. Monsieur Laprise prévoit participer prochainement à la réunion de la «Society of Automotive Engineers » au Centre Cobo de Détroit.

Les agriculteurs qui voudraient se renseigner sur la culture du chanvre industriel peuvent visiter ces deux sites Internet: www.kenex.org (un site bilingue) ou encore www.hempline.com, le site de la compagnie Hempline Incorparated.

Ref.: Le Rempart le 4 février 1998

P.T.A. Association - Grande Pointe

Left to right: Rosalie Van-Damme (Secretary), Carmelle L'Écuyer (President), Michelle Vanden Enden (Vice-President), Diane Martin (Treasurer).

Société des dames Ste-Anne - Grande Pointe

1ère rangée: Shirley Carroll, Alice Brown,
2e rangée: Marie-Anne Brown, Anna Benoit, Gloria Benoit, Diana Martin et Clara Cartier.

"WOMEN TO REMEMBER"

Mrs. Dora Bourdeau Tuck, a lifelong resident of Grande Pointe married Murray Tuck, August 2, 1958. She is the daughter of Harry Bourdeau and Délia Laprise. Since 1960 she has given close attention to all ladies who passed through the doors of her beauty shop for the last 37 years. Even after retirement she still catered to the special needs of the physically challenged and older ladies in their nineties unable to obtain accessible services provided by the beauty shop.

Dora, you are well remembered for the tender loving care you gave to your aging mother. With your energetic and cheerful disposition you have uplifted the spirits of hundreds of women over the years. I hereby present to you a simple "Thank You," dear Dora.

Mrs. Teresa Rivard, a resident of Pain Court for seventeen years. She married Bernard Rivard and they have four beautiful children, three boys and one girl. Teresa is an extremely devoted and loving wife and mother. She was the director of the french folk music church choir in Pain Court for many years, leading us in song and worship with her guitar and beautiful voice. Teresa is still the leader of the music ministry for the prayer meetings at the "Pines" in Chatham.

"Affordable Elegance" was started in 1983. She is involved in manufacturing and sales of custom draperies and valance designing. Bed coverings as well as many types of blinds is also part of Teresa's business. A love of sewing and ongoing education keeps Teresa updated in her field. She has attained specialist level in home decorating.

Teresa, thank you for sharing your gifts and talents with us, and for making our windows so beautiful.

Mrs. Helen Jack Gagner,

Helen Jack was born and raised in Dover Township - Baldoon Road - close to the new St. Andrew Presbyterian Church. She was the daughter of Gordon Jack and Ella Bacheldor and had twin brothers and one sister. In 1944, she married Armand Gagner of Pain Court at St. Joseph Church, Chatham.

They have lived and farmed most of their lives on the outskirts of Chatham in Harwich Township. They raised a family of four boys and three girls: Dan in real estate, Dave in Pro Hockey, Kathy and Lynn both teachers, Rick in business, Larry a lawyer, Lisa in business.

In 1998, Dave Gagner their son, one of Chatham's most beloved hockey athlete has been recognized and named recipient of the Chatham and Kent Sports Achievement Award. Dave had just completed his 13th season with the National Hockey League.

He declared "he grew up dreaming about a life in the N.H.L," having played for such teams as Minnesota, Dallas Stars, New York Rangers, Toronto Maple Leafs, Calgary Flames, the Florida Panthers and his current team the Vancouver Canucks. As he grows older, he realizes he's been fortunate to have maintained good health and success in his career.

To this day, Helen monitors her children's success with great pride.

Mrs. Gagner has parleyed her skill, and considerable energy into a successful farm-based business. Helen is the woman behind "Helen's Country Harvest," a thriving home-based business of canned pickles, sauces, beets and assorted jams with its basic ingredients grown on the Gagner farm in Harwich. To ensure the taste is unique, Helen uses her own recipes like the small batches mothers and grandmothers used to make when canning season rolled around.

Now in her early seventies she has a lifetime experience putting up food for her own family. As the children grew up and began their own families she continued to work in the kitchen. Her children express much pride in the wonderful flavours Mom comes up with.

Today her products can be found from Windsor to Toronto. With a few reliable and conscientious workers she produces approximately 4000 cases of preserves yearly. It is a hands on operation. She overseas the growing of the crop, the preparation and canning of the preserves and once a week loads up and personally delivers to her customers.

In 1990, Helen lost her husband, Armand, who for quite sometime had suffered from a heart condition. This handsome couple worked side by side for some 50 years.

Mrs. Gagner, a very classic and lovable person, has other priorities as well. She attends hockey games across the country, visits her family and friends far and near. Her yearly visits to Florida were most welcome by her relatives and friends like me. At a time in her life when most people want to slow down, Helen seems to have an abundance of physical energy and drive stored up and retirement is nowhere in sight.

Jeanne Wright Trudell "Honoured in Nursing Career"

She is known as Jean Trudell loving wife of Bernard Trudell of Pain Court. She deserves being honoured for a distinguished career in nursing.

Jean worked for many years as a nurse, then became instructress at St. Clair College School of Nursing in Chatham for 20 years.

We commend you Jeanne, in your success in nursing and in teaching.

Doreen Stallaert, née Delrue, a lifelong resident of this area has opened a new tanning salon "Tropical Paradise" at 49 Keil Dr., Chatham. As a certified hairstylist and aesthetician Doreen has been in business since the early 1980's and is now the owner and manager of "Tropical Paradise." She has been an active organizer for several charity events for the Chatham Kent Women's Centre. Doreen has more than 15 years of experience in hairdressing and other aesthetic services.

Pat Pinsonneault, opened the doors of her "Gift Boutique" to the community March 17 1986 at its present location 65 Thames St. next to Forsyth Travel Bureau. She is the wife of Real Estate broker Yvon Pinsonneault formerly of Pain Court.

She strives to give you a wide variety of quality choices in gifts for all occasions. She has a friendly courteous staff and invites you to browse at your leisure.

À la douce mémoire

Claire Jeanne Roy

(Née Pinsonneault)
décédée le 1 avril, 1998

Nous l'avons aimée durant sa vie, ne l'oublions pas après sa mort.

* * *

The Sisters of the Holy Names of Jesus and Mary,
of the Ontario Province wish to express their profound
gratitude for your donations in memory of Claire Roy.
Sister Suzanne Mailloux received a total of $1,045.00 for
her mission works in Brazil.

"Elles célèbrent leurs 95 ans"

Dame Vélina Maillet Béchard âgée de 95 ans est l'épouse de Henri Béchard décédé à Pain Court janvier 1993. Il était le fils de Médard Béchard et Emma Benoit qui épousa Vélina Maillet de Grande Pointe, le 24 novembre 1924. Elle est la fille de Régis Maillet et Maria Simard de Grande Pointe. Henri et Vélina furent bénis et récompensés pour leurs efforts à l'égard de leurs sept enfants: Verne, Ivan, Beverly, Jeanette, Jérôme, Gérard et Norbert. Félicitations!

Edna Robert Peltier

Dame Edna Peltier a épousé William Pelletier le 26 décembre 1927, à Pain Court. Elle est la fille de Joseph Robert et Célina Caron. Willie Peltier fils de George Peltier et Lucie Bourassa, est décédé le 20 avril 1970 à l'âge de 68 ans.

Edna, sa femme survit. Elle est âgée de 95 ans et figure dans le vidéo de la paroisse de Pain Court publié en 1995. C'est une mère modèle, douée de patience et de compassion. Elle est la chère maman de Clara Cleeve, Fernande Gray et Roland.

A tribute to forgotten secretaries

Contrary to secretaries who work in business offices and for whom there is a day of recognition set aside each year, this tribute is for all past and present secretaries who have toiled, and dedicated much of their time and knowledge for the welfare of the parish communities of Pain Court, Grande Pointe and St. Peters.

Have we forgotten your efforts? Not really, but we have forgotten to show some appreciation. Seldom do you see accolades for a secretary. Presidents yes, treasurers yes as they are involved with monies to offer, but secretaries? I have known secretaries who have dedicated themselves for some 15 - 20 years. Yet, we have somewhat failed to recognize that they are the personnel behind all correspondence, all the invitations, all the thank you cards, all recorded documents initiated, all committee briefings, all historical data and furthermore sacrificing their own priorities.

Let's try to show our appreciation by recognizing them in a tangible way for their dedication, their perseverance in serving the various committees of our three communities.

Birthplace of the Dionne Quintuplets, North Bay, Ontario, Canada
Old postcard of their homestead

A tribute to the surviving "Dionne Quints" Cécile, Yvonne and
Annette who so valiantly fought for their rights in 1998 against
the Harris government. The "Dionne sisters' message directed
at all children:

> "Never be afraid to speak out against injustice,
> Never be afraid to fight for what is right,
> Never be afraid to hug your parents."

Special message to my daughters-in-law

Front row, left to right: Colette, Rose-Marie, Coline.
Second row: Aline, Bernadette, Penny, Lucille and Caroline.

I want to voice my appreciation to my daughters-in-law, Aline Cartier, Rose-Marie Houle, Bernadette Pinsonneault, Marie-Reine Masse, Penny McDonald and Lucille Benoit for the help and constant devotion towards my sons. They are very special to me.

They have known how to be a friend and a partner. Marriage can be a peaceful island in a world of turmoil and strife, therefore they continually strive to maintain a pleasant atmosphere of loving support for their family life.

They learned to listen and hear not only words but also the non-language of tone, mood and expression. Rest assured, I did not raise angels. They are ordinary boys.

They have respect for each other's rights . . . everyone is a person of flesh and blood, entitled to his or her own choices and mistakes. Each has the right to equality.

They have love for their husbands . . . love is the measure of life:
<u>Only so far as we love, do we really live.</u>

They have raised families which I cherish.

Kindly accept my love and may God shower upon you His blessings.

À la douce mémoire des membres défunts de ma famille

Bernard Roy - mon frère

Né le 24 octobre 1928, il est décédé le 2 février 1996. Il laisse dans le deuil son épouse Irène Bourdeau, et ses trois filles, Becky, Germaine, Kathy, ainsi que sept petits-enfants: Angela, Jennifer, Rachel, Kala, Jordan, Sara et Steve.

Marc Roland Lucier - mon neveu

Né le 3 février 1950 et décédé le 17 mai, 1994. Il laisse dans le deuil ses parents M. et Mme Félix Lucier, ses frères Robert et Rosaire ainsi que sa soeur Claudette.

Félix Lucier - mon beau-frère

Né le 28 septembre 1921, et décédé le 4 juin 1996. Il laisse dans le deuil sa femme Yvonne Roy Lucier et ses trois enfants Robert, Rosaire et Claudette, ainsi que quatre petits-enfants, Rob, Gregg, Brian et Jean-Paul.

Edmond Roy - mon frère

Né le 24 novembre 1932, décédé le 27 décembre 1996. Il laisse dans le deuil sa femme Yvette Delrue Roy et ses trois enfants Vincent, Raymond, Colette, ainsi que six petits-enfants: André, Adrian, Eric, Ashwin, Kristopher et Kaelyse.

Les organistes de la paroisse de Grande Pointe

Dans la paroisse St-Philippe de Grande Pointe, plusieurs musiciens et musiciennes se sont dévoués au sein des cérémonies religieuses au cours des années. La musique et le chant ont toujours rehaussé les célébrations liturgiques grâce aux organistes dévoués qui ont su sacrifier leur temps pour maintenir la grandeur et la beauté des offices divins depuis la fondation de la paroisse.

De 1882 à 1917, je n'ai pu obtenir aucun renseignement concernant les organistes qui ont pu avoir assumé cette tâche. Par contre, en 1918, c'est le Père Joseph Emery qui dessert la paroisse pour une période de 10 ans et l'organiste à cette époque se trouve Mlle Laurentia Houle jusqu'à son mariage en 1923. Quand celle-ci déménage à Québec, Mme Délima Emery Houle, soeur du Père Joseph Emery, la remplace et occupe le poste d'organiste aidée de sa fille, Marie-Jeanne, surtout pour les célébrations du soir. À son tour, Marie-Jeanne quitte en 1933 pour poursuivre ses études.

Vers 1941, Mme Laurentia Perreault revient dans la paroisse et reprend sa place à l'orgue jusqu'en 1946 lorsque Dorothée Martin, nièce du Père Oscar Martin, curé de la paroisse dans le temps, prend la relève jusqu'en 1949.

Avec l'arrivée du Père Chevalier en 1949, Mme Marie-Jeanne Cartier s'engage comme organiste et maintient le poste pendant plusieurs années. À différentes reprises, M. Amédée Emery, en plus d'être organiste, s'occupe de faire chanter les élèves surtout pour les célébrations du dimanche.

Au départ de Mme Marie-Jeanne Cartier, Mme Clara Benoit prend la rèleve partageant la tâche avec Mme Stella Delanghe.

Vers les années '50, M. Amédée Emery, un enseignant dans la paroisse, donne son appui surtout pour les fêtes spéciales.

Un peu plus tard, vers les années '65, Mme Gloria Benoit partage ses talents au service de sa communauté.

Au début des années '70, Mme Thérèse Gagnon, enseignante à l'école St-Philippe de Grande Pointe, dirige la chorale de l'école et de l'église en plus de toucher l'orgue quand l'occasion s'y prête.

Par contre, c'est depuis 1979 que Mme Thérèse Gagnon a choisi de servir volontairement dans un domaine qu'elle aime beaucoup et qu'elle s'y connaît bien: la musique. À cet égard, Thérèse remplit une tâche démésurée dans la paroisse où la multiplicité de ses actes ne se mesure qu'avec le résultat de sa générosité et le fruit de son dévouement. Vous n'avez qu'à contempler les célébrations liturgiques françaises et anglaises si minutieusement préparées et chacunes relatives au thème que constitue la liturgie propre à chaque dimanche du calendrier liturgique. Et tout cela, elle le fait pour animer davantage le sens du message de l'Évangile.

Depuis un quart de siècle, Thérèse est restée fidèle à son engagement comme organiste, directrice et ajoutons en plus, compositeure et appui constant des guitaristes.

Depuis 1997, Mme Thérèse Gagnon partage la responsablilité d'organiste avec M. Joseph Benoit, un musicien de grande renommée de la paroisse même.

L'orgue garde toujours sa priorité, bien entendu, cependant, petit à petit la guitare et le violon sont devenus un ajout au répertoire musical des cérémonies religieuses et la paroisse de Grande Pointe déborde de talents dans ce domaine.

C'est grâce à vous, musiciennes et musiciens de chez nous: organistes, guitaristes, violonistes, et choristes, la paroisse St-Philippe de Grande Pointe continue de nous édifier en manifestant la parole et l'amour du Seigneur à travers ses célébrations musicales réchauffant et faisant vibrer tous les coeurs qui cherchent un réconfort spirituel.

"Festival de la Moisson"

Félicitations aux organisateurs du 21e "Festival de la Moisson" qui a eu lieu à Pointe-aux-Roches du 1er au 5 novembre, 1998.

Fêtons dans la gaieté - les récoltes sont terminées. C'est grâce à CBEFT, le centre culturel St. Cyr, et le soutien financier du Conseil des arts de l'Ontario que nous nous réjouissons avec Angèle Arsenault accompagnée de Charles Johnson au violon. Elle nous revient pour la 5e fois car elle a toujours été appréciée. Elle communique une sincérité et une joie de vivre qui sèment la gaieté partout où elle se présente sur la scène.

La président du centre culturel St-Cyr, Ursule Rondot Leboeuf, nous accueille et nous souhaite la bienvenue.

"Temple de la Renommée"

Le centre culturel Tournesol, Windsor, Essex, Kent, investira dix nouveaux membres au Temple de la renommée Francophone du sud-ouest, le 29 novembre, 1998 au Salon Richelieu de la Place Concorde.

Parmi la dizaine de personnes on retrouve trois couples qui ont été actifs au palier régional, avec quatre autres personnes très militantes.

Ils sont: Ursule et Paul Leboeuf, Claire et Jérémie Beaulne, Pauline et Jean-Paul Gagnier, Mlle Elmira Sylvestre, Messieurs Eugène Grandin, Emile Lamarsh et Lucien Frappier.

DON   TETRAULT

Don Tetrault, owner of Tatro Group of Companies, which totals 17 businesses, was honoured as the 1997 Entrepreneur of the Year. His entrepreneurial accomplishments include being the largest exporter of used truck parts in Canada, with products being shipped to places such as Cuba, Holland, China and Hong Kong.

He also has business ventures in leasing, farming and manufacturing. He recently opened a fork lift operation in Chatham, opened a marina complex,   transformed the former Campbell's building into a business operation; he also has business operations in Toronto and Texas.

Although he has achieved much in business, Tetrault's philosophy is very basic and straight-forward. "Just work hard, be honest and have good people." He added, "You start that way and you finish that way."

In accepting his award Tetrault said the honour "belongs to all of us. Chatham, be a part of it."

Ref. Ellwood Shreve   Chatham This Week

The Chatham and District Chamber of Commerce honoured Mr. Don Tetrault March 24, 1998 as 1997 Entrepreneur of the Year. He is the oldest son of Orville Tetrault and Leona Blondeel of Grande Pointe. People in our area acknowledge your entrepreneurial ventures and trust that your wisdom and integrity will continue to forge ahead in the next millennium.

Caroline Roy Laprise

SOUPER CHAUD! - Les membres du club de l'Amitié de Pain Court ont bien apprécié le souper de chili auquel on les a conviés après leur partie de cartes hebdomadaire, le mercredi 7 octobre 19 . Alexina Graff, Léonard Charron, qu'on voit à peine, loin derrière, Rita King, Alex Trahan, Paul-Émile Raymond, Edmond Chauvin et Léona Lozon ont arrosé le tout, précaution oblige, de bonne bière.

Tous les membres du dernier conseil d'administration, à l'exception du vice-président dont le poste demeure d'ailleurs vacant, ont été reportés à leur fonction. Ce sont: Edmond Gagner, président, Marguerite Gagnier, secrétaire, Adeline Bélanger, trésorière, Marie-Anne et Régis Caron, Bernard Gagnier, Angela Gagner, Thérèse et Raymond Thibodeau, Bernice et Raymond Couture, Mae et François Caron, ainsi que Madeleine et Fernand Pinsonneault, conseillères et conseillers.

Le souper de Noël du club de l'Amitié de Pain Court se déroula le jeudi 17 décembre 1998. Marguerite Gagnier, secrétaire

Ref. - Vivre + - Journal des âgés

Conseil scolaire francophone catholique

LA VOIX DU SUD-OUEST
Mars 1998

Nous désirons offrir un chaleureux accueil et exprimer notre vive reconnaissance à ces personnes dévouées qui ont généreusement accepté de   diriger le premier conseil scolaire francophone du sud-ouest.

Francophone du Sud-ouest:

Père Robert Couture   -   Président
Joseph Bisnaire   -   Vice-président
Conseillers et conseillères - Louise Aitken, Jean Brulé, Lucille Guillenette, Gérard Couture, Euclide Forgues, Didier Marotte, Diane Normand, Joseph Séguin, Céline Vachon.

Cadres administratifs:

Michel Serré	Directeur Général
George Groulx	Surintendant d'affaires
Paul Bélanger	Surintendant de l'éducation
Michel Cyze	Surintendant de l'éducation
Janine Griffore	Surintendant de l'éducation
Denis Levert	Surintendant de l'éducation
Camille Thomas	Surintendant de l'éducation

Discours prononcés lors de la cérémonie inaugurale
Place Concorde - le mardi 6 janvier 1998

Père Robert Couture, Président
Mes chers amis, Est-ce possible que le rêve soit enfin devenu réalité? Oui, mes chers amis, non seulement est ce possible mais il est évident que nous nous trouvons devant le rêve devenu réalité.

**Les francophones partout en Ontario
ont finalement la pleine gestion
de leurs écoles, gérées PAR et
POUR les francophones.**

N'oublions pas de reconnaître que ce n'est qu'un début. Il reste de multiples questions à régler: Comment bien desservir 26 écoles sur un territoire dépassant 28,000 kmz?   Comment assurer l'accès aux contribuables?   Quel sera le site permanent du siège social? Comment harmoniser les six sections de langue française? Y aura-t-il assez d'argent pour assurer une éducation de qualité aux 7000 élèves?

Au lieu de s'attarder sur l'inconnu, il faut mettre l'accent sur ce que l'on connaît et bâtir sur cette fondation. Premièrement, nous avons maintenant la pleine gestion de nos écoles! Deuxièmement, nous avons sur notre territoire 26 écoles francophones catholiques qui oeuvrent de façon excellente, reflétant un système qui sait se prendre en main grâce aux multiples intervenantes et intervenants. Troisièmement, nous avons un cadre administratif sous le leadership de M. Michel Serré, prêt à se dévouer et à relever le défi. Quatrièmement, nous avons autour de cette table onze conseillers et conseillères scolaires nouvellement élus qui sont prêts à se donner corps et âme pour bâtir ensemble un conseil scolaire dont nous serons fiers. Et en tout lieu, nous avons notre Seigneur Jésus-Christ qui nous accorde sa grâce, le courage et la persévérance pour surmonter tout défi.

> We stand before the threshold opportunity rather than trial. I am reminded of the story of Pandora's box which was opened out of curiosity and all the ills of the world came out. I refuse to place emphasis on the ills that education is now facing, but rather call to mind what came out of Pandora's Box last, and that was hope. Hope transcends all ills and draws strength from challenge. It is our God who alone can give us such hope.

J'ai l'honneur de desservir ce nouveau conseil à titre de son premier président et humblement, je vous demande votre appui, vos conseils et vos prières. Je suis heureux que M. Joseph Bisnaire ait accepté le poste de vice-président et je suis certain qu'il jouera un rôle très important pour le bon fonctionnement du conseil. Je remercie les neuf conseillers et conseillères scolaires d'avoir accepté le défi au moment où leur rôle n'est pas encore clair.

Je suis heureux et fier que mes parents, Lionel et Évelyne Couture, soient parmi nous ce soir car ce sont eux qui ont inculqué en moi la fierté pour ma langue et pour ma foi. Je suis aussi fier de voir les membres du Comité local d'amélioration de l'éducation ainsi que les multiples partenaires scolaires et communautaires. Je souligne en particulier la présence de Mgr. Sherlock, notre évêque, qui a pu être des nôtres ce soir, ainsi que la présence des prêtres francophones qui sont appelés à garder intact l'aspect spirituel de nos écoles.

Ma mère m'a souvent dit qu'on rêve quand on dort et qu'on travaille quand on est réveillé. Ce soir, nous francophones catholiques du sud-ouest ontarien, nous sommes réveillés: c'est le temps de travailler, le temps de bâtir!

**L'élève n'est pas la principale raison
d'être d'un conseil scolaire, il/elle
est sa SEULE raison d'être.**

Michel Serré, Directeur général

Monsieur le Président, chers conseillers et conseillères scolaires, Monseigneur Sherlock et bien chers invités du Conseil de district des écoles catholiques de langue française n° 63.

Après plusieurs années d'attente, ou même plusieurs décennies d'attente, nous voici à la réunion inaugurale de notre nouveau conseil scolaire. Oui, un nouveau conseil géré pour des francophones.

Cet événement historique marque la pleine gestion scolaire pour tous les catholiques francophones du sud-ouest de la province d'Ontario. Et un peu partout en Ontario cette semaine, d'autres conseils scolaires francophones tournent aussi une page d'histoire franco-ontarienne.

Je tiens à remercier sincèrement les nouveaux élus et les nouvelles élues, représentants et représentantes du district 63, d'avoir eu confiance en moi en me nommant directeur général du conseil scolaire.

J'espère bien être à la hauteur de la situation. Les défis à surmonter sont énormes mais je demeure convaincu qu'ensemble, nous pourrons bâtir un conseil scolaire francophone catholique digne de tous les parents et les élèves de notre région.

Le travail qui nous est confié est de fusionner six sections de langue française en un seul conseil scolaire. C'est certainement un défi à relever à court et à long terme. Il faudra être patient et ne pas cesser d'espérer le meilleur pour tous les élèves de notre système scolaire.

À mon avis, pour que l'école en soit une de la réussite, il faut aussi comprendre que l'éducation de l'élève francophone catholique est une responsabilité partagée entre le foyer, l'école, la paroisse et la communauté.

Ce milieu de vie est rendu possible grâce à une étroite collaboration entre l'école, la paroisse, les parents, les éducateurs et éducatrices et le clergé.

Un de nos plus grands défis sera sûrement la restructuration financière des systèmes scolaires ontariens. Il sera donc très important d'établir nos priorités le plus tôt possible. Nous devons faire preuve de flexibilité tout en ne perdant jamais de vue notre raison d'être.

> To our English speaking parents and friends, welcome to this historic occasion. I can assure you that this Board is very committed to French language Catholic Education. I sincerely hope that you will always be very proud of your children's schools.

En terminant, je vous assure de ma disponibilité en tout temps. Je suis à votre service et mon plus grand souhait est de bâtir et de maintenir avec votre aide, le meilleur système scolaire francophone catholique de la province.

Board of Trustees –
We wish to express our thanks to the dedicated persons who have generously accepted to direct the activities of the first French language school board in Southwestern Ontario.

Highlights of opening ceremony

"Students are not the main reason for a school board's existence, they are the only reason."

Father Robert Couture   Board Chair

"Our objective is to create an environment where everything centres around the students."

Michel Serré, Director of Education

Ordinateurs pour les salles de classe

Les conseillers scolaires du Conseil scolaire de district des écoles catholiques du Sud-Ouest ont récemment annoncé l'allocation d'environ 2 000 000$ pour l'achat de 767 ordinateurs Pentium II pour ses six écoles secondaires.

Suivant l'orientation du ministère de l'Éducation et de la formation qui désire mettre l'accent sur la salle de classe, cette première dépense importante touchera directement les élèves du palier secondaire et permettra de réaliser un objectif clé du Conseil qui est d'offrir un ordinateur pour chaque deux élèves.

Ce projet d'envergure, issu d'un partenariat avec la compagnie Bell Canada, placera les écoles secondaires du Conseil scolaire de district des écoles catholiques du Sud-Ouest au premier rang parmi toutes les écoles secondaires anglophones et francophones de la province et permettra non seulement de maintenir, mais également d'augmenter nos inscriptions à ce palier.

Ouverture sur le Monde

L'ouverture officielle du Programme d'accès communautaire (PAC) a eu lieu à l'École secondaire de Pain Court, le jeudi 24 septembre 1998. Le PAC a pour objet d'aider la population, les groupes et les entreprises de Pain Court, du canton de Dover et des régions avoisinantes à découvrir et à faire usage de l'outil essentiel que représente le réseau Internet dans le monde d'aujourd'hui. Deux étudiants ont été embauchés durant les mois d'été pour faire la promotion du PAC et assurer la formation des participants. Ce projet a vu le jour grâce à l'appui financier d'industrie Canada et aux efforts d'une formidable équipe de personnes et d'entreprises locales. Entre autres, étaient présents à la soirée d'ouverture, Bill Weaver, conseiller de Chatham-Kent, ainsi que Paul Bélanger qui a été l'âme de ce projet communautaire. Le PAC est ouvert le mercredi et le jeudi soir, de 19 h à 21 h, et le samedi, sur demande.

Le saviez-vous?

Pour l'année scolaire 1998 - 1999, le Conseil scolaire de district des écoles catholiques du Sud-Ouest compte un total de 429,05 enseignants et enseignantes (310,05 au palier élémentaire et 119 au palier secondaire). Ce chiffre comprend 46 nouveaux enseignants et enseignantes. Nous desservons une clientèle de 6947 élèves (5320 au palier élémentaire et 1627 au palier secondaire), à compter du 11 septembre 1998, et nous avons 27 écoles. Nous avons raison d'être fiers.

Marks 50th year in priesthood

May 25, 1998

CUTTING ANNIVERSARY CAKE – Father Earl Pare celebrates the 50th anniversary of his ordination to the priesthood with his family, friends and parishioners from all over southwestern Ontario on Sunday. Marcel Roelandt looks on.

With far fewer than 50 years in any calling, most people are thinking of retirement. Not Father Earl Pare. He seems to prefer a good round number, like the end of the millennium. "Two more years," the 74-year-old Roman Catholic priest told his friends, family and parishioners as he celebrated the 50th anniversary of his ordination to the priesthood on Sunday. Pare said he never planned to be serving past 1990 when he was ordained on May 22, 1948.

"I thought if I made about 42 it would be good," he said.

Earl Donald Pare was born in Windsor, the youngest of three children. His elder sister Loreeda Mousseau of LaSalle was also at St. Peter's Church to celebrate his day, after Pare celebrated mass with parishioners.

Shortly after he was ordained, Pare celebrated his first mass at Blessed Sacrament Church in Windsor. He served at nine other parishes since, including ones in Tecumseh, LaSalle, two in the Wheatley area, two in Windsor, Wallaceburg, Sarnia and finally at St. Peter's Church in Tilbury East Township for the past six years.

A lot has changed in the church over half a century. But some things remain.

Take the stone inscription near the river bank of the cemetery that Pare designed and built himself. And the stone inscriptions and designs in all the borders around the parish house and the church that Pare took pride in constructing.

And there are the parishioners, many of whom feel that Pare is a very important part of their own families.

St. Peter's is the second oldest Roman Catholic Church in Essex County and Chatham-Kent.

As a gift, parishioners bought Pare an authentic hospital bed, which elevates to help him breathe. He prefers to sleep sitting up a little, because of an asthmatic condition.

By Bill Currie
The Chatham Daily News

The Wonderful Grace of Sharing

HELPING OUT: Pain Court Knights of Columbus Grand Knight Vincent Pinsonneault and Yvette Roy, president of the Ladies of Ste-Anne, present a donation of $2,500 to Roland Robert, a man who was injured in a helicopter accident in August. The money was raised at a Nov. 22 benefit dinner at Immaculate Conception Church. Robert injured his spinal cord in the crash near Tecumseh, which left him in hospital for more than two months. About 300 family members and friends joined in the benefit at the church hall. Robert joined the Knights last spring.
Chatham Daily News, Staff Photo

A large group of citizens have experienced an exhilarating feeling of happiness, sharing the joys, the fears, the griefs of special friends. An added feeling of compassion and love came about with the opportunity to be able to share financially, to feel that we are part of this world cosmos.

This is what I and many friends shared from far and near, in the last week.
Family and friends of Richard Laprise and Bonnie Sheets rejoiced together at a beautiful wedding ceremony November 14, 1998. The music was performed by Joseph and Denise Benoit close friends of the bride and groom. Guests were entertained at a reception with dinner and dancing.

*   *   *

The November 21, 1998 weekend was spent with friends and family in sharing with Roland Robert, a 35 year old Pain Court pilot, who is back home after a helicopter crash near Tecumseh. He's in a wheelchair with L1 and L2 spinal cord injury. He is optimistic that eventually he will be able ot walk with braces.

The Knights of Columbus and the Ladies of Ste-Anne of Pain Court were happy to host an event for one of their own. Some 300 members, family and friends joined him at a dinner at Immaculate Conception Church Hall. "It feels good" he said to be surrounded by well wishers at the party. "Its great to be here with a bunch of friends."

A substantial sum of money was raised by the Knights for Roland , his wife Janice, their son Christopher and their daughter Danielle. This will serve well for rehabilitation equipment and other costs incurred to date by his family.

What's Wrong with A. J.?

Family hopes specialized US tests will help find a diagnosis. The four year old André- James Laprise has suffered from a severe gastrointestinal disorder. His parents, André and Laurie, managed to find a pediatric mobility specialist in Pittsburgh a year ago but O.H.I.P approval wasn't in. These specialized tests are priced at $16,000.00 U.S. and are not available in Canada.

Rose and Bob Branquet of the Central Tavern in Pain Court . . . hosted a benefit dinner Sunday November 22, 1998 for the son of their employee, Laurie Laprise. The Laprise family is most grateful for the support of the Community, the Dover Kinsmen, Grande Pointe Fire Fighters, Ladies of Ste-Anne, Knights of Columbus, Dover Rod and Gun Club, Amherstburg Optimist Club and a host of merchants who contributed and also a special mention to Frank Létourneau as well as numerous and generous private donations. A sold-out benefit dinner was hosted at the Central Tavern. They hoped to raise over four thousand dollars to help cover additional expenses. Rose and Bob Branquet have done this many times before helping children with special needs. An auction was held with gifts contributed by local merchants and individuals.

The Laprises said it was a bit tough to be on the receiving end of such a benefit, saying "this is unbelievable."

It is really heart warming to feel the spirit of compassion and sharing in our community.

Une nouvelle école catholique française nommée
d'après feu Monseigneur Augustin Caron

Sa première nomination après son ordination, a été à Wallaceburg comme assistant au curé dans la paroisse de "Our Lady of Christians." Ensuite, il a exercé son ministère à l'Immaculée Conception, Windsor, à l'Annonciation de Pointe-aux-Roches et a occupé le poste d'administrateur et curé dans la paroisse de St-Joseph, Rivière-aux-Canards. Par la suite, il a été transféré à St-Joachim, où il a accueilli les Soeurs de la Charité d'Ottawa pour habiter un tout nouveau couvent qu'il a fait construire pour elles. En septembre 1962 le titre de prélat honorifique lui a été conféré pendant son mandat à la paroisse de St-Joachim. De McGregor , il a pris sa retraite en 1968 pour se revoir encore une fois dans sa paroisse d'origine de Pain Court.

Lors de sa retraite pendant sa convalescence d'une maladie sérieuse, il a fait construire une maison avec une chapelle privée sur la ferme paternelle de Pain Court. Au besoin, il rendait service aux curés des paroisses. Il est décédé le 8 mars 1983 et les funérailles ont été présidées par Monseigneur Jean Michel Sherlock.

Cinq de ses soeurs sont religieuses et enseignantes de la Communauté des Saints Noms de Jésus et de Marie.

Aujourd'hui, trois de ces religieuses sont vivantes et ont enseigné à l'Écoles du Sacré-Coeur à LaSalle et Saint Joseph de Rivière-aux-Canards.

Pour honorer et montrer la reconnaissance de la part des parents et élèves touchés par le ministère de ce noble prêtre, le Conseil de district des écoles catholiques du sud-ouest, a cru bon de nommer la nouvelle école élémentaire catholique et française d'après lui, à Rivière-aux-Canards. (La rédaction-d'après les renseignements obtenus des archives du diocèse de London)

Monseigneur Augustin Caron, d'heureuse mémoire, est né à Pain Court, le 17 novembre 1902. Il a été ordonné au sacerdoce le 25 mai 1929. Grand patriote, homme zélé et infatigable pour la foi et la culture française dont il en a fait ses deux plus grandes préoccupations au cours de sa vie.

" Ensemble nous faisons un bout de chemin."

Au début de mai 1988, voici qu'un ami Aimé Guay, bafoué par la maladie et la perte de son épouse Emérentienne âgée de 82 ans, s'arrête à ma porte afin de puiser un peu de compassion pour alléger sa peine. Je connaissais ce gentil couple depuis une dizaine d'années déjà, Aimé était doué d'une personnalité douce et un coeur rempli d'humilité.

Né le 17 juillet 1904 à Thetford Mines Québec, ce fut dans ce patelin qu'il fini ses études primaires et secondaires ainsi que ses années de Collège. À 18 ans, il s'embarque en train avec son père pour aller faire les récoltes dans l'ouest Canadien.

À l'hiver en 1925, il demande à son père un billet de chemin de fer en direction de Détroit où déjà il connaît des amis et son oncle qui travaillent à l'usine de Ford. Il faillait bien se loger et se nourrir, alors n'importe quel emploi fassait l'affaire. Il se contente d'accepter une position avec un salaire minimum- balayer et nettoyer dans l'usine. Après trois mois, les chefs de Ford constatent qu'il est gradué d'un collège et spécialiste en dactylo manuel, 92 mots la minute avec diplôme. À cet instant, il devient membre du personnel bilingue et y demeure pendant 41 ans. Il prend sa retraite bien méritée à 62 ans, en 1966.

Pendant cinq années il voyage avec sa femme à travers les États-Unis et le Canada où ils visitent leur quatre garçons et la parenté. Âgé de 68, il prend domicile en Floride à Zephirhills pendant un certain temps puis en 1977 construit une nouvelle demeure à Port Richey, Floride. C'est ici qu'ils anticipent passer leur vieillesse dans un beau climat chaud et recevoir leur famille, leur parenté et leurs amis à l'abri des hivers rigoureux du Nord.

Après la mort de son épouse en février 1988, et lui-même hospitalisé, il demande pas plus qu'un peu de support morale de sa soeur Germaine afin de récupérer. À peu près au même temps, Germaine aussi prend domicile en Floride, en face de mon foyer. Le 23 février 1989 lorsque nous fêtons l'anniversaire de deux de ses garçons, Harold de Californie et Norman de Floride, nous avons saisi l'occasion pour échanger des voeux nuptiaux. Nous nous sommes engagés à s'aider, à s'encourager et à se supporter mutuellement pour les années qui suivront.

Ensemble, nous avons parcouru un bout de chemin. Nos enfants ont été témoins de notre amour et de nos sentiments mutuels. Nous avons été choyés par Dieu et nous en sommes reconnaissants. Pendant sept ans nous nous sommes supportés mutuellement dans un atmosphère de tranquilité et de fidélité en s'aidant l'un et l'autre.

J'étais à ses côtés lorsque Dieu l'a rappellé à lui le 5 mai 1995 pour recevoir sa récompense au centuple. Il était âgé de 89 ans.

C'est Noël 1998. Trois années se sont écoulées depuis son départ mais il reste gravé dans mon coeur à jamais. En ce jour de fête cher Aimé, je te présente le plus beau cadeau que je puisse te faire . . . "Mes sept années de mémoires inoubliables."

Caroline Roy Laprise

A Word of Appreciation
to
Dr. J. Boekhoud
Dr. L. Clement
Dr. D. Aerssen
for overseeing my health
and welfare over a period
of twenty-five years.

1932 Duesenberg Model J

Antique car shows are a real attraction. Being an antique car buff, I attend many shows and parades in our area as well as in Florida. Lately, I dropped in at RM. Classic Cars restoration Company, Park Ave. West to extend my congratulations to Mr. Myers.

Success in his business has become an international business venture. I'm closely related to his family being first cousin with his mother Rita. His personal family status is as follows:
- Robert Joseph Myers
- Born April 30, 1956
- Youngest of 4 children
- Married with 2 children
- Wife, Cathy Van Raay-Myers
- Son, Shelby Myers 15 years old
- Daughter, Jessica Myers 14 years old
- Father, Arsene Myers
- Mother, Rita Ouellette
- Grandparents: Paul Ouellette and Magdelena Caron of Grande Pointe.
           : Alphy Myers and Eliza Charron of Grande Pointe.

Robert has been in the antique car business for 21 years and as you know his father, Arsene, was a hobbyist that was very supportive and helpful in his business. After Arsene's retirement from Eaton Springs in Chatham he became quite active in Robert's business and with family support the company has become an international company doing business all over the world.

RM employs over 50 people with office locations in Toronto, Michigan, and California. The company's most recent addition is a new head office location that will combine a restoration shop and a 100-car classic auto museum located on the 401 highway at 40 highway. This move comes along after being located on Park Avenue West in Chatham for nearly 20 years. Grand opening June 1999.

More Democracy Is Needed

I'm privileged to present to you a visionary, Lawrence Kerr a retired 92 year old farmer and lifelong area resident. His column appears regularly in the Chatham Daily News. I'm pleased to share his views on the farm, on the economic, educational and political institutions.

Lawrence Kerr

When one assesses economic opportunity, Canada appears to be the most favoured nation on earth. We are rich in mineral resources. Our food producing capacity ranks very high. Our energy resources include oil wells, gas wells, water power and the material for atomic energy. Our fresh water supply is probably the best on earth. Our population make up is exceptional.   We have attracted abilities from dozens of nations. Our primary language is English which is a substantial advantage in business, science and travel.

We have excellent ports on both oceans. Our inland waterways serve so much of our industry. We enjoy a 3,000 mile peaceful border with the richest economy on earth, and we have the NAFTA to make that market singularly available. Canada enjoys a stimulating climate that begets energy and originality. Twenty-nine years ago we ranked fifth in the world's per capita production. We possessed every advantage required to propel us towards the number one spot.

Actually, in the last three decades we have slipped from fifth place in per capita production to 19th. Our currency has fallen in value. Unemployment is still 8.3%. Interest on our national debt takes a huge bite out of every tax dollar. Crime and drugs have been increasing persistently. Most serious of all our problem is the brain drain to the USA. Definitely we have missed the world's finest opportunity to have it flow in the opposite direction.

Our problems must almost entirely be credited to successive governments and parties in opposition. Their vision and foresight for the sake of re-election have not been focussed further ahead than attracting voters in the next election, and our voters are not well informed.

Our failures must be attributed to the system and not the individual elected members. When I was a new graduate of the Ontario agricultural College I spent five years in the employ of the Department of Agriculture. I served for one month or more in 11 different counties of Ontario. I was advised to get to know the local members. They usually have valuable knowledge and their acquaintance may help to get things done locally. I have always kept track of the local members in Kent and Lambton. At age 92 I have sized up a lot of parliamentarians. With 99 per cent of them I have considered that the local people had made excellent choices.

Definitely the system needs assistance.

It appears probable that Canada could greatly benefit from the farsighted leadership for public opinion by a network of discussion groups made up of carefully selected individuals. We would suggest groups of 15 to 19 members chosen for a two-year term or more by the heads of local governments and by the presidents of local universities in the district. Ontario might merit four or five such groups and the other provinces and districts proportionately fewer.

Prospective members should be requested to fill out a questionnaire inquiring if the individuals would be willing and able to serve without remuneration and without expenses paid. Generally, members required to stay overnight might be eligible for expenses.

Public confidence would be high if a substantial portion of councillors were able and willing to serve Canada without expense to the taxpayer.

Canada has a wealth of well experienced, well qualified individuals in all geographic areas and in all universities. Care should be taken that the fair sex and youth are suitably represented. Twenty or 30 such discussion groups, meeting the first of each month or of every other month, could provide forward looking vision and priceless leadership of public opinion.

Members would be free to think and speak without concern for reelection of the individual or the party. They would be expected to have no party allegiance except Canada.

A substantial portion of discussion time at each meeting should be devoted to the topic suggested by the Ottawa office. Results of a vote on each topic should be forwarded to Ottawa along with outstanding logic brought out in discussion. Each council should have a part-time secretary. The Ottawa office should have an economist or, if necessary, several economists that are capable writers to summarize and publicize the best arguments of the area councils.

Recommendations that are new and different to current public thinking should be represented along with the percentage of councillors voting in favour. Novel ideas should be discussed over a number of months with the changing percentage of councillors in favour shown each time.
"Democracy is a form of government in which the power resides in all the people."
(Funk and Wagnalls Dictionary)

It is important that "all the people" be informed and forward looking.
All of our levels of governments have shown themselves eager to follow the dictates of the majority. Our rapidly changing modern democracy needs the leadership of our most talented, our most sound, far-sighted and public spirited individuals. This is necessary to keep "all of the people" firmly in control.

With experience and adaptation, a national network of discussion groups should have the potential to put Canada back on the road to achieving her God given potential in standard of living and in quality of living.

Le vicaire épiscopal
francophone est nommé évêque

(C&PR) Sa Sainteté le Pape Jean-Paul II vient d'annoncer la nomination du Père Donald Thériault comme évêque de l'Ordinariat militaire du Canada, un poste qui était vacant depuis le départ de Mgr. André Vallée, nommé évêque du diocèse de Hearst en 1996.

Mgr. Thériault est actuellement curé de la paroisse Saint-François-Xavier à Tilbury. En plus d'être, depuis un an, le vicaire épiscopal pour la com munauté francophone, il cumule plusieurs autres postes au sein du diocèse: juge au Tribunal ecclésiastique, vice-président de la Commission diocésaine liturgique, membre de l'équipe diocésaine pour le ministère des prêtres de London.

Né en 1946 à Paquetteville, au Nouveau-Brunswick, il a été élevé à Sarnia car ses parents s'y sont établis lorsqu'il n'avait que deux ans. Mgr. Thériault a été ordonné prêtre en 1971 après avoir terminé ses études théologiques au Séminaire St. Peter de London. Il détient aussi un baccalauréat en arts de l'université Western Ontario et une maîtrise en liturgie de l'institut catholique de Paris.

Mgr. John Sherlock, évêque du diocèse de London, se dit à la fois heureux et peiné par cette nomination. «Nous sommes très fiers du travail que Mgr. Thériault a généreusement fourni au diocèse mais nous allons véritablement ressentir un vide avec son départ. Les prières de tout le diocèse l'accompagnent au moment où il entreprend de nouvelles responsabilités dans l'Église.» Rejoint par le REMPART dès son retour d'Ottawa où il a dû assister à une rencontre avec des militaires, et ce immédiatement après l'annonce officielle de sa nomination, Mgr. Thériault avait ce message pour les francophones du diocèse. «Je les remercie de leur appui, de leur gentillesse à mon égard, avant même que je devienne vicaire épiscopal. Je commençais à peine à faire tourner la roue de ce nouveau poste, de rencontrer les prêtres et les paroissiens. Je voulais travailler avec le nouveau conseil scolaire, je voulais me rendre à Windsor et à la Place Concorde mais le temps m'a manqué. Si possible, lors de vos célébrations du tricentenaire, je viendrai célébrer avec vous car les francophones restent près de mon coeur.»

Mgr. Thériault devrait officiellement entrer en fonction dans environ trois mois, comme évêque de l'Ordinariat militaire où il y a un grand nombre de militaires, y compris les militaires catholiques de rite oriental, ainsi que le personnel civil soumis à la foi de la Défense nationale. Avec un effectif catholique se chiffrant à 75,183 personnes, l'évêque est responsable de 33 paroisses et missions. «Pour moi c'est un territoire pas mal connu car j'ai travaillé comme aumônier capitaine pendant l'été pour treize ans,» ajoutait Mgr.Thériault, en même temps qu'il enseignait au Séminaire St. Peter de London. «J'avais les étés de libre, alors j'ai fait partie des Forces armées.»

Le Rempart 1er avril 1998

Tilbury priest now a CAF bishop

The Chatham Daily News by Andrew Cornell

TILBURY - When the Vatican's representative in Canada, the Papal Nuncio, requested a personal meeting with Rev. Donald Theriault last week, the Tilbury priest knew it was not to talk about the weather.

"I kind of braced myself," Theriault said in an interview Wednesday, hours after Pope John Paul II announced his appointment as the Roman Catholic bishop for the Canadian Armed Forces.

"There were rumblings that something could be developing. But that was over the last year, or a year and a half. I certainly had no ambitions to become a bishop."

Sometime in the next few months, once a date has been set, the pastor of St. Francis Xavier Parish will be ordained Bishop for Military Ordinary of Canada, and will pack his bags for Ottawa.

Going from a small town in southwestern Ontario to a posting that could involve intercontinental travel is a major jump. But Theriault will have no trouble trading in his cloth for green fatigues, figuratively speaking. He is a former armed forces chaplain and was a captain in the armed forces reserves.

"I'll miss the community here that I'm going to leave . . . but I couldn't ask for a better appointment. It's going to be a good ride."

As bishop, he will lead a far-flung diocese of more than 75,000 Catholics and their families, plus 40 priests across Canada and overseas.

"My duties are to be in touch with all the parishes. Part of the duty of bishop is to keep close to priests and support them and help them along, see to their welfare and exercise good ministry for the people."

He expects he will be spending a significant amount of time on the road.

He has been in Tilbury since 1991. Prior to that, he was a professor at St. Peter's Seminary in London for 14 years. He has been a priest since 1971.

He was born in Paquetteville, New Brunswick. His family moved to Sarnia when he was two.

He is the second Military Ordinary appointed by the Roman Catholic Church for its adherents in the Canadian Armed Forces. The post was created in 1986 but has been vacant since August 1996, when Bishop Andre Vallee was appointed to the Diocese of Hearst.

In addition to his parish duties, Theriault is episcopal vicar for the Francophone community in the Diocese of London. He is a former president of the London Council of Priests, vice-president of the London Liturgical Commission, judge of the London Marriage Tribunal, chaplain to French-language public schools in the London area and a member of the Ontario Liturgical Commission.

Father Eugène Roy

Father Roy succeeded Father Donald Thériault who was appointed Roman Catholic Bishop for the Canadian Armed Forces in 1998.

Father Roy was born and educated in Pain Court and is the son of Norman Roy and Helen Tremblay.

Parish cluster members arrived at a consensus regarding the new Sunday Mass schedule for our clustered parish communities of St. Francis Xavier, Tilbury; St. Charles, Stevenson; St. Peter's, Raleigh; St. Patrick, Merlin. The recommendations have been approved by their respective parish councils and it is my duty and obligation as moderator of the cluster to submit to our final agreement for our Sunday Mass schedule for the cluster. Effective October 3, 1998 the Saturday evening mass will alternate every month between the parish of St. Peter's and St. Patrick.

With the millennium around the corner it seems ironic that St. Peter's Raleigh, the second oldest church in the Diocese of London built in 1802 is now established as a cluster parish with Father Roy as pastor and Father Rocheleau associate pastor St. Francis Xavier parish Tilbury.

Nouveau vicaire épiscopal

Le poste, resté vacant depuis le départ de Mgr. Donald Thériault nommé aumonier des forces armées canadiennes il y a quelques temps. Le nouveau vicaire épiscopal du diocèse de London, le Père Eugène Roy est nommé à ce poste le 22 juin, 1999.

Ce nouveau vicaire a pour objectif de resserver les liens de collégialité parmis les prêtres de langue française du diocese afin de mieux desservir la population de cette langue. Le Père Roy natif de Pain Court a été ordonné prêtre en mai 1984. Il se dit fier de la nomination car elle représente la reconnaissance de la communauté francophone et invite les membres de cette communauté à communiquer leurs préoccupations à leur curé afin qu'on en tienne compte aux réunions des prêtres de langue française.

Père Roy est conscient de l'ampleur de la responsbilité et anticipe voué tous les efforts nécessaires afin de voir les fruits.

Rév. Robert L. Champagne

Ordination
Le 11 mai - May 11, 1974

**Un temps
d'espérance**

**Il y a des guerres ...
Il y a de la souffrance ...
Des tourments ....
La méchanceté ...
Des pauvres ...
Et il y a ...**

Des gens s'étonnent: « Serons-nous capables un jour de rendre ce monde meilleur? Sera-t-il rempli de paix, de bonheur pour tous? » Parfois, nous perdons l'espoir quand les temps sont difficiles.

À Noël, les chrétiens célèbrent la naissance de Jésus, le fils de Dieu. Il est venu annoncer au peuple : « Ne perdez pas de courage: Regardez. Je suis avec vous jusqu'à la fin des temps. »

Dieu vient parmi nous pour rendre notre monde meilleur, rempli de bonté et nous montrer l'Amour.

Joyeux Noël
Bonne Heureuse Année 1999

Père Robert Champagne
Communauté de l'Immaculée Conception et de St-Philippe.

Du rêve à la réalité

Je veux partager ma joie de vivre avec mes collègues avec qui j'ai travaillé pendant au delà de 65 ans. Nous avons partagé nos ambitions, nos rêves et nos peines.

Aujourd'hui je veux partager mes joies et les honorer davantage en parlant d'eux dans mes écrits.

"Mon Héritage, Ma Cutlure, Mes Souvenirs"

Ensemble nous avons constatés le progrès dans nos paroisses et nos écoles. Les progrès techiniques, scientifiques, industiels et économiques ont améliorés notre style de vie. J'espère que les générations future porterons haut le flambeau avec fierté et dignité.

À l'aube du millénaire j'anticipe que Dieu répondre Ses bénédictions sur vous, vos familles et toutes entreprises familiales et paroissiales.

Faite nous cadeau de votre histoire. L'amour ça mène loin.

The Clock of Life

The clock of life
Is wound but once.
And no man has the Power
To say just when
The clock will stop
At late or early hour.
The present only is our own
Live, Love, toil with a will
Place no trust in tomorrow
For the clock may then be still.

Ref - January 1963 WJBK "With this Ring" Mgr. Sheen.

What is life?

Life is a challenge . . . . perform it.

Life is a gift . . . . accept it.

Life is a sorrow . . . . overcome it.

Life is a tragedy . . . . face it.

Life is a duty . . . . .perform it.

Life is a game . . . . .play it.

Life is a mystery . . . . unfold it.

Life is a song . . . . sing it.

Life is an opportunity . . . . take it.

Life is a journey . . . . complete it.

Life is a promise . . . . fulfill it.

Life is a beauty . . . . praise it.

Life is a struggle . . . . fight it.

Life is a goal . . . . achieve it.

Life is a puzzle . . . . solve it.

Life is beautiful . . . . enjoy it.

Conclusion

SOEUR EUCHARIA

100

1898 -1998

Seigneur, bénis les gens qui consacrent leur vie pour le bien-être de la société.

Seigneur, bénis les gens, qui, par leur sourire, leur belle humeur et leur générosité, savent apporter au coeur un peu de chaleur.

Ces mots représentent l'âme de Soeur Eucharia, née Victoria Nellie Trudell, fille de M. Régis Trudell et de Euphrasie Béchard de Pain Court. Elle entra en communauté chez les "Soeurs Ursulines," le 4 janvier 1920. Elle suivit les traces de sa soeur aînée, Ellen, qui, déjà avait fait son entrée chez les Ursulines le 5 août 1915 et connue sous le nom de Soeur Rosalie.

Elle me raconte, en mai 1997, que sa vocation comme religieuse était bien établie en octobre 1919.

"Deep in my heart, I knew that I wanted to become a nun," declared Sister Eucharia.

Elle a passé sa vie dans les environs de Chatham au couvent des "Ursulines." Comme postulante, elle a fait un stage à Windsor où elle s'est occupée de faire la cuisine et les lavages pendant plusieurs années pour une dizaine de soeurs enseignantes. Elle souligne qu'à cette époque-là les cordes à linges étaient installées d'un arbre à l'autre et que le lavage se faisait le lundi et le samedi.

De cette intelligence vive se dégage une personnalité attachante embrassant dans sa totalité le sens de l'être humain d'où émane une disposition débordante de tendresse afin d'apporter un peu de confort à ses soeurs en communauté. Presque "centenaire," elle démontre ce même attachement envers sa parenté, ses amis, ses neveux et nièces en assistant aux fêtes spéciales et en secourant les malades avec ses visites régulières et sympatiques.

Pour ses 99 ans, cette grande vivante garde un coeur alerte, indépendant et libre. Le 26 avril 1997, elle se déplace obligeamment pour assister à la fête du 50e anniversaire de mariage de sa nièce Angela Trudell, mariée à Edmond Gagner.

Toujours vaillante et courageuse, elle entreprend des tournées à l'hospice "Copper Terrace" pour visiter Blanche Caron Foy, sa nièce, afin d'alléger son sort dans la maladie. Elle a un don rare: le génie du coeur guidé par l'intelligence du coeur rempli de compréhension et d'affectueuse sagesse.

Elle a le sens de l'humour et son coeur de mère reste imprimé dans le coeur de ceux qui la côtoient. Elle a vécu totalement pour les autres ... cela se voit.

C'est elle qui entreprenait l'organisation des pique-niques au parc Rondeau pour les bonnes soeurs Ursulines accommodant les jeunes et les moins jeunes. Pour une dizaine d'années consécutives et approchant ses 85 ans, Soeur Eucharia avait un itinéraire toujours bien rempli pour le rendez-vous au chalet Laprise. Pour la pause du midi, un brunch bien garni suffisait pour rassasier les appétits; pour le souper, c'était un repas chaud avec garniture habituelle servi en présence de la maîtresse de maison et se terminant toujours avec quelque chose de spécial préparé exclusivement pour l'hôtesse du chalet.

La journée en villégiature laissait parfois sa marque. Souvent les bonnes Soeurs retournaient chez elle le visage brûlé par le soleil et les pieds brûlés par le sable chaud de la plage. Disons que les joies d'enfants régnaient en maître prenant pour acquis que le lac Erié leur épargnerait toutes inconvéniences.

Encore une fois, l'anticipation d'une vacance au chalet Laprise était mise en veilleuse jusqu'à l'été prochain pour Soeur Eucharia et ses compagnes.

Récemment, j'ai eu le plaisir de jaser avec elle lors de sa fête d'anniversaire. Jugez vous-mêmes la présence d'esprit et la mémoire prodigieuse de cette femme remarquable, jeune de 99 ans. En voici quelques anecdotes:

"Un bon jour ma mère était absente et je décide de faire des biscuits," déclare Soeur Eucharia. "Laissez-moi vous dire que les gars ont eu du plaisir avec mes biscuits. En effet, ils jouaient à la boule avec mes biscuits. Vous devinez comment durs ils étaient? On a bien ri."
Ensuite, elle raconte l'aventure du voyage en sleigh chez les "Houle" au printemps:
"La famille Houle nous accueille pour la nuit," raconte-t-elle. "Mais quelle détresse le lendemain matin! Toute la neige était disparue avec la tempête de pluie. Ça c'était pas drôle! Un vrai embarras pour retourner à la maison, je vous en assure."

Soeur Eucharia nous parle ensuite du levage de la grange chez son père, là où se trouve aujourd'hui la demeure de son neveu Bernard Trudell. Comme c'était la coutume beaucoup d'hommes se rendaient pour aider. De dire Soeur Eucharia:

"Imaginez, à douze ans, j'étais curieuse et je voulais savoir ce qui se passait mais ma mère mit fin à tout cela: "Ma petite fille," dit-elle, "tu fais ta première communion demain. Monte en haut et dis ton chapelet. Ce n'est pas ta place de regarder tous ces hommes-là..." et Soeur Eucharia s'éclate de rire.

Sur un ton plutôt sombre, Soeur Eucharia parle de la grippe espagnole, une épidémie mortelle qui a sévi au début du siècle et toute la famille de son oncle Isidore Trudell a été frappée par cette grippe. Les sept enfants y ont échappé bel; c'est sa tante Marie qui en a été victime.

"Après la mort de cette chère tante," dit-elle "nous avions une mission à remplir... celle de secourir oncle Isidore et ses sept enfants privés de soins maternels.

À une autre reprise, elle me raconte un incident, celui-ci humoristique, concernant la rentrée des religieuses enseignantes. Comme les soeurs avaient un grand verger et que ce jardin comportait plusieurs âcres, il y avait tout à leur disposition pour se bien nourrir: beurre, lait, porc, volailles et cetera. Donc, il y avait beaucoup de "cannage" à faire dans la cuisine comme par exemple embouteiller le jus de pommes et le jus de raisin.

"De temps à autre," dit-elle, "nous avions du plaisir car plusieurs d'entre elles n'étaient pas au courant des opérations de la cuisine mais ce qui mit le comble aux expériences du "cannage" is when Sister Anthony commented: "Look she's drunk. Look she's holding the post. Well, well, she's tasted the wine too much. Put her away."
"What a humorous interlude, and one never to be forgotten," relates Sister Eucharia.

"According to "Chatham This Week," Sister Bernadette Laporte is the last of the Ursuline teaching sisters to teach at the Pines. An era will come to an end at Ursuline College when the final bell rings in June. After teaching French for 18 years at the city's only Roman Catholic high school known as "The Pines," Sister Laporte had spent 26 years in total, teaching. At 64 years old, she has earned her retirement. Sister Bernadette credits the Ursulines for having a great impact on

Catholic education, locally. She noted when many of the Ursuline Sisters taught "it was work of charity... it was not for monetary reasons." [1]

As a former boarder at the Pines in 1935 and 1936, I feel a tinge of sadness when I think that such a privileged era has come to an end. It seems only yesterday that my father, Adolphe Roy, paid my tuition and board not with cash money, but with loads of hay and sometimes it was a load of oats which helped to feed the livestock and the chickens.

Sister Anne Denomy, daughter of Lawrence Denomy, a prominent druggist in the city, served as the last Ursuline principal at the Pines until retiring a few years ago. "She believes that the values which the Ursuline sisters have cultivated over their 137 year history in Chatham will remain with the school.

"It's not going to come to an end," she said.

As a principal for 15 years and before that as a teacher of chemistry, physics and algebra, Sister Anne has wonderful memories of her time at the Pines.

"The young people and the staff are the two things I missed the most about the school," she said." [2]

Former students often mention her name with reverence and fond memories as they were fortunate to experience her loving and caring understanding.

For many devoted sisters of the Ursuline College "The Pines" it was definitely a phenomenal adjustment and yes, even in their church life, having lived through practically a century of technological revolution, academic advancements and industrialization.

Sister Eucharia has been a living example as she has readily adjusted with an amazing serenity. May God bless you with love and happiness in your apostolate. May He transform you and all the Sisters into beings of peace, love, health, happiness, tenderness and compassion, and that you, dear Sister Eucharia, will faithfully continue to express your admirable sense of humour towards mankind.

Both, my sister Yvonne and I are very grateful to our cousin, Sister Thérèse May, for having assisted us and having welcomed us to a sumptuous dinner after a most enjoyable and rewarding visit with Sister Eucharia.

Hopefully, we will continue to appreciate and witness the survival of "The Pines" as a school of continuing education throughout the next millennium.

                                                    Caroline Laprise

1. Chatham This Week,
2. Chatham This Week

Sister Eucharia is 100 years old. A special celebration was held at the Pines on April 25th, 1998. In the new millennium on January 4th, 2000, this will mark her 80th year of devotion, compassion and love as a member of the "Ursuline Sisters" in Chatham.

À l'École secondaire de Pain Court . . .

. . . Un rêve devient une réalité

L'ouverture officielle de la nouvelle aile se fait ce soir, le 1er mai, 1996

Historique de l'E.S.P.C.

En 1986, l'École Secondaire de Pain Court devient une école catholique du Conseil des écoles catholiques du comté de Kent. À ses débuts en 1953, l'école s'appelait École H.J. Payette Contiuation School.

Cette section spéciale sur l'École Secondaire de Pain Court a été préparée avec la collaboration de Mme Janet Cadotte et de M. Jean-Paul Gagnier que nous remercions sincèrement.

1. Réf. Gracieuseté Le Rempart

À l'École secondaire de Pain Court, le rêve est devenu la réalité. L'ouverture officielle à E.S.P.C. donnera l'occasion de célébrer le succès et la réussite qui couronnent des années de rêves d'une communauté.

Aujourd'hui l'école fleurit. Avec 250 élèves projetés pour l'année 1996 - 1997, la construction et les rénovations terminées, et le placement récent de l'E.S.P.C. parmi les 20 écoles exemplaires au Canada, il faut dire que notre école connaît la réussite. Mais elle n'a pas toujours été tellement prospère. Il n'y a pas longtemps, la petite école luttait pour sa survie et songeait à des temps meilleurs.

En 1972, elle prend officiellement le nom É.S.P.C. et se compose de 120 élèves. L'inscription chute pendant les prochaines années et en 1986, l'année du transfert de l'école du conseil public au Conseil catholique, il n'y a que 53 étudiants. L'école offre peu de cours et le risque de fermeture se fait de plus en plus menaçant. C'est grâce à un octroi du gouvernement provincial d'environ 2,5 millions de dollars que l'école a pu mieux répondre aux besoins des élèves et enfin se moderniser. L'octroi est le résultat d'une demande faite par la section de langue française, suite aux efforts et à la vision commune de Jacques Meilleur-Lamoureux, Paul Bélanger et de la directrice à l'époque Janine Griffore.

Après l'ajout des portatives, la future construction est planifiée en trois étapes. La première étape commence en 1991 avec l'addition d'un nouveau gymnase et de nombreuses rénovations au parc et au terrain de l'école. Une nouvelle piste de course est aménagée et le parc comprend aussi une terre et une prairie, qui s'étendent sur un total de 14 acres.

La deuxième étape commence deux ans plus tard avec la construction de deux laboratoires de science et de deux salles de classe. Pour cette étape, la municipalité de Dover, le Conseil des écoles catholiques de Kent et le Ministère des parcs et loisirs rassemblent les fonds nécessaires.

La troisième étape est la plus considérable. Une aile technologique est ajoutée au bâtiment; cette aile contient une salle technologique, une bibliothèque communautaire, deux salles de classe et une salle d'ordinateurs. Il y a des rénovations à plusieurs locaux dont la salle de musique, le salon du personnel, la salle d'arts et la salle de vidéo. La cafétéria est rénovée pour avoir une cuisine. Le secrétariat et le bureau d'orientation sont aussi refaits. Aussi, on ajoute une chapelle au coeur du bâtiment.

Les trois étapes apportent des changements qui modifient complètement le visage de l'école. Après des années de construction, la métamorphose est enfin complète. Selon Shannon Green, étudiante de la 12e année et membre du comité organisateur de l'ouverture officielle de l'école, c'est à peu près temps.

"Pendant toutes mes années à l'école secondaire, il y a toujours eu de la construction. C'est bon de l'avoir finalement terminée," a dit Shannon. Elle a dit que même si les dérangements de la construction ont parfois créé des inconvénients de toutes sortes, les élèves sont fiers et heureux de leur 'nouvelle' école. "Il y a de nouveau une fierté et une énergie nouvelle dans l'école. Nous grandissons et fleurissons comme jamais auparavant. C'est quelque chose qu'on devrait célébrer," a dit Shannon.

C'est l'idée de célébration qui fait naître celle de l'ouverture officielle de l'école. La cérémonie, qui a lieu le 1er mai, donnera la chance aux élèves, au personnel et à la communauté de fêter leur partenariat et les buts qu'ils ont atteints ensemble. Ils célébreront non seulement la fin de la construction et des rénovations mais aussi l'épanouissement et la réussite de la petite école qui, il y a à peine 10 ans, doutait de sa survie. C'est une célébration qui couronne des années d'efforts et qui est amplement méritée. À l'E.S.P.C., le rêve est devenu la réalité!

Un milieu qui permet de s'épanouir

À l'occasion de l'ouverture officielle de l'École secondaire de Pain Court, j'aimerais remercier tous les partenaires qui ont contribué de près ou de loin à la réalisation d'un rêve. En 1986, notre école ne comprenait que 56 élèves mais le désir d'avoir une école de langue française secondaire dans Kent a toujours été présent. Grâce à la vision de notre conseil scolaire et des membres de l'administration ainsi que de l'appui des parents, nous comptons en 1996 plus de 230 jeunes francophones qui bénéficient d'une grande variété de programmes et de cours à ESPC. La transformation de notre édifice a eu lieu en trois étapes avec l'addition d'une aile technologique, de laboratoires de sciences, de salles de classe, d'une chapelle, d'une bibliothèque et d'un gymnase. Le partenariat entre le canton de Dover, le Ministère de l'Éducation et le Conseil des écoles séparées de Kent nous a permis d'atteindre notre but qui était d'offrir aux jeunes francophones une éducation catholique française de qualité dans un milieu qui leur permet de s'épanouir pleinement et de développer leur fierté au niveau de la langue et de la culture.

Un rêve de cette envergure ne se réalise pas sans les efforts de plusieurs. Aux membres de la direction qui ont occupé le poste avant mon arrivée et les enseignants/tes qui ont toujours su maintenir un enthousiasment contagieux pour la tâche malgré la poussière, le bruit et les centaines de boîtes, merci de votre appui et de votre excellent travail! Mes sincères remerciements vont aussi au comité de la construction qui a su incorporer les besoins et les désirs de tous, lors du design des salles et le choix d'équipement. Je tiens aussi à remercier Mme Janet Cadotte et le comité de l'ouverture officielle qui a préparé une merveilleuse célébration en l'honneur de cette occasion. Mais je dois féliciter de façon particulière les élèves, qui malgré les inconvénients n'ont pas perdu de vue le rêve d'une école qui offre non seulement l'excellence au niveau des programmes dans une ambiance familiale mais aussi un endroit où tout est possible et dans lequel ils/elles peuvent réaliser leur plein potentiel. C'est aux Patriotes d'aujourd'hui et de demain que je lance le défi - c'est maintenant à votre tour de continuer à faire vivre le rêve!

Denise Couture-Bell
Directrice

Rien n'est impossible

Le 1er mai de cette année, l'École secondaire de Pain Court célèbre l'ouverture officielle de ses nouvelles installations qui comprennent, entre autres, une aile technologique et une magnifique bibliothèque scolaire/communautaire. Le Père Thériault de la paroisse St-Francis de Tilbury ainsi que des représentants du ministère de l'Éducation et de la Formation se joindront à la communauté scolaire et environnante en cette heureuse occasion.

L'histoire de l'École secondaire de Pain Court est réellement extraordinaire. D'une population estudiantine de 50 élèves en 1986, les effectifs dépassent 250 élèves en 1996. C'est une véritable joie de constater que tous ces jeunes finissants et finissantes francophones apporteront une grande richesse culturelle et linguistique au comté de Kent et à la grande famille franco-ontarienne du sud-ouest de l'Ontario.

Nous adressons nos félicitations et nos remerciements les plus sincères à tous ceux et celles qui ont contribué à ce succès, en particulier Janine Griffore, directrice 1989-1993, Paul Bélanger, Adjoint au directeur de l'éducation, et Denise Couture-Bell, directrice actuelle de l'ÉSPC, ainsi que tous les membres de la grande famille scolaire, le personnel enseignant, les élèves et la communauté entière. Si l'on se donne la main, rien n'est impossible!

Jacques Meilleur-Lamoureux
Surintendant des écoles de langue française

Une école réellement communautaire

"Les écoles franco-ontariennes sont à l'image des milieux qu'elles desservent" (Aménagement linguistique, Ministère de l'Éducation et de la formation 1994). Rien n'est plus vrai dans le cas de l'École secondaire de Pain Court, qui est réellement une école de la communauté du comté de Kent, une communauté florissante et innovatrice.
À titre de Présidente du Conseil des écoles séparées catholiques de Kent, j'ai le plaisir de féliciter et de remercier tous ceux et celles qui ont travaillé sans relâche pour réaliser ce rêve. Nous avons raison d'être fiers.

Marie Cadotte
Présidente du CÉSC de Kent

Les Patriotes ont réalisé leur rêve

Félicitations!
Enfin, après cinq ans de planification et de labeurs intensifs, les Patriotes ont réalisé leur rêve! C'est grâce à un travail d'équipe dont les membres sont très nombreux que nous pouvons jouir des additions et des rénovations qui se sont ajoutées à notre petite école de campagne. L'an 2000 s'annonce bien!

Erin Jenkins
Première ministre 1995-1996
Conseil des élèves
ESPC

Une école des plus modernes

À titre de Présidente de la Section de langue française du Conseil des écoles séparées catholiques de Kent, j'ai l'honneur d'annoncer l'ouverture officielle de la "nouvelle" École secondaire de Pain Court. Avec l'ajout d'une aile technologique et d'une bibliothèque scolaire/communautaire, suivant un projet de rénovation considérable, notre école secondaire de langue française se révèle toute fraîche et des plus modernes. Après plusieurs années de pour parlers et d'innombrables soumissions, grâce aux multiples partenariats formés avec la communauté, nous les Franco-Ontariens et Franco-Ontariennes du comté de Kent avons enfin une école secondaire de langue française dont nous pouvons être fiers. Nos nouvelles installations avec des ressources et de l'équipement de pointe nous permettent d'offrir toute une gamme de cours que l'on ne retrouve normalement que dans les très grandes écoles secondaires.

Au nom de la Section de langue française, je saisis cette occasion pour féliciter le personnel enseignant, les élèves et la communauté entière pour cette initiative collective qui sera officiellement célébrée le mercredi 1er mai.

Louise Aitken,
Présidente de la SLF

Le personnel enseignant 1995 : Première rangée: Mme Laroche, Mme Caron, Mme Létourneau, Mme Larche, Mme Dixon, Mme L'Écuyer et Mlle Trépanier; deuxième rangée : M. Ouellette, Mlle Lavergne, M. Goulet, Mme Couture-Bell, M. Gobbi et Mme Cadotte; troisième rangée : Mme Schinkelshoek, M. St-Louis, M. Mainville, Mme Shymanski, M. Myers et M. Gagnier; quatrième rangée : M. Robert, M. Mayer, M. Arago, M. Thomas, M. Griffore et Mlle Bondy. Absent: M. Brisson.

Nous exprimons nos meilleurs voeux à l'administration, au personnel et aux élèves de
l'École Secondaire de Pain Court
et nous les félicitons de leur apport remarquable à la vie de la communauté francophone de Kent!

AEFO Kent secondaire
Paroisse Immaculée-Conception
Paroisse St-Philippe de Grande-Pointe
AEFO Kent élémentaire
Les Dames de Ste-Anne de Pain Court
Le Conseil Immaculée-Conception des Chevaliers de Colomb

Des chansons françaises

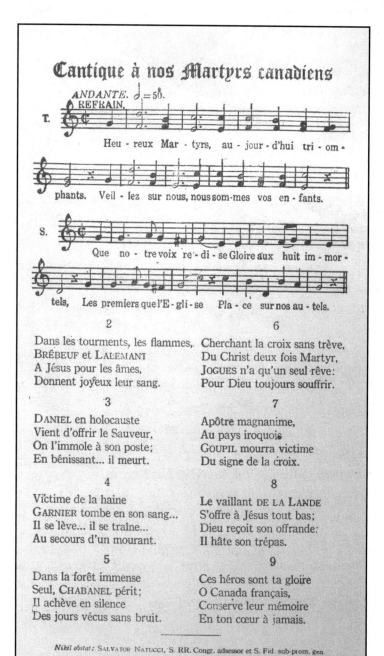

Cantique à nos Martyrs canadiens

ANDANTE. ♩=5δ.

REFRAIN.

T.

Heu - reux Mar - tyrs, au - jour - d'hui tri - om -

phants. Veil - lez sur nous, nous som - mes vos en - fants.

S.

Que no - tre voix re - di - se Gloire aux huit im - mor -

tels, Les premiers que l'E - gli - se Pla - ce sur nos au - tels.

2

Dans les tourments, les flammes,
BRÉBEUF et LALEMANT
A Jésus pour les âmes,
Donnent joyeux leur sang.

3

DANIEL en holocauste
Vient d'offrir le Sauveur,
On l'immole à son poste;
En bénissant... il meurt.

4

Victime de la haine
GARNIER tombe en son sang...
Il se lève... il se traîne...
Au secours d'un mourant.

5

Dans la forêt immense
Seul, CHABANEL périt;
Il achève en silence
Des jours vécus sans bruit.

6

Cherchant la croix sans trève,
Du Christ deux fois Martyr,
JOGUES n'a qu'un seul rêve:
Pour Dieu toujours souffrir.

7

Apôtre magnanime,
Au pays iroquois
GOUPIL mourra victime
Du signe de la croix.

8

Le vaillant DE LA LANDE
S'offre à Jésus tout bas;
Dieu reçoit son offrande:
Il hâte son trépas.

9

Ces héros sont ta gloire
O Canada français,
Conserve leur mémoire
En ton cœur à jamais.

Nihil obstat: SALVATOR NATUCCI. S. RR. Congr. adsessor et S. Fid. sub-prom. gen.

O CANADA.

1

O Canada, terre de nos aïeux
Ton front est ceint d'un fleuron glorieux,
Car ton bras sait porter l'épée
Il sait porter la croix
Ton histoire est une épopée
Des plus brillants exploits
Et ta valeur de foi trempée
Protégera nos foyers et nos drots (Bis)

II

Sous l'oeil de Dieu, près du fleuve géant,
Le Canadien grandit en espérant.
Il est né d'une race fière,
Béni fut son berceau;
Le ciel a marqué sa carrière
Dans ce monde nouveau
Toujours guidé par sa lumière,
Il gardera l'honneur de son drapeau (Bis.)

III

Amour sacré du trône et de l'autel,
Remplis nos coeurs de ton souffle immortel!
Parmi les races étrangères,
Notre guide est la loi:
Sachons être un peuple de frère,
Sous le joug de la foi,
Et répétons comme nos pères
Le cri vainqueur: "Pour le Christ et le roi."

O CANADA! MES PAYS! MES AMOURS!

I

Comme le dit un vieil adage,
Rien ne'st si beau que son pays!
Et de le chanter c'est l'usage
Le mien je chante à mes amis (Bis.)
  En te voyant. (Bis)
  Terre chérie (Bis)
  Dans mon coeur je dis tous les jours (Bis)
  O Canada belle patrie, O Canada sois mes amours (Bis.)

II

Le Canadien comme ses pères.
Aime à chanter, à s'égayer.
Doux, aisé, vif en manières
Poli, galant, hospitalier (Bis)
Répéter: En te voyant.

III

Chaque pays vante ses belles;
Je crois bien que l'on ment pas;
Mais nos canadiennes comme elles
Ont des grâces et des appas. (Bis)

Choeur. Maints ruisseaux (Bis)
  Et maintes rivières (Bis)
  Arrosant nos fertiles champs (Bis)
  Et de nos montagnes altières
  On voit le loin les longs penchants (Bis).

C'EST QUELQUE CHOSE.

(Nom.)

......................c'est quelque chose
......................c'est bien.
Monsieur le curé l'a dit dimanche au prône
......................c'est quelque chose
......................c'est bien, bien, bien.

IL A GAGNE SES EPAULETTES.

Il a gagné ses épaulettes,
Maluron, malurette.
Il a gagné ses épaulettes,
Maluron, maluré,
Maluron, malurette,
Maluron, maluré.

VIVE LA CANADIENNE.

I

Solo. Vive la canadienne,
Refrain. Vole, mon coeur, vole
Solo. Vive la canadienne
  Et ses jolis yeux doux,
Refrain. Et ses jolis yeux dous
  Et ses jolis yeux doux.

II

Femme forte et chrétienne,
Vole, mon coeur, vole
Femme forte et chrétienne,
Elle nous charme tous.

III

Nous l'aimons à l'extrême
Vole, mon coeur, vole
Nous l'aimons à l'extrême
D'amour tendre et jaloux.

IV

Elle est fine et gentille,
Vole, mon coeur, vole
Elle est fine et gentille
Belle dans tous les goûts.

V

C'est à qui la marie,
Vole, mon coeur, vole
C'est à qui la marie,
Les garçons en sont fous.

VI

La famille foissonne,
Vole, mon coeur, vole
La famille foissonne.
En petits manitous.

VII

Elle fait à l'éguille,
Vole, mon coeur, vole.
Elle fait à l'éguille
Nos habits, nos surtouts.

VIII

Elle apprend à sa fille,
Vole, mon coeur, vole.
Elle apprend à sa fille,
A ménager les sous.

IX

Elle est bien sans pareille,
Vole, mon coeur, vole
Elle est bien sans pareille,
Pour soigner rhume et toux.

X

Elle a toujours aux cartes,
Vole, mon coeur, vole
Elle a tourjours aux cartes
Les mains pleines d'atouts.

XI

Jusqu'à l'heure dernière
Vole, mon coeur, vole
Jusqu'à l'heure dernière
Sa vie est toute à nous.

XII

Ce n'est qu'au cimetière,
Vole, mon coeur, vole.
Ce n'est qu'au cimetière
Que son règne est dissous.

BIENVENUE
AUX ANCIENS DE PAIN COURT.
CANTATE

Introduction et choeur.

En cet anniversaire
Si cher à notre coeur
Montez, chants et prière,
Montez vers le Seigneur.
Déployez-vous, joyeux drapeaux,
Sur notre campagne en liesse;
Par vos carillons les plus beaux,
Cloches chantez notre allégresse.

Choeur. Pour chanter ce jour de bonheur
Nous attendions votre venue,
Et vous acceuillons de tout coeur:
Bienvenue! Bienvenue!
Fils de Pain Court, hôtes d'honneur,
A tous joyeuse bienvenue!

I

O ma paroisse, entends la voix
De tous tes enfants chantant ta gloire,
Tes belles années d'autrefois,
Noble page de notre histoire,
Tu sus garder avec amour
Ton doux parler, ta foi chr. tienne,
Tu sus rester jusqu'à ce jour
Une paroisse canadienne.

II

Sur le sol qui fut ton berceau,
L'on vit dans la première aurore
Un apôtre, un saint, un héros
Annoncer le Dieu qu'on adore.
Brébeuf, daignez du haut des cieux
Vous souvenir de notre terre;
Veillez encore sur ces lieux
Où l'on vous aime et vous révère.

III

Seigneur, vous nous avez comblé
De biens et de magnificence:
Chemins fleuris, champs fortunés,
Zélés pasteurs, foi et vaillance.
Bénis encore dans ta bonté
Les enfants ainsi que leurs pères.
Nous maintiendrons notre passé
Inscrits aux plis de nos bannières.

Choeur. Encore un souhait de bonheur
Dans l'allégresse jubilaire:
Fils de Pain Court, hôtes d'honneur
Au revoir, au centenaire!

ALLOUETTE.

Allouette, gentille allouette,
Allouette je te pleumerai (Bis.)
Je te pleumerai la tête, (Bis.)
Et la tête, (Bis). Allouette, (Bis.)
Ah!

Je te pleumerai les yeux.
Je te pleumerai le bec.
Je te pleumerai le cou.
Je te pleumerai les ailes.
Je te pleumerai les pattes.
Je te pleumerai les dos.
Je te pleumerai la queue.

BON SOIR MES AMIS.

Bon soir mes amis, bon soir (Bis)
Mes cousins et mes cousines,
Mes cousins et mes cousines
Mes amis, bon soir.
Au revoir.

II

Bonsoir..........................(Bis)
Mon grand père et ma grand'mère
Mes amis bon soir (Bis)
Au revoir.

III

Bonsoir..........................(Bis)
Et puis mon oncle et puis ma tante
Mes amis bonsoir. (Bis)
Au revoir.

IV

Bonsoir..........................(Bis)
Et puis les autres et puis c'est tout
Mes amis bonsoir (Bis)
Au revoir.

Rebel Grandma of the 90s

I'm 80 years old and unwilling to trade my fundamental family values for the modern ones of today's generation. My top priority is to be true to myself, to my beliefs and to my traditions. My story isn't really one of achievements in the sense of being awarded special honours. My accomplishments are small by comparison to others. My story is really that of an ordinary but gutsy woman, who has survived the roaring 20s, the depression, World War II, the hardships of raising a family, the progressive years that followed and now the computerized era of the nineties.

With all these changes also came the change in values which I partly accept, but like a stubborn old mule, I tend to reject today's modern philosophies and ideologies. My hope lies in my children, my grandchildren, my relatives and my friends. This is what is important: people, their lives, their hopes, their dreams. It's for them that I'm trying to tell my story, in my own words, plain and simple but alive with the truth.

There is no fiction in this book only facts as seen by me. There is a vast difference between life in the 30s and the 90s. In the 30s nobody bought things they did not need, with money they did not have, to impress people they did not really care for. Nobody tried to keep up with the Jones'. Our neighbours and friends meant so much to us, especially in our early years. We never had poor neighbours, just some who were a bit better off than others.

Before I sign off, I want to thank all of them once again.

As I witness the global devastation of floods, fires, crippling ice storms, threats of war, murders, famine, diseases, and earthquakes, chemical warfare of all descriptions, I realize that today's values are distorted, that we have failed to some extent to believe in the infinite wisdom and mercy of God.

As the millennium draws ever closer, we hear of dire predictions that are somewhat disturbing. A number of factors arouse sudden fears, even consternation and panic over impending alarming dangers, but life must go on.

If I had my life to do over, there probably would be little change. I enjoyed the challenge, the ups and the downs of finances. It was interesting to fight the whims of the weather year after year on the farm, learning from our grandfathers' predictions and studying the effects of the moon on our planet. Life is worth living and a real challenge.

Scientific advances aren't all good. Perhaps in our modern world we know too much. Because science is so much more capable of answering
questions, we tend to look for clinical answers while ignoring the more spiritual features of life.

Children born into such an environment of illusions are unlikely to thrive and grow up emotionally strong and secure.

"Social change which caused a shift in focus from the rights of the community to the rights of the individuals has damaged our society," says Serge Leclerc. The Me-ism philosophy which surfaced in the 60s and 70s, has caused people to start looking out for themselves rather than the rights of the community. This has resulted in diminishing the distinction between right and wrong and a "lack of moral and ethical certainty." [1]

One hundred years is a very long time. Fifty years is a long time to even try to cover details of the word "evolution." So much has happened in this last century of history. New problems, new lifestyles and new challenges have appeared. In our new world, it is natural to ask: "What does it mean to be a good parent? What does it mean to have a meaningful relationship in marriage? What does it mean to be a good layperson in one's apostolate? What does it mean to be a good priest, a good minister in this time of constant change as we approach the Third Millennium?"

Everyone needs to be attentive and sympathetic but also critical and watchful of historical developments and new ideologies. Contemporary men and women have but one great expectation

697

from priests, ministers and lay persons who work with clergy: "help and understanding in their thirst for Christ and His teachings." All other needs, whether economic, political or social needs can be met by any number of other people. The priest has a mysterious awesome power over the Eucharistic Body of Christ. Celebrating the Eucharist is his most sublime and most sacred function. By reason of this power he becomes the steward of the greatest treasure of the Redemption, for he gives people the Redeemer in person. Hope, Love, and Charity guided pilgrims a century ago and will continue to do so in this new millennium. [1]

Science may provide answers in particular instances, but we should ponder for a while whether our dependency on science and laws risk diminishing one of the most unscientific features of humanity. That is "Faith."

[1] Ref. Yvonne Bendo
Chatham News

Caroline Roy Laprise

Good Morning Neighbours

This message is for all my good neighbours, young and old. Those from Pain Court, those in Rondeau Park, as well as all those in Florida for the last 20 years.

Everyone is special in their own way. I have vivid memories of those, who have extended love and compassion to me and my family throughout the years.

A special tribute for my elder neighbours: Mr. and Mrs. Jean-Baptiste Therrien, Josephat Laprise, Erminie Sterling, Denis Goure, Eugène Primeau, Orville Pinsonneault, Alex Trahan, Réginald Blair, Origène Faubert, Calixte Therrien, Médore Béchard, Hector Béchard, John and Julie Faubert, Norman Goure and Carl Sterling. Last but not least, to Wilfrid Laprise and his wife Carmel, who were always there to share the joys and sorrows throughout the years. To all, I owe a debt of gratitude. You were special people to me.

In Rondeau, watching for my well-being over some 10 - 40 years; the Foote Family, The McNeilage Clan, The Savards, The Coopers, The Chilshoms, The Barhydes and the Davises. I've appreciated your tender loving care and your compassion. May God keep you and shower you with His Gifts of Love, Peace, and Health.

For the last 20 years, I've enjoyed the loving care of my neighbours in Florida. I thank you all for enhancing my life over the years. You were all very special in your own way. Accept my best wishes: Percy and Yvonne (Gagner) Nugent, Frank and Bunny Kacyznski, Germaine St. Pierre, Vernice Price, Tom d'Aurio, Len and Sylvia, Frank and Betty Mulvihill, my relatives, Diane Guay and Guy- Norman Guay. Aimé Guay's neighbours; the Bushways, Joseph and Lottie Beaudoin, Henry and Edith Bremer.

My first neighbour in Senate Manor, Bert and Beverly Heider, and later, Herb and Beverly Anthony.

Friends from Canada made our days, also. To mention a few - Réal and Adèle Charron, Sylva and Marion Létourneau and Cécile Kovalt, Alphonse and Alma Pinsonneault together with Gérard and Alice Roy, Anne Brown, Louella Caron, Esther Cartier, Elsie Demars and Ovéline Demars. Rosalie and Robert Côté, Jean-Paul Caron and Rita, Aleta Wills, and Edmond and Angela Gagner. We all enjoyed everyone's company.

Marc and Thérèse Donlon, also joined in our parties along with Jerry Cavanagh, Marie-Jeanne Caron and Angela Lynch who came to Florida every year until 1998 when she was 94 years old. Florence Hatton whom I visited regularly, died two months before her 100th birthday in 1995. I love also Jean Kaiser (Pelletier) and Marie with whom I visited the flea markets, regularly. Best regards to Kay Davis and Paul, long time friends since 1975; Kay has retired in Pennsylvania, after Paul died.

Last but not least Fernand and Juanita Gervais who purchased my home in 1987. At the time I had decided to settle into a mobile home, so I would cope with less work. They returned from a three year posting to Japan in 1990 and occupied the home.

How could I ever forget all the great parties, the weekly get-together's. Life is what you make it and rest assured it was a pleasant and exhilarating way of life to reside in Florida with all these pleasant loving people. I do count my blessings everyday.

ME - ISM

A new generation of individuals with a self serving attitude has emerged in the last quarter of the 20th century. It is the "Me - ism" generation. The Me - ism phenomenon has affected people of all races, genders, ages, social and financial status with no specific group of individuals necessarily forming a majority of the group. The exception to this, is that the younger generation is moving towards Me - ism at an alarming pace. This devastating mind set that may be transmitted to the first generation of the 21st century will have consequences that reach far beyond our current scope of realization.

To understand and attempt to correct this generational flaw, we must go back to the source of the problem. To place the entire blame on the younger generations would be irresponsible and unfair. The term "selfish" and the individuals described by this term have been in existence for centuries. The percentage of individuals categorized as such, has been very small in the past. Since the end of the great depression and World War II, the growth, prosperity and technological advances in our country have lead to greater independence for all individuals. On the surface, this is a good thing. However, without the proper guidance to channel this independence effectively, the baby boomers become the first link in the evolving Me - ism generation.

Many other factors have contributed to the current explosion in Me - ism, none of which were necessarily bad or even inappropriate when evaluated independently. The problem most often lies in the excess, exaggeration, abuse or just plainly going overboard on any one issue. Television, entertainment and particularly talk shows as well as commercials are a significant influence on promoting "Do whatever you want to do" or "I'm worth it" attitude. A key factor is the lack of respect for the sanctity of marriage and the family unit. The declining level of respect for other people has also had an influence. The "woman's lib" movement, although quite necessary and beneficial to women in general, is another example where going overboard has accentuated the Me - ism attitude. The high divorce rate and mixed families have caused many individuals to lose faith and trust in other people. The result is that these individuals and particularly the children in single parent homes, have had to look after themselves to survive emotionally. This has had a significant impact in the propagation of Me - ism.

In summary, Me - ism is a selfish attitude brought on by a series of events and cultural changes. These changes developed more rapidly than the educational process required to inform people how to make good choices in unfamiliar situations. It is certainly not fair to say that all of human kind has become selfish because there is indeed a great deal of kindness, generosity and unselfish people in the world. The development of a youth with good judgement, common sense and a strong sense of value will be the key to changing this unproductive generational flaw. In addition to the personal satisfaction derived from giving, acts of kindness are usually twice rewarded in ways you may least expect. It is hopeful that a series of world wide catastrophes will not be required for all of us to realize that we all need each other in one form or another.

Jean-Marie Laprise

New Endeavours in Farming

"We are on the leading edge in hemp research and production," Jean said. "And like any other business, success doesn't come overnight. But I have to say there have been significant gains over the past 24 months."

Laprise said he was first introduced to the crop in 1995 by his business partner, Claude Pinsonneault.

A Farmer

There once was a farmer who turned entrepreneur,
Even won awards for his innovative ideas, for sure!
He toiled with his hands and calculated in his head
Til' one day people heard and believed what he said.

He had a dream, a vision, or perhaps quite a few,
And projected an image of optimism to the crew.
When others said, you're taking a very big chance
Your smile is all it took to offer some reassurance.

For you are a true leader who did more than most
In pursuing a dream (or two) from coast to coast.
Ah! But alas my dear brother, you should remember
This until your life's December, and each day treasure

The privilege you experienced in sharing your life
With a confidante and a friend, yes that's your wife.
Because a great woman's love is something to cherish
And when all is said and done she'll still be a dish.

Colette Laprise

Farmer's Future in Fields of Hemp
By Bob Boughner The Daily News, July 22, 1997

JEAN AND LUCILLE LAPRISE, KENT HEMP FARMERS
. . . with some items made from the crop

North American agricultural history is being chalked up on a Dover Township farm located less than six kilometres from downtown Chatham.

And the farmer behind it all is Jean Laprise, a young, unassuming vegetable growing specialist, who was named entrepreneur of the year in 1995 by the Chatham and District Chamber of Commerce.

Laprise's claim to fame in recent years has been his success in Brussel Sprouts and vegetable transplant crops. In addition to being Ontario's
largest grower of Brussel Sprouts, he produces at least 10 different varieties of vegetable transplants and hundreds of acres of top quality seed corn.

But now the attention of the graduate of Ridgetown College of Agricultural Technology has turned to an old crop that is being re-discovered, due, in large measure, to relaxed federal laws.

Laprise has spent the past two years and "tons of dough" on research of the hemp crop. And he's about to get involved in the processing of the crop for the industrial market.

"This is the largest project I have ever been involved with," he said.

Laprise envisions a huge market for industrial hemp in North America. He is confident that acreage will climb above the 20,000 mark by early in the next century.

Right now he is busy organizing North America's first-ever industrial hemp day, which will be held on his farm August 7. Guest speakers will include Ontario Agriculture Minister Noble Villeneuve.

And during the event, Laprise will reveal production and processing plans for his new hemp company known as Kenex Ltd. for 1997, 1998 and 1999.

Rose-Marie Ur & Agriculture Minister Vanclief toured the Kenex hemp production facilities in Pain Court. Jean Laprise, President, and Bob l'Écuyer, General Manager, explain the harvesting process, with bales of hemp behind them. The M.P.s tasted cheese, seeds and other products made from hemp, a new export product helping to diversify our agricultural operations. Farmers in Essex, Lambton, Kent & Middlesex counties are growing hemp under contract to Kenex, or Hempline in Delaware

Laprise will also display, for the first time in Canada, a state-of-the-art hemp harvesting machine, which he recently purchased in Europe.

Laprise is convinced that hemp is the crop of the future and he intends to be on the ground floor of its development.

He is currently growing more than 100 acres of hemp and says the uses for its products are "endless."

Moreover, it will create many new job opportunities in southwestern Ontario.

Hemp, he said, can be used for everything from making chocolate bars to throat lozenges to clothing, shoes, insulation, paper, animal bedding, automotive parts and even in the manufacture of ethanol.

The Dover farmer says there is considerable interest in the crop, not only right across Canada but in the United States where hemp production is presently not permitted by government regulation.

Soybeans are now the crop of choice for seed corn rotation.

However, soybean cyst nematodes are increasing at an alarming rate in southwestern Ontario causing many soybean growers to rethink their planting strategies due to the financial losses resulting from nematode damage.

Laprise claims that industrial hemp is an excellent alternative crop for soybeans.

Another important factor involving hemp is the fact the crop does not require herbicides - "that's great for the environment."

"The cost of production is higher than for corn but the net returns should be comparable to corn and beans. And the added advantage is the elimination of herbicides."

Laprise said the most extensive research on hemp in Canada is taking place in Kent County and depending on the success of that research, acreage could easily reach the 20,000 mark early in the next century.

The Dover farmer farms 1,500 acres of land and has a staff of more than 40 employees.

From Caroline's Family

Born and raised in a farming community, Caroline developed a sense of adventure at an early age. Her enquiring mind, tenacity to reach her goals and natural ability to confront challenges proved to be assets during her life's work. Armed with a plethora of knowledge, she could be considered an expert in many fields.

To say that Caroline enjoys travelling is an understatement. Some might even say she has a transient nature because she always has things to do and places to go. Maintaining a second home most of her life was difficult but forced her to refine her packing techniques to an extraordinary level. Those of us who know her can attest that she can meticulously pack a truckload of items into her car. Oh! and that includes a hearty lunch for the road.

However, there is one place her spirit feels truly at home. She is drawn to this sanctuary, a place for rejuvenation and peace, and where she connects with the splendour of nature. Imagine an early morning walk to the beach, watering the lawn and flower gardens, relaxing in a rocking chair on the veranda and offering an expression of gratitude for the ever-changing view of the lake and the wonders of nature. This is part of Caroline's routine before making breakfast at her most treasured place, the cottage.

The time has come to gain a better understanding and appreciation of "Maman's" relentless efforts to collect articles and save all those old boxes of memorabilia. She used to say "J' va mettre cela dans le scrapbook" and when asked why, she would add "Because some things are worth remembering."

Maman, it is with pride in our hearts that we accept this anthology and collection of lifelong memories. Thank you for having the courage to undertake this project, the perseverance to continue it, the determination to finish it and most of all, thank you for having the vision to preserve our heritage.

Colette Laprise

De la famille Roy

À la fête de l'exploit de ton livre, nous offrons des souhaits extraordinaires de beauté, de reconnaissance, de célébration, de foi profonde et de sérénité. Puisse les années qui viennent être un temps de repos et d'action de grâces! Bonne santé . . . pour que cela dure assez longtemps et te prépare un temps semblable pour toujours!

Merci Caroline de tout ce que tu as fais pour nous. C'est cette prière de la Bible que nous faisons pour toi!

"Que la Seigneur te bénisse et te garde,
Qu'il te révèle son visage et t'accorde sa grâce,
Qu'il t'illumine de son regard de bienveillance,
Et te donne la paix, le plénitude du bonheur."

Livre des nombres 6: 22-27

*   *   *

Caroline, you have reached a milestone along life's way. This moment to stop and think of your special accomplishments. It's a time of pride down deep inside in all you have achieved.

A time of "émerveillement" for all you have meant
to those around you, family and friends.
A time of openness for us to "thank you."
A time of rest and inner peace with your God.
It is a time for fond reflection and a time to savour memories,
then to look ahead with joy on all you've yet to accomplish.

We embrace you with all our hearts,

Loretta Roy

Acknowledgements

As I turn the last pages of this book before it goes to print, I realize that the family institution has received overwhelming importance. Our society revolves on the driving influence all the institutions have on our cosmos, be it family, education, religious, economic, political or recreational. All constitute a force, and one cannot thrive and develop without each element and each other.

Rest assured, in my 80th year, I am proud to present to you this anecdotal journal of sorts through which your goodwill and thoughtfulness abound. It is the milestone of four generations who, in different ways, have contributed knowledge, time and nohow; to others who have graciously and willingly presented various photos and written articles, to all I am most humble.

At the threshold of this new millennium I wish to acknowledge the help I received from my children and my grandchildren. They have encouraged me to understand and accept the formidable advances in computerized technology associated with the publishing of this book.

To Richard Laprise the computer repair man, who executed his workmanship whenever my daughter Coline experienced computer breakdowns. I also recognize his skills for writing and transferring all photos and text onto a CD for the printers copy and permanent use for future generations.

To Vincent Laprise who did some scanning and worked magic on some old photos, for giving us advice and for helping me as much as he could, considering he was extremely busy.

It's heart warming to salute the delivery girl Christie Trudell who carried papers for her mother and her two years of coping with the disturbance of a peaceful household transformed into a hubbub of a print shop.

To all the people I love who have so graciously contributed articles, photos, eulogies, or suggestions in order to enhance the quality of information for this project, I thank you.

I wish to acknowledge Laprise Farms Ltd, whose employees were so gracious to me, especially to Angela Couture Pawlak who for two years 1995-96 was doing my secretarial work and recorded it on computer for future references.

My project was further enhanced through the relentless efforts and indispensable help of Angéline Marentette who had the courage to spend tedious hours to edit and polish my work and to present an acceptable version of it. Furthermore, it was through her cooperation that we met with Marty Gervais, writer in residence at the University of Windsor.

Through Mr. Gervais's briefing and counselling we acquired a much deeper understanding of the work involved in publishing this book. His expertise as a writer and publisher was important and appreciated.

A long time friend and relative, Paul Richer, I'm very thankful that he gladly prepared the layout of the book cover, which is my pride and joy.

A special favour was granted when Lucile Caron and her sister Aline Bondy, both retired teachers who taught at our local schools, visited my home. They are the daughters of Mr. and Mrs. Alcide Caron of Pain Court.

Lucile has retired after teaching for thirty-five years. She candidly offered me her assistance by doing proofreading, a task that requires a sharp eye for details, adroitness and finesse. You amaze me and I'm most grateful.

I've appreciated verifying data with the special reference books published by "La Société Franco-Ontarienne d'Histoire et de Généalogies" de Pain Court et de Grande Pointe, compiled by Amédée Emery, Omer Charron, Claudette Piquette-Bibeau and Agathe Saumure as director.

I hereby acknowledge with enthusiasm, Mrs. Madeleine Leal who graciously accepted the task of proofreading this exposé in a very limited time frame before presenting it to the publisher. Your help was invaluable.

To the host of persons who have graciously accepted to grant me permission to publish some of their work, thank you very much.

Special regards to my sister Yvonne Lucier who cared to watch over me and call me every-day thereby bringing her support and understanding.

To my daughter, Colette, who twice a year travelled from Nova Scotia to give the cart a push in order for us to keep rolling, I love you.

A special thank you to my ailing daughter Coline who has been at the helm of the computer desk over two years, dispatching all the paper work to a conscientious crew of workers. I cannot find adequate words to describe her efficiency in handling this task so well. Furthermore she has displayed unknown creative talents in word processing, manuscript formatting, design concepts and the scanning of the nearly 400 photos displayed in this book ready for the printer.

It is most touching to establish the degree of close cooperation displayed by all the personnel involved in the publishing of these memoirs.

I also want to acknowledge that everyone who worked so diligently on this book are amateurs (except for the printer). We all strived to do our best, but if there are any errors I wish to apologize in advance.

To the good Lord for always being there for me, for inspiring me, for giving me the health and the patience to endure this most exhausting but fulfilling work. Whenever I needed help, he would create a situation to open doors for me or send a good Samaritan to help.

Last but not least, to everyone who, in any small way, have contributed articles or information towards this project, I hereby say thank you.

Caroline Roy Laprise

Semi-conclusion

En cette fin du deuxième millénaire après Jésus-Christ, notre humanité oscille entre l'optimisme et l'angoisse. D'un côté nous avons plusieurs raisons de nous réjouir. Les découvertes scientifiques et technologiques libèrent de plus en plus ouvriers et ouvrières d'un travail abrutissant. Les avances médicales et de meilleures conditions hygiéniques prolongent l'espérance de la vie. Les moyens de transport nous permettent des déplacements de plus en plus rapides; en quelques heures nous passons d'un froid nordique à la chaleur des Antilles.[1]

Des milliers de "gadgets"nous facilitent la vie quotidienne alors que les communications nous relient en quelques instants à n'importe quel lieu du monde.

Seigneur me voici au soir de ma vie, apprends-moi à t'aimer d'avantage dans la peine, la joie ou l'ennui. Aide-moi à saluer les vieillards et reconnaître tes bienfaits au sein des malades.

Seigneur, reste avec moi afin que je puisse te rendre grâce. Accorde-moi de persévérer dans mes croyances, mes valeurs et par là grandir dans ton amour.

Vis-à-vis le travail, j'ai maintenu ma famille de huit enfants au meilleur de mes connaissances et j'ai épaulé mon mari Trefflé dans toutes ses entreprises. Je me suis engagée dans les projets paroissiaux et diocésains ainsi que ceux de la province dédiés aux causes catholiques et françaises tout en préservant un équilibre raisonnable envers mes frères de différentes cultures de la région.

Aujourd'hui, j'anticipe de vivre au ralenti et je désire passer mes heures de loisirs à partager les joies et les peines de mes confrères les aidant à les consoler dans la mesure possible.

Caroline Roy Laprise

Bonne Heureuse Année 1999
Pour le millénaire, paix, joie, santé et le paradis à la fin de vos jours.

1. Référence - Révérend Père Bernard Lacroix   Éditions Fides 1997

DESIDERATA

Va paisiblement ton chemin à travers le bruit et la hâte, et souviens-toi que le silence est paix. Autant que faire se peut, et sans courber la tête, sois amis avec tes semblables; exprime ta vérité calmement et clairement; écoute les autres, même les plus ennuyeux ou les plus ignorants. Eux aussi ont quelque chose à dire. Fuis l'homme à la voix haute et autoritaire; il pèche contre l'esprit. Ne te compare pas aux autres par crainte de devenir vain ou amer, car toujours tu trouveras meilleur ou pire que toi.

Jouis de tes succès, mais aussi de tes plans. Aime ton travail, aussi humble soit-il, car c'est un bien réel dans un monde incertain. Sois sage en affaires, car le monde est trompeur. Mais n'ignore pas non plus, que verrue il y a, que beaucoup d'hommes poursuivent un idéal et que l'héroïsme n'est pas chose si rare. Sois toi-même et surtout ne feins pas l'amitié: n'aborde pas non plus l'amour avec cynisme, car malgré les vicissitudes et les désenchantements, il est aussi vivace que l'herbe que tu foules. Incline-toi devant l'inévitable passage des ans, laissant sans regret la jeunesse et ses plaisirs. Sache que pour être fort, tu dois te préparer, mais ne succombe pas aux craintes chimériques qu'engendrent souvent fatigue et solitude. En deçà d'une sage discipline, sois bon avec toi-même.

Tu es bien fils de l'univers, tout comme les arbres et les étoiles. Tu y as ta place. Quoi que tu en penses, il est clair que l'univers continue sa marche comme il se doit. Sois donc en paix avec Dieu, quel qu'il puisse être pour toi; et quelles que soient ta tâche et tes aspirations dans le bruit et la confusion, garde ton âme en paix. Malgré les vilenies, les labeurs, les rêves déçus, la vie a encore sa beauté. Sois prudent.

ESSAIE D'ÊTRE HEUREUX

Épilogue

"Fais-moi Cadeau de ton Histoire"

"Chacune de nos vies, sans exception,
est un trésor à raconter pour soi, pour
ses enfants, pour tous ceux que l'on
aime." Mon plus bel héritage, c'est mon
histoire. La réprésentation écrite de
moi-même et de ma vie, décrit simultané-
ment des actes éminemment personnels
et fondamentalement sociaux. Il existe
un modelage culturel de la mémoire qui
fait que le passé personnel ne peut être
relu qu'à travers les représentations
qu 'une génération particulière se fait de
son histoire passée.
À votre tour, faites nous cadeau de votre
histoire, de vos souvenirs ou de quelque
chose semblable.

Caroline Roy Laprise

Index
Alphabetical Order - Ordre Alphabetique
Italiques = en français

AGMV
MARQUIS

Québec, Canada
1999